P9-CLC-759

AN AMERICAN CIVIL LIBERTIES UNION HANDBOOK

THE RIGHTS OF EMPLOYEES AND UNION MEMBERS

THE BASIC ACLU GUIDE TO THE RIGHTS OF EMPLOYEES AND UNION MEMBERS

SECOND EDITION
Completely Revised and Updated

Wayne N. Outten
Robert J. Rabin
Lisa R. Lipman

General Editor of the Handbook Series
Norman Dorsen, President, ACLU 1976–1991

SOUTHERN ILLINOIS UNIVERSITY PRESS
CARBONDALE AND EDWARDSVILLE

344.01
089⊤

Copyright © 1994 by the American Civil Liberties Union
All rights reserved
Printed in the United States of America
Production supervised by Natalia Nadraga

97 96 95 94   4 3 2 1

Library of Congress Cataloging-in-Publication Data

Outten, Wayne N.
    The rights of employees and union members : the basic ACLU
guide to the rights of employees and union members / Wayne N.
Outten, Robert J. Rabin, Lisa R. Lipman.
        p.   cm. — (An American Civil Liberties Union handbook)
    1. Labor laws and legislation—United States. 2. Employee rights—
United States. I. Rabin, Robert J. II. Lipman, Lisa R.
III. Title.   IV. Series.
KF3319.3.O965   1994
344.73′012596—dc20
[347.30412596]   93-16895
ISBN 0-8093-1913-6   CIP
ISBN 0-8093-1914-4 (pbk.)

The paper used in this publication meets the minimum requirements of
American National Standard for Information Sciences—Permanence of
Paper for Printed Library Materials, ANSI Z39.48-1984. ∞

Contents

Preface

This guide sets forth your rights under present law and offers suggestions on how they can be protected. It is one of a continuing series of handbooks published in cooperation with the American Civil Liberties Union (ACLU).

Surrounding these publications is the hope that Americans, informed of their rights, will be encouraged to exercise them. Through their exercise, rights are given life. If they are rarely used, they may be forgotten and violations may become routine.

This guide offers no assurances that your rights will be respected. The laws may change, and in some of the subjects covered in these pages, they change quite rapidly. An effort has been made to note those parts of the law where movement is taking place, but it is not always possible to predict accurately when the law *will* change.

Even if laws remain the same, their interpretation by courts and administrative officials often varies. In a federal system such as ours there is a built-in problem since state and federal laws differ, not to speak of the variations among states. In addition, there is much diversity in the ways in which particular courts and administrative officials interpret the same law at any given moment.

If you encounter what you consider to be a specific abuse of your rights, you should seek legal assistance. There are a number of agencies that may help you, among them ACLU affiliate offices, but bear in mind that the ACLU is a limited-purpose organization. In many communities there are federally funded legal service offices that provide assistance to persons who cannot afford the costs of legal representation.

In general, the rights that the ACLU defends are freedom of inquiry and expression; due process of law; equal protection under the law; and privacy. The authors in this series have discussed other rights (even though they sometimes fall outside the ACLU's usual concern) in order to provide as much guidance as possible.

These books have been planned as guides for the people directly affected: thus the question-and-answer format. (In some areas there are more detailed works available for experts.) These guides seek to raise the major issues and inform the nonspecialist of the basic law on the subject. The authors of these books are themselves specialists who understand the need for information at "street level."

If you encounter a specific legal problem in an area discussed in one of these handbooks, show the book to your attorney. Of course, he or she will not be able to rely exclusively on the handbook to provide you with adequate representation. But if your attorney hasn't had a great deal of experience in the specific area, the handbook can provide helpful suggestions on how to proceed.

Norman Dorsen, General Editor
Stokes Professor of Law
New York University School of Law

Acknowledgments

This book is a melding and major updating of two earlier books in this series. The larger portion is derived from *The Rights of Employees*, by Wayne N. Outten (with Noah A. Kinigstein). The parts dealing with the rights of employees within their unions is based on *The Rights of Union Members*, by Clyde W. Summers and Robert J. Rabin. We thank those who helped create those initial works. We make a special bow to Professor Summers, whose pioneering work in this field continues to influence current writing and legal developments.

We are most grateful to three lawyers who joined us relatively late in the enterprise to enable us to complete our work in several important areas. Jack A. Raisner of Lankenau Kovner & Kurtz and of St. John's University (New York City) drafted the chapters on AIDS and whistleblowing and made major contributions to the chapters on privacy, disability discrimination, and hiring. He also coordinated the entire project during its final stages. Rob Leibross (Denver, Colorado) is responsible for the chapters on pensions and on employee welfare benefits, while Lionel Postic, assistant professor, Regent University School of Law, developed the chapter on wrongful termination.

We also thank our long-suffering research assistants who did the initial leg work on earlier drafts, and who tracked down endless leads and additional authorities. They are Douglas Hollowell, Patricia King, Lisa Bellew, Darlene Addie, Patrick Zabatta, Benjamin C. Rabin, John Sahady, Virginia Piekarski, Jeanne Vasaleck, Philippe Zimmerman, Janet Shanks, Ori Karev, and Hal Gilenson. We also acknowledge the constant help, support, and good humor of Joyce Robertson and Clare Doerle and the editorial and other technical assistance of Shannan Hudgins, who was always cheerful and gracious.

Additionally, we thank several practicing lawyers for providing helpful information or for making valuable suggestions on drafts of some of the chapters. They are Max Zimny, Daniel Kosanovich, Mimi Satter, Leonard Flamm, Lucas Guttentag,

Ronald Dean, and Robert Stulberg. None of them, however, bears any responsibility for the final product.

Work is an important part of our lives. This book, which is our work, gives us pride and satisfaction. We hope it enhances the dignity, the security, and the pleasure of your own work.

PART 1
The Employment Relationship

I

An Overview

Why is my job important?

Work is a central part of our lives. Many of us define ourselves by the work that we do. Work can be ennobling or oppressive. Think of its place in literature. Lenny tells George in John Steinbeck's *Of Mice and Men*, "Guys like us, that work on ranches, are the loneliest guys in the world." Willie Loman, in Arthur Miller's *Death of a Salesman*, cries out to his boss, "There were promises made across this desk! I put in thirty-four years in this firm and now I can't pay my insurance! You can't eat the orange and throw the peel away—a man is not a piece of fruit!" Upton Sinclair describes the horrors of the meat packing plant in *The Jungle*. "The great packing machine ground on remorselessly, without thinking of green fields, and the men and women and children who were part of it never saw any green thing, not even a flower." Studs Terkel's *Working* chronicles the hopes and frustrations of workers in more recent times.

Not only does work provide fulfillment, but it is usually the economic foundation for our existence. It is the main income stream for most of us, and the source of other important financial benefits as well. Many workers enjoy comprehensive health insurance, with the employer paying most if not all of the premium. Most employers provide some sort of sick leave, supplemented by a disability program, so that if you are unable to work because of illness, you'll continue to receive your regular income for some fixed period of time. If you are injured on the job you'll receive pay under the Worker's Compensation system. Everyone who enters the workforce builds up credit for Social Security, which provides the primary retirement benefit for many of us. In addition, many employers establish their own pension plans, so that your retirement income is tied to your years of work for your employer. When your work stops, many of these benefits are lost or diminished. It is no wonder people are often devastated, spiritually and economically, if they are out of work.

What are the downsides of work?

The workplace can wear you down. Constant exposure to carcinogens or repetitive motions in your work may disable you. Accidents can happen. Time slowly takes its toll. And as you spend more and more time at one job, your ability to move may be lessened. Your dependence on your employer grows as your marketability declines.

You develop skills and knowledge at your work that will help you become a more productive worker. But your employer may seek to restrict you in the use of this knowledge and ability if you leave the workplace. He may also require you to turn over royalties from the fruits of your inventions or creative work on the job.

What is the relationship of the workplace to the rest of society?

Because of the central place our work occupies in our lives, the workplace may play a surprisingly large role in accomplishing objectives society finds important. Under the Americans with Disabilities Act, accommodations must be made by employers and other employees to allow workers with disabilities to function effectively in the workplace. In the nation's war on drugs, the workplace often becomes a primary arena in which your activities may be monitored. Your employer may be the principal enforcer of laws regulating immigration. Because your family, both old and young, may depend on you for care, society has a vital interest in seeing that you have adequate time off from work to provide care. Federal law now guarantees parental leave and other family leave, and many states provide similar coverage. As the person closest to the scene, the worker is often in the best position to bring to public attention things that are wrong in the workplace—unsafe working conditions, defective products, adulterated food. In a just society, protection must be given against reprisal to the worker who reports these problems.

What is my relationship with my other workers?

The workplace may be crowded. With constant contact, difficult encounters may occur. You may have the bad luck to be subjected to an unpleasant boss. You may be harassed by fellow workers or by management. You may feel your work performance or advancement is not judged fairly and on its merits, but turns on irrelevant considerations like your race, gender, age, sexual preference, or disability. You may think that others get better treatment because of favoritism to individuals or groups.

What do you mean by the term *employee* in the title of this book?

Almost all of us are workers in one way or another, but not all of us are employees. An *employee* is a worker who is employed by somebody else. That somebody else, the employer, puts up the capital and takes the risk that the business will succeed or fail, although the employee shares in that risk to some extent. The employer offers to hire the employee at fixed terms. When the employee agrees, a relationship is formed on those terms. Many of your workplace rights depend on how this relationship is defined.

Some workers work for themselves. Think of the difference between a trio of musicians who hire themselves out for gigs and a single violinist who is hired by a symphony orchestra. Those who work for themselves are responsible for their own well being. An eloquent portrait of the self-sustaining worker is Richard Rhodes's book, *Farm*, the story of an actual farm family that must fend for itself. The farmer decides how much to invest in seeds and equipment, what crops to plant, how much money to borrow, what equipment to repair or replace, whether to rely on government subsidized farm programs, how much to put aside for the future, how much to spend for health insurance, and so on. But even the self-employed worker can have workplace disputes. Our farmer may have a product safety claim against the manufacturer of a combine that breaks down or injures him, he may have a dispute with his insurance carrier, or even with an investment counsellor who has helped him set up a pension. He may have disputes with the government over crop allocations under a government subsidy program, or he may have a claim for disability payments under the Social Security Act.

We have not included in this book the rights of self-employed workers. Nor do we discuss whether greater recognition should be given to the employment status of homemakers. Part-time workers, although they may paste together a full-time week from a variety of jobs, are given marginal protections by the laws, and as a result we have little to say about them in this book. Nor do we address the problems of those groups that are excluded from some of the statutes we cover, for example, agricultural workers, public employees, and professionals.

Does our nation have a workplace policy?

No. Even though work is so central to our lives, we have not developed a societal consensus about the obligations and rights that belong in the workplace. Neither our laws nor our cultural traditions systematically reflect the basic attributes of a civilized workplace policy. The ingredients of a sound workplace policy would include protection against unjust dismissal and against economic dislocation, recognition of the personal integrity of the worker, fair treatment in workplace decisions such as job assignments, a say in how the workplace is governed, adequate health insurance, proper retirement coverage, adequate parental and medical leave protections and other family-friendly policies, and safeguards against workplace illness and injury.

In short, we have not fully recognized in this country that the job relationship carries with it basic rights and responsibilities on both sides. The traditions and laws of other countries have given their workers greater rights of security, dignity, and participation. In our country the basic model of work is that the employee has no duties to the employer and the employer no obligations to the employee, except those that are reached by agreement or imposed by specific laws. The essential model is one of employment at will: the employee may quit at any time and the employer may terminate the employee for any reason or no reason at all. Our country does not recognize that the worker builds up an equity and a stake in the job through long years of faithful service.

The actual employment situation isn't, however, as hopeless as the model appears. There are a number of judicial and legislative measures that secure many of the features of a just workplace as described above. For example, federal laws forbid employers from making employment decisions based on race, national origin, sex, religion, age, or disability. A proposed uniform state law would protect employees from dismissals that are not for cause. Yet, these developments are often the result of political forces or even luck. We lack a systematic, comprehensive view of workplace policy that rests on some common understanding of the work relationship.

What are the sources of law that regulate the workplace?
The laws regulating the workplace come from a variety of sources, often overlapping or conflicting and sometimes not applicable at all to a particular workplace or situation. We discuss here the broad categories of legal regulation of the workplace.

The first source of law is the law of contracts. It consists of those rights and obligations that a court is willing to find in the agreement made by the worker and his employer. Individual employees with strong bargaining power, like baseball players, are often able to negotiate a written contract that governs the full range of workplace obligations. Self-employed workers who work together, such as lawyers, may define their relationship through partnership agreements. Workers who do not have written contracts may be able to develop rights through other written documents, such as an employee handbook. In some circumstances, oral representations and commitments, such as Willie Loman claimed in *Death of a Salesman*, can also be the basis of contractual claims. Naturally you are much better off if you can capture your employer's representations in writing. Not only is it easier to prove that these representations were made, but sometimes an oral contract is not enforceable.

Some courts have begun to find contractual obligations in the employment relationship itself, even if the employer and worker have made no specific agreement. These rights may be found in representations or commitments made by the employer, or simply in the notion that the work relationship carries with it some basic obligations of "good faith" on both sides.

The law of contracts is state not federal law. In some states, courts have gone far to secure employees' contract rights; in other states, the employment-at-will doctrine is still the mainstay of the employment relationship. Thus, your rights are determined in part by where you live or work.

The second source of workplace law derives from a variety of state and federal statutes. In these circumstances, society, through its elected representatives, has decided that certain basic workplace rights must be secured and not left to the abilities of individual employees to make good agreements with their employers. The list of these rights grows constantly and is the subject of continuing debate as this book goes to press. Laws regulating worker health and safety (OSHA), preventing discrimination based on gender, race, age, and disability (for example, Title VII of the Civil Rights Act of 1964, the Civil Rights Act of 1991 and the Americans with Disabilities Act), providing workers' compensation, protecting pensions that are established at the workplace (ERISA), giving rights to older workers (OWBPA), and guaranteeing job security to parents who need time off to care for a newborn, newly adopted, or seriously ill child are typical examples that will be discussed in this book.

The third set of laws covers workers who are represented by unions. Initially, our nation did not regulate the workplace through specific workplace standards, except in such basic areas as maximum hours of work, child labor, and even, at one time, restrictions on the work women could perform. Then, in the late 1930s, Congress decided to allow workers to join together and determine their own conditions of work through collective bargaining with their employers. These basic labor laws are designed to foster the process of collective bargaining but not to dictate the actual terms of employment.

The early labor laws were especially important as a check on a judiciary that was generally hostile to the labor movement. The strength of unions in the United States is declining, as substantially less than 20% of all workers are now represented by unions. But even for that small segment of the workforce, the rights obtained through collective bargaining are significant. Collective bargaining sets terms and conditions of employment that usually are not regulated or provided by other laws, for example, protection against unjust dismissal and other discipline and fair procedures for workplace advancement, usually based on seniority. Collective bargaining provides for a quick and easy way to enforce your workplace rights. The unionized worker usually has far greater voice in the governance of the workplace than does his nonunion counterpart. As described further below, some companies have set up systems of employee communication that may be viewed as alternatives to union representation, but they do not provide the worker with the power of collective bargaining.

A fourth set of workplace rights comes from the law of torts. This body of law basically sets minimum standards of conduct that persons owe to one another. It is significant in the workplace in the law regarding unjust dismissal, especially in terminations that violate public policy or are carried out in an offensive or humiliating manner, under the tort of intentional infliction of emotional distress. Tort law can give rise to defamation actions over things that are said or written about employees. It may be of value too in seeking economic redress for workplace injuries.

A final set of workplace protections comes from the United States Constitution or from state constitutions. Guarantees of due process may be a further source of protection against unjust dismissal. The First Amendment protects your right to speak out. And Fourth Amendment protections may empower you to resist unreasonable intrusions into your privacy, such as drug testing or monitoring of work. The United States Constitution applies only to the conduct of government and not of private employers. Thus, constitutional rights are of importance primarily to public employees. However, parallel sorts of rights may be developed in the private workplace, for example, by incorporating constitutional notions of fairness into just cause provisions of a collective bargaining agreement or by state tort doctrines that recognize a right of privacy.

Does it make a difference in my rights if I am represented by a labor union?

Yes. The worker who is represented by a union is entitled to all the benefits that are negotiated by his union in his workplace. These rights are set out in a collective bargaining agreement. The represented worker can enforce these rights, although he must depend on the union to advance his claim. In addition, the organized worker is governed by almost all the statutory protections discussed in this book. There may be situations where rights overlap, and where the worker must first look to his collective bargaining agreement, or even where his rights under the agreement take precedence over statutory rights, but these situations are not common. While an attempt has been made to balance the presentation in the chapters below on the advantages of choosing union representation, we make the assumption is that most workers will find it beneficial to support their union.

Will I need a lawyer to help me secure the rights discussed in this book?

Yes, in most cases. This book is designed to introduce you to your rights as an employee. It is meant to open your eyes to situations where you can demand protection. If you think you've encountered a problem in the workplace where this book suggests you may have some rights, that is the time to find a good lawyer. This book is only a first step.

It isn't easy to obtain a lawyer. Good lawyers are expensive, and experienced lawyers are hard to find. Included in this book is an appendix that lists ways to go about finding a lawyer. Employment law is a specialized field, and you are advised to find a lawyer who is an expert in it. Do not rely on a lawyer's word that he is an expert, but try to obtain references from somebody who has had a good experience with a lawyer or from the sources listed in the appendix. In some cases you will be able to turn to an administrative agency, which will provide you with legal assistance at no cost. Some administrative agencies are so overloaded, however, that it may take years before your claim will be resolved. While legal representation is costly, there are ways to finance the fees; some attorneys will consider contingent fee arrangements and some statutes require the employer to pay the employee's counsel fees if the employee prevails. You should discuss these alternatives with your lawyer.

One of the groups listed in the appendix is NELA, an organization of lawyers practicing in this field. Lisa Lipman, Jack Raisner, and Wayne Outten are active in this group. So is one of our contributing authors, Robert Liebross. We list NELA not to increase the trade of these good people but because their organization can provide valuable references to you.

How should lawyers use this book?

Cautiously. This is not a book for lawyers, in the sense that it even begins to take the place of careful research, thorough reading of the leading treatises, and experience. We flatter ourselves to think that some lawyers will use this book for general guidance and initial research leads. We welcome that. However, we warn lawyers that this is not an exhaustive research tool. It is written for an audience of workers, persons not schooled in the subtleties of the law. We've tried to speak plainly, something lawyers don't always do. In saying things simply and clearly we do not always emphasize important distinctions and qualifications in the law. Nor is our research intended to be complete. We've tried to provide current cases that best illustrate our text. They are chosen in part for their usefulness in conveying the law to the reader. The practicing lawyer must go beyond these starting cases to adequately represent his or her client.

II

The Hiring Process

Getting a job is a very important subject in a book on employment rights. Without a job, many of the other subjects are academic. This chapter provides an overview of the hiring process, with many of the topics discussed in greater detail in subsequent chapters. For example, chapter 23 on privacy discusses employment issues that often occur at the hiring stage (such as drug testing and honesty testing), and chapters 8 through 17 cover discrimination in employment, including in the hiring process.

Does an employer have an absolute right to refuse to hire me?

No. Although employers have wide discretion in hiring, they cannot intentionally discriminate against certain protected classes of applicants. Nor may employers make hiring decisions based on factors that seem to be neutral, but that disproportionately exclude such protected workers.[1] For instance, an employer may not refuse to hire an applicant because she is a Hispanic female (disparate treatment). Nor may the employer arbitrarily impose a height requirement that excludes applicants who are, for example, less than 5 feet 5 inches tall since this may disproportionately exclude Hispanic females (disparate impact). Employers engage in unlawful disparate treatment when they base hiring decisions upon an applicant's race, color, religion, sex, pregnancy, national origin, disability, or (if you are over 40 years old) age.[2] In some states, it is unlawful to discriminate on the basis of an applicant's sexual orientation,[3] romantic relationship,[4] arrest record,[5] political affiliation,[6] marital status,[7] color blindness,[8] unfavorable military discharge,[9] alien status,[10] sickle-cell trait[11] or because the applicant is bankrupt or subject to a childcare support withholding order.[12] Employers are not required, however, to hire a "protected" applicant (a minority or female for example) just because he or she is in a protected class. The employer may choose the most qualified applicant, or between equally qualified applicants, or even a less qualified applicant, as long as unlawful criteria are not used.[13]

What may a prospective employer ask on a job application form or at a job interview?

Most questions that a prospective employer may ask you probably do not violate the law. Therefore, if you choose not to answer a question that you find offensive, the prospective employer may, as a result, decide not to hire you. However, preemployment inquiries that directly reveal your race, color, sex, age, religion, national origin, pregnancy, or disability usually do violate the law. You should also be wary of questions that indirectly reveal protected characteristics since these too may be treated as evidence of discrimination. Such inquiries may include non-job-related matters such as marital status, number of children, friends or relatives working for the company, criminal records, credit rating, garnishments, terms of military discharge, and availability for work on weekends and holidays. The Equal Employment Opportunity Commission (EEOC), which has enforcement authority, has determined that inquiries into otherwise improper areas are not unlawful if made in compliance with fair employment practice laws.[14] For instance, an airline may ask applicant pilots their age if it has established a bona fide occupational qualification that pilots be under 60 years of age.

In some occupations, such as banking or childcare, the employer has a legal duty to screen out dangerous individuals through preemployment inquiries and background checks.[15] The EEOC has issued a "Guide to Pre-Employment Inquiries,"[16] and similar publications are issued by state authorities.[17]

What are some examples of permissible and impermissible questions?

A prospective employer may not ask your race (unless given permission by a government agency as part of an affirmative action program) or the color of your skin, hair, or eyes, but it may ask about distinguishing physical characteristics for identification purposes.[18] An employer may ask your sex but may not ask whether you are pregnant or plan to be, except in the rare instance when nonpregnancy is a bona fide occupational qualification (BFOQ).[19] A BFOQ exists when an employer is able to demonstrate that all members of the excluded class are unable to satisfy the job requirements. For example, gender is a BFOQ for a job modeling bathing suits but not for a job involving heavy physical labor.[20] An employer may not ask your age or date of birth before hiring but may require proof that you are above the minimum legal working ge.[21] Once hired, however, you may be required to supply proof of age. An employer may not discriminate on the basis of national origin; thus an inquiry into your birthplace may be unlawful if you were denied a job on that basis.[22] An employer can refuse to hire an alien, however, and may therefore ask whether you are a United States citizen.[23]

An employer may not ask about your religious beliefs or affiliations but may inform you of normal work hours so as to avoid potential conflicts with religious obligations.[24] Nonetheless, employers must make "reasonable accommodations" for the religious practices of employees, unless undue hardship to the efficient running of the business can be shown.[25] In jurisdictions that prohibit job discrimination on the basis of marital status, employers may not ask your marital status, but may ask whether you have outside commitments or responsibilities that may hinder your meeting work schedules.[26] Also, an employer cannot require that you supply names and addresses of relatives but may ask for the names and addresses of any relatives already employed by that employer.[27] Similarly, an employer is not permitted to ask you whether you have any health impairments or to require you to take a physical but may ask whether you are physically able to perform the particular tasks of the job.[28]

In all of the illustrations above the assumption is that the employer is covered by federal or state antidiscrimination laws. Smaller employers (with less than 15 employees), however, may be immune from these laws.

Employers commonly ask other preemployment questions that raise legal questions that are discussed elsewhere in this book. Briefly, these include inquiries involving

- *Credit ratings.* Due to their discriminatory impact, credit ratings questions generally are considered unlawful at the hiring stage.[29] (See chapter 23 on privacy for a fuller discussion.)

- *Arrests and convictions.* Unless they involve specific, job-related offenses, questions about arrests or convictions raise issues of discriminatory impact and invasion of privacy. (See chapters 23 on privacy and 8 on discrimination.) The reason an employer's questions about arrests and convictions are considered discriminatory is that it has been shown that certain protected classes of employees are statistically more likely to have criminal records than the general population. The use of such criteria would tend to disqualify more of these minority job applicants than nonminority applicants. Nevertheless, an employer may ask you about arrests if it can show that such information is essential to the safe and efficient operation of the business.[30]
- *Height and weight.* An employer may not ask about these factors unless it can demonstrate that they are essential to the safe performance of the position; otherwise they may have a discriminatory impact (by eliminating members of protected classes). For example, a requirement that prison guards be at least five feet two inches tall and 120 pounds was unlawful because it disproportionately impacted on women and did not correlate with physical strength, a valid hiring factor.[31]
- *Disabilities.* (See chapter 14 on disability discrimination.)
- *Union membership.* You cannot be required to be a union member to get a job because such "closed shop" hiring practices are illegal. But you may be required to join a union or pay dues after you start work. (For a fuller discussion, see chapter 19 on union membership.)
- *Smoking.* (See chapter 23 on privacy for a fuller discussion.)

May an employer request that I submit a photograph with my job application?

Probably not. This practice could be deemed discriminatory if you could show that it caused you to be rejected (or if it caused a disproportionate number of applicants in your protected class to be excluded from the employer's workforce). After hiring, you may be required to submit a photograph for identification purposes.

Must I give my social security number?

Yes. Nothing prohibits an employer or prospective employer from asking for or using your social security number at any time. If you do not disclose it as requested, the prospective employer may reject your application, but you will not have violated any law. Once you have been hired, your employer is entitled to know your security number in order to satisfy income tax requirements.

Can a prospective employer require that I take a polygraph or psychological stress evaluator test?

In most cases, no. Because they are often unreliable, Congress has banned the use of polygraphs and other mechanical honesty testing devices in the vast majority of workplaces.[32] Many states have laws that further restrict the use of polygraphs[33] (and in a few instances, psychological stress evaluators).[34] Applicants or employees may nevertheless still be subject to polygraph testing if they either work in government, in the pharmaceutical or security industries, or if they are being investigated for workplace theft. (For further discussion of this subject, see chapter 23 on privacy.)

Do I get any preference if I am a veteran?

Yes, for jobs with companies that do significant business with the government. (For a full discussion, see chapter 17 on veterans and reservists.)

If the employer is hiring through an employment agency, is the agency bound by antidiscrimination laws?

Yes. Federal laws prohibiting discrimination on the basis of race, national origin, color, religion, and sex apply to every public or private employment agency that procures employees for an employer, or that provides job opportunities for applicants, if the relationship with the employer is ongoing, and if the employer has 15 or more employees and is in an industry affecting commerce.[35] Similar standards apply under the federal law against age discrimination, with some minor differences: one or more employers for whom employees are procured must be engaged in an industry affecting commerce and have 20 or more employees; federal government employment agencies are not covered; and agencies that help employees find jobs probably are not covered.[36]

Employment agencies are covered by the Americans with Disabilities Act if they have more than 25 employees after July 1992 and more than 15 after 1994.[37] An employment agency may be found to have engaged in unlawful activities if it discriminates against, fails to refer for employment, or otherwise classifies a person based on race, sex, color, religion, national origin, disability, or age (when the person is over the age of 40). Also, agencies that deal with only one sex (unless sex is a BFOQ) or that provide information concerning the ages of prospective employees may be found to have violated antidiscrimination laws. Finally, an agency that seeks to satisfy a job order that it knows is illegal (for example, one requesting a young, white male for a particular position) shares responsibility for any illegal act that results from its referral of applicants.[38]

What restrictions are there on a potential employer's ability to check any reference I provide?

There are few legal restrictions on the ability of an employer to check references or on the methods used. Typically, a prospective employer will ask an applicant to sign a form authorizing the employer to request information on the applicant's employment and educational background. Many schools and prior employers will refuse to divulge such information without such a signed authorization. Employers may not, however, ask for references to gain information from a former employer that the law bars them from receiving directly from the applicant. For example, a prospective employer may not seek information as to an applicant's creditworthiness from a former employer if that inquiry would be unlawful on a job application form or preemployment interview. (See chapter 23 on privacy for a fuller discussion of information collection.)

Can I do anything about bad references from former employers?

In general, prospective employers are entitled to contact an applicant's former employer to verify information given during the application process and to request any job-related information or opinions. Any reference that is not intentionally inaccurate or defamatory is qualifiedly privileged and not subject to legal challenge. But if the reference is intentionally inaccurate and it injures your employment possibilities, you may have a remedy, if you can show that the statements made by the former employer constitute libel or slander.[39] Employees are seldom able to demonstrate that the former employer exceeded the bounds of the qualified privilege and rarely prevail in such legal challenges. Nonetheless, at least seven states (California, Connecticut, Indiana, Kansas, Missouri, Montana, and Nevada) allow suits against former employers who tender intentionally inaccurate employment references.[40] (See chapter 23 on privacy for a fuller discussion of defamation.)

During a job interview can I refuse to answer a question I think is improper or not job-related?

Yes, but it may cost you the job. If you think a question is improper, it may be wise to inquire first into the relevance of the question and, before answering, express your opinion that the question may be illegal. Do tell the truth. Your untrue answer to a preemployment question may be sufficient grounds for later discipline or discharge or may cause you to lose a valid discrimination claim, even if the untruth was not discovered until after you ceased employment.[41]

In general, how should I prepare to protect my rights during the hiring process?

First, try to find out as much as possible about the duties of the job for which you are applying and the skills needed to perform them successfully. This will permit you to spot improper, non-job-related inquiries more easily. Second, check the law in your state to see whether a prospective employer may request or require that you take a drug or written honesty exam as part of the hiring process (see chapter 23 on privacy). Keep a record of any occurrences or inquiries that you find questionable and preserve any paperwork the employer provides you. Finally, carefully assess your needs, how important the position is to you, and how far you would be willing to challenge questionable pre-employment inquiries and practices.

If during the hiring process your employer makes promises to you or demands promises from you regarding terms of employment, either orally or in writing, or if your employer presents you with a formal contract, you will want to familiarize yourself with the contractual terms discussed in chapter 3 of this book. You would be well-advised to consult an attorney before agreeing to work under terms you do not like or fully understand.

NOTES

1. *Griggs v. Duke Power Co.*, 401 U.S. 424 (1971).
2. 42 U.S.C. §§ 2000e *et seq.*; 29 U.S.C. §§ 621 *et seq.*, as amended by the Civil Rights Act of 1991. *Also see* Americans with Disabilities Act of 1990, 42 U.S.C. §§ 12101, *et seq.*, and Vocational Rehabilitation Act of 1973, 29 U.S.C. §§ 701 *et seq.*; Cal. Lab. Code § 1102.
3. Wis. Stat. Ann. § 111.32(5). Twenty-four states offer guide booklets designed to steer employers away from questions impermissible under state law. They include Arizona, California, Colorado, District of Columbia, Delaware, Hawaii, Idaho, Illinois, Indiana, Maine, Michigan, Maryland, Nevada, New Hampshire, New Jersey, New York, Ohio, Pennsylvania, Rhode Island, South Dakota, Vermont, Washington, West Virginia, Wisconsin.
4. *E.g.*, *Wilson v. Taylor*, 733 F.2d 1539 (11th Cir. 1984).
5. *E.g.*, 31 Conn. Gen. Stat. § 57:31-511. For a complete list of state laws, see 8 FEP Manual 499:502 (BNA).
6. Cal. Lab. Code § 1102; *see Novosel v. Nationwide Ins. Co.*, 721 F.2d 894 (3d Cir. 1983).
7. *E.g.*, N.H. Rev. Stat. Ann. 31:354-A; N.Y. Exec. Law § 296.
8. *E.g.*, Cal. Government Code, art. 2, ch. 10, § 19701, in 8A FEP Manual 453:836 (BNA).
9. *E.g.*, Illinois Fair Employment Practices Commission, "Guidelines on Discrimination in Employment," Art. 6, in 8A F.E.P. Manual 453:2757 (BNA).
10. *E.g.*, Mass. Gen. Laws. Ann. ch. 149, § 19C.
11. *E.g.*, Fla. Stat. Ann. ch. 448, § 075.
12. *See*, Mich. Comp. Laws Ann. §§ 552-623 (1987).
13. *Hopkins v. Price Waterhouse*, 490 U.S. 228 (1989).
14. Uniform Guidelines on Employment Selection Procedures, 29 C.F.R. § 1607 (1990); *also* "EEOC Guide to Pre-Employment Inquiries," 8 FEP Manual 443 (BNA) at 65; 2 EPG ¶ 4120 (CCH) [hereinafter referred to *EEOC* Guide].
15. *E.g.*, Ala. Code § 26-20-1(1) (1986) requiring criminal record checks for daycare workers and others who attend children; *also see EEOC Guide*, 8A FEP Manual 443:65 (BNA); 2 EPG ¶ 4120 (CCH).
16. 8A FEP Manual 443:65 (BNA); 2 EPG ¶ 4210 at 2251-42 (CCH).

17. *See supra* note 3.
18. *See e.g.*, *EEOC v. Spokane Communicate Products*, 534 F. Supp. 518 (E.D.Wash. 1982). *E.g.*, West Virginia's Human Rights Commission "Pre-employment and Inquiry Guide," in 8A FEP Manual 457:3075 (BNA).
19. *Rosenfeld v. Southern Pac.*, 444 F.2d 1219 (9th Cir. 1971); *but see Int. Union of U.A.W. v. Johnson Controls*, 113 L.Ed.2d 158, 111 S.Ct. 1196 (1991), where the Supreme Court held that employers cannot reject fertile female employees due to the risk of fetal harm stemming from hazardous workplace conditions.
20. *Backus v. Baptist Medical Center*, 510 F. Supp. 1191 (D.D.C. 1981).
21. *Mohammed v. Callaway*, 698 F.2d 395 (10th Cir. 1983).
22. *See* Immigration Reform and Control Act of 1986, 8 U.S.C. § 1324A.
23. *See Ansonia Board of Education v. Philbrook*, 479 U.S. 60 (1986).
24. *Espinoza v. Farah Mfg. Co. Inc.*, 414 U.S. 86, 95 (1973).
25. *Howard v. Haverty Furniture Cos. Inc.*, 615 F.2d 203 (5th Cir. 1980).
26. *Local 53 v. Volger*, 407 F.2d 1047 (5th Cir. 1969).
27. *EEOC Guide*, 8A FEP Manual 443:68 (BNA); 2 EPG ¶ 4120 (CCH).
28. *See* Americans with Disabilities Act of 1990, 42 U.S.C. §12101 *et seq.*
29. See Federal Credit Reporting Act, 15 U.S.C. §§ 1681, *et seq.*
30. *See Gregory v. Litton Systems, Inc.*, 316 F. Supp. 401 (C.D. Cal. 1970), *aff'd as modified*, 472 F.2d 631 (9th Cir. 1972); *Kinoshita v. Canadian Pac. Airlines*, 803 F.2d 471 (9th Cir. 1986).
31. *Dothard v. Rawlinson*, 433 U.S. 321 (1977).
32. *See* 29 U.S.C. §§ 2001, *et seq.* (the Employee Polygraph Protection Act took effect Dec. 27, 1988).
33. For a complete list, see 8A FEP Manual 499:505 (BNA).
34. *E.g.*, Pa. Cons. Stat. 18:7507.
35. 42 U.S.C. § 2000e. *See also* EEOC "Guidelines on Discrimination Based on Sex," 29 C.F.R. § 1604.
36. *See* EEOC regulations to the Age Discrimination in Employment Act, 29 C.F.R. §§ 621, 623(b)(d).
37. 42 U.S.C. §§ 12101, *et seq.*
38. 29 C.F.R. §§ 1604, 1604(b).
39. *Pirre v. Printing Developments, Inc.*, 468 F. Supp. 1028 (S.D.N.Y), *aff'd*, 614 F.2d 1290 (2d Cir. 1979).
40. Cal. Lab. Code §§ 1050, 1053, 1054; Conn. Gen. Stat. Ann. § 31-51; Ind. Code §§ 22-6-3-1 and 2; Kan. Stat. Ann. 44-808(3); Mo. Ann. Stat. § 290.140; Mont. Rev. Code Ann. 39-2-801-804; and Nev. Rev. Stat. §§ 613.210 *et seq.*
41. *Trapp v. State University College at Buffalo*, 30 FEP Case 1499 (W.D.N.Y. 1983); *Summers v. State Farm Mut. Auto. Ins. Co.*, 864 F.2d 700 (10th Cir. 1988).

III

Discipline and Termination

Much of the friction between labor and management stems from discipline and termination issues. In fact, the most frequent claims before labor arbitrators are termination disputes, with disciplinary issues as the second most frequent.[1] In the employment relationship, nothing is so disquieting to an employee as apprehension about being laid off or terminated or the less severe—but often no less traumatic—threat of being disciplined on either proper or improper grounds.

Historically, the relationship between management and its employees has been a private consensual relationship not generally subject to legal remedies when problems arose. Legal remedies for discipline and termination issues were provided only when there was a union setting, a public sector employee, or a written employment contract. Now, however, the rights and responsibilities of the parties to the employment relationship are increasingly becoming subject to statutory regulation. Furthermore, the courts are defining the terms and conditions (in ways not considered) by the parties to the relationship. For instance, statements that the parties did not consider to form contracts are not being held to be contractual in nature. Although the relationships between employers and employees is now more equitable, they have also become more complex.

This chapter considers discipline and termination issues, with a particular focus on the increased recognition by the courts of an employee's right to challenge a termination considered to be wrongful because it violates public policy or the employment contract between the employee and employer. The chapter, however, gives only broad general trends in this area of law that may or may not be applicable in the state in which you are employed. If you believe that your employer has wrongfully disciplined or terminated you, you should contact an attorney who specializes in employment litigation.

What limits my employer's ability to discipline or terminate me?

Your legal right to challenge your employer's ability to discipline or terminate you depends on numerous factors. Public employees (e.g., employees of federal, state, or local governmental units) are protected by constitutional and statutory provisions, by civil service systems, and sometimes by union contracts. Generally, a government employee cannot be disciplined or terminated without "just cause." For a full discussion of the just cause and due process protections of such employees, see "The Rights of Government Employees," another handbook in this series. Employees of nongovernmental employers (private employees) have some legal protections against discipline and termination. Protections that may apply to them fall into the following categories:

- antidiscrimination laws (federal and state prohibitions on discipline or termination based on race, sex, religion, age, national origin, etc.);
- antiretaliation laws (federal and state prohibitions on retaliation against employees for certain protected activities, such as union activity and reporting job safety violations);
- collective bargaining agreements (union contracts containing just cause and due process provisions—applicable to less than 20% of American workers);
- individual employment contracts (relatively rare, except for high-level employees);
- company policies (personnel manuals describing good cause or due process policies); and
- termination in violation of established public policies.

Each of these categories is discussed in this book. Antidiscrimination laws are discussed in chapters 5 through 12, and collective bargaining agreements are discussed in chapter 18. The other categories are covered in this chapter.

If you do not fall under the protection of one of these categories, you cannot successfully challenge your discipline or termination even if it is arbitrary, unreasonable, and unfair.

Why do I have such little protection against my employer's actions?

The generally unlimited right of your employer to discipline or terminate an employee is grounded in the judicially established *employment-at-will* doctrine, considered by some to be the cornerstone of American employment law. Simply stated, this doctrine recognizes an employer's authority to discipline or terminate, with impunity, an employee for any reason—even a bad one—or for no reason at all.[2] The rationale for this century-old rule is that both parties to an employment contract should be able to terminate the relationship freely, allowing each to gain the benefit of an unexpected opportunity or to escape an unsatisfactory work situation. When formulated, the doctrine flowed logically from the prevailing legal and economic notion of the time—freedom of contract. The United States Supreme Court viewed the situation in the following manner in the early twentieth century: "The right of a person to sell his labor upon such terms as he deems proper is . . . the same as the right of the purchaser of labor to prescribe the conditions upon which he will accept such labor from the person. . . . [T]he employer and the employee have equality of right, and any legislation that disturbs that equality is an arbitrary interference with the liberty of contract."[3]

One generation's logic, however, has a way of becoming another's fallacy. The assumption underlying the at-will doctrine is that an employee can move easily from one job to another—either voluntarily or by necessity—without suffering substantial injury as a result. Few today believe that employment can be lost without significant financial and emotional cost.[4] As a nation of wage earners, most Americans depend on their salary as their primary means of support. Continued employment is no longer merely desirable; it is essential. Society also has an interest in the continued employment of individual workers—first, in assuring that its citizens are self-sufficient; and second, in encouraging stable work relationships.

In time, society in general and the legal system in particular recognized that as employers' power over their workers grew, so did the opportunity to abuse the absolute right to discipline and terminate. The first major intrusion on this authority came in the 1930s when Congress enacted the Railway Labor Act[5] and the National Labor Relations Act,[6] which prohibited employer retaliation against workers who joined in union activity. The Supreme Court rejected the employers' challenges to the constitutionality of those statutes.[7] The number of unions and unionized workers grew substantially in the following years. One of the first rights sought and obtained by unionized employees through the collective bargaining process was the requirement that management have just cause for any disciplinary action taken against a union employee.

Union employees today constitute less than one fifth of the American workforce. Most American workers—unlike employees in the rest of Western industrial society—have no generalized protection against discipline or termination.[8]

What legitimate interests does the at-will rule serve in modern society?

Employers argue that they need, and are entitled to, unbridled authority to hire and retain the best personnel they can find.[9] America's economic success is often traced to the unfettered manner in which corporate management is allowed to conduct business. These advocates argue that the less management prerogatives are restricted, the more management is able to run an efficient and profitable business. At this theory's core is the at-will doctrine, allowing managers to place the best available employee in the most suitable position in the company. Employers often point to the inefficiencies of government bureaucracies as the inevitable result of imposing limitations on an employer's right to discipline and terminate employees.

Few dispute that management flexibility is essential to running a business efficiently and in turn to a healthy economy. Those who challenge the continued vitality of the at-will doctrine, however, contend that unfair or improper discipline or termination works counter to corporate success. A termination rooted in nonbusiness-related considerations (such as an employee's race or age or rejection of a supervisor's sexual advance) may result not only in the loss of a valuable employee but may seriously injure employee morale. Those who seek to limit an employer's authority to discipline or terminate employees cite management's experience in Europe and in unionized settings in the United States to illustrate that just cause discipline requirements can coexist comfortably with profitable business operations.[10]

Few on either side of the argument believe that an incompetent or unqualified employee must be kept on the job, and few contend that a termination on improper discriminatory grounds should be condoned or permitted. The debate concerns whether an employee disciplined or terminated for no reason should be afforded a remedy against his or her employer.[11] Employers argue that, so long as the decision does not violate a clear legal prohibition, the decision is theirs alone to make. Employee-rights advocates insist that a person should not be denied his or her livelihood unless just cause exists for the disciplinary action or termination.

Nevertheless, as discussed earlier, if the disciplinary action or termination does not violate an antidiscrimination or antiretaliation law, the terms of an employment contract, or public policy, there is generally no legal basis for challenging the employer's action. Private employers are entitled to discipline or terminate nonunion employees without being required to offer a job-related reason or any reason.

Do some companies provide due process mechanisms?

Yes. Collective bargaining agreements virtually always provide for procedures for handling grievances. Interestingly, a growing number of companies are establishing grievance procedures for their nonunion employees; many of those procedures mimic the systems established for union employees under collective bargaining agreements. Other policies established to resolve worker disputes include corporate *open-door policies,* which allow an employee to raise a work-related matter with any management person at any time, and the establishment of ombudsman offices in companies to receive and act on complaints from their employees.

Two justifications are often cited for the unilateral creation of such procedures and policies for nonunion employees. First, they aid management in discovering and resolving employee complaints at an early stage. Second, the existence of procedures and policies to resolve disputes in a nonunion setting inhibit an incipient or as yet unformulated union drive.

The nature and effectiveness of these procedures varies with the company and the personnel administering them. Among the actual and potential shortcomings of these nonunion grievance procedures are a lack of administrative and moral support for a single, inexperienced grievant; inadequate assurances of protection against reprisal; and the lack of a neutral third party to resolve the dispute finally. Some of the potential benefits to employers are that employees have a clear and officially sanctioned place to take their problems; those in authority may become less arbitrary in their behavior toward employees and may feel the need to support their actions more carefully; and, in general, these procedures may assist in establishing an atmosphere in which employees' views and problems are treated with more dignity and care.

In recent years, Congress and state legislatures have prohibited and regulated employment decisions based on an applicant's or employee's race, color, national origin, sex, age, disability, handicap, and in some states, political affiliation, sexual orientation, marital status, height, weight, arrest record, or genetic trait.[12] If, however, an employee has a claim against his or her employer (e.g., a race, sex, or age discrimination claim), the employee need not seek to resolve the claim through internal company procedures before starting a lawsuit.

Courts in an increasing number of jurisdictions have also permitted employees to challenge terminations that violate a clear and significant public policy or an implied or express term of a just cause employment agreement.[13] The first such court decision appeared in 1959, when a California court allowed an employee terminated by his employer for refusing to commit perjury before a legislative committee to recover damages.[14] The court reasoned, "it would be obnoxious to the interests of the state and contrary to public policy and sound morality to allow an employer to discharge any employee, whether the employment be for a designated or unspecified duration, on the ground that the employee declined to commit perjury, an act specifically enjoined by statute."[15] Since then courts in other jurisdictions have adopted this view and recognized wrongful, retaliatory, or abusive discharge suits brought by employees.

What is the theory behind a wrongful termination action?

There are three basic types of wrongful termination claims: an action claiming retaliatory termination in violation of public policy; a breach of an express or implied just cause employment contract; and a breach of the implied covenant of good faith an fair dealing.

Terminations that violate public policy. A frequent challenge to the at-will rule is the claim that the termination violated an express and significant public policy. In this type of lawsuit, the employee asks the court to recognize a narrow exception to the at-will doctrine, based on the facts of the particular case and a clearly articulated public policy. Before a court in your state is willing to adopt such an exception in your case, you must show that (1) you did something that the law encourages or protects or refused to do something that the law says that you should not do and that (2) your employer disciplined or terminated you in response to your action or inaction. Listed below are circumstances of some recent cases in which employees were terminated and brought and won lawsuits based on the public policy exception:

- refusal to commit perjury or testify falsely;[16]
- service of jury duty;[17]
- an attempt to get his company to comply with the state's food, drug, and cosmetic act;[18]
- the filing of a workers' compensation claim against a current employer;[19]
- the filing of a workers' compensation claim against a previous employer;[20] and
- refusal to participate in a price-fixing scheme in violation of the antitrust laws.[21] In this case, the California Supreme Court noted that this trend in the case law of allowing employees to sue for wrongful discharge demonstrates "that the employer is not so absolute a sovereign of the job that there are not limits to his prerogative."[22]
- A court looked to the state consumer credit protection act as a course of public policy in declaring unlawful the termination of a bank employee for furnishing information to bank auditors regarding improperly overcharged accounts.[23] The court concluded that an employer's otherwise absolute right of discharge must be tempered "where the employer's motivation for the discharge contravenes some substantial public policy principle."[24]

Challenges to terminations contrary to a clearly mandated public policy will typically succeed. However, it is still uncertain as to what constitutes "public policy" in wrongful discharge cases. Given the potential breadth of this concept, courts have been rather conservative in applying the term. The courts in most states require that the public policy be found in a constitutional provision or a state statute.[25] The Illinois Supreme Court attempted to provide a definition of public policy.[26] That court concluded:

> In general it can be said that public policy concerns what is right and just and what affects the citizens of the State collectively . . . . Although there is a precise line of demarcation dividing matters that are the subject of public policies from matters purely personal, a survey of cases in other states involving retaliatory discharges shows that a matter must strike at the heart of a citizen's rights, duties, and responsibilities before the tort will be allows.[27]

Although most courts would agree with the Illinois Supreme Court's definition, a number of them have held that the failure to identify a specific constitutional provision or statute is fatal to a claim of wrongful termination in violation of public policy.

Breach of express or implied contract. Courts are more willing to hold employers to their promises of job security and benefits and have begun to enforce those written or oral promises as contractual rights. Some courts have enforced promises of job security made in employee handbooks[28] and orally during interviews.[29] In the past, courts dismissed employees' lawsuits that sought enforcement based on such promises on the grounds that the promises were not bargained for and were therefore not part of the employment contract.[30]

The courts, however, have recently recognized that the promises of job security made by an employer to an employee should be enforced against that employer. That the employee did not negotiate over the terms contained in an employee handbook does not affect the enforceability of the promise as a contractual right of the employee. The promises can take a number of forms and can range from an explicit statement that an employee can be terminated only for just cause[31] to a progressive disciplinary procedure that implies that termination will occur only when just cause exists.[32] A contract based on a promise contained in a written employee handbook or policy statement is typically known as an *implied contract.*

Oral statements about job security also create just cause employment contracts in some jurisdictions. An oral statement of job security is usually made in response to an employee's question or concern about job security. A statement that an employee will have his or her job as long as he or she does a good job may form a just cause employment contract.[33] If that occurs, the contract formed is know as an *express contract.*[34]

Either an implied contract or an express contract may be changed, or modified, if both the employee and the employer agree to change.[35] Such a change can include the issuance of a new handbook and the requirement that you, as an employee, agree to any changes in the handbook. These types of agreements are typically found in preprinted forms that state that you agree that you are an "at-will employee" or that you agree that you can be terminated by your employer "with or without cause." Signing that type of agreement changes your just cause employment contract—even an express one—to an at-will employment contract.[36]

The difference between an implied contract and express contract becomes important if the employer tries to change the employment contract without your agreement. This is known as a *unilateral modification*. A federal court in South Carolina held that under South Carolina law, the employer does not have the power to unilaterally modify an implied contract.[37] The Michigan Supreme Court, on the other hand, has held that an implied employment contract may be changed by the employer without the employee's assent so long as reasonable, uniform notice of the change is given to all affected employees.[38] The Michigan Supreme Court has also held that an express employment contract can be changed only if the employee agrees to the change and that merely continuing to work after the change is not to be construed as agreement to that change.[39]

Implied covenant of good faith and fair dealing. A basic principle of contract law is that every contract contains an implied covenant of good faith and fair dealing. Under this principle, all contracts contain an implied obligation that both parties will act in good faith and deal fairly with each other. Until recently, however, this obligation did not apply to employment contracts or act as a limitation on an employer's right of termination. Nonetheless, the courts in a number of states have endorsed the view that both parties to an employment contract may be obligated under certain circumstances to treat the other fairly and in good faith, even when terminating the contract.[40]

Courts have held that the following situations constitute a breach of the implied covenant of good faith and fair dealing:

- The obligation existed in the employment contract of a salesman of forty years of service who allegedly was terminated so that his employer could avoid paying a substantial commission to him.[41]

- The employer violated an implied covenant of good faith and fair dealing when it summarily terminated a long-term employee without holding an impartial hearing as provided for under its personnel policies.[42]

- The dismissal of a worker who refused the sexual advances of her superior was wrongful, and a dismissal "motivated by bad faith or malice or based on retaliation is not in the best interest of the economic system or the public good" and constitutes a breach of the employment contract.[43]

Although jurisdictions that have considered the claim are almost evenly divided on whether to imply the covenant of good faith and fair dealing into employment contracts, it presents a potentially strong weapon for a court inclined to limit the perceived arbitrariness of employer personnel policies.[44]

Nevertheless, despite these developments, the at-will rule is still very much alive and continues to dominate the law of discipline and termination. The cases described above are examples of narrow exceptions carved into the doctrine. In almost all states, an employee is presumed to be employed as an at-will employee unless that employee establishes one of the exceptions described in this chapter.

Are there other limitations on an employer's authority to discipline or discharge employees?

Yes, to summarize, the three basic limitations on the discretion of an employer to discipline and terminate are: (1) just cause requirements in public sector employment and under union collective bargaining agreements; (2) statutory restrictions on employment related discrimination based on age, sex, race, national origin, disability, or related categories and on retaliation against employees for protected activity; and (3) judicially established limitations rooted in public policy or in a broad view of an employee's rights under a just cause employment contract.

Management's prerogatives have been further limited by a broadening of classes of individuals protected from employment discrimination by state law, typically through fair employment practice legislation enforced by state human rights agencies. Such state fair employment practice laws parallel federal law and in some states extend further job security to applicants or employees discriminated against as a result of marital status, color blindness, genetic trait (such as sickle cell anemia), unfavorable military discharge, sexual orientation, arrest history, alien status, marital status, height, weight, and disability. A number of states also bar employment discrimination based on political affiliation or the fulfillment of civic obligations, such as serving on jury duty.[45]

Perhaps the newest development in this area has been the extension of job protection to whistleblowers, i.e., employees who report violations of laws or dangers to public health or safety to those in authority. (See chapter 25) Whistleblower protection has taken three forms. First, in a few notable cases courts have recognized an exception to the at-will doctrine on the basis that employer retaliation for an employee reporting a violation of law or a danger to public health or safety violates public policy and is prohibited. For example, the West Virginia Supreme Court of Appeals allowed a bank employee who furnished information to bank auditors about improperly overcharged accounts to sue for wrongful dismissal.[46] Second, two states, Michigan and Connecticut, have enacted whistleblower protection acts that bar discrimination against employees who report violations of law to government bodies.[47] A handful of states have enacted similar legislation but have restricted its coverage to state employees.[48] Finally, Congress and a growing number of states have attached to specific public safety, health, and environmental statutes antireprisal provisions that prohibit retaliatory personnel actions against employees who report violations of those acts to appropriate authorities or who pursue their rights under the acts.[49] For example, an employee who reports an imminently dangerous situation on the worksite to OSHA and requests an inspection is entitled to protection against any reprisal taken by the employer.[50] Title VII of the Civil Rights Act of 1964, the centerpiece of employment discrimination law, provides protection against retaliation for having pursued rights under that law.[51] Similarly, many state workers' compensation laws seek to alleviate the fear of filing a workers' compensation claim by assuring that no harm to a worker's employment will occur as a result.[52]

Perhaps the purest whistleblower antireprisal protection can be found in environmental protection statutes such as the Clean Air Act and federal Water Pollution Control Act.[53] The type of claim sought to be protected there is one primarily in the public interest—e.g., "my company is emitting poisonous gas into the air"—rather than one primarily in the employee's self-interest—e.g., "the factory roof may fall on my head."[54] In providing this protection, Congress and state legislatures seek to promote the purposes of the particular legislation, i.e., to safeguard our environment or otherwise promote public health or safety.

If you are covered by a collective bargaining agreement in a unionized workplace, management will almost certainly have to demonstrate just cause for any personnel action taken against you. Also, veterans who have received an honorable discharge and have returned to their former positions may not be discharged without cause for a period of a year following reemployment.[55] Employment contracts for a fixed term generally require just cause for dismissal as well.[56]

What constitutes *just cause*?

Over the years, some basis principles have emerged from the efforts of arbitrators to determine what constitutes *just cause.*[57] First, the company rule or policy that the company accuses you of violating must be reasonably related to the company's safe and efficient operation and must have been made known to you before your actions, unless the rule or policy is self-evident. Next, management must adequately and fairly investigate the charges made against you before disciplining or terminating you. You must also have been adequately warned beforehand of the consequences of breaching the rule or policy. Management's response must be corrective in nature, and not punitive, and must be reasonably responsive to the severity of the offense. Finally, the punishment must be consistent with prior practices and must not be discriminatorily or arbitrarily applied.

Employee offenses that are generally viewed as constituting just cause include chronic absenteeism; violation of plant safety rules; inefficient or incompetent work performance; insubordination; disloyalty; dishonesty; disclosure of trade secrets; intoxication; gambling; gross negligence; fighting; and participating in an illegal strike. What constitutes just cause for discipline in a particular unionized employment setting is ultimately for an arbitrator to decide.

What is the difference between being laid off and being terminated?

Sometimes it is hard to distinguish being laid off from being terminated. This confusion results either because management has not clearly communicated its intention to the employee or because management is unsure of the nature of its action. Simply put, a termination is intended to be a permanent severing of the employment relationship. A layoff, on the other hand, is the temporary disruption of a still-existing relationship. The focus is on the employer's intentions and actions. For example, if your company tells you on Friday not to come to work the next Monday because of a temporary slowdown in business but states or implies that you will be recalled when business picks up, you have been laid off. On the other hand, if your company eliminates your position and takes other actions indicating that the relationship is permanently ended, then you have been terminated. Some employer actions that tend to indicate termination rather than layoff are: a cash settlement of accrued benefits, such as unused vacation or sick days; instructions to fellow employees or company security agents that you are not allowed back on company grounds; or an exit interview in which the basis of the discharge is discussed and during which you agree on termination benefits. After a period of time, a layoff may become a termination if reinstatement is no longer being considered.

The distinction between a termination and a layoff is not merely semantic, but may determine your rights upon release. For example, you might be entitled to severance pay under a collective bargaining agreement or employment contract if you are terminated but not if you are laid off. Further, the ability to file a discriminatory or retaliatory discharge suit under federal or state law may depend on whether you were terminated or laid off. If your company tells you not to return to work for an unspecified period of time, you may want to insist that management be more specific about the possibility of reinstatement so you can better gauge your rights.

Am I entitled to advance notice before being laid off or terminated?

Before the enactment of the federal WARN statute, American workers were not entitled to any notice before termination. The WARN statute, which is discussed further in chapter 26, provides that notice of certain closings of businesses must be given. Generally, when a union worker covered by a collective bargaining agreement suffers a disciplinary termination, he or she learns of management's displeasure well in advance of termination under the progressive discipline procedures of the agreement, unless serious misconduct is the basis of the termination. Unions have sought to negotiate notice periods but have made little progress.

Company practices on giving notice differ substantially: some companies terminated with little or no notice; others provide adequate notice; some even keep soon-to-be-terminated employees on the payroll for a while to facilitate a search for future employment; and some provide a generous severance settlement to ease the financial burden caused by termination. You should know your company's policy about notice of termination before you actually need to know.

What are my rights if I am laid off or terminated?

That depends, of course, on the particulars of your employment agreement. You should keep in mind some basic matters. You are generally entitled to unemployment insurance if you have been laid off or terminated for a reason other than misconduct and have worked long enough to qualify under the laws of your state.[58] You should immediately explore with your employer the termination benefits to which you are entitled. For example, you should determine the amount of accrued wages and commissions not yet paid, the number of unused vacation and sick days you have accumulated, and the amount of any severance pay owed to you. You should ask about, and obtain in writing, the length of your coverage under the company's group hospital, surgical, dental, and life insurance plans and information on the extent to which you can convert those plans into individual policies. If you are married and your spouse is employed, you should also explore the extent to which you may be covered under your spouse's company's insurance plans. Finally, you should read carefully the terms of the company's pension and profit-sharing plans; you are entitled to prompt and specific information on such benefits under federal law.[59]

If your company terminates you, it may conduct an exit interview to discuss the reasons for the action and to answer any questions you may have. This is a good time to ask any questions you may have as to your rights on termination. For example, in addition to learning what benefits are owed you, you may want to ask about the use of office staff and facilities while you seek new employment. You should ask your employer to provide you with all of the reasons for the termination and whether or not your employer will provide you with a letter of recommendation. Try to assess the type of reference your now ex-employer may make to your potential employers, and ask your employer to speak frankly about how your termination will be characterized in response to inquiries from those potential employers.

What are exit agreements or releases and covenants not to sue?

In some instances, when management fears that you may bring a lawsuit, the company may ask you to sign a document stating that you will not bring any claims against your employer in a lawsuit as a result of your termination. In return for your agreement not to sue the company, the company provides you with benefits or severance pay that you would not ordinarily receive. Courts generally uphold the release of common law claims, such as in a case of wrongful termination or if you signed the agreement because of duress or of company-committed fraud in getting you to sign the agreement. Courts are less willing to allow the release of statutory claims but will most likely do so if a fair settlement is made. The Supreme Court has allowed the waiver of an employee's Title VII claim when the waiver was voluntary and knowing.[60] Federal law also now requires that claims arising under the Age Discrimination in Employment Act may be waived only in a specified manner. The written release, must provide you with benefits to which you are not already entitled; make reference to rights arising under that act; afford you twenty-one days in which to consider the agreement; advise you to consult an attorney before signing it; and allow you seven days from the date you sign the agreement to revoke your acceptance of the agreement. The agreement does waive claims that arise after the date on which you sign the agreement.[61]

If your employer asks you to sign a release or a covenant not to sue following your notification of termination, you should seek the advice of your lawyer or of a union official *before* you sign.

What are my remedies in a wrongful termination case?

If you believe that you have been wrongfully terminated, you may bring a lawsuit in the state courts of the state where you were employed. You should contact an attorney as soon as you are terminated as possible to avoid having the lawsuit dismissed because too much time has elapsed between the termination and the start of the lawsuit. The law also requires that you make reasonable efforts to obtain employment that is substantially similar to the job from which you were terminated. In determining whether or not to accept employment, the effect of accepting employment on your potential lawsuit should be considered.

If you win a wrongful termination claim, you are entitled to compensatory damages (i.e., lost wages and fringe benefits). You may be reinstated to your former position, or an equivalent position within the company. The monetary damages award will be reduced by any income you earned, or could have earned with reasonable effort, in the period between your termination and the court judgment.

If your claim is that your company breached an employment contract with you (a contract claim), you may not be able to receive any additional damages. If you allege that your company violated public policy in terminating you, you may recover additional damages, including punitive damages if the discharge was wanton and malicious. In addition to recovering damages from the company, you may be able to sue your supervisor if he or she had the authority to terminate you and did so with the intent to injure you in a way that violates public policy.[62] You may also be able to sue for mental distress or pain and suffering, however, such awards are rare.[63]

Where should I go to seek assistance in obtaining alternative employment?

You should first inquire at your employment insurance office about how they may assist you in finding a new job. That office may be able to steer you to public or private employment agencies, or you may want to seek out those agencies on your own. You may ask at union recruiting halls whether they know of any employment opportunities. Of course, you may apply directly to potential employers. Perhaps the first, least expensive, and most sensible approach is to ask friends and relatives whether they know of any openings that you are qualified to fill.

NOTES

1. Wall Street Journal, Aug. 31, 1982, at 1.
2. *Payne v. Western & Allegheny R.R. Co.*, 81 Tenn. 507, 519–20 (1884), *overruled on other grounds, Hutton v. Watters*, 132 Tenn. 527, 179 S.W. 134 (1915).
3. *Adair v. United States*, 208 U.S. 161, 174–75 (1908).
4. *See* Summers, *Individual Protection Against Unjust Dismissal: Time for a Statute*, 62 Va. L. Rev. 481 (1976); *At-Will Employment and the Problem of Unjust Dismissal*, 36 N.Y.C.B.A. Rep. 170 (Apr. 1981).
5. 45 U.S.C. §§ 151–88.
6. 29 U.S.C. § 158(a)(1).
7. *Texas & New Orleans R.R. Co. v. Brotherhood of Ry. & Steamship Clerks*, 281 U.S. 548 (1930); *NLRB v. Jones & Laughlin Steel Corp.*, 301 U.S. 1, 33–34 (1937).
8. *See* Peck, *Unjust Discharges for Employment: A Necessary Change in the Law*, 40 Ohio St. L.J. 1 (1979).
9. *See, e.g., Martin v. Platt*, 386 N.E.2d 1026 (Ind. Ct. App. 1979); *Geary v. United States Steel Corp.*, 456 Pa. 171, 319 A.2d 174 (1974).
10. *Peck, supra* note 8, at 46–49; *Summers, supra* note 4, at 508–19.
11. Note, *Defining Public Policy Torts in At-Will Dismissals*, 4 Stan. L. Rev. 153, 170–72 (1981).
12. For a fuller discussion of these issues, see chapters 5 through 12.
13. *See* Note, *Public Policy Limitations on the Retaliatory Discharge of At-Will Employees in the Private Sector*, 14 U.C. Davis L. Rev. 809, 820 (1981).
14. *Peterman v. International Bhd. of Teamsters*, 174 Cal. App. 2d 184, 344 P.2d 25 (195).

15. *Id.* at 188–89, 34 P.2d at 27.

16. *See, e.g., Cronk v. Intermountain Rural Elec. Ass'n,* 765 P.2d 619 (Colo. Ct. App. 1988); *Jackson v. Minidoka Irrigation,* 98 Idaho 339, 563 P.2d 54 (1977); *DeRose v. Putnam Management Co.,* 398 Mass. 205, 496 N.E.2d 428 (1986); *Sides v. Duke Hosp.,* 74 N.C. App. 331, 328 S.E.2d 818 (1985.)

17. *Jackson v. Minidoka Irrigation,* 98 Idaho 339, 563 P.2d 54 (1977); *Nees v. Hocks,* 272 Or. 210, 536 P.2d 512 (1975); *Reuther v. Fowler & Williams, Inc.,* 255 Pa. Super. 28, 386 A.2d 119 (1978).

18. *Sheets v. Teddy's Frosted Foods, Inc.,* 179 Conn. 471, 427 A.2d 385 (1980).

19. Courts in the following states have held that a claim for wrongful termination in violation of public policy is stated when an employer allegedly terminates an employee for filing a workers' compensation claim: California, *Meyer v. Bryon Jackson, Inc.,* 120 Cal. App. 3d 59, 174 Cal. Rptr. 428 (1981); Florida, *Smith v. Piezo Technology & Professional Administrators,* 427 So. 2d 182 (Fla. 1983); Illinois, *Kelsey v. Motorola,* 74 Ill. 2d 172, 384 N.E.2d 353 (1978); Indiana, *Frampton v. Central Indiana Gas Co.,* 260 Ind. 249, 297 N.E.2d 425, 63 A.L.R. 3d 973 (1973); Kansas, *Chrisman v. Philips Industries, Inc.,* 242 Kan. 772, 751 P.2d 140 (1988); Maryland, *Pope v. Bethesda Health Center,* 628 F. Supp. 797 (D. Md. 1986), *rev'd on other grounds,* 813 F.2d 1306 (4th Cir. 1987); Michigan, *Sventko v. Kroger Co.,* 69 Mich. App. 644, 245 N.W.2d 151 (1976); Missouri, *Henderson v. St. Louis Housing Auth.,* 605 S.W.2d 800 (Mo. Ct. App. 1979); Nevada, *Hansen v. Harrah's,* 100 Nev. 60. 675 P.2d 394 (1984); New Jersey, *Cerracchio v. Alden Leeds, Inc.,* 233 N.J. Super. 435, 538 A.2d 1292 (1988); Oklahoma, *Thompson v. Medley Material Handling, Inc.,* 732 P.2d 461 (Okla. 1987); Oregon, *Stocking v. Fred Meyer, Inc.,* 68 Or. App. 598, 683 P.2d 1021 (1984); Pennsylvania, *Rettinger v. American Can Co.,* 574 F. Supp. 306 (M.D. Pa. 1983); Tennessee, *Clanton v. Cain-Sloan Co.,* 677 S.W.2d 441 (Tenn. 1984); West Virginia, *Stanholtz v. Monongahela Power Co.,* 165 W. Va. 305, 270 S.E.2d 178 (1980); Wyoming, *Griess v. Consolidated Freightways,* 776 P.2d 752 (Wyo. 1989).

    The Alabama Supreme Court refused to recognize a claim of wrongful termination under these circumstances. The Alabama legislature, therefore, created a claim by enacting a statute prohibiting employers from terminating their employees for filing workers' compensation claims.

20. *See Darnell v. Impact Industries, Inc.,* 105 Ill. 2d 158, 473 N.E.2d 935 (1984); *Goins v. Ford Motor Co.,* 131 Mich. App. 185, 347 N.W.2d 184 (1983).

21. *Tameny v. Atlantic Richfield, Co.*, 27 Cal. 3d 167, 164 Cal. Rptr. 839 (1980).

22. *Id.* at 171, 164 Cal. Rptr. at 845.

23. *Harless v. First National Bank in Fairmont*, 162 W. Va. 116, 246 S.E.2d 270 (1978).

24. *Id.* at 275.

25. *See, e.g., Washington v. Union Carbide Corp.*, 870 F.2d 957 (4th Cir. 1989) (applying West Virginia law); *Russ v. Pension Consultants Co., Inc.*, 182 Ill. App. 3d 769, 538 N.E.2d 693 (1989); *Traught v. Richardson*, 78 N.C. App. 758, 338 S.E.2d 617 (1987).

26. *Palmateer v. International Harvester Co.*, 85 Ill. 2d 124, 421 N.E.2d 876 (1981).

27. *Id.* at 130, 421 N.E.2d at 878–79.

28. Courts in the following states have held that an employee handbook or personnel policy may, under certain circumstances, constitute an employment contract: Alabama, Arizona, Arkansas, California, Colorado, Connecticut, District of Columbia, Hawaii, Idaho, Kansas, Maryland, Massachusetts, Michigan, Minnesota, Mississippi, Nebraska, Nevada, New Jersey, New Mexico, New York, Ohio, Oklahoma, Oregon, Pennsylvania, South Carolina, South Dakota, Tennessee, Utah, Vermont, Virginia, Washington, Wisconsin, and Wyoming.

29. Courts in the following states have held that oral promises of job security may form a just cause employment contract: California, Illinois, Indiana, Kansas, Kentucky, Michigan, Ohio, Pennsylvania, South Dakota, Texas, Virginia.

30. *See Johnson v. National Beef Packing Co.*, 220 Kan. 52, 551 P.2d 779 (1976); *Shaw v. S.S. Kresge Co.*, 167 Ind. App. 1, 328 N.E.2d 775 (1975).

31. *Toussaint v. Blue Cross & Blue Shield of Michigan*, 408 Mich. 579, 292 N.W.2d 880 (1980).

32. *See, e.g., Dalton v. Herbruck Egg Sales Corp.*, 164 Mich. App. 543, 417 N.W.2d 496 (1987).

33. *See, e.g., Hetes v. Schefman & Miller Law Office*, 152 Mich. App. 117, 393 N.W.2d 577 (1987).

34. *See Bullock v. Automobile Club of Michigan*, 432 Mich. 472, 444 N.W.2d 114 (1989).

35. *See Ledl v. Quik Pik Food Stores Inc.*, 133 Mich. App. 583, 349 N.W.2d 529 (1984).

36. *See Scholz v. Montgomery Ward & Co.*, 437 Mich. 83, 468 N.W.2d 845 (1991).

37. *Toth v. Square D Co.*, 712 F. Supp. 1231 (D.S.C. 1989).

38. *In re Certified Question (Bankey v. Storer Broadcasting Co.)*, 432 Mich. 438, 443 N.W.2d 112 (1989).

39. *Bullock v. Automobile Club of Michigan*, 432 Mich. 472, 444 N.W.2d 114 (1989).

40. Courts in the following states have held that employment contracts have implied in them a covenant of good faith and fair dealing: Alaska, *Milford v. deLascala*, 666 P.2d 1000 (Alaska 1983); Arizona, *Wagenseller v. Scottsdale Memorial Hosp.*, 147 Arz. 370, 710 P.2d 1025 (1985); California, *Foley v. Interactive Data Corp.*, 47 Cal. 3d 654, 765 P.2d 373, 254 Cal. Rptr. 211 (1988); Idaho, *Metcalf v. Intermountain Gas Co.*, 116 Idaho 622, 778 P.2d 744 (1989); Iowa, *Hugh v. Sperry Corp.*, 581 F. Supp. 1246 (S.D. Iowa 1984) (applying Iowa law); Massachusetts, *Fortune v. National Cash Register Co.*, 364 N.E.2d 1251 (Mass. 1971); Montana, *Hobbs v. Pacific Hide & Fur Depot*, 771 P.2d 125 (Mont. 1989); Nevada, *Savage v. Holiday Inn Corp.*, 603 F. Supp. 311 (D. Nev. 1985).

41. *Fortune v. National Cash Register Co.*, 373 Mass. 96, 364 N.E.2d 1251 (1977).

42. *Cleary v. American Airlines, Inc.*, 111 Cal. App. 3d 443, 168 Ca. Rptr. 722 (1980).

43. *Monge v. Beebe Rubber Co.*, 114 N.H. 130, 133, 316 A.2d 549, 551 (1974). *Cf. Howard v. Dorr Woolen Co.*, 120 N.H. 295, 414 A.2d 1273 (1980).

44. *See* Comment, *Protecting At-Will Employees Against Wrongful Discharge: The Duty to Terminate Only in Good Faith*, 93 Harv. L. Rev. 1816 (1980).

45. For a fuller discussion of these issues, see chapters 8 through 16, 24, and 25.

46. *Harless v. First National Bank in Fairmont*, 162 W. Va. 116, 246 S.E.2d 270 (1978).

47. Mich. Comp. Laws § 15.361 *et seq.*; 1982 Conn. Pub. Acts 82–89.

48. Ind. Code Ann. §§ 4–15–10–1 *et seq.* (Burns 1981); Md. State Gov't Code Ann. § 12G–K.

49. See Appendix A.

50. Occupational Safety and Health Act of 1970, 29 U.S.C. § 660(c) (1).

51. 42 U.S.C. § 2000c-3(a).

52. *See, e.g.*, Conn. Gen. Stat. Ann. § 31–379; Ill. Ann. Stat. ch. 48 § 138.4(h).

53. Clean Air Act Amendments of 1977, 42 U.S.C. § 7622(a); federal Water Pollution Control Act of 1972, 33 U.S.C. § 1367(a).

54. *Cf.* Federal Water Pollution Control Act of 1972, 33 U.S.C. § 1367(a), with Occupational Safety and Health Act of 1970, 29 U.S.C. § 660(c)(1).

55. See chapter 17.

56. *See* DeGiuseppe, *The Effect of the Employment-at-will Rule on Em-*

ployee Rights to Job Security and Fringe Benefits, 10 Ford. Urban L.J. 1, 14–16 (1981–82).

57. *See Policy and Practice Series: Personnel Management* (BNA) 203:25–29 (1982).
58. For further discussion, see chapter 7.
59. For further discussion, see chapter 5.
60. *Alexander v. Gardner-Denver Co.*, 445 U.S. 36 (1974).
61. 29 U.S.C. §§ 626(f)(1)(A)–H).
62. *Harless v. First Nat'l Bank in Fairmont*, 162 W. Va. 116, 289 S.E.2d 692 (1982).
63. *Id.* at 702.

PART 2
Compensation and Benefits

IV

Wages and Hours

This chapter covers the laws that set minimum standards for wages, overtime, child labor, and equal pay for equal work. These laws on wages and hours place certain limitations on the terms and conditions of employment that employers and employees may legally adopt.

The most important wage and hour law is the federal Fair Labor Standards Act (FLSA).[1] This comprehensive statute applies to all enterprises and industries involving interstate or foreign commerce. It requires that employees covered by the law be paid a minimum hourly wage and time and a half for overtime hours. It also sets rules on child labor and requires equal pay for equal work.

Certain other federal wage and hour laws that set special standards for persons employed under public works contracts and under government supply and service contracts. These are the Davis-Bacon Act,[2] which determines wage rates for federally financed or assisted construction; the Walsh-Healey (Public Contracts) Act[3] and the McNamara-O'Hara Service Contract Act,[4] which determine wage rates for contracts to provide supplies and services to the federal government; and the Contract Work Hours and Safety Standards Act,[5] which sets overtime standards for federal contracts. Another similar law, the Migrant and Seasonal Agricultural Workers Protection Act,[6] protects migrant farm workers.

Finally, there are various federal and state laws that affect your take-home pay, such as garnishment, bankruptcy, and tax deductions. Other laws affecting wages are discussed elsewhere in this book. For example, prohibitions against wage discrimination on the basis of race, sex, religion, age, disability, and other factors are covered in chapters 8 through 17, and laws pertaining to collective bargaining concerning wages are discussed in chapter 18. The laws discussed in this chapter are very detailed. For brevity and clarity, this chapter provides only an overview of the laws —many limited rules, special provisions, and exceptions are necessarily omitted. You should consult the appropriate agency for more specific information.

THE FAIR LABOR STANDARDS ACT

The Fair Labor Standards Act (FLSA)—popularly known as the federal Wage and Hour Law—is the overall federal wage-hour law regulating employment. It was enacted in 1938, and amended several times since to create labor conditions assuring a minimum standard of living necessary for the health, efficiency, and general well-being of employees and to eradicate the burdens on commerce caused by substandard labor conditions.[7]

The FLSA is administered and enforced by the Wage and Hour Division of the U.S. Department of Labor.[8] The division has ten regional offices and hundreds of district offices throughout the country to monitor compliance with FLSA requirements. More detailed information about the FLSA and other federal laws administered by the Wage and Hour Division is available from your local wage and hour office. Also, employers of employees subject to the FLSA must display a poster informing the employees of their FLSA rights and of where they may get more information.

What does the FLSA provide?

Under the basic wage standards of the FLSA, a covered, nonexempt employee is entitled to (1) a prescribed minimum wage[9] and (2) overtime pay at not less than one and a half times the employee's regular rate after 40 hours of work in the week.[10] The act also sets rules for child labor[11] and requires equal pay for equal work regardless of gender.[12]

The FLSA does *not* require vacation, holiday, or sick pay; rest periods, holidays off, sick days, or vacations; premium pay for weekend or holiday work; severance pay; fringe benefits; or a limit on hours of work for employees 16 years of age or older. These other matters depend on agreement between the employer and the employees, or their authorized representatives. Additionally, some states have laws covering some of these benefits.

Does the minimum wage cover all private employees?

No. The FLSA covers any employee who (1) is personally engaged in commerce[13] or the production of goods for commerce;[14] (2) handles, sells, or otherwise works on goods or materials that have moved in or been produced for commerce by any person;[15] or (3) though not personally engaged in the activities described in (1) or (2), works in an enterprise that has employees who are so engaged.[16] Some employees who are covered by the FLSA, however, are exempt from the minimum wage, overtime pay, equal pay, or child labor provisions; these exemptions are discussed below with the appropriate provisions.

Employees who are personally engaged in interstate commerce include communication and transportation workers; clerical or other workers who regularly use the mails or telephone for interstate commerce or who keep records on interstate transactions; employees who regularly cross state lines in the course of their work; and employees of independent employers who perform clerical, custodial, maintenance, or other work for firms engaged in commerce or in the production of goods for commerce.[17]

Employees in the following enterprises are covered by the act because the enterprises are presumed engaged in commerce: hospitals or residential institutions for the sick, aged, or mentally ill; schools;[18] and public agencies.[19] The employees in all other enterprises will be covered if the enterprises meet a minimum annual gross volume of sales or business of at least $500,000.[20] When the only regular employees of an enterprise are the owner or members of the owner's immediate family, these employees are not covered even though the enterprise is engaged in commerce or the production of goods for commerce.[21]

The FLSA has been amended to include most federal and state public employees,[22] domestic service workers in households,[23] agricultural employees,[24] and in certain circumstances, employees of employers providing contract services to the federal government.[25]

An employee who is not covered by the FLSA, or who is exempt under some FLSA provision (as discussed below), may be entitled to similar rights under a state wage and hour law. The FLSA and other federal wage and hour laws have not completely preempted state regulation in the area of fair labor standards. For example, employers engaged in purely intrastate commerce are beyond the jurisdiction of federal fair labor laws, but remain subject to state laws and regulations. In addition, states may enact labor standards laws that apply to employers that are covered by the federal laws, as long as the state standards are consistent with federal standards. Where state law differs from the FLSA, employers must comply with whichever law is more beneficial to employees. For example, if a state's minimum wage is higher than that required by the FLSA, the employer must pay the higher state wage. Thus, the FLSA provides a minimum, but not the maximum, level of protection for employees.

Are all covered employees entitled to the minimum wage?

No. The FLSA and the regulations of the Wage and Hour Division set forth numerous partial and complete exemptions from the minimum wage law. These exemptions are specific and narrowly defined, with exacting terms and conditions. The following examples are illustrative only. Detailed information is available from your local wage and hour office.

The following employees are partially exempt from the minimum wage and may be paid subminimum wages: learners; apprentices; handicapped workers; messengers; and full-time students working in retail or service establishments, in agriculture, in institutions of higher education, and for schools.[26] Subminimum wages may be paid to such employees only after the employer has obtained specific authorization from the Wage and Hour Administration.[27] In Puerto Rico, the Virgin Islands, and American Samoa, industry wage orders may set wage rates below the minimum wage.[28]

In addition, the following employees are completely exempt from the minimum wage provisions of the FLSA:[29]

- executives, administrators, or professionals (including academic administrative personnel or teachers in elementary or secondary schools);
- outside salespersons;
- casual babysitters or companions to ill or aged persons;
- seamen on non-American vessels;
- employees of amusement and recreational establishments having seasonal peaks;
- agricultural workers whose employer used no more than 500 man-days of agricultural labor during any quarter of the preceding year; and agricultural employees who are

members of the employer's immediate family, minors working as harvesters on a farm with their parents, or "cowboys" (working on the range producing livestock);
- employees engaged in the fishing industry (including offshore processing of seafood);
- employees of weekly, semiweekly, and daily newspapers with circulations of less than 4,000, most of which are in the county of publication or contiguous counties;
- switchboard operators of independently owned public telephone companies having no more than 750 stations.

Nevertheless, many of these employees may be covered by state minimum wage laws. Approximately 80% of the states have laws that either establish a statutory minimum wage or authorize the creation of wage boards to create minimum wages on an industry-by-industry basis. A few of these states have minimum wages that are higher than that provided by the FLSA.[30] Employers must pay the highest applicable wage rate.

How is the minimum wage determined?

The minimum wage is determined by Congress, which has amended the FLSA's minimum wage provision 6 times since the act was originally passed in 1938. Currently, the minimum wage is $4.25 per hour. A subminimum training wage of $3.60 per hour may be paid to first-time workers between the ages of 16 and 19, for up to 6 months. Usually, any compensation to be received beyond the minimum wage arises either from a private agreement between the employee and employer or from a collective bargaining agreement between the employer and the union representing the employee. In the absence of such an express agreement, the law will assume that the employer promised to pay for work performed and will require the employer to pay for the reasonable value of services rendered. The reasonable value of services rendered is based on such factors as the nature of the work, the customary rate of pay, and the amount of time. As explained above, in states where the state minimum wage is higher than that mandated by the FLSA, employers must pay the higher rate.

When and how must my employer pay me?

A covered employee must be paid for all hours worked in a workweek,[31] but the payroll period need not coincide with the workweek. The FLSA places no restrictions on the length of the payroll period; it could be weekly, biweekly, semimonthly, or monthly. Some states, however, have laws limiting the length of the payroll period; these laws typically require payment at least every two weeks or semimonthly. In computing the pay due during a particular payroll period, the beginning day of the workweek may not be changed for purposes of evading the FLSA's overtime requirements.

While the FLSA does not specify acceptable forms of wage payment, every state does specify acceptable forms—most require payment in cash or by negotiable check.

For which hours must I be paid?

Under the FLSA, you are entitled to be paid for all "hours worked."[32] This includes the time you must be on duty, on the employer's premises, or at any prescribed place of work. It also includes any additional time you are "suffered or permitted" to work, whether or not requested to do so. As discussed more fully below, hours worked may include time spent in idleness and in incidental activities, as well as in productive work.[33]

Can my employer consider the value of room, board, meals, etc., as part of my wages?

Usually. Your employer may meet the minimum wage standard by adding together the money paid as wages and the "fair value" of certain goods or services given to you.[34] The Wage and Hour Administration determines the proper amount. Significantly, the goods or services must be furnished customarily and voluntarily accepted.[35]

Generally, your employer may not deduct the value of anything provided to you that either is necessary to or an incident of the work itself. For example, if your employer sends you on a business trip, the cost of your transportation may not be deducted as "wages" for the purposes of meeting the minimum wage requirement. On the other hand, if your employer provides you with transportation to and from work during nonwork time, the value of the transportation may be deducted, even if this causes your wages to fall below the minimum.[36] Similarly, the value of tools needed to perform your job may not be deducted, nor may the costs of purchasing or laundering a required uniform reduce your wages below the minimum. Nor may you be compelled to purchase these necessities if doing so reduces your income below minimum wage.[37] The value of an employer-furnished automobile that is indispensible to the performance of your job may not be deducted from wages, even if you use the car for nonwork purposes.[38] Your employer may, however, deduct the value of furnished meals, housing, or merchandise from the company store, if these items are for your primary benefit and are independent from the requirements of your job. On the other hand, discounts on merchandise purchased from your employer may not be deducted.

Must my employer pay me for incidental activities, such as maintaining equipment or changing my clothes?

Maybe. Whether time spent by employees on activities incidental to their principal duties is compensable depends on the particular facts of each case.[39] Such incidental activities may include setting machinery for work, supplying a workbench, changing clothes and washing, waiting for work, rest periods, meal periods, civic and charitable activities, and traveling to and from work.

Time spent on incidental activities that are an integral part of the principal duties is compensable.[40] It does not matter when such integral activities are performed (before, during, or after the workday) or whether any contrary contract, custom, or practice exists. Thus, setting machinery for work and supplying a workbench are compensable activities. On the other hand, time spent changing clothes and washing, even though an integral part of the employee's duties, may be made noncompensable by a union contract or by custom or practice under such a contract.[41]

Time spent on incidental activities that are not an integral part of the principal duties is compensable when performed during the workday if the time spent is for the employer's benefit; controlled by the employer so the employee cannot use it for his own purposes; "suffered or permitted" by the employer; or at the employer's request.[42] Thus, compensation is due for short rest periods and coffee breaks, for being on call on or near the employer's premises, and for doing charitable work at the employer's request. You are not entitled to pay for meal periods during which you are completely relieved of work, though you are entitled to pay for such periods if you do any work then or if you are on call.

Time spent on incidental activities that are not an integral part of the principal duties is not compensable when performed before or after the principal duties are done. The only exception is when such activities are made compensable by a contract between the employer and the employees or their union or by the employer's custom or practice.[43] Thus, traveling to and from work and waiting in a timeclock or paycheck line are not compensable in the absence of a contrary contract, custom, or practice.

Must my employer pay me for holidays, sick days or vacations?

No. The FLSA does not require your employer to pay you for absence due to holidays, vacations, illness, or other similar causes.[44] Nor does the FLSA require an employer to include such absences as part of straight-time hours in determining whether overtime pay is due.[45] Additionally, while many states have laws requiring that you be given time off on certain designated holidays (such as the Fourth of July), these laws do not require that you be paid for these days.

On the other hand, many employers do pay for such absences. They sometimes are required to do so by employment contracts or collective bargaining agreements. They sometimes do so voluntarily as a matter of policy. If your employer has such a policy, such pay may be considered part of your contract of employment, and your employer may be liable to you for breach of contract if it fails to abide by the policy.[46] If your employer does pay for such absences, those absences may be considered part of straight-time, and that pay may be ignored when computing your regular pay rate for overtime pay purposes.[47]

Must my employer pay me for absences due to voting or jury duty?

Although no federal law requires that you be given time off to vote with pay, about half of the states have enacted statutes with this requirement.[48] Typically, the state law will specify the maximum amount of time off that must be granted and will provide that such time off is to be granted without loss of pay.[49] A few states require an employer to give an employee time off to vote without pay.[50] Many state laws contain penalties that may be assessed against an employer who refuses to grant voting-time privileges or who penalizes employees for exercising such privileges.[51]

A number of states[52] have laws that require your employer to give you time off for jury duty. These statutes prohibit your employer from discriminating against you because you have been summoned to serve on a jury. Most states do not require an employer to pay an employee for the duration of the jury duty.[53] Connecticut, for example, limits the employer's monetary responsibility to the first three days of the worker's jury duty.[54] Finally, a few states require an employer to pay the employee's salary for the entire term of jury duty.[55]

May my employer lower my wages?

Sometimes. If you do not have a contract (personally or through a union) with your employer, your employer may lower your future wages and benefits. Your wages and benefits may not be lowered retroactively, may not be lowered below the minimum wage, and may not be lowered because of illegal discrimination (see chapters 8 through 15) or in retaliation for certain lawful acts on your part (see chapter 3).

If your wages and benefits are established in a collective bargaining agreement, any effort to reduce them may be a violation of that agreement, and you should consult your union representative; a grievance may be filed. If your wages and benefits are fixed in a written or oral contract directly between you and your employer, any attempt to reduce them may be a breach of that contract. If you cannot resolve the problem with your employer, you could sue for that breach.

These considerations also apply to a promised bonus. If your employer promised to pay you a bonus and you performed the services required to earn the bonus, your employer's failure to pay it would be a breach of the contract or the collective bargaining agreement, and you could take proper measures to enforce your rights.

May my employer pay me less than a person of the opposite sex for the same or substantially similar work?

No. The Equal Pay Act of 1963 added to the FLSA a requirement of equal pay for equal work regardless of sex.[56] An employer must give equal pay and benefits to men and women employed in the same establishment on jobs that require "equal skill, effort, and responsibility" and that are "performed under similar working conditions."[57] The application of the Equal Pay Act is discussed in detail in chapter 11 on sex discrimination.

May my employer reduce my wages for tips I receive?

Sometimes. Your employer may consider tips as part of your wages if you customarily and regularly receive more than $30 a month in tips.[58] However, such a tip credit may not exceed 50% of the minimum wage. An employer who elects to use the tip credit must tell you in advance[59] and must be able to show that you receive at least the minimum wage when direct wages and the tip credit are combined. Also, you are entitled to keep all of your tips, except to the extent that you participate in a tip pooling arrangement with other employees who customarily and regularly receive tips.[60]

When am I entitled to overtime pay and to how much am I entitled?

Under the FLSA, the basic rule is that you are entitled to overtime pay after 40 hours of work in the workweek, and the overtime pay rate must be at least one-and-a-half times the regular pay rate.[61]

The workweek is defined as a period of 168 hours over 7 consecutive 24-hour periods.[62] The employer may begin the workweek on any day of the week and at any hour of the day. Each workweek stands alone: no averaging of 2 or more workweeks is allowed. Hospitals or nursing homes are an exception to this averaging prohibition;[63] these employers may adopt, by agreement with the employees, a 14-day overtime period in lieu of the usual 7-day workweek, provided the employees are paid at least time and a half their regular pay rate for hours worked over 8 in a day or 80 in a 14-day work period.[64] Other exceptions are seamen on American vessels and police and firefighters.[65]

The 1985 amendments to the FLSA provided an alternative form of overtime compensation for state and local governments.[66] The government, by prior arrangement with the employee, may agree to compensate hours of overtime with compensatory time off (comp time) in lieu of monetary compensation.[67] Comp time must be provided at a rate not less than one and a half hours for each hour of overtime worked.[68]

The FLSA does not require overtime pay for working more than a certain number of hours in a day; it does not require premium pay for working on a Saturday, Sunday, or holiday, and it does not require premium pay for preshift, postshift, or night work.[69] You may, of course, be entitled to such premium pay under an employment contract or a collective bargaining agreement. The FLSA requires only extra pay for weekly overtime hours—generally, those hours in excess of 40 in a week.

In addition to the FLSA, about half of the states have their own requirements for overtime pay.[70] In a number of these states, however, the employee must work in excess of 45 or more hours before the overtime pay provisions apply.[71] A number of states also have maximum hour restrictions that limit the number of hours an employee may work during a shift or a week.

Are all covered employees entitled to overtime pay?

No. As with minimum wage requirements, numerous categories of employees are partially or completely exempt from overtime pay requirements. And as with the minimum wage exemptions, overtime pay exemptions are specific and narrowly defined. The exemptions described below are illustrations only; more detailed information is available from your local wage and hour office.

All employees who are completely exempt from the minimum wage provisions of the FLSA are also completely exempt from its overtime pay provisions. The following additional employees are completely exempt from overtime pay provisions:[72]

- agricultural employees generally;
- employees engaged in the local transportation of fruits or vegetables or of harvest workers;
- live-in household employees;
- taxicab drivers;
- drivers and drivers' helpers on local deliveries when paid on the basis of trip rates;
- firefighters and law enforcement personnel working for small agencies (less than 5 such employees);

- employees of federally regulated motor carriers, railroads, express companies, water carriers, and air carriers;
- salesmen, partsmen, or mechanics employed by automobile, truck, or farm implement dealers; and salesmen employed by trailer, boat, or aircraft dealers;
- seamen;
- employees of motion picture theaters;
- outside buyers of poultry and dairy products;
- certain employees who process maple syrup;
- employees of nonprofit agricultural irrigation systems;
- employees of country elevators with less than 6 employees;
- forestry or logging employees for an employer with less than 9 such employees;
- certain resident houseparents at nonprofit educational institutions;
- announcers, news editors, and chief engineers of radio and television stations in small communities.

Under a partial exemption, certain employees are entitled to overtime pay under a standard different from the normal standard of time and a half for hours in excess of 40 in a workweek. For example, hospital and nursing home employees are entitled to overtime at time and a half on the basis of a 14-day period rather than the usual 7-day workweek, if the employee agrees to the arrangement and receives overtime for hours in excess of 8 daily and 80 during the period. The following categories of employees are partially exempt from overtime pay provisions:[73]

- commission employees at retail or service establishments;
- hospital and nursing home employees;
- employees of certain wholesale petroleum distributors;
- employees working under certain collective bargaining agreements;
- employees who gin cotton, make sugar or syrup, or process or handle leaf tobacco; and cotton or sugar service employees;
- employees of private concessionaries in national parks, forests, and wildlife refuges.

If I earn a salary, am I ineligible to receive overtime pay at the time-and-a-half rate?

Employees who do not fall within the foregoing narrow exemptions often wonder whether the time-and-a-half overtime pay provisions of the FLSA apply to them. At the outset, the law presumes that you are nonexempt, that is, entitled to draw time-and-a-half overtime pay for the hours you work beyond 40 per week. To *deny* you this entitlement, your employer must demonstrate that you are exempt, by showing that you (1) are paid on a salary or fee basis, rather than on an hourly basis, and (2) perform the duties of an executive, administrator, professional, or outside salesperson, as those positions are defined by the FLSA regulations.[74]

Therefore, you are entitled to overtime pay at a time-and-a-half rate, if you do not draw a salary. If your paycheck is reduced by the days, or fractions of days, that your miss, you are generally considered nonsalaried, nonexempt and, thus, entitled to time-and-a-half overtime pay. (Under certain circumstances, employers may reduce the pay of salaried employees for absences taken for personal or nonmedical reasons and for full weeks in which they do no work at all.)[75] You are generally considered salaried, however, if you receive your full weekly pay without regard to the number of days or hours worked.

As a salaried employee, you are still entitled to time-and-a-half overtime pay under the FLSA, unless your employer can prove that you perform the work of a bona fide executive, administrator, professional, or outside salesperson (or work in one of the exempt categories above). Anyone earning less than $170 per week cannot be considered as being within any of these four important classifications.[76]

Executive. To be an executive, and thus exempt under the FLSA regulations, your primary duty must consist of the management of the enterprise or of a subdivision or department of it. You must also customarily and regularly direct the work of two or more other employees, and have a say in the hiring, firing, and evaluating of these employees. To be exempt, executives may not spend more than 50% of their time performing functions other than management.[77]

Administrator. To be an exempt administrator, your primary duty must require the exercise of discretionary and independent judgment[78] and must consist of either (1) the performance of office or nonmanual work directly related to management policies or the general business operations of your employer or your employer's customers or (2) the performance of administrative functions in an educational setting in work directly related to the academic instruction or training carried on there.[79]

"White-collar" and other office workers, such as computer programmers and bookkeepers who do work related to general business operations are not administrators unless they customarily exercise independent judgment and discretion.

Doing routine clerical work is not administrative. To be exempt, employees must make decisions of importance by themselves and influence and have responsibility for carrying out management policies, even if they do not formulate them.[80]

Professional. An employee is exempt if his or her primary duty consists of the performance of a learned, artistic, or educational profession, e.g., medicine, law, theatre, and teaching. In addition, the work must require the consistent exercise of discretion and judgment in its performance and must be predominantly intellectual and varied in character so that its output or accomplishments cannot be standardized in relation to time.[81]

Outside salesperson. To be exempt, the salesperson must (1) work customarily and regularly away from the employer's place of business while making sales; and (2) spend no more than 20% of the hours worked in the week (by the employer's nonexempt employees) engaged in work of another nature.[82] Indications of outside salesperson status are little direct supervision, large commissions, special sales training, and a job title.[83]

Whether you are salaried or not, if you fall outside these four categories, you are probably entitled to be paid at time-and-a-half for the hours your work over 40 per week.

How is overtime pay computed?

The method of computation depends on whether you are paid on an hourly, piecework, or salary basis. Under each method, the first step is determining your regular hourly pay rate.[84] Basically, this regular rate is your total weekly pay less statutory exclusions, divided by the total weekly hours worked for which you were paid. The following kinds of payments are excluded when computing your regular rate: expense reimbursements; gifts; Christmas and discretionary bonuses; pay for absences due to holidays, vacations, illness, voting, jury service, weather conditions, or a sick family member; profit-sharing, savings plan, and welfare plan payments; and premium pay for hours worked in excess of normal daily or weekly standards or on holidays or normal days off.[85] Normally, the kind of premium pay just mentioned not only can be excluded in computing regular pay but also can be credited by your employer against overtime pay required by the FLSA.[86] Premium pay for hazardous work, for undesirable working conditions, and for undesirable working hours may not be excluded from regular pay or credited against overtime pay.[87]

If you are paid by the hour, the computation is simple. For each hour over 40 that you worked in the workweek, your employer must pay you at least one-and-a-half times the regular hourly rate. Assume, for example, that you are paid $5.00 per hour and worked 45 hours in a workweek. For the first 40 hours, you would be entitled to $5 an hour times 40 hours, or $200. For each of the 5 hours over 40, your hourly rate would be 1½ times $5.00, or $7.50; and your overtime pay would be $7.50 an hour times 5 hours, or $37.50. Your total pay for the week would be $200 plus $37.50, or $237.50.

If you are paid on a piecework basis, your regular pay rate is determined by dividing your total weekly earnings by the total number of hours you worked that week.[88] For each hour over 40 worked in that week, you are entitled to overtime pay of at least one-half the regular rate, in addition to your full piecework earnings.[89] Suppose, for example, that you produced enough units to earn $225 during a 45-hour week. The regular pay rate for that week would be $225, divided by 45, or $5. You would be entitled to overtime pay of $2.50 (half the regular rate) for each of the 5 overtime hours, or $12.50. Your total pay for the week would be $225 plus $12.50, or $237.50.

Alternatively, before the work is performed, a pieceworker and an employer may agree to compute overtime at the rate of one-and-a-half times the piece rate for each piece produced during overtime hours. The piece rate used in this overtime computation must be the one actually paid during the straight-time and must be enough to yield the minimum wage for each straight-time hour.[90]

If you are paid a salary for a specified number of hours each week, your regular pay rate is determined simply by dividing your salary by the specified number of hours. If, however, you are paid a salary for an unspecified or varying number of hours each week, the regular pay rate is determined by dividing your salary by the number of hours actually worked each week.[91] For each hour over 40 worked in a workweek, you are entitled to one-half the regular rate, in addition to the salary.[92] Assume, for example, that your hours of work vary each week and that you are paid $300 a week for whatever hours you actually work. If you worked 50 hours in a workweek, the regular pay rate for that week would be $300 divided by 50 hours, or $6 an hour. For each of the 10 overtime hours, you would be entitled to $3 an hour (one-half the regular rate), for a total of $30 in overtime pay. Your total pay for the week would be $300 plus $30, or $330.

If you are paid a salary on other than a weekly basis, your weekly pay must be determined before computing the regular rate and overtime. If the salary is for a half month, your weekly pay is determined by multiplying your salary by 24 (the number of pay periods in a year) and then dividing the product by 52 (the weeks in a year). Similarly, for a monthly salary, multiply by 12, and divide the product by 52.[93]

May children work?

Yes, under certain conditions. The FLSA contains provisions regulating the ages at which children may work and the hours they may work.[94] A few other federal laws have special provisions regarding child labor, and every state has laws regulating child labor. Many of these state laws require that a child be a certain age before being allowed to work in certain industries, particularly hazardous industries, and many of them have provisions governing such matters as schooling and rest periods that must be followed when children are employed. An employer is required to abide by the highest child labor standards that are applicable to it.

These provisions are designed to protect the educational opportunities of children and to prohibit their employment in jobs detrimental to their health or well-being.[95]

In what circumstances may a child work?

Whether a child may work depends on numerous factors, including the child's age, the kind of work involved, who the employer is, and when the work is performed. The only exemptions from the child labor provisions of the FLSA are performing in radio, television, movie, or theatrical productions and working in certain agricultural jobs.[96] The FLSA regulations on child labor differ for nonfarm and farm work, generally being more lax for farm work.

Nonfarm work. A person 18 years of age or older may do any job, whether hazardous or not, for unlimited hours.[97] A 16- or 17-year-old may do any nonhazardous job for unlimited hours.[98] Lists of nonfarm jobs deemed too hazardous for anyone under 18 are available from your local wage and hour office.

A 14- or 15-year-old may work outside of school hours in a nonhazardous, nonmanufacturing, nonmining job under certain conditions.[99] The child may work no more than 3 hours on a school day, 18 hours in a school week, 8 hours on a nonschool day, or 40 hours in a nonschool week.[100] The child may not begin work before 7:00 A.M. or end work after 7:00 P.M., except from June 1 through Labor Day, when work must end by 9:00 P.M.[101]

Farm work. A person 16 years of age or older may do any farm job, whether hazardous or not, for unlimited hours. A 14- or 15-year-old may do any nonhazardous farm job outside of school hours;[102] lists of farm jobs deemed too hazardous for anyone under 16 are available from your local wage-and-hour office.

A 12- or 13-year-old may work in a nonhazardous farm job outside of school hours either with parental consent or on the same farm as a parent or guardian.[103] Under age 12, a child may work only outside of school hours on a farm owned or operated by a parent or guardian or with the parent's written consent in a nonhazardous job on a farm exempt from minimum wage requirements.[104] Under limited circumstances prescribed by the secretary of labor, a 10- or 11-year-old may hand-harvest short season crops, outside of school hours and for no more than 8 weeks between June 1 and October 15, for a local employer who has received approval from the secretary of labor.[105]

A child of any age may work at even a hazardous job for a parent or guardian on a farm owned or operated by that parent or guardian.[106]

What should I do if I think my wage-hour rights have been violated?

You should contact your local wage and hour office, which may provide you with free information and advice. Furthermore, an FLSA compliance officer may investigate your complaint to determine whether your employer's practices comply with the FLSA. These compliance offices have broad powers to enter upon the employer's premises to inspect and copy records and to question employees and employers.[107] Even in the absence of an employee complaint, FLSA compliance officers investigate employers by periodically inspecting employer records, by spot checking suspected violators, and by reinspecting past violators.

If an FLSA official finds a violation, several things could happen. Generally, the official will try to bring the employer into voluntary compliance with the law by recommending changes in employment practices and by inducing the employer to pay any backwages due to employees.[108] The Wage and Hour Division may supervise payment of these backwages.

If the employer does not voluntarily comply with the FLSA, the secretary of labor may sue for backpay and an equal amount of liquidated damages.[109] The secretary may also sue for an injunction to restrain an employer from future violations of the law, including the unlawful failure to pay proper minimum wage, overtime, and equal pay compensation.[110] The secretary may bring a lawsuit for backpay, or an injunction suit, or both, without employee consent.[111]

As an employee, you may file a private lawsuit for backpay and an equal amount as liquidated damages, plus attorney's fees and court costs.[112] In such a private suit, the court may deny or reduce the liquidated damages if your employer acted in good faith.[113] You may not sue, however, if you have been paid backwages under the supervision of the Wage and Hour Division or if the secretary has already filed a suit to recover the wages.[114]

An FLSA wage suit, whether brought by the secretary of labor or by an employee, must be started within 2 years of a nonwillful violation, or within 3 years for a willful violation.[115] The 2- or 3-year period begins when the wages become due and the employer fails to pay them.[116] A willful violation is one where the employer knew or showed reckless disregard for the matter of whether its conduct was prohibited by the act.[117]

In addition to the above sanctions, an employer who willfully violates the FLSA may be criminally prosecuted and fined up to $10,000 for a first conviction.[118] A second conviction may result in a 6-month prison term, in addition to the fine. Criminal prosecutions may be brought any time within 5 years after the violation.[119] An employer who violates the child labor provisions is subject to a $1,000 civil penalty for each violation.[120]

It is illegal for an employer to fire or otherwise discriminate against an employee for filing a complaint, or for instituting, or causing to be instituted, any proceeding under or related to the FLSA, or for participating in any proceeding under or related to the FLSA.[121]

OTHER FEDERAL WAGE-HOUR LAWS

This section briefly discusses the federal laws regulating the wages and hours of employees working under public works contracts, government supply and service contracts, and contracts for federally financed and assisted projects. These laws exhibit considerable interlocking with each other and with the FLSA. The result is a complex patchwork of coverage, with some overlapping coverage and some anomalous gaps in coverage. Generally, these laws and the FLSA are supplementary, not mutually exclusive. Thus, an employer may be subject to one or more of these wage and hour laws while still being subject to all of the requirements of the FLSA.

This section also covers special provisions pertaining to migrant farm workers.

What are the wage and hour laws for employees under a public works contract?

The Davis-Bacon Act,[122] enacted in 1931, guarantees minimum wages and fringe benefits for laborers and mechanics employed by contractors or subcontractors on federal contracts for more than $2,000 to construct, alter, or repair public buildings or public works.

Employees under such a public contract must be paid at least the wage rate found by the secretary of labor to be prevailing for corresponding workers employed on similar projects in the locale in which the work is to be performed. The act was passed to protect employees from substandard earnings by fixing minimum wages and benefits; it also protects local union workers from being displaced or undercut by nonunion workers willing to work for less.

Employees under a public contract must be paid not only the prevailing wage rates but also the prevailing fringe benefits—or equally valuable fringe benefits or supplemental wages equivalent to the value of those benefits. Thus, any fringe benefit prevailing in the area must be matched, including medical or hospital care; pensions; life, disability, sickness, and accident insurance; vacation and holiday pay; unemployment benefits; and training programs. When an employee receives supplemental wages in lieu of fringe benefits, these supplements are excluded from the base pay rate used for overtime pay purposes.

The Contract Work Hours and Safety Standards Act,[123] enacted in 1962, requires, among other things, that all laborers and mechanics covered by the Davis-Bacon Act receive overtime pay of at least one-and-a-half times the basic rate of pay for hours in excess of 40 per week.[124]

The Miller Act[125] requires the prime contractor on a public contract exceeding $25,000 to furnish a bond protecting the payment of wages to all workers not only laborers and mechanics on the project. An employee who is not paid within 90 days after finishing work on a project can sue directly on these bonds. Also, trustees of an employees' health and welfare fund can recover delinquent employer contributions under these bonds. The government can waive these bonds on certain foreign, "cost-plus," or military projects.

If an employer violates the law covering employment under a public contract, the government may terminate the contract, withhold payment on the contract in order to pay the workers, and blacklist the employer. In addition, if the withheld payments are insufficient to pay the amounts owed to the laborers and mechanics as minimum wages, the workers may sue the contractors and their sureties (which are required by the Miller Act) directly for recovery.

What are the wage and hour laws for employees under contracts for federally financed or assisted projects?

Contracts for projects that are wholly or partly financed or assisted by federal money are covered by the Contract Work Hours and Safety Standards Act (regarding overtime); but such contracts are not automatically covered by the Davis-Bacon Act (regarding prevailing wage rates) or the Service Contract Act (discussed below). As a result, dozens of statutes pertaining to specific federally financed or assisted projects contain provisions extending the Davis-Bacon wage standards to laborers and mechanics employed on such projects. These statutes include the Federal-Aid Highway Act of 1956, the Area Redevelopment Act, the federal Airport Act, the Equal Opportunity Act of 1964, and statutes for the construction of hospitals, schools, and community facilities. [126] In addition, the National Foundation on the Arts and Humanities Act of 1965 [127] effectively extends the Davis-Bacon Act provisions not only to laborers and mechanics but also to professionals retained under programs financed under that act by the National Foundation on the Arts and the Humanities, or any of its subdivisions or agents.

What are the wage-and-hour laws for employees under government supply contracts?

The Walsh-Healey Act [128] (also known as the Public Contracts Act), enacted in 1936, provides that all employees (except executives, administrators, professionals, and office, custodial and maintenance employees) who work under a contract to supply the federal government with materials, supplies, articles, or equipment for more than $10,000 are protected by minimum wage and overtime pay requirements and by safety and health standards. This act was designed to use the leverage of the government's immense purchasing power to raise labor standards.

Under the Walsh-Healey Act, the secretary of labor fixes specific minimum hourly rates for particular industries and a general minimum hourly rate for all other industries. These minimum rates are fixed on the basis of prevailing minimum rates in the industry or in similar industries. This act also provides that employees under a government supply contract must receive overtime pay of at least one and a half times the basic rate of pay for hours in excess of 40 per week. Unlike the Davis-Bacon Act and the Service Contract Act (discussed below), the Walsh-Healey Act provides no right to prevailing fringe benefits.[129]

In addition to the minimum wage and overtime pay standards, the Walsh-Healey Act prohibits the employment of boys under age 16 and girls under age 18[130] and of convict labor under the contract; it also requires safe and sanitary working conditions.[131]

If an employer violates the Walsh-Healey Act, the government can cancel the contract and blacklist the employer.[132] Unlike the FLSA, the Walsh-Healey Act does not authorize employees' suits for recovery of unpaid compensation, liquidated damages, or attorney's fees, but it does provide for collection by the federal government of unpaid compensation for the benefit of employees.[133]

What are the wage and hour laws for employees under government service contracts?

The Service Contract Act (SCA), sometimes called the McNamara-O'Hara Act,[134] was enacted in 1965 and amended in 1972. The act requires payment of minimum wages and fringe benefits to employees who work under a contract with the federal government when the principal purpose of the contract is to furnish services through service employees; the SCA also requires safe and sanitary working conditions under such contracts. Regardless of the contract amount, all service and nonservice employees under the contract must be paid at least the minimum wage specified by the FLSA. If the contract amount exceeds $2,500, the service employees must be paid minimum wages and fringe benefits at rates determined by the secretary of labor to be the prevailing rates and benefits for such employees in the locality where the services are performed. If the employees under the contract are covered by a collective bargaining agreement, the secretary must take into account the agreement's wages and fringe benefits. As under the Davis-Bacon Act, the fringe benefits obligation may be fulfilled by any combination of fringe benefits or supplemental cash wages equal to the value of the standard fringe benefits.

The SCA itself does not provide for overtime pay, but the service employees covered by the SCA may be entitled to overtime pay under other federal laws, including the Contract Work Hours and Safety Standards Act (for laborers and mechanics), the Walsh-Healey Act (for employees of supply contractors), and the FLSA (for employees who are covered and not exempt under this general law).

What protections exist for farm workers?

The Migrant and Seasonal Agricultural workers Protection Act (MSPA)[135] is designed to protect migrant and seasonal agricultural workers, producers of agricultural products, and the general public from abuse by "irresponsible" farm labor contractors.[136] A farm labor contractor is someone paid to recruit, solicit, hire, furnish, or transport migrant or seasonal agricultural workers (excluding members of the worker's immediate family). Migrant agricultural workers are workers who are employed in agricultural employment of a seasonal or other temporary nature and who are required to be away from their permanent homes overnight; seasonal agricultural workers are workers who are employed in agricultural employment of a seasonal or other temporary nature and who are not required to be away from their permanent homes overnight when employed in certain field work or in certain related canning or processing operations.[137] Labor unions are explicitly exempt from the act.[138]

The MSPA requires a farm labor contractor and a farm labor contractor employee to obtain a certificate of registration from the secretary of labor and to comply with all provisions of the MSPA.[139] Administration and enforcement of the MSPA is handled by the Wage and Hour Division of the Department of Labor.[140]

To qualify for a certificate of registration, an applicant must file an affidavit stating the applicant's permanent place of residence and conduct and method of operation as a farm labor contractor;[141] a set of fingerprints;[142] a statement identifying all vehicles to be used for transporting migrant workers and all property to be used for their housing, together with proof that the property conforms with federal and state safety and health standards; and a designation of the secretary as agent for service of process in any action against the farm labor contractor who has left the jurisdiction in which the action is commenced or who is otherwise unavailable.[143]

A certificate will not be issued to a person who has done any of the following: made false statements in the application; failed to comply with the act or any regulation under the act; failed to perform agreements entered into or to comply with the terms of any working arrangements made with migrant workers, without justification; recruited or employed, or assisted another in recruiting or employing, illegal aliens; given misleading or false information to migrant workers regarding employment; failed to perform agreements entered into or to comply with the terms of any working arrangements made with migrant workers, without justification; or been convicted of any crime involving gambling or the sale of alcoholic beverages incident to activities as a farm labor contractor, or been convicted of robbery, extortion, bribery, or similar crimes.[144]

After a certificate has been issued, each farm labor contractor and each farm labor contractor employee must carry it at all times while engaging in farm labor contracting activities and must display it upon request.[145] Each pay period, the farm labor contractor is required to give workers detailed information, in the workers' own language, concerning wages and deductions.[146] The MSPA also governs housing controlled by farm labor contractors for farm workers[147] and requires such contractors to fulfill other obligations designed to protect the interests of farm workers. A farm labor contractor who is found to have knowingly violated the MSPA may be liable for civil damages of $500 per plaintiff per violation[148] and for criminal fines (not to exceed $1,000 for a first offense or $10,000 for any subsequent offenses) and penalties.[149]

If you are aggrieved by the violation of any provision of the act, you may sue in federal court. You need not exhaust your administrative remedies first.[150] The court may appoint an attorney for you. If the contractor is found to have intentionally violated the act, the court may award damages up to the amount of your actual damages or $500 for each violation (with a $500,000 limit in class actions) and may grant equitable relief.[151]

Retaliation for filing a complaint or for instituting any proceeding under the act is prohibited.[152] If you believe that you have been discriminated against, you can file a complaint with the secretary of labor.[153] Any attempted waiver of your rights against a farm labor contractor is void.[154]

The MSPA is intended to supplement other state[155] and federal laws which protect migrant and seasonal workers. Specifically, migrant workers are protected by the FLSA, and an employer who violates the regulations of the MSPA and FLSA may be liable for liquidated damages under both acts.[156]

OTHER LAWS AFFECTING WAGES AND HOURS

Your wages and hours are also directly and indirectly affected by other federal and state laws.[157] The amount of your take home pay may be substantially affected by such things as tax deductions and wage garnishments. Some of the laws that may affect your paycheck are discussed in this final section on wages and hours.

What can my employer deduct from my gross pay?

Virtually all employers are required to withhold federal and state income taxes and social security taxes from your wages. The amount of the income tax deducted from your wages depends upon your marital status, the number of exemptions you claim, and your income bracket. Also deducted is your social security tax, currently 7.65% (for 1992, $55,500 is the maximum amount of earnings on which taxes are due).[158] Your employer must contribute an equal percentage of your earnings to your social security account and may not deduct his share of social security taxes from your salary.[159]

Although most employers are required to pay for unemployment insurance, a few states allow an employer to deduct such unemployment insurance contributions from your wages.[160] If you do not live in one of these states, and your employer is deducting for unemployment compensation, your employer may be violating your state's wage and hour law. No state allows deductions for worker's compensation.

Almost all states have statutes protecting your wages from unauthorized deductions. For example, Connecticut prohibits an employer from withholding wages unless a law requires it or you authorize it in writing.[161] Also, some states expressly limit an employer's right to deduct from or otherwise adjust your salary because of defective workmanship or lost or stolen property.[162]

Your employer may not take a deduction from your wages to satisfy a debt you owe your employer. Like any other creditor, your employer must obtain a court order authorizing such a deduction, and the garnishment has to comply with the Federal Wage Garnishment Law, which is discussed below.[163] Of course, you may voluntarily assign a portion of your wages and authorize your employer to make a deduction for this purpose.

May I assign my wages?

Generally, yes. An assignment is a voluntary agreement whereby you give your rights to something to another. For example, you may assign part of your wages to a person to whom you owe a debt. Or you may assign a certain amount of your wages to your union for dues or to an employment agency as payment for getting you your job. Upon receiving notice of an assignment, your employer must deduct the assigned sum from your wages and pay it directly to your creditor.

Most states have laws that restrict the assignment of wages. For example, Minnesota forbids an assignment of the future wages of a married person without the written consent of the spouse.[164] Vermont imposes a limit of 10% on the amount of your wages that can be assigned as security for a loan.[165] In New York, you may not assign any part of your wages if you earn less than $85.00 per week.[166] If you are asked to assign part of your wages to a third party, you should check with an office of your state employment agency.

May my wages be garnisheed?

Yes. Garnishment occurs when a court orders your employer to withhold a portion of your earnings for the payment of your debts. Usually, to get a garnishment order from a court, your creditor must prove that you, in fact, owe the money and that you have failed to make payments on the debt.

Federal and state laws restrict the garnishment of wages. The Federal Wage Garnishment Law[167] (FWGL) limits the amount of your wages that may be garnisheed and prohibits your being discharged on the ground that your wages are subject to a garnishment order. The FWGL states that a garnishment may not exceed 25% of your disposable earnings for the workweek, or the amount by which disposable earnings for a workweek exceed 30 times the federal minimum hourly wage, whichever is less.[168] The FWGL defines *disposable earnings* as the income that remains after deductions required by law (such as federal, state, and local income taxes and social security taxes) are made. Deductions that are not mandated by law (such as for union dues, health insurance, etc.) are included in disposable earnings for purposes of garnishment.

The FWGL also contains a special provision for the garnishment of wages for the payment of child support and alimony. Under these sections, 50% of your disposable earnings may be garnisheed for child support or alimony if you are supporting another person; if you are not responsible for the support of another, up to 60% of you earnings may be garnisheed.

In addition to the Federal Wage Garnishment Law, many states have laws that impose further restrictions on the garnishment of wages. Many of these laws establish a maximum percentage of your wages that may be garnished. For example, in New York 90% of your salary is exempt from garnishment, unless a court determines part of the salary to be unnecessary for the reasonable requirements of the debtor and debtor's dependents.[169] If the state rule on garnishment is stricter than the federal rule, the state rule governs.[170]

The IRS is entitled to levy against your wages to collect unpaid taxes. The Federal Wage Garnishment Law limitations on the amount of your earnings that may be garnisheed do not apply to a garnishment to pay back taxes.[171]

Am I entitled to unpaid wages if I am terminated?

Yes. The vast majority of states specifically require that an employee who is discharged must be paid any unpaid wages very shortly after termination, usually the next business day.[172] If an employee dies and is owed wages or other remuneration, most states specifically require that the employer pay these monies to the employee's estate. If your employer fails to pay you accrued wages upon termination, you should contact the Wage and Hour Division of the United States Department of Labor.

Am I entitled to payment for accrued fringe benefits upon termination of my employment?

Generally your employer is not required to pay you for unpaid fringe benefits (such as vacation, holidays, sickdays, etc.) when your employment ends; but a strong argument can be made that such benefits are a form of deferred wages for services and that payment should be made on a pro rata basis. Frequently such a provision will be part of a union employment contract or a voluntarily adopted employer policy. In recognition of this, many states have enacted laws requiring an employer to pay a terminated employee accrued fringe benefits within a certain period if the employer has such a policy or if the union contract contains such a clause.

Am I entitled to severance pay if I am terminated?

Maybe. Severance pay is a sum of money, in addition to unpaid wages, that is paid to an employee upon the termination of employment. Severance pay is considered an employee benefit under the Employee Retirement and Income Security Act (ERISA) and is discussed in chapter 6.

What happens if my employer goes bankrupt and I am owed wages?

When a company goes bankrupt, the company's employees are typically among those who compete for payment from the remaining assets of the company. The Bankruptcy Code of 1978[173] establishes a priority list of those persons who seek the repayment of debt incurred by the bankrupt company.[174]

Under the code, employees' claims for wages, salaries, and commissions are given a very high priority. The purpose of this provision is to protect those who are dependent upon their wages and who, upon losing their jobs, especially need legal protection.[175] Unfortunately, the actual amount you may be able to recover is limited. For example, this high priority applies only to compensation earned within 90 days prior to the date your employer filed for bankruptcy, or within 90 days before your employer ceased doing business, whichever occurred first. Also, only the first $2,000 of wages owed to you is entitled to priority; additional amounts are general, unsecured claims against the employer's assets. As a practical matter, you probably won't have to do anything to exercise your rights.

The bankruptcy judge handling your employer's case will simply order your employer to comply with the priorities established under the code. Some states make officers or major shareholders of corporate employers personally liable for unpaid wages.[176]

Finally, your state may have a special provision to protect the employees of a partnership that goes bankrupt. For example, in New York, the wages of an employee of a partnership must be paid before the payment of any other claim.[177] Additionally, partners are personally liable for the debts of the partnership, so a judgment for unpaid wages may be enforced against the personal assets of any of the partners.

NOTES

1. 29 U.S.C. § 201 *et seq.*
2. 40 U.S.C. § 276a *et seq.*
3. 41 U.S.C. § 35 *et seq.*
4. 41 U.S.C. § 351 *et seq.*
5. 40 U.S.C. § 327 *et seq.*
6. 29 U.S.C. § 1801 *et seq.*
7. 29 U.S.C. § 202.
8. 29 U.S.C. § 204(a).
9. 29 U.S.C. § 206.
10. 29 U.S.C. § 207(a)(1).
11. 29 U.S.C. § 212.
12. 29 U.S.C. § 206(d).
13. 29 U.S.C. § 203(b).
14. 29 U.S.C. § 203(s).
15. *Id*
16. *Id.*
17. *See* 29 C.F.R. § 776.0 *et seq.*
18. 29 U.S.C. § 203(s)(1)(B).
19. 29 U.S.C. § 203(s)(C).
20. 29 U.S.C. § 203(s)(1)(A)(ii).
21. 29 U.S.C. § 203(s)(2).
22. 29 U.S.C. § 203(e)(2)(C). *See Garcia v. San Antonio Metro Transit Authority,* 469 U.S. 528 (1985), *overruling National League of Cities v. Usery,* 426 U.S. 833 (1976).
23. 29 U.S.C. § 206(f).
24. 29 U.S.C. § 206(a)(5).

25. 29 C.F.R. § 541.1.
26. 29 U.S.C. § 214.
27. 29 U.S.C. § 214.
28. 29 U.S.C. §§ 206(a)(2) and (3).
29. *See* 29 U.S.C. §§ 213(a) and (d).
30. As of 1992 the following states have minimum wage requirements higher than those set by the FLSA: Alaska ($4.75), Hawaii ($4.75), New Jersey ($5.05), Oregon ($4.75), Rhode Island ($4.45).
31. 29 U.S.C. § 206.
32. *Id.*
33. 29 U.S.C. § 203(o).
34. 29 U.S.C. § 203(m).
35. 29 C.F.R. § 531.30.
36. 29 C.F.R. § 531.32(a).
37. *Schultz v. Hinojosa,* 432 F.2d 1092 (5th Cir. 1970).
38. *Brennan v. Modern Chevrolet Co.,* 363 F. Supp. 327 (N.D. Tex. 1973), *aff'd,* 491 F.2d 1271 (5th Cir. 1974).
39. 29 C.F.R. § 790.7(b).
40. *Steiner v. Mitchell,* 350 U.S. 247 (1956); *Mitchell v. King Parking Co.,* 350 U.S. 260, *reh'g denied,* 350 U.S. 983 (1956).
41. 29 U.S.C. § 203(o). *See Hoover v. Wyandotte Chemicals Corp.,* 455 F.2d 387 (5th Cir. 1972), *reh'g denied,* 409 U.S. 847 (1972); *Nardone v. General Motors, Inc.,* 207 F. Supp. 336 (D.N.J. 1962).
42. 29 C.F.R. § 785.7; *Leone v. Mobil Oil Corp.,* 523 F.2d 1153 (D.C. Cir. 1975).
43. 29 U.S.C. § 254. This is part of the Portal-to-Portal Act of 1947, which amended the FLSA in relation to compensation for incidental activities. *See* 29 C.F.R. pt. 790.
44. *Boll v. Federal Reserve Bank,* 365 F. Supp. 637 (E.D. Mo. 1973), *aff'd,* 497 F.2d 335 (8th Cir. 1974).
45. Wage and Hour Field Operation Handbook para. 32d 03C.
46. *See, e.g., Olson v. Rock Island Bank,* 339 N.E.2d 39 (Ill. App. Ct. 1975).
47. 29 C.F.R. § 778.216.
48. ·The following states have laws requiring that employees be given a specified amount of time off to vote: Alaska, Ariz., Ark., Cal., Colo., Ga., Haw., Ill., Iowa, Kan., Ky., Md., Mass., Minn., Mo., Neb., Nev., N.M., N.Y., Ohio, Okla., S.D., Tenn., Tex., Utah, Wash., W. Va., Wis., Wyo.
49. The following states prohibit employers from deducting pay for time spent voting: Alaska, Ariz., Ark., Cal., Colo., Haw., Iowa, Kan., Md., Minn., Mo., Neb., Nev., N.M., N.Y., Ohio, Okla., S.D., Tenn., Tex., Wash., Wyo.

50. The following states, which require an employer to allow an employee to vote, do not require an employer to provide an employee with paid time off to vote: Ga., Ill., Ky., Mass., Utah, W. Va., Wis.
51. Alaska, Ariz., Ark., Colo., Haw., Iowa, Kan., Md., Mass., Minn., Mo., Neb., Nev., N.M., N.Y., Ohio, Okla., S.D., Tex., Utah, W. Va., Wis.
52. Alaska, Alabama, Ark., Ariz., Cal., Del., D.C., Fla., Ga., Haw., Idaho, Ill., Ind., Iowa, Ky., La., Maine, Md., Mich., Minn., Missouri, Neb., Nev., N.H., N.J., N.C., N.D., Ohio, Okla., Or., Pa., R.I., S.C., S.D., Tenn., Tex., Utah, Vt., Va., Wash., W. Va., Wis., Wyo.
53. Of the states requiring employers to give employees time off for jury duty, the following states require no compensation for time spent on a jury: Alaska, Ariz., Ark., Cal., Del., D.C., Fla., Ga., Haw., Idaho, Ill., Ind., Iowa, Ky., La., Me., Md., Mass., Mich., Minn., Mo., N.H., N.Y., N.C., N.D., Ohio, Okla., Or., Nev., Pa., R.I., S.C., S.D., Tex., Utah, Vt., Va., Wash., W. Va., Wis., Wyo.
54. Conn. Gen. Stat. § 51-247(b)(1).
55. Ala., Neb., N.J., Tenn.
56. 29 U.S.C. § 206(d).
57. 29 U S.C. § 206(d)(1).
58. 29 U.S.C. §§ 203(m) and (t).
59. 29 U.S.C. § 203(m)(1).
60. 29 U.S.C. § 203(m)(2).
61. 29 U.S.C. § 207(a)(1).
62. 29 C.F.R. § 778.105.
63. 29 C.F.R. § 778.601(a).
64. 29 C.F.R. § 778.601(d).
65. 29 U.S.C. §§ 213(b)(20) and 207(k).
66. Fair Labor Standard Amendments of 1985, Pub. L. No. 99-150.
67. 29 U.S.C. § 207(o)(2).
68. *Id.*
69. 29 C.F.R. § 778.102.
70. The following states have their own requirements for overtime pay: Ala., Alaska, Ariz., Ark., Cal., Colo., Conn., Haw., Idaho, Ill., Ky., Me., Md., Mass., Mich., Minn., Mo., Mont., Nev., N.H., N.J., N.M., N.Y., N.C., N.D., Ohio, Or., Pa., R.I., Tex., Vt., Wash., W. Va., Wis., Wyo.
71. The following states require work in excess of 45 or more hours per week prior to providing for overtime pay: Kan., N.M., Okla., Pa., Vt., Wyo.
72. *See* 29 U.S.C. § 213(b).
73. 29 U.S.C. § 206(d).

74. 29 U.S.C. § 213(1)(1); 29 C.F.R. § 541.1–3.
75. 29 C.F.R. §§ 541.118(a) and (2).
76. 29 C.F.R. §§ 41.(1)(f), 541.2(e)(2), and 541.3(e).
77. 29 C.F.R. § 541.103.
78. 29 C.F.R. § 541.2(e)(2).
79. 29 C.F.R. § 541.2(a).
80. 29 C.F.R. §§ 541.205(a)–(c).
81. 29 C.F.R. §§ 541.3(a)–(c).
82. 29 C.F.R. §§ 541.5(a); 541.500.
83. *Hodgson v. Krispy Creme Doughnut Co.*, 346 F. Supp. 1102 (M.D. N.C. 1972).
84. *Masters v. Maryland Management Co.*, 493 F.2d 1329 (4th Cir. 1974).
85. 29 U.S.C. § 207(e).
86. 29 U.S.C. § 207(h).
87. 29 U.S.C. § 207(e)(6).
88. 29 C.F.R. § 778.111(a).
89. *Walling v. Alaska Pacific Consol. Mining Co.*, 152 F.2d 812 (9th Cir. 1945), *cert. denied*, 327 U.S. 803 (1945).
90. 29 U.S.C. § 207(g).
91. 29 C.F.R. § 778.114.
92. *Id.*
93. *General Electric Co. v. Porter*, 208 F.2d 805 (9th Cir. 1953), *cert. denied*, 347 U.S. 951 (1954).
94. 29 U.S.C. § 212.
95. *Lenroot v. Western Union Tel. Co.*, 52 F. Supp. 142 (S.D.N.Y. 1943), *aff'd*, 141 F.2d 400 (2d Cir. 1944), *rev'd on other grounds*, 323 U.S. 490 (1944).
96. 29 U.S.C. § 213(c).
97. 29 U.S.C. § 203(l).
98. *Id.*
99. 29 U.S.C. § 203(l)(1).
100. 29 C.F.R. § 570.119.
101. *Id.*
102. 29 U.S.C. § 203(1).
103. 29 U.S.C. § 213(c)(1).
104. 29 U.S.C. § 213(c)(1)(A).
105. 29 U.S.C. § 213(c)(4)(A).
106. 29 U.S.C. § 213(c)(2).
107. 29 U.S.C. § 211(a).
108. Wage and Hours Field Operations Handbook § 53c14(a).
109. 29 U.S.C. §§ 216(b) and (c).
110. *Id.*

111. *Id.*
112. *Id.*
113. 29 U.S.C. § 258.
114. 29 U.S.C. § 216(b).
115. 29 U.S.C. § 255(a).
116. 29 C.F.R. § 790.21.
117. *McLaughlin v. Richland Shoe Co.*, 486 U.S. 128 (1988).
118. 29 U.S.C. § 216(a).
119. *Id.*
120. *Id.*
121. 29 U.S.C. § 215(a)(3).
122. 40 U.S.C. §§ 276a *et seq.*
123. 40 U.S.C. §§ 327 *et seq.*
124. 40 U.S.C. § 328.
125. 40 U.S.C. §§ 270a *et seq.*
126. *See* 29 C.F.R. § 5.1.
127. 20 U.S.C. § 954(j).
128. 41 U.S.C. §§ 35 *et seq.*
129. 41 U.S.C. § 35(c).
130. 41 U.S.C. §§ 35(d) and (e).
131. 41 U.S.C. § 35(d).
132. 41 U.S.C. §§ 36 and 37.
133. 41 U.S.C. § 36.
134. 41 U.S.C. §§ 351 *et seq.*
135. 29 U.S.C. §§ 1801 *et seq.*
136. 29 U.S.C. § 1801.
137. 29 U.S.C. § 1802.
138. 29 U.S.C. § 1803(a)(3)(B).
139. 29 U.S.C. § 1811.
140. 29 U.S.C. § 1862.
141. 29 U.S.C. § 1812(1).
142. 29 U.S.C. § 1812(4).
143. 29 U.S.C. § 1812.
144. 29 U.S.C. § 1813.
145. 29 U.S.C. § 1811(c).
146. 29 U.S.C. § 1831.
147. 29 U.S.C. § 1821.
148. 29 U.S.C. § 1854.
149. 29 U.S.C. § 1851.
150. 29 U.S.C. § 1854.
151. *Id.*
152. 29 U.S.C. § 1855(a).
153. 29 U.S.C. § 1855(b).

154. 29 U.S.C. § 1856.
155. 29 U.S.C. § 1871.
156. *Maldonado v. Lucca*, 636 F. Supp 621 (D.N.J. 1986).
157. For a thorough discussion of state fair labor standards laws on a state-by-state basis, see BNA, *Labor Policy and Practice Series, Wages and Hours* (1982).
158. 26 U.S.C. §§ 3101; 3111; 1402(b).
159. 29 C.F.R. § 531.38.
160. Ala. Code § 25-4-54; Alaska Stat. § 23.20.165; Ill. Ann. Stat. Ch. 216(c); Mass Gen. Laws Ann. Ch. 149 § 150(a); N.J. Stat. Ann. § 43:21-7(d).
161. Conn. Gen. Stat. § 31-71e.
162. *E.g.*, Wis. Stat. §§ 103.455; 134.57.
163. *Sears, Roebuck & Co. v. A.T. & G. Co. Inc.*, 239 N.W.2d 614 (Mich. App. 1976).
164. Minn. Stat. § 181.07.
165. 12 Vt. Stat. Ann. § 2229.
166. N.Y. Lab. Law art. 19, ch. 41, § 48-b.
167. 15 U.S.C. §§ 1671 *et seq.*
168. 15 U.S.C. § 1673(a).
169. N.Y. Civ. Prac. L. R. § 5231(d).
170. 15 U.S.C. § 1677(1).
171. 15 U.S.C. § 1673(b)(1)(C).
172. All states except the following require an employee be paid shortly after termination: Ala., Fla., Ga., Miss., Ohio, Tenn.
173. 11 U.S.C. §§ 101 *et seq.*
174. 11 U.S.C. § 507.
175. *In re Bauer Co.*, 3 B.C.D. 1147 (S.D. Ohio 1977).
176. N.Y. Bus. Comp. Law. § 630.
177. *See, e.g.*, N.Y. Partnership Law § 71-a.

V

Pensions

If you are covered by a pension plan, you should know certain facts about your pension. Your plans for retirement probably depend largely on the income you can expect from your pension and social security benefits. It's important to know what these benefits will be and what you must do to qualify for them, so you can plan intelligently for your retirement years. Just because you are covered by a pension plan does not mean that you will automatically get a pension—you must meet the requirements of your plan.

This chapter explains some aspects of pension plans generally so you can better understand your own plan. It does not cover every aspect of every plan. Pension plans vary greatly, and it's important to understand the provisions of your particular plan. As explained more fully later, you are entitled to a summary of your plan's provisions and to periodic reports on your rights under the plan. If you do not understand any provision of the plan or how it applies to you, ask your plan administrator, union representative, or employer to explain it to you.

The federal government publishes several very useful free booklets on pensions. These booklets and other information are available at area offices of the U.S. Pension and Welfare Benefit Administration, which are listed in this chapter. Another useful reference is the ACLU handbook *The Rights of Older Persons* by Robert N. Brown, *et al.* A significant portion of this chapter is based on the "private pensions" chapter of that handbook.

Does the law guarantee me a pension?

No. An employer is not required to establish a pension plan or to continue a plan once it has been established. Nonetheless, more than 40 million private employees—about half of the private workforce—work for employers with pension plans. In addition, as explained later, federal income tax law now encourages employees to establish *individual retirement accounts*, which are like personal pension plans.

What is a pension?

The term *pension* describes an agreement or program under which an employer, an employee, a union, or all of these contribute money to a fund during an employee's working years to provide income for the employee upon retirement. The term really involves three separate ideas: a pension plan, a pension fund or trust, and a pension benefit. A *pension plan* is the agreement or program established by the employer, employee, or union. A *pension fund or trust* is the collection of money contributed by these parties held for the benefit of employees under the pension plan. And a *pension benefit* is the money from the pension fund that is paid, usually monthly, to the employee after retirement. In this chapter we use the term *pension* loosely, sometimes referring to pension benefits, sometimes to all three concepts—plans, funds, and benefits.

To understand your rights under your pension plan, you must first understand what kind of plan you have.

What kinds of pension plans are there?

There are two basic types of pension benefit plans. In a *defined contribution* plan (for example, a profit sharing plan), the employer contributes a fixed amount into the plan each year. The money is invested, and the contributions and earnings are allocated each year to an individual account for each employee. An employee's benefit at retirement is based on the amount in the employee's individual account.

In a *defined benefit* plan, the plan benefit formula sets, or defines, the amount of the monthly benefit payable at retirement. For example, a benefit formula might provide a monthly pension of 1% of final average pay times years of service or $20 per month times years of service. Each year the employer contributes an amount that, when added to past and future contributions and earnings, will be sufficient to provide employees with their defined monthly pensions at retirement.

Many rules apply to both types of plans, but there are differences. The most important difference is that if a defined benefit pension plan terminates without sufficient funds to provide monthly pensions, a federal government agency, the Pension Benefit Guaranty Corporation (PBGC), will insure, or guarantee, these monthly pension benefits up to a set amount. For plans terminating in 1992, the amount is $2,352.27, payable at age 65. The PBGC is discussed later in this chapter.

What laws govern pension plans?

Although an employer does not have to set up a pension plan, any plan that is established must meet certain minimum standards. Most of these standards stem from the Employee Retirement Income Security Act (ERISA)[1] of 1974. The purpose of ERISA is to protect the interests of workers who participate in pension plans, and their beneficiaries. The balance of this chapter discusses ERISA in more detail.

ERISA applies to almost all private employer pension plans. The main exceptions are plans of religious institutions, such as a church, synagogue, or mosque (unless the institution elects to have the plan covered by ERISA) and plans set up to provide additional benefits only to a few of the employer's highest paid people.[2] For each of the ERISA basic protections, there may be a few additional exceptions. ERISA does not apply to federal, state, or local government pension plans.

Most ERISA protections generally apply to employees who worked or were on paid leave for at least one hour on or after the first day of their pension plan's 1976 plan year. Most plan years start on January 1st, but they do not have to. The plan summary states which day the plan year starts. However, some ERISA rules take effect before 1976. The two most important are the rules requiring plan officials to comply with strict standards of loyalty and care in carrying out their duties under the plan, which took effect on January 1, 1975.[3] Also, the PBGC insurance protections generally apply to defined benefit pension plans that terminated after June 30, 1974.[4]

In addition to ERISA, a number of other laws regulate private pensions. These include the Labor Management Relations Act, the Age Discrimination in Employment Act of 1967, the Securities Act of 1933, the Securities Exchange Act of 1934, the Civil Rights Act of 1964, and the Internal Revenue Code.

Am I automatically entitled to participate in the pension plan where I work?

No. Employees working in jobs covered by a company pension plan can be required to meet specific age and service requirements to enter the plan. Generally, you must have completed one year of service with the sponsoring employer and must be over 21 years old to participate.[5] ERISA defines a year of service as a 12 month period that begins when the employee starts work and during which the employee has 1,000 hours of service.[6] One thousand hours equals about 6 months of full-time (40 hours per week) or 12 months of part-time (20 hours per week) work.

As an alternative to the 1,000-hour rule, plans may require employees to complete a continuous year of employment beginning when the employee starts work, before an employee must be allowed to participate. If the plan uses this rule, continuous periods of full- or part-time work must be counted. Absences from work of less than one year do not break your continuous service and must also be counted.

Can older workers be kept from participating in pension plans?

Generally, no. However, before 1988, certain plans, called *defined benefit plans*, were permitted to exclude employees who began work within 5 years of normal retirement age from participating in the plan.[7] Defined-benefit plans are those which provide a definite benefit for each employee at retirement. An example of a defined benefit plan is one that promises a benefit of $5 a month per year of service to a retiring participant so that a retiree with 20 years of service would receive a benefit of $100 per month. But because of the rule permitting exclusion of employees beginning work within 5 years of their plan's normal retirement age (frequently 65), a worker hired 4 years before retirement might receive nothing. Starting in 1988, employees cannot be excluded from participating in a plan because they were hired within 5 years years of the plan's normal retirement age. Employees can be required to complete 5 years of service, though, to have the right to a pension.[8] Many pension plans covering low-income workers are defined benefit plans.

After entering the plan, you can earn credits toward your pension. Your plan may have more generous rules, such as permitting all employees to participate in the plan from date of hire, for example. In addition, different rules will determine whether you have worked long enough to have a right to a pension and the amount of that pension.

How can I find out about my plan?

You cannot enforce your rights in your plan unless you know what those rights are. ERISA therefore includes detailed reporting and disclosure requirements.

The plan administrator is required to file various reports with the Department of Labor. These include, in addition to copies of all documents that must be furnished to you, a plan description giving information on what the plan provides and how it operates and an annual report containing financial statements and schedules of the plan.

The information that must be disclosed to participants and beneficiaries falls into four categories: (1) information that the administrator of the plan must furnish automatically; (2) information that must be furnished free within 30 days of written request; (3) information that must be furnished within 30 days of written request and payment of a reasonable charge; and (4) information that must be made available at the principal office of the administrator and other places. The information that must be supplied in each category is as follows.

1. The administrator must furnish automatically to each participant and to each beneficiary receiving benefits:[9]

- the summary plan description, within 90 days after a person becomes a participant or beneficiary or within 120 days after the plan was initiated;
- a summary of any change in the plan description or a summary of a material change in the terms of the plan within 210 days after the end of the plan year in which the change is adopted;
- an updated summary plan description every 5 years integrating all amendments if there have been any; and, if no amendments have been adopted, another summary plan description every 10 years;
- a summary of the annual report, within 9 months after the end of the plan year;
- a statement of total benefits earned, and the percentage of such benefits that are vested, upon termination of employment or a one-year break in service;

- a statement upon termination of employment of the nature, form, and amount of deferred vested benefits;
- if a claim for benefits is denied, a written explanation;
- a written explanation before the annuity starting date of the terms and conditions of any joint and survivor annuity and the effect of electing against such an option.

2. The administrator must furnish to any pension plan participant or beneficiary, within 30 days of written request, a statement of total benefits accrued and whether those benefits are vested. If benefits have not yet vested, the statement must indicate the earliest date on which the accrued benefits will become vested. This statement need not be furnished more than once in a 12-month period.[10]

3. The administrator must furnish to any participant or beneficiary, within 30 days of written request and payment of a reasonable charge, the latest updated summary plan description, the plan description, the latest annual report; the documents under which the plan was established or is operated, and any terminal reports.[11]

4. The administrator must make available to any participant or beneficiary at the principal office of the administrator and other places the plan description, the latest annual report, and the documents under which the plan was established or is operated, such as the collective bargaining agreement or trust agreement.[12]

If you stop working you may be entitled to receive pension information only if you have qualified for benefits, have a reasonable belief that you have qualified for benefits, or expect to return to work for your former employer.[13] Therefore, if you know you will soon be leaving your job and have not yet qualified for a pension, you should make sure that you have a copy of the current plan summary before you stop working.

The Internal Revenue Service informs the Social Security Administration that a plan participant who terminates employment before retirement age has a right to pension benefits at retirement age. The Social Security Administration keeps this information to provide to employees and their beneficiaries upon request, or automatically when they apply for Social Security benefits.

In addition to the foregoing, the public may inspect and

copy all plan documents filed with the Department of Labor and many documents filed with the Treasury Department.

If your employer is not providing this information to you, contact the Office of Public Affairs within the Department of Labor for assistance. The address and telephone number are Room N-5666, U.S. Department of Labor, Washington D.C. 20210; (202) 219-8921. The plan's annual financial report and summary plan description are on file in the Labor Department's Division of Public Disclosure and can be obtained from that office. That address is Room N-5507, U.S. Department of Labor, Washington, D.C. 20210. The telephone number is (202) 219-8771.

If you have doubts about the information you are receiving about your plan, contact the Pension and Welfare Benefit Administration, U.S. Department of Labor, 200 Constitution Ave., N.W., Room N-5619, Washington, D.C. 20210, (202) 219-8776 or the Department of Labor office nearest you. The department has offices in the following cities: Boston, Mass.; New York, N.Y.; Philadelphia, Pa.; Atlanta, Ga.; Fort Wright, Ky.; Detroit, Mich.; Kansas City, Mo.; St. Louis, Mo.; Chicago, Ill.; Dallas, Tex.; Los Angeles, Ca.; San Francisco, Ca.; and Seattle, Wash. Consult a phone directory for the address and telephone number of the office nearest you.

What is benefit accrual?

Once you have satisfied the requirements for participation in a pension plan, you begin to accumulate or accrue credits that will determine the amount of your pension. Normally, the size of the pension is based largely on the number of years of service you have after becoming a participant in the plan. Under ERISA, if you have worked at least 1,000 hours during a year, you must be credited as having accrued at least some benefits that year. An employer is permitted by ERISA to require you to work more than 1,000 hours to obtain credit for a full year of accrued benefits, but credit for at least a partial year of accrued benefits must be given if you work at least 1,000 hours.

The *accrued benefit* is the benefit that you have earned to a particular point in time.[14] Benefit accrual is the process of accumulating pension credits or, in the case of a defined contribution plan, accumulating funds in your individual pension account. ERISA limits defined-benefit plans from "backloading" benefits or from providing that you earn benefits at a faster rate during later years of work.[15] However, the law permits plans to use a benefit formula that provides full benefits only if you work until normal retirement age and reduces benefits if you do not.[16]

To illustrate this point, a plan might provide that all employees working through the plan's normal retirement age (for example, age 65) receive a flat benefit of $100 per month. However, if a worker leaves employment before reaching that age, that benefit would be multiplied by a fraction: years of service divided by years of service that would have been completed if the employee had worked through the normal retirement age. Thus, the worker hired at age 45 who leaves work at age 55 would receive, at age 65, a monthly benefit of $100 multiplied by 10/20, or $50 per month. However, the worker hired at age 55 who works through age 65 would receive the full $100 per month at age 65.

Prior to 1988, many pension plans provided that pension amounts were frozen once an employee reached the plan's normal retirement age and would not increase for work after that age. Starting in 1988 for most pension plans,[17] a pension plan cannot deny benefit credit to an employee for any year of service simply because the employee has reached a particular age. This rule generally applies to workers employed in 1988 and thereafter.

What is vesting?

Although you accrue retirement benefits while participating in a pension plan, you are not entitled to receive those benefits unless they are vested.

Vesting is an employee's legal right to receive a pension at retirement age. A pension "vests" after you have worked for a specified period of time for an employer that has a pension plan.

Vesting is different from benefit accrual, as can be seen from the following example. Joe Smith began working for Ford Motor Company when he was 30 years old. After working there full time for 4 years, he quit his job at Ford and went to work for General Motors. Because Joe worked more than 1,000 hours per year while at Ford and because he was over 21 years old when he went to work there, he was a participant in Ford's pension plan after his first year. And he has 3 years of accrued pension benefits. Nevertheless, he may never receive these benefits. Why? Because current law permits a company to require a worker to be employed for 5 years before his benefits vest. A worker who leaves before his benefits vest may never receive them. On the other hand, if Joe stayed at Ford for 5 years (including his first year when he was not a participant in the plan), his benefits would vest, and he would receive them at retirement age even though he quit Ford long before retirement age.

Before ERISA, plans could provide for extremely stringent vesting requirements or for none at all. ERISA remedied these problems by establishing minimum vesting rules and requiring that plans provide for vesting prior to retirement.[18] From 1976 to 1988, a plan was allowed to provide for a more generous vesting schedule, but through 1988 its vesting schedule must be at least as good as one of the three called for by ERISA— 10-year, 100% vesting; 15-year, graded vesting; and the "rule of 45."[19] In addition, ERISA requires that an employee become 100% vested if the employee works up to the plan's normal retirement age, regardless of the number of years worked.[20]

For most workers, the vesting rules changed in 1989, but the changes only apply to employees who were working under the plan in 1989 when the new rules took effect, and thereafter. If you stopped working under a plan before the new rules applied, the old vesting rules apply.

Since 1989, plans have been required to comply with one of two vesting rules: 5-year, 100% vesting or 7-year, graded vesting.[21] The 7-year rule requires that employees be 20% vested after completing 3 years of service, increasing 20% per year until the employee is 100% vested after completing 7 years of service.

Nevertheless, union-negotiated multiemployer pension plans may continue to use the 10-year, 100% rule.[22]

How does vesting work?

If your employment terminated before ERISA took effect in 1976, the ERISA vesting rules do not apply to you. The terms of the plan in effect when you stopped working will apply.

If you terminated employment after ERISA first applied to your plan in 1976, benefits derived from your contributions are always 100% vested. The plan must provide that your accrued benefit based on your employer's contributions will vest under one of three vesting formulas.

Between 1976 and 1988, most plans used either 10-year, 100% "cliff" vesting or "graded" vesting—5-year, 25% vesting gradually increasing to 100% after 15 years. Less common but permissible was the "rule of 45." Under 10-years, 100% vesting, you must complete 10 years of service to be vested, and vesting is 100%.

Graded vesting. Under graded vesting, at least 25% of an employee's accrued benefits from employer contributions must be vested after 5 years of service. An additional 5% must be vested for each of the next 5 years of service, and again another 10% must be vested for each year of the third 5-year period. After 15 years, the employee is fully vested. The operation of this schedule can be seen in table 5.1.

Table 5.1
Graded Vesting, by Years of Service and Nonforfeitable Percentage

Years of Service	Nonforfeitable Percentage
5	25
6	30
7	35
8	40
9	45
10	50
11	60
12	70
13	80
14	90
15 or more	100

To illustrate the way graded vesting works, assume that Mary Green works for a company with a defined benefit plan paying $15 per month at retirement for each year of service. If she worked 15 years, her pension would be fully vested and she would receive $210 per month at retirement (100% × $15 × 14 years). If she left after only 5 years, she would receive a pension at retirement (whereas under 10-year, 100% vesting she would not). But her pension would be only 25% vested and would be only $15 per month (25% × $15 × 4 years). (Again remember that the first year of service is counted for vesting but not for accrual purposes.)

The rule of 45. Under the "rule of 45," an employee with 5 years of service must be at least 50% vested when the sum of his age and years of service totals 45. For each additional year, the employee's vested percentage is increased by 10% so that not later than 5 years after meeting the threshold 45 requirement, the participant is 100% vested. The option further provides that the participant who has completed at least 10 years of service regardless of age must be 50% vested in accrued benefits at the end of the 10 years and must be vested in an additional 10% for each of the next 5 years of service. Most plans have not used this vesting rule, and it no longer may be used for current employees since the start of the 1989 plan year.

Can plans be made to provide more rapid vesting schedules than those just described?

Yes. The ERISA schedules are the minimum permitted by law. A plan can create a more generous vesting schedule. In addition, if the plan is top heavy (i.e., where officers and owners have accumulated more than 60% of the benefits in the plan), the plan must provide participants with a minimum benefit each year and fast vesting.[23] The top heavy rules apply for the 1984 plan year and thereafter. Plans in small offices are the most likely to be top heavy.

How are years of service counted for the different vesting schedules?

For vesting purposes, the definition of a year of service is basically the same as for participation purposes. The general rule is that all years of service in which at least 1,000 hours are worked are to be counted. As a result, plans may no longer disregard long periods of service because short breaks have occurred, but must recognize the aggregate of all years of service. There are some exceptions, however, and it is important to note that certain years of service before the enactment of ERISA may not count.[24]

Treasury Department regulations also allow plans to calculate years of service by counting continuous years of employment, instead of using the 1,000 hour rule.[25] For example, if you started work on February 1, 1988, you need to work through January 31, 1998 (ten full years) to complete ten years of service. If you miss work for less than twelve months, there is no break in your continuous service. You must be given vesting credit for all days you are paid or are entitled to be paid for working, including sick leave and vacation time. If you are laid off, you must be given vesting credit for one year after your date of layoff.

What is a break in service?

Prior to ERISA, many pension plans had restrictive rules which prevented employees from receiving credit for all of the years they worked. Called *break in service rules*, these provisions dictated that an employee's service prior to a period of absence from work would be disregarded in computing pension benefits. For example, one woman worked for a firm for 30 years, with occasional layoffs for short periods of time, the longest being May 1966 to May 1968. When she applied for a pension, she found that none of her service before 1968 counted toward retirement because her absence during 1966 through 1968 was over 18 months. The employer took no account of the 25 years she had worked prior to the break.[26]

ERISA limits the ability of an employer to exclude some years of service in determining the amount of a pension, and whether the employee has a vested right to it. ERISA requires that a plan participant accumulate one half-year's worth of benefits for each year he or she works at least 1,000 hours. If an employee works between 500 and 1,000 hours during a year, the employer need not give the employee credit for accruing benefits, but the employer cannot declare that a break in service has occurred.[27] Only if an employee has worked 500 or fewer hours during the year can the employer declare that a break in service has occurred, thus potentially affecting credit for benefits accrued in past years.[28]

ERISA also protects workers by preventing pension plans

from taking away credit for years worked before a break in service. Only if (1) you have 5 consecutive break years, and (2) the number of break years is greater than or equal to the number of years worked before the break, can you lose credit for years worked before the break.[29] For example, if you have 4 years of credited service and are laid off for 2 years after which you return to work for your old employer, ERISA requires that you be given credit for the 4 years of service you accumulated before being laid off. Only if you were laid off for 5 or more years could your years of work prior to the break be disregarded. And your years of service prior to the break will be disregarded only if your benefits are not vested.[30] For employees with vested benefits, an employer may not disregard years of service before the break. When a break occurs, however, an employee may be required to complete a year of service after returning to work before the prior years will be counted.[31] Once your benefits have been vested, they cannot be taken from you no matter how long you are away from your job.

Can I still get benefits from a pension plan if I leave my job and compete with my employer?

If you have met the requirements of one of the ERISA vesting schedules, you cannot lose your vested rights by competing with your employer. Benefits vested more quickly than required by ERISA may, however, be forfeited if the plan contains a noncompetition clause.[32]

Can my employer deprive me of vested benefits by amending my pension plan?

Before ERISA, an employer was free to change the vesting schedule of a pension plan in a way that would deprive workers of vested benefits. Under ERISA this is illegal.[33] For example, an employer cannot switch from a plan under which an employee with 3 years of service has partially vested benefits to a plan that requires all workers to be employed for 5 years before any benefits vest. However, pre-ERISA amendments depriving workers of benefits are not outlawed by ERISA; only amendments after the effective date of ERISA are illegal.

ERISA prevents plan amendments from taking away an employee's vested right to receive his accumulated retirement benefits at normal retirement age. However, as originally enacted, ERISA did not prevent employers from taking away an employee's options under the plan to receive benefits before normal retirement age, benefits in any form of payment other than a lifetime annuity beginning at normal retirement age, or special retirement benefits if the employee had not qualified for the option before the amendment.

Plan amendments (made after July 1984) cannot eliminate an existing form of payment for previously accumulated benefits or the employee's right to receive a special benefit that the employee presently has partially qualified for, as long as the employee later satisfies the preamendment eligibility requirements for the benefit.[34] Nevertheless, since a plan amendment can limit how benefits are accumulated in the future, the amendment can limit this right to the amount accumulated on the date of amendment. Supplements to pensions that are paid only until the employee becomes eligible for Social Security are not protected and may be eliminated by a plan amendment.[35] For example, the Retirement Equity Act (REA) requires plans that terminate after July 30, 1984 to provide employees with the right to take early retirement according to the terms of the plan before termination.[36] Before the REA, a terminating plan that provided that an employee could retire at 55 instead of 65 with either a full or reduced pension had only to provide employees not yet 55 with a full pension at 65. The REA now requires plans, if they terminate, to provide these early retirement benefits if the employee qualifies for them either before or after the plan terminates.

A plan may, however, limit the value of these early retirement benefits to the value of the benefits the employee has accumulated on the date the plan is amended. An amendment can change how benefits earned in the future may be taken. The REA makes no change in the law concerning the benefits the Pension Benefit Guaranty Corporation (PBGC) guarantees will be paid in case the plan terminates without the money to provide them.[37]

Will years of service accumulated while working for one employer be lost if the business is acquired by a new employer?

No. ERISA requires that all years of service with the "employer or employers maintaining the plan" must be counted. The result is that when a new employer continues an old plan—

in the case of a merger, for example—years of service from the previous employer's period of control must be counted.[38] If the new employer does not continue the old employer's plan but instead uses his own plan, the old years might not be counted.[39]

When do pension payments begin?

A pension plan will provide when monthly pension payments start, and the plan must follow its rules. Most pension plans provide that monthly pension payments start the month you retire. However, ERISA allows the plan to provide that monthly payments will start slightly later than the month you retire but no later than 60 days after the close of the plan year in which the *latest* of the following events occur: (1) you reach age 65 or the normal retirement age stated in your plan (if less than 65); (2) the 10th anniversary of the year you begin to participate in the plan or (3) you terminate service with the employer maintaining the plan.[40]

"Normal retirement age"[41] is significant for two important reasons. First, ERISA requires full vesting of pensions if a worker is employed on reaching normal retirement age.[42] Second, payments must start within a certain time period after the retiree reaches normal retirement age.

Since there are fewer years in which to fund an older employee's pension than a younger employee's pension, larger yearly payments may be needed to fund that pension. Consequently, ERISA permitted, but did not require, pension plans to provide that employees would not reach normal retirement age and automatically vest in their pensions until at least ten years[43] after they entered and started to participate in the plan. Thus, some pension plans simply define normal retirement age as a particular age (typically, age 65). Other pension plans, to make certain that pensions do not fully vest and soon become payable for older employees until ten years after the employer started funding that pension, define normal retirement age as *the later of* age 65 or the 10th anniversary of the date that the employee entered the plan.

For most persons employed after the start of the 1988 plan year, the 10-year requirement is reduced to 5 years.[44]

However, for persons who turn 70½ years of age after December 31, 1987, the Internal Revenue Service rules now require monthly pension payments to start no later than April 1st of the year after the person turns 70½, whether or not he or she is still working for his or her employer.[45] For persons who turned 70½ before December 31, 1987, the pension plan may have a rule that payments do not start until retirement.

How do I file a claim to receive a pension?

Before ERISA, a worker whose claim for a pension was denied often had no way to find out the reason for denial, no procedure to appeal the denial, and no right to sue in court to obtain a pension. ERISA remedies this situation.

Under ERISA, all pension plans are required to have a procedure by which a plan participant can submit a claim to receive a pension.[46] ERISA requires that all participants be given a plan summary that explains the procedure to be followed by anyone filing a claim.[47] ERISA also requires that an appeal procedure be established, including the following provisions.

> The plan must give you written notice of the decision on your claim for benefits within 90 days. The plan may have one 90 day extension if you are given written notice of the extension before the first 90 days are up. If your claim is denied, the specific reasons for the denial must be stated, with specific reference to the plan provision on which the denial is based. If no decision is reached within the permitted 90 or 180 day period, the claim will be treated as if denied, and you can proceed to appeal. Appeals under ERISA are to be in writing. You have 60 days, from notice that your claim was denied, in which to file an appeal. In most plans, a decision on your appeal is to be reached within 120 days of the time your appeal is received. The decision on appeal must be in writing and refer to the plan provisions on which it is based. To assist your appeal, ERISA requires that plan administrators allow you to review important pension documents affecting your claim for benefits and to allow you to submit written material in support of your appeal.[48]

ERISA does not require plans to permit you to appear in person to support an appeal. In other words, no hearing is required, although the statute does require a "full and fair review." One court has stated that for a review to be "full and fair," the plan must, at a minimum, tell you on what evidence the initial denial of your claim was based, let you respond as to whether the evidence was accurate and reliable, and on review, consider the evidence you submit as well as the evidence used to deny the claim.[49]

ERISA also entitles you to go to either state or federal court to sue your pension plan if your claim for benefits is denied,[50] but you must go through the plan's claims and appeals procedure before filing a lawsuit.[51] ERISA does not specify what the court will consider while hearing your appeal. If your pension plan provides the plan administrator or plan trustees with discretionary authority to interpret the plan and decide claims (and almost all do), then the courts generally will defer to their interpretations of the plan or the facts unless you can show that they "abused their discretion" in reaching a decision.[52] This generally means that if their interpretation is reasonable, it will be upheld even if another interpretation would be reasonable also. This means the court, more likely than not, will defer to the plan trustees' determination of what the facts of the case are or what the plan intends. But the court will determine what the plan's legal obligations are and whether the plan has complied with those obligations. And the court will focus on the evidence the plan trustees considered and might not consider further evidence that was not submitted to them.[53]

Can I work and still receive my pension?

Generally, yes, but there are some exceptions. A person entitled to receive a pension generally will not lose his pension because he decides to open a business or go to work full or part time.[54] ERISA, however, does permit a pension plan to suspend payment of pension benefits after a participant reaches the plan's normal retirement age if a recipient returns to work for his former employer.[55] ERISA also permits the suspension of benefits to a recipient who was a participant in a multiemployer plan if the retiree returns to work in the same industry, trade, and geographical area covered by the pension plan.[56] But in either case, your benefits can be suspended only if you work forty or more hours per month.[57] Of course, you can contest a decision by your plan that you are working in the same industry, trade, or locality. This was done by a former maritime worker whose pension benefits were suspended when he accepted a job with the government. The court ruled that government service was not work in the same industry.[58] If you have not yet reached the plan's normal retirement age, ERISA's vesting rules do not prevent the plan from enforcing a plan rule suspending your pension until normal retirement age if you go back to work.[59]

Also, a multiemployer plan's trustees cannot adopt a rule taking away your right under the plan to receive a pension before normal retirement age because you also work for a nonunion employer unless there is proof that the rule was adopted to enhance the financial integrity of the plan or to benefit plan members.[60]

Can I receive both Social Security and a pension?

Yes, but a plan may provide pensions only to workers earning above a certain income[61] or may reduce pensions of all workers by part of the amount a worker will receive[62] as a Social Security benefit.[63] This is called "integrating" a pension plan with Social Security. Since Social Security payments are weighted in favor of lower income workers, pension integration can have the effect of substantially reducing or eliminating the pension benefits of these workers.[64] For example, a plan that reduces your pension benefits by part of what you receive as a Social Security benefit (called an *offset plan*) typically might provide that you will receive 1% of average final earnings, multiplied by your years of service, minus 50% of the Social Security benefit you will receive at age 65. If your average final earnings are $18,000 ($1,500 per month), you have worked 30 years for your employer under the plan, and if your monthly Social Security benefit at age 65 would be $600, your monthly pension from the plan at normal retirement age would be: $1\% \times \$1,500 \times 30 - 50\% \times \$600 = \$150$ per month. ERISA, however, forbids a pension plan from reducing your pension because of cost-of-living increases in Social Security.[65]

Does ERISA protect my pension if my employer goes out of business or terminates my pension plan?

Yes, in part. Before ERISA, many workers lost their pensions because an employer went out of business or decided to discontinue its pension plan. While ERISA does not require that an employer have a pension plan nor that it continue to operate a plan already established, it does provide partial protection for workers whose pension plan is terminated and cannot pay those benefits. The principal protection offered by ERISA is an insurance program that guarantees the payment of some pension benefits to retirees if their defined benefit pension plan is terminated. The Pension Benefit Guaranty Corporation (PBGC)[66] was established by ERISA; defined benefit pension plans[67] (with very limited exceptions)[68] are required to pay insurance premiums to the PBGC. In return for these premiums, the PBGC guarantees that participants of defined benefit plans will be paid at least some of their pension if their plan folds or is terminated.[69] Only participants in defined benefit plans are protected;[70] participants in defined contribution plans are not protected. Moreover, only vested benefits are guaranteed.[71] So participants in a defined benefit plan whose benefits had not vested when the plan terminated are not protected either. And even those with vested benefits have no guarantee that they will receive all of their benefits.[72] For example, if the plan increased benefits within 5 years of plan termination, the increase is not fully insured.[73] Also, many pension plans pay death, medical, and disability benefits in addition to normal retirement benefits. ERISA requires the PBGC to guarantee only basic retirement benefits, so you may lose other kinds of benefits in the event your plan is terminated.[74]

If your plan is a multiemployer plan (i.e., a plan negotiated by a union with more than one employer), additional rules will determine what your benefit is under the plan and how much of your benefit is insured if the plan becomes insolvent.[75] If your employer stops contributing to the plan, you may lose benefits that are based on your service before the employer began contributing to the plan.[76] If the plan is in financial difficulty, benefits established or increased under the plan in the last 5 years may be eliminated.[77] And if the plan becomes insolvent, only part of your basic benefit is insured by the PBGC.

The address and telephone number of the Pension Benefit Guaranty Corporation are 2020 K Street, N.W., Washington, D.C., (202) 778-8800.

What happens to my vested benefits if I leave my job before retirement?

You have a legal right to receive your benefits on reaching normal retirement age under the plan. Also, if you have met the service requirements under the plan to qualify for receiving benefits at early retirement age, you may elect to do so on reaching that age.

If the lump sum present value of your monthly benefits is $3,500 or less, the plan has the right to pay you that lump sum when you terminate employment under the plan. If the value is over $3,500, you cannot be "cashed out" without your consent.

Some plans provide that benefits may be provided in a lump sum when employment under the plan terminates. The terms of the plan determine whether or not you have this right.

What standards of conduct regulate the investments of pension plan assets?

Before ERISA, a major problem faced by participants and beneficiaries of pension plans was the irresponsible way in which the assets of the plan were managed. Pension plan trustees, managers, and others sometimes used fund assets to benefit themselves and invested fund assets in real estate deals and other high-risk schemes that often went broke.

Under ERISA, plan trustees and others who exercise control over the management of the plan or the disposition of its assets or who render investment advice for a fee are required to discharge their duties solely in the interest of plan participants and beneficiaries.[78] They also are required to use care, skill, and prudence in managing the plan's assets,[79] and they must minimize the risk of losses to the fund by diversifying their investment of fund assets.[80]

ERISA also prohibits these persons from engaging in a wide range of practices harmful to the fund, such as lending the fund's money to friends; borrowing money from the fund for their personal use; selling their own property to the fund; or buying property from the fund. In addition, a pension plan may not have more than 10% of the fair market value of its assets invested in the employer's stock or real property.[81] If you suspect that plan assets are being invested in violation of these rules, you should contact an office of the U.S. Department of Labor.

May I sue my plan for violations of ERISA?

Yes. One of the most important features of ERISA is the fact that it substantially strengthens the ability of plan participants, retirees, and the government to sue their pension plans. Under ERISA, participants and beneficiaries may bring lawsuits against plans and those who manage them to enforce rights created by ERISA and by their pension plan.[82] The actions available include the following.

1. Participants and beneficiaries may sue plan administrators who fail or refuse to comply with proper requests for information. Administrators may be personally liable to the participant or beneficiary for up to $100 per day from the date of the failure or refusal.[83] Any person who fails to furnish information or maintain records in accordance with the requirements of the law may be liable for a civil penalty of $10 for each employee with respect to whom failure occurs.[84] And there may be criminal liability for willful violations of disclosure requirements. For violations by a private individual, the law provides for a $5,000 fine or imprisonment for not more than one year or both; corporate violations may result in a fine of up to $100,000.[85]

2. Participants and beneficiaries may sue to recover benefits due, to enforce existing rights, or to clarify rights to future benefits under the terms of the plan.[86]

3. Suit may be brought against persons who have any discretionary control over the management of a plan for breach of their duties under ERISA and the plan.[87] The law provides that these people will be personally liable for restoration of any losses to the plan that result from a breach of their duties.[88]

4. Participants may sue to prevent any act that violates any provision of the law or to enforce any provision of the law or the plan.[89]

5. Participants may also request the secretary of labor to exercise his authority to enforce the participation or vesting provisions of ERISA.[90] And the secretary may also sue to prevent improper practices or to enforce ERISA.[91]

6. Finally, it is important to emphasize that under ERISA, courts may allow reasonable attorney's fees and costs of the action to either party.[92] This provision may encourage plan participants to bring lawsuits to vindicate their rights by making it economically possible to obtain a lawyer. Some, but not all, courts have ruled a worker who wins a lawsuit to recover benefits unlawfully denied by a pension plan will ordinarily be awarded an attorney's fee, unless such an award would be unjust.[93] However, a worker who brings a frivolous lawsuit

could be required to pay the other side's attorney's fee.[94] If you believe the pension plan is not complying with its legal obligation either to provide you with information or benefits you are entitled to, you can also contact the Office of Technical Assistance within the Department of Labor, Room N-5619, U.S. Department of Labor, Washington, D.C. 20210, (202) 219-8776.

Can sex discrimination in pension plans be challenged?

Yes, the federal courts have been consistent in holding that the Civil Rights Act of 1964, Title VII applies to retirement funds.

Does the Age Discrimination in Employment Act of 1967 apply to pension plans?

Yes. On April 15, 1991, the Older Workers Benefit Protection Act[95] (OWBPA) began to apply to most private employer pension plans. That act amended the Age Discrimination in Employment Act of 1967 (ADEA) and overturned the Supreme Court's 1989 decision[96] that the ADEA generally did not apply to employee benefits. The OWBPA applies also to state and local government employees and benefit plans as of October 16, 1992.[97]

The ADEA applies to employers with 20 or more employees and protects employees who are at least 40 years of age. As amended by OWBPA, the ADEA now prohibits arbitrary age discrimination in providing employee benefits. An employer may not provide older employees with less benefits than younger employees unless the employer can show that the cost of providing benefits to older employees is greater than the cost of providing the same benefits to younger employees.[98]

Can I establish my own pension plan?

Yes. An individual may deduct up to $2,000 per year from gross income to contribute to an Individual Retirement Account (IRA).[99] Workers and nonworking spouses may contribute up to $2,250 to a joint IRA. However, under certain circumstances, you may not be able to deduct the full amount of your contribution. The most common exceptions are if you participate in your employer's pension plan or your income exceeds $25,000 ($40,000 for married couples).

What rights do widows and widowers have to pensions?

Before ERISA, private pension plans did not have to offer benefits for widows and widowers. Those plans that did usually required the worker to sign a form and agree to take a reduction in his or her own pension. Often the worker simply never got around to signing the form, and despite good intentions, the widowed spouse received no pension benefits when the working spouse died. ERISA made some important changes, and the Retirement Equity Act of 1984 (REA), amending ERISA, requires plans to provide a survivor's benefit if a spouse has a vested right to a pension and worked or was on paid leave on or after August 23, 1984.[100] Under the REA, a survivor's pension is protected once the worker becomes vested.[101] Whether the worker dies while still employed or after retirement, the worker's spouse will collect a survivor's pension unless he or she gives written consent to waive that survivor's pension.[102] The amount of the worker's pension is reduced at retirement to provide for the survivor's pension, which must be 50% of the reduced amount the worker received or would have received had he lived to retirement age.[103]

Technically, the survivor's protection comes at two points: protection before the worker retires and protection at retirement. The worker's spouse can waive either of these protections. The plan must tell employees within three years of the plan year in which the employee turns 32[104] of their spouse's right to receive a survivor's benefit if, as a vested worker, he or she dies before retiring.[105] Nevertheless, even if the worker's spouse waives the protection at some point before the worker retires he or she will automatically have the protection again once the worker retires and starts collecting a pension.[106] If the worker's spouse waives the protection at the time the worker retires, the plan can provide that this decision is irrevocable.

In general, a plan must begin paying the survivor's pension immediately if the worker died after reaching retirement age and, if the worker died before retiring, in the first year the worker could have retired under the plan (usually age 55)[107] A basic survivor's pension must be paid for the survivor's life, even if the survivor remarries. A spouse will have a right to this survivor's benefit if he or she was married at least one year before the worker's pension started or before he died, whichever is earlier.[108]

If an employee was not working or on paid leave under the plan on or after August 23, 1984, the rules are more complex. Generally, if you worked under the plan between 1976 and August 23, 1984, had ten years of service, and have not started to receive your pension, you may elect that your spouse receive survivor's benefits if you die before starting to receive a pension.[109] The plan is required to have told you by September 30, 1985 of this right to elect survivor's benefits.[110] Also, if you worked under the plan on or after September 2, 1974, but left work before ERISA was first applied to the plan (generally, in 1976), and have not started to receive your pension, you may elect to provide your spouse with survivor's benefits if you die while receiving your pension.[111]

Before the Retirement Equity Act of 1984, ERISA did not require plans to provide survivor's benefits if workers earned pensions but died before retirement. To receive a survivor's pension, the plan had to have a provision allowing for early retirement.[112] Also before the REA, ERISA did not require plans to pay a spouse a survivor's benefit if the worker signed a form before starting to receive his pension saying he did not want his pension reduced to provide for a survivor's benefit. If a person was working under a plan when ERISA was first applied to it and started to receive his pension before the 1985 plan year began, a surviving spouse will receive a benefit unless a worker signed such a form before starting to receive a pension.

NOTES

1. 29 U.S.C. § 1001, *et seq.* (1985).
2. 29 U.S.C. § 1003(b) (1985).
3. 29 U.S.C. § 1114(a) (1985).
4. 29 U.S.C. § 1461 (1985).
5. 29 U.S.C. § 1052(a) (1985). Prior to 1985, pension plans could require employees to be at least 25 years old in order to enter the plan. ERISA section 202(a)(1)(A)(i), Pub. L. No. 93-406, 88 Stat. 853.
6. 29 U.S.C. § 1052(a)(3)(A) (1985).
7. ERISA § 202(a)(2)(B), Pub. L. No. 93-406, 88 Stat. 853.
8. 29. U.S.C. § 203(a) (1985).
9. 29 U.S.C. §§ 1024(b)(1), 1025, 1055(c)(1) (1985). 29 C.F.R. § 2560.503.
10. 29 U.S.C. §§ 1025(a), 1132(c) (1985).

11. 29 U.S.C. §§ 1024(b)(4), 1132(c) (1985).
12. 29 U.S.C. § 1024(b)(2) (1985).
13. *Firestone Tire & Rubber Co. v. Bruch*, 489 U.S. 101 (1989).
14. 29 U.S.C. § 1054(b)(1)(C) (1985).
15. 29 U.S.C. § 1054(b)(1) (1985).
16. 29 U.S.C. § 1054(b)(1)(C) (1985).
17. 29 U.S.C. § 1054(b)(1)(H); 26 U.S.C. § 411(b)(1)(H); 29 U.S.C. § 623(i) (1985).
18. 29 U.S.C. § 1054(b)(l) (1985).
19. 29 U.S.C. § 1053(a)(2) (1985). The Rule of 45 generally required that an employee with five years of service be 50% vested when the sum of age and years of service totalled 45. After that, each additional year increased vesting by 10%. The rule was not commonly used and may not be used for current employees after the start of the 1989 plan year.
20. ERISA § 203(a)(2); Pub. L. No. 93-406, 88 Stat. 854.
21. 29 U.S.C. § 1053(a)(2) (1985).
22. *Id.*
23. 26 U.S.C. §§ 416(g), (i) (1985).
24. 29 U.S.C. § 1053(b)(l) (1985) (Years of service in which an employee fails to contribute to a plan requiring employee contributions and years of service in which an employer does not maintain a plan may be disregarded). 29 U.S.C. § 1053(b)(l)(B), (C) (1982)(Years of service before age 18 also may be disregarded, except that plans adopting the rule of 45 schedule may not disregard years of service before age 25 during which the employee was a participant). 29 U.S.C. § 1053(b)(l)(A) (Supp. III. 1985). ERISA required plans to count an employee's years of service after age 22 for vesting purposes. The REA amends ERISA to require plans to count years of service after age 18.
25. 26 C.F.R. § 1.410(a)–7(d). A plan using this "elapsed time" method of counting service must add together nonsuccessive periods of service and give you credit for interruptions in employment of less than one year, 26 C.F.R. § 1.410(a)–7(d)(1); and give you up to 12 months additional credit if you are laid off or placed on a leave of absence. 26 C.F.R. §§ 1.410(a)–7(a)(3), (b)(2).
26. R. Nader & K. Blackwell, *You and Your Pension* (1973).
27. 29 U.S.C. § 1052(b); 29 C.F.R. § 2530.204.
28. 29 U.S.C. § 1053(b)(3)(A,B).
29. 29 U.S.C. §§ 1052(b)(4), 1053(b)(3)(D)(Supp. III 1985). Int. Rev. Code of 1954, §§ 410(a)(5)(D), 411(a)(6)(D). The plan may require a full year of service after the break before crediting years of service prior to the break. 29 §§ U.S.C. 1052(b)(3), 1053(b)(3)(B)(1982); Int. Rev. Code

of 1986, §§ 410(a)(5)(C), 411(a)(6)(B). The minimum "five year break rule" added to ERISA by § 102(d)(2) of the Retirement Equity Act of 1984, Pub. L. No. 98-397, 98 Stat. 1427, generally applies only to workers employed in 1985 and thereafter. 29 U.S.C. § 1001(note) added by Pub. L. No. 98-397, § 302(a), 98 Stat. 1451.

30. After 1984 a worker who takes a year off from work because she is pregnant or because he or she cares for a newly born or adopted child cannot be charged with a break in service for that one year. In other words, whatever the length of the break, it will be reduced by one year if leave is taken for these reasons. 29 U.S.C. §§ 1052(b)(5), 1053(b)(3)(E)(Supp. III 1985). A plan negotiated by a union may wait until the agreement in effect on Aug. 23, 1984 terminates but only until Jan. 1, 1987 to comply with this rule and the five year break rule. These rules are amendments to ERISA added by the Retirement Equity Act of 1984, 29 U.S.C. § 1001 (note)(Supp. III 1985). The rule that breaks in service be at least 5 years before you lose credit, added by the REA, will not restore pre break years of credit lost before the rule applies.

31. 29 U.S.C. § 1052(b)(3)(1982), 1053(b)(3)(B).

32. *Noell v. American Design Profit Sharing Plan,* 764 F.2d 827 (11th Cir. 1985); *Hepple v. Roberts & Dybadahl, Inc. Profit Sharing Plan,* 622 F.2d 962 (8th Cir. 1980); *Hummell v. S.E. Rykoff & Co.,* 634 F.2d 446 (9th Cir. 1980).

33. 29 U.S.C. § 1053(c)(1)(A).

34. 29 U.S.C. § 1054(g)(2)(Supp. III 1985); Pub. L. No. 98-397, § 301(a)(2), 98 Stat. 451.

35. 130 Cong. Rec. S9671, S9679-80 (daily ed. Aug. 2, 1984) (S. Rep. on H.R. 4280, 98th Cong., 2d Sess.).

36. 29 U.S.C. § 1054(g)(2)(Supp. III 1985); Pub. L. No. 98-397, § 301(a)(2), 98 Stat. 1451.

37. 130 Cong. Rec. H87656 (daily ed. Aug. 6, 1984) (remarks of Sen. Dole); 130 Cong. Rec. H8756 (daily ed. Aug. 9, 1984) (remarks of Rep. Clay).

38. 29 U.S.C. § 1053(b)(1)(Supp. III 1985). Similarly, plans must provide that participants will be entitled to receive benefits equal to or greater than the benefits they would have been entitled to receive immediately before the merger had the plan been terminated. 29 U.S.C. § 1058.

39. ERISA § 1015, 26 U.S.C. § 401(a)(2)(provides that service for a former owner, under a new owner's plan shall, to the extent provided by the Treasury Department regulations, be treated as service for the new owner. To date, the Treasury Department has not issued any

regulations under this provision). *See Phillips v. Amoco Oil Co.*, 799 F.2d 1464 (11th Cir. 1986), *cert. denied*, 481 U.S. 1016 (1987).

40. 29 U.S.C. § 1056(a).
41. 29 U.S.C. § 1002(24) (1985).
42. 29 U.S.C. § 1053(a) (1985).
43. ERISA § 3(24), 88 Stat. 837.
44. Pub. L. No. 101-239, Tit. VII, § 7871(b)(2), 103 Stat. 2435 (Dec. 19, 1989); OBRA '86, Pub. L. No. 99-509, § 9203(b), 100 Stat. 1979. The effective date can be delayed for participants in union-negotiated pension plans. Pub. L. No. 99-509, § 9204(a)(2), 100 Stat. 1979.
45. 26 U.S.C. § 401(a)(9)(C) (1985).
46. 29 U.S.C. § 1022(b)(1985). *See generally* Pillsbury, *Employee Benefit Plan Claims Under ERISA*, 8 Journal of Pension Planning and Compliance 49 (1982).
47. *Id.*
48. 29 U.S.C. § 1133 (1985); 29 C.F.R. § 2560.503-1.
49. *Grossmuller v. UAW*, 715 F.2d 853 (3d Cir. 1983).
50. 29 U.S.C. § 1132(e) (1985).
51. *Mason v. Continental Group, Inc.*, 763 F.2d 1219 (11th Cir.) *cert. denied* 474 U.S. 1087 (1985); *Amato v. Bernard*, 618 F.2d 559 (9th Cir. 1980).
52. *See supra* note 13.
53. 29 U.S.C. § 1053(a)(3)(B)(i)(1985); 29 C.F.R. § 2530.203-3(c)(1).
54. *Riley v. MEBA Pension Trust*, 570 F.2d 406 (2d Cir. 1977).
55. 29 U.S.C. § 1053(a)(3)(B)(i) (1985); 29 C.F.R. § 2530.203-3(c)(1).
56. 29 U.S.C. § 1053(a)(3)(B)(ii) (1985); 29 C.F.R. § 2530.203-3(c)(2).
57. 29 C.F.R. § 2530.203-3(c)(1,2).
58. *Riley v. MEBA Pension Trust*, 570 F.2d 409–13 (2d Cir. 1977); 586 F.2d 968 (2d Cir. 1978). These rules limiting when the plan can suspend your pension only apply to plans that employers contribute to. If the plan is run by a union and funded entirely by employee contributions, these limitations do not apply. 29 U.S.C. § 1051(4) (1985).
59. *Geib v. N.Y. Teamster's Pension Fund*, 758 F.2d 973 (3d Cir. 1985); *Johnson v. Franco*, 727 F.2d 442 (5th Cir. 1984).
60. *Chambless v. Masters, Mates, and Pilots Pension Plan*, 772 F.2d 1032 (2d Cir. 1985), *cert. denied* 475 U.S. 1012 (1985); *Deak v. Masters, Mates, and Pilots Pension Plan*, 821 F.2d 572 (11th Cir. 1987).
61. For your service during and after 1989, a plan may subtract only up to 50% of the pension benefit you accumulate because of the amount of your Social Security benefit. For service before 1989, the 50% cap does not apply, and pension benefits for some lower paid workers for

these years could legally be wiped out because of the amount of their Social Security benefit. Internal Revenue Code § 401(l)(4)(B), as amended by the Tax Reform Act of 1986, Pub. L. No. 99-514, § 1111(a). The permissible cut-off point is determined by the Internal Revenue Service under a complex formula based on the part of your Social Security benefits attributable to employer contributions. *See* Schulz and Leavitt, *Pension Integration: Concepts, Issues, and Proposals,* 5–6 (Employee Benefits Research Institute 1983). *See generally* Rev. Rul. 71-446, 1971-2 C.B. 187.

62. Pension plans are permitted to estimate a participant's Social Security benefits in calculating their pensions but then must recalculate benefits based on actual Social Security payments once the participant begins receiving Social Security, at the request of the participant. Rev. Rul. 84-45, 1984-1 C.B. 115; *Dameron v. Sinai Hospital of Baltimore, Inc.,* 626 F. Supp. 1012, (D. Md., 1986) *aff'd,* 815 F.2d 975 (4th Cir. 1987).

63. 26 U.S.C. § 401(a)(5)(1985); 26 C.F.R. § 1.411(c)(4). *See generally Alessi v. Raybestos-Manhatten, Inc.,* 451 U.S. 504 (1981). Fifty-six percent of all plan participants in medium- and large-sized companies are in plans that are "integrated" with Social Security. *Employee Benefits in Medium and Large Firms, 1984* United States Dep't. of Labor, Bureau of Labor Statistics, Bulletin 2237 at 11 (1985).

64. The fairness of pension integration formulas is currently in controversy. *See Schulz and Leavitt, supra* note 61; "The Case of the Disappearing Pension," Pension Rights Center, 1984.

65. 29 U.S.C. § 1056(b)(1985).

66. 29 U.S.C. § 1302(a) (1985); PBGC is a unit within the Department of Labor.

67. 29 U.S.C. § 1321(a), (b) (1985). Defined benefit plans are defined above in this chapter.

68. One exception is an employer providing professional services that has a plan covering 25 or fewer active participants.

69. 29 U.S.C. § 1321(b)(13)(1985); 29 U.S.C. § 1306 (1985); 29 U.S.C. § 1322 (1985). Termination is defined by 29 U.S.C. § 1341–43 (1985). Events causing termination include the failure of the plan to meet ERISA funding requirements, the inability of the plan to pay benefits when due, and a significant reduction in the number of plan participants. *Id.*

70. Disputes have arisen between PBGC and pension plans over whether the plan is a defined benefit or defined contribution plan. PBGC has sought to protect workers by finding a plan to be a defined benefit plan where the status of the plan is unclear. *Connolly v. PBGC,* 419

F. Supp. 737 (C.D. Cal. 1976) *rev'd* 581 F.2d 729 (9th Cir. 1978), *cert. denied*, 440 U.S. 935 (1979); *on remand*, No. 84-1555 (C.D. Cal., May 1, 1984), *aff'd*, 106 S. Ct. 1018 (1986).

71. 29 U.S.C. § 1322 (1985).
72. 29 U.S.C. § 1322(b) (1985).
73. 29 U.S.C. § 1322(b) (1985).
74. *Id.*
75. 29 U.S.C. § 1322a (1985).
76. 29 U.S.C. § 1053(a)(3)(E) (1985).
77. 29 U.S.C. § 1425(a)(1); 26 U.S.C. § 418D(a)(1) (1985).
78. 29 U.S.C. § 1104(a)(1)(A) (1985).
79. 29 U.S.C. § 1104(a)(1)(B) (1985). These individuals are called fiduciaries. *Id.*
80. 29 U.S.C. § 1104(a)(1)(C) (1985). Pension plan assets are the nation's largest single source of capital. In 1985, they were estimated at $1 trillion. Ippolito, *Pension, Economics & Public Policy,* at table 1-1 (1985).
81. 29 U.S.C. §§ 1106, 1107 (1985).
82. 29 U.S.C. § 1132(a) (1985). The act further provides that federal district courts shall have jurisdiction, without respect to jurisdictional amounts or diversity requirements, to redress grievances under the law. 29 U.S.C. § 1132(f) (1985). The General Accounting Office estimates that the Labor Department can monitor only 1% of plans.
83. 29 U.S.C. §§ 1132(a)(1)(A), 1132(c) (1985).
84. 29 U.S.C. § 1059(b) (1985).
85. 29 U.S.C. § 1131 (1985).
86. 29 U.S.C. § 1132(a)(1)(B)(1985). If you are attempting to obtain benefits or enforce your rights under the terms of the plan, you may bring a lawsuit in state or federal court. If you are claiming, however, that the plan has violated legal obligations imposed by ERISA, you must file the lawsuit in federal court, 29 U.S.C. § 1132(e)(1)(1985). In either case, all claims relating to the plan will be decided by federal law under ERISA. State law will not apply. 29 U.S.C. § 1144(a)(1985); *Shaw v. Delta Air Lines*, 463 U.S. 85 (1983).
87. 29 U.S.C. § 1132(a)(2) (1985).
88. 29 U.S.C. § 1109(a) (1985). *See Massachusetts Mutual Life Ins. Co. v. Russell*, 473 U.S. 134 (1985). In addition, a fiduciary may be held liable, under certain conditions, for the breach of duty of a cofiduciary. See 29 U.S.C. § 1105 (1985).
89. 29 U.S.C. § 1132(a)(3) (1985).
90. 29 U.S.C. § 1132(b)(2) (1985).
91. 29 U.S.C. § 1132(a)(5) (1985). Moreover, in order to determine

whether a violation has occurred, the secretary of labor is empowered to launch investigations into the administration of plans. 29 U.S.C. § 1134(a) (1985).

92.   29 U.S.C. § 1132(g)(1) (1985).

93.   *Smith v. CMTA-IAM Pension Trust*, 746 F.2d 587 (9th Cir. 1984); *Landro v. Glendenning Motorways, Inc.*, 625 F.2d 1344 (8th Cir. 1980).

94.   *Bittner v. Sadoff & Rudoy Industries*, 728 F.2d 820 (7th Cir. 1984). A worker, however, who reasonably brings a lawsuit to recover benefits should ordinarily not be punished by having to pay an opponent's attorney's fee. *Marquardt v. North American Car Corp.*, 652 F.2d 715 (7th Cir. 1981).

95.   Pub. L. No. 101-433, 104 Stat. 978 (Oct. 16, 1990).

96.   *Public Employees Retirement System of Ohio v. Betts*, 492 U.S. 158 (1989).

97.   Federal employees are not covered by the OWBPA.

98.   Exceptions to this general rule may apply to severance pay, long-term disability benefits and some early retirement incentive payments.

99.   Int. Rev. Code § 219.

100. 29 U.S.C. § 1055(a) (Supp. III 1985), 29 U.S.C. § 1001 (note)(Supp. III 1985); Pub. L. No. 98-397, § 303(v).

101. 29 U.S.C § 1055(a) (Supp. III. 1985).

102. 29 U.S.C § 1055(c)(2) (Supp. III. 1985).

103. 29 U.S.C § 1055(d) (Supp. III. 1985).

104. 29 U.S.C § 1055(c)(3)(B) (Supp. III. 1985).

105. 50 Fed. Reg. 29,371 (1985), codified as 26 C.F.R. § 1.401-11T (Q&A 30).

106. 29 U.S.C § 1055(c) (Supp. III. 1985).

107. 29 U.S.C § 1055(e)(1) (Supp. III. 1985).

108. 29 U.S.C § 1055(f) (Supp. III. 1985).

109. 29 U.S.C. § 1001 (note) (Supp. III 1985); Pub. L. No. 98-397, § 303(e)(2) (1984).

110. 50 Fed. Reg. 29,371 (1985), codified as 26 C.F.R. § 1.401-11T (Q&A 28).

111. 29 U.S.C. § 1001 (note) (Supp. III 1985); Pub. L. No. 98-397, § 303(c)(1) (1984).

112. Employee Retirement Income Security Act of 1974, Pub. L. No. 93-406, §§ 205(b), (c)(1); 88 Stat. 862 (1974).

VI
Welfare Benefits

What is severance pay?

Severance pay is money paid to a worker when employment terminates under certain circumstances.[1] Severance pay may be designed to serve the same purpose as unemployment benefits; to protect the worker from the risks of not having an income for a period of time after employment ends.[2] However, some employers provide severance pay on termination of employment simply as a reward for past service, whether or not there is any period of unemployment.[3] One court described separation pay as "a kind of accumulated compensation for past services and a material recognition of their past value."[4] Traditional sick leave and vacation wages paid by an employer from its general funds are not severance pay.[5]

What is employee health insurance?

Employee health insurance is protection against the risk that present or former employees and their families will not be able to obtain or afford the cost of paying for medical treatment in the event of illness or injury. The benefit typically provides payment for part or all of certain expenses incurred in obtaining such treatment.

Employee health insurance might be provided not only during a period of employment, but also for a period of time after employment ends, under certain circumstances. Federal law now requires most private employers with 20 or more employees to offer employees and their beneficiaries the opportunity to remain covered by the company health insurance plan for 18 months after coverage would otherwise end because employment terminates.[6] Under other circumstances, coverage must be offered for up to 18, 29, or 36 months. The employee can be required to pay for the full cost of continued coverage under the plan. A booklet describing "COBRA continuation coverage" can be obtained from the United States Department of Labor by writing COBRA, Consumer Information Center, Pueblo,

CO 81009. COBRA rights are described at the end of this chapter.

Aside from COBRA rights, some employers provide health insurance benefits for workers eligible to retire when employment ends. Whether the employer may reduce or eliminate retiree health insurance benefits or increase the cost of coverage charged to retirees is discussed later in this chapter.

Employers generally provide employees with health insurance in one of four ways:[7]

1. purchasing a policy of insurance from an insurance company to provide health insurance benefits to its employees. This is the most common method used by an employer to provide benefits to its employees.[8]

2. a relatively new concept is the Multi-Employer Welfare Arrangement (MEWA)[9] where several unrelated employers contribute to a privately arranged plan that attempts to create the advantages of a large employer's ability to spread risk. In the last several years, the Department of Labor has found a number of these MEWAs to be simply pyramid schemes that leave employers and workers with hugh unpaid medical bills when the MEWA goes bankrupt. ERISA provides that MEWAs are subject to some state regulation,[10] but to date the states have not been very effective in such regulation. The employee is better protected by arguing that the MEWA itself is not a "plan" and, in the case of an MEWA bankruptcy proceed directly against the employer's "plan."[11]

3. self-insuring, in which the employer acts as its own insurance company. Large employers are much more likely to self-insure than small employers, who generally cannot afford to take the risk that employees will make very large claims for benefits for treatment of serious medical conditions. Employers who generally self-insure sometimes purchase insurance to cover large claims.[12]

4. by bargaining with a union to pay a specific amount of money, generally measured by the hours worked by an employee, into a multiemployer trust fund,

which pays benefits to plan members and beneficiaries under the trust fund benefit formula.[13]

What laws govern severance pay and employee health insurance benefits?

Before 1976, private employer denials of severance pay and employee health insurance were generally reviewed under principles of contract law, whether the denial was under a plan established by the employer or negotiated with a union through collective bargaining.[14] If the benefit was negotiated by a union with a private employer in collective bargaining, denials were reviewed for breach of the labor agreement under the Labor Management Relations Act of 1947 (Taft-Hartley Act).[15]

For workers employed in 1976 and thereafter, severance pay and employee heath insurance benefits are considered to be welfare benefits under the Employee Retirement Income Security Act of 1974 (ERISA).[16]

ERISA does not require severance pay plans or health insurance plans to provide for any particular level of benefits. Instead, the law leaves it up to the employer, either by itself or through collective bargaining with a union, to set the terms of the plan. ERISA does require that the terms of the plan be disclosed to all employees it covers[17] requires that the plan be operated in the interests of the plan members and for their exclusive benefit,[18] and provides that an employee or beneficiary's right to benefits under the plan is legally enforceable.[19]

A group insurance program offered by an insurer to employees may not be considered an employee health insurance plan regulated by ERISA if:

- neither the employer nor a union make contributions;
- employee participation is voluntary;
- the employer or union simply collect employee premiums for the insurance company and publicize the policy; and
- the employer or union do not benefit.[20]

With very limited exceptions, ERISA prevents state laws from applying to claims for benefits from severance pay or employee health insurance plans.[21] Thus, even if an insurance company denies a claim in bad faith, you will be entitled to the benefits under the terms of the plan, but no remedy for any harm suffered as a result.[22] Moreover, one federal appeals court has ruled that a pension plan participant could recover extra federal income taxes he was required to pay from a pension plan administrator who failed to comply with instructions to transfer funds from one account to another.[23]

However, if the state law creates the obligation to provide a one-time severance payment, the law might apply. For example, a Maine law requires employers who close a plant to provide a lump sum severance payment to employees who lose their jobs. The Supreme Court ruled that the state plant closing benefits law was enforceable.[24]

One general exception to this rule that state laws do not apply to employee welfare benefit plans are state insurance laws that require insurance policies issued by companies licensed to do business in that state to contain specific provisions or provide specific benefits.[25] To fit within the exception, the state law must regulate the business of insurance; it must not only have an impact on the insurance industry but also be specifically directed toward that industry.[26] For example, Massachusetts law requires any general health insurance policy that provides hospital and surgical coverage to provide also a certain minimum level of coverage for mental illness. The Supreme Court ruled that this type of state law minimum benefit requirement could be enforced.[27] This means that group insurance policies purchased by employers for their employees, which constitutes an employee health insurance plan, can be subject to this type of state insurance law.

However, if an employer decides not to buy a group health insurance policy from an insurance company and instead chooses to write a benefit plan for its employees and act as its own insurance company (self-insure), then the state insurance laws that might have applied to the purchase of an insurance policy will not apply.[28] Some employee health insurance plans require they be subrogated to the participant's claims against others. For example, if the participant is injured in an auto accident and recovers money from a negligent driver, the fund will make a claim on that money to the extent of the plan's payments. Pennsylvania law prevented a health insurance plan from enforcing such a reimbursement rule. The Supreme Court ruled that the Pennsylvania law could not apply where the employer did not buy an insurance policy, but was self-insured.[29]

Large employers are more likely to take on the risks of self-insuring than small employers. Even when an employer self-insures, it may hire an insurance company to administer the plan and decide benefit claims. Simply because an insurance company denies a claim does not mean that there is an insurance policy. You need to determine whether the insurance company sold the employer an insurance policy or simply is administering the employer's self-insured plan. You should write the plan administrator, listed in your plan booklet to obtain this information.

Must my employer have a severance pay plan or an employee health insurance plan?

No. While employers are not required by law to offer these benefits, many do in order to attract and retain good employees. Whether or not your employer has such a plan for its employees is determined by the employer or negotiated with a union through collective bargaining. Except for many small businesses, most employers offer their employees a health insurance plan.

If your employer has decided to provide its employees with a severance or health insurance plan, ERISA requires the plan providing those benefits to comply with minimum standards for disclosing the terms of the plan to employees[30] and requires the person operating the plan (called the *plan administrator*) to operate the plan carefully, in the interest of plan members, and to carry out the plan's terms.[31]

Must any plan apply to all Employees?

No. An employer is not required to provide the same benefit plan to all employees. The plan will state to which groups of employees the plan applies. If your employer has a benefit plan that applies to you, the employer is required to follow the terms of the plan in determining whether you have a right to benefits.[32]

How can you tell if your employer has a benefit plan that applies to you?

Once you are covered by an employee benefit plan, such as a severance pay plan or a health insurance plan, the employer is required to provide you with a plan summary. The summary must be "written in a manner calculated to be understood by the average plan participant and . . . sufficiently accurate and comprehensive to reasonably apprise such participants and beneficiaries of their rights and obligations under the plan."[33] In enacting this requirement, Congress reasoned, "It is grossly unfair to hold an employee accountable for acts which disqualify him from benefits if he had no knowledge of these acts or if these conditions were stated in a misleading or incomprehensible manner in plan booklets."[34]

However, situations arise where employers may provide specific benefits to one or more employees, yet deny that it has any general benefit plan that applies to other employees. There may not be any written benefit plan. Informal company policies or arrangements can be enough to create an employee benefit plan.[35] If, from the employer's past conduct, you can determine the amount of benefits, who is intended to receive and who is intended to pay for the benefits, and procedures for receiving benefits, then the employer will not be able to deny that it has a benefit plan.[36]

What rules apply in making claims for benefits?

ERISA requires employee pension and welfare benefit plans to have a claims procedure,[37] which is described more fully in chapter 5. Briefly, you make a written claim for benefits with the plan administrator, whose name and address is in your summary plan booklet. If no administrator is listed, your employer is considered to be the plan administrator.[38] Make sure you have written proof that the claim was received—such as by sending the claim by certified mail, return receipt requested.

If your claim is denied or not answered within the required time (generally, 90 days), you must file an appeal with the administrator. Only after the administrator has denied your appeal or not answered the appeal within the required time (generally, 60 days) can you file a lawsuit in court seeking your benefits. Generally, you must give the administrator two chances to provide you with benefits before you can go to court.

Which edition of a plan applies to me?

Unlike pension plans, ERISA does not require severance pay plans or health insurance plans to provide that employees have a legal right to benefits simply by working for a certain number of years or through retirement age.[39] Instead, ERISA generally leaves it up to employers, either individually or through collective bargaining with a union, to set the plan's rules for qualifying for benefits.

Under ERISA, an employer has a legal obligation to follow the terms of the plan. Over time, however, the terms of benefit plans change, and an issue that frequently arises is which version of the plan applies to you. One general rule is that when an employee terminates employment, the terms of the benefit plan in effect at that time determine legal rights to benefits immediately due and payable. As a result, once you have qualified for benefits under a plan, new rules cannot be added to deprive you of that benefit.[40]

However, if you have not terminated employment and have not qualified for a benefit, an employer generally may change the terms of the plan to reduce or eliminate a benefit or add new rules to qualify for the benefit.[41]

How do you determine if you have qualified for a benefit?

After we determine which benefit plan applies to you, the next question asked frequently is how do we determine whether an employee has qualified for a benefit. The issue usually arises after a claim for benefits is denied or when an employer changes a plan and notifies employees that only certain persons will qualify for benefits under the old rules. Often the meaning of the plan is disputed, and the question boils down to who decides what the plan means and what guidelines are usually applied in making that decision.

First, who has the right to decide what the plan means. ERISA allows employers to give themselves the discretion to interpret the plan.[42] If the plan provides that the plan administrator has the discretionary authority to interpret the plan, the courts will not overturn that interpretation unless it is an "abuse of discretion." The courts generally allow this authority to be described in many ways; all that is required is some specific indication that the administrator has been given the power to construe disputed or doubtful terms.[43] If the plan does not provide for discretionary review, the court will review the plan's denial under the *de novo* standard of review—that is, it will conduct an independent review for the "most reasonable" interpretation of the plan language or evidence in support of the claim without giving any deference to the plan's decision.

While almost all pension plans (that are not negotiated with a union) now provide the plan administrator with this authority, some severance pay plans and health insurance plans still do not. Thus, when disputes arise, it is important to review the terms of the plan document to see if it gives the plan administrator the discretionary authority to interpret the plan document. You have a legal right to obtain a copy of the plan document simply by writing the plan administrator and asking for a copy. You may be charged up to $0.25 per page for the copy.

After the plan administrator has interpreted the plan to deny the claim, determining whether the administrator has "abused its discretion" in interpreting the plan is complicated and involves questions of judgment. The most that can be said fairly here is to list some of the many factors that courts have looked at in making this decision.[44]

- Is the interpretation inconsistent with the plain meaning of the plan (how the plan language is commonly understood)?[45]
- Is the interpretation inconsistent with the goals of the plan?
- Does the interpretation render some language in the plan documents superfluous?
- Is the interpretation inconsistent with other parts of the plan?
- Is the interpretation at odds with the requirements of ERISA?
- Is the interpretation inconsistent with how that plan language has been interpreted in the past?[46]

In specific cases, courts have issued decisions favorable to employees. For example, the federal court of appeals in California ruled that ambiguities in health insurance policies purchased by employers must be construed in favor of coverage of employees.[47] There, a plan could not apply a policy limit on treatment of mental illness to deny benefits for treatment of autism because the plan was ambiguous whether autism was a "mental illness." However, another federal appeals court has rejected this general approach of interpreting ambiguities.[48]

In addition, another federal court of appeals has ruled that where an insurance company representative authorized to provide information about coverage under a plan interprets an ambiguous provision in a plan and states that certain expenses are covered, and an employee then incurs expenses in reliance on those representations, the insurance company will not be allowed to deny payment.[49] That same court has also ruled that where an insurance company has a financial incentive to deny a claim for health insurance benefits, such as where it determines claims under a policy it has issued to an employer, the court will overturn the denial unless the insurance company shows that its decision was not tainted by self-interest.[50]

A third federal court of appeals has ruled that where an employer makes a misleading offer of welfare plan benefits (which includes severance pay or health insurance) from an "unfunded plan" (where the money comes out of the employer's assets and not out of an employer benefit trust fund) to an employee, who reasonably relies on the offer, the employer will not be allowed to profit from the misrepresentation by later adding new conditions and denying the benefit.[51]

Finally, a fourth federal court of appeals has ruled that when an employee health insurance plan terminates and a plan member asks about his status and options for continuing insurance coverage, the plan officials must provide him with correct and complete information.[52]

Different courts have reached different conclusions whether representations that benefits are provided by a health insurance plan are binding and prevent the employer from applying what may be the contrary, but written, terms of the plan. Where the court concludes that the terms of the plan are clear, the court is less likely to permit those terms to be modified by such representations.[53] However, where the court concludes that the plan is ambiguous, courts are more likely to rule that oral and written representations made by employers or by plan officials are binding.[54]

What are some common situations in which disputes arise over severance pay?

Disputes over severance pay are common when an employer sells all or part of a business to another employer. In these situations, the workers may find that they terminate their employment relationship with the selling company and are hired by the buying company the next day.[55] The day-to-day details of the work often remains the same, and even compensation and benefits may not be greatly affected. The former employer and its former employees may disagree over whether the workers are entitled to severance pay now that their employment relationship has ended.

The first step is to review the terms of the plan summary and the plan document. Severance pay plans generally are interpreted like any other contract.[56] The plan legally might provide that severance benefits are paid only to workers not hired by the buyer, or only to those who, even if hired, do not remain employed with the buyer for a specific length of time.

Many courts have permitted denials of severance pay to workers hired by the new owner of their workplace, even where the plan does not expressly require a period of unemployment to qualify for benefits.[57] These courts apply the reasoning that severance pay is essentially an unemployment benefit and that to provide the benefit where there is no unemployment would result in a windfall to the employees.[58]

Many severance pay plans, however, are not written to address all the different circumstances in which disputes may arise, and employers may try to add new requirements for benefits just before workers would qualify under the existing terms of the plan. Courts have permitted employers, on the eve of the sale, to amend a severance pay plan to add the requirement that its employees not be hired by the buyer to qualify for severance pay.[59] However, any such amendment may have to be in writing; a court has stated that it would not enforce an oral amendment[60] or an attempt to add orally new requirements that are not contained in the plan.[61] However, in sale of business situations, what one court may view as implied in the plan may be seen by another court as adding a new condition.

What if the plan summary and the plan documents are different?

In describing the terms of a plan, it is quite common for a summary to provide that "in the event of a conflict between the summary and the terms of a plan, the terms of the plan will control." Such language may not be enforceable, however, where an employee reasonably relies on the summary.[62] Moreover, one federal appeals court recently ruled that statements in the summary plan description are binding and that any language in the summary to the contrary has no effect.[63] Some courts have required employees to show that they acted in reliance on the terms of the summary before the court will give priority to the summary over a conflicting rule in the plan document.[64] However, other courts have ruled that in the event of a conflict, the summary is enforceable and the employee need not show that he or she acted in some way in reliance on the summary.[65]

What general rules apply to retiree health insurance claims?
As a result of the rapidly rising cost of healthcare in recent years, many employers have reduced or eliminated health insurance benefits provided to future or already retired employees or have increased the premiums charged for the coverage. Many lawsuits have been filed over whether the employer may do so.

There is a general consensus on only a few basic points; many other decisions are sharply criticized by employers, employees, unions, retirees, or insurance companies. First, the points of general agreement. ERISA does not require an employer to have a health insurance plan or for that plan to provide that employees can be covered by health insurance after retirement.

Employees covered by a plan must be given summary plan descriptions (SPDs), and the SPD must set forth all the rules to qualify for benefits and circumstances that might disqualify a person from receiving benefits.

Moreover, if the plan provides for retiree health insurance coverage, the terms of the plan in effect at retirement determine rights and obligations, and the terms of that plan are legally enforceable.[66] Simply working through retirement age will not prevent the employer from changing retirement benefits if the plan authorizes the employer to change the benefits provided workers after they retire.[67]

Whether your plan is negotiated with a union or simply put into effect by the employer makes a difference in the kinds of legal issues likely to arise. For example, many plans for non-union employees provide that the employer reserves the right to amend or terminate the plan at any time. Many lawsuits revolve around what this language means and how it applies to retirees.

Also, whether your employer purchased a policy of insurance from an insurance company or self-insures may make a difference. For example, many policies generally provide that coverage under the policy ends on the earliest of the following: the date of termination of employment; the date the employee fails to make a required premium payment; the date the coverage ends; or the date the policy is terminated. Where the policy elsewhere provides for continuing coverage for retirees, the question frequently arises how the two sections interact. Where the employer self-insures and does not purchase an insurance policy, this question does not arise.

Major questions that can arise are:

1. What documents determine legal rights. In addition to the legal plan document and/or collective bargaining agreement, what legal significance should be given to the plan summary and any insurance policy?

2. What legal significance should be given to written or oral statements by company officials, in formal presentations or in informal discussions, that benefits would not be changed or that costs would not be increased after a person has retired? The question becomes especially important when the statements are inconsistent with the plan document or the plan summary.

3. Can any inference be made that benefits provided at retirement were intended to be lifetime benefits unless specific language in the plan indicates the inference is unwarranted?

4. What legal significance should be given to language in a plan document or summary that the employer reserves the right to change the plan's benefits and that the plan may be discontinued at any time?

5. In determining what the plan means, do we only look at the intent of the employer offering the plan, or do we also consider the reasonable expectations of the employees?

Generally, courts first look to the written plan document or documents to determine whether or not they clearly and unambiguously provide that retiree benefits cannot be changed. Most courts will review both plan summaries and legal plan documents in making such a determination.[68] If the answer is clear, courts generally will not consider other evidence. Where the plan is not negotiated, courts have ruled that by reserving the right to terminate the plan, the employer may change retiree benefits under the plan.[69]

In one case, an employer repeatedly made oral and written representations to employees that retiree benefits would be for life at no cost. However, the legal plan document and the plan summary provided employees expressly reserved the company's right to amend or terminate the benefits offered. A federal court of appeals disregarded the presentations and allowed the employer to reduce the retiree benefits.[70]

Where retiree benefits are negotiated with a union, the simple fact that the contract has expired does not determine whether the retiree benefits continue.[71] An agreement may provide that benefits continue after the agreement expires.[72]

Moreover, one federal court of appeals has ruled that specific language that "benefits will continue" after retirement takes precedence over general language establishing that the contract lasts only for a certain period of time.[73] In that case, the court found it important that while some benefits were provided only for a specific period of time, the contract did not limit the time the retiree benefits would be provided. In addition, courts have ruled that the parties to the contract may have intended that retiree benefits be "for life" even if they did not expressly say so in the contract.[74]

In addition, where the answer is not clear from the face of the contract and other plan documents, a court generally will consider other writings and statements and other conduct as evidence of what was intended,[75] including prior negotiations or dealings between the union and the employer. The type of evidence that courts have considered significant includes oral and written statements made to workers in exit interviews at retirement; continuing retiree insurance while stopping the active employees' insurance when a contract expires; preparing an estimate, upon discontinuing a plan, of the future cost of providing lifetime insurance to retirees.[76]

However, where a contract states that the employer generally reserved the right to amend or terminate a plan, another federal court of appeals has ruled that lifetime benefits are not created by other sections of the agreement that provide that retiree benefits "will continue" after retirement[77] or that retirement benefits will continue "until death of retiree."[78] Even though a plan summary distributed to employees provided that "benefits will continue for the remainder of your life," a court still ruled that other evidence justified the conclusion that there was no intent to provide lifetime benefits to retirees."[79]

How do general rules in health plans apply to common issues that arise in healthcare cases?

"Experimental." Many times plans will deny payment on the basis that the treatment was "experimental." A controversial cancer treatment called ABMT generated a number of cases on this issue.[80]

"Reasonable and necessary." Usually the opinion of the treating doctor as to reasonableness will be upheld unless clearly wrong.[81]

"Preexisting condition." Many plans exclude payment for medical conditions that existed prior to the effective date of coverage. The plan may provide coverage for such conditions after a period of time if no treatment is rendered during that time; in some cases, usually after a longer period, whether or not treatment is provided. A good rule of thumb as to what is a "preexisting condition" is "there is a distinct symptom or condition from which one learned in medicine can with reasonable accuracy diagnose the illness."[82]

"Mental or nervous disorder." Many plans exclude or reduce coverage for a mental or nervous disorder. Three different definitions of what is a mental or nervous disorder have developed: (1) whether the medical problem is "caused" by a mental disorder; (2) whether the manifestation of the problem is "mental"; and (3) whether the problem, whatever its nature, is normally treated by professionals in the mental health field.[83]

What are long-term disability policies?

Many employers provide long-term disability insurance that pays a certain percentage of the salary of an employee who becomes "totally disabled." This percentage is usually 60 to 70% of the income and is reduced by monies received from other sources such as workers' compensation and Social Security disability. For the typical wage earner, after such deductions, the disability policy usually pays little or nothing.

The definition of "total disability" in such policies usually means that the worker must be disabled from the normal duties of her own job. After a period of time, usually one to two years, the definition changes so that the worker must be disabled from all work for which the worker is qualified by "age, education and experience."[84] For this definition most plans simply follow the ruling of the Social Security Administration—if you qualify for Social Security disability benefits you will continue to receive benefits under the policy.[85] The use of vocational experts to establish the fact of disability is a good idea.[86] Where the worker's treating doctor and the plan's "one time" doctor disagree, the courts will usually find in favor of the opinion of the treating doctor by analogy to Social Security cases.[87]

Sometimes the denial of benefits will force the person to return to work, but this will not always defeat the claim for benefits.[88]

What are COBRA health insurance continuation rights?

In 1986, Congress enacted the health insurance continuation law in response to "reports of the growing number of Americans without any health insurance coverage and the decreasing willingness of our Nation's hospitals to provide care to those who cannot afford to pay."[89] Included in the budget authorization act (the Consolidated Omnibus Budget Reconciliation Act of 1985 or COBRA),[90] COBRA applies to employers—both private and state and local government[91]—with 20 or more employees.[92]

COBRA provides that employees and their families who would otherwise lose health insurance coverage under an employer's group health insurance plan have the right, under certain circumstances, to elect to continue that coverage for at least 18 months and possibly up to 36 months. The employee or family member who elects continuation coverage can be required to pay the full cost of the continued coverage under the plan (plus 2% for administrative expenses). For example, if you have paid $50 per month for health insurance coverage under your employer's plan, but the full cost of your coverage was $150 per month (the employer paid the rest), you can be charged $150 per month plus 2% for COBRA continuation coverage. Evidence of insurability cannot be required as a condition of providing COBRA coverage.[93]

What triggers the right to elect COBRA continuation coverage?

The right of a covered employee or family member to elect COBRA continuation coverage is triggered by a loss of coverage (which need not be immediate) under an employee group health insurance plan resulting from the

- death of the covered employee;[94]
- termination of employment of the covered employee (except for gross misconduct);[95]
- reduction of hours of the covered employee;[96]
- divorce or legal separation of the covered employee from the employee's spouse;[97]
- covered employee becoming entitled to benefits under Medicare;[98] or
- dependent children ceasing to meet the plan's definition of a dependant.[99]

How long can COBRA continuation coverage last?

If the end of regular coverage is triggered by the termination of the worker's employment or a reduction of hours of employment, the person losing coverage must be notified of their right to and may elect to continue his or her coverage under the group health plan for up to 18 months from the date coverage would otherwise end.[100] The 18-month period is extended to 29 months if the person losing coverage is totally disabled.[101] Coverage that would otherwise end as a result of a different triggering event may be continued for up to 36 months.[102]

Can the length of COBRA continuation coverage be cut short?

Yes. The period of COBRA continuation coverage can be ended if one of the following circumstances occurs:

- the employer terminates group health insurance coverage for all employees;[103]
- the covered person fails to pay required premiums within 30 days after the due date (or whatever longer period might apply under the terms of the plan);[104] or
- the covered person becomes covered under another group health insurance plan or entitled to Medicare.[105]

What notice must I receive about COBRA continuation rights?

When an employee or spouse first becomes covered by an employee group health insurance plan, the plan must provide written notice of COBRA continuation rights to both the employee and the spouse.[106] COBRA rights must be described in the summary plan description provided all covered employees.

When an event occurs that will cause the employee or family member to lose coverage under the plan, the plan administrator must be notified. If the event is a divorce, legal separation, or a dependant becoming ineligible for coverage under the terms of the plan, the employee or family member must notify the health plan administrator (named in the summary plan description) within 60 days after the event ccurs.[107] If the event is the covered employee's death, termination of employment, reduction of hours, or entitlement to Medicare, the employer must notify the plan administrator within 30 days after the event.[108]

Within 14 days of receiving such notice, the plan administrator must provide notice of the right to elect COBRA continuation coverage for each person who might otherwise lose coverage.[109] From the date that coverage would otherwise end (or if later, from the date of receiving notice from the plan administrator that coverage will soon end and that there are rights to elect COBRA continuation coverage), the employee or family member has at least 60 days to elect COBRA coverage.[110] Payment of the first premium must be made within 45 days after COBRA coverage is elected.[111] If COBRA coverage is elected, there will not be any gap in coverage—coverage will be continuous. However, payment for coverage prior to the election must be made with the first payment, due within 45 days after coverage is elected.[112]

NOTES

1. *See generally* Daniels, *Creating, Administering and Terminating Severance Plans in an Era of Economic Dislocation,* 6 Labor Lawyer 905 (1990).
2. *See Gilbert v. Burlington Industries,* 765 F.2d 320 (2d Cir. 1985);

aff'd mem., 477 U.S. 901 (1986); *Sly v. P.R. Mallory & Co.*, 712 F.2d 1209, 1211 (7th Cir. 1983).

3. *See, e.g., Bennett v. Gill & Duffus Chemicals, Inc.*, 699 F. Supp. 454 (S.D.N.Y. 1987).

4. *Chapin v. Fairchild Camera and Instrument Corp.*, 31 Cal. App. 3d 192, 198 (1973), *quoting Willets v. Emhart Manufacturing Co.*, 208 A.2d 546 (Conn. 1965).

5. 29 C.F.R. § 2510.301(b)(2,3). *See Shea v. Wells Fargo Armored Service Corp.*, 810 F.2d 372 (2d Cir. 1987).

6. This obligation was created by the Consolidated Omnibus Budget Reconciliation Act of 1985, Pub. L. No. 99-272, Title X, 100 Stat. 222 (1986) and took effect, for non-collectively bargained plans, on the first day of the first plan year starting on or after July 1, 1986. For collectively bargained plans, the obligation took effect on the later of first day of the 1987 plan year, or for plans maintained under a collective bargaining agreement in effect on April 7, 1986, on the first day of the first plan year starting after the expiration of that agreement. The Internal Revenue Service has proposed regulations to administer COBRA. Prop. Treas. Reg. § 1.162-26, 52 Fed. Reg. 22716 (June 15, 1987), *modified,* 52 Fed. Reg. 26122 (July 10, 1987). Congress has amended COBRA in part, and those changes may have different effective dates.

7. *See* Perritt, *Health Care Plans and ERISA*, 6 Labor Lawyer 949, 952 (1990).

8. *Id.* at 957.

9. 29 U.S.C. § 1002(40) (Supp. III 1985).

10. 29 U.S.C. § 1144(a)(6) (1985).

11. *Credit Managers v. Kennesaw Life*, 809 F.2d 617 (9th Cir. 1987).

12. *Id.* at 962.

13. Multiemployer welfare benefit trust funds are subject to § 302(c)(5) of the Labor Management Relations Act of 1947, 29 U.S.C. § 186(c)(5).

14. *See generally* J. Vogel, "Until Death Do Us Part: Vesting of Retiree Insurance," 9 Ind. Rel. L.J. 183, 189 n.25 (1987).

15. 29 U.S.C. § 185 (1985).

16. Most states have laws regulating insurance companies doing business in that state. Those state laws might regulate group health insurance policies sold by insurance companies to employers in that state. Those state laws may apply. ERISA § 514(b)(2)(A), 29 U.S.C. §§ 1144(b)(2)(a) (1985).

17. 29 U.S.C. § 10245.

18. 29 U.S.C. § 1104(a)5.

19. 29 U.S.C. § 1132(a)(1)(B)5.

20. Labor Department regulation 2510.3-1(j), 29 C.F.R. § 2510.3-1(j).

21. 29 U.S.C. § 1144(a)5. *FMC Corp. v. Holliday*, 111 S. Ct. 403 (1990); *Shaw v. Delta Air Lines*, 463 U.S. 85 (1983).

22. *Pilot Life Insurance Co. v. Dedeaux*, 481 U.S. 41 (1987). Bills were introduced into the 102d Congress to reverse this result. *See* § 794 (ERISA Preemption Amendments of 1991); H.R. 1602. No bill was signed into law.

23. *Warren v. Society National Bank*, 905 F.2d 975 (6th Cir. 1990), *cert. denied*, 111 S. Ct. 2256 (1991). The *Warren* holding was rejected in *Harsch v. Eisenberg*, 956 F.2d 651 (7th Cir. 1992) and *Novak v. Andersen Corp.*, 962 F.2d 757 (8th Cir. 1992), and placed in doubt by *Mertens v. Hewitt Associates*, 113 S. Ct. 2063 (1993).

24. *Fort Halifax Packing Co. v. Coyne*, 482 U.S. 1 (1987).

25. ERISA § 514(b)(2)(A), 29 U.S.C. § 1144(b)(2)(A) (1985).

26. *Pilot Life Insurance Co. v. Dedeaux*, 481 U.S. 41 (1987). The Supreme Court has relied on three factors in separating out those practices that constitute the business of insurance and that may remain subject to state insurance laws: "*First*, whether the practice has the effect of transferring or spreading a policyholder's risk; *second*, whether the practice is an integral part of the policy relationship between the insurer and the insured; and *third*, whether the practice is limited to entities within the insurance industry." *Metropolitan Life Insurance Co. v. Massachusetts*, 471 U.S. 724, 744 (1985).

27. *Metropolitan Life Insurance Co. v. Massachusetts*, 471 U.S. 724 (1985).

28. *Id.*

29. *FMC Corp. v. Holliday*, 111 S. Ct. 403 (1990).

30. 29 U.S.C. § 1024 (1985).

31. 29 U.S.C. § 1104 (1985).

32. 29 U.S.C. § 1104(a)(1)(D) (1985).

33. 29 U.S.C. § 1022(a)(1) (1985).

34. H.R. Rep. 533, 93d Cong., 2d Sess., *reprinted in* 1974 U.S.C.C.A.N. 4639, 4646.

35. *See, e.g., Brown v. Armco-Pittsburgh Corp.*, 876 F.2d 546 (6th Cir. 1985); *Scott v. Gulf Oil Corp.*, 754 F.2d 1499 (9th Cir. 1981).

36. *Donovan v. Dillingham*, 688 F.2d 1367 (11th Cir. 1982)(*en banc*).

37. 29 U.S.C. § 1133 (1985).

38. 29 U.S.C. § 1002(16) (1985).

39. *See Hansen v. White Motor Corp.*, 788 F.2d 1186 (6th Cir. 1986).

40. *Egert v. Connecticut General*, 900 F.2d 1032 (7th Cir. 1990); *Brug v. Pension Plan of the Carpenters*, 669 F.2d 570 (9th Cir. 1982).

41. *See, e.g., Reichelt v. Emhart Corp.*, 921 F.2d 425 (2d Cir. 1990), *cert. denied*, 111 S. Ct. 2854 (1991); *Adams v. Avondale Industries, Inc.*, 905 F.2d 943 (6th Cir. 1990), *cert. denied*, 111 S. Ct. 517 (1990).

42. *Firestone Tire & Rubber Co. v. Bruch*, 489 U.S. 101 (1989).

43. *See, e.g., DeNobel v. Vitro Corp.*, 885 F.2d 1180 (4th Cir. 1989).

44. *DeNobel v. Vitro Corp.*, 885 F.2d 1180 (4th Cir. 1989).

45. *Blau v. Del Monte Corp.*, 748 F.2d 1348 (9th Cir. 1984), *cert. denied*, 474 U.S. 865 (1985).

46. *Taylor v. The Continental Group Change in Control Severance Pay Plan*, 933 F.2d 1227 (3d Cir. 1991).

47. *Kunin v. Benefit Trust Insurance Company*, 910 F.2d 534 (9th Cir.), *cert. denied*, 111 S. Ct. 581 (1990).

48. *Brewer v. Lincoln National Life Insurance Co.*, 921 F.2d 150 (8th Cir. 1990).

49. *Kane v. Aetna Life Insurance*, 893 F.2d 1283 (11th Cir. 1990).

50. *Brown v. Blue Cross and Blue Shield of Alabama, Inc.*, 898 F.2d 1556 (11th Cir. 1990).

51. *Black v. TIC Investment Corp.*, 900 F.2d 112 (7th Cir. 1990).

52. *Eddy v. Colonial Life Insurance Company*, 919 F.2d 747 (D.C. Cir. 1990).

53. *See Moore v. Metropolitan Life Insurance Co.*, 856 F.2d 488 (2d Cir. 1988)(oral and written representations of company officials that health insurance plan provided "lifetime benefits at no cost" do not override clear and unambiguous terms of plan reserving right of employer to amend or terminate the plan); *Musto v. American General Corp.*, 861 F.2d 897 (6th Cir. 1988), *cert. denied*, 490 U.S. 1020 (1989).

54. *See infra* n.67.

55. *See, e.g., Bennett v. Gill & Duffus Chemicals, Inc.*, 699 F. Supp. 454 (S.D.N.Y. 1987).

56. *Jacobs v. Picklands Mather & Co.*, 933 F.2d 652, 659 (8th Cir. 1991).

57. *See, e.g., Lakey v. Remington Arms Co.*, 874 F.2d 541 (8th Cir. 1989); *Schwartz v. Newsweek, Inc.*, 827 F.2d 879 (2d Cir. 1987); *Jung v. FMC Corp.*, 755 F.2d 708 (9th Cir. 1985).

58. *See Sly v. P.R. Mallory & Co.*, 712 F.2d 1209, 1211 (7th Cir. 1983).

59. *Adams v. Avondale Industries, Inc.*, 905 F.2d 943 (6th Cir. 1990), *cert. denied*, 111 S. Ct. 517 (1990); *Young v. Standard Oil (Indiana)*, 849 F.2d 1039 (7th Cir.), *cert. denied*, 488 U.S. 981 (1988).

60. *Hozier v. Midwest Fasteners, Inc.*, 908 F.2d 1155 (3d Cir. 1990).

61. *Blau v. Del Monte Corp.*, 748 F.2d 1348 (9th Cir. 1984), *cert. denied*, 474 U.S. 865 (1985).

62. *McKnight v. Southern Life and Health Insurance Company*, 758 F.2d 1566 (11th Cir. 1985).

63. *Hansen v. Continental Insurance Co.*, 940 F.2d 971 (5th Cir. 1991).

64. *See, e.g., Anderson v. Alpha Portland Industries, Inc.*, 836 F.2d 1512 (8th Cir. 1988).

65. *Heidgerd v. Olin Corp.*, 906 F.2d 903 (2d Cir. 1990); *Edwards v.*

State Farm Mutual Automobile Insurance Company, 851 F.2d 134 (6th Cir. 1988).

66. *See Pratt Petroleum Production Management Employee Savings Plan;* 920 F.2d 651 (10th Cir. 1990).

67. *See, e.g., Moore v. Metropolitan Life Insurance Co.*, 856 F.2d 488 (2d Cir. 1988); *Hansen v. White Motor Corp.*, 788 F.2d 1186 (6th Cir. 1986).

68. *See, e.g., Alday v. Container Corp. of America*, 906 F.2d 660 (11th Cir. 1990). *But see Gridley v. Cleveland Pneumatic Co.*, 924 F.2d 1310 (3d Cir. 1991)(participant cannot recover benefits allegedly due under plan summary, but not plan document).

69. *See, e.g., Musto v. American General Corp.*, 861 F.2d 897 (6th Cir. 1988), *cert. denied*, 490 U.S. 1020 (1989).

70. *Moore v. Metropolitan Life Insurance Co.*, 856 F.2d 488 (2d Cir. 1988).

71. *See, e.g., United Paperworkers v. Champion International Corp.*, 908 F.2d 1252 (5th Cir. 1990); *see generally John Wiley & Sons, Inc. v. Livingston*, 376 U.S. 543 (1964).

72. *Keefer v. H.K. Porter Co., Inc.*, 872 F.2d 60 (4th Cir. 1989); *United Steelworkers v. Connors Steel Co.*, 855 F.2d 1510 (11th Cir. 1988). In almost all of the cases where the employer has attempted to terminate, rather than reduce, retiree benefits, the retirees' workplace had been permanently closed. Rogers, *Rethinking Yard-Man: A Return to Fundamental Contract Principles in Retiree Benefits Litigation*, 37 Emory L.J. 1033, 1045 n.54 (1988).

73. *UAW v. Yard-Man, Inc.*, 716 F.2d 1476 (6th Cir. 1983), *cert. denied*, 465 U.S. 1007 (1985).

74. *See, e.g., Smith v. ABS Industries, Inc.*, 890 F.2d 841 (6th Cir. 1989); *UAW Cadillac Malleable Iron Co.*, 728 F.2d 807 (6th Cir. 1984).

75. *See, e.g., United Paperworkers v. Champion International Corp.*, 908 F.2d 1252 (5th Cir. 1990); *Smith v. ABS Industries, Inc.*, 890 F.2d 841 (6th Cir. 1989); *Bower v. Bunker Hill Co.*, 725 F.2d 1221 (9th Cir. 1984).

76. *See Local 150, United Food & Commercial Workers Int'l Union v. Dubuque Packing Co.*, 756 F.2d 66 (8th Cir. 1985).

77. *DeGeare v. Alpha Portland Industries, Inc.*, 837 F.2d 812 (8th Cir.), *vacated and remanded*, 489 U.S. 1049 (1989).

78. *Anderson v. Alpha Portland Industries, Inc.*, 836 F.2d 1512, 1514 (8th Cir. 1988).

79. *Id.* at 1519.

80. Compare *Wilson v. Group Hospitalization*, 91 F. Supp. 309 (D.D.C. 1992) with *Clark v. K-Mart*, 16 E.B. Cas (BNA) 1523 (3d Cir. 1992)

(*en banc*). *See also Johnson v. District 2 MEBA*, 857 F.2d 514 (9th Cir. 1988).

81. *Sarchett v. Blue Shield*, 43 Cal. 3d 1 (Cal. S. Ct. 1987). *But see Jett v. Blue Cross*, 890 F.2d 1137 (11th Cir. 1989).

82. *Marek v. AMBA Marketing*, 1989 WL 4141 (unpublished) (9th Cir. 1989). *See also Eley v. Boeing Co.*, 945 F.2d 276 (9th Cir. 1991).

83. *See, e.g., Phillips v. Lincoln National*, 774 F. Supp. 494 (D. Ill. 1991); *Kunin v. Benefit Trust Life*, 696 F. Supp. 1342 (D. Cal. 1988); *Simons v. Blue Cross*, 536 N.Y.S.2d 431, 144 A.D.2d 28 (N.Y. 1989).

84. *See* cases collected in *James v. Equicor*, 92 Los Angeles Daily Journal DAR 6283 (D. Cal. 1992); *Farrow v. Montgomery*, 167 Cal. App. 3d 648 (Cal. 1986).

85. *Govindarajan v. FMC Corporation*, 932 F.2d 634 (7th Cir. 1991); *Bova v. American Cyanamid Co.*, 662 F. Supp. 483 (D. Ohio 1987); *Pierce v. American Waterworks Co.*, 683 F. Supp. 996 (W.D. Pa. 1988).

86. *Jenkinson v. Chevron*, 634 F. Supp. 375 (D. Cal. 1986).

87. *Murry v. Heckler*, 722 F.2d 499 (9th Cir. 1983).

88. *Mabry v. Travelers*, 193 F.2d 497 (5th Cir. 1952). "Pinched by poverty, beset by adversity, driven by necessity, one may work to keep the wolf away from the door though not physically able to work."

89. H.R. Rep. No. 241, 99th Cong., 2d Sess., 44.

90. Pub. L. No. 99-272, Title X, 100 Stat. 227 (April 10, 1986).

91. *See* Prop. Treas. Reg. § 1.162-26 (Background Q&A 8), 52 Fed. Reg. 22716 (to be codified at 26 C.F.R. 1.162-26 (Background Q&A 8) (Proposed June 15, 1987).

92. 29 U.S.C. § 1161(b) (Supp. III 1985).

93. 29 U.S.C. § 1162(4) (Supp. III 1985).

94. 29 U.S.C. § 1163(1) (Supp. III 1985).

95. 29 U.S.C. § 1163(2) (Supp. III 1985).

96. 29 U.S.C. § 163(32) (Supp. III 1985).

97. 29 U.S.C. § 1163(3) (Supp. III 1985).

98. 29 U.S.C. § 1163(4) (Supp. III 1985).

99. 29 U.S.C. § 1163(5) (Supp. III 1985).

100. 29 U.S.C. § 1162(2)(A)(i) (Supp. III 1985).

101. 29 U.S.C. § 1162(2)(A) (Supp. III 1985).

102. *Id.* (Supp. III 1985).

103. 29 U.S.C. § 1162(2)(B) (Supp. III 1985).

104. 29 U.S.C. § 1162(2)(C) (Supp. III 1985).

105. 29 U.S.C. § 1162(2)(D) (Supp. III 1985).

106. 29 U.S.C. § 1166(a)(1) (Supp. III 1985).

107. 29 U.S.C. § 1166(a)(3) (Supp. III 1985).

108. 29 U.S.C. § 1166(a)(3) (Supp. III 1985).
109. 29 U.S.C. § 1166(a)(4)(c) (Supp. III 1985).
110. 29 U.S.C. § 1165(1) (Supp. III 1985).
111. 52 Fed. Reg. 22716 (Q&A 47, 48) (1987) to be codified at 26 C.F.R. 1.162 (Q&A 47, 48) (June 15, 1987).
112. *Id.*

VII
Statutory Benefits

Numerous federal and state statutes provide compensation for employees and their families for wages lost due to retirement, disability, or unemployment. This chapter provides a very brief overview of three major statutory benefits: workers' compensation, Social Security, and unemployment insurance. No attempt is made here to provide detailed or specific information on which you can rely. For more specific information on how these benefit programs apply to you, you should consult the appropriate state or federal agency listed in your telephone directory.

WORKERS' COMPENSATION

The familiar phrase workers' compensation refers to a type of insurance coverage that compensates workers and their families for lost wages and medical expenses incurred due to injury, disease, or death arising out of and in the course of employment.[1] Since 1949, every state has had a statute governing workers' compensation coverage. By 1990, workers' compensation covered approximately 90% of the American workforce. Although state statutes differ in many regards and change frequently to meet economic conditions, all provide medical expenses, rehabilitation expenses and cash benefits for work-related injuries and diseases.

What are the typical features of a workers' compensation statute?

1. You must be an employee.
2. You are automatically covered and can receive compensation for injuries arising out of and in the course of employment.
3. Negligence and fault are irrelevant to the determination of benefits.

4. In return for the guaranteed compensation, you relinquish any common law right to sue your employer for negligence.

5. Although workers' compensation generally is an exclusive remedy, you still retain, in many states, the right to sue negligent third parties, such as manufacturers whose defective products injure you at work. You may even be able to sue your employer if he or she causes you harm intentionally or recklessly.

6. The usual rules of procedure and evidence are relaxed at workers' compensation hearings in order to quickly resolve workers' claims.

7. The employer alone bears the expense of providing workers' compensation coverage.

What benefits are included in the typical workers' compensation statute?

The most important benefits include

- weekly disability income, based on your previous earning history; this disability income is generally between one-half and two-thirds of your average weekly wages;
- "scheduled" benefits for the loss or incapacity of a body member or organ, such as a leg, hand, or eye;
- hospital, surgical, nursing, and medical expenses, which may include rehabilitation expenses;
- burial expenses and death benefits to the family and dependents of a worker who dies from a work accident.

Each of these benefits is described more fully later.

Who is covered by workers' compensation?

Virtually every employee who is accidentally injured at work. Even in the three states in which coverage is elective (New Jersey, South Carolina, and Texas), most employees are covered. However, in certain states, coverage may be compulsory only on certain employers (e.g., those with more than a specified number of workers) or in certain industries or jobs (e.g., hazardous jobs). Typically, no coverage is required for domestic workers, agricultural laborers, or freelancers.

Whether compulsory or elective, a bona fide employer-employee relationship must exist for the worker to be covered.

An independent contractor is not covered; usually, neither is a partner or volunteer. In almost every workers' compensation statute, a general contractor will be considered the employer of employees of its subcontractors and is therefore liable for compensation benefits to injured employees of the subcontractor.

If you are not covered by workers' compensation, your remedy against your employer is based on the common law; that is, you can sue your employer.

Does workers' compensation cover all injuries or diseases?

No. Only injuries or diseases "arising under and in the course of employment" are covered. In other words, a disability that is not causally related to the job is not covered by workers' compensation.

Generally, the phrase "arising under and in the course of employment" is construed very broadly. If you can show that your injury was a result of being present at the job—that is, "but for" being at work, you would not have been injured—compensation will be awarded. Even when the risk that caused the injury is remote from the job itself and the chain of causation is attenuated, the courts have awarded compensation. For example, a delivery driver would probably be compensated if he accidently trips on his shoelace while carrying packages and is injured. Yet a driver would not be compensated for injuring his back when he rested his foot on the rear of his truck to tie his shoelace since this just as easily could have occurred off the job.

If you are injured going to or from work, the pivotal question is whether you were within the "zone of danger" associated with the job site. Compensation may be awarded if the risk that caused the injury was an integral condition of the job site that had to be confronted when going to or from work. Injuries that occur away from the job site are usually not compensable, though there are exceptions.

A problem in proving causation arises when you had a preexisting illness that was the cause of injury or death. You generally have the burden of proving that the preexisting illness was aggravated by conditions at the job. If you cannot prove this, benefits may be denied.

Even if a disability is not covered by workers' compensation, it might be covered by other disability income insurance. Many employees—particularly those in unions—are covered by private disability income insurance. In fact, several states—including California, Hawaii, New Jersey, New York, Rhode Island, and Puerto Rico—require employers to provide temporary disability income insurance coverage to all workers who are covered by workers' compensation. Furthermore, for a serious disability, you may qualify for disability benefits under Social Security.

Does workers' compensation cover all injuries on the job?
Yes, except for injuries caused by your own willful conduct. Generally, however, you may be entitled to compensation even if your injury is caused by your own negligent or reckless conduct, as long as the injury arose out of your employment.

Willful misconduct may include acts involving prohibited overstepping of the boundaries defining your job, therefore placing a resulting injury outside the "course of employment." Examples include using company property for personal purposes contrary to clearly stated company policy performing acts expressly prohibited by company rules, or doing work your employer has specifically stated to be outside the scope of your job. Also, some statutes provide that your compensation will be forfeited or reduced for injuries caused by your deliberate violation of known policies designed to prevent injuries or for your refusal to use safety devices or observe safety rules.

Generally, you do not automatically forfeit compensation if you were intoxicated at the time of your injury, unless you were too intoxicated to perform your job; in that event, you in effect abandoned your employment. If you were sober enough to perform your job when you were injured, whether you get benefits and whether they are reduced generally depend on the extent to which your intoxication caused your injury.

What if I have a preexisting condition that aggravates the injury?
You may still be eligible for benefits. Some states apportion the amount of benefits based on the preexisting condition and the aggravation of the injury. Generally, an employer takes a worker "as is"; the risk of employing a person with a preexisting

disease or disability is assumed by the employer. However, some states encourage employers to hire disabled workers through a *second injury rule*. In that situation, a worker with a preexisting disability may be eligible for workers' compensation benefits for only a limited period of time (e.g., two years).

Can I recover for pain and suffering?

Not usually. The only time you can recover for this is when the pain impairs your ability to earn a living.

Can I sue my employer even though I receive workers' compensation benefits?

Generally, no. One of the rules of the workers' compensation system is that the standard benefits for the injured worker are the worker's exclusive claim against the employer; that is, the employer that provides workers' compensation coverage to its workers is immune from civil lawsuits by its workers for damages.

Nonetheless, you may not be entirely without remedy. Most jurisdictions permit suit against an employer for injuries or death caused by the employer's intentional misconduct, such as an assault on a worker. In addition, a few jurisdictions permit suit for injuries or death caused by an employer's willful, wanton, or reckless conduct. Several states allow increased workers' compensation awards if injury or death is caused by failure to provide safety devices, to obey safety regulations, or to comply with duties imposed by statute or regulation; and two states allow increased awards for serious and willful misconduct of the employer.

Generally, you retain the right to sue negligent third parties. For example, if you were injured by a malfunctioning machine at work and you were covered by your state's workers' compensation law, you would receive a set weekly income but could not sue your employer. Nevertheless, in most states, you could still sue the manufacturer of the machine on a negligence, strict liability, or product liability theory of recovery. If you recover damages from a third party, your employer's workers' compensation insurance carrier generally has a lien against that recovery to the extent of all wages and medical expenses for which it has paid.

Under what is known as the *dual capacity theory*, you might be able to sue your employer, not in its capacity as employer, but in some other capacity. For example, the employer may happen to be the manufacturer of a tool that injures one of its employees; the employee can sue, not as an employee, but as a user of the product. The dual capacity theory has been adopted in several states and rejected in several others.

How do I start my workers' compensation claim?

You must give notice of the injury to your employer as soon as possible, preferably as soon as you learn of it. This notice may be verbal or written, as long as it meets state requirements, letting your employer know that an investigation will occur and that you will file a claim.

You must also file a notice advising involved parties that a claim exists. The claim will usually be heard by a hearing officer, who may be a referee, arbitrator, or commissioner. The hearing process is generally simple and informal.

If you are unhappy with the hearing officer's decision, you may appeal to a full tribunal, which can review the entire record. If you are dissatisfied with the tribunal's decision, you can appeal to the state courts. The court will review the issues of law as applied to the facts and decide whether the tribunal's decision was justified. In some states, the court has the power to reexamine the factual issues in considering your appeal.

Can a closed claim be reopened?

Possibly. The workers' compensation administrator has the discretionary authority to reopen your case if your condition has changed significantly or if fraud, mistake, or abuse of discretion occurred in handling your claim.

Who pays for workers' compensation?

Employers. An employer cannot deduct the cost of workers' compensation coverage from your wages.

An employer may provide workers' compensation in three ways: (1) by buying a private workers' compensation and employer liability policy from a commercial insurance carrier; (2) by buying coverage through a state workers' compensation fund; or (3) by setting aside reserves sufficient to cover the risks involved. Most benefits are financed by the first two methods.

Are the benefits taxable?
Workers' compensation benefits are not subject to income or payroll taxes. Also, in most states, such benefits are exempt from claims of your creditors and may not be assigned. These exemptions may not apply, however, to unpaid taxes, alimony, child support, or attorney's fees.

What is the time limit for filing a claim?
Each state has a statute of limitations for filing a workers' compensation claim, but the statutes vary greatly. In some states, the statute of limitations begins to run from the time you were injured. In other states, the statute starts to run when you realize that you were in fact injured. If you have an occupational disease, the statute generally starts to run when you know (or should know) that you have a disease and that it was connected with your job. Also, the statute of limitations may be tolled during any period that you receive benefits before filing a claim.

What if the statute of limitations has already run?
You *may* still be able to pursue your workers' compensation claim. For example, your lateness may be excused if you had thought your injury was minor, if your injury was latent, if you were intimidated not to file a claim, or if there was a misrepresentation or mistake of fact.

Can I be discharged or disciplined for filing a workers' compensation claim?
Generally no. Many workers' compensation statutes contain provisions specifically forbidding retaliation against employees for filing claims. In some other states, the courts allow workers to sue for retaliation, even in the absence of an antiretaliation provision in the statute, holding that it is against public policy to permit retaliation for the exercise of the statutory right to compensation. (For a fuller discussion of such cases, see chapter 3 on termination.) Be aware, however, that not all states provide such protection and that, even in those that do, retaliation may be hard to prove and the process for obtaining protection relief can be difficult and uncertain.

SOCIAL SECURITY

Social Security is the popular name for the Old Age, Survivors, and Disability Insurance Program (OASDI), which was created in 1935 as part of the Social Security Act. The three types of benefits covered by Social Security are old age and disability benefits, which are payable to the worker; benefits for the dependents of a retired or disabled worker; and benefits for the surviving family of a deceased worker, including a lump-sum death benefit. Social Security protects workers and their dependents from the loss of income due to the worker's disability, old age, or death. Social Security is administered by the Social Security Administration (SSA), a federal agency.

For far more detailed information regarding Social Security, see *The Rights of Older Persons,* another book in the ACLU series.[2]

Who can receive social security benefits?

Social Security is a form of income insurance, not welfare, and thus is based on work experience and eligibility, not need. The benefit is based on the worker's average monthly salary in employment that is "covered" by the Social Security system. In addition, the worker must have worked long enough in the covered employment to have become "fully insured."

Is all work "covered employment"?

Almost all types of work count toward establishing eligibility for Social Security benefits. This includes part-time, freelance, and self-employed workers. Approximately 90% of U.S. workers are covered. Most workers who are not covered by Social Security are covered by another type of retirement plan.

Some workers, however, may not realize that they are not covered by Social Security. For example, workers may be ineligible if their employer failed to comply with reporting requirements or did not pay Social Security taxes for them. The responsibility for withholding Social Security tax and paying it lies with the employer. Self-employed individuals pay a percentage of their yearly earnings equal in amount to the percentage assessed against both an employer and employee.

Unlike workers' compensation, domestic workers (e.g.,

housekeepers, cooks, and gardeners) and agricultural workers are covered by Social Security.

How do I become "fully insured"?

To become fully insured, you must work in covered employment for a sufficient number of calendar quarters. A "calendar quarter" is a three-month period beginning on January 1, April 1, July 1, or October 1.

The number of quarters necessary to be eligible for benefits depends on the type of benefit involved. Generally, survivor benefits require the fewest quarters of coverage and retirement benefits, the most.

Do I have to be a certain age to receive retirement benefits?

To be entitled to any retirement benefits you must also be fully insured (i.e., have enough quarters of coverage), and you must have retired from your job. If you retire at age 65, you will be eligible to receive your full benefit. (This retirement age will gradually increase to age 67 beginning in the year 2000). If you delay retirement beyond age 65, the amount of your benefit will increase for every month you continue working until age 70; the longer you delay retirement, the greater your benefit will be. This increase is known as the *delayed retirement credit*. If you have reached 62, you are eligible for reduced retirement benefits that increase as you reach age 65.

Can my family receive my benefits?

Yes. You, your spouse, and your children may be eligible for retirement benefits. Your spouse is entitled to benefits based on your work record if your spouse is at least 62 years of age. Likewise, a former spouse is entitled to benefits if you and your former spouse were married at least ten years before divorcing and your former spouse remains unmarried at the time of application. The basic benefit of a spouse or former spouse is one half of the primary benefit.

A child who is age 17 or younger, single, and dependent upon a retired worker is eligible for benefits. An 18-year-old child is eligible if he or she is a full-time high school student. The term *child* includes adopted children, stepchildren, and (under some circumstances) grandchildren. If the insured worker is alive, the child will receive half of the primary benefit.

If the insured worker is deceased, the child will receive three-quarters of the primary benefit. In the case of spouse and child benefits, the claimant's benefits may be reduced if their total amount exceeds the family maximum.

Can I work while I am receiving benefits?
Yes. Persons age 70 or older may earn any amount of money without any loss of benefits. Persons under age 70 may earn a limited income. As of 1992, you may still receive full Social Security benefits if you are between ages 65 and 70 and earn under $850 a month ($10,200 per year) or are between ages 62 and 65 and earn less than $620 a month ($7,440 a year). If you are over age 65 and exceed the limit, your benefit will be reduced $1 for every $3 earned over the limit. If you are under age 65 your benefit will be reduced by $1 for every $2 earned over the limit. These limits change periodically and there are exceptions to them, so you should contact your local Social Security office for current figures.

Who can receive disability benefits?
You are eligible for disability income benefits if you are disabled, you are "fully insured," and you accumulated 20 quarters of coverage in the last 40 quarters before becoming disabled. The provisions discussed earlier governing the eligibility of your spouse and children to receive your retirement benefits also govern their eligibility to receive your disability benefits.

How can I prove that I am disabled?
The Social Security Act defines disability as the "inability to engage in any substantial gainful activity by reason of medically determinable physical or mental impairment which can be expected to result in death or which has lasted or can be expected to last for a continous period of not less than 12 months." Establishing that you are disabled within the meaning of that provision will be the most difficult problem you face in applying for disability benefits. You have the burden of demonstrating to the SSA that you are disabled. The existence of a disabling, medically determinable physical or mental impairment can be proven in several ways.

Some diseases (e.g., rheumatoid arthritis in major parts, advanced tuberculosis, acute epilepsy) are considered so serious as to be deemed "disabling" automatically. The SSA has complied a list of diseases considered to be disabling called the *list of impairments*. If you can establish that you suffer from a listed impairment, you will automatically be found disabled. You also can be found disabled if you can demonstrate that the disease that you have is the medical equivalent of a disease on the list of impairments. If your medical findings indicate that your condition is equal, in terms of severity and duration, to a listed impairment, you will be presumed disabled.

If you are not presumed disabled, you can be found disabled if your physical or mental impairment is so severe that you cannot do your previous work and cannot (considering your age, education, and work experience) engage in *any other kind of substantial gainful work*. This means any form of labor that exists *anywhere* in the national economy, regardless of whether that work exists near where you live, or whether a specific job vacancy exists, or whether you would actually be hired if you applied for work.

In trying to prove that you are disabled, you should assemble detailed evidence of your medical problems, age, education, and work history and submit this information to the SSA. A statement from your doctor is particularly important. It should outline your medical condition in detail and explain why your doctor believes your condition prevents you from engaging in any substantial gainful employment; a short statement that he thinks you are disabled without explaining why, will not be enough. If you have been treated by several doctors, obtain a statement from each. In addition to doctors' statements, you can submit statements from family and friends to verify, for example, that you are frequently tired and in pain and are therefore unable to work.

If you prove that you are unable to engage in your previous occupation, the SSA will try to show that you are able to perform some type of "work that exists in the national economy." A "vocational expert" may testify at your hearing that jobs exist that a person of your age, experience and medical condition can do. Because the rules governing disability benefits are complex, the assistance of a lawyer or other representative experienced in Social Security cases often is essential. Obtain help before you apply for disability benefits, and do not hesitate to appeal an initial determination by the SSA that you are ineligible—such decisions often are overturned.

Who is eligible for survivors' benefits?

Survivors' benefits are payable to the spouse of the deceased worker or to the worker's parents and children. The survivors' benefits provide monthly cash benefits and a lump-sum payment upon the worker's death.

To receive survivors' benefits, a surviving spouse (or an eligible divorced spouse) must be age 60 or older or between ages 50 and 60 and totally disabled, and the worker must have been fully insured at death. To be considered a surviving spouse by the SSA, you must have been married to the deceased worker for at least nine months, or have borne him a child, or have adopted his or her child. A widow may be eligible for mother's insurance benefits if her husband died fully or currently insured or if she is unmarried and is caring for the deceased worker's child. For a surviving divorced spouse to receive benefits, he or she must have been married to the worker for 10 years and be over age 60 (age 50 if totally disabled).

How do I obtain social security benefits?

You must fill out an application for the Social Security Administration and provide documents to prove your identity, age, and other relevant information. Visit or write the nearest Social Security Administration office for forms and for more specific information.

Your claim will be processed more quickly if you provide all the necessary documents with your initial filing. Therefore, you should find out as much as possible about SSA requirements.

Is the information in my SSA file private?

Generally, yes. With a few exceptions, it is illegal for an SSA employee to disclose information from your file to the public. These exceptions include providing information about your coverage to past and present employers and giving information to other government agencies for legitimate governmental purposes.

UNEMPLOYMENT INSURANCE

Unemployment insurance (UI) provides you with benefits when you become unemployed through no fault of your own.[3] You receive a weekly benefit based on your regular pay. Unemployment insurance is administered by both federal and state agencies. Although the benefits only partly offset lost wages, they can help keep you and your family going while you look for a new job or wait to resume your old one.

Are all workers covered by unemployment insurance?

No. Generally, to be covered by UI, you must have been an employee of a covered employer. In general, this excludes independent contractors, self-employed persons, and freelance workers. Also, certain kinds of employment are usually exempt; these include workers for nonprofit organizations, student nurses and interns, newsboys, casual laborers, certain government employees, some salespersons and brokers, minors working for parents, and parents working for children. Under certain conditions, domestic workers and agricultural workers may be covered. Sometimes an employer may elect to cover exempt employees voluntarily.

UI laws vary from state to state. You should contact your local UI office to answer specific questions.

Who is eligible for unemployment insurance benefits?

Basically, you will get UI benefits if you were a covered employee and then, through no fault of your own, you became and remained unemployed. Specifically, you are eligible for UI benefits if you meet each of the following five conditions: (1) you had "qualifying employment"; (2) you are "ready, willing, and able" to work; (3) you register for work with the state employment security office; (4) you file for benefits; and (5) the waiting period for benefits has elapsed.

Even if you meet these eligibility conditions, you may be *disqualified* for benefits if any of the following applies: (6) you refuse suitable employment; (7) you were discharged for misconduct; (8) you quit your job without good cause; (9) your unemployment was caused by a labor union dispute; or (10) you earned more than a specified amount of money.

How do I file for benefits?

You must go in person to your state employment security office. With special permission, you may be able to file your claim by mail. You will receive no credit until you have actually filed your claim. Therefore, it is crucial that you file as soon as possible.

As with filing for Social Security and Workers' Compensation benefits, you should have all supporting documents with you when you file; but don't delay filing just because you don't have all the records you need. File right away, and then get the records. The information you will need to provide includes your recent employers, your salary, where you worked (address, city, state), and why you left your job. You can be penalized for providing false or misleading information.

How long do unemployment benefits run?

In most states, the benefits run for 26 weeks. However, under unusual circumstances, this period is sometimes extended. The period may be less if you barely qualified.

How is "ready, willing, and able" defined?

To be eligible for benefits, you must show that you are "ready, willing, and able" to work. That is, you must prove that you are actively in the job market. This may be proven in several ways.

1. Keep a written record of the name, address, date, and other pertinent data for each job application you make and each job interview you have.
2. Apply for jobs in which you have previous experience or for which you have received specific training or education; that is, you must seek "suitable work."
3. Do not refuse an offer of "suitable work"; to do so may disqualify you from UI benefits.
4. Show that you are in fact looking for a job on your own. This may be done by checking want ads, contacting unions, following leads, and visiting employers. Also, you must register with your local employment security office.

The phrase "ready, willing, and able" is not always easy to prove or define. Various states have interpreted the term differently.

When you register with your local UI office, ask a counselor to give you specific, up-to-date information on the applicable standards.

How much is the weekly benefit?

Your weekly UI benefit amount is based in part on how much you earned when you were working. Each state has its own formula for this computation, and it is often complicated. The weekly benefit determined by these computations is not necessarily what you will actually receive. Some states add a few dollars to the weekly benefit for each dependent. Every state has minimum and maximum benefits. As of 1992, weekly benefits range from $5 to $335.

Can I collect unemployment insurance benefits in addition to benefits from a pension plan, workers' compensation, or social security?

Generally, no. Most states eliminate or reduce UI benefits for any week in which you receive certain "disqualifying income." Typically, this includes dismissal pay, retirement pay, workers' compensation for temporary partial disability, and old-age benefits under the Social Security Act.

What constitutes "misconduct" as a ground for disqualifying me from receiving benefits?

Generally, you are disqualified from UI benefits if you were discharged for misconduct. The definition of misconduct varies from state to state, but some basic principles apply.

The concept of misconduct is aimed at disqualifying the claimant whose voluntary and intentional behavior brought about the discharge. The misconduct must indicate an intentional disregard for the employer's business. It need not violate the law or a moral code.

Most states require that employee's misconduct be job related. In those states, conduct off the premises of employment or after working hours usually cannot be grounds for disqualification. Some of those states, however, allow disqualification if the claimant was discharged due to conviction for a crime that makes continued employment a detriment to the employer.

An isolated violation of a company rule is generally not considered misconduct, unless the violation had particularly serious consequences. But repeated violations of an employer's rule, particularly after warnings, is considered to be evidence of misconduct in most states. Thus, being absent or late for work frequently would be considered misconduct, while isolated instances of either generally would not.

Mere inefficiency or the commission of an error in judgment may be sufficient grounds for discharge, but are generally not enough to disqualify the claimant from UI. Rather, poor performance is grounds for disqualification only if it is a result of gross negligence or if it reflects an intentional disregard for the interests of the employer. Intoxication is generally not grounds for disqualification if the claimant is an alcoholic and thus the intoxication is a function of that disease rather than a result of the employee's free choice.

What constitutes good cause for quitting a job?

Generally, you cannot qualify for UI benefits if you quit your job voluntarily. On the other hand, if you quit voluntarily, but with "good cause," many states will allow you UI benefits. Basically, you are considered to have quit for good cause when you were virtually compelled to leave the job. The definition of good cause varies among the states. Some states include in their definition only factors relating to employment, while others have a more expansive definition that includes personal reasons. Personal reasons held to constitute good cause for quitting include moving with a spouse who has been transferred, caring for a sick relative in another state, and taking a higher-paying job that fails to materialize. On the other hand, some states deny UI benefits if you quit due to your marriage or to following your spouse to another place.

What can I do if my benefits are denied or terminated?

If you are denied UI benefits or if your benefits are terminated, you are entitled to a hearing before an administrative hearing officer. You should request such a hearing in writing; your local office may provide a form. You may be deemed to have waived your right to a hearing if you do not request it promptly.

The hearings are usually informal; formal rules of procedure and evidence are generally not applicable. At the hearing, you and your employer may give testimony and may present witnesses and documentary evidence. You may be represented by counsel. If you are unhappy with the decision of the hearing officer, you can appeal to the board or other tribunal set up for the purpose by your state. If you are still dissatisfied with the results, you can appeal to the state courts.

During the pendency of any appeal of denial or termination of benefits, you should continue reporting to your local UI office. This will establish your continuing eligibility if you receive a favorable decision on appeal.

NOTES

1. For more details you should consult a treatise on the subject. The best known are Larson, *Workmen's Compensation Law*; Schneider, *Workmen's Compensation*, and Blair, *Reference Guide to Workmen's Compensation. Also see*, Chamber of Commerce of the United States, *Analysis of Worker's Compensation Laws.*
2. Brown, *The Rights of Older Persons* (Southern Illinois University Press, 1989). Treatises to consult for more information on Social Security include *Social Security Coordinator*, Warren Graham Lamont (publ.) and McCormick, *Social Security Claims & Procedures*, 2d ed.
3. For more information on the Unemployment Insurance Benefits consult *Comparison of State Unemployment Insurance Laws*, U.S. Dept. of Labor, Washington, D.C.

PART 3
Discrimination

VIII

Discrimination: An Overview

Various federal and state statutes, as well as administrative regulations and local ordinances, forbid discrimination in employment based on race, sex, religion, age, national origin, and disability. In addition, discrimination is illegal in some jurisdictions on the basis of sexual orientation, marital status, arrest or conviction records, and other grounds.

Of course, an employer "discriminates" whenever it treats one employee differently from another, but such different treatment is generally legal. Unless a private employee is protected by a union or an employment contract, an employer has almost unlimited discretion to play favorites. In general, an employer lawfully may promote an inexperienced relative over a more competent person or pass over a person with an abrasive personality in favor of a less productive but passive person. An employer may even hire sports fans instead of movie lovers.

The law of discrimination as it affects private employees is very complex. This chapter introduces the subject of employment discrimination and covers various procedures, remedies, and other matters that pertain to employment discrimination in general. In the chapters that follow, the law applicable to discrimination based on race, national origin, sex, religion, age, disability, veteran or reservist status, AIDS, and sexual orientation will be discussed. Therefore, to thoroughly understand the law that applies to your particular situation, you should read this introductory chapter, plus the chapter or chapters that pertain to you.

What laws prohibit employment discrimination?

It is helpful to begin with a brief overview of the laws pertaining to discrimination in private employment. Many people think that the U.S. Constitution protects them against discrimination in private employment. This is not the case. For example, the Equal Protection Clause of the Fourteenth Amendment to the U.S. Constitution prohibits the states from making laws that deny the equal protection of the law to similarly situated persons. This prohibition, however, applies to discriminatory actions that are taken by governments or parties acting under governmental authority, and not to discrimination by private employers. The Thirteenth Amendment to the U.S. Constitution, which prohibits slavery, does apply to private employers. However, it has been narrowly interpreted to prohibit only the institution of slavery itself, and not the more subtle forms of discrimination that survived the abolition of slavery in the mid-nineteenth century.

The most potent antidiscrimination law in the area of private employment is Title VII of the Civil Rights Act of 1964[1] which was recently amended by the Civil Rights Act of 1991.[2] Title VII prohibits discrimination in private employment on the basis of race, sex, religion, color, or national origin, with respect to compensation for and the terms, conditions, or privileges of employment. Title VII prohibits discrimination in hiring, firing, promotion, transfer, job training, and apprenticeship decisions. It makes it illegal for labor organizations (e.g., unions) to exclude from membership, limit, segregate, classify, fail to refer for employment, limit employment opportunities, or cause an employer to discriminate against an employee on the basis of race, sex, religion, color, or national origin.[3] Title VII also covers referrals by employment agencies and prohibits employment agencies from discriminating on the basis of race, sex, religion, color, or national origin.

Title VII is administered by the Equal Employment Opportunity Commission (EEOC), an agency of the federal government.[4] The EEOC is responsible for enforcing Title VII and has the power to adjudicate and resolve charges of discrimination. As explained in greater detail later in this chapter, you may find that your rights under Title VII can only be effectively protected in court; however, before you can go to court you must file a charge complaining of discrimination with the EEOC or a comparable state agency.

Other federal laws pertain to discrimination by employers in the private sector. Section 1981 of the Civil Rights Act of 1866,[5] designed to implement the constitutional amendment abolishing slavery, guarantees all persons "the same right . . . to make and enforce contracts . . . as is enjoyed by white citizens."[6] Since 1975, Section 1981 has been read to prohibit intentional discrimination on the basis of race in private employment.[7] Additionally, "race" as it is used in Section 1981 has been interpreted broadly to include certain ethnic groups in some circumstances.[8] Section 1981 is discussed in chapter 9 on race. Section 1981's broad scope was limited by a 1989 Supreme Court decision;[9] however, the Civil Rights Act of 1991 (CRA 1991) has repudiated that narrow view of the law, and Section 1981 now expressly prohibits intentional discrimination on the basis of race in the "making, performance, modification, and termination of contracts, and the enjoyment of all benefits, privileges, terms, and conditions of the contractual relationship."[10] There are also federal laws that prohibit employment discrimination on such grounds as age, disability, and veteran status. Some state and local laws prohibit discrimination on the basis of sexual orientation. These and other laws are discussed later in this book.

In addition, in 1965, President Johnson issued Executive Order (E.O.) 11246 (later amended by E.O. 11375),[11] which requires that all federal contracts include an "equal opportunity clause." By signing a contract containing such a clause, the private contractor promises not to discriminate in hiring and to take affirmative action to eliminate discrimination. Additionally, firms with at least 50 employees that contract with the U.S. government for $50,000 or more must file an affirmative action plan setting forth specific steps for achieving equal employment. These Executive Orders are enforced by the Office of Federal Contract Compliance Programs (OFCCP) in the Department of Labor.[12]

One other federal law deserves mention. Section 1983 of the Civil Rights Act of 1871[13] provides that every person acting under the color of state law can be liable for acts of racial discrimination. Essentially, Section 1983 is aimed at prohibiting employment discrimination by public officials and other persons acting as representatives of the state. Further discussion of Section 1983 is beyond the scope of this book.

The federal civil rights laws are supplemented by state and local civil rights laws, regulations, and ordinances. All states except Alabama, Arkansas, Georgia, and Mississippi have state civil rights statutes affording some protection to private employees. In many situations, the EEOC (which enforces Title VII) must defer to or cooperate with the agency created to enforce the state civil rights law.[14] Many counties and cities have enacted civil rights laws that provide additional protection against particular kinds of discrimination.

Are there important limitations to these laws that I should know at the outset?

Yes. First, different laws have different time limits for asserting your rights. A court must dismiss your claim if you bring it to court or file your charge with the EEOC after the applicable time limit (called a statute of limitations). These and other procedural requirements are discussed in greater detail later in this chapter and in the chapters that follow.

Second, different laws cover different employers. Title VII applies only to employers that have 15 or more employees and that are engaged in interstate commerce (the transfer of goods and services between two or more states).[15] On the other hand, your state fair employment practice law may cover employers with as few as 4 employees, and Section 1981 applies to claims of discrimination based on race without any qualification as to the size of the employer. Therefore, in some circumstances, a victim of racial discrimination may be able to assert claims under Title VII, Section 1981, and a state employment law. In other circumstances, that same individual may have no remedy; for instance, the individual may have waited too long before asserting a Section 1981 claim, may work for an employer who employs fewer than 15 employees and may live in a state (e.g., Georgia) that does not have a state law prohibiting employment on the basis of race.

The laws also differ in terms of their procedural requirements and the relief they provide. For example, Title VII permits only limited damages for emotional distress (compensatory damages); and although it now provides for limited punitive damages as well, these are permitted only under certain circumstances. On the other hand, many state fair employment laws permit unlimited damages for emotional distress. Therefore, employees often claim violation of their state's fair employment law in conjunction with their Title VII claim. While this list is by no means comprehensive, it should give you an idea of some of the factors to consider.

Is there anything about the history of Title VII that I should know?

Yes. Since Title VII's enactment more than 25 years ago,

many important precedents have been established by employees seeking to enforce their rights under it. Title VII became a powerful tool for eradicating employment practices that were intentionally discriminatory as well as those that, however they may have been intended, were discriminatory in effect. These important precedents were called into question by a series of Supreme Court decisions issued between 1989 and 1991. These decisions seriously changed and severely limited the scope of Title VII's protection and struck a near-lethal blow to victims of employment discrimination. In reaction, major civil rights organizations marshalled their forces. On November 21, 1991, after a two year struggle, the Civil Rights Act of 1991 (CRA 1991) was signed into law.[16] This landmark legislation undid much of the damage caused by those Supreme Court decisions. It also extended new relief (such as jury trials and compensatory and punitive damages in certain circumstances) to victims of discrimination, including victims of discrimination based on disability.

A number of issues are still unresolved in light of these developments. One such issue is whether CRA 1991 will govern cases that were already pending when CRA 1991 was enacted and whether it will govern cases involving acts that occurred prior to its enactment.[17] Therefore, Title VII must be discussed both in the context of these recent Supreme Court decisions and in terms of CRA 1991. If your case was already pending on November 21, 1991, or if the discriminatory acts occurred prior to that date, it will be important for you to consult with an attorney knowledgeable in this area of law.

How do I prove discrimination under Title VII?

How you prove discrimination under Title VII depends on what you can prove about what happened to you. While the facts of each case are different, discrimination cases are usually based on one of two theories: disparate treatment and disparate impact. If you are to succeed in court, the facts of your situation usually must conform to the general outlines of a disparate impact or disparate treatment theory. This section provides an overview of what constitutes a disparate treatment case, including the stages involved in litigating such a claim, and the kinds of evidence required. The next sections do the same for a disparate impact case.

Thinking about your own situation in light of these sections will give you a clearer idea of the strengths and weaknesses of your case. It is important to remember that an attorney who specializes in this area of law will often see the facts of your case differently from the way you see them. Moreover, as a case develops, the strength of various facts often changes, making certain claims more easily provable than others.

A *disparate treatment* case is based on the idea of different treatment. In a disparate treatment case, you are claiming that you were treated less favorably because you are a member of a certain race, sex, religion, color, or national origin (called a *protected group*). For example, suppose you are a member of one of these protected groups and were terminated for failing to adhere to your employer's policy concerning lateness. At the same time, individuals who are not members of a protected group violate that policy all the time but are not terminated. In such a case, you could say you were being treated differently and less favorably. You must show that your employer intended to discriminate against you because you are a member of a protected group. If the other elements described later in this section are present, you may have a meritorious claim for discrimination under the disparate treatment theory.

Sometimes the discriminatory treatment has become the employer's standard operating procedure. This is a form of a disparate treatment case and is called a *pattern and practice* case. In pattern and practice cases, you allege that the employer engages in systematic disparate treatment of a protected class.[18]

There are three stages to litigating a Title VII disparate treatment claim. It is important to remember that ultimately the burden of proving your case rests with you, the plaintiff employee. The litigation begins when you file a complaint in court asserting that your rights have been injured. (Before you can file your complaint, you must have completed certain proceedings before the EEOC. These pre-lawsuit requirements are described later in this chapter.) In your complaint you must state facts you believe you can prove and that, when proven, will allow a court to infer that there has been unlawful discrimination.[19] Usually, you state facts that show that (1) you belong to a protected group; (2) you applied and were qualified for a job the employer was seeking to fill; (3) despite these qualifications, you were denied the position; and (4) after rejecting you, the employer continued to seek applications from people with qualifications like yours.[20] Of course, you adapt the facts in your complaint to reflect the particular adverse employment action, e.g., discipline, layoff, promotion, transfer, retaliation, or wages.[21] Upon proving these elements you are said to have established your *prima facie* case.

Once you have established your prima facie case, the defendant (employer) then has the burden (and opportunity) to rebut your claim of discrimination by offering a legitimate, nondiscriminatory reason for its adverse employment decision. The employer's task at this second stage of litigation is not difficult; the employer need not *prove* that the legitimate, nondiscriminatory reason was the real reason for its decision or that, for instance, the person hired instead of you was really more qualified. Legitimate reasons are *any* reasons that are not discriminatory. Employers are given broad authority in their employment decisions. As long as their decisions are not based on prohibited reasons, they will stand. Thus, an employer can claim it made the decision based on business conditions or because it simply liked a different applicant or employee better. The employer need not prove the absence of discriminatory motive.[22]

In the third stage of litigation you must prove that the employer's stated reason for the action is in fact merely pretext to conceal the real discriminatory reason for the employment decision. You can do this directly, by demonstrating that a discriminatory reason more likely motivated the employer, or indirectly, by "showing that the employer's proffered explanation is unworthy of credence."[23]

There are three kinds of evidence you can use to prove your position: direct evidence, comparative evidence, and statistical evidence. Generally, you should use all the evidence you can muster in each of these categories. Direct evidence includes derogatory remarks or statements by the employer or its representatives. Usually, discrimination takes more subtle forms and there is little, if any, direct evidence. Even when there is direct evidence, it may not be of sufficient magnitude to prove your case. Often, such evidence will be supportive, but not sufficient.[24]

Comparative evidence is evidence that shows either (1) that in a similar factual situation others were treated more favorably than you; or (2) that the employer acted contrary to its own policies in the way it treated you. Often, the employer will try to show that your situation is not really the same or comparable to those of the employees you cite. If the court agrees with the employer, it will rule against you; it may even exclude the evidence. For example, in one case,[25] the plaintiff maintained she had been denied tenure because she was a woman and that similarly situated males had been granted tenure. The court disagreed with the plaintiff's assessment that there were similarly situated males. The court found that to qualify for tenure, teachers had to demonstrate excellence in either scholarship or teaching. The plaintiff had not been rated excellent in either of these categories. In contrast, the male teachers had received excellent ratings in either teaching or scholarship. The court concluded the male teachers were not similarly situated because they possessed a degree of excellence the plaintiff lacked. As a result, the court excluded the information concerning them from evidence thereby undercutting the plaintiff's case.

Alternatively, the employer will try to show that you were treated the same as others not in the protected group. For example, suppose you claim you were terminated for filing a charge with the EEOC. The employer may counter by showing that other employees who filed charges with the EEOC were not disciplined or terminated. This will make it harder for you to prove that you were terminated for filing with the EEOC.

Finally, when an employment practice affects a large number of employees, statistics may help you prove your case. For example, an inference of discrimination can be raised by showing a significant statistical disparity between the number of protected group members in the employer's workforce as compared to the number of qualified members within the geographical area from which the employer recruits employees.[26]

It is important to emphasize that even when the defendant has produced enough evidence to raise a genuine issue of fact as to whether it was motivated by a legitimate, nondiscriminatory reason, the plaintiff may still prevail. To prove pretext, you should look for evidence that the employer departed from its usual practice, applied different criteria to minority workers, has a history of discriminating, or created a hostile work environment.

Can I prove discrimination under Title VII if the employer's policy appears neutral but has a discriminatory effect on a protected group?

Yes. Such cases are called *disparate impact* cases and were first recognized by the Supreme Court in its 1971 decision in *Griggs v. Duke Power Co.*[27] Under *Griggs*, a disparate impact case arises where a seemingly neutral employer policy (such as requiring employees to obtain a certain score on a preemployment test or requiring them to have a college degree) is applied uniformly but nonetheless has a disproportionate negative impact on a protected group (such as women or minorities). Since Title VII is aimed at "the *consequences* of employment practices, not simply the motivation,"[28] an employer who has no intention to discriminate, but who engages in a practice that has a discriminatory effect, violates Title VII.

Therefore, unlike disparate treatment cases, disparate impact cases require no proof of discriminatory motive.[29] Because disparate impact cases focus on the consequences of employment practices, statistics are extremely important and often figure prominently as the evidence of discrimination. Likewise, because the employment practice is one that affects large numbers of employees, disparate impact cases have more often been class action lawsuits rather than cases involving one individual. Disparate impact cases have challenged the use of aptitude and intelligence tests, degree requirements, length of experience requirements, physical requirements (such as height, weight, and strength standards) and requirements concerning arrest, garnishment, and credit histories. Disparate impact cases have also been used to challenge subjective employment practices, such as promotions based on a supervisor's subjective feelings about who can do a job better.[30]

The requirements for proving discrimination under a disparate impact theory were made much more stringent by the Supreme Court's decision in *Wards Cove Packing v. Atonio* in 1989.[31] CRA 1991 reversed, in part, and modified, in part, the new requirements established in *Wards Cove*. As this book goes to press it is not yet clear whether CRA 1991 will govern pending or pre-CRA 1991 cases.[32] Under the Civil Rights Act of 1991 disparate impact is established if the employees demonstrate that an employment practice causes a disparate impact and the employer fails to demonstrate that the challenged policy is job related and consistent with business necessity.[33] The employees need not prove intent. Employees are required to prove that each challenged practice causes a disparate impact; however, where the employer's "decision-making processes are not capable of separation for analysis, the decision-making process may be analyzed as one employment practice."[34] If your case is pre-CRA 1991, you should consult an attorney knowledgeable in this area of law.

Can an employer whose employment decisions are based on subjective criteria violate Title VII?

Yes. Many employment decisions are made wholly or partially on the basis of subjective criteria. These may include personal preference, judgment, or knowledge of candidates and recommendations, as well as such subjective categories as "ability to get along with people." An employer may not escape the reach of Title VII by basing its employment decisions on such subjective criteria. This is true for both disparate treatment and disparate impact cases.[35]

Can there be a violation of Title VII if discrimination was one of several reasons for the adverse employment decision?

Yes. Cases that contain both discriminatory and nondiscriminatory reasons for the adverse employment decision are called *mixed motive* cases. In its 1989 decision in *Price Waterhouse v. Hopkins*,[36] the Supreme Court articulated the burdens of proof of the respective parties in mixed motive cases. *Price Waterhouse* is itself a "mixed" blessing for employees.

In *Price Waterhouse*, the female employee, Hopkins, applied for partnership at Price Waterhouse, a major accounting firm. When the firm decided not to make her a partner, she brought a Title VII suit claiming that it based its decision on her gender. The facts clearly showed that some of the decision-makers based their decision on gross stereotyping (asserting that Hopkins should "walk more femininely, talk more femininely, dress more femininely, wear make-up, have her hair styled and wear jewelry").[37] The facts showed that the decision was also based on legitimate reasons (Hopkins's lack of interpersonal skills).[38]

The Court (in separate opinions) ruled as follows. A plaintiff who establishes that discrimination was one motive for the employer's decision shifts the burden of proof to the employer. The employer must then prove that there were legitimate reasons for the decision. In this sense, the case is good for employees. However, if the employer shows that it would have made the same decision even absent the discriminatory motive, then the court must find that there has been no violation of Title VII. This is bad for employees because it means that even the most blatant discrimination will be permitted if it occurs alongside legitimate, nondiscriminatory behaviors. This is what happened in *Price Waterhouse*. The employer was found not liable even though gender was a motivating factor because the employer established that the same result would have been reached for legitimate, nondiscriminatory reasons.

The rule in *Price Waterhouse* has been modified by the Civil Rights Act of 1991. Now, an employee who proves that an employment decision was motivated in part by an illegal consideration will prevail but will not win backpay, reinstatement, or damages if the employer can prove that it would have taken the same action even absent the discriminatory motive. If the employer can prove that, the prevailing employee only is entitled to attorneys' fees, declaratory relief, and certain injunctive relief.[39] Again, whether *Price Waterhouse* or CRA 1991 applies to pending cases is an open issue.

Is a seniority system illegal if it perpetuates the effects of past discrimination?

No, unless the seniority system itself was created with the specific intent to discriminate. As previously explained, Title VII does not require the plaintiff to prove that the employer intended to discriminate; it is enough if the employment decision has a discriminatory effect. In the area of seniority systems, however, Title VII creates an exception to this rule. Section 703(h) states[40] that it

> shall not be an unlawful employment practice for an employer to apply different standards of compensation, or different terms, conditions, or privileges of employment pursuant to a bona fide seniority . . . system . . . *provided that such differences are not the result of an intention to discriminate because of race, color, religion, sex, or national origin.*

In other words, even if a seniority system locks in the effect of past discrimination, it will not be found to violate Title VII, unless it was adopted because of its discriminatory impact.[41]

The Supreme Court ruled that there must be a finding of actual intent to discriminate on the part of those who negotiated or maintained the system. Furthermore, the Court has ruled that a discriminatory motive cannot be inferred from anything less than a factual showing of actual motive.[42] Thus, it is extremely difficult to prove that a seniority system violates Title VII.

Can an employer ever base its employment decisions on sex, religion, race, or national origin?

It depends. An employer may make employment decisions on the basis of sex, religion, or national origin in those limited circumstances where the characteristics are bona fide occupational qualifications (BFOQs) reasonably necessary to the normal operation of the employer's business.[43] There is no BFOQ exception that allows employment decisions to be based on race. The Supreme Court has ruled that the BFOQ exception is extremely narrow. Particular BFOQ situations are discussed in the succeeding chapters when appropriate.

Can I bring a Title VII action if discrimination at work makes it so intolerable that I resign?

Sometimes. If the work environment is so intolerable that it would force anyone to resign, you may have an action for discrimination based on constructive discharge. However, courts are reluctant to recognize such situations. Therefore, you should be sure to check with an attorney familiar with employment discrimination law before you resign with the idea that you could bring this kind of discrimination claim.

Can I be punished for protesting discriminatory conditions?

No. The Civil Rights Act of 1964 prohibits discrimination against you "because [you have] opposed any practice made . . . unlawful . . . by [Title VII], or because [you have] made a charge, testified, assisted, or participated in any manner in an investigation, proceeding or hearing under [Title VII]."[44] Similarly, Executive Order (E.O.) 11246 (as amended by E.O. 11375) penalizes employers who do not prevent the intimidation or coercion of employees who aid in investigations of alleged discrimination by contractors.[45] These provisions clearly provide you with a remedy if your employer retaliates against you (for example, by firing you) for filing a discrimination charge or for otherwise participating in formal proceedings. They also afford some protection against mistreatment or discharge in response to making an informal complaint.

On the other hand, not all forms of protest against discrimination are protected by Title VII. To determine the limits of protected protest activity, a balance will be struck between the intention of the fair employment laws "to protect persons engaging reasonably in activities opposing . . . discrimination" and the right of employers to fairly select and supervise personnel.[46] For example, an employee who had filed a discrimination charge with the EEOC was not protected from discharge by the antiretaliation provision when his employer demonstrated that he had a long record of unexcused absences and that other employees with similar records of absenteeism had also been discharged.[47]

In determining whether an employer's action amounts to illegal retaliation, a court might also ask whether the employee has simply gone "too far" in an on-the-job pursuit of one's rights.[48] One court stated that an action protesting discrimination is unreasonable and therefore outside of Title VII if it is "calculated to inflict needless economic hardship on the employer."[49] For example, an employer could properly fire an employee whose conduct went beyond legitimate complaints of alleged discrimination to the point of disclosing confidential information to newspaper reporters and circulating rumors that the company was in financial jeopardy.[50] An employee was protected from retaliation, however, for writing and circulating a petition that protested racial discrimination and for organizing employees to assert their legal rights.[51] Many courts would protect the employee against retaliation, even if the underlying charge of discrimination is found to be without merit, if the employee had a reasonable belief that the opposed practice constituted illegal discrimination.[52] Even though retaliation is illegal, if you file a charge you can expect to face a chilly work environment and, possibly, some form of retaliation. This is discussed later in this chapter under "What Should I Do If I Believe I Have Been the Victim of Illegal Discrimination?"

What types of employee recruitment practices violate Title VII?

An employer whose workforce consists predominantly of white males and who relies on its employees for word-of-mouth recruiting, may be practicing a form of indirect racial and/or sexual discrimination. Such a policy has been found to be unlawful because it tends to perpetuate the composition of the existing workforce and to limit the opportunities available to women and minority job seekers. While courts have recognized their inability to halt grapevine recruitment by a company's employees, they have ordered that specific job openings be advertised in media that reach other communities, and that the company publicize the fact that it is an equal opportunity employer.[53] Other recruitment practices that violate Title VII are discussed, where applicable, in the succeeding chapters.

Can an employer's use of tests during the hiring process violate Title VII?

Yes. Title VII explicitly approves the use of "ability tests" in the hiring process.[54] Under CRA 1991, however, an employer may not "adjust the scores of, use different cutoff scores for, or otherwise alter the results of, employment related tests on the basis of race, color, religion, sex or national origin."[55] The validity of these tests is discussed in the context of discrimination based on race (chapter 9) and sex (chapter 11), since that is where testing practices have been challenged the most.

Does Title VII prohibit discrimination in working conditions?

Yes. The antidiscrimination laws afford some protection against an employer who creates a hostile work environment for employees who are members of a protected group (e.g., women or minorities). An employer may not permit on-the-job harassment, such as the use of racial ephithets, the closer supervision of minority workers, and the uneven application of disciplinary rules. Nor may an employer permit other discriminatory work conditions, such as discriminatory promotion practices or job assignments. The EEOC has held that an employer must take reasonable steps to maintain an atmosphere free of intimidation of, and insults to, protected group members.[56]

To support a hostile work atmosphere claim, you must prove that management was, or should have been, aware of the offensive or discriminatory conduct but failed to correct the situation.[57] Therefore, in most cases, you should complain to your employer about the condition before initiating any legal action. Such a complaint will give your employer an opportunity to remedy the discriminatory working conditions and may help establish that your employer was aware of and failed to remedy the discriminatory practice.[58]

Can my employer prevent me from recovering under Title VII even if I prove that I have been a victim of unlawful discrimination?

Perhaps. In the last several years, we have seen the increasing use of a theory known as the *after-acquired evidence doctrine*.[59] The after-acquired evidence doctrine permits the employer to use evidence of misconduct that was unknown at the date of termination to prevent the employee from receiving relief or remedy on his or her meritorious Title VII claims. Thus, by using this doctrine, employers have been able to have otherwise meritorious suits against them dismissed. The employee's misconduct must be such that, had it been known, it would have resulted in immediate termination. The theory is that, since the employee would have been terminated immediately anyway, the employee is not entitled to claim relief under the discrimination statutes.

The number of courts adopting this theory is growing, and we can expect to see it continue to grow.[60] In many cases, plaintiffs have been unable to defeat the employer's argument to show that the employer would not have fired them even if it had known about the misconduct.[61] The following example is typical of these cases. Suppose an employee who has been terminated has a valid claim that the decision to terminate her was based on her sex. Suppose, however, that the employee lied about her educational background and age on her employment application. The employer does not know this information at the time it terminated the employee, and the information therefore did not enter into the employer's decision. During the course of the lawsuit, the employer discovers that the employee lied on her application. If the case is being brought in a jurisdiction that has adopted after-acquired evidence doctrine, the employee may not be able to recover on her valid sex discrimination claim. Instead, the employer will be able to have the case dismissed if it can demonstrate that it would have terminated the employee immediately had it known about the misrepresentation on the employment application—either because the employer terminates employees who lie or because the job called for an individual with certain experience or education.

On the other hand, in at least one case, the plaintiff successfully raised questions as to whether the employer would have refused to hire him.[62] There, the plaintiff failed to disclose both a prior felony conviction and his tardiness record from his previous employer. As to the felony conviction, the plaintiff presented evidence that the felony conviction was based on a law that was later struck down as unconstitutional and that his conviction was purged by a presidential pardon. Thus, it was unclear whether the employer would have refused to hire him had it known about the conviction, the unconstitutionality of the law, and the presidential pardon. As to the tardiness record with the prior employer, the plaintiff presented evidence that the tardiness record was compiled during a period of tension between the prior employer and the union and did not necessarily reflect the plaintiff's dependability. To bolster his argument, plaintiff presented evidence that he had "100%" dependability and "outstanding" attendance records with the employer during his temporary employment period of three months. Therefore, if you think that your claim may be defeated by this type of after-acquired evidence, you should consider how you might demonstrate that the employer would not necessarily have terminated you even had it known about the misconduct at the time it made the decision.

Can I be forced to arbitrate my claim of employment discrimination instead of bringing it to court?

Sometimes. In 1991, in *Gilmer v. Interstate/Johnson Lane Corp.*,[63] the United States Supreme Court ruled that a compulsory arbitration provision could force an employee to bring his claim of age discrimination to arbitration instead of to court. The court reasoned that there was no evidence that Congress intended ADEA (Age Discrimination in Employment Act) claims to be brought only in court. Since *Gilmer*, other lower courts have ruled that Title VII also allows for the enforcement of compulsory arbitration provisions.[64] It is likely that employment applications will begin to include arbitration clauses. You may wish to consult with an attorney before you accept employment where your claims will have to be arbitrated.

Although arbitration may be cheaper and faster, an employee is probably less protected in arbitration than in court. It may be harder to get from the employer the documents that will prove your discrimination claim. The arbitrator may be unfamiliar with the applicable law and, in any event, need not apply the law the way a court is required to apply the law. Worse still, the arbitrator may be biased. In addition, arbitration procedures generally do not provide for broad equitable relief and class actions. Therefore, the purpose of the antidiscrimination laws—eliminating discrimination in the workplace—will be frustrated. Finally, there already is unequal bargaining power between employees and employers; in many respects, arbitration will increase the disparity because the employee will lack the protection afforded by court procedures.

What should I do if I believe I have been the victim of illegal discrimination?

If you believe that you have been the victim of employment discrimination you must decide whether the problem can be solved by simply bringing it to the attention of the appropriate person within your company or whether to seek help from governmental agencies and the courts. This section outlines some issues you might consider in deciding how to proceed.

You do not have to hire an attorney to bring an EEOC complaint or even a lawsuit against your employer. Unfortunately, given the complexity of this area of the law and the backlog of cases filed with the EEOC, pursuing a discrimination claim solely through administrative agencies (like the EEOC or the state or city fair employment practice agency) is typically time-consuming and frustrating. Because this area of the law is so complicated and is constantly changing, you should consult an attorney experienced in equal employment law if possible even if you then choose to proceed without an attorney.

Whether or not you retain an attorney, the first action you should take if you suspect that you have been a victim of discrimination is to keep a written record of all incidents and facts relating to your complaint. For instance, if the discrimination involves the hiring process, as soon as possible after the job interview, you should prepare a summary of the names, comments, and questions of the employer's representatives during your discussions with them. If you were subjected to discriminatory remarks, you should note the name of the person who made them, the precise words used, and the names of coworkers who heard the remarks and could be called as witnesses on your behalf. You should also observe and record the numbers of minorities and women employed by the company and their status. You should gather copies of any employer evaluations of your job performance, and you should record any informal comments by your supervisors. You should list dates, times, and locations of incidents. You should not keep these records at work in order to prevent discovery by supervisory personnel. On the other hand, if you pursue your claim and file a lawsuit, you should be aware that the employer and its attorneys will eventually have the opportunity to review these records. The more scrupulously accurate and careful your notes, the better your evidence in support of your case.

You should speak to any other employees in your company who may have experienced discriminatory treatment from your employer. These employees may wish to participate in an action against the employer. A joint protest by employees is more likely to pressure an employer into making desired changes than an individual complaint. In addition, workers engaged in any collective action to improve their working situation are protected against retaliation by their employer under the National Labor Relations Act, which prohibits retaliation against employees for their participation in "concerted activities for . . . mutual aid or protection."[65] Rights of union members are discussed elsewhere in this book.

Before filing a formal charge, you should determine whether you can achieve your immediate goals without taking action outside of the company. Even if a lawsuit eventually results in success, the emotional and financial expense may be greater than the relief you are awarded by the court. Also, if you file a charge, you can expect to face a chilly work environment and, possibly, some form of retaliation. (Even though Title VII permits you to pursue claims for retaliation based on discrimination, you should decide ahead of time if this is something you are willing to endure.) Therefore, you may wish to try to inform your superiors of the substance of your charge and explore with them the internal measures that could be taken to solve the problem. If time permits, it is often a good idea to consult an attorney experienced in equal employment law before you file a charge; the attorney may be able to give you some understanding of the likely strengths and weaknesses of your case and the comparative advantages or disadvantages of the various federal, state, and local agencies.

If your company is covered by Executive Order 11246, you should direct your complaint to the Equal Employment Opportunity (EEO) officer in your company. You should remember, however, that the EEO officer is not impartial, since he or she is an employee of your company. Therefore, when meeting with the officer, you have none of the procedural rights associated with a governmental hearing, such as the right to call witnesses or to be represented by an attorney. Your object during your discussions with the EEO officer should be to present the facts of your claim clearly and completely. Nevertheless, during these discussions, you should consider the EEO officer a representative of your employer and should not disclose information that you do not want passed along to your employer.

If your attempts at resolving your complaint internally fail, or if the statute of limitations for filing a complaint is about to run, you should file a formal complaint of employment discrimination. Generally, it is best to file a complaint under all of the laws that apply to your situation. For example, you could file a complaint with a state agency or with the EEOC under Title VII, bring a court action under Section 1981, and file a complaint under E.O. 11246. Since the remedies under these laws are independent, you may pursue claims under these laws simultaneously.[66]

How do I file a Title VII complaint?

Title VII requires that you file a formal charge of discrimination with the EEOC or a state or local fair employment agency before you may file a suit in federal court. The charge itself is simply a description of the employer's conduct that resulted in the illegal discrimination. In filling out a charge form, whether with a local or state agency or with the EEOC, you should be careful to include *all* possible allegations of discriminatory conduct. Later proceedings will focus *only* on those issues that are related to the allegations stated in the charge.[67] At the same time, however, you should carefully avoid stating *any* unnecessary facts. Inconsistencies between the charge and later testimony may undermine the strength of your claim. All persons or companies potentially responsible for the discriminatory practice should be named in the charge because it is difficult to add additional defendants later in the lawsuit.[68] If you think that the employer's discriminatory actions may be typical of how it treats other members of your protected group (e.g., women or minorities) you may wish to state in your charge that you are filing it on behalf of yourself and other similarly situated employees.

What does the EEOC do after a charge has been filed?

Within 10 days after receiving the charge, the EEOC must notify your employer of the allegations of illegal conduct.[69] The EEOC will then investigate the charge to determine whether there is "reasonable cause" to believe that the allegations are true. These investigations, carried out by EEOC personnel, are supposed to last no longer than 120 days after the filing of the charge or after the 60-day local or state agency deferral period. Because of the backlog of cases filed with the EEOC, however, many investigations drag on for several years.

If the EEOC finds "reasonable cause" to believe that your employer has violated Title VII, it will try "conciliation," that is, to convince both sides to settle their differences informally. If no agreement can be reached, the EEOC may choose to file a lawsuit in federal court against your employer.[70] In such a court action, the EEOC will be seeking to enforce the federal antidiscrimination laws by obtaining relief for you. The EEOC will be represented by its own attorneys at no cost to you. You can limit your role to that of a witness, or you may join the lawsuit as an *intervenor*.

If the EEOC decides not to bring a lawsuit or if the EEOC does not find probable cause, it will issue you a *right-to-sue letter*, giving you the right to begin your action in court.

Can I bring a lawsuit in court without filing with the EEOC?

No. You may bring your own lawsuit in federal court under Title VII, but only after the EEOC has had an opportunity to examine your charge[71] and has issued you a right-to-sue letter. You have a right to obtain this letter 180 days after you file your charge with the EEOC,[72] regardless of whether the EEOC has taken any action on your complaint. EEOC regional offices may issue this letter before the expiration of 180 days, if requested.

If you wish to pursue your case privately, you must file suit in federal district court within 90 days after receipt of notice that the EEOC has dismissed the charge, or after receipt of the right-to-sue letter.[73] If you do not file within 90 days, you lose your right under Title VII to sue on your claim. It is extremely important that you decide whether you are going to seek the assistance of an attorney *before* you get your right-to-sue letter. Although 90 days may seem like adequate time to prepare a complaint, it may take that long just to find an attorney. An attorney will want to review the facts carefully before initiating a lawsuit. Of course, as previously stated, you may bring a private Title VII lawsuit in federal court without a lawyer.

Title VII allows a court to appoint an attorney for you if you need help. Title VII also permits the court to allow the lawsuit to proceed without the usual payment of various court fees and security bonds[74] and allows the court to award attorney's fees to the successful party.[75]

Are there time limits for filing my charge with the EEOC or local agency?

Yes, and they are very important. If your state or locality does not have an appropriate fair employment agency, you must file your charge with the EEOC within 180 days of the discriminatory act.[76] If there is an appropriate state or local fair employment agency designed to enforce a state or local law, the charge must be brought to that agency within the time limits specified by the local law. In general, in these states (called *deferral states*) the charge must be filed withing 240 days of the discriminatory act.[77]

You should be aware that you may lose your right to sue if you miss these time limits. The Supreme Court has ruled that no extensions of the time will be granted merely because you pursued your discrimination complaint through contract grievance machinery,[78] through arbitration procedures,[79] or through a federal court action under Section 1981.[80] In a 1989 case, *Lorance v. AT&T Technologies,*[81] the Supreme Court further limited the right of some plaintiffs to recover by ruling that the time in which to sue on a facially neutral seniority system that may have had an impermissible disparate impact begins on the date an adverse policy is adopted, not on the date it actually affects you. In *Lorance,* the company adopted a policy in which seniority was determined by time in a certain position, rather than length of plantwide service. The plaintiffs brought suit when they were demoted under the terms of the seniority policy, some three to four years after the policy had been adopted. The Court ruled that their claims were time-barred because the time to sue had begun on the date the policy was adopted. The Court rejected the *continuing violation* theory discussed in the next section of this chapter. Under the Court's ruling, employees who think a change in policy might affect them may be well-advised "to sue anticipatorily or forever hold their peace."[82] Therefore, no matter how you choose to pursue your claim, if your claim may be covered by *Lorance,* you should be sure to file a formal complaint within the time frame as specified.

The Civil Rights Act of 1991, however, reversed *Lorance* by providing that the time for asserting challenges to such laws begins (1) when the seniority system is adopted; (2) when an individual becomes subject to the seniority system; or (3) when an individual is injured by the system.[83]

What can I do if more than 180 days have elapsed since I was discriminated against?

If the discriminatory practice occurred more than 180 days ago, your action may be time barred. But you can still file your complaint after the 180-day limitations period has expired if the discriminatory practice is "continuing." Continuing acts of discrimination are those actions of the employer that cause you to suffer discrimination repeatedly. For example, if an employer has set wages according to gender (an illegal practice), each paycheck constitutes another act of discrimination; the 180- or 240-day limitations period will begin to run anew with the receipt of each paycheck. If your suit is barred by the statute of limitations, other avenues may be available. For example, you may be able to bring a Section 1981 or Section 1983 action.

How do I pursue a claim against my employer if it has contracts with the federal government?

Complaints of discrimination that come under E.O. 11246 (as amended by E.O. 11375) must be filed with the U.S. Department of Labor's Office of Federal Contract Compliance Programs (OFCCP) within 180 days of the violation.[84] The OFCCP has full responsibility for the administration and enforcement of that executive order. In racial discrimination cases, however, the OFCCP has restricted its role to reviewing the employment records of companies that have contracts with the federal government. Individual complaints filed with the OFCCP are transferred to the EEOC for investigation and processing under Title VII. If E.O. 11246 applies, you should file a complaint with the OFCCP, even if you plan to file a Title VII charge with the EEOC, since your employer will be subject to losing its federal contracts if a violation is found.

What is a class action?

A class action is a lawsuit brought by one or more persons who are named in the complaint and who bring the action on behalf of themselves and all others subjected to similar treatment. If certain procedural requirements are satisfied, the named plaintiffs in a class action may obtain relief for others who have suffered discrimination, even though these individuals do not file claims of discrimination themselves.

In a Title VII class action, only one person must run through the Title VII-EEOC charge processing before the whole class commences suit. The other class members need not file a charge or obtain a right-to-sue letter.[85] The class may not, however, include persons whose Title VII claims would have been time barred when the class representative's charge was filed.[86]

Many lawsuits under Title VII have been class actions because claims of discrimination based on an inborn characteristic are particularly well suited for litigation in that form. Over the years, however, the courts have made it more difficult to fulfill the requirements for certification to proceed as a class action.

In one case, for example, a plaintiff who did not suffer *hiring* discrimination was not allowed to represent workers who suffered from that particular type of discrimination.[87]

What remedies are available if I win a Title VII case?

Remedies authorized under Title VII are designed to place you in the financial and career position you would have been in had the discrimination not occurred. Remedies can take the form of an order to hire, reinstate, or promote you; an injunction forbidding continuation of the practice found to be discriminatory; or an award of backpay, i.e., the wages that would have been earned had the discrimination not occurred.[88] Backpay awards may also include interest, overtime, shift differentials, vacation and sick pay, and pension plan contributions.[89] A backpay award is recoverable, however, only for the two years preceding the filing of the EEOC charge; and the court must reduce the amount of any backpay award by any amounts you earned or reasonably could have earned during the period in question.[90]

The Civil Rights Act of 1991 authorizes compensatory and punitive damages in some circumstances.[91] For claims arising after the enactment of CRA 1991 (and for pending claims if the courts decide CRA 1991 is retroactive), these additional damages may be recovered in cases of intentional discrimination (that is, disparate treatment cases). Compensatory damages are available for "future pecuniary losses, emotional pain, suffering, inconvenience, mental anguish, loss of enjoyment of life, and other non-pecuniary losses."[92] To receive punitive damages, you must prove that the discriminatory acts were done with "malice or reckless indifference to the federally protected rights of an aggrieved individual."[93]

The amount of compensatory or punitive damages is limited by the size of the employer. The maximums are $50,000 for employers of 15 to 100 employees; $100,000 for employers of 101 to 200 employees; $200,000 for employers of 201 to 500 employees; and $300,000 for those employing over 500 employees.[94]

As previously stated, these Title VII remedies are available to the successful Title VII plaintiff even if actions brought under different laws result in sanctions against the employer. For example, an employer found to have violated E.O. 11246 and

Title VII may not only be required to pay damages to the individual employees but may also lose its right to be awarded future contracts with the federal government.[95]

If I win a discrimination case, can I obtain attorney's fees from the losing side?

As noted before, an employee involved in a discrimination case should try to obtain counsel whenever possible. It is often difficult to retain an attorney, however, because discrimination suits are usually lengthy and may not involve much money. Title VII provides a partial remedy, granting the federal courts the discretion to award attorney's fees to the successful party.[96] Courts have generally awarded these fees to prevailing employees even where they are represented by legal services and nonprofit organizations.[97] No fees are assessed for representation by the EEOC.[98] Fees have not been granted to employees' attorneys in cases brought under state law if the state law does not authorize payment.

Can a court require an employer to hire or promote a certain number of employees from a certain group?

Yes. This is commonly referred to as *affirmative action.* Voluntary and court-ordered affirmative action remedies are discussed in the next chapter, "Race," because that is the context in which these remedies arise most often. It is clear, however, that affirmative action may also be used to remedy the effects of discrimination on the basis of sex.

NOTES

1. 42 U.S.C. §§ 2000e *et seq.*, as amended.
2. Pub. L. No. 102-166 was signed into law on November 21, 1991.
3. 42 U.S.C. §§ 2000e-2(a)(1), (b).
4. 42 U.S.C. § 2000e-4.
5. 42 U.S.C. § 1981.
6. *Id.*
7. *Johnson v. Railway Express Agency, Inc.*, 421 U.S. 454, 460 (1975).
8. *St. Francis College v. Al-Khazraji*, 481 U.S. 604 (1987); *Shaare Tefila Congregation v. Cobb*, 481 U.S. 615 (1987).
9. *Patterson v. McLean Credit Union*, 491 U.S. 164 (1989).

10. Pub. L. No. 102-166 § 101(1)(b).
11. Exec. Order No. 11246, 30 Fed. Reg. 12319, 3 C.F.R. 1964–1965, Comp. p. 339, as amended by Exec. Order No. 11375, 32 Fed. Reg. 14303, 3 C.F.R. 1966–1970, Comp. p. 684.
12. 41 C.F.R. §§ 60-1.2 *et seq.*
13. 42 U.S.C. § 1983.
14. 42 U.S.C. § 2000e-5(e).
15. 42 U.S.C. § 2000e(b).
16. Pub. L. No. 102-166.
17. *Compare Mozee v. American Commercial Marine Service Co.*, No. 90-2660, 5/7/92 (7th Cir.) (CRA 1991 not retroactive) *with Robinson v. Davis Memorial Goodwill Industries*, 58 FEP Cases 887 (D.D.C. 1992) (CRA is retroactive). The United States Supreme Court has granted *certiorari* on cases involving this issue and, by the time this book is published, probably will have resolved the issue.
18. *Hazelwood School Dist. v. U.S.*, 433 U.S. 299 (1977).
19. *Texas Dep't of Community Affairs v. Burdine*, 450 U.S. 248 (1981).
20. *McDonnell Douglas Corp. v. Green*, 411 U.S. 792 (1973).
21. *See generally* 2 Larson, *Employment Discrimination* § 50.22 (1990). *See Loeb v. Textron*, 600 F.2d 1003, 1014 n.12 (1st Cir. 1979).
22. *Bd. of Trustees of Keene State College v. Sweeney*, 439 U.S. 24, 25 n.2 (1978).
23. *Texas Dep't of Community Affairs v. Burdine*, 450 U.S. 248, 256 (1981). *See St. Mary's Honor Center v. Hicks*, 61 V.S.L.W. 4782 (1993). The impact of *Hicks* has yet to be assessed as this book goes to press. An attorney knowledgeable in this area of law will be able to assess whether you will carry your burden of proof.
24. *See, e.g., Cariddi v. Kansas City Chiefs Football Club, Inc.*, 568 F.2d 87 (8th Cir. 1977).
25. *Lieberman v. Gant*, 630 F.2d 60 (2d Cir. 1980).
26. *Wards Cove Packing Co. v. Atonio*, 490 U.S. 642 (1989). *See Int'l Brotherhood of Teamsters v. U.S.*, 431 U.S. 324 (1977).
27. 401 U.S. 424 (1971).
28. *Id.* 432 (emphasis in original).
29. *Int'l Brotherhood of Teamsters v. U.S.*, 431 U.S. 324, 349 (1977).
30. *Watson v. Fort Worth Bank and Trust*, 487 U.S. 977 (1988).
31. *Wards Cove Packing v. Atonio*, 490 U.S. 642 (1989).
32. The United States Supreme Court agreed to consider the issue of retroactivity and by the time this book is published, will likely have resolved this issue.
33. CRA § 105(k)(1)(A).
34. CRA § 105(k)(1)(B)(i).
35. *E.g., Furnco Construction Corp. v. Waters*, 438 U.S. 567 (1978)

(disparate treatment); *U.S. Postal Service Bd. of Governors v. Aikens*, 460 U.S. 711 (1983) (disparate treatment); *Watson v. Fort Worth Bank and Trust*, 487 U.S. 977 (1988) (disparate impact).

36. 490 U.S. 228 (1989).
37. *Id*. at 235.
38. *Id*. at 236.
39. CRA § 107(b)(3)(B)(i) and (ii).
40. 42 U.S.C. § 2000-2(h) (emphasis added).
41. *TWA v. Hardison*, 432 U.S. 63, 81 (1977).
42. *Pullman Standard v. Swint*, 456 U.S. 273 (1982).
43. 42 U.S.C. § 2000e-(2)(e)(1).
44. 42 U.S.C. § 2000e-3(a).
45. 32 C.F.R. § 191.50.
46. *Hochstadt v. Worcester Foundation for Experimental Biology*, 545 F.2d 222 (1st Cir. 1976).
47. *Brown v. Ralston Purina Co.*, 557 F.2d 570 (6th Cir. 1977).
48. *Hochstadt v. Worcester*, 545 F.2d 222, 234 (1st Cir. 1976).
49. *EEOC v. Kallir, Philips, Ross, Inc.*, 401 F. Supp. 66, 71 (S.D.N.Y), *aff'd*, 559 F.2d 1203 (2d Cir.), *cert. denied*, 434 U.S. 920 (1977).
50. *Hochstadt v. Worcester*, 545 F.2d 222 (1st Cir. 1976).
51. EEOC Dec. No. 70-119, 10 FEP 811 (1969).
52. *Berg v. La Crosse Cooler Co.*, 613 F.2d 1041 (7th Cir. 1980); *Sias v. City Demonstration Agency*, 588 F.2d 692 (9th Cir. 1978).
53. *U.S. v. Georgia Power Co.*, 474 F.2d 906, 926 (5th Cir. 1973).
54. 42 U.S.C. § 2000e-2(h).
55. CRA § 106.
56. *Rogers v. EEOC*, 454 F.2d. 234 (5th Cir. 1972), *cert. denied*, 406 U.S. 957 (1972).
57. 2 Larson, *Employment Discrimination* § 84.10 n.12 (1990).
58. *Watkins v. Scott Paper*, 530 F.2d 1159 (5th Cir.), *cert. denied*, 429 U.S. 861 (1976).
59. *Summers v. State Farm Mutual Automobile Insurance Co.*, 864 F.2d 700 (10th Cir. 1988).
60. *O'Day v. McDonnell Douglas*, 58 FEP Cases 535 (D. Ariz. 1992); *Churchman v. Pinkerton's*, 756 F. Supp. 515 (D. Kan. 1991); *O'Driscoll v. Hercules, Inc.*, 745 F. Supp. 656 (D. Utah 1990).
61. *See, e.g., O'Day*, 58 FEP Cas. 535.
62. *Punahele v. United Air Lines*, 756 F. Supp. 487 (D. Colo. 1991). *See also Kristufek v. Hussman Food Service Co.*, 61 FEP Cas. 72 (7th Cir. 1993).
63. *Gilmer v. Interstate Johnson Lane Corp.*, 111 S. Ct. 1647 (1991).
64. *E.g., Mago v. Shearson Lehman Hutton, Inc.*, 58 FEP Cases 178 (9th Cir. 1992); *Alford v. Dean Witter Reynolds, Inc.*, 939 F.2d 229

(5th Cir. 1991); *Willis v. Dean Witter Reynolds, Inc.*, 948 F.2d 305 (6th Cir. 1991).

65. 29 U.S.C. § 157.
66. *Johnson v. Railway Express Agency, Inc.*, 421 U.S. 454 (1975).
67. *Jenkins v. Blue Cross Mutual Hosp. Ins., Inc.*, 538 F.2d 164 (7th Cir.), *cert. denied*, 429 U.S. 986 (1976).
68. *See Williams v. General Foods Corp.*, 492 F.2d 399 (7th Cir. 1974). *But see Bowe v. Colgate-Palmolive Co.*, 416 F.2d 711 (7th Cir. 1969).
69. 42 U.S.C. §§ 2000e-5(b),(e); 29 C.F.R. § 1601.14.
70. 42 U.S.C. §§ 2000e-5(b),(f)(1).
71. *Mohasco Corp. v. Silver*, 447 U.S. 807 (1980).
72. 29 C.F.R. § 1601.28.
73. 42 U.S.C. § 2000e-5(f)(1).
74. *Id.*
75. 42 U.S.C. § 2000e-5(k).
76. 42 U.S.C. § 2000-5(e).
77. Although Title VII considers charges timely if they are filed within 300 days of the discriminatory act, under agreements with local agencies the charges are automatically deferred to the local agencies for 60 days. The EEOC then takes jurisdiction again only *after* the 60-day deferral period. Therefore, to come within the 300-day requirement, you must file with the EEOC within 240 days.
78. *Int'l Union of Elec. Radio & Machine Workers v. Robbins & Meyers, Inc.*, 429 U.S. 229, 236 (1976).
79. *Alexander v. Gardner-Denver Co.*, 415 U.S. 36 (1974).
80. *Johnson v. Railway Express Agency, Inc.*, 421 U.S. 454 (1975).
81. *Lorance v. AT&T Technologies, Inc.*, 490 U.S. 900 (1989).
82. *Id.* (Marshall, J., dissenting).
83. CRA § 112(2).
84. 41 C.F.R. § 60-1.21.
85. *Albemarle Paper Co. v. Moody*, 422 U.S. 405, 414 n.8 (1975). *See Hicks v. Crown-Zellerbach Corp.*, 49 F.R.D. 184 (E.D. La. 1968).
86. *See, e.g., East Texas Motor Freight Systems Inc. v. Rodriguez*, 431 U.S. 395 (1977).
87. *Wetzel v. Liberty Mutual Insurance Co.*, 508 F.2d 239 (3d Cir. 1975), *cert. denied*, 421 U.S. 1011 (1975).
88. 42 U.S.C. § 2000e-5(g). *See generally Albemarle Paper Co. v. Moody*, 422 U.S. 405 (1975).
89. *E.g., Royal v. Bethlehem Steel Corp.*, 636 F. Supp. 833 (E.D. Tex. 1986) (value of overtime); *Boomsma v. Greyhound Food Mgmt. Inc.*, 639 F. Supp. 1448 (W.D. Mich. 1986) (value of pension contributions, vacation pay, and medical insurance).

90. 42 U.S.C § 2000e-5(g). *See Pettway v. American Cast Iron Pipe Co.*, 494 F.2d 211 (5th Cir. 1974), *cert. denied,* 439 U.S. 115 (1979).
91. Section 1977A of the Revised Statutes *as added by* CRA § 102.
92. Section 1977A(b)(3) of the Revised Statutes *as added by* CRA § 102.
93. Section 1977A(b)(1) of the Revised Statutes *as added by* CRA § 102.
94. Section 1977A(b)(3) of the Revised Statutes *as added by* CRA § 102.
95. 30 Fed.Reg. 12319.
96. 42 U.S.C. § 2000e-5(k).
97. *Id.*
98. *EEOC v. Enterprise Ass'n Steamfitters Local No. 638,* 542 F.2d 579 (2d Cir. 1976), *cert. denied,* 430 U.S. 911 (1977).

IX
Race

What federal laws protect private employees from racial discrimination?

Numerous laws protect employees from discrimination on the basis of race. These laws overlap in some ways and are very different in other ways. Understanding their interrelationship will help you protect and enforce your rights.

On the federal level, there are the following protections. First, Title VII of the Civil Rights Act of 1964 (Title VII),[1] furnishes the most comprehensive protection to the private sector worker as it specifically outlaws racial discrimination in private employment. Title VII is discussed at great length in the preceding chapter, "Discrimination: An Overview." Second, the Civil Rights Act of 1866 (Section 1981),[2] designed to implement the constitutional amendment abolishing slavery,[3] guarantees to all persons "the same right . . . to make and enforce contracts . . . as is enjoyed by white citizens."[4] Section 1981 prohibits racial discrimination in both the private and public sectors.[5] Section 1981 is discussed later in this chapter. Third, some private employees are protected by Executive Order 11246.[6] Under E.O. 11246, any private employer that has a contract with the federal government must agree not to discriminate on the basis of race. Such employers also may be required to make affirmative efforts to recruit and promote minority workers. The order is enforced by the Office of Federal Contract Compliance Programs (OFCCP) in the Department of Labor[7] and is discussed in the preceding chapter.

Additional protections exist on the state and local levels. Most states have enacted fair employment practice laws that, to some extent, prohibit racial discrimination by employers in the private sector.[8] Many cities have ordinances forbidding racial discrimination by local private employers or by municipal contractors or agencies. These state and local laws often create agencies that investigate complaints, grant relief, or institute criminal proceedings. Where such agencies meet federal standards, the EEOC will not act upon any discrimination charge that has not been previously examined at the local level.[9] Therefore, it is important to check the law in your area.

Discriminatory practices in general are discussed in the preceding chapter. This chapter discusses the issues that arise more frequently in the context of discrimination based on race and the federal laws prohibiting such discrimination.

What is the significance of having different laws?

Different laws cover different situations, have different procedural requirements (including different time limitations) and provide different remedies. Some of the main differences among the federal laws are discussed in greater detail in the preceding chapter. Using all of the legal remedies available to you on the federal, state, and local levels will allow you to obtain the most complete relief possible. Avoiding claims under laws that do not protect you is likewise important. Courts must dismiss such claims, and, in some instances, an employer might even seek sanctions against you for having brought "frivolous" claims to court. In addition, the Civil Rights Act of 1991 prohibits you from obtaining duplicate relief for compensatory and punitive damages for race discrimination under both Title VII and Section 1981.[10]

What racial groups are protected by the federal laws against racial discrimination?

Antidiscrimination laws protect all racial groups—not only African-American workers, but also Hispanic, Asian, and American Indian workers. White workers are also protected.[11]

Additionally, the laws against racial discrimination prohibit discrimination on the basis of association with minorities or minority organizations. Courts have found violation of federal laws where an employer denied employment to an applicant on the grounds of the applicant's interracial marriage, where an employer denied promotion to a union steward who represented an African-American man in a series of discrimination claims, and where an employee was "forced" into early retirement for selling a home to an African-American coworker.[12] The courts considered these employees victims of racially discriminatory employment practices and allowed them relief under these laws.

What forms of employer conduct violate the prohibition against racial discrimination?

The federal and state fair employment laws prohibit all forms of overt racial discrimination. An employer may not pursue a "whites only" hiring policy or maintain segregated facilities, such as restrooms, lockers, dressing rooms, eating areas, or employer-provided housing.[13] An employer may not assign jobs along racial lines. For example, it may not assign more dangerous or unpleasant jobs to African Americans,[14] assign African-American police officers only to African-American residential areas, or assign African-American salespersons to so-called African-American accounts.[15]

An employer may not consider race in determining employee compensation. Thus, pay rates or raises[16] and the allocation of such benefits as vacations and bonuses[17] may not be apportioned on the basis of race. An employee's hours may not be reduced or an employee be assigned less desirable hours because of race. Employees must have equal opportunity to work overtime[18] and to obtain favorable overtime hours.[19] They must have equal opportunity to obtain promotions or transfers.[20] An employer may not make employment decisions on the basis of stereotypes about abilities or traits, for example, failing to promote a given minority to a certain job on the grounds that minority members would not be interested in the job.[21]

If an employer has practiced racial discrimination in the past, its current policies may operate in a biased fashion even though they appear neutral. Any compensation plan based on an employer's job-assignment policy is suspect if the underlying policy itself is discriminatory. For example, a company may properly compute retirement benefits based on past levels of compensation. But if the company previously paid lower wages to minority workers based on racially discriminatory job classifications, the apparently neutral retirement plan will operate illegally to lock in the effects of past discrimination.[22]

Courts will generally uphold an employer's evenhanded application of its grooming and dress requirements, even where the employees maintain that the policy has an adverse effect on cultural identification or pride. Thus, prohibitions against moustaches or against wearing hair "corn row" style have been upheld.[23] However, discrimination on the basis of immutable characteristics associated with race may violate Title VII, even where not all members of the race share the characteristic.

In addition to these distinct discriminatory acts, an employer is responsible for preventing a hostile work environment. A hostile work environment is created by on-the-job harrassment, such as the use of racial ephithets, the closer supervision of minority workers, and the uneven application of disciplinary rules. The EEOC has held that an employer must take positive steps, where necessary, to address or eliminate employee intimidation.[24]

To support a hostile work environment claim under Title VII, you must show a pattern, such as the continuous use of racial epithets or the telling of racial jokes, coupled with an insufficient response by the employer.[25] Sporadic or isolated incidents are insufficient to support a claim. You must be able to prove that management was or should have been aware of the offensive conduct but failed to correct the situation.[26] Therefore, in most cases, you should complain to your employer about the condition before initiating any legal action. Not only will this give your employer an opportunity to remedy the discriminatory working conditions, but it may also help establish that your employer was aware of and failed to remedy the discriminatory practice.

Are there particular practices that, although neutral on their face, have been found to violate Title VII's prohibition against racial discrimination?

Yes. As explained more fully in chapter 8, employment practices that have the appearance of being evenhanded may have a discriminatory effect. Title VII prohibits such employment policies unless they are justified by business necessity.[27] Since Title VII strives to eliminate the discriminatory consequences of employment practices you need not prove discriminatory intent in such cases. Such cases are called *disparate impact cases*.

Over the years, courts have found that a wide variety of requirements may have a disproportionate adverse impact on minority applicants and employees. Courts will examine the use of degree requirements;[28] employment and aptitude tests;[29] height and weight requirements;[30] and length of service, seniority, or prior experience requirements[31] to see if they are discriminatory. To a lesser extent, courts will scrutinize an employer's practice of requiring arrest or conviction records[32] or of requiring information concerning garnishment, bankruptcy, and credit ratings.[33]

There is nothing illegal about any of these requirements in and of themselves. As discussed in chapter 8, if it can be shown that they were instituted with the *intent* of discriminating against a minority group they would, of course, violate Title VII. Similarly, under the disparate impact theory, the job requirement would still violate Title VII if it can be shown that (1) it has the *effect* of discriminating against minority applicants or employees and (2) there is no business necessity that justifies it. A practice will be deemed a business necessity if it is related to job performance in such a way that an applicant who did not meet the requirement would be unable to perform the job successfully. An employer hiring an electrical engineer, for example, could legitimately require that an applicant hold a degree from a school of electrical engineering because such a degree is considered a valid indicator of a skill related to the job. The requirement of a twelfth grade education for applicants to all office and clerical jobs, on the other hand, has been found to violate Title VII.[34]

Many significant cases benefiting minorities were litigated under the disparate impact theory. As explained more fully in chapter 8, the Supreme Court's 1989 decisions have made litigating such cases significantly more difficult. However, the Civil Rights Act of 1991 (CRA 1991)[35] changed the harsh results of those decisions, reviving the disparate impact theory.

What types of recruitment practices violate Title VII's prohibition against racial discrimination?

Although Title VII does not explicitly cover recruitment practices, courts have found violations of Title VII in recruitment practices that perpetuate or create a labor force of one race or that prevent minorities from learning about job opportunities.

The following practices have been prohibited. An employer may not have a policy of preferentially hiring the relatives of present employees if the workforce contains few minority workers.[36] An employer that owns two companies may not recruit workers for one company from the ranks of the other if the hiring policies of that other company discriminate against minorities.[37] Nor may an employer use a referral source that it knows discriminates in referring applicants[38] or recruit from predominantly white sources, such as educational institutions, if the employer's present workforce is racially imbalanced.[39] Such employers have been ordered to advertise specific job openings in media that reach the minority community, to list employment vacancies with state employment commissions, and to publicize the fact that they are equal opportunity employers.[40]

Title VII also prohibits discrimination by private and public employment agencies. An employment agency may neither refuse to refer a person for employment nor classify applicants for job openings on the basis of race.[41] In some circumstances, an employer has an affirmative duty to recruit minorities. E.O. 11246 imposes on an employer an affirmative duty to recruit minorities in order to remedy past discrimination. The same is true of affirmative action programs, which are discussed later in this chapter.

Can an employer's use of tests during the hiring process violate Title VII's prohibition against racial discrimination?

Yes. Title VII explicitly approves the use of "ability tests" in the hiring process.[42] Nevertheless, such a test will be invalid if it operates to disqualify a disproportionately large number of minority applicants, unless the employer can demonstrate that it "reliably predicts which applicants possess the reasonably necessary job skills and traits."[43]

The two most common methods of establishing that a test is job-related are called *content-validity* and *criterion-related validity*. A test meets the content validity requirement if it directly measures a skill or knowledge necessary to perform the job. For example, a typing test is an appropriate examination for prospective typists. Criterion-related validity refers to the accuracy of a test in predicting an applicant's level of job performance. The employer must show that the test reliably identifies those applicants who will function successfully on the job. The use of a written aptitude test, for example, would be suspect if, while it tended to screen out minority applicants, a significant number of those who passed the test failed to perform the job adequately. Such a result would suggest that the test measured abilities irrelevant to job performance. The EEOC's Employment Selection Guidelines establish minimum standards for the validation of tests used for hiring or promotion.[44]

The Civil Rights Act of 1991 changed the way in which these tests can be scored by banning the practice of adjusting the test scores to benefit those protected by Title VII.[45] This practice, known as *race norming,* though often secretive, was widespread and was used to eliminate the disparate impact of many tests. Now that race norming is unlawful, an employer may not adjust test scores, use different cutoff scores, or otherwise alter the outcome of employment-related tests in order to benefit members of any race, national origin, religion, or sex. Presumably, if you are denied an employment opportunity as a result of race norming by your employer, you may sue for discrimination under Title VII. Nor can employers defend against charges of test alteration by claiming it is being carried out as part of an affirmative action program.[46]

How do I prove that my employer's promotion practices discriminate on the basis of race?

An employer that does not discriminate in its hiring policies may nevertheless discriminate in its promotion practices. The first step in ascertaining whether this is happening is the most obvious: determine whether more minority workers are in lower level positions than in higher level positions of the company. For example, statistics indicating that African Americans are promoted at half the rate of white employees may, when combined with other evidence, show illegal discrimination under Title VII.[47]

The next step is to look for a particular practice that hampers the advancement of minority employees. For example, if African Americans are concentrated in certain positions, it may be because they are denied equal access to training. A company's training programs, whether formal or informal, must be available equally to all employees. All personnel must receive adequate notice of such programs and of promotion opportunities.

Evaluations of employees that are used to determine promotions must meet the same standards that are applied to hiring practices. Test and degree requirements for a promotion that have a discriminatory impact must be job related if they are to withstand a Title VII challenge. Subjective evaluations of employee work performance are particularly suspect since racial bias may influence such evaluations.

How can I prove that I was fired on the basis of my race?

An employer will often contend that an employee has been discharged for incompetence, insubordination, or other misconduct. A minority worker in such a situation should seek to determine whether similar behavior by white workers also resulted in termination. If whites were not terminated, the antidiscrimination laws may have been violated. For example, a trucking company could not legally discharge an African-American driver upon its learning that his license had previously been suspended when a white driver was not fired after the employer learned that he had lied on his job application about numerous traffic citations.[48]

The fair employment laws do not, however, prohibit an employer from discharging a worker for valid business reasons, as long as company policy is applied evenhandedly. Therefore, a minority employee may be terminated or demoted for engaging in disruptive acts against his employer—even if those acts have been designed to protest the employer's racial polices—if whites were terminated for engaging in disruptive events of the same magnitude.[49]

Is a seniority system illegal if it perpetuates the effects of past discrimination?

No, unless the seniority system itself was created with the specific intent to discriminate. This issue is discussed more fully in the preceding chapter, "Discrimination: An Overview."

Can an employer voluntarily adopt a plan to hire or promote a certain number of employees from a certain group?

Yes. The goal of Title VII is to eliminate employment discrimination. It would be ironic if courts prohibited employers from voluntarily adopting plans to eradicate the results of practices that, intentionally or unintentionally, have led to disparities in their workforces. Thus, Title VII leaves it to the discretion of the private employer "voluntarily to adopt affirmative action plans designed to eliminate conspicuous racial imbalance in traditionally segregated job categories."[50] There need not be a prior finding of discrimination in order for an employer to create and adopt such a plan. The Civil Rights Act of 1991 expressly protects "court-ordered remedies, affirmative action, or conciliation agreements that are in accordance with the law."[51]

The validity of affirmative action plans has been upheld when they are designed to attain, not maintain, a workforce whose composition better reflects the proportion of qualified minorities and women in the area labor force and when the interests of nonminority members of the workforce (e.g., white males) are not unnecessarily trammeled.[52] As contradictory as it seems, a court is more likely to uphold an affirmative action plan that addresses hiring and promotion than one that tries to maintain prior affirmative action gains in the context of a layoff.[53] Those challenging affirmative action plans have the burden of proving that they are not valid. They must prove that the employer could achieve its goal by alternative means that would have less impact on nonprotected group members (i.e., nonminorities).[54]

Two examples illustrate these principles. In *Steelworkers v. Weber*,[55] the employer recognized that it had very few African Americans employed in skilled craft positions at one of its plants, even though approximately 39% of the local workforce was African American. On its own initiative, the employer created the following plan to remedy the situation. It reserved for African-American employees 50% of the openings in in-plant, craft-training programs until the percentage of African-American craftworkers in the plant was comparable to the percentage of African Americans in the local laborforce. The Court upheld the plan, noting that it conformed with the purpose of Title VII. The Court stated that the plan did not unnecessarily trammel the interests of white employees since it neither required their discharge nor created an absolute bar to their advancement. The Court also noted that the plan was a temporary measure that would cease once the employer attained a racially balanced workforce.

The Supreme Court also upheld the voluntary affirmative action program in *Johnson v. Transportation Agency, Santa Clara County*.[56] That program allowed the employer to consider the gender of qualified applicants as one of a number of factors in making promotions within traditionally segregated job categories in which women had been "significantly underrepresented." It did not set aside a specific number of positions for women. Instead, it looked for yearly improvement with a long-term goal of attaining a "work force whose composition reflected the proportion of minorities and women in the area labor force."[57] The Court concluded that the plan did not unnecessarily trammel the rights of the white male employees and was a remedial, not a permanent, measure.

Sometimes litigation is settled by means of a consent decree, a decree to which the parties (usually the victims of discrimination and the employer or union whom they have sued) agree and that a court, in effect, adopts. Such consent decrees are considered voluntary. Therefore, those consent decrees that contain affirmative action plans are governed by the principles outlined above.[58] In 1989 the Supreme Court limited the effectiveness of such consent decrees by ruling that they could be challenged years after they have been approved by the court.[59] The Civil Rights Act of 1991 severely limits such attacks. Now, persons who had actual notice of the proposed judgment and a reasonable opportunity to object to it or individuals whose interests were adequately represented by another party may not attack such consent decrees.[60] There will, however, continue to be attacks by persons claiming that such consent decrees deny them due process of law; the court will have to decide the scope of the due process to be afforded.[61]

Can a court require an employer to hire or promote a certain number of employees from a certain group?

Yes. Mandatory affirmative action programs are also legal. Title VII authorizes courts to order appropriate affirmative action to remedy past discrimination.[62] Such plans may include requirements for hiring and promotion goals. As with voluntary plans, it does not matter whether the employer practices that resulted in the disproportionate underrepresentation of minorities were intentional or unintentional. At the same time, Title VII prohibits courts from requiring the hiring or promotion of an individual if the employment decision was made for any reason other than discrimination (for example, if the individual was not qualified for the job).[63] Thus, affirmative action does not mean that a minority person who is not qualified for a job must be given that job. Rather, it means that qualified minority persons must be recruited and be considered fully for employment and promotion.

Courts are given broad latitude to fashion an affirmative action remedy that is appropriate to the facts of the particular situation before it. Where appropriate, courts have ordered employers to hire and promote workers according to formulas that favor identified minority applicants until certain hiring goals are met. Such remedies need not be limited to actual victims of discrimination. For example, in *Local 28 of the Sheet Metal Workers' Int'l Assoc. v. EEOC*,[64] the Court directed the discriminating union to pay a fine that would be used to support affirmative action and to meet a membership goal of 29% African Americans and Hispanics by 1987. The Court noted that where the record showed "pervasive and egregious discrimination" and the "egregious violation of Title VII" it was not necessary to limit affirmative relief (in this case union membership) to actual victims of discrimination. Rather, the relief extended to the class of African Americans and Hispanic applicants for union membership. Notably, in this case, there had been over twenty years of rulings by various state and federal court and administrative agencies finding that the union had excluded minorities for discriminatory reasons. The union had disregarded repeated court orders to adopt the 29% African American and Hispanic membership goal.[65]

How do I bring a lawsuit for racial discrimination under Title VII?

The procedures under Title VII are discussed in the preceding chapter "Discrimination: An Overview."

Do federal laws other than Title VII prohibit discrimination on the basis of race by private employers?

Yes. The most important of these (and the only one covered in this book)[66] is Section 1981 of the Civil Rights Act of 1866.[67] Section 1981 was designed to implement the Thirteenth Amendment to the United States Constitution (the amendment abolishing slavery). Section 1981 guarantees "all persons" the same rights as "white persons" when it comes to making and enforcing contracts. Section 1981 has long been interpreted to prohibit discrimination in private employment based on race.[68] Exactly what "race" means has been a matter of some controversy, as discussed in the next section. Although the meaning and usefulness of the statute was complicated (and greatly limited) by the United States Supreme Court's decision in 1989 in *McLean v. Patterson Credit Union*,[69] the Civil Rights Act of 1991 has restored the prior law.

Who can sue under Section 1981?

Obviously, Section 1981 includes African Americans. Other groups have also been able to claim protection under the statute. The Supreme Court has held that whites have a claim under Section 1981 for (1) discrimination against them and in favor of African Americans;[70] (2) discrimination against them because of their association with or activities on behalf of African Americans;[71] and (3) discrimination by one white against another.[72] Hispanics and noncaucasians can sue under Section 1981.[73] Finally, although most courts that have considered the question have held that Section 1981 does not support a claim for discrimination on the basis of national origin, other courts have upheld such claims where national origin is in fact indistinguishable from race.[74] Recent Supreme Court decisions maintain that race under Section 1981 is to be understood in the same manner as the 39th Congress understood it in 1866.[75] Therefore, certain groups, such as Jews and Arabs, that would have been considered separate races in 1866 are considered separate races for purposes of Section 1981 and can sue under it.

Which private employers are covered by Section 1981?

Section 1981's prohibitions apply to all persons and to legal entities (such as corporations). Under Section 1981, an aggrieved employee can bring suit in federal court against any employer, no matter how large or small. Therefore, even if your employer is too small to be covered by Title VII, you still may be able to bring a federal lawsuit if you can satisfy the other requirements of a Section 1981 claim as discussed in the next section.

What must I prove in a Section 1981 case?

To prove your Section 1981 claim, you must show discrimination on account of race. This could include a claim of retaliatory discharge.[76] You must prove that the employer intended to discriminate.[77] A variety of direct and circumstantial evidence may be used to prove intent. Circumstantial evidence of intent may include statistics or other evidence of the employer's selective enforcement of its procedures or policies.[78] Unlike Title VII, however, you cannot state a Section 1981 claim based solely on disparate impact. If you fail to establish discriminatory intent, your claim will be dismissed.[79]

Finally, since the statute provides "all persons" with the same right "to make and enforce contracts . . . as is enjoyed by white citizens" it would be likely to assume that it protected employees in most aspects of the employment relationship. This was true until the Supreme Court decided *Patterson v. McLean Credit Union*[80] in 1989. In *Patterson*, the plaintiff claimed she had been harassed, denied promotion, and terminated because of her race. The Court ruled that Section 1981 protects employees from discrimination only in the *formation* of the employment contract, not from problems that may occur later in the employment relationship. Therefore, the court concluded, Section 1981 does not protect employees from harassment on the job and only covers promotions if the promotion would create a "new and distinct relation between the employee and the employers." The Civil Rights Act of 1991 completely reversed *Patterson* and restored the prior law. Therefore, unless your claim is based on facts that occurred after *Patterson* and before November 21, 1991, and the court rules that CRA 1991 is not applicable to claims arising during that time, you will be able to assert a Section 1981 claim based on the "making, performing, modification and termination of contracts, and the enjoyment of all benefits, terms and conditions of contractual relationships."[81]

How do I enforce my rights under Section 1981?

Lawsuits under Section 1981 are properly commenced directly in federal district court. Private employees do not have to complete any administrative procedures first (such as filing with the EEOC). A Section 1981 claim is, for the most part, totally independent from a Title VII claim. An exception may exist where an employer has already litigated all the issues in state court under a state law claim that would be litigated in the employee's Section 1981 claim.[82]

The time period in which to file a Section 1981 claim is set by state statutes of limitations, not federal law.[83] Therefore, the length of time available to initiate a suit under Section

1981 varies from state to state; you should check carefully to make sure you find out the correct statute of limitations in your state. Because filing a Title VII claim does not alter the time limits for filing a Section 1981 suit, you should not wait for the EEOC to rule on a Title VII charge before filing a complaint based on Section 1981. If you wait, the time period for the Section 1981 lawsuit might expire while the EEOC is still investigating your Title VII claim.

What remedies are available under Section 1981?

Unlike Title VII, Section 1981 provides the following relief: (1) compensatory damages (those that compensate for pain and suffering or emotional distress); (2) punitive damages (those that are intended to punish the employer); (3) preliminary injunctions to prevent an employer from continuing the disputed practice while the case is being litigated (in Title VII cases, no injunction may arise while the charge is being processed by the EEOC or state administrative agency); and (4) backpay that, unlike Title VII backpay awards, is not limited to two years.[84] Additional monetary relief under Section 1981 may include an award to compensate for loss of work benefits.[85]

Under Section 1981 you may also obtain other appropriate equitable (nonmonetary) relief such as an order directing hiring, promotion, reinstatement, or retroactive seniority. Finally, courts have imposed affirmative action programs under Section 1981.

Will my Section 1981 suit be tried before a jury?

It depends on the kind of relief sought. If you are seeking only equitable (nonmonetary) relief, such as reinstatement, the case is tried before a judge, not a jury. If you are seeking legal relief (monetary damages), you have a right to a jury trial. It is unsettled, however, whether backpay is considered legal or equitable relief.[86]

NOTES

1. 42 U.S.C. §§ 2000e *et seq.*, as amended.
2. 42 U.S.C. § 1981.
3. U.S. Constitution, Amendment XIII.
4. 42 U.S.C. § 1981.
5. *Johnson v. Railway Express Agency, Inc.*, 421 U.S. 454 (1975).

6. Exec. Order No. 11246, 30 Fed. Reg. 12319, 3 C.F.R. 1964–1965, Comp. p. 339, as amended by Exec. Order No. 11375, 32 Fed. Reg. 14303, 3 C.F.R. 1966–1970, Comp. p. 684.
7. 41 C.F.R. §§ 60–1.1 *et seq.*
8. Alabama, Arkansas, Georgia, and Mississippi are the only states that have no law prohibiting racial discrimination. Moreover, the extent of the protection provided by the various state laws varies markedly from state to state.
9. 42 U.S.C. § 2000e-5(c).
10. CRA § 102.
11. *McDonald v. Santa Fe Trail Transportation Co.*, 427 U.S. 273 (1976).
12. *Chacon v. California Dept. of Corrections*, No. SACV 90-679-GLT, 12/31/91 (D. Cal.). *Faraca v. Clements*, 10 FEP Cas. 718 (N.D. Ga. 1973), *aff'd*, 506 F.2d 956 (5th Cir.), *cert. denied*, 422 U.S. 1006 (1975) (interracial marriage); *Sperling v. United States*, 515 F.2d 465 (3d Cir. 1975), *cert. denied*, 426 U.S. 919 (1976) (promotion); *DeMatteis v. Eastman Kodak Co.*, 511 F.2d 306 (2d Cir.), *aff'd in relevant part*, 520 F.2d 409 (2d Cir. 1975) (retirement).
13. *Firefighters Institute for Racial Equality v. City of St. Louis*, 588 F.2d 235 (8th Cir. 1978), *cert. denied*, 443 U.S. 904 (1979) (eating facilities); *DeMatteis v. Eastman Kodak Co.*, 511 F.2d 306 (2d Cir.), *aff'd in relevant part*, 520 F.2d 409 (2d Cir. 1975) (housing); *EEOC v. H.S. Camp & Sons*, 33 FEP Cas. 330 (M.D. Fla. 1982) (restrooms).
14. *Segar v. Civiletti*, 508 F. Supp. 690 (D.D.C. 1981); *Eubanks v. Pickens-Bond Construction Co.*, 635 F.2d 1341 (8th Cir. 1980).
15. *Baker v. City of St. Petersburg*, 400 F.2d 294 (5th Cir. 1968).
16. *Paxton v. Union National Bank*, 688 F.2d 552 (8th Cir. 1982), *cert. denied*, 460 U.S. 1083 (1983); *Eubanks v. Pickens-Bond Construction Co.*, 635 F.2d 1341 (8th Cir. 1980).
17. *Rice v. Litton Systems Inc.*, 8 FEP Cas. 763 (D.C. Cir. 1974) (workloads, vacations).
18. *E.g., Sanders v. Sherwin-Williams Co.*, 495 F. Supp. 571 (E.D. Mich. 1980).
19. *Eubanks v. Pickens-Bond Construction Co.*, 635 F.2d 1341 (8th Cir. 1980).
20. *Newman v. Avco Corp.*, 313 F. Supp. 1069 (M.D. 1970), *reversed*, 451 F.2d 743 (6th Cir. 1971), *on remand*, 491 F. Supp. 89 (M.D. Tenn. 1973).
21. *Lams v. General Waterworks Corp.*, 766 F.2d 386 (8th Cir. 1985) (supervisor failed to recommend African Americans for promotion based on subjective belief that they were not interested in being promoted to other jobs).

22. *But see Carpenter v. Stephen F. Austin State University,* 706 F.2d 608 (5th Cir. 1983).

23. *Rogers v. American Airlines,* 527 F. Supp. 229 (S.D.N.Y. 1981) (hair).

24. *See, e.g.,* EEOC Dec. 72-0779, 4 FEP Cas. 317 (1971).

25. *Hunter v. Allis-Chalmers Corp., Engine Div.,* 797 F.2d 1417 (7th Cir. 1986); *Snell v. Suffolk County,* 782 F.2d 1094 (2d Cir. 1986).

26. *See Edwards v. Foucar, Ray & Simon, Inc.,* 23 FEP Cas. 1644 (N.D. Cal. 1980) (plaintiff fails to meet criteria).

27. *Griggs v. Duke Power Co.,* 401 U.S. 424 (1971).

28. *Id.*

29. *Id.*

30. *Davis v. County of Los Angeles,* 566 F.2d 1334 (9th Cir. 1977), *vacated on grounds of mootness,* 440 U.S. 625 (1979) (height requirements disproportionately affecting Hispanics). *See Dothard v. Rawlinson,* 433 U.S. 321 (1977) (height and weight requirements disproportionately affecting women).

31. *Fisher v. Proctor & Gamble Mfg. Co.,* 613 F.2d 527, 541 n.27 (5th Cir. 1980), *cert. denied,* 449 U.S. 1115 (1981) (length of prior experience).

32. *Green v. Missouri Pacific Railroad Co.,* 523 F.2d 1290 (8th Cir. 1975); EEOC Dec. No. 71-797, 3 FEP Cas. 266.

33. *Williams v. St. Louis Diecasting Corp.,* 470 F. Supp. 1205 (E.D. Mo.), *appeal dismissed,* 611 F.2d 1223 (8th Cir. 1979) (garnishment); *EEOC v. American National Bank, aff'd in part, reversed in part, vacated in part,* 21 FEP Cas. 1532 (E.D. Va. 1979) *cert. denied,* 459 U.S. 923 (1982) (credit records).

34. *Griggs v. Duke Power Co.,* 401 U.S. 424 (1971).

35. Pub. L. No. 102-166 was signed into law November 21, 1991.

36. *McCoy v. Safeway Stores, Inc.,* 5 FEP Cas. 628 (D.D.C. Cir. 1973); EEOC Dec. No. 71-797, 3 FEP 266.

37. *EEOC v. N.Y. Times Broadcasting Service Co.,* 542 F.2d 356 (6th Cir. 1976).

38. *E.g., United States v. Sheet Metal Workers Int'l. Assoc., Local No. 36,* 416 F.2d 123 (8th Cir. 1969).

39. *United States v. Georgia Power Co.,* 474 F.2d 906 (5th Cir. 1973).

40. *E.g., Id.* at 926 (5th Cir. 1973). *See Stamps v. Detroit Edison Co.,* 365 F. Supp. 87 (E.D. Mich. 1973), *reversed on other grounds,* 515 F.2d 301 (6th Cir. 1975).

41. 42 U.S.C. § 2000e-2(b).

42. 42 U.S.C. § 2000e-2(h).

43. *United States v. Georgia Power Co.,* 474 F.2d 906, 912 (5th Cir. 1973).

44. 29 C.F.R. § 1607.14.

45. CRA § 106.
46. *See Bridgeport Guardians, Inc. v. City of Bridgeport*, 933 F.2d 1140 (2d Cir. 1991).
47. *Rowe v. GM*, 457 F.2d 348 (5th Cir. 1972).
48. *Johnson v. Ryder Truck Lines, Inc.*, 575 F.2d 471 (4th Cir. 1978), *cert. denied*, 440 U.S. 979 (1979).
49. *McDonnell Douglas Corp. v. Green*, 411 U.S. 792 (1973).
50. *United Steelworkers of America v. Weber*, 443 U.S. 193, 209, *reh'g denied*, 444 U.S. 889 (1979).
51. CRA § 116.
52. *Johnson v. Transportation Agency, Santa Clara County*, 480 U.S. 616 (1987).
53. *Compare Firefighters Local Union No. 1784 v. Stotts*, 467 U.S. 561 (1984) *and Wygant v. Jackson Board of Education*, 476 U.S. 267 (1986) *with Johnson v. Transporation Agency, Santa Clara County*, 480 U.S. 616 (1987) *and United Steelworkers of America v. Weber*, 443 U.S. 193, 209, *reh'g denied*, 444 U.S. 889 (1979).
54. *Johnson v. Transporation Agency, Santa Clara County*, 480 U.S. 616 (1987).
55. *United Steelworkers of America v. Weber*, 443 U.S. 193, *reh'g denied*, 444 U.S. 889 (1979).
56. 480 U.S. 616 (1987).
57. 480 U.S. at 616.
58. *Local No. 93, Int'l Ass'n of Firefighters v. City of Cleveland*, 478 U.S. 501 (1986).
59. *Martin v. Wilks*, 110 S. Ct. 11 (1989).
60. CRA § 108(2).
61. *Id.*
62. 42 U.S.C. § 2000e-5(g).
63. 42 U.S.C. § 2000e-5(h).
64. *Local 28, Sheet Metal Workers' Int'l Ass'n v. EEOC*, 478 U.S. 421 (1986).
65. *See also U.S. v. Paradise*, 480 U.S. 149 (1987) (upholding court-ordered affirmative action remedy based on Equal Protection Clause of Fourteenth Amendment to U.S. Constitution arising from similarly egregious facts).
66. Depending on the circumstances of your case, your attorney may also consider 42 U.S.C. §§ 1983 and 1985.
67. 42 U.S.C. § 1981.
68. *Johnson v. Railway Express Agency, Inc.*, 421 U.S. 454 (1975).
69. 491 U.S. 164 (1989).
70. *McDonald v. Santa Fe Trail Transportation Co.*, 427 U.S. 273 (1976).
71. *Des Vergnes v. Seekonk Water Dist.*, 601 F.2d 9 (1st Cir. 1979),

vacated on other grounds, 454 U.S. 807 (1981). *See Alizadeh v. Safeway Stores, Inc.,* 802 F.2d 111 (5th Cir. 1986), *reh'g denied,* 1990 U.S. App. LEXIS 18753.

72. *St. Francis College v. Al-Khazraji,* 107 S. Ct. 2022 (1987).

73. *See St. Francis College v. Al-Khazraji,* 107 S. Ct. 2022 (1987); *Manzanares v. Safeway Stores, Inc.,* 593 F.2d 968 (10th Cir. 1979); *Bullard v. OMI Georgia Inc.,* 640 F.2d 632 (5th Cir. 1981).

74. *Hiduchenko v. Minneapolis Medical & Diagnostic Center,* 467 F. Supp. 103 (D. Minn. 1979); *Bhandari v. First National Bank of Commerce,* 829 F.2d 1343 (5th Cir. 1987), *cert. denied,* 110 S. Ct. 1539 (1990).

75. *St. Francis College v. Al-Khazraji,* 107 S. Ct. 2022, *reh'g denied,* 107 S. Ct. 3244 (1987); *Shaare Tefila,* 107 S. Ct. 640 (1987).

76. *See Greenwood v. Ross,* 778 F.2d 448 (8th Cir. 1985).

77. *Firefighters Local Union No. 1784 v. Stotts,* 467 U.S. 561, 583 n.16 (1984); *General Building Contractors Ass'n Inc. v. Pennsylvania,* 458 U.S. 375, 389 (1982).

78. *See, e.g., Anderson v. Group Hospitalization,* 820 F.2d 465 (D.C. Cir. 1987).

79. *General Building Contractors Ass'n Inc. v. Pennsylvania,* 458 U.S. 375 (1982).

80. 491 U.S. 164 (1989).

81. CRA § 101.

82. *See Kremer v. Chemical Construction Corp.,* 456 U.S. 461, *reh'g denied,* 458 U.S. 1133 (1982) (Title VII claim); *Mitchell v. National Broadcasting Co.,* 553 F.2d 265 (2d Cir. 1977) (Section 1981 claim).

83. *Goodman v. Lukens Steel Co.,* 482 U.S. 656 (1987).

84. *Johnson v. Railway Express Agency, Inc.,* 421 U.S. 454, 460 (1975) (compensatory and punitive damages); *Johnson v. Goodyear Tire & Rubber Co.,* 491 F.2d 1364 (5th Cir. 1974) (backpay awards). *See also Claiborne v. Illinois Central R.R.,* 583 F.2d 143 (5th Cir. 1978), *cert. denied,* 442 U.S. 934 (1979) ($50,000 punitive damages award).

85. *See Brown v. A.J. Gerrard Mfg. Co.,* 715 F.2d 1549 (11th Cir. 1983).

86. *See Novack Investment Co. v. Setser,* 454 U.S. 1064, 1066 (1981) (White, J., dissenting from denial of *certiorari*).

X

National Origin

America is a nation of immigrants. Historically, relationships among the various immigrant groups have been far from smooth; successive groups of immigrants have often treated newer arrivals with hostility, perceiving in them a real or imagined threat to the status quo in the form of "cheaper labor" or tougher competition for jobs. This chapter addresses discrimination against private employees on the basis of national origin and, to a lesser extent, citizenship status. To learn more about national origin and citizenship status discrimination in general, see *The Rights Of Aliens and Refugees* by Lucas Gutentag, a recently revised book in this series.

Which federal laws prohibit discrimination on the basis of national origin?

Various laws prohibit discrimination on the basis of national origin. These include Title VII of the Civil Rights Act of 1964[1] (Title VII), Section 1981 of the Civil Rights Act of 1866[2] (Section 1981), and the Immigration Reform and Control Act of 1986[3] (IRCA). Additionally, Executive Order (E.O.) 11246 (as amended by E.O. 11375) protects certain employees against discrimination on the basis of national origin.[4] For a fuller discussion of Title VII and E.O. 11246 see chapter 8. Section 1981 is discussed more completely in chapter 9. The IRCA is discussed in greater detail later in this chapter. For convenience, all of these laws are briefly summarized here.

Title VII, which applies to employers with 15 or more employees and specifically prohibits discrimination in employment based on national origin, affords the broadest protection. Title VII applies to decisions concerning the compensation, terms, conditions, or privileges of employment, as well as decisions concerning hiring, firing, promotion, or demotion. Title VII also makes it illegal for a labor organization to exclude from membership, limit, segregate, classify, fail to refer for employment, limit employment opportunities, or cause an employer to discriminate against an employee on the basis of national origin.[5] For purposes of Title VII, national origin means both the country "where a person was born, or, more broadly, the country from which his or her ancestors came,"[6] as well as "the physical, cultural, or linguistic characteristics of a national origin group."[7]

Section 1981 (which prohibits discrimination in employment based on race) may also be used to fight discrimination based on national origin in those situations where "national origin" is synonymous with "race" as "race" is defined for purposes of Section 1981.[8] For purposes of Section 1981, races are "identifiable classes of persons who are subjected to intentional discrimination solely because of their ancestry or ethnic characteristics."[9]

The IRCA makes it unlawful for an employer to hire individuals who are not legally authorized for employment in the United States.[10] It also contains a provision that expressly prohibits national origin discrimination.[11] The IRCA applies to all employers with 4 or more employees.[12] Thus, employers who are not covered by Title VII may be covered by the IRCA. The Department of Justice is responsible for enforcing the IRCA.[13] The IRCA applies only to hiring, discharge, recruitment, or referral for a fee.[14] It does not cover discrimination in any other terms or conditions of employment, such as wages or benefits.

Finally, E.O. 11246 (as amended by E.O. 11375) requires all federal contracts to include an "equal opportunity clause" and prohibits discrimination on the basis of national origin.

Who is legally authorized for employment?

You are authorized for employment if you are a United States citizen, a national, or an alien whose visa status allows you to work or who has been given work authorization from the Immigration and Naturalization Service (INS). The INS usually grants work authorization to legal permanent residents, students, temporary agricultural workers (e.g., migrant farmers), refugees seeking political asylum, and many others.

Not having a green card does not automatically exclude you from the authorization to work.[15]

Which national origins are protected?

All national origins are protected under the IRCA and Title VII. Under Section 1981, members of ethnic groups that would have been considered separate races in the nineteenth century should be considered separate races for purposes of Section 1981 today.[16] Under recent Supreme Court decisions, this includes Arabs and Jews, and may also include Germans and the English.[17] However, to sustain a Section 1981 claim you must prove that the intentional discrimination you suffered was based on your ethnic identity, not on your religion or on your place or nation of origin.[18]

Must I be a citizen in order to be protected by these laws?

It depends on the law. You need not be a citizen to be protected by Title VII. Title VII protects both citizens and aliens (noncitizens) from discrimination on the basis of national origin (and other characteristics such as race, religion, and sex).[19] Section 1981 protects lawfully admitted aliens, legal residents ineligible for citizenship, and temporary residents.[20] It is less clear whether illegal aliens are also protected under Section 1981 when they, for obvious reasons, are unlikely to bring their claims to court.[21]

The IRCA protects only those aliens who are authorized to work in the United States by specifically prohibiting discrimination against them both on the basis of national origin and on their citizenship status.[22] On the other hand, the IRCA *requires* an employer to discriminate against illegal aliens by refusing to employ them;[23] these individuals could not state a discrimination claim under the IRCA. The IRCA and Title VII are interrelated in that an employer who has employed illegal aliens must afford them the protections of Title VII.[24]

Can an employer discriminate against me based on my status as a noncitizen?

It depends. Title VII, the IRCA and Section 1981 differ in this area. Title VII does not forbid discrimination based on citizenship. Title VII does prohibit a citizenship requirement or preference, however, where it is "but one part of a wider scheme of unlawful national-origin discrimination"[25] or where an employer uses "a citizenship test as a pretext to disguise what is in fact national origin discrimination."[26] Therefore, under Title VII it is unlawful to discriminate against aliens "because of race, color, religion, sex or national origin—for example, by hiring aliens of Anglo-Saxon background but refusing to hire those of Mexican or Spanish ancestry . . . but nothing in the Act makes it illegal to discriminate on the basis of citizenship or alienage."[27]

The IRCA *requires* employers to discriminate against undocumented aliens seeking employment after November 6, 1986. On the other hand, the IRCA prohibits employers from discriminating on the basis of national origin (as discussed earlier in this chapter) or against those noncitizens who have declared their intent to become a citizen. These "intending citizens" are lawfully admitted aliens who have completed a Declaration of Intent to Become a Citizen form.[28]

It is unsettled whether Section 1981 would support a discrimination claim by a private employee based on alienage;[29] public employees do appear to be protected from such discrimination.[30]

Must I fill out Form I-9?

Yes. At the time of hiring, you and your employer must complete Form I-9. In it, you must state that you are authorized to work, and your employer must state that it has reviewed your work authorization documents and that they appear to be valid.[31] Your employer will provide you with the form. An employer may dismiss or refuse to hire anyone who refuses to complete this form.[32]

An employer has 30 business days after hiring you to review the documentation proving your identity and authorization for work and to complete its portion of Form I-9.[33] If you cannot provide documentation but can show your employer a receipt indicating that you have applied for it, you then have 21 business days from the date you were hired to obtain the necessary documentation.[34] Acceptable documentation includes a United States passport, a United States citizenship or naturalization certificate, or a temporary resident or employment authorization card.[35] You may also provide a combination of two documents, such as a state driver's license and an INS reentry permit.[36] Your employer may not request more or different documents than are required by the IRCA or refuse to honor your documents that appear genuine on their face.[37] For further information about Form I-9 requirements, contact your local

200 The Rights of Employees and Union Members

INS office or call the INS office of Special Counsel for Immigration-Related Unfair Employment Practices, (800) 255-7688, toll free.

May an employer seek working papers only from those individuals who "look foreign"?

No. The IRCA requires an employer to verify the status of *all* its employees. An employer who seeks to verify the citizenship status or authorization-to-work status of only some of its employees violates the IRCA's clear requirement to verify the status of all employees hired after November 6, 1986. Moreover, such conduct would violate both the IRCA's and Title VII's prohibitions against discriminating on the basis of presumed national origin (which the employer would be doing by making judgments based on appearance). Obviously, many individuals who may "look foreign" are in fact either citizens or aliens authorized to work.[38]

May an employer discriminate against me because of my inability to speak English or because of my accent?

It depends. Requiring English fluency or lack of a noticeable accent may violate Title VII if done for discriminatory reasons or applied unequally. To be lawful, the language requirement must not be overly broad in coverage and must have a reasonable business justification.

In general, where your accent does not interfere with your ability to perform duties of the position in question, it will not be considered a legitimate justification for an adverse employment decision. For example, one court found discrimination where the employee's accent would not have interfered with his ability to act as a supervisor.[39] By contrast, another court upheld a decision denying employment to an individual with a heavy accent where the position (at the Department of Motor Vehicles) required dealing with irate and impatient members of the public. There the court ruled that the employer's requirement of excellent English language communication skills was important to adequate performance of the job, and that its employment decision was not motivated by discriminatory intent.[40] Once can expect to see further litigation in this area.[41]

May an employer require that only English be spoken on the job?

It depends. An individual's primary language is often an essential national origin characteristic. The EEOC has taken the position that requiring an individual to speak only English at the workplace is "unduly burdensome," "disadvantages an individual's employment opportunities on the basis of national origin," and may impermissibly create an "atmosphere of inferiority, isolation and intimidation based on national origin which could result in a discriminatory working environment."[42] Therefore, the EEOC will closely scrutinize the employer's requirements concerning speaking English on its premises. This issue will see increasing litigation since some courts have upheld such rules based on a showing of business necessity, but others have rejected the employer's business necessity argument.[43]

Employers who have such rules should inform their employees of the rules in a clear manner.[44] An employer's failure to do so, coupled with an adverse employment action against an employee for not speaking English at a particular time, may be evidence of discrimination on the basis of national origin.

May an employer assign jobs on the basis of national origin?

Maybe. Title VII probably does not bar an employer from making such assignments provided that national origin is clearly related to the assignment, and the employees' contributions to the workplace result in appropriate compensation, promotions, and other benefits.[45] This is dramatically illustrated by *Perez v. FBI*,[46] a class action suit against the FBI. There, the plaintiffs, Latino FBI agents, claimed that Latino agents were disproportionately assigned to certain duties (such as monitoring wiretaps) because of their presumed Spanish language expertise. These assignments prevented them from obtaining the experience and achievements necessary for promotions.

The FBI argued that the use of the Latino agents' Spanish language skills was crucial to its mission. It cited the emergence of the national drug problem which, it claimed, caught the FBI with a severe shortage of agents with sufficient Spanish language skills. The FBI noted that it clearly told its agents at their time of hire that, to accomplish its mission, it would use their skills at any time and in any way it saw fit.

The court rejected the FBI's defense. It found the following: Non-Latino agents hired because of their Spanish language skills were not given the same Spanish language duties that were given to Latino agents. Latinos whose first language was English, not Spanish, were incorrectly presumed to have Spanish language expertise. The FBI's practices prevented Latino agents from completing their assigned investigations since they often had to turn them over midstream in order to monitor wiretaps. As a result of these discriminatory practices, Latino agents received neither the training nor credits needed to advance within the FBI. Nor did they receive promotions commensurate with their years of experience or the full benefits that others were receiving. The court directed the FBI to correct this pattern and practice of discrimination.

Are height and weight requirements lawful?

Generally not. Height and weight requirements tend to exclude individuals on the basis of national origin. Therefore, where they disproportionately disqualify individuals of a particular national origin and are not related to successful job performance they are generally not lawful.[47]

Are there any exceptions to Title VII's prohibition against discrimination on the basis of national origin?

Yes. An employer may lawfully deny employment opportunities to anyone who does not fulfill the national security requirements stated in section 703(g) of Title VII.[48] Additionally, an employer may lawfully deny employment opportunities in those very limited circumstances where national origin is a bona fide occupational qualification.[49] The meaning of bona fide occupational qualification is defined narrowly but may allow, for example, Chinese restaurants to hire Chinese waiters and waitresses for authenticity's sake.[50]

As an American, am I protected against discrimination by Japanese or other foreign employers who are doing business in the United States?

America is the national origin of those born in the United States. In most circumstances, Title VII protects Americans from being discriminated against by foreign nationals here, just as it protects those of other origins. For example, in Japanese-run businesses operating in the U.S., Americans of non-Japanese origin are protected from discrimination in favor of persons of Japanese origin.[51] However, treaty obligations between the United States and Japan allow Japanese-controlled firms in the United States to discriminatorily select executive-level personnel who are Japanese citizens, despite Title VII. For the employer to be exempt from Title VII, the work must be supervisory or executive in character, the company must be at least half-owned by Japanese nationals and must have substantial trade or investment relations with Japan, and the work must be authorized by the Treaty of Friendship, Commerce, and Navigation between the United States and Japan.[52]

Are Native Americans protected against discrimination?

Yes. Native Americans are protected by Title VII on the bases of national origin, race, or both.[53] Additional protection may be had under the Civil Rights Acts of 1866 and 1871. See chapter 9 on race discrimination.

On the other hand, Title VII does not apply to tribal groups. They are not considered "employers" covered by Title VII and thus may favor their own members in employment to the exclusion of others.[54]

What should I do if I believe I have been discriminated against on the basis of national origin?

The procedures for enforcing your rights under Title VII and E.O. 11246 are discussed in chapter 8; chapter 9 describes the procedures for Section 1981. Those chapters also explain the time limits you must observe in order to preserve your rights.

The IRCA is enforced by the Department of Justice, which has created a "special counsel" to receive and process claims for unfair immigration-related employment practices.[55] You, someone else on your behalf, or an officer of the Immigration and Naturalization Service must file your charge with the special counsel.[56] You can obtain information concerning the content and form of the charge through the special counsel's regional office.[57]

You must file your charge with the special counsel within 180 days of the occurrence of the unfair immigration-related employment practice.[58] A charge that is filed by mail is deemed filed on the date of the postmark.[59]

The special counsel's office will serve the employer with notice of the charge within ten days of receiving it.[60] The special counsel has 120 days to investigate the charge and has the authority to obtain access to evidence it believes is necessary for its investigation.[61] It then determines (1) whether there is "reasonable cause" to believe the charge is true and (2) whether it will file a complaint with an administrative law judge (ALJ).[62] If the special counsel decides it lacks reasonable cause to believe the charge is true, and decides not to file a complaint with an ALJ, it issues a letter of determination notifying the employer and the charging party of its decision.[63]

You may file a complaint with an ALJ if the special counsel (1) issues a letter of determination that there is no "reasonable cause," (2) fails to issue a letter of determination within the 120-day period, or (3) fails to bring a complaint before an ALJ within 120 days of receipt of the charge.[64] If you file a complaint, the special counsel may intervene and also participate in the proceeding. You must file your complaint within 90 days after the expiration of the 120-day period or within 90 days of the special counsel's decision not to prosecute, whichever is sooner.[65]

Both the employer and charging party have a right to a hearing before an ALJ who will issue a decision.[66] The hearing may not be held sooner than 5 days after the complaint is served.[67] Any person may appeal an ALJ's order to a federal court of appeals,[68] but the appeal must be filed within 60 days after the ALJ's order.[69]

If you believe you have been discriminated against on the basis of both Title VII and the IRCA, you should be aware that both claims cannot be pursued simultaneously. However, you should be sure to file both charges within the applicable time periods.

What are my remedies if I succeed in proving my claims?

For a discussion of the remedies available under Title VII and E.O. 11246, see chapter 8, "Discrimination: An Overview"; see chapter 9, "Race," for a discussion of remedies under Section 1981.

The following relief is available under the IRCA. The ALJ

may order the employer to cease and desist and may impose fines and record-keeping requirements. In addition, the ALJ may order reinstatement or hiring of the individuals adversely affected.[70] There may also be an award of backpay from a date not more than two years prior to the date the charge was filed with the ALJ (but no earlier than November 6, 1986).[71]

The losing party may be ordered to pay attorney's fees to the prevailing party if the losing party's argument was "without reasonable foundation in law and fact."[72]

NOTES

1. 42 U.S.C. §§ 2000e *et seq.*, as amended.
2. 42 U.S.C. § 1981.
3. Pub. L. No. 99-603, 100 Stat. 3359 (1986) (codified throughout 8 U.S.C. § 1101 *et seq.*). *See* 8 U.S.C. § 1324a, b.
4. Exec. Order No. 11246, 30 Fed. Reg. 12319, 3 C.F.R. 1964-1965, Comp. p. 339, as amended by Exec. Order No. 11375, 32 Fed. Reg. 14303, 3 C.F.R. 1966–1970, Comp. p. 684.
5. 42 U.S.C. § 2000e-2(a)–(c).
6. *Espinoza v. Farah Manufacturing Co. Inc.*, 414 U.S. 86, 88 (1973).
7. 29 C.F.R. § 1606.1.
8. *Saint Francis College v. Al-Khazraji*, 481 U.S. 604 (1987).
9. *Id.* at 613.
10. 8 U.S.C. § 1324a(a)(1).
11. 8 U.S.C. § 1324b(a)(1).
12. 8 U.S.C. §§ 1324b(a)(1) and (2).
13. 8 U.S.C. § 1324b(c)(1).
14. 8 U.S.C. § 1324b(a)(1) and (2).
15. 8 C.F.R § 274a.12.
16. *Saint Francis College v. Al-Khazraji*, 481 U.S. 604, 612 (1987).
17. *Id.; Shaare Tefila Congregation v. Cobb*, 481 U.S. 615 (1987). *See Bennun v. Rutgers State University*, No. 90-5638 (July 25, 1991) (3d Cir.).
18. *Saint Francis College v. Al-Khazraji*, 481 U.S. 604 (1987).
19. *Espinoza v. Farah Manufacturing Co., Inc.*, 414 U.S. 86 (1973).
20. *Graham v. Richardson*, 403 U.S. 365 (1971); *Takahashi v. Fish and Game Commission*, 334 U.S. 410 (1948); *Yick Wo v. Hopkins*, 118 U.S. 356 (1886).
21. *Commercial Standard Fire and Marine Co. v. Galindo*, 484 S.W.2d

635 (Tex. Civ. App. 1972). *See Phyler v. Doe*, 458 U.S. 1131 (1982); *Bolanos v. Kiley*, 509 F.2d 1023 (2d Cir. 1975).

22. 8 U.S.C. § 1324b(a)(1).

23. 8 U.S.C. § 1324a(a).

24. EEOC: "Policy Statement on the Relationship of Title VII to the 1986 Immigration Reform and Control Act," adopted February 26, 1987. *See EEOC v. Tortilleria La Mejor*, 55 FEP Cas. 217 (E.D. Cal. 1991).

25. *Espinoza v. Farah Manufacturing Co., Inc.*, 414 U.S. 86, 92 (1973).

26. *Id.*

27. *Id.*

28. 8 U.S.C. § 1324b(a)(3).

29. *Bhandari v. First Nat. Bank of Commerce*, 829 F.2d 1343 (5th Cir. 1987) (en banc) *vacated and remanded*, 109 S. Ct. 3207 (1989), *original judgment reinstated*, 887 F.2d 609 (5th Cir.) (en banc), *cert. denied*, 110 S. Ct. 1539 (1990) (White, J., dissenting); *Ben-Yakir v. Gaylinn Associates, Inc.*, 535 F. Supp. 543 (S.D.N.Y. 1982); *De Malherbe v. International Union of Elevator Constructors*, 438 F. Supp. 1121, 1136-42 (N.D. Col. 1977). *But see Vietnamese Fishermen's Association v. Knights of the Ku Klux Klan*, 518 F. Supp. 993 (S.D. Tex. 1981).

30. See cases cited *supra* n.20.

31. 8 U.S.C. §§ 1324a(b)(1) and (2).

32. 8 U.S.C. § 1324a(a)(1)(B).

33. 8 C.F.R. § 274a.2(b)(1)(ii).

34. 8 C.F.R. § 274a.2(b)(1)(vi).

35. 8 C.F.R. § 274a.2(b)(1)(v).

36. 8 C.F.R. §§ 274a.2(b)(1)(v)(B) and (C).

37. 8 U.S.C. § 1324(a)(b).

38. EEOC: "Policy Statement on the Relationship of Title VII to the 1986 Immigration Reform and Control Act," adopted Feb. 26, 1987.

39. *Carino v. University of Oklahoma Bd. of Regents*, 750 F.2d 815 (10th Cir. 1984).

40. *Fragante v. City and County of Honolulu*, 699 F. Supp. 1429 (D. Hawaii 1987), *aff'd*, 888 F.2d 591 (9th Cir. 1989), *cert. denied*, 110 S. Ct. 1811 (1990).

41. For example, the EEOC has filed suit against a hotel chain that made employment decisions based on accent. *EEOC v. Madison Hotel*, No. 92-718A (E.D. Va.).

42. 29 C.F.R. § 1606.7(a).

43. *See, e.g., Gutierrez v. Municipal Court*, 51 FEP Cas. 435 (9th Cir. 1988), *vacated*, 51 FEP Cas. 457 (1989); *Garcia v. Gloor*, 618 F.2d 264 (5th Cir. 1980), *cert. denied*, 449 U.S. 1113 (1981); *Dimaranan v. Pomona Valley Hospital*, 57 FEP Cas. 315 (D.C. Cal. 1991); *Garcia v. Spin Steak Co.*, No. C91-1949 RHS, (Oct. 4, 1991) (N.D. Cal.).

44. 29 C.F.R. § 1606.7(c).
45. *Cota v. Tucson Police Dept.*, 58 FEP Cas. 1565 (D. Ariz. 1992); *Perez v. FBI*, 707 F. Supp. 891 (W.D. Tex. 1988).
46. *Perez v. FBI*, 707 F. Supp. 891 (W.D. Tex. 1988).
47. 29 C.F.R. § 1606.6(a)(2); *Dothard v. Rawlinson*, 433 U.S. 321 (1977).
48. 42 U.S.C. § 2000e-2(g).
49. 42 U.S.C. § 2000e-2(c).
50. *See* remarks of Rep. Dent, 110 Cong. Rec. 2549 (1964).
51. *Fortino v. Quasar Co.*, 950 F.2d 389 (7th Cir. 1991).
52. *Id.* at 392.
53. *Brito v. Zia Co.*, 478 F.2d 1200 (10th Cir. 1973).
54. 42 U.S.C. § 2000e(b); *see also Wardle v. Ute Indian Tribe*, 623 F.2d 670 (10th Cir. 1980).
55. 8 U.S.C. § 1324b(c).
56. 8 U.S.C. § 1324b(b)(1).
57. Office of Special Counsel for Immigration-Related Unfair Employment Practices, P.O. Box 65490, Washington, D.C. 20035-5490; (800) 255-7688 (toll free) or (202) 653-8121.
58. 8 U.S.C. § 1324(d)(3).
59. 28 C.F.R. § 44.300(b).
60. 8 U.S.C. § 1324b(b)(1); 28 C.F.R. § 44.301(e).
61. 8 U.S.C. § 1324b(d)(1); 28 C.F.R. §§ 44.302(a) and (b).
62. 8 U.S.C. § 1324b(d)(1).
63. 28 C.F.R. § 44.303(b).
64. 8 U.S.C. § 1324b(d)(2); 28 C.F.R. § 44.303(c)(1).
65. 28 C.F.R. §§ 44.303(c)(1) and (2).
66. 8 U.S.C. § 1324b(e)(1).
67. *Id.*.
68. 8 U.S.C. § 1324b(i).
69. *Id.*
70. 8 U.S.C. § 1324b(g).
71. 8 U.S.C. § 1324b(g)(2)(C).
72. 8 U.S.C. § 1324b(j)(4).

XI

Sex

Discrimination in employment on the basis of sex was made illegal with the enactment of the Civil Rights Act of 1964.[1] While the law protects both genders, the chief purpose of the law was to create equal opportunity for women. Despite the significant strides women have made in the workplace during the quarter century since its enactment, much discrimination remains, and often it remains difficult to convince a court that your employer has discriminated against you on the basis of sex.[2] Most women find themselves locked into lower paying jobs that provide little or no opportunity for advancement or receive less pay than their male counterparts for performing substantially equal work.[3] Those in higher management positions find themselves bumping up against a "glass ceiling."[4] While sexual harassment in the workplace is now undisputably illegal, it is still too often the usual course of business. Similarly, although discrimination on the basis of pregnancy is illegal, many women who take pregnancy leave find their jobs adversely affected when they return. The effectiveness of federal and state laws providing job security for parents taking childcare leave remains to be seen. (See chapter 27, "Family and Medical Leave.")

This chapter outlines some of the key laws that prohibit employment discrimination on the basis of sex and discusses some of the basic issues that arise in this area. Because of the evolving nature of this area of law, if you believe you are being mistreated, you should consult the EEOC or an attorney knowledgeable in this area.

What laws prohibit sex discrimination?

The most far-reaching law that protects private employees against sex discrimination is Title VII of The Civil Rights Act of 1964, as amended by the Pregnancy Disability Act of 1978.[5] Title VII outlaws discrimination based on sex, except when an employer can prove that it is absolutely necessary to have an employee of a certain gender perform the job. Usually, it is difficult for an employer to prove that being of a certain gender is a bona fide occupational qualification (BFOQ) for the performance of a certain job.[6] In practice, the only types of jobs that have been protected by the BFOQ defense are jobs such as wet-nurse, washroom attendant, model, and actor/actress.[7]

Other laws that are important in the area of sex discrimination in employment are the Equal Pay Act,[8] E. O. 11246 (as amended by E.O. 11375), the Age Discrimination in Employment Act,[9] and state sex discrimination laws. The Equal Pay Act is discussed later in this chapter. The executive order is discussed in chapter 8, and the Age Discrimination in Employment Act is discussed in chapter 13, "Age."

Is it ever legal to segregate jobs by sex?

Apart from the narrow BFOQ exception mentioned above, such job segregation is almost never legal.[10] This means it is illegal under Title VII to give "light" (and lower paying) work to women and "heavy" (and higher paying) work to men;[11] to assign women "heavy" jobs that they cannot manage in an attempt to force them to resign; to hire men and women for separate departments in a company; or to prohibit transfers between departments that, prior to the enactment of Title VII, were segregated by sex.[12] Also, an employer may not refuse to hire women on the grounds that state laws require certain extra benefits for women that an employer does not want to pay or purportedly cannot afford.

Can an employer use height or weight as a selection criteria?

Generally, no. Such standards inevitably screen out more women than men and thus are discriminatory. In *Dothard v. Rawlinson*,[13] the Supreme Court specifically declared this practice illegal. However, in the rare case where the employer can demonstrate business necessity, a court may allow the use of these criteria.[14]

Can an employer use tests that measure physical ability or strength as a selection criteria?

Generally, no. Courts will closely scrutinize such tests to see if they accurately measure the ability to perform essential job functions. Only where the test is sufficiently related to an essential aspect of job performance will a court uphold it. For example, one court[15] upheld a firefighters' physical exam on which men clearly performed better than women. That test measured speed and strength. The court concluded the test was valid because the defendant demonstrated that speed and strength (rather than stamina, for example) are critical in the first stages of a fire. In the more usual case, the exams that have been challenged do not contain sufficient job relatedness and courts have invalidated them.[16]

Can an employer deny jobs, promotions, or overtime work to women because of state "protective" labor laws?

No. State "protective" laws passed at the beginning of the twentieth century regulated the type of jobs that women were allowed to hold and their working conditions. Protective legislation has included weight-lifting limitations, mandatory rest periods, and maximum hours restrictions. It was intended to protect women "from the greed as well as the passion of man."[17] Such laws have been held to violate Title VII,[18] and employers may not use them to defend discriminatory employment decisions.

May an employer discriminate against me because I am pregnant?

No. In 1978, Congress amended Title VII to make it illegal to discriminate on the basis of pregnancy, childbirth, or any related medical condition (e.g., abortion). That law, referred to as the Pregnancy Discrimination Act (PDA),[19] makes clear that pregnant women who are able to and want to work must be treated like other workers.

The PDA prohibits an employer from refusing to hire or refusing to promote a woman because she is pregnant. It also prohibits an employer from turning away female applicants who are likely to become pregnant (unless the employer similarly rejects males who are likely to become fathers). An employer cannot fire a woman because of her pregnancy or force her to take a leave of absence.[20] An employee must be permitted to continue working as long as she is physically able to perform the duties of her position and must be permitted to return to work as soon as she is able to do so in the same manner as other employees who are reinstated after taking a medical leave. A doctor's note should be considered sufficient evidence of a woman's disability.[21] If the employer grants leaves of absence for medical disability, it must also grant maternity leaves. Women disabled by pregnancy, childbirth, or related medical conditions must be treated like other workers who are temporarily disabled by short-term medical disability. When and if a medical leave becomes necessary, the employer may not impose a certain length leave on the woman but must hold open her job on the same basis that it holds open jobs for employees on sick or disability leave for reasons not related to pregnancy. It should be noted, however, that state laws that allow pregnant employees greater disability leave than other disabled employees are permissible and do not violate Title VII.[22]

Additionally, Title VII requires that health insurance and disability benefits policies treat pregnancy or pregnancy-related conditions the same way they treat other medical conditions.[23] Thus, pregnancy-related expenses should be reimbursed on the same basis as expenses for non-pregnancy-related medical conditions, and health insurance policies may not require a greater deductible for pregnancy than they require for other medical conditions. Similarly, a health insurance plan may not exclude pregnancy for female employees and for the spouses of its male employees.[24] The only exception concerns abortion. Health insurance benefits may (but need not) exclude abortion as a covered expense except in cases of life endangerment to the mother or where medical complications have arisen because of an abortion.[25] The EEOC has published "Questions and Answers on the Pregnancy Discrimination Act, Pub. L. No. 95-555, 92 Stat. 2076 (1978)," containing further information on the treatment of pregnant workers.

One final note. Title VII covers pregnancy only to the extent that the woman is physically disabled because of the pregnancy or pregnancy-related condition. Title VII does not require employers to provide time off to care for a newborn, newly adopted, or sick child. Laws providing job security if you take time off to care for your child are discussed in greater detail in chapter 27.

Are different retirement ages or benefits for men and women legal?
No. Since women generally live longer than men, it costs

employers more to provide women with certain retirement and pension benefits. Employers used to pass along these extra costs to their women employees. The Supreme Court has ruled that to do so violates Title VII. In *Los Angeles Department of Water & Power v. Manhart*,[26] the court ruled that an employer could not require female employees to make larger contributions to their pension plans than their male counterparts in order to receive equal benefits. In *Arizona Governing Committee for Tax-Deferred Annuity v. Norris*,[27] the court ruled that, where the employer contributed equal amounts for all its employees, it could not provide lesser retirement benefits to women employees than to their male counterparts.

May an employer advertise jobs as "male" or "female"?

No. Title VII prohibits employers and employment agencies from placing help-wanted ads in sex-segregated newspaper columns.[28] Although Title VII does not prohibit newspapers from having such columns, employers would be unable to use them. Additionally, many state fair employment laws prohibit newspapers from having sex-segregated help wanted columns.[29]

May an employer exclude women from certain jobs because of potential injury to the fetus if the employee became pregnant?

No. The Supreme Court has ruled that Title VII forbids sex-specific "fetal protection" policies. In *United Auto Workers v. Johnson Controls, Inc.*,[30] the Court invalidated a policy that prohibited all women (but not men) between the ages of 17 and 70 from working in jobs involving lead exposure and in jobs that could lead to promotions to jobs involving lead exposure. Nor may an employer require sterilization as a prerequisite for obtaining or keeping a certain job.

May an employer make employment decisions that are based in part on stereotyped assumptions concerning women's behavior or women's work?

No. Such intentional discrimination violates Title VII. In *Price Waterhouse v. Hopkins*,[31] Ann Hopkins applied for, and was denied, partnership in Price Waterhouse, a large accounting firm. Hopkins was denied partnership for a variety of reasons, some of which involved her failure to conform to stereotyped notions about women. Indeed, she had been advised that she could improve her chances for partnership if she would "walk more femininely, talk more femininely, dress more femininely, wear make-up, have her hair styled and wear jewelry." The court held that this comment, along with other evidence, proved that gender played a motivating part in the employment decision. Accordingly, the employer violated Title VII. In the Civil Rights Act of 1991, Congress clarified this rule by stating that an employer can escape liability for compensatory and punitive damages under Title VII by proving that it would have made the same decision even if sex had not been a motivating factor. But once an employee proves that such biased conduct occurred, the employer may be held liable for attorney's fees and may be subject to injunctive relief to prevent such conduct from influencing future decisions.[32]

By the same token, an employer may not single women out for questions regarding family circumstances and childcare arrangements as if they are the only sex concerned with the impact of family responsibilities on job demands.[33]

Is sexual harassment legal?

No. Under Title VII sexual harassment—unwelcome sexual advances or conduct—is prohibited.[34] Sexual harassment includes unwelcome sexual advances, animosity that is gender based, whether it is sexual or nonsexual, and a sexually charged workplace. Title VII sexual harassment claims usually fall into two categories: *quid pro quo* and *hostile work environment*. In quid pro quo harassment situations a supervisor demands sexual favors from an employee in exchange for a job benefit over which the supervisor has some control. In hostile work environment situations the employee is forced to endure any form of conduct that is unpleasant because of his or her gender; the conduct need not include a direct invitation to engage in sexual activity. While many complaints involve both forms of harassment, there are some important differences between these two theories of sexual harassment.

What is quid pro quo harassment?

In quid pro quo harassment, sexual favors are demanded in exchange for job benefits (i.e., "If you go to bed with me, you'll get a promotion, be hired, be retained, etc."). It can be a single demand. Moreover, the sexual favors can be demanded in exchange for a benefit the employee already has (i.e., "If you go to bed with me you will be able to keep your job.") In quid pro quo sexual harassment the demand need not be express; rather the demand can be implied from physical conduct such as fondling.[35] To prove quid pro quo harassment, you must show that you were deprived of a job benefit as part of your claim, i.e., that "submission to such [sexual] conduct is made either explicitly or implicitly a term or condition of [your] employment" or that "submission to or rejection of such conduct by [you] . . . is used as the basis for employment decisions affecting [you]."[36] In quid pro quo cases, you may recover damages from the employer if the harasser is someone with the authority to affect your work opportunities.[37] If the demand is made by a coworker with no power to affect your job status then you cannot claim quid pro quo harassment; however, you may have a hostile work environment claim. Under the EEOC guidelines, an employer is liable for conduct of nonsupervisory personnel only if it "knows or should have known of the conduct."[38]

What is "hostile" or "offensive work environment" harassment?

This form of harassment deprives an employee of the right to work in an environment free from discrimination, intimidation, ridicule, or insult. You may have a claim for hostile environment sexual harassment if the sexual "advances, requests for sexual favors, and other verbal or physical conduct of a sexual nature . . . unreasonably interfere with [your] work performance or create an intimidating, hostile or offensive working environment."[39]

Generally, but not always, a single incident is an insufficient basis for a hostile work environment claim. The harassment can take the form of gender-based animosity of a sexual nature such as when the victim is made the butt of crude sexual jokes and pranks or is grabbed or whistled at, or it can take the form of nonsexual gender baiting, such as when the victim is the target of physical aggression or theft. Conduct that makes the workplace sexually charged need not be directed specifically toward the victim for it to be unlawful. Such conduct can include the condoning of pornographic posters, profanity, and sexual activity between others that creates favoritism. You can recover damages even if the harassment did not result in tangible job consequences (for example, you were not fired or demoted); however, you must demonstrate that the unwelcome sexual conduct is so severe or pervasive that it alters your conditions of employment by creating a psychologically "abusive working environment."[40] The offensive conduct may be perpetrated by coworkers or nonemployees, that is, those who lack supervisory power. The employer is liable in these cases only if it "knew or should have known of the harassment in question and failed to take prompt remedial action" to stop the harassment.[41]

How do I prove sexual harassment?

Obviously, the proof is different and depends on the facts of your case. The EEOC has stated that "[b]ecause sexual attraction may often play a role in the day-to-day social exchange between employees, the distinction between invited, uninvited-but-welcome, offensive-but-tolerated, and flatly rejected advances may well be difficult to discover."[42] Courts (and the EEOC) evaluate the merits of sexual harassment claims on a case-by-case basis by looking at the totality of the circumstances. The following are among the factors that are considered. First, they will consider whether the conduct was unwelcome. If you are a victim of sexual harassment, you will have a stronger case if you unequivocally rejected the advances and complained to the employer while the harassment was going on or shortly after it ceased. Obviously, the extent to which you can demonstrate unwelcomeness depends on the facts and circumstances of your situation.

Second, the courts and EEOC will look to see if the employer has a procedure for handling sexual harassment grievances. You will have a stronger case if (assuming there is a procedure) you know and follow it. This will prevent your employer from escaping liability (in hostile environment cases) by claiming it did not or could not have known about the harassment. It will also put you in a better position for proving the inappropriateness or inadequacy of the employer's response. You should monitor the employer's response closely, and, to the extent possible, document the sequence of events. An employer who fails to respond adequately is more likely to be found liable by the court.

Finally, most victims of harassment are women. Many courts have begun to recognize that what may seem inoffensive to men may constitute harassment to women. Although most courts view the proper standard for evaluating a hostile environment claim as whether the claimant was "at least as affected as the reasonable person under like circumstances,"[43] a growing number of courts have adopted the "reasonable woman standard."[44] Thus, as one court has summarized, "well-intentioned compliments by co-workers or supervisors can form the basis of a sexual harassment cause of action if a reasonable victim of the same sex as the plaintiff would consider the comments sufficiently severe or pervasive to alter a condition of employment and create an abusive working environment."[45] It is the job of the employer, the court noted, to "educate and sensitize" its workforce to eliminate objectionable conduct.[46]

If I quit because of intolerable conditions, can I still sue for sexual harassment?

Yes. Under Title VII, employees who quit to avoid sexual harassment that can no longer be endured are entitled to the same relief available to those who are fired. Quitting under such circumstances is called *constructive discharge*. Before you quit a job with the idea that you can claim constructive discharge, however, you should consult an attorney knowledgeable and experienced in this area of law. Generally, employees who claim constructive discharge must be able to *prove* that a reasonable person would have felt compelled to resign because of the aggravating conduct. Additionally, some courts require that the employee also prove that the employer *intended* to force the employee to resign or at least deliberately created the unendurable working environment.[47]

Until a constructive discharge can be proved, an employee's "voluntary" resignation may render him or her ineligible to receive unemployment compensation. To overcome this, the sexual harassment victim must, again, show that she had "good cause for resigning." In some courts this means demonstrating evidence of intolerable harassment, that the employer knew about the harassment, and that the harassment caused her to quit.[48]

Can I have a claim if the sexual harassment does not involve me directly?

It depends. If a coworker succumbs to unwanted sexual advances and receives a job benefit which you deserved, you may be able to claim sexual harassment.[49] Similarly, at least one court has recognized a sexual harassment claim if a benefit denied to one employee was given to someone who had a consensual romantic relationship with a supervisor.[50] Likewise, a court may recognize a sexual harassment claim if the sexual conduct of some members of the workforce creates an environment that "affect[s] the motivation and work performance of those who [find] such conduct repugnant and offensive."[51]

Are there laws other than Title VII that protect against sexual harassment?

Yes. Though Title VII offers jury trials and the possibility of compensatory and punitive damages to victims of sexual harassment, the common law can still offer protection and compensation that may not be available under Title VII (See chapter 8). In several states, a sexual harassment victim may also bring claims under various tort theories, such as intentional infliction of emotional distress (for outrageous conduct that exceeds all bounds of decency),[52] invasion of privacy,[53] and defamation.[54] The availability of remedies under these theories should be discussed with an attorney knowledgeable in the area.

May an employer impose certain requirements on one subclass of men or women and not on others?

It depends. An employer who treats a subclass of men or women differently may violate Title VII when the different treatment is based on sex plus a neutral factor. Courts call this kind of discrimination *sex-plus discrimination*. Under this theory, courts have struck down employer practices of refusing to hire women—but not men—with preschool-age children;[55] prohibiting or limiting the hiring of married women—but not men;[56] and requiring women—but not men—to use their husband's names.[57] As seen from these examples, a Title VII violation arises where the neutral factor involves a characteristic that cannot be changed or a trait that involves fundamental rights.

May an employer impose a dress code?

Generally, yes. Generally, courts will uphold dress codes that are applied even-handedly to all employees.[58] On the other hand, dress codes that are significantly more burdensome for women, or found to be demeaning, will be struck down.[59]

What should I do if I believe I have been discriminated against on the basis of my sex?

You should consult the EEOC or an attorney to see whether you have any legal recourse. The procedures for filing a Title VII charge of sex discrimination are the same as the procedures for filing a charge of any other form of discrimination prohibited by Title VII. Those procedures are described in chapter 8 of this book.

What is the equal pay act?

The Equal Pay Act makes it illegal for an employer to pay women less than men for the same work.[60] The guiding principle is "equal pay for equal work." This provision was added to the Fair Labor Standards Act (FLSA) in 1963.

To determine whether the Equal Pay Act has been violated, the courts first analyze the type of work performed by the men and women. Only workers engaged in "substantially similar" work can be compared to determine inequalities in salary. The term *substantially similar* work means that the men and women work in the same establishment (i.e., the same physical space or location) and perform the same type of job requiring comparable "skill, effort, and responsibility."[61] In addition, the jobs must be equal in terms of working conditions, and the tasks of each job must be very similar.

The jobs compared need not be identical. Jobs may be compared despite insubstantial or minor differences in the skill, effort, or responsibilities required.[62] Jobs may not be compared, however, if they are substantially different. For example, the pay of a female bookkeeper can be compared to that of a male bookkeeper working on a different ledger but cannot be compared to that of a male clerk. A comparison may be made when employees of one sex are doing work formerly done by employees of the opposite sex. For example, if male bank tellers were replaced by female bank tellers and the women were paid at a lower rate than the men, the equal pay provisions would have been violated. But no comparison is possible when only men are employed in one job and only women are employed in a dissimilar job. Thus, an employer would not be found in violation of the equal pay standard if it paid telephone operators, all of whom were women, less than telephone repairmen, all of whom were men.

Pay differentials are permitted, however, if they are attributable to bona fide seniority or merit systems or to incentive systems that reward productivity or if they are attributable to a factor other than sex.[63] Whether a difference in pay is based on a factor "other than sex" has been an issue in many cases.[64]

An employer may not correct an equal pay violation by reducing anyone's pay rate; rates can be equalized only by pay increases.[65] Thus, a woman who is paid a lower rate than a man for the same work is entitled to have her pay raised to the man's level; the man's pay cannot be lowered to the woman's level. Also, the employer cannot remedy a violation by firing or transferring the higher paid persons.

The equal pay provisions apply to all private employees covered by the FLSA, except that employees who are completely exempt from the minimum wage laws (discussed in chapter 23) are also exempt from the equal pay law; nonetheless, executives, administrators, professionals, and outside salesmen are not exempt from the equal pay law. Labor organizations are bound by the equal pay law and may not cause or attempt to cause any employer to violate it. The equal pay requirement in the FLSA applies concurrently with other state and federal laws pertaining to sex discrimination in employment. In addition to Title VII, most states have equal pay laws. An employer must comply with any federal, state, or local law that establishes equal pay standards higher than those under the FLSA. On the other hand, compliance with any other applicable law does not excuse noncompliance with the equal pay law.

What if there are no men doing the same work for more pay?

For years, some courts took the position that in a wage discrimination claim under Title VII, the plaintiff had to satisfy the Equal Pay Act requirement that a man be performing the same act for a higher wage. In 1981, in *County of Washington v. Gunther*,[66] the Supreme Court rejected this view and ruled that women can sue under Title VII for sex discrimination in wages where the wages were initially set at a lower rate than for men, even if no men were performing the same work for more pay at the time of the suit. *Gunther* thus supports an action for equal pay even if no man is doing the same work for more money.

In *Gunther* the plaintiffs also sought to advance a theory of comparable worth. Under that theory employees are entitled to equal pay for jobs that, although not substantially similar, are nonetheless *comparable* in their intrinsic value to the employer. The *Gunther* court expressly avoided endorsing the concept of comparable worth although it effectively laid the groundwork for a comparable worth standard. Because of the absence of the endorsement, however, subsequent cases based on a comparative worth standard have been largely unsuccessful.[67]

What should I do if I feel I'm not getting equal pay for equal work?

If you feel you are being discriminated against in violation of the Equal Pay Act, you can either proceed through the EEOC or go directly to court. Unlike Title VII, you need not file a charge before going to court.

If you go through the EEOC, it will conduct an investigation. If a violation is found, the EEOC will try to collect the wages that are due and to persuade the employer to raise your wages. If a voluntary agreement between the employer and the EEOC cannot be reached, the EEOC may bring a lawsuit on your behalf to secure lost pay and to require that the employer change its policy.[68]

If you decide instead to go directly to court without filing a charge with the EEOC, you should at least consult with an attorney. You must bring such an action within two years of the discrimination, or within three years if the discrimination was willful.

What can I recover if my action is successful?
You can be awarded up to three years of backpay, a similar amount as punitive damages to punish the employer for engaging in a discriminatory practice, and attorney's fees and court costs.[69]

NOTES

1. 42 U.S.C. §§ 2000e *et seq.*, as amended.
2. *See, e.g.*, *Halbrook v. Reichhold*, No. 89 Civ 952 (KC), (July 8, 1991) (S.D.N.Y.).
3. Recent studies show full-time women workers earn 66 cents for every dollar earned by men.
4. The Civil Rights Act of 1991 established a glass ceiling commission to study and make recommendations concerning the underrepresentation of women and minorities in top-level positions. CRA §§ 203–4.
5. 42 U.S.C. §§ 2000e *et seq.*, as amended.
6. 42 U.S.C. § 2000e-2(e).
7. *Rosenfeld v. Southern Pacific Co.*, 444 F.2d 1219 (9th Cir. 1971); *Diaz v. Pan American World Airways*, 442 F.2d 385 (5th Cir.), *cert. denied*, 404 U.S. 950 (1971); *Jennings v. New York State Office of Mental Health*, 90 Civ. 5633, (Mar. 16, 1992) (S.D.N.Y.).
8. 29 U.S.C. § 206(d)(1).
9. 29 U.S.C. §§ 621 *et seq.*
10. *E.g.*, *Adair v. Beech Aircraft*, 58 FEP Cas. 85 (D. Kan. 1992).
11. *Bowe v. Colgate-Palmolive Co.*, 416 F.2d 711 (7th Cir. 1969).
12. *See, e.g.*, *Chrapling v. Uniroyal, Inc.*, 15 FEP Cas. 795 (D. Ind. 1977).
13. 433 U.S. 321 (1977).
14. *See Boyd v. Ozark Airlines, Inc.*, 568 F.2d 50 (8th Cir. 1977) (height); *Jarrell v. Eastern Air Lines, Inc.*, 430 F. Supp. 884 (E.D. Va. 1977), *aff'd*, 577 F.2d 869 (4th Cir. 1978).
15. *Zamlen v. Cleveland*, 906 F.2d 209 (6th Cir. 1990), *cert. denied*, 111 S. Ct. 1388 (1991). *See Berkman v. City of New York*, 812 F.2d 52 (2d Cir.), *cert. denied*, 484 U.S. 949 (1987).
16. *See* 29 C.F.R. §§ 1607.4–5.
17. *Muller v. Oregon*, 208 U.S. 412, 422 (1908).

18. *Kober v. Westinghouse Electric Co.*, 480 F.2d 240 (3d Cir. 1973); *Rosenfeld v. Southern Pacific Co.*, 444 F.2d 1219 (9th Cir. 1971).

19. Pub. L. No. 95-555, 92 Stat. 2076 (1978), *amending* 42 U.S.C. § 2000-(k).

20. Nor may an employer discriminate against the husband whose wife is pregnant on the basis of her pregnancy. *See Nicol v. Imagematrix*, 56 FEP Cas. 1533 (E.D. Va. 1991).

21. *EEOC v. Ackerman, Hood & McQueen*, 55 FEP Cas. 668 (W.D. Okla. 1991).

22. *California Federal Savings and Loan Association v. Guerra*, 479 U.S. 272 (1987).

23. *See EEOC v. Wooster Brush Co. Employees Relief Association*, 727 F.2d 566 (6th Cir. 1984).

24. *Newport News Shipbuilding & Dry Dock Co.*, 462 U.S. 669 (1983).

25. 42 U.S.C. § 2000e-(k).

26. 435 U.S. 702 (1978).

27. 436 U.S. 1073 (1983).

28. *See* 42 U.S.C. § 2000e-3(b).

29. *See, e.g., Pittsburgh Press Co. v. Pittsburgh Commission on Human Relations*, 413 U.S. 376 (1973).

30. 499 U.S. ____, 111 S. Ct. 1196, 113 L. Ed. 2d 158, 55 FEP Cas. 365 (1991).

31. 490 U.S. 228.

32. CRA § 107(a).

33. *Bruno v. Crown Point Ind.*, 57 FEP Cas. 623 (7th Cir. 1991).

34. 29 C.F.R. § 1604.11(a). *See generally Meritor Savings Bank v. Vinison*, 477 U.S. 57 (1986).

35. *See, e.g., Pease v, Alford Photo Indus.*, 667 F. Supp. 1188 (W.D. Tenn. 1987).

36. 29 C.F.R. § 1604.11(a)(1)(2).

37. *See Meritor Savings Bank v. Vinson*, 477 U.S. 57, 106 S. Ct. 2399, 2407–8 (1986); *Horn v. Duke Homes*, 755 F.2d 599 (7th Cir. 1985); *Henson v. City of Dundee*, 682 F.2d 897 (11th Cir. 1982).

38. 29 C.F.R. § 1604.11(d).

39. 29 C.F.R. § 1604.11(a)(3).

40. *Meritor Savings Bank v. Vinson*, 477 U.S. 57, 67 (1986). *See Scott v. Sears, Roebuck & Co.*, 798 F.2d 210 (7th Cir. 1986).

41. *See, e.g., Hall v. Gus Construction Co.*, 842 F.2d 1010 (8th Cir. 1988).

42. EEOC Policy Guidance, Empl. Pctc. Guide ¶ 5258 (March 19, 1990).

43. *Burns v. McGregor Electronic Industries*, 57 FEP Cas. 1373 (8th Cir. 1992).

44. *E.g.*, *Ellison v. Brady*, 924 F.2d 872 (9th Cir. 1990); *Andrews v. City of Philadelphia*, 895 F.2d 1469 (3d Cir. 1990); *Yates v. Avco Corp.*, 819 F.2d 630 (6th Cir. 1987).

45. *Ellison v. Brady*, 924 F.2d 872 (9th Cir. 1990).

46. *Id.*

47. These include courts found in the D.C. Second, Fourth, and Eighth Circuits. *E.g.*, *Paroline v. Unisys Corp.*, 879 F.2d 100 (4th Cir. 1989), *aff'd in part and rev'd in part*, 900 F.2d 27 (4th Cir. 1990) *en banc.*

48. *See Tedesco v. Commonwealth*, 122 Pa. Commw. Ct. 549, 552 A.2d 759 (1989); see also chapter 7, "Statutory Benefits."

49. EEOC Policy Guidance on Sexual Favoritism, 8 Fair Empl. Prac. Man. (BNA) 405:6817–21 (Jan. 2, 1990).

50. *See King v. Palmer*, 778 F.2d 878 (D.C. Cir. 1985), *in remand*, 641 F. Supp. 186 (D.C. Cir. 1986); *Toscano v. Nimmo*, 570 F. Supp. 1977 (D. Del. 1983). *But see De Cintio v. Westchester County Medical Center*, 807 F.2d 304 (2d Cir. 1986), *cert. denied*, 484 U.S. 965 (1987).

51. *Broderick v. Ruder*, 685 F. Supp. 1269 (D.D.C. 1988). *But see Drinkwater v. Union Carbide*, 904 F.2d 853 (3d Cir. 1990).

52. *Priest v. Rotary*, 634 F. Supp. 571 (N.D. Cal. 1986) (man exposed himself to female); *Dias v. Sky Chefs*, 979 F.2d 1370 (9th Cir. 1990) (supervisor criticized employee's looks and had her discharged).

53. *Rogers v. Loew's L'Enfant Plaza Hotel*, 526 F. Supp. 523 (D.D.C. 1985) (sexual invitations and leering).

54. *Dwyer v. Smith*, 867 F.2d 189 (4th Cir. 1989) (sexually harassed police officer claimed she was falsely accused of lying).

55. *Phillips v. Martin Marietta Corp.*, 400 U.S. 541 (1971).

56. *E.g.*, *Sangster v. United Air Lines*, 438 F. Supp. 1221 (S.D. Cal. 1977), *aff'd*, 633 F.2d 864 (9th Cir. 1980), *cert. denied*, 451 U.S. 971 (1981).

57. *See, e.g.*, *Allen v. Lovejoy*, 553 F.2d 522 (6th Cir. 1977).

58. *Earwood v. Continental Southeastern Lines, Inc.*, 539 F.2d 1349 (4th Cir. 1976).

59. *Carroll v. Talman Federal Savings & Loan Association*, 604 F.2d 1028 (7th Cir. 1979), *cert. denied*, 445 U.S. 929 (1980).

60. 29 U.S.C. § 206(d)(1).

61. *Thompson v. Sawyer*, 678 F.2d 257 (D.C. Civ. 1982).

62. *See Corning Glass Works v. Brennan*, 417 U.S. 188 (1974); *Aldrich v. Randolph Central School District*, No. 91-7566, May 5, 1992 (2d Cir.); *Hodgson v. City Stores*, 479 F.2d 235 (5th Cir. 1973); *Hodgson v. Miller Browning Co.*, 457 F.2d 221 (7th Cir. 1972).

63. 29 U.S.C. § 206(d).

64. *See, e.g.*, *Ende v. Board of Regents*, 757 F.2d 176 (7th Cir. 1985);

Laffrey v. Northwest Airlines, Inc., 567 F.2d 429 (D.C. Cir. 1976), *cert. denied*, 434 U.S. 1086 (1978); *Hodgson v. Robert Hall Clothes, Inc.*, 473 F.2d 589 (3d Cir.), *cert. denied*, 414 U.S. 866 (1973).

65. 29 U.S.C. § 206(d)(1).
66. 452 U.S. 161 (1981).
67. *E.g., International Union, United Automobile, Aerospace & Agricultural Implement Workers of America v. Michigan*, 886 F.2d 766 (6th Cir. 1989); *American Nurses Association v. Illinois*, 783 F.2d 716 (7th Cir. 1986); *AFSCME v. Washington*, 770 F.2d 1401 (9th Cir. 1985).
68. 29 C.F.R. § 1620.19.
69. 29 C.F.R. § 1620.22.

XII

Religion

Many immigrants to this country, including some of the first settlers, came to escape religious persecution and to live equally with others. Nevertheless, while the concept of religious freedom is deeply cherished in our country, religious prejudice has been present throughout our history, particularly in employment.

The First Amendment to the United States Constitution guarantees freedom of religion and prohibits the establishment of any official religion. Consequently, religious discrimination is forbidden in employment by federal, state, and local governments. However, the First Amendment does not reach private employment.

Is religious discrimination illegal in private employment?

Generally, yes. Title VII of the Civil Rights Act of 1964 specifically prohibits discrimination in private employment on the basis of religion. Under Title VII, it is unlawful for an employer to refuse to hire, to discharge, or to otherwise discriminate against anyone with respect to compensation, terms, conditions, or privileges of employment because of the person's religion.[1] The term *religion* refers not only to religious beliefs but also to religious observance and practice.[2] Title VII also requires an employer to "reasonably accommodate" an employee or applicant's religious observance and practice unless such accommodation would cause it "undue hardship."[3] These terms are discussed later in this chapter. Additionally, certain ethnic groups may have additional protection under Section 1981, a federal statute that prohibits racial discrimination in the making of private contracts, including employment contracts.[4] Section 1981 is discussed in chapter 9.

Religious discrimination cases usually fall into two categories: those based on your employer's failure to "reasonably accommodate" your religious needs and those based on disparate treatment. Disparate treatment (discussed in general in chapter 8) occurs when you are treated in a discriminatory fashion because of your religious beliefs and practices. It may take the form of blatant intentional persecution, such as an employer refusing to hire you or firing you because of your religious heritage or beliefs, or it can be more subtle or unintentional. Such discrimination is clearly prohibited under Title VII.[5] A duty to "reasonably accommodate" your religious needs may arise if your work schedule requires you to work on your sabbath; or if a company dress code precludes the wearing of a veil, which is required by your religious beliefs;[6] or if your religion prohibits medical examinations that an employer requires. These employer actions may be illegal under Title VII if your religious needs prevail over your employer's business needs.

Can an employer ever consider religion when making an employment decision?

Yes. An employer may consider religion when making an employment decision if the employer is a religious group or organization and the work involved is connected with the "carrying on" of such an organization;[7] religion is a bona fide occupational qualification (BFOQ) of the position as defined by statute;[8] the employer is an educational institution, that is in whole or substantial part, owned, supported, controlled, or managed by a particular religion or religious organization;[9] or the employer is an educational institution directed towards the propagation of a particular religion.[10] The scope of these exceptions is increasingly litigated; such litigation meets with varying results.[11]

What is a "religious belief"?

The phrase "religious belief" in Title VII has been given a broad definition. It is not confined to theistic concepts or to traditional beliefs but includes ethical and moral beliefs that are sincerely held with the strength of traditional religious views.[12] Some courts have also held that discrimination against an atheist is prohibited, thereby including under Title VII the freedom not to believe.[13]

A person can be deemed to have a religious belief even if no religious group espouses the belief or even if the religious group to which the person professes to belong does not accept such a belief. On the other hand, a mere personal preference based on economic or social ideology does not constitute religious belief.[14] For example, membership in the United Klans of America has been held to be outside the protection of Title VII.[15]

Must my employer accommodate my religious beliefs?

Yes and no. Your employer must offer to "reasonably accommodate" your religious observances, practices, and beliefs when they conflict with job-related duties. On the other hand, your employer need not make accommodations that would impose "undue hardship" on it. As Section 701(j) of Title VII itself states:[16]

> The term "religion" includes all aspects of religious observance and practice, as well as belief, unless an employer demonstrates that he is unable to reasonably accommodate to an employee's or prospective employee's religious observance or practice without undue hardship on the conduct of the employer's business.

The tension between these opposing concepts determines the extent to which your employer must make accommodations.

The Supreme Court has construed an employer's obligation to accommodate an employee's religious observance or practice narrowly. In *Trans World Airlines, Inc. v. Hardison,*[17] Hardison's religion required him to refrain from working on Saturday, its sabbath. When Hardison was assigned to work on Saturdays, he suggested various alternatives. TWA and the union rejected them, claiming his alternatives would increase TWA's operating costs and would violate the negotiated system under which Saturday work was assigned on the basis of seniority. Hardison refused to work on Saturdays and was fired for insubordination.

The Supreme Court held that TWA and the union did not have to accommodate Mr. Hardison's religious beliefs in the circumstances.

> To require TWA to bear more than a *de minimus* cost in order to give Hardison Saturdays off is an undue hardship. Like abandonment of the seniority system, to require TWA to bear additional costs when no such costs are incurred to give other employees the days off that they want

would involve unequal treatment of employees on the basis of their religion. By suggesting that TWA should incur certain costs in order to give Hardison Saturdays off the Court of Appeals would in effect require TWA to finance an additional Saturday off and then to choose the employee who will enjoy it on the basis of his religious beliefs. While incurring extra costs to secure a replacement for Hardison might remove the necessity of compelling another employee to work involuntarily in Hardison's place, it would not change the fact that the privilege of having Saturdays off would be allocated according to religious beliefs.[18]

Under *Hardison*, therefore, your employer need not accommodate your religious beliefs if to do so would require incurring more than a minimal cost, directly or indirectly.

Nine years later the Supreme Court had the opportunity to reconsider Section 701(j). In *Ansonia Board of Education v. Philbrook*,[19] the Court ruled that *any* reasonable accommodation offered by the employer is sufficient to meet its accommodation obligation under Title VII and that the employer need only demonstrate that it has offered a reasonable accommodation to the employee. An employer need not accept the employee's preferred accommodation(s) and need not demonstrate that it has rejected the employee's proposed alternative accommodation(s) because they would result in undue hardship to the employer.[20] An employee should not brush aside an employer's good faith and reasonable attempts to accommodate his or her religious beliefs and insist that the employer adopt the employee's solution.[21]

The Equal Employment Opportunity Commission (EEOC) guidelines incorporate and supplement the *Hardison* and *Philbrook* standards.[22] Those guidelines provide, for example, that in determining whether an accommodation would require more than a *de minimus* cost and therefore constitute undue hardship, due consideration must be given to the identifiable cost in relation to the size and operating costs of the employer and the number of employees who may actually need the ccommodation.[23] Also, an employer may not use the fact that it has other employees with the same religious beliefs as the employee requesting an accommodation as evidence of undue hardship.[24]

The scope of the employer's duty to accommodate is a developing area of law. If an employer makes no attempt to accommodate, a court will more likely than not find that Title VII has been violated.[25] One court has ruled that the employer must offer to accommodate the employee's religious need prior to taking the adverse employment action.[26] Moreover, whether an accommodation is reasonable depends on, among other factors, whether a benefit is being doled out in a discriminatory fashion, even if the employer would be free not to provide the benefit at all.[27] For example, granting unpaid leave for religious purposes is not a reasonable accommodation by an employer who grants paid leave for all purposes except religious ones, even though paid leave is a benefit that an employer is free not to provide at all. On the other hand, it is not clear how far the employer must go to accommodate religious holiday schedules. Plaintiffs have met with mixed success where their coworkers have complained that the employer's varying its neutral work scheduling system to accommodate the religious observance of some amounts to unfair preferential treatment.[28]

Occasionally, courts have considered whether Title VII and other state laws that require private employers to accommodate certain religious beliefs and practices violate the First Amendment to the United States Constitution either by "establishing" a religion or preventing its free exercise.

Title VII has survived these challenges, but state laws have met with mixed success.[29] Finally, when the religious discrimination grows out of a collective bargaining agreement, the union's duty to accommodate is the same as that of the employer.[30]

May my employer require my participation in religiously-oriented activities?

It depends. A secular employer may not treat you adversely for refusing to participate in employer-sponsored religious activities.[31] Nor may an employer harass you for your lack of specific religious beliefs.[32] Refusing to participate in nondenominational meditation exercises or "New Age"-type training activities, however, is less likely to be protected by antidiscrimination laws because the court may not regard such activities as religious.[33] Nor is the employer's requirement that you participate in such activities likely to infringe upon your constitutionally based right of freedom of religion since such training generally neither prevents you from practicing your religion nor imposes on you the practice of another religion.[34]

Does Title VII apply to job applicants?

Yes. Under EEOC guidelines, employers must accommodate the religious needs of job applicants as well as employees. Thus, an employer may not schedule preselection tests during a period that conflicts with an applicant's religious practices. Furthermore, an employer, in asking about availability for work, cannot make any reference to religious practices, unless justified by business necessity.[35]

What should I do if I believe I am being discriminated against because of my religion?

You should promptly notify your employer (and your union, if you have one) of your religious views and of the need for accommodation.[36] Once notified, your employer is required to consider accommodations. Although you are not required to propose acceptable accomodations to your employer,[37] and your employer is not required to accept the accommodations you propose,[38] it may be a good idea to propose something.

If your employer does not make acceptable accommodations and you are discharged or otherwise disciplined for failure to comply with your employer's requirements, you may institute proceedings against your employer under Title VII; the procedures are discussed in chapter 8 of this book.

To prevail in a Title VII religious discrimination case, you must plead and prove that (1) you have a bona fide belief that conflicts with an employment requirement, (2) you informed your employer of your views and of the need for accommodation, and (3) you were discharged or otherwise disciplined for failure to comply with the conflicting employment requirement.[39]

Can I collect unemployment compensation if I quit my job due to my religious beliefs?

Yes. In 1981 the Supreme Court held in *Thomas v. Review Board of the Indiana Employment Security Division*[40] that the First Amendment prohibits a state from denying you unemployment compensation when you have been forced to quit your job because of your religious beliefs. In that case, Thomas (a Jehovah's Witness) quit his job after he was transferred to a job making tank turrets, because making instruments of war violated his religious beliefs. The Court held, in effect, that his sincerely held religious beliefs must be deemed "good cause" for him to quit his job and that he could therefore collect unemployment compensation. This First Amendment protection also applies to religious converts[41] but may not apply where the religious practice violates a "neutral law of general application" such as the prohibition against ingesting peyote[42] or engaging in polygamy.[43] For more on unemployment compensation, contact your local unemployment insurance board.

NOTES

1. 42 U.S.C. § 2000e-2(a)(1).
2. 42 U.S.C. § 2000e(j).
3. *Id.*
4. 42 U.S.C. § 1981; *Saint Francis College v. Al-Khazraji*, 481 U.S. 604 (1987); *Shaare Tefila Congregation v. Cobb*, 481 U.S. 615 (1987).
5. *Stoller v. Marsh*, 682 F.2d 971 (D.C. Cir. 1982), *cert. denied*, 460 U.S. 1037 (1983). *See Rosen v. Thornburgh*, 55 FEP Cas. 580 (2d Cir. 1991).
6. *Cf. Bhatia v. Chevron U.S.A., Inc.*, 734 F.2d 1382 (9th Cir. 1984) (employer permitted to require plaintiff to shave off facial hair in order to meet safety regulations requiring face seal while wearing respirator required by job function).
7. 42 U.S.C. § 2000e-1. *See Corporation of Presiding Bishop v. Amos*, 483 U.S. 327 (1987) (exemption applies to the secular, nonprofit activities of a religious organization). *See generally* EEOC Dec. 83-6, 31 FEP Cas. 1858 (1983) (discussing what constitutes a religious organization).
8. 42 U.S.C. § 2000e-2(e)(1). *See Kern v. Dynalectron Corp.*, 577 F. Supp. 1196 (N.D. Tex. 1983), *aff'd*, 746 F.2d 810 (5th Cir. 1984); *Pime v. Loyola University of Chicago*, 585 F. Supp. 435, 442–43 (N.D. Ill. 1984), *aff'd*, 803 F.2d 351 (7th Cir. 1986).
9. 42 U.S.C. § 2000e-2(e)(2). *See Pime v. Loyola University of Chicago*, 803 F.2d 351 (7th Cir. 1986) (university not exempt as an education institution because church did not control its decisions concerning university matters).

10. 42 U.S.C. § 2000e-2(e)(2).
11. *See Matter of Klein*, 57 FEP Cas. 1047 (Ct. App. N.Y. 1991); *Black v. Snyder*, No. C5-91-71, (June 18, 1991) (Minn. Ct. App.) (First Amendment does not bar clergy member from suing her former church under Title VII for sexual harassment by its pastor); *Little v. Wuerl*, 55 FEP Cas. 786 (3d Cir. 1991) (application of Title VII to church decision to fire teacher would create excessive enlargement with religion); *DeMarco v. Holy Cross High School*, No. CV-91-2551, (July 17, 1992) (E.D.N.Y.).
12. 29 C.F.R. § 1605.1.
13. *Young v. Southwestern Savings & Loan Association*, 509 F.2d 140, 144 (5th Cir. 1975); EEOC Dec. 72-1114, 4 FEP Cas. 842 (1972); 110 Cong. Rec. 2607 (1964) (remarks of Rep. Caller).
14. 29 C.F.R. § 1605.1; *Edwards v. School Board*, 483 F. Supp. 620 (W.D. Va. 1980), *vacated and remanded on other grounds*, 658 F.2d 951 (1981). *See United States v. Seeger*, 380 U.S. 163 (1965); *Welsh v. United States*, 398 U.S. 333 (1970).
15. *Bellamy v. Mason's Stores, Inc.*, 368 F. Supp. 1025 (E.D. Va. 1973), *aff'd*, 508 F.2d 504 (4th Cir. 1974).
16. 42 U.S.C. § 2000e(j).
17. 432 U.S. 63 (1977).
18. *Hardison*, 432 U.S. at 65.
19. 479 U.S. 60 (1986).
20. In so ruling, the Court specifically noted that regulations providing that "when there is more than one means of accommodation which would not cause undue hardship, the employer . . . must offer the alternative which least disadvantages the individual with respect to his or her employment opportunities" [29 C.F.R. § 1605.2(a)(2)(ii)(1986)] was inconsistent with the plain meaning of Title VII to the extent it "require[d] the employer to accept any alternative favored by the employee short of undue hardship." 479 U.S. at 70 n.6.
21. *Miller v. Drennon*, No. 91-2166 (June 19, 1992) (4th Cir.).
22. EEOC Guidelines on Discrimination Because of Religion, 29 C.F.R. 1605; EEOC Policy Statement N-915-025 (May 9, 1988).
23. 29 C.F.R. § 1605.2(e)(1).
24. 29 C.F.R. § 1605.2(c)(1).
25. *Wangsness v. Watertown School Dist.*, 541 F. Supp. 332 (D.S.D. 1982).
26. *Toledo v. Nobel-Sysco, Inc.*, 892 F.2d 1481 (10th Cir. 1981).
27. *Ansonia Board of Education v. Philbrook*, 479 U.S. 60, 71, (1986) *quoting Hishon v. King & Spalding*, 467 U.S. 69, 75 (1984).
28. *E.g.*, *Brener v. Diagnostic Center Hospital*, 671 F.2d 141 (5th Cir. 1982); *Pinsker v. Adams Joint Dist. No. 28J of Adams & Arapahoe*,

735 F.2d 388 (10th Cir. 1984). *But see McGuire v. General Motors,* No. 91-3238, (Feb. 2, 1992) (6th Cir.).

29. *See, e.g., Thornton v. Caldor, Inc.,* 472 U.S. 703 (1985) (state may not require employers to provide sabbath observers with an absolute and unqualified right not to work on their chosen sabbath day); *Nottelson v. Smith Steel Workers, D.A.L.V. 1980,* 643 F.2d 445 (7th Cir. 1981); *Gavin v. Peoples National Gas Co.,* 464 F. Supp. 622 (W.D. Pa. 1979), *vacated and remanded on other grounds,* 613 F.2d 482 (3d Cir. 1980). *But see Cook v. Chrysler Corp. and UAW Local 110,* No. 87-1985C(5), (Dec. 31, 1991) (E.D. Mo.).

30. *E.g., Moore v. A.E. Staley Manufacturing Co.,* 727 F.§ Supp. 1156 (N.D. Ill. 1989); *EEOC v. University of Detroit,* 701 F. Supp. 1326 (E.D. Mich. 1988).

31. *See, e.g., Townley Engineering & Mfg. Co.,* 859 F.2d 610 (9th Cir. 1988).

32. *Matter of Meltebeke,* Or. Bur. of Lab. Ind., No. 29-90 (Feb. 2, 1991).

33. *See, e.g., Kolodziej v. Smith,* 7 IER Cas. 778 (Mass. Sup. Ct. 1992).

34. *Id.*

35. 29 C.F.R. § 1605.3(b).

36. 29 C.F.R. § 1605.2(c); *Brown v. General Motors Corp.,* 601 F.2d 956 (8th Cir. 1979).

37. *Redmond v. GAF Corp.,* 574 F.2d 897 (7th Cir. 1978).

38. *Ansonia Board of Education v. Philbrook,* 479 U.S. 60 (1986).

39. *Turpen v. Missouri-Kansas-Texas Railroad Co.,* 736 F.2d 1022, 1026 (5th Cir. 1984); *Brown v. General Motors Corp.,* 601 F.2d 956 (8th Cir. 1979); *Anderson v. General Dynamics Convair Aerospace Division,* 589 F.2d 397, 401 (9th Cir. 1978), *cert. denied,* 442 U.S. 921; *Edwards v. School Board of City of Norton, Va.,* 483 F. Supp. 620 (W.D. Va. 1980), *vacated and remanded on other grounds,* 658 F.2d 951 (4th Cir. 1981).

40. 450 U.S. 707 (1981).

41. *Hobbie v. Unemployment Appeals Commission of Florida,* 480 U.S. 136 (1987).

42. *Employment Div., Dept. of Human Resources v. Smith,* 494 U.S. 872 (1990).

43. *Reynolds v. United States,* 98 U.S. 145, 25 L. Ed 244 (1878).

XIII
Age

The most important statute prohibiting age discrimination is the Age Discrimination in Employment Act (ADEA).[1] The act was originally enacted by Congress in 1967 and amended to extend coverage in 1974, 1978, and 1986. ADEA is currently the only federal law specifically banning age discrimination in private employment, whereas the Age Discrimination Act of 1975 prohibits age discrimination in programs or activities receiving federal assistance.[2]

In addition to these federal laws, most states have laws against age discrimination. Under ADEA's express terms, where a state's age discrimination laws are more protective, those laws will govern;[3] but where a state law, local law, or a collective bargaining agreement is less protective than ADEA, the federal law takes precedence.[4] Thus, you should find out whether, in addition to the protections outlined in this chapter, you have further protection under your state's law. For additional discussion of age discrimination in employment see the ACLU handbook, *The Rights of Older Persons* by Robert N. Brown and others. Some portions of this chapter are based on that book.

What is the scope of ADEA?

ADEA prohibits discrimination on the basis of age in all aspects of the employment relationship, including hiring, promotion, termination, demotion, terms and conditions of employment, referrals by employment agencies, and membership in labor unions. ADEA also outlaws discriminatory employment advertising as well as retaliation against persons who have asserted their rights under ADEA.[5]

ADEA applies to the following employers, employment agencies, and labor organizations:[6] employers engaged in an industry affecting interstate commerce who have had 20 or more employees for each working day in each of 20 or more calendar weeks in the current or preceding calendar year;[7]

employment agencies that regularly seek to produce employees for an employer subject to ADEA; and most labor organizations with more than 25 members connected with interstate commerce.

ADEA protects all persons who are at least 40 years old[8] and who are either applicants for employment with or employees of an employer covered by ADEA. ADEA does not protect persons under age 40, although they may be protected by applicable state law. Exceptions include certain bona fide executives or employees holding high policy-making positions whose retirement benefits total more than $44,000;[9] employees at institutions of higher learning who have contracts for unlimited tenure;[10] independent contractors (i.e., those whose daily activities are not controlled by the employer);[11] and, in some cases, firefighters and law enforcement officers.[12] Moreover, ADEA permits age-based restrictions on entry into bona fide apprenticeship programs.[13]

May an employer consider my age if I am 40 years old or older?

Sometimes. Discrimination on the basis of age is not illegal in every circumstance.[14] In addition to the exceptions listed in the previous section, an employer may discriminate based on age when "age is a bona fide occupational qualification [BFOQ] reasonably necessary to the normal operation of the particular business, or where the differentiation is based on reasonable factors other than age."[15]

Also (with certain qualifications) certain employee benefit plans—including retirement, pension, or insurance plans—may treat older and younger employees differently.[16] In such cases a plan may provide less generous benefits to older employees based on the increased cost to the employer in providing those benefits. Plans created before ADEA was enacted are not exempt. Plans may not require or permit the involuntary retirement of an employee or serve as an excuse not to hire someone over the age of 40. Of course, an employer does not have to hire or keep you if you are not qualified for the job or there is no position for you, and ADEA expressly permits termination or discipline for "good cause."[17] These exceptions and others are discussed later in this chapter.

How do I prove age discrimination?

This depends on the theory of your case. Generally, age discrimination cases use a disparate impact or a disparate treatment theory or both. These theories are discussed in detail in chapter 8 and are reviewed only briefly here. A disparate impact case claims that an employer's policy or practice, even if seemingly age neutral, is discriminatory because it has a numerically disproportionate adverse impact on members of the protected class, that is, employees over 40 years of age.[18] In a disparate impact case, you must identify the specific employer practice or criterion that has caused the discriminatory impact.[19] These practices or criteria may be objective (e.g., a screening test or degree requirement) or subjective (e.g., "slowness" or "lacks potential").[20] Disparate impact cases are discussed later in this chapter in response to the question "Can I Prove Age Discrimination if the Employer's Action Appears 'Neutral' On Its Face But Has Had a Disparate Impact on Older Workers?"

A disparate treatment case claims that the employer treated the employee adversely because of age. In this case the plaintiff must prove that the employer consciously intended to discriminate because of age.[21] Disparate treatment cases may be based on direct evidence, and/or circumstantial evidence. Direct evidence includes comments to the effect that employees over the age of 40 are "too old to work here"[22] or that the employer is "going to get rid of the good 'old Joes' and get some younger folks in."[23] Not surprisingly, there are few cases of direct evidence of discrimination. Circumstantial evidence may include statistical proof of a pattern of discrimination; however, as discussed later, some courts are wary of statistics in disparate treatment cases. Circumstantial evidence may also include other acts of the employer against older workers.[24]

At the outset of the litigation, you, as the employee, must first make out a *prima facie case*. In a disparate treatment case, you must show that (1) you are a member of the protected class (i.e., over 40 years old); (2) an adverse action was taken against you (e.g., you were terminated or demoted); (3) you were replaced either by someone under 40 or by someone significantly younger than you; and (4) you were qualified for another open position or the position was given to the younger person.[25] The third factor of the prima facie case may be modified in certain circumstances.[26] For example, in a large scale reduction in a workforce situation, where many qualified employees may be laid off and not replaced, a showing that younger employees with less skills were retained will satisfy the third factor. Other modifications of the prima facie case are discussed later in this chapter.

To establish your prima facie case you need evidence that would permit a reasonable jury to find that age was a significant factor in the employer's decision.[27] That is, you must show that each element of the prima facie case is more probably true than not.[28] In legal parlance, you are required to prove your prima facie case by a "preponderance of the evidence," which may be direct or circumstantial. Courts will dismiss those cases where the plaintiff cannot establish a prima facie case.[29]

Once you establish your prima facie case, the employer can show that even though age was used it would have made the same decision even absent any discriminatory intent.[30] Some of these defenses, called *affirmative defenses*, are discussed later in this chapter. More typically, the employer may try to dispel the adverse inference of discrimination by articulating "some legitimate, nondiscriminatory reason" for its decision.[31] Here, the employer does not need to *prove* this was its reason by a preponderance of evidence. It needs only to show evidence that it was its actual reason.[32]

Once the employer produces a legitimate, nondiscriminatory reason for the adverse employment decision, the employee is given an opportunity to persuade the court either "that a discriminatory reason more likely motivated the employer or . . . that the employer's proffered explanation is unworthy of credence."[33] In other words, you can prove age discrimination by discrediting the employer's stated reason for its decision, that is, by showing that it is pretext. If you show the employer's articulated reason is false or not the real reason, you need not also prove the real reason for the decision was age. Under this so-called indirect method of proof once a court finds the employer's stated reasons to be not credible or not the true reasons, it may infer that age was the real reason for the employment decision. Of course, if you have direct evidence that the reason was age, it becomes even more likely that the court will find in your favor.

A good way to discredit an employer's articulated reason

is by showing that its decision is internally inconsistent. For example, suppose an employer stated that a certain promotion was based on performance evaluations, but the employer did not previously use evaluations to determine promotions or that younger employees were consistently promoted. This would be good circumstantial evidence that the performance evaluation reason was pretextual and, accordingly, that age was the factor in the promotion decision. On the other hand, courts will not overrule business decisions, even if unwise or unfair, as long as age was not a factor in making those decisions. Therefore, if an employer states that it reorganized its sales force out of business necessity, the mere fact that profits remained flat or even decreased after the reorganization does not, in and of itself, prove age discrimination. Rather, the court may conclude that the employer used poor business judgment.[34] Thus, the more different pieces of evidence you can muster, the stronger your case.

To prove age discrimination, you need only prove that age was a "determinative" factor in your employer's decision. You need not show that age was the sole or even the main factor motivating the employer. It is enough to show that were it not for the presence of age discrimination, the employer would not have made the discriminatory decision.[35] In other words, you must show that age was a factor that "made a difference" in the decision.[36]

Can I prove age discrimination if the employer's action appears neutral on its face but has had a disproportionate adverse impact on older employees?

Yes. Courts have long recognized that policies and practices that appear neutral on the surface may have a disproportionate adverse impact on employees over 40 years of age. Challenges to practices that fall more harshly on one group than on another that cannot be justified by business necessity are called disparate impact cases. All sorts of tests, qualifications, and criteria may be challenged under the disparate impact theory, such as degree requirements,[37] limitations on the number of positions available for senior faculty,[38] and subjective selection processes.[39] Disparate impact cases are discussed in chapter 8.

Plaintiffs have succeeded in proving disparate impact concerning a variety of policies and practices. These include the denial of severance pay to employees eligible for early retirement;[40] the reservation by a college of a certain number of positions for nontenured faculty;[41] and a policy of not considering work experience in excess of ten years.[42] Additionally, some courts have held that it is unlawful to accomplish economic savings by discharging higher paid older employees where the higher pay is a result of long experience, service, or age; these courts have concluded that actions based on such high pay factors are directly related to age.[43]

Can I prove age discrimination if I was replaced by another person who is also over the age of 40?

Generally, yes. Courts have generally accepted the notion that 60-year-olds will seldom be replaced by persons in their twenties.[44] Instead, the likely replacements for those in their sixties will be other members of the protected age group, i.e., those over 40 years of age. On the other hand, when those in their forties suffer discrimination, the likely replacements are those outside the protected class, i.e., those under age 40.[45] Discrimination based on replacement of an older member of the protected class by a younger one is well established, especially in disparate treatment cases.[46]

Can statistics play an important role in proving age discrimination?

Yes. Statistics have been used in both disparate impact and disparate treatment cases. They form the backbone of disparate impact cases described in the previous section. In disparate treatment cases, statistics have also been used to demonstrate that the employees adversely affected by an employer's action are disproportionately older or that the employees treated more favorably were disproportionately younger.[47] Statistics have been used to prove both the prima facie case and to prove pretext.[48] However, a plaintiff who relies exclusively on statistical evidence will rarely succeed in proving discrimination.[49] Nonetheless, even if the statistics are insufficient in and of themselves, they can offer valuable support to your case. For example, one court took notice of statistics indicating that all those hired in new jobs (33 individuals) were under the age of 50, while all those dismissed (11 individuals) were over the age of 50.[50] Although the court carefully stated that it would not evaluate the strength of the statistics, it found them worthy of favorable comment and ruled in the plaintiff's favor.

On the other hand, it is easy to understand why courts are wary of cases that rely mainly on statistics. Since the average age of a workforce always changes, such change does not prove discrimination in and of itself. Even where there is no employee turnover, the average age of a given workforce will increase over time as each member of the workforce ages. Second, in many cases the sample may be too small to be statistically significant.[51] Finally, plaintiffs sometimes fail to provide an adequate context for the statistical evidence. Courts have rejected such evidence as meaningless. For example, one plaintiff sought to prove age discrimination by showing that all seventeen employees who left the employer during the relevant period were in the protected age group.[52] The court rejected the plaintiff's proof because of his failure to compare the employees who were discharged with those retained or to compare retention levels between employees over the age of 40 with those under the age of 40.[53] Similarly, the court rejected the plaintiff's statistics showing that 94.2% of the employees hired in the two years following his termination were under age 40.[54] The plaintiff failed to provide (1) the relative qualifications of those hired and the positions to which they were assigned and (2) information regarding the labor pool of applicants, including whether qualified older applicants were available for or applied for the jobs.[55]

Can I prove age discrimination if age is not the only reason for the employer's action?

Yes. Age need not be the sole or predominant reason for the employer's action. Rather, age need only be a determining factor in the decision.[56] This means that were it not for the employee's age, the employer would not have taken the allegedly discriminatory action.[57] At least one court has explained the standard as meaning that age "made a difference" in the decision.[58] Thus, where there can be several reasons for the employer's decision, the plaintiff will succeed by showing that age was one of these factors. If the plaintiff proves that age was among the reasons for the decision, the plaintiff need not prove that the reasons offered by the employer are pretextual.[59]

What defenses may be used by an employer, employment agency, or labor organization that has been accused of age discrimination?

A defendant in an age case can use many defenses to defeat an age discrimination claim. These include discharge or discipline for cause or reasonable factors other than age; action taken pursuant to a bona fide employee benefit plan or bona fide seniority system; and a corporate reorganization or job elimination. These defenses are discussed in this section. Other defenses, including the bona fide occupational qualification (BFOQ), procedural defects, reduction in force, and waiver, settlement, or release are discussed separately thereafter.

Good cause and reasonable factors other than age. ADEA provides that it is not unlawful for an employer, employment agency, or labor organization to make an employment decision based on "reasonable factors other than age"[60] or to "discharge or otherwise discipline an individual for good cause."[61] Courts have upheld employment decisions based on an employer's administration of its personnel policies,[62] performance evaluations,[63] as well as on subjective factors such as personality[64] or friendship.[65] On the other hand, where the reasons for the adverse employment decision are linked to age or have a disproportionate impact on older employees, the decision may violate ADEA. For example, one employer's denial of severance pay to employees who also were eligible for early retirement was found "inoxorably linked to age" and therefore violated ADEA.[66] Similarly, favoring nontenured faculty members was found to have a disproportionate impact on older employees and therefore violated ADEA.[67]

Bona fide employee benefit plans. ADEA prohibits discrimination in the payment of benefits on the basis of age.[68] Benefits may be made pursuant to retirement, pension, and insurance plans or may be made on an *ad hoc* basis.

An employee benefit plan is lawful as long as the employer conforms to its terms in administering it,[69] it provides real benefits,[70] and it is not intended to evade the purposes of the ADEA.[71] To comply with ADEA, all plans (including those that were adopted before ADEA was enacted)[72] may not discriminate on the basis of age in the payment of benefits unless it is based on the cost of paying for those benefits for the older workers. Thus, employers may reduce benefit levels for older workers to the extent necessary to achieve approximate equivalency in the cost of providing the benefits for older and younger workers.[73] In other words, if certain benefits cost an employer more as employees get older (e.g., life insurance or disability insurance), the employer does not violate the ADEA by providing reduced benefits for older employees if the employer incurs at least as much of a cost in providing these lesser benefits as it does for providing greater benefits for younger employees.[74]

An employer may not deny severance benefits merely because an employee is also eligible for retirement when the time for paying severance occurs. Nonetheless, the employer may deduct from severance payments the cost of certain retiree medical benefits and the value of certain early retirement benefits.[75] To deduct the latter, the retirement benefits must be made available due to a contingency not based on age, such as the closing or sale of a business, and the employee must be eligible for an immediate and unreduced retirement benefit.[76] Additionally, benefits under a long-term disability plan may be reduced by pension benefits that the employee voluntarily elects to receive and by payments the employee is eligible to receive if the employee has attained the later of normal retirement age or age 62.[77]

Questions about discrimination often arise in the context of early retirement plans. It is lawful to offer employees incentives in the form of additional benefits if they retire early.[78] Courts have viewed this as a permissible carrot, not a prohibited stick. Even though the decision to retire early may be a very difficult one, there is no ADEA violation as long as the employee has the free choice of retiring or not retiring.[79] Retirement plans may have minimum ages for normal and early retirement benefits.[80] Defined benefit pension plans can subsidize early retirement benefits or supplement retirement benefits until employees qualify for Social Security benefits.[81]

Bona fide seniority systems. ADEA expressly allows an employer "to observe the terms of a bona fide seniority system."[82] The system may not require or permit the involuntary retirement of an employee because of age.[83]

A system is considered "observed" if it is implemented without regard to age.[84] Seniority should not be confused with age. A 35-year-old may have more seniority (i.e., more years on the job) than a 55-year-old. ADEA prohibits discrimination on the basis of age, not seniority.[85] A seniority system will be considered bona fide when, for example, it is based on years of experience or on skill and ability.[86] In contrast, a system that includes a policy or practice that differentiates solely on the basis of age is not bona fide.[87] Finally, a system that "permits" retirement (in violation of ADEA) is one that allows employees to be retired involuntarily under its terms.[88]

Corporate reorganization. Often employees are told that their terminations are the result of a corporate reorganization. Where there is an actual reorganization, based on business related considerations, there is no ADEA violation.[89] One court has explained that the "mere termination of a competent employee when an employer is making cutbacks due to economic necessity is insufficient to establish a prima facie case of age discrimination."[90] Therefore, an employer may succeed in establishing this defense where it makes decisions based on uniformly administered scoring systems or even on the dismissal of more expensive employees—provided the expense does not correlate with age.[91]

On the other hand, where the plaintiff produces direct, circumstantial, or statistical evidence that age was a factor in the employer's decision[92]—either because the employer refused to consider the employee's retention or relocation because of age, or because the employer regarded age as a negative factor[93]—the plaintiff can establish a case.

The plaintiff's evidence may include statistics showing disproportionate discharge in the protected age group;[94] disproportionate retention of younger employees;[95] consistent replacement of those discharged by younger employees, even if the replacements are also in the protected age group;[96] or inconsistencies in the employer's actions, thereby demonstrating that the proffered reason of "corporate reorganization" is merely pretext.[97]

When is age a bona fide occupational qualification?

ADEA permits employers to make decisions based on age where age is a "bona fide occupational qualification [BFOQ] reasonably necessary to the normal operation of the particular business."[98] The BFOQ defense is intended to be an "extremely narrow" exception to ADEA.[99] To prove this defense, the employer must meet both prongs of a two-pronged test. First, the employer must prove that the job qualifications it invokes to justify discriminating on the basis of age are reasonably necessary to the "essence or central mission of the employer's business."[100] This is to prevent the use of qualifications that are peripheral to the employer's business as a pretext for discriminating on the basis of age.[101]

Second, since age qualifications must be more than for an employer's convenience, the employer must demonstrate that it is compelled to rely on age as a "proxy" for the necessary job qualification discussed above.[102] The employer can meet this second prong by establishing (a) that it "had reasonable cause to believe that all or substantially all [persons over its age limit] would be unable to perform safely the duties of the job involved" or (b) that it is highly impractical to deal with the older employees on an individualized basis.[103] As one court has explained, "employers are entitled to articulate the qualifications they consider essential to their businesses and to exercise substantial discretion in judging [their] reasonableness. . . . Yet such decisions must be supported by objective fact in order to comply with the ADEA."[104]

Whether a given employer has established a BFOQ defense is a question of fact. Evidence may be drawn from such diverse areas as expert medical testimony, industry practice, and government regulation.[105] If the employer succeeds in proving age is a BFOQ, an individual employee's qualifications may be irrelevant.[106]

Employers have used the BFOQ defense to support mandatory retirement rules. They have frequently argued that age is a BFOQ because it is a proxy for the physical fitness demanded by a particular job, such as law enforcement officer, and that individualized screening is prohibitively expensive or otherwise impractical. Defenses such as this have met with mixed success. In these cases the issue is whether an employer must implement and enforce standards of "physical strength and stamina" and "the ability to withstand stress" in order to prove that the mandatory retirement age is a BFOQ.[107] Some courts have ruled that unless there is a minimum fitness standard that must be maintained by all employees, a mandatory retirement rule cannot be enforced as a BFOQ.[108] Other courts have not required testing and monitoring of employees as long as the employer can provide "objective evidence on whether the older employees can perform their duties."[109]

Can I still prove age discrimination when the employer is reducing its work force?

Yes. Courts have modified the prima facie case requirements for reduction in force (RIF) situations where many qualified employees may be dismissed and not replaced. As a result, the usual formulation of the prima facie case is inappropriate; a plaintiff could rarely show that the employer sought a replacement. Courts have disagreed, however, on what alternative proof will constitute the plaintiff's prima facie case. In one circuit court, for example, the prima facie case consists of showing that others not in the protected class were treated more favorably.[110] In other circuits, the plaintiffs must show that they were qualified to assume other positions at the time of discharge or must produce evidence that the employer intended to discriminate when it made its employment decision.[111]

In some ways, a RIF may be a harder case for a plaintiff trying to prove discrimination. The employer, by economic necessity, is forced to lay off many workers. Some courts may be more sympathetic to the employer because of this. Additionally, if the employer can show that it carefully decided who to let go and who to retain, it may be more difficult for the plaintiff to demonstrate that the employer's articulated reason is merely a pretext.

To make out a prima facie case in a RIF case, is it sufficient to show I was qualified for a lower position that was vacant at the time of the reduction in force?

It depends. In some courts it is sufficient for plaintiffs to show that they were qualified to assume any other available job.[112] Nevertheless, some courts also examine the employer's policies and defer to them. For example, where an employer has consistently refused to allow employees in such situations to accept demotions, the court will defer to the employer's legitimate business concerns about morale.[113] Moreover, it is important for potential plaintiffs to inform their supervisors if they are willing to accept other available positions (including demotions or transfers to new locations). An employer is not required to monitor the changes and development of its employees' interests in specific jobs at specific locations over time; in one case, an employee who failed to inform her supervisor of her willingness to relocate found herself without a job and without an age discrimination claim.[114]

Must an employer that is reducing its work force cause older workers to "bump" or replace younger, less senior employees?

No. ADEA requires that an employer, even in a RIF situation, reach employment decisions without regard to age; however, ADEA does not require an employer to give special and better treatment to individuals over the age of 40 simply because they are members of the protected class.[115] As a general matter, absent a policy or contract that provides otherwise, an employer instituting layoffs or a RIF, may prohibit the affected older employees from "bumping" or replacing less senior employees.[116] An employer that has a policy allowing bumping privileges must be sure that those privileges are not administered in a way that discriminates on the basis of age, for example, by allowing employees only under a certain age to bump.[117] Finally, if an employer deviates from its bumping policy (even if that policy is informal and was discontinued prior to the layoffs), an employee may use that deviation to show that the employer's proffered reason for the termination is merely a pretext.[118]

Can I be forced to retire because of my age?

Generally, no. ADEA prohibits mandatory retirement for most employees. Your employer cannot force you to retire, and no seniority system or employee benefit plan (e.g., retirement, pension, or insurance plan) can require you to retire.[119] Moreover, even an otherwise bona fide retirement system will be held to violate ADEA if it incorporates a mandatory discharge policy. In *Trans World Airlines v. Thurston*,[120] the Supreme Court examined two related retirement policies. The first policy required pilots to retire at age 60 for safety reasons. The parties did not contest that this was a BFOQ. The second policy allowed pilots who became disqualified from flying for any reason other than age to bump less senior flight engineers. As a result, pilots under the age of 60 were given a bumping privilege that was denied to pilots age 60 or older. The Supreme Court concluded that this bumping policy violated ADEA. The

Court ruled that a retirement system that incorporates this discriminatory bumping policy likewise violates ADEA because it effectively forces the retirement of certain pilots on the basis of age.

As mentioned earlier, in certain circumstances, imposing a mandatory retirement age may be a BFOQ.[121] Also, ADEA permits the mandatory retirement of executives or high level policymakers who are age 65 or older and entitled to a nonforfeitable retirement benefit of $44,000 or more a year.[122] Additionally, until January 1, 1994, the act allows the involuntary retirement of tenured employees of institutions of higher learning once they reach the age of 70[123] and the retirement of firefighters and law enforcement officers under certain circumstances.[124]

May my employer offer me incentives to retire?

Generally, yes. Courts have upheld the right of employers to offer employees added benefits if they agree to retire early. The decision to retire, however, must be truly voluntary. That is, the employee must be free to retire or not to retire.[125] Courts have taken the position that the added incentives are a "permissible carrot" for employees.[126] However, courts have disagreed on how much time should be provided to employees to think about such offers.[127]

Can my employer force me to choose between severance pay and an early retirement package?

No. An employer who is severing the employment relationship may not give severance pay to other younger employees who are ineligible for retirement and simultaneously deny severance pay to those who are eligible for retirement benefits.[128] On the other hand, an employer may offer the choice of accepting early retirement or severance pay or continuing to work.[129] In the latter example, the employee is not being forced to do anything and can continue to work.

May an employer offer me less benefits because of my age?

Yes. The Older Workers Benefit Protection Act, amending section 4(f)(2) of ADEA, allows an employer to provide reduced benefits to older employees if those reduced benefits cost the employer as much as the greater benefits provided to younger employees.[130] Thus, for example, if an employer spends as much for life insurance for each employee between the ages of 60 and 65 as for each employee between the ages of 55 and 64, the employer will satisfy ADEA's requirements even if the older employees end up with less life insurance coverage than the younger ones.

May my health benefits be different from those of a younger employee?

No. The ADEA has been amended to require employers to provide employees age 65 and older and their spouses age 65 or older with the same health benefits as are provided younger employees.[131]

Can I waive my rights to sue an employer under the ADEA?

Generally, yes. Before the Older Workers Benefit Protection Act (OWBPA) was enacted on October 16, 1990, many courts had endorsed the proposition that a person could waive or release his or her rights under ADEA if done in a "knowing and voluntary" manner.[132] OWBPA codified and supplemented the standards developed by the courts. To be considered a knowing and voluntary waiver, the waiver must meet the following minimum standards.[133]

1. The waiver must be in writing and must be written in a way that is calculated to be understood by the individual to whom it applies. When the waiver is part of a benefit package or program applicable to more than one employee, it must be in writing and calculated to be understood by the average individual eligible to participate.

2. The waiver must specifically refer to rights or claims arising under ADEA.

3. The waiver may not require employees to waive rights or claims that may occur after the date the waiver is executed.

4. The employee must receive valuable consideration for the waiver in addition to any benefits or amounts the employee was already entitled to receive.

5. The employee must be advised in writing to consult with an attorney before signing the waiver.

6. The employee must be given at least 21 days to consider the waiver. If the waiver is requested in connection with a

termination or severance program offered to a group or class of employees, each employee must be given at least 45 days to consider the waiver.

7. The waiver must be part of an agreement that is revocable for at least seven days following the employee's signing and the waiver cannot become effective or enforceable until the seven-day period has expired.

8. When the waiver is requested in connection with a termination or severance program offered to a group or class of employees, the employer must, at the outset of the 45-day waiting period, inform each eligible employee in writing of (a) the class of employees who are eligible, the specific eligibility requirements for participation in the program, and any applicable time limits on participation and (b) the job titles and ages of all employees eligible or selected for the program and the ages of all employees in the same job classification or organizational unit who are not eligible or selected.

9. If a charge of age discrimination has been filed with the EEOC or a lawsuit has been commenced, the waiver requirements are relaxed. Under those circumstances, a waiver is considered voluntary and knowing if, at a minimum, in addition to satisfying the first five points above, the employee has been given "a reasonable period of time" to consider the waiver agreement. That reasonable period could be less than 21 days.

Some additional protections may still be available for employees who sign releases. First, one court has ruled that an employee who has signed a waiver or release may still file an age discrimination charge with the EEOC. Even if the waiver or release is valid, the EEOC has notice of the employer's practice and may investigate it if it chooses. The court reasoned that a waiver of the right to file the charge was void because it violated public policy.[134] Second, an employer may not retaliate against an employee for challenging the validity of an executed waiver, for example, by terminating the pension of a retiree who, despite his signed release, files a claim for age discrimination.[135] Courts are split on whether an employer may require you to return the money received in exchange for the release before allowing you to proceed with an ADEA claim.[136] As a general matter, a waiver or release should be discussed with an attorney *before* being signed.

What should I do if I believe I have been discriminated against because of age?

To ensure that your rights are fully protected, you should take two actions immediately.

1. File a "charge" with the Equal Employment Opportunity Commission (EEOC) alleging age discrimination. You must file your charge within the proper length of time. In states that have not established a state agency to handle violations of state discrimination laws, you must file with the EEOC within 180 days after the discriminatory action occurred. In other states, provided you have filed a complaint with the appropriate state agency, you must file your federal charge with the EEOC within 300 days after the discriminatory action occurred, or within 30 days after the termination of the state administrative agency proceedings, whichever is earlier. Generally, if you fail to file your charge in a timely fashion, you will be prohibited from asserting your rights under federal law.

The period within which to file your charges begins on the day you knew or should have known of the discriminatory act. Suppose, for example, your employer told the people in your division on January 1 that the division would cease operations as of March 31.

The period within which to file with the EEOC starts to run on January 1, not March 31. A charge is filed when the EEOC receives it, not when the charging party mails it.

There is no fee for filing a charge with the EEOC. Although some offices allow you to file a charge by mail or telephone, it may be in your interest to go to the EEOC office personally.

2. If your home state or state of employment has an agency authorized to deal with age discrimination, contact that agency and file a charge with it. To find that agency, contact the EEOC, the state Department of Labor, or state employment services offices. Filing with both the EEOC and the state agency are prerequisites to pursuing your rights in court.

You must file with *both* agencies to preserve your rights under ADEA. However, you should also be aware that the EEOC regulations provide that a charge filed with the federal or the state agency is deemed filed with both agencies where a worksharing agreement is in effect. You can check with the local EEOC or state agency office to see if such a worksharing agreement is in effect.

Are there exceptions to the time limits for filing a charge?
Generally, no. Courts have been reluctant to keep the time limits from running unless there has been misconduct, bad faith, or other egregious behavior by the employer. The courts will examine whether the employee's failure to file is the consequence either of "a deliberate design by the employer or of actions that the employer should unmistakably have understood would cause the employee to delay filing his charge."[137] Although this is a hard standard to meet, occasionally employees succeed. One court tolled the filing period because the employer's misrepresentations for terminating the employer, if relied upon, warranted tolling.[138] Another court found tolling warranted where an employer offered the employee a substantial severance package provided the employee did not discuss his termination with anyone prior to his termination 4½ months later.[139] Some courts would reject tolling because this conduct of the employer was not the cause of the employee's failure to file on time with the EEOC.[140] Employers who have provided lengthy severance pay and benefits to employees during the transition will not have tolling imposed upon them.[141]

What should I include in the charge filed with the EEOC?
The purpose of the charge is to provide the EEOC and the employer with enough information so that the EEOC can attempt to eliminate the unlawful practices through conciliation. It is in the plaintiff's interest to be as broad but brief as possible in the charge. Therefore, it is sufficient to include: the nature of the alleged act (i.e., the termination or demotion); its date (or if it is discrimination that is continuing, it is very important to say so); and the fact that others who were younger were treated more favorably or that this practice has adversely affected older employees. It is also helpful to say, if appropriate, that the employer's actions adversely affected "other similarly situated employees." This may enable other plaintiffs to "piggyback" onto your charge if they decide to assert their rights at a later time and have missed the filing period themselves.

What do I do after I file the charge?
After you have filed the charge, you must wait 60 days before you take further legal action. You cannot bring a lawsuit under ADEA until the end of the 60-day waiting period.[142] This wait-

ing period is intended to give the EEOC an opportunity to resolve the dispute through "conciliation, conference and persuasion."[143] ADEA and most state laws require that the EEOC or state agency to attempt conciliation, that is, to settle the charge without litigation.[144]

What happens if the discrimination complaint cannot be settled by conciliation?

Under ADEA, you may bring a lawsuit 60 days after filing with the EEOC or state agency.[145] A federal lawsuit supersedes any pending state action.[146] The EEOC is authorized to bring a suit either in its name or that of the discrimination victim;[147] the EEOC's suit preempts any suit by the victim unless the private suit has already been started.[148] Alternatively, you can allow the EEOC or state agency to investigate the claim and seek to obtain a letter finding a "violation." An employer may be more likely to conciliate if the EEOC or state agency finds a violation; however, in the vast majority of charges filed, the agency finds that no violation has occurred. Regardless of the EEOC's or a state agency's investigatory results, you are always entitled to file a lawsuit, provided you file the suit within the proper time period, as discussed below. A court is not bound by the EEOC or state agency determination, and their findings are not to be given preclusive effect.[149]

Under state laws, a formal adversary proceeding may follow the failure of conciliation if the state agency has made a preliminary finding in favor of the employee. In some states there may be a hearing before the appropriate administrative agency;[150] in other states, you may be able to bypass the administrative procedure and sue in state court.[151] Sometimes the state agency may represent you in either the administrative hearing and/or state court.[152]

How soon must a lawsuit be started under ADEA?

Under the Civil Rights Act of 1991, the latest time to start a lawsuit is 90 days after you receive notice from the EEOC stating that it will take no further action on your case and that you may take your case to court. Thus, the time for filing a lawsuit runs from no sooner than 60 days after filing your charge to no later than 90 days after receiving notice from the EEOC.[153]

There may be a question as to the time to file a lawsuit for those cases involving events prior to November 21, 1991. Under the prior law, federal litigation must have been started with a federal court within 2 years of the discriminatory practice.[154] If the discrimination was "willful," then the period to file was three years.[155] For the discriminatory practice to be considered "willful," the plaintiff needed to show that the employer either knew or showed "reckless disregard" in determining its obligations under ADEA.[156] Since this was often hard to prove, employees were better off filing within 2 years if possible. It is not clear whether this longer (2 to 3 year period) will apply to cases involving acts that occurred prior to November 21, 1991; for these cases, you are better off filing your lawsuit in court within 2 years of the date of the discrimination or 90 days of receipt of the EEOC letter, whichever is earlier.

Can I join a class action?

Yes. A class action is a lawsuit brought by one or more individuals as representatives of a class of individuals who have common interests in the matter being litigated. Under ADEA, you must personally and affirmatively consent to "opt-in" or join the action; otherwise, the outcome of the action will not apply to you.[157] To join, however, you must be "similarly situated" to the class representatives (i.e., the named plaintiffs).

What remedies can I receive if I have been discriminated against because of my age?

ADEA allows a court to "grant such legal or equitable relief as may be appropriate to effectuate the purposes of the legislation."[158] Those purposes are "to promote employment of older persons based on their ability rather than their age" and "to prohibit arbitrary age discrimination in employment."[159] The relief is intended to "make whole" the victims of age discrimination; that is, to place them in the position they would have been in but for the discrimination. The following forms of relief are available to successful plaintiffs, depending on the particular facts of each case.

Backpay. This constitutes the direct and actual out-of-pocket monetary losses arising from the discrimination. Backpay includes all benefits and other compensation-related sums. For example, if you are terminated, you would be entitled to all the wages (and wage increases) you would have received from the date of your termination up to the date of your reinstatement by that employer. This amount is reduced by any wages and compensation earned at any other job during that time period. Even though you are a victim of discrimination, you have a strict obligation to use reasonable efforts to mitigate your damages by looking for other work. It is very important that you keep written records of your efforts to find other suitable employment. Losses in wages that could have been avoided by you can be deducted from your backpay award, or your backpay award can be lost entirely.

Reinstatement or frontpay. In addition to backpay, courts may require the employer to reinstate you. Where this option is impractical, courts have awarded frontpay.[160] Frontpay consists of your future earnings from the job you are not reinstated to minus what you could be expected to earn from other future employment. This sum is projected forward and then reduced to present value.[161] The preferred remedy is reinstatement since then the calculations are not speculative; where reinstatement is not feasible (because of animosity or similar circumstances), frontpay will be awarded. Generally, an employee's preference is not considered.

Liquidated damages. Statutory damages are available to victims of "willful violations" of ADEA for acts that occurred prior to November 21, 1991.[162] This results in a doubling of the backpay (but not the frontpay) award. For the violation to be "willful" you must show that the employer somehow acted recklessly in disregarding its obligations under ADEA. This is the same "willfulness" test as is used to determine the two-year versus three-year statute of limitations.[163] In general, the employer's actions must be flagrant in their disregard of ADEA. For acts that occurred after November 21, 1991, it is unclear whether there are any liquidated damages; it will depend on whether the Civil Rights Act of 1991 is retroactive.

Fringe benefits. Because ADEA strives to make the victim of discrimination "whole," it may be appropriate to award a variety of fringe benefits. These have included pension, health, and insurance benefits, as well as sick leave or seniority rights.

Equitable relief. Equitable relief is nonmonetary relief. In addition to reinstatement, it includes hiring, promotion, and retroactive seniority or credited service. In appropriate cases, it may also include injunctive relief—for example, a court order to prevent your employer from laying you off rather than retiring you. Injunctive relief is special relief and is awarded only in special cases.

Pain and suffering or emotional distress. ADEA does not provide for compensatory or emotional and mental distress damages. However, many state discrimination laws do provide for this relief. Therefore, in certain circumstances you may decide to pursue your state claim even if this means starting a separate lawsuit. Generally, federal courts allow you to append your state claim to your federal claim so that you can secure compensatory damages.

In addition to damages for emotional and mental distress, the remedies typically available under state age discrimination statutes are the same as those available under ADEA.

NOTES

1. 29 U.S.C. §§ 621 *et seq.*
2. 42 U.S.C. §§ 6101 *et seq.*
3. 29 U.S.C. § 633.
4. *Michael v. Majority of Board of Trustees of N.Y.C. Emp. Retirement System*, 80 A.D.2d 147, 437 N.Y.S.2d 977 (1st Dep't 1981) (ADEA overrides conflicting state law); *Johnson v. Mayor and City Council of Baltimore*, 515 F. Supp. 1287 (D. Md. 1981), *reversed*, 731 F.2d 209 (4th Cir. 1984), *reversed*, 469 U.S. 1156 (1985) (ADEA priority over city ordinance); *Levine v. Fairleigh Dickinson University*, 646 F.2d 825 (3d Cir. 1981) (ADEA precedence over collective bargaining agreement).
5. 29 U.S.C. §§ 623(d) and (e).
6. 29 U.S.C. §§ 623(a)–(c) and 630.
7. *See Thurber v. Jack Reilly's, Inc.*, 717 F.2d 633 (1st Cir. 1983), *cert. denied*, 466 U.S. 1904 (1984) (part-time workers should be included in determining the number of employees).
8. 29 U.S.C. § 631. As enacted in 1967, the ADEA covered only private employers. In 1974 the act was amended to cover federal, state, and local government employers.
9. 29 U.S.C. § 631(c)(1). *See Passer v. American Chemical Society*, 56 FEP Cas. 88 (D.D.C. 1991).
10. 29 U.S.C. § 631(d).
11. *Garrett v. Phillips Mills, Inc.*, 721 F.2d 979 (4th Cir. 1983); *EEOC*

v. Zippo Mfg. Co., 713 F.2d 32 (3d Cir. 1983); *Hickey v. Arkla Industries, Inc.*, 699 F.2d 748, 751 (5th Cir. 1983).

12. 29 U.S.C. § 623(i).

13. 29 C.F.R. § 1625.13. However, *see Quinn v. New York State Elec. and Gas Corp.*, 569 F. Supp. 655 (N.D.N.Y. 1983), *summary judgment granted*, 621 F. Supp. 1086 (N.D.N.Y. 1985).

14. 29 U.S.C. § 623(f).

15. 29 U.S.C. § 623(f)(1).

16. *See generally* Older Workers Benefit Protection Act, §§ 101–2, Pub. L. No. 101-433, 104 Stat. 978 (Oct. 16, 1990).

17. 29 U.S.C. § 623(f)(3).

18. *See Leftwich v. Harris-Stowe State College*, 702 F.2d 686 (8th Cir. 1983); *Geller v. Markham*, 635 F.2d 1027, 1032 (2d Cir. 1980), *cert. denied*, 451 U.S. 945 (1981).

19. *Wards Cove Packing Co., Inc. v. Atonio*, 490 U.S. 642 (1989).

20. *Watson v. Fort Worth Bank & Trust*, 487 U.S. 977 (1988).

21. *Duffy v. Wheeling Pittsburgh Steel Corp.*, 738 F.2d 1393, 1395 (3d Cir. 1984) *quoting Texas Dept. of Community Affairs v. Burdine*, 450 U.S. 248, 253 (1981).

22. *Cooper v. Asplundh Tree Expert Co.*, 836 F.2d 1544, 1545 (10th Cir. 1988).

23. *Hedrick v. Hercules, Inc.*, 658 F.2d 1088, 1092 (5th Cir. 1981). *See also Beshears v. Asbill*, 55 FEP Cas. 1383 (8th Cir. 1991) (older workers have problems adapting to change).

24. *Herman v. National Broadcasting Co.*, Inc., 744 F.2d 604 (7th Cir. 1984).

25. *Ramsey v. Chrysler First, Inc.*, 861 F.2d 1541 (11th Cir. 1988); *Coburn v. Pan American World Airways, Inc.*, 711 F.2d 339 (D.C. Cir. 1983).

26. *McDonnell Douglas Corp. v. Green*, 411 U.S. 792, 802 n.13 (1973); *Duffy v. Wheeling Pittsburgh Steel Corp.*, 738 F.2d 1393 (3d Cir. 1984); *Williams v. General Motors Corp.*, 656 F.2d 120 (5th Cir. 1981), *cert. denied*, 455 U.S. 943 (1982).

27. *Rose v. National Cash Register Corp.*, 703 F.2d 225 (6th Cir. 1983). *See Giacoletto v. Amax Zinc*, 57 FEP Cas. 1273 (7th Cir. 1992); *Taggart v. Time*, 54 FEP Cas. 1628 (2d Cir. 1991).

28. *Sutton v. Atlantic Richfield Co.*, 646 F.2d 407 (9th Cir. 1981).

29. *Ramsey v. Chrysler First, Inc.*, 861 F.2d 1541 (11th Cir. 1988).

30. *Young v. General Foods Corp.*, 840 F.2d 825, 828 (11th Cir. 1988) *citing Buckley v. Hospital Corp. of America*, 758 F.2d 1525, 1529-30 (11th Cir. 1985).

31. *Texas Dept. of Community Affairs v. Burdine*, 450 U.S. 248 (1981).

32. *Id.*

33. *Id.* at 256.

34. *See, e.g., Metz v. Transit Mix, Inc.*, 828 F.2d 1202 (7th Cir. 1987) (Easterbrook, J., dissenting).

35. *Chappell v. GTE Products Corp.*, 803 F.2d 261 (6th Cir. 1986); *Hagelthorn v. Kennecott, Corp.*, 710 F.2d 76 (2d Cir. 1983); *Cancellier v. Federated Dept. Stores*, 672 F.2d 1312 (9th Cir. 1982), *cert. denied*, 459 U.S. 859 (1982); *Loeb v. Textron Inc.*, 600 F.2d 1003 (1st Cir. 1979).

36. *Paolillo v. Dresser Industries, Inc.*, 865 F.2d 37 (2d Cir.), *modified*, 884 F.2d 707 (2d Cir. 1989).

37. *Lester v. Olin Corp.*, 50 FEP Cas. 1468, 51 Empl. Pctc. Dec. ¶ 39,452 (N.D. Fla. 1989).

38. *Leftwich v. Harris-Stowe State College*, 702 F.2d 686 (8th Cir. 1983).

39. *Rose v. Wells Fargo & Co.*, 902 F.2d 1417 (9th Cir. 1990).

40. *EEOC v. Borden's, Inc.*, 724 F.2d 1390 (9th Cir. 1984).

41. *Leftwich v. Harris-Stowe State College*, 702 F.2d 686 (8th Cir. 1983).

42. *Haskins v. Dep't of Health & Human Services*, 35 FEP Cas. 256 (E.D. Mo. 1984).

43. *Metz v. Transit Mix, Inc.*, 828 F.2d 1202 (7th Cir. 1987); *Geller v. Markham*, 635 F.2d 1027 (2d Cir. 1980); *Marshall v. Arlene Knitwear, Inc.*, 454 F. Supp. 715 (E.D.N.Y. 1978), *aff'd*, 608 F.2d 1369 (2d Cir. 1979). *But see Bay v. Times Mirror Magazine*, 56 FEP Cases 407 (2d Cir. 1991). *See also Wilson v. Firestone Tire & Rubber Co.*, No. 89-3801, (May 6, 1991) (6th Cir.).

44. *McCorstin v. United States Steel Corp.*, 621 F.2d 749, 753–54 (5th Cir. 1980).

45. *See Lowe v. Commack Union Free School District*, 886 F.2d 1364 (2d Cir. 1989) (Pierce, J., dissenting); *Maxfield v. Sinclair Intern.*, 766 F.2d 788 (3d Cir. 1985), *cert. denied*, 474 U.S. 1057 (1986).

46. *E.g., Chipollini v. Spencer Gifts, Inc.*, 814 F.2d 893 (3d Cir. 1987).

47. *E.g., Herman v. National Broadcasting Co., Inc.*, 744 F.2d 604 (7th Cir. 1984).

48. *E.g., Hollander v. American Cyanamid Co.*, 895 F.2d 80, 84 (2d Cir. 1990); *Goldstein v. Manhattan Industries*, 758 F.2d 1435 (11th Cir.), *cert. denied*, 474 U.S. 1005 (1985); *Pirone v. Home Insurance Co.*, 559 F. Supp. 306 (S.D.N.Y.), *aff'd*, 742 F.2d 1430 (2d Cir. 1983).

49. *Rose v. Wells Fargo & Co.*, 902 F.2d 1417 (9th Cir. 1990); *EEOC v. Sandia Corp.*, 639 F.2d 600 (10th Cir. 1980).

50. *Herman v. National Broadcasting Co., Inc.*, 744 F.2d 604, 610 (7th Cir. 1984).

51. *Parker v. Federal National Mortgage Association*, 741 F.2d 975 (7th Cir. 1984).

52. *Simpson v. Midland-Ross Corp.*, 823 F.2d 937 (6th Cir. 1987).

53. *Id.* at 943.
54. *Id.*
55. *Id.*
56. *Krodel v. Young*, 748 F.2d 701 (D.C. Cir. 1984), *cert. denied*, 474 U.S. 817 (1985); *Kiel v. Goodyear Tire & Rubber Co.*, 575 F. Supp. 847 (N.D. Ohio 1983), *aff'd*, 762 F.2d 1008 (6th Cir. 1985).
57. *Cancellier v. Federated Dep't Stores*, 672 F.2d 1312 (9th Cir.), *cert. denied*, 459 U.S. 859 (1982).
58. *Paolillo v. Dresser Industries, Inc.*, 865 F.2d 37 (2d Cir.), *modified*, 884 F.2d 707 (2d Cir. 1989).
59. *EEOC v. Prudential Savings and Loan Ass'n*, 741 F.2d 1225, 1230 (10th Cir. 1984); *Chipollini v. Spencer Gifts*, 814 F.2d 893 (3d Cir. 1987).
60. 29 U.S.C. § 623(f)(1).
61. 29 U.S.C. § 623(f)(3).
62. *See, e.g., Johnson v. Perkins*, 815 F.2d 1220 (8th Cir. 1987).
63. *Moore v. Sears, Roebuck & Co.*, 683 F.2d 1321 (11th Cir. 1982).
64. *Grubb v. W.A. Foote Memorial Hospital*, 741 F.2d 1486 (6th Cir. 1984) (discharge based on personality conflict).
65. *Allison v. Western Union Telegraph Co.*, 680 F.2d 1318 (11th Cir. 1982) (upholding decision based on terminating "person you will miss the least").
66. *EEOC v. Westinghouse Electric Corp.*, 869 F.2d 696 (3d Cir. 1987).
67. *Leftwich v. Harris-Stowe State College*, 702 F.2d 686 (8th Cir. 1983).
68. 29 U.S.C. § 623(f)(2) as amended by the Older Workers Benefit Protection Act, Pub. L. No. 101-433, 104 Stat. 978 (Oct. 16, 1990).
69. *Patterson v. Independent School District*, 742 F.2d 465 (8th Cir. 1984).
70. *United Air Lines v. McMann*, 434 U.S. 192 (1977).
71. 29 U.S.C. § 623(f)(2) as amended by the Older Workers Benefit Protection Act § 103(1).
72. 29 U.S.C. § 623(k).
73. 29 C.F.R. § 1625.10 (1988).
74. 29 U.S.C. § 623(f)(2)(B)(i).
75. 29 U.S.C. § 623(l).
76. 29 U.S.C. § 623(l)(2)(A).
77. 29 U.S.C. § 623(l)(3).
78. *Patterson v. Independent School District*, 742 F.2d 465 (8th Cir. 1984).
79. *See Henn v. National Geographic Society*, 819 F.2d 824 (7th Cir. 1987); *Patterson v. Independent School District*, 742 F.2d 465 (8th Cir. 1984).
80. 29 U.S.C. § 623(l)(1).

81. *Id.*
82. 29 U.S.C. § 623(f)(2)(A).
83. *Id.*
84. *Ayala v. Mayfair*, 831 F.2d 1314 (7th Cir. 1987) *overruled on other grounds by Oxman v. WLS-TV*, 846 F.2d 448 (7th Cir. 1988).
85. *Reilly v. Friedman's Express, Inc.*, 556 F. Supp. 618 (M.D. Pa. 1983).
86. *Morelock v. NCR Corp.*, 586 F.2d 1096 (6th Cir. 1978). *See Arnold v. United States Postal Service*, 649 F. Supp. 676 (D.D.C. 1986).
87. *Trans World Airlines v. Thurston*, 469 U.S. 111 (1985).
88. *Id.*
89. *Rose v. Wells Fargo & Co.*, 902 F.2d 1417 (9th Cir. 1990).
90. *La Grant v. Gulf & Western Manufacturing Co.*, 748 F.2d 1087, 1090 (6th Cir. 1984).
91. *See Metz v. Transit Mix, Inc.*, 828 F.2d 1202 (7th Cir. 1987).
92. *McMahon v. Libbey-Owens-Ford Co.*, 870 F.2d 1073 (6th Cir. 1989); *Williams v. General Motors Corp.*, 656 F.2d 120 (5th Cir. 1981), *cert. denied*, 450 U.S. 943 (1982); *Rosengarten v. J.C. Penney Co., Inc.*, 605 F. Supp. 154 (E.D.N.Y. 1985).
93. *Stendebach v. CPC International, Inc.*, 691 F.2d 735 (5th Cir. 1982).
94. *Uffelman v. Lone Star Steel Co.*, 863 F.2d 404 (5th Cir. 1989).
95. *Id.*
96. *Id. quoting McCorstin v. United States Steel Corp.*, 621 F.2d 749, 754 (5th Cir. 1980) ("Because of the value of experience rarely are sixty-year-olds replaced by those under forty. The replacement is more subtle but just as injurious to the worker who has been discharged. That the person is replaced by a person ten years younger rather than twenty years does not diminish the discrimination; the subtlety only tends to disguise it").
97. *Lockhart v. Westinghouse Credit Corp.*, 879 F.2d 43 (3d Cir. 1989).
98. 29 U.S.C. § 623(f)(1).
99. *Western Air Lines v. Criswell*, 472 U.S. 400, 412 (1985).
100. *Id.* at 413; *Usery v. Tamiami Trail Tours, Inc.*, 531 F.2d 224, 235–236 (5th Cir. 1976).
101. *Western Air Lines v. Criswell*, 472 U.S. 400, 412 (1985).
102. *Id.* at 414.
103. *Id.*
104. *EEOC v. Mississippi*, 837 F.2d 1398, 1400 (5th Cir. 1988).
105. *Western Air Lines v. Criswell*, 472 U.S. 400 (1985). *See Johnson v. Mayor of Baltimore City Council*, 472 U.S. 353 (1985).
106. *Williams v. Hughes Helicopters, Inc.*, 806 F.2d 1387 (9th Cir. 1986).
107. *EEOC v. City of East Providence*, 798 F.2d 524, 528 (1st Cir. 1986).
108. *EEOC v. Mississippi*, 837 F.2d 1398 (5th Cir. 1988); *EEOC v. Penn-*

sylvania, 829 F.2d 392 (3d Cir. 1987); *EEOC v. New Jersey*, 631 F.
Supp. 1506 (D.N.J. 1986), *aff'd*, 815 F.2d 694 (3d Cir. 1987).

109. *EEOC v. Missouri State Highway Patrol*, 748 F.2d 447, 454 (8th
Cir. 1984), *cert. denied*, 474 U.S. 828 (1985). *Accord EEOC v. City
of East Providence*, 798 F.2d 524 (1st Cir. 1986).

110. *Oxman v. WLS-TV*, 846 F.2d 448, 455 (7th Cir. 1988). For other
courts using this or a similar approach see *Thornbrough v. Columbus
and Greenville Railroad Co.*, 700 F.2d 633, 642 (5th Cir. 1985);
Duffy v. Wheeling, 738 F.2d 1393 (3d Cir.), *cert. denied*, 469 U.S.
1087 (1984); and *Coburn v. Pan American World Airways, Inc.*, 711
F.2d 339 (D.C. Cir.), *cert. denied*, 464 U.S. 994 (1983).

111. *Williams v. General Motors Corp.*, 656 F.2d 120 (5th Cir. 1981),
cert. denied, 455 U.S. 943 (1982).

112. *Ayala v. Mayfair Molded Products Corp.*, 831 F.2d 1341 (7th Cir.
1987).

113. *Ridenour v. Lawson Co.*, 791 F.2d 52 (6th Cir. 1980) *quoting Parcinski v. The Outlet Co.*, 673 F.2d 34 (2d Cir. 1982).

114. *Foster v. Arcata Assoc., Inc.*, 772 F.2d 1453 (9th Cir.), *cert. denied*,
475 U.S. 1048 (1985).

115. *Tice v. Lampert Yards*, 761 F.2d 1210 (7th Cir. 1988); *Parcinski v.
The Outlet Co.*, 673 F.2d 34 (2d Cir. 1982).

116. *Tice v. Lampert Yards*, 761 F.2d 1210 (7th Cir. 1988); *Moore v.
McGraw Edison*, 804 F.2d 1026 (8th Cir. 1986); *Simpson v. Midland-
Ross Corp.*, 823 F.2d 937, 942 n.6 (6th Cir. 1987); *Ridenour v.
Lawson Co.*, 791 F.2d 52 (6th Cir. 1986).

117. *Trans World Airlines v. Thurston*, 469 U.S. 111, 124 (1985). *See
Ayala v. Mayfair Molded Products Corp.*, 831 F.2d 1314 (7th Cir.
1987). *Cf. Barnes v. GenCorp.*, Inc., 896 F.2d 1457 (6th Cir. 1990).

118. *Herold v. Hajoca Corp.*, 864 F.2d 317 (4th Cir. 1988).

119. 29 U.S.C. § 623(f)(2).

120. 469 U.S. 111 (1985).

121. *See, e.g., EEOC v. Mississippi*, 837 F.2d 1398 (5th Cir. 1988).

122. 29 U.S.C. § 631(c). *See Passer v. American Chemical Society*, 56
FEP Cas. 88 (D.D.C. 1991).

123. 29 U.S.C. § 631(d).

124. 29 U.S.C. § 623(i).

125. *Britt v. E.I. DuPont de Nemours & Co., Inc.*, 768 F.2d 593 (4th
Cir. 1985); *Parker v. Federal National Mortgage Association*, 741
F.2d 975 (7th Cir. 1984); *Herbert v. Mohawk Rubber Co.*, 47 EPD
para. 38,139 (D. Mass. 1988).

126. *Schuler v. Polaroid Corp.*, 848 F.2d 276, 278 (1st Cir. 1988); *Karlen
v. City College of Chicago*, 837 F.2d 314 (9th Cir. 1988); *Bodnar*

v. Synpol, Inc., 843 F.2d 190 (5th Cir.), *cert. denied*, 109 U.S. 260 (1988).

127. *See Henn v. National Geographic Society*, 819 F.2d 824 (7th Cir. 1987). *Cf. Paolillo v. Dresser Industries, Inc.*, 821 F.2d 81 (2d Cir. 1987).

128. *See EEOC v. Westinghouse Electric Corp.*, 725 F.2d 211 (3d Cir. 1983), *cert. denied*, 469 U.S. 820 (1984); *EEOC v. Borden's, Inc.*, 724 F.2d 1390 (9th Cir. 1984).

129. *Parker v. Federal National Mortgage Association*, 741 F.2d 975 (7th Cir. 1984).

130. 29 U.S.C. § 623(f)(2)(B)(i).

131. 29 U.S.C. § 623(g). This section was added to the ADEA by the Tax Equity and Fiscal Responsibility Act of 1982 (Pub. L. No. 97-248). It was subsequently amended by § 2301(b) of the Deficit Reduction Act of 1984 (DEFRA), Pub. L. No. 98-369 and by § 9201(b) of the Consolidated Omnibus Budget Reconciliation Act of 1986 (COBRA), Pub. L. No. 99-272.

132. *Coventry v. U.S. Steel Corp.*, 856 F.2d 514 (3d Cir. 1988); *Lancaster v. Buerkle Buick Honda Co.*, 809 F.2d 539 (8th Cir. 1987); *Runyan v. National Cash Register Corp.*, 787 F.2d 1039 (6th Cir. 1986).

133. 29 U.S.C. § 626(f).

134. *EEOC v. Cosmair, Inc., L'Oreal Hair Care Division*, 821 F.2d 1085, 1090 (5th Cir. 1987).

135. *EEOC v. U.S. Steel Corp.*, 671 F. Supp. 351 (W.D. Pa. 1987).

136. *Isaacs v. Caterpillar*, 55 FEP Cas. 1639 (D.C. Ill. 1991).

137. *Price v. Litton Business Systems, Inc.*, 694 F.2d 963, 965 (4th Cir. 1982).

138. *Meyer v. Riegel Products Corp.*, 720 F.2d 303 (3d Cir. 1983), *cert. denied*, 465 U.S. 1091 (1984).

139. *Felty v. Graves-Humphreys Co.*, 785 F.2d 516 (4th Cir. 1987).

140. *Felty v. Graves-Humphreys Co.*, 818 F.2d 1126 (4th Cir. 1987).

141. *Price v. Litton Business Systems, Inc.*, 694 F.2d 963 (4th Cir. 1982), *Kriegesmann v. Barry-Wehmiller Co.*, 739 F.2d 357 (8th Cir. 1984).

142. 29 U.S.C. § 626(d).

143. 29 U.S.C. § 626.

144. 29 U.S.C. § 626(c). *Cf.* N.Y. Exec. Law § 297-3a.

145. 29 U.S.C. § 626(d).

146. 29 U.S.C. § 633(b).

147. 29 U.S.C. § 626(b).

148. 29 U.S.C. § 626(c).

149. *Astoria Federal Savings & Loan Assoc v. Solimino*, 55 FEP Cas. 1503 (U.S. 1991).

150. *E.g.*, Conn. Gen. Stat. §§ 31-127–32 (1977).

151. *E.g.*, N.Y. Exec. Law § 297-9.

152. *E.g.*, Conn. Gen. Stat. § 31-127; Del. Code Ann. tit. 19, § 712; N.J.S.A. 10:5-6 (1976).

153. CRA § 115.

154. 29 U.S.C. § 626(e), incorporating § 6 of the Portal-to-Portal Act of 1947, 29 U.S.C. § 255 (1984).

155. 29 U.S.C. § 626(e).

156. *Trans World Airlines v. Thurston*, 469 U.S. 111 (1985).

157. 29 U.S.C. § 216(b).

158. 29 U.S.C. §§ 626(b) and (c).

159. 29 U.S.C. § 626(b).

160. *Lewis v. Federal Prison Industries*, 58 FEP Cas. 127 (11th Cir. 1992); *Whittlesey v. Union Carbide Corp.*, 742 F.2d 724 (2d Cir. 1984).

161. *Loeb v. Textron, Inc.*, 600 F.2d 1003 (1st Cir. 1979).

162. 29 U.S.C. § 626(b), incorporating FLSA § 16, 29 U.S.C. § 216(a).

163. *Trans World Airlines v. Thurston*, 469 U.S. 111 (1985).

XIV
Disability

By 1990 there were approximately 8.2 million unemployed Americans with disabilities. Most wanted to work but could not find jobs. Many were not working because they were rejected by employers on account of their disabilities. The cost of this discrimination, in terms of human anguish and economic waste, spurred the enactment of the Americans with Disabilities Act of 1990 (ADA).[1] This sweeping federal law has been called the most significant civil rights legislation since 1964.

Before 1990 Congress had dealt with discrimination against individuals with disabilities in a piecemeal fashion. It enacted the Rehabilitation Act of 1973.[2] That act covered only the federal government as an employer and private employers having substantial contracts with or receiving financial assistance from the federal government. Congress also had enacted the Vietnam Era Veteran's Readjustment Assistance Act of 1972,[3] which paralleled the Rehabilitation Act. Other federal legislation provided federal assistance or grants to states for the purpose of educating children with disabilities[4] and aiding states in eliminating educational and architectural barriers to employing persons with disabilities.[5] These laws required states to make some efforts to employ persons with disabilities. This chapter discusses Title I of the ADA and the Rehabilitation Act.

What does the ADA do?

Title I of the ADA declares that employers must offer individuals with disabilities equal employment opportunities. This means employers must enable people with disabilities to attain the same level of performance as employees without disabilities and to enjoy equal benefits and privileges.

To comply with Title I, employers must learn what job skills people with disabilities possess and hire those individuals with appropriate skills. This may sometimes entail making accommodations to help the disabled person obtain and perform a job. Under the ADA, employers who discriminate outright or who do not attempt to make such reasonable accommodations may be subject to lawsuits similar to those brought under Title VII. A finding of discrimination may result in the imposition of backpay awards, reinstatement, compensatory and punitive damages, and other forms of relief.

If the ADA seems complex, it is because it is so ambitious. It seeks to equalize the employment opportunities of millions of individuals, each of whom brings to the requirements of a given job a unique set of skills and disabilities. To break down the psychological and physical barriers disabled individuals face, the ADA requires employers to adjust their jobs, and perhaps themselves, until the qualified disabled person is provided with working conditions that are on par with everyone else's. The ADA's rules and procedures provide a workable framework for this enormous task. You must therefore familiarize yourself with these procedures in order to take full advantage of the opportunities opened up by the ADA. The process begins by answering several of the key questions that are discussed here.

Does the ADA cover the place where I work (or seek to work)?

Most employers must comply with the ADA. Employers with 15 or more employees are covered by the law (until July 26, 1994, employers with fewer than 25 employees are exempt).[6] If the business in question employs less than these numbers, you will have to determine whether any state antidiscrimination laws apply. Many states offer ADA-like protections to those in smaller businesses.

The ADA does not apply to the federal government.[7] Federal government workers, however, are covered by Section 501 of the Rehabilitation Act of 1973;[8] that law is discussed later in this chapter. Also exempt are certain private membership clubs and Indian tribes.[9]

What rights does the ADA protect?

The ADA makes it unlawful for employers to discriminate against protected individuals with respect to virtually every aspect of employment. Once you can establish that the ADA applies, the law prohibits discrimination in regard to hiring, promotion, transfer, layoff, termination, pay, assignments, seniority, medical examinations, disciplinary action, leaves of absence, benefits, training, and the use and enjoyment of workplace facilities. In short, it covers virtually every aspect of work.[10]

The ADA prohibits the employer from limiting, segregating, or classifying a job applicant or employee in a way that adversely affects employment opportunities for that person because of his or her disability.[11] It prohibits discrimination against individuals who have a relationship or association with a person with a disability.[12] Like Title VII, it also protects the rights of anyone who opposes a discriminatory employment practice or who files a complaint, testifies, assists, or participates in some form of enforcement of the act.[13]

Who is protected by the ADA?

The ADA prohibits discrimination against persons with a disability who are qualified to perform the essential functions of the job, without or without reasonable accommodation.[14] As can be seen, this sentence has several parts. To be covered under the ADA, you must first establish that you have a disability. You must then show that you are qualified to do the job in question. You are not qualified if you are unable to perform the essential functions of the job. However, if you would be able to perform those functions with the aid of an accommodation, you are covered and must be provided that accommodation, as long as doing so would not impose an "undue hardship" on the employer. All of these important concepts are explained further below.

What is considered a disability under the ADA?

As mentioned, the ADA applies only to individuals with disabilities. The definition of a disability under the ADA is "an impairment, physical or mental, that substantially limits one or more major life activities."[15] A physical impairment can be any physiological disorder or condition, even a cosmetic disfigurement.[16] A mental impairment is any mental or psychological disorder, such as mental retardation, emotional or mental illness, or a learning disability.[17] A person is considered to have an impairment regardless of whether medication or a prosthesis might alleviate the condition. Under the ADA, characteristics within the normal range are not considered impairments, such as lefthandedness, height, weight, nearsightedness, and eye or hair color. Nor are temporary conditions such as the flu or a broken limb considered impairments, unless they become abnormally prolonged, for instance a broken leg that does not heal. Nor are personality traits such as a quick temper or irresponsible behavior impairments. Stress and depression are conditions that may be considered impairments, however, if they stem from a documented psychological disorder. Under the ADA, these impairments by themselves do not make a person disabled unless they "substantially impair a major life activity."[18]

In any event, these impairments must substantially limit a "major life activity" to be considered disabilities under the ADA. Major life activities include caring for oneself, performing manual tasks, walking, seeing, hearing, speaking, breathing, learning, eating, and reproduction. Working may also be considered a major life activity. If an impairment does not limit one's ability to walk or see, for instance, but does substantially limit one's ability to perform a class of jobs, or a broad range of jobs in various classes, then one is disabled. For instance, a jet pilot with a slight vision defect who is barred from flying passenger aircraft but may still fly cargo planes is not substantially impaired in the activity of working. But a laborer whose back injury prevents the performance of most laborer jobs, would be considered disabled under the ADA.

Homosexuality and bisexuality are not considered impairments and thus are not disabilities covered by the ADA. The ADA also excludes from coverage sexual and other behavioral disorders such as transvestism, pedophilia, and transsexualism, compulsive gambling, kleptomania and pyromania.[19]

Is drug or alcohol dependence a disability covered by the ADA?

An alcoholic is considered a person with a disability under the ADA. Such a person cannot be discriminated against because of alcoholism and may be entitled to consideration of accommodation, if it will allow him or her to perform the essential functions of the job. If the alcohol use adversely affects the person's job performance, however, the employer may discipline or discharge the person. For example, an employee who reports late to work due to alcoholism can be reprimanded for tardiness but not more so than any other latecomer.

Drug use, however, is not protected the way alcoholism is under the ADA. The ADA states that an individual who is currently using drugs illegally is not considered disabled. An employer may test for drugs under the ADA and discharge those found using them illegally. An employer may not discriminate, however, against a drug addict who is not currently using drugs and who has been rehabilitated or is receiving treatment for drug addiction.[20]

Does the ADA protect me if an employer mistakenly thinks that I have a disability and treats me accordingly?

Yes. Some people are discriminated against based on their past medical record. Suppose, for example, you once suffered from a heart attack. Even though you are in perfect health now, you are nevertheless protected by the ADA if your employer regards you as disabled or simply decides not to promote you because of your medical history. Any person without a disability who is *perceived* as having one is covered by the ADA. For instance, a person who is rumored to have the HIV virus and is treated adversely because of it will be protected as will a person with an unpleasant looking scar or birthmark. The purpose of the ADA is to eliminate groundless fears, myths, and stereotypical attitudes that have blocked the employment opportunities of individuals with disabilities.[21]

How can I tell whether I am "qualified" and thus covered under the ADA?

To be "qualified" and therefore protected by the ADA, you must meet the necessary job prerequisites. These typically include education, experience, training, skills, licenses and other work-related requirements. For instance, if a job requires four years of work experience and the individual with a disability has only two, he or she would not be qualified and therefore not able to bring a claim under the ADA.

In addition to satisfying the prerequisites, you will be considered qualified only if you are able to perform the essential functions of the job, with or without reasonable accommodation.[22]

What are the essential functions of the job?

To be considered qualified under the ADA you must be able to perform the "essential functions" of the job, with or without accommodation. The "essential functions" depend on the job and are usually identified by the employer. For the job of proofreading, for example, an essential function would be the accurate reading of documents. If you have an eye disorder that renders you unable to read under normal lighting conditions, you would still be qualified if you were able to accurately proofread with an accommodation, such as a high-intensity lamp.[23]

"Essential functions" are distinct from "marginal functions." With respect to our example, if the job of proofreading entails the occasional filing of documents on a high shelf, that task would be considered marginal. If you were a good proofreader but were unable to reach high shelves due to a back injury, you would be considered qualified because you are able to perform the essential functions of the job, though not a marginal one. As a qualified individual with a disability you cannot be discriminated against for your inability to perform nonessential job functions.

Generally, the employer's judgment is considered important evidence of what the essential functions are, especially when the employer has written job descriptions that accurately reflect the way the job is actually being performed.[24]

When it appears that the employer has mislabeled marginal functions as essential—perhaps in order to disqualify persons who cannot perform them due to disability—the court will scrutinize that determination. For a function to be labeled essential, the ADA, as interpreted by the EEOC, requires first that employees in the position are actually required to perform the function. Next, the employer must show that by removing that function, the job would "fundamentally change" or that the "position exists to perform the function." The court will also inquire as to whether other employees are available to perform the function, whether it can be distributed, or whether it is a highly specialized function. A rarely performed function may be considered essential where the stakes are high. For instance, a pilot may never have to crash-land a plane, but that function is essential because of the disaster that might occur if the pilot could not perform that function.

What is a "reasonable accommodation" and when must an employer consider providing it?

A reasonable accommodation is anything related to a person's disability that will be effective in reducing barriers to employment. It can be a job modification, a change in work environment, or an adjustment in the way things are done.[25] For example, a ramp that allows a person using a wheelchair to attend a job interview and then have access to the work area would be a reasonable accommodation. Providing an assistant to someone with manual dexterity limitations would also be a reasonable accommodation.

An employer must consider making such accommodations when the person with a disability would be able to perform the essential functions of the job with the reasonable accommodation, as well as when they are necessary to enabling the employee to enjoy employment benefits (such as use of the cafeteria). Employers who refuse to discuss accommodations or to provide them where the circumstances so warrant, are liable for discrimination under the ADA. However, if an accommodation would not enable a disabled person to meet the qualification requirements of a job or would not enable the employee to obtain job benefits and privileges, then the accommodation would not be considered "reasonable" and the employer need not provide it.

Other examples of reasonable accommodations identified by the EEOC are making facilities readily accessible, restructuring a job by reallocating marginal job functions, altering the essential job functions performed, modifying work schedules, obtaining assistive devices, modifying examinations, providing readers and interpreters, permitting changes in leave policies, and allowing an employee to provide his or her own assistive devices that the employer might not be required to provide (for example, a seeing-eye dog).[26] Generally, personal assistive devices must be provided by the employee, such as hearing aids and eyeglasses, while nonpersonal equipment modifications are the obligation of the employer under the reasonable accommodation rule.

When am I entitled to a reasonable accommodation?

Qualified individuals with disabilities may demand a reasonable accommodation and employers now have the duty to tell applicants and employees that they can request them. If the employer does not know of your limitations the obligation may not arise. Thus, it is up to the employee to notify the employer of his or her nonobvious limitations. Such requests should be backed up with medical documentation indicating the employee's limitations.[27]

How are reasonable accommodations determined?

Once an employer recognizes that the employee requires an accommodation a "flexible, interactive process" to find the appropriate accommodation should begin between the employer and employee. The employer who refuses to make the effort to identify accommodations with the person with a disability violates the ADA. The EEOC recommends that, as a first step, the employer should consult with the employee and exchange suggestions about ways to overcome the barrier. Together they should identify potential accommodations and assess their relative effectiveness in enabling the individual to attain the desired qualification or benefit. The objective is to select the accommodation that would best serve the needs of the individual and the employer. If more than one accommodation would be effective, the employer may consider the preferences of the individual but may choose the one that is less expensive or easier to provide.[28]

An illustration of how this process works is provided by the EEOC's "sack-handler" example. Here, a job currently entails the carrying of 50-pound sacks. An employee who has a back impairment requests an accommodation. An analysis of the job reveals that the essential functions of the job are lifting and moving the sacks but not necessarily carrying them. The employee has medical documentation showing he is able to lift the 50-pound sacks but unable to carry them. Thus, he would be qualified for the job as long as he has an accommodation that helps him in moving the sacks. At this point the employer is obligated to consult with the employee to consider effective accommodations and to select the best one. Three accommodations are identified: the use of a dolly, a hand truck, or a cart. The employee may prefer the dolly, but if the employer finds the hand truck is as efficient and preferable due to cost or other factors, then the employer may fulfill its duty by providing the hand truck. If the individual refuses to accept the employer's choice, however, and is therefore unable to perform the job, the individual may no longer be considered "qualified" and may lose protection under the ADA.

When you engage in the reasonable accommodation process with an employer remember that the employer bears the burden of making reasonable efforts to consider and provide an effective accommodation. The threat of a lawsuit hangs over the employer who does not. To help you secure your rights and achieve the most desirable accommodation, there are many sources for advice, such as the Jobs Accommodation Network, and you may benefit from legal counsel with expertise in this area.[29]

Can an employer refuse to provide a reasonable accommodation?

Yes. The employer is not required to make a reasonable accommodation if it would impose an "undue hardship" on the operation of the business. The question of what is an "undue hardship" must be addressed on a case-by-case basis. If the employer can prove that there is no alternative to the reasonable accommodation suggested, and that the suggested accommodation would impose an undue hardship, then you may be unable to pursue your rights further under the ADA.[30]

Generally, an undue hardship is an action that requires "significant difficulty or expense" in relation to the size of the employer and the nature of the operation. For the employer to deny you a reasonable accommodation on the basis that it imposes an "undue hardship" the employer might have to demonstrate that it would be "unduly costly, extensive, substantial, disruptive, or . . . would fundamentally alter the nature or operation of the business," according to the EEOC's definition of that term.[31]

For example, a person in a wheelchair may apply for a checkout counter position in a small grocery. If the wheelchair cannot fit in the space behind the cash register, a reasonable accommodation might be reconstruction of the checkout counter to make it accessible. But if such alterations would be unduly extensive and costly, then the owner might be able to successfully claim that the accommodation imposes an undue hardship. By comparison, the same alteration in a nationwide supermarket chain probably would not be an undue hardship because the cost in comparison to the size of the operation would be much less substantial.

Do reasonable accommodations have to be made in the job application process?

Yes. An employer must provide an equal opportunity for an individual with a disability to participate in the job application process and to be considered for a job. This may include providing a TDD (telecommunication device for the deaf) number with job advertisements. Preemployment applications and exams should be in a form that persons with visual impairments or learning disabilities can comprehend and complete.[32]

May an employer inquire into my medical condition when I apply for a job?

No. The ADA bans all preemployment questions relating to medical conditions and disabilities until an offer of employment is made. Therefore, job applications and interviews must be free of any reference to your medical condition or history.[33] This prohibition bars questions such as: "Do you have any disabilities or impairments which may affect your performance in the position for which you are applying?" "Have you ever been hospitalized?" "Have you ever filed for worker's compensation insurance?" "Are you taking prescribed drugs?" "Have you been treated for drug addictions or alcoholism?"

At the pre-offer stage the employer is permitted to ask whether you are able to perform a specific job function that is needed for the job, even if it is not an essential function. An employer may ask all applicants to describe or demonstrate how they will perform a job, with or without an accommodation. If an applicant has an obvious or known disability, an employer may ask him or her to describe or demonstrate how these functions will be performed, even if other job applicants are usually not asked to do so—but only if the known disability would interfere with those functions. Otherwise, an employer may not ask for such a demonstration unless it asks it of everyone.

For example, if a person has only one arm and an essential function of the the job is driving a car, the interviewer should not ask if or how the disability would affect the person's driving.

The employer may ask if he or she has a valid driver's license and whether he or she can perform the driving required, with or without an accommodation. The applicant may be asked to describe or demonstrate how the driving will be performed, even if this is not required of everyone, since this is a known disability that would interfere with the performance of the driving.

There are other rules that govern the application process. At the pre-offer stage, the employer may not ask whether an applicant will need or request leave for medical treatment or for other reasons related to a disability. Nor may an employer request information about the job applicant from anyone else. Any test used in the recruitment or hiring process that tends to screen out individuals with disabilities will be discriminatory unless it is job related and consistent with business necessity. For instance, a reading examination that screens out dyslexic applicants will be unlawful if used to hire agricultural workers who need not read on the job. An employer may condition the eventual hiring on a medical exam once a job offer has been made, as discussed below.

There are a few instances when an employer may be permitted or even required to make an inquiry into your medical condition in the pre-offer state. Federal contractors may invite applicants to self-identify their disabilities, in order that the contractor may fulfill its affirmative action commitments under Section 503 of the Rehabilitation Act. The contractor is prohibited, however, from using this information in its hiring decision. Several other federal laws may require that disability information be gathered, such as certain veterans' assistance programs offered by the Department of Labor.

May an employer inquire into my medical condition after offering me a job but before hiring me?

Yes. Before an employee starts work, the employer may condition the job offer on the satisfactory result of a full investigation of your medical status. The only restriction on the employer is how it uses the information gathered at this stage. The post-offer medical exam need not be job related and questions may be asked about your medical history and past workers' compensation claims.[34]

If you are not hired because a post-offer medical examination or inquiry reveals a disability, the reason for not hiring you must be job related and necessary for the business. The employer must also show that no reasonable accommodation was available that would enable you to perform the essential job functions or that accommodation would impose an undue hardship, as discussed above.

A post-offer medical examination may be used to disqualify a person with a disability who would pose a "direct threat" to health and safety. (See below). It may not be used, however, to disqualify a person who is currently fit but whom the employer thinks poses a future threat to health and safety in the workplace.[35]

May my employer inquire into my medical condition after I am hired?

Yes, as long as the inquiry is limited to job-related matters and is consistent with business necessity. The examination or inquiry may be triggered by the necessity of determining whether an employee is physically fit to do the job, either after the employee becomes disabled or has difficulty performing the job effectively. An employee who has a disability and who requests an accommodation can be required to submit to a medical examination to determine if he or she has a disability covered by the ADA and is entitled to an accommodation.

Is the information collected in medical exams confidential under the ADA?

Yes, but with several exceptions. The ADA imposes very strict limitations on the use of information obtained from post-offer and post-hire medical examinations. It should be kept under lock in a file separate from the employee's personnel file. All medical-related information must be kept confidential by the employer except under the following circumstances: (1) supervisors and managers may need to know the information in order to make accommodations; (2) first aid and safety personnel may need to know the information in case of emergency; (3) certain government officials investigating ADA compliance may be provided the information; (4) state workers' compensation boards may require relevant information; and (5) relevant information may be provided to insurance companies where required for coverage purposes.[36]

May I submit false answers to medical inquiries?

It depends. The ADA provides that an employer may refuse to hire or may fire you if you knowingly provide a false answer to a lawful post-offer inquiry about your condition or workers' compensation history. Presumably, the fact that you submitted false information in an unlawful inquiry cannot be used against you. For example, an employer would not be justified in not hiring you for lying on a preemployment medical questionnaire since that premature inquiry would be unlawful.[37]

Can my employer deny me a position because it thinks I pose a safety threat to myself or others?

Sometimes. An employer may require as a qualification for employment that an individual not pose a "direct threat" to the health and safety of the individual or others. An employer must, however, meet very specific and stringent requirements in establishing that such a direct threat exists. The employer must be prepared to demonstrate that: (1) there is significant risk of substantial harm, (2) the specific risk has been identified, (3) the risk is current, not speculative or remote, and (4) the assessment of the risk is objective and based on medical or other factual evidence regarding the particular individual.[38]

Even if there is a genuine significant risk of substantial harm, the employer must consider whether the risk can be eliminated or reduced below the level of a "direct threat" by reasonable accommodation.

The "direct threat" standard is also applicable to individuals with communicable diseases that may be transmitted through the handling of food.[39] The United States Department of Health and Human Services prepares lists of contagious diseases that fall into this category. An employer would not be required to hire a job applicant with one of these diseases where no reasonable accommodation could eliminate the risk of transmitting the disease through the handling of food. The Centers for Disease Control maintains, however, that proper personal hygiene and sanitation in food-handling jobs are the most important measures to prevent transmission of disease. It should be noted that AIDS/HIV is *not* considered a disease transmittable through food handling.

Can my employer reduce my pay if I cannot do certain job functions due to my disability?

Generally, not. Under the ADA, an employer cannot reduce the pay of an employee with a disability because of the elimination of a marginal job function or because it has provided a reasonable accommodation. An employee who is reassigned to a lower paying job or provided a part-time job as an accommodation, however, may be paid the lower amount that would normally apply to such positions.[40]

Can my employer discriminate against me with regard to my health insurance or pension plan if I have a disability?

No. The ADA demands that employers give disabled employees equal access to whatever insurance or benefit plans the employer provides. It prohibits employers from denying insurance to individuals with disabilities or subjecting them to different terms or conditions based on their disability alone if the disability does not pose increased insurance risks.[41] An employer cannot fire or refuse to hire an individual with a disability because the employer's current health insurance plan does not cover the individual's disability or because the individual may increase the employer's future health care costs. Nor may an employer so treat an employee because of a family member whose disability is not covered or may increase the costs of the plan.[42]

Nevertheless, the ADA permits employers to conform their plans to other federal or state regulations, even if employees with disabilities are adversely affected, as long as such compliance is not used as a means to evade the purpose of the ADA. Similarly, if an employer has an insurance plan that excludes coverage for certain preexisting conditions or limits coverage for certain procedures or treatments, these restrictions may adversely affect employees with disabilities without violating the ADA as long as the employer is not seeking to evade the intent of the ADA by excluding such coverage. These exclusions must, however, apply to all insured individuals, regardless of disability in order to be allowable under the ADA.

Similarly, a uniformly applied leave policy does not violate the ADA because it has a more severe impact on an individual because of his or her disability. However, if an individual with a disability requests a modification of such a policy as a reasonable accommodation, an employer may be required to provide it, unless it would impose an undue hardship.[43]

Can I be discriminated against because of my relationship with a person with a disability?

No. Under the ADA an employer may not treat you adversely because you associate with a person with a disability. For example, if you live with someone who has a communicable disease, such as a person with HIV, your employer cannot deny you work for that reason. However, an employer is not required to give you a leave of absence as a reasonable accommodation so that you can care for that individual.[44]

What do I do if I have been discriminated against because of my disability?

Under the ADA you can enforce your rights by following the steps described with respect to other discrimination claims brought under Title VII. The same remedies are available. See chapter 8, "Discrimination: An Overview." Basically, you must file a charge with the EEOC or state civil rights agency. Your nearest office can be found by calling (800) 669-4000 (voice) or (800) 800-3302 (TDD). The procedures to follow and the remedies available under the Rehabilitation Act are described later in this chapter.

What employers are covered by the rehabilitation act?

The Rehabilitation Act applies to the federal government as an employer and to those private employers who receive federal funding or assistance. Three sections of the Rehabilitation Act provide protection against discrimination in employment based on disability. The rights and remedies available vary widely and depend on which particular section of the Rehabilitation Act governs each case.

1. The section most widely used by individuals is Section 504.[45] Section 504 prohibits discrimination against otherwise qualified handicapped[46] individuals in "any program or activity receiving federal financial assistance or under any program or activity conducted by any Executive agency or by the United

States Postal Service."[47] This section is a direct ban on discrimination against handicapped persons.

2. Section 503[48] requires every contract in excess of $2,500 entered into by a department or agency of the federal government to contain a clause requiring the contractor to take affirmative action toward employing qualified handicapped persons. This section applies to any private employer who has such a contract with the federal government. In addition, Section 503 requires any private employer who has a contract with the federal government for $50,000 or more and who has 50 or more employees to file a written affirmative action plan.[49]

Under the required affirmative action plans, contractors must review their employee selection procedures to insure careful consideration of the job qualifications of handicapped applicants.[50] Employers must review their selection criteria to make sure that the stated job qualifications are in fact necessary to perform the particular job.[51] Section 503 is intended to prohibit employers from establishing discriminatory job qualifications that are not necessary for the particular positions and that will effectively bar handicapped people from employment because they cannot meet these requirements.

Most courts that have considered the question have ruled that individuals may not seek to remedy a violation of Section 503 by filing a private lawsuit.[52] Instead, individuals may file a complaint with the Department of Labor which must then investigate it.[53] If its Office of Federal Contract Compliance Programs decides there has been a violation that cannot be corrected through conciliation and persuasion, the Department of Labor may pursue an action in court or in an administrative proceeding.[54]

3. Section 501[55] requires every department, agency, and instrumentality of the executive branch of the federal government to adopt an affirmative action plan for the hiring, placement, and promotion of handicapped persons. These plans must be updated every year and must be reviewed by an interagency committee designed to monitor the employment of handicapped persons by the federal government.

What does the rehabilitation act require of covered employers?

Both the Rehabilitation Act and the ADA prohibit covered

employers from discriminating in employment against a qualified individual with a disability because of the individual's
disability and requires covered employers to make reasonable
accommodations for the individual with the disability unless
doing so would impose an undue hardship on the employer.

The Rehabilitation Act does not explain where, in the employment process, discrimination is prohibited and does not
define "discrimination."

The Rehabilitation Act defines a "handicapped individual"
as one who (1) has a physical or mental impairment that substantially limits one or more of the major life activities of the
individual; (2) has a record of such an impairment; or (3) is
regarded as having such an impairment.[56] Those with a record
of an impairment that limits a major life activity are included
within the definition of "handicapped" in order to protect individuals who have recovered from an impairment that substantially limited them in the past. Those who are regarded as
having an impairment that limits a major life activity are included within the definition of "handicapped" in order to protect individuals whose physical or mental impairments do not
substantially limit major life activities but who are treated by
employers as having such limitations. As the Supreme Court
explained, "such an impairment might not diminish a person's
physical or mental capabilities, but could nevertheless substantially limit that person's ability to work as a result of the negative
reactions of others to the impairment. . . . [Congress's inclu-
sion of this language is an acknowledgement] that society's
accumulated myths and fears about disabilities and disease are
as handicapping as are the physical limitations that flow from
actual impairment."[57]

Is an employer covered by the Rehabilitation Act required to make accommodations for my disability?

Yes, if you are qualified for the job and if the necessary
accommodations are reasonable ones that would not cause the
employer undue hardship. You are qualified if you can perform
the essential functions of the employment position you seek
or hold, either with or without reasonable accommodation.
The Supreme Court has explained that this means being "able
to meet all of a program's requirements in spite of [your] handicap."[58] The Court illustrated this by using the example of a

blind person seeking the position of bus driver. Since that individual would be unable to perform the job of bus driver with or without accommodation, that individual would not be considered qualified.[59]

Employers may require that all applicants and employees be able to perform the essential functions of the job but may not discriminate based on an individual's inability to perform marginal (i.e., nonessential) job functions. For example, because deafness is not related to performing the essential functions of being a bus driver an employer may not discriminate against an applicant who is deaf merely because the applicant is deaf.[60]

What kinds of accommodations are reasonable under the rehabilitation act?

Reasonable accommodations are those accommodations that will not cause the employer "undue hardship." "Undue hardship" is determined on a case-by-case basis. However, under Section 794 of the Rehabilitation Act "undue hardship" has been construed narrowly, in part because it was based on the Supreme Court's decision in *Hardison v. Trans World Airlines*.[61] That case discussed the meaning of the employer's need to accommodate the religious beliefs of an employee under Title VII of the Civil Rights Act. The Court construed the employer's burden narrowly and ruled that the employer need not make more than minimal accommodations. The use of the *Hardison* reasoning in the context of individuals with disabilities has effectively prevented the employment of many individuals with disabilities. Generally, required accommodations have been minimal. For example, allowing the use of a hearing aid has been found a reasonable accommodation for a deaf individual whose job was to drive a bus.[62]

Regulations governing Section 501 of the Rehabilitation Act, on the other hand, impose more expansive duties on federal agencies, including job restructuring and the acquisition or modification of equipment. Whether the required accommodation is reasonable depends, in part, on the resources available to the agency in question.

What kinds of disabilities are covered under the Rehabilitation Act?

The Rehabilitation Act does not list the disabilities covered;

however, blindness, epilepsy, prior mental illness, back problems, and diabetes have all been covered in certain circumstances.[63]

The Rehabilitation Act recognizes alcoholism as a disability but excludes individuals whose current alcohol abuse prevents performance of the duties of the particular job or threatens the property or safety of others.[64] The Rehabilitation Act excludes current illegal drug users from their coverage[65] and does not protect drug abusers whose addiction prevents them from performing the job's duties or who pose a threat to the safety of others.[66]

As to AIDS and other infectious diseases, the Supreme Court has ruled that coverage of the Rehabilitation Act extends to a contagious disease that substantially limits one or more major life functions of an otherwise-covered handicapped person.[67] Therefore, under the Rehabilitation Act, an individual with AIDS or with an impairment caused by another communicable disease may be considered "handicapped." However, if the individual creates a substantial risk of infecting others in the workplace, that individual may not be considered "otherwise qualified." As a result, some individuals with communicable diseases may not be protected because they are not "otherwise qualified." The Supreme Court has cautioned that rather than considering all employees with contagious diseases as having a disability, each case must be analyzed to see whether the particular individual is otherwise qualified.[68]

What do I do if I believe I have been discriminated against in violation of the Rehabilitation Act?

Under the Rehabilitation Act, relief is available as follows. If you are employed by the federal government and your agency violates Section 501, by failing to engage in affirmative action hiring of handicapped persons, for example, your only remedy is to complain to the Equal Employment Opportunity Commission; you cannot sue your employer directly. You must file your complaint with the EEOC within 180 days of the alleged violation. The EEOC will investigate the charge and try to resolve the matter. If it is unsuccessful at informal conciliation, the EEOC can sue and seek the same remedies as afforded by Title VII.[69]

As a general rule, if your employer contracts with the federal government and violates Section 503, you must complain to the Department of Labor.[70] Most courts that have considered the question will not allow you to sue your employer directly under Section 503. The Department of Labor will investigate your claim; if informal conciliation fails, the department can recommend that the director of the Office of Federal Contract Compliance bring a court action against your employer or discontinue payments on any outstanding contracts. Also, contractors found to have discriminated can be declared ineligible to receive future contract awards from the federal government.

Section 504 confers on private individuals the right to sue the employer directly.[71] You should commence a Section 504 action by filing a complaint with the agency that provides federal assistance to your employer. Although most courts have held that plaintiffs suing under Section 504 are not required to exhaust administrative channels before filing a court action, you may be able to resolve your problem through an administrative complaint and thus avoid the expense and time associated with litigation.[72]

What remedies are available if I win a discrimination action under the Rehabilitation Act?

If you bring an action under Sections 501 or 504 of the Rehabilitation Act, you can recover the same remedies as are recoverable under Title VII of the Civil Rights Act of 964.[73] These remedies are intended to make victims of discrimination "whole" and include backpay for individuals who allege intentional discrimination[74] and appropriate injunctive relief, such as instatement or reinstatement or a retroactive award of seniority rights.[75] In addition, compensatory damages may be available.[76] These are explained in chapter 8. In the few cases allowing private suits under Section 503, the courts have awarded individually tailored relief; there is some authority that individuals should be entitled to the same damages as those allowed under Section 504.[77] Additionally, courts have directed the contractor to take affirmative steps to accommodate that individual's disability.[78] In most cases, however, sanctions for violating Section 503 are confined to loss of federal contracts and future ineligibility to receive federal contracts.

NOTES

1. 42 U.S.C. §§ 12101 *et seq.* Much of the discussion in this chapter is based on the Final Rules and Regulations of the Equal Employment Opportunity Commission; 29 C.F.R. §§ 1630 *et seq.*, and the Technical Assistance Manual of the Employment Provisions (Title I) of the Americans with Disabilities Act (TAM).
2. 29 U.S.C. §§ 701–96(i).
3. 38 U.S.C. §§ 2011–14.
4. Education for All Handicapped Children Act, 20 U.S.C. §§ 1400–85.
5. The Developmentally Disabled Assistance and Bill of Rights Act of 1975, 42 U.S.C. §§ 6000–83.
6. 29 C.F.R. § 1630.2(e).
7. *Id.* at § 1630.2(e)(2)(i).
8. 29 U.S.C. § 701–96(ii).
9. 29 C.F.R. § 1630.2(e)(2)(i).
10. 29 C.F.R. § 1630.4.
11. 29 C.F.R § 1630.5.
12. 29 C.F.R § 1630.8.
13. 29 C.F.R § 1630.12.
14. *See* TAM chapter 2.
15. 29 C.F.R. § 1630.2(g).
16. 29 C.F.R. § 1630.2(h)(1).
17. 29 C.F.R. § 1630.2(h)(2).
18. 29 C.F.R. § 1630.2(j).
19. 29 C.F.R. §§ 1630.2(g)(2), 1630.3(d).
20. 29 C.F.R. §§ 1630.3(a)–(c).
21. 29 C.F.R. §§ 1630.2(k), (l).
22. 29 C.F.R. §§ 1630.2(m), (n).
23. 29 C.F.R. §§ 1630.2(n)(1), (2).
24. 29 C.F.R. § 1630.2(n)(3).
25. 29 C.F.R. §§ 1630.2(o)(1), (2).
26. *See* TAM chapter 3.
27. *Id.*
28. *See* Appendix to Part 1630—Interpretative Guidance on Title V of the Americans With Disabilities Act on § 1630.9.
29. Job Accommodation Network. Phone: (800) 526-7234.
30. 29 C.F.R. § 1630.9.
31. *See* TAM chapter 3.
32. *Id.*
33. *See* TAM chapters 4 and 5.
34. 29 C.F.R. §§ 1630.13–14.
35. *Id.* *Also see* TAM chapters 5 and 6.
36. *Id.*

37. *Id.*
38. 29 C.F.R. § 1630.14(b).
39. 29 C.F.R. § 1630.14(c)(3); *see* TAM chapter 6.
40. 29 C.F.R. § 1630.3(r).
41. 29 C.F.R. § 1630.16(e).
42. *See* TAM chapter 7.
43. 29 C.F.R. § 1630.14(f); *see* TAM chapter 6.
44. *Id.* However, you may be entitled to a leave under the Family Leave Act discussed in chapter 27.
45. 29 U.S.C. § 794.
46. The Rehabilitation Act uses the phrase "individuals with handicaps," a phrase that is offensive to the individuals the act is intended to benefit. The ADA uses the phrase "individual with a disability." This phrase is more accurate and carries with it none of the perjorative connotations of "handicap." The word "handicap" is used in this chapter only when discussing the Rehabilitation Act and the cases interpreting it.
47. 29 U.S.C. § 794.
48. 29 U.S.C. § 793(a).
49. 41 C.F.R. § 60-741.5(a).
50. 41 C.F.R. § 60-741.6(a).
51. 41 C.F.R. § 60-741.6(b).
52. *See, e.g., Beam v. Sun Shipbuilding & Dry Dock Co.*, 679 F.2d 1077 (3d Cir. 1982); *Hodges v. Atchison, Topeka and Santa Fe Ry.*, 728 F.2d 414 (10th Cir.), *cert. denied*, 469 U.S. 822 (1984); *Ernst v. Indiana Bell Tel. Co.*, 717 F.2d 1036 (7th Cir. 1983), *cert. denied*, 464 U.S. 1041 (1984); *Meyerson v. Arizona*, 709 F.2d 1235 (9th Cir. 1983), *vacated on other grounds*, 465 U.S. 1095 (1984); *Hoopes v. Equifax Inc.*, 611 F.2d 134 (6th Cir. 1977).
53. 29 U.S.C. § 793(b); 41 C.F.R. § 60.741.26(e).
54. 41 C.F.R. §§ 60.741, 60.741.26(g)(2), 60.741.28(b), 60.741.29.
55. 29 U.S.C. § 791(b).
56. Rehabilitation Act, 29 U.S.C. § 706(7)(A).
57. *School Bd. of Nassau County v. Arline*, 480 U.S. 273, 283–84, *reh'g denied*, 481 U.S. 1024 (1987).
58. *Southeastern Community College v. Davis*, 442 U.S. 397, 406 (1979).
59. *Id.* at 407 n.7.
60. *Strathie v. Department of Transp.*, 716 F.2d 227 (3d Cir. 1983).
61. 432 U.S. 63 (1977).
62. *Strathie v. Department of Transp.*, 716 F.2d 227 (3d Cir. 1983).
63. *Doe v. Syracuse School Dist.*, 508 F. Supp. 333 (N.D.N.Y. 1981); *E.E. Black Ltd. v. Marshall*, 497 F. Supp. 1088 (D. Haw. 1980),

vacated on other grounds, 26 FEP Cas. (BNA) 1183 (D. Haw. 1981); *Bentivegna v. U.S. Dep't of Labor*, 694 F.2d 619 (9th Cir. 1982).

64. ADA, § 512(a)(v) (amending Rehabilitation Act § 7(8)).
65. *Id.*
66. *Heron v. McGuire*, 803 F.2d 67 (2d Cir. 1986).
67. *School Bd. of Nassau County v. Arline*, 480 U.S. 273, *reh'g denied*, 481 U.S. 1024 (1987).
68. *Id.*
69. 29 U.S.C. § 794a(a)(1).
70. 29 U.S.C. § 793(b).
71. *Consolidated Rail Corp. v. Darrone*, 465 U.S. 624 (1984).
72. *Miener v. Missouri*, 673 F.2d 969, 978 (8th Cir.), *cert. denied*, 459 U.S. 909 (1982); *Pushkin v. Regents of Univer. of Colorado*, 658 F.2d 1372, 1381 (10th Cir. 1981).
73. 42 U.S.C. §§ 2000e-5(g).
74. *Consolidated Rail Corp. v. Darrone*, 465 U.S. 624 (1984).
75. *E.g., Duran v. City of Tampa*, 451 F. Supp. 954 (M.D. Fla. 1978).
76. *See, e.g., Gelman v. Department of Educ.*, 544 F. Supp. 651 (D. Colo. 1982).
77. *See California Paralyzed Veterans Ass'n. v. FCC*, 496 F. Supp. 125 (C.D. Cal. 1980), *aff'd*, 721 F.2d 667 (9th Cir. 1983), *cert. denied*, 469 US 832 (1984) and cases cited therein. *See* C.R. Richey, *Manual on Employment Discrimination Law and Civil Rights Actions in the Federal Courts* F2-8 (1988).
78. *See Prewitt v. United States Postal Serv.*, 662 F.2d 292 (5th Cir. 1981).

XV

AIDS

The AIDS/HIV epidemic presents an urgent and serious public health problem.[1] In the United States, millions of people have been infected by the HIV virus and hundreds of thousands have died of AIDS. Medical costs of AIDS, in the United States alone, are rising into the tens of billions of dollars.

Although AIDS raises many new and difficult moral and legal questions, some of the answers are remarkably clear and straightforward. For example, as discussed later, fears by employers and coworkers of the AIDS virus spreading on the job are generally unfounded because the AIDS virus simply is not communicable in the context of virtually all normal workplace activities and practices. Accordingly, no medical or legal justification exists for excluding infected persons from such workplaces. Similarly, with few exceptions, no legitimate purpose is served by contravening an employee's privacy and confidentiality concerns by revealing the employee's AIDS-related condition to anyone without a real "need to know."

Employers should deal with the issues raised by AIDS in the workplace by setting up policies that deal with disabilities generally (not just AIDS) and by establishing procedures to deal with disputes that may arise. Most importantly, the consensus of experts is that the best response to the problems raised by AIDS in the workplace is *education.* The answer lies not in testing applicants or employees for AIDS or in refusing to hire or in discharging persons infected with the AIDS virus but in disseminating to everyone concerned basic medical information about the disease.

Can I be discriminated against if I have AIDS?
Generally, no, because if you carry the HIV virus you probably will be considered disabled and protected by any disability statute that covers your workplace.[2]

Certain employers haved claimed that the job protections that go along with disability status should not extend to HIV-positive employees who show no outward signs of the viral infection. This argument has been rejected by most legislatures and courts.[3] Even where no visible signs of the infection are present, the courts have held that the HIV infection substantially limits major life activities such as socializing[4] and reproduction.[5] The ADA regulations confer protected status on all AIDS carriers because being HIV-positive is "inherently substantially limiting."[6] Even individuals who are perceived to have AIDS but in fact are not HIV-positive are also covered under most statutes.[7] Nevertheless, in states such as Texas, the courts have held that those carrying the virtually undetectable early stages of the HIV infection do not warrant discrimination protection and thus can be fired for testing HIV-positive.[8] You may be subject to such a state law if your employer is not covered by the Americans with Disabilities Act (see chapter 14).

Under most disability antidiscrimination laws, employers may not refuse to hire, treat differently, or discharge an HIV-positive employee who is otherwise able and qualified to work. This means that you may not be treated adversely just because you have AIDS as long as you can still do the job, with or without a reasonable accommodation. If your condition prevents you from performing the essential functions of the job, however, your employer may be permitted to terminate or demote you if (a) there is no reasonable accommodation that will allow you to perform those functions, or (b) providing such an accommodation would impose an "undue hardship" on your employer (see chapter 14).

When is an employer justified in firing a person with AIDS?

Under most federal and state disability laws, the answer is almost never, as long as the employee is able to perform the essential functions of the job with or without reasonable accommodation, unless the accommodation imposes an undue hardship on the employer. HIV-infected employees such as pharmacists[9] and restaurant workers[10] who were fired because their employers feared transmission of the virus have won back their jobs or have won money damages by bringing discrimination claims. Similarly, fired HIV-positive plaintiffs have defeated their employers' claims that workers would be demoralized by having to work with an HIV-infected person.[11] Today, employers are rightfully more terrified of AIDS discrimination lawsuits than they are of transmission of the disease.

Medical science is still concerned, however, over the risk of transmission where so-called "exposure-prone" medical workers are involved. Several cases of accidental transmission of the virus, through needle-sticks and the like, have been documented. The controversial issues of whether to test medical personnel for HIV infection and whether to retain those who test positive and perform invasive procedures is likely to provoke debate for some time. One court, however, upheld the firing of a hospital nurse who, after his live-in companion died of AIDS, refused to reveal to the hospital the results of his AIDS test.[12] Another court upheld the suspension of a surgeon diagnosed with AIDS, although the court also found that the hospital was liable for invading his privacy when it failed to keep his condition confidential.[13] These early cases may reflect society's initial overreaction to fears about AIDS. For the most part, those seeking to prevent HIV virus transmission consider reassignment or discharge only as a last resort.

As mentioned, disability statutes such as the Americans with Disabilities Act allow employers to refuse to hire or terminate HIV-infected employees under certain conditions. If you cannot perform the essential functions of the job even with a reasonable accommodation or if such an accommodation imposes an undue hardship on your employer, your employer may be permitted to discriminate against you. Similarly, your employer may be permitted to treat you adversely if you pose a significant risk of harm to yourself, other employees, or customers. Such a direct threat, however, must be demonstrated with valid medical analysis or other objective evidence. It cannot be based on speculation. As mentioned, there are few instances where such a risk is genuinely posed. For instance, a school teacher with AIDS won the right to remain in the classroom since no health risk was created.[14]

Can my employer reduce my medical insurance coverage if I have AIDS?

Perhaps. While ERISA, the federal law governing benefits, prohibits employers from firing employees with HIV disease because of increased insurance costs, it does not require that the employer provide medical insurance for any particular illness. Hence, employers may consider limiting or excluding insurance coverage for HIV-related healthcare. Although cap-ping HIV-related benefits certainly appears to be discriminatory, courts have suggested that the Americans with Disabilities Act permits employers to set such policies as long as there is a "sound actuarial basis" for doing so and the reduction is not "a subterfuge for discrimination."[15] Therefore, if an employer decides that it simply cannot afford to pay the premiums for the coverage of a given illness (such as AIDS) beyond a certain point, then the employer would claim that it does not violate the ADA by reducing or eliminating the coverage with respect to that illness. The U.S. Supreme Court has allowed to stand a Texas federal court's interpretation of ERISA as permitting an employer to reduce its cap on AIDS-related health benefits from $1 million to $5,000 when an employee with the disease filed a claim.[16] This case predates the ADA, however. By contrast, the EEOC has taken the position that health plans may not exclude HIV-related diseases from their coverage because it is discriminatory.[17] To clarify employees' rights, Congress is addressing the obviously devastating effects such sudden withdrawals of coverage have on the HIV-infected individual.[18]

Can I be forced to work alongside a person with AIDS?

Yes, because for the most part, AIDS-phobia will not be tolerated in the workplace (although, no one can *force* you to work, of course). If you are assigned to share space or tools with a person with AIDS, the risk of transmission occurring is virtually nonexistent. For transmission to occur, a sizeable amount of blood or sperm must be passed from the infected person directly to the bloodstream or mucous membrane of the recipient.[19] According to the Centers for Disease Control, no one has ever contracted AIDS from sharing telephones, tools, typewriters, water fountains, toilet seats, or even toothbrushes.

Even in the healthcare industry where several cases of accidental transmission have occurred, the risks are considered minimal and safety precautions are being instituted that limit the risk to acceptable levels. For instance, the Occupational Safety and Health Administration (OSHA) has published guidelines that require healthcare facilities to provide special training and other protections to healthcare workers to guard against infection by AIDS or hepatitis.[20]

Under OSHA guidelines, you may refuse to work if in good

faith you believe that your job involves an unreasonable risk of serious injury or death. But as mentioned, the fear that casual contact will cause HIV infection is not reasonable. If, however, there is a possibility of blood or other bodily fluid passing into your blood stream from an HIV-infected person where you work, you should bring this to the attention of the employer. Even in high-risk situations, you are not likely to have a right to refuse to work as long as your employer adheres to OSHA guidelines and to any other state law precautions that pertain (see chapter 24). In such situations it is safe to say that little or no danger exists.

Can my employer insist that I take the HIV antibody test?

In most cases, yes, but not at the prehiring stage. If you are applying for a job, any medical testing—including an AIDS testing—is prohibited unless your employer is *not* covered by the Americans with Disabilities Act. Nor should you be tested if you are covered by a collective bargaining agreement that does not permit it. Once you have been offered the job, however, or have been hired, your employer may test you for the HIV virus if your employer does so for everyone. But your employer may not take any adverse action against you based on the results unless it is job related and nondiscriminatory (see chapters 14 and 23). Any test you take must be accurate, and steps to protect your privacy must be taken. A growing number of states and municipalities have addressed these concerns in laws and ordinances. Among the states with specific guidelines governing AIDS testing are Arizona, California, Colorado, Hawaii, Iowa, Kentucky, Maine, Massachusetts, Missouri, Nebraska, New Mexico, North Carolina, Rhode Island, Texas, Washington, and Wisconsin.[21]

While privacy law, for the most part, does not protect private sector employees from being tested for AIDS, privacy-based actions have been successful against employers who mishandle HIV test results and expose a person's status to others.[22]

Public sector employers may be protected against mandatory HIV testing under the Fourth and Fourteenth amendments to the Constitution and under state constitutional and statutory law[23] (see chapter 23). Nevertheless, one court has ruled that a fire department's mandatory HIV testing of firefighters was not an unreasonable search and seizure and thus was constitutional.[24] Similarly, where a governmental body or agency such as a public hospital reasonably suspects that an employee is HIV infected, confirmatory testing will not likely be deemed an invasion of privacy.[25] Meanwhile, mandatory AIDS testing for workers is finding little favor, even in the healthcare industry. The National Commission on AIDS has found that there is "no current justification for restricting the practice of health care professionals on the basis of HIV status alone."[26]

Can my employer disclose to others that I am HIV-positive?
Yes, but generally only within your business and on a "need-to-know" basis. As mentioned, employers who negligently mishandle HIV-status information may be liable as well as those who report it unnecessarily. For instance, an employee made a worker's compensation claim and underwent a medical examination. Concerned that he might contaminate the medical instruments, the claimant disclosed to the doctor's nurse that he was HIV-positive. Otherwise, his HIV status was irrelevant to his worker's compensation claim. Nevertheless, the doctor reported it anyway. The court held that the doctor could be liable for improperly disclosing confidential information. (For a fuller discussion, see chapter 23.)[27]

Can I collect unemployment insurance if I have left employment because of an AIDS-related condition?
To be eligible for unemployment compensation, an employee must be "ready and able" to work. Thus, an employee who left employment because AIDS made him unable to work would not be eligible for such compensation, though he may be eligible for disability benefits. Nevertheless an employee was able to collect unemployment after he was fired for lying to his employer about his condition. The court held that the employee's deception was designed to protect his privacy and did not harm the employer.[28]

If an employee refuses to work because a coworker has AIDS, the employer could consider it a "voluntary quit" or a termination for misconduct (i.e., insubordination). If the employee can prove he left for "good cause," he may qualify for benefits. But if his reason for leaving is safety related, that concern must be reasonable. In view of the medical evidence on AIDS in the workplace, such an employee probably would be found to have left for other than "good cause" and would not be eligible for benefits.

NOTES

1. For an in-depth discussion of this subject, *see Rights of People Who Are HIV Positive,* an ACLU handbook in this series (forthcoming 1994).
2. Americans with Disabilities Act of 1990, 42 U.S.C. §§ 12101 *et seq.*
3. *E.g., Doe v. District of Columbia,* 796 F. Supp. 559 (D.D.C. 1992) (department violated the Rehabilitation Act by rescinding an employment offer to an asymptomatic HIV-positive firefighter who was "otherwise qualified"). A few state courts such as those of Texas do not consider AIDS a disability, *e.g., Hilton v. Southwestern Bell Telephone Co.,* 936 F.2d 823 (5th Cir. 1991); for the disability laws of other states see chapter 14.
4. 42 U.S.C. §§ 12101 *et seq.;* 29 C.F.R §§ 1630 *et seq.*
5. *Benjamin R. v. Orkin Exterminating,* (W.V. Sup. Ct. 1990).
6. 29 C.F.R § 1630.2(j).
7. *School Bd. of Nassau County v. Arline,* 480 U.S. 273 (1987); *Petri v. Bank of New York,* 582 N.Y.S.2d 608 (N.Y. Sup. Ct. 1992); *but see Rose City Oil Co. v. Missouri Commission on Human Rights,* N90. 60270 (Mo. Ct. App. 1992).
8. *Hilton v. Southwestern Bell Telephone Co.,* 936 F.2d 823 (5th Cir. 1991); *Chevron Corp. v. Redmon,* 745 S.W.2d 314 (Tx. Sup. Ct. 1987).
9. *Doe v. A Medical Center,* Case Nos. 1B-E-D-86-116054 and 1B-P-S-87-117683, N.Y.S. Div. Human Rights decided June 27, 1990; *aff'd sub nom., in the Matter of Westchester County Medical Center,* 2 EPG Prac. Guide (CCH) ¶ 5362 (Dep't of Health and Human Services, Civil Rights Reviewing Authority, Sept. 25, 1992).
10. *Club Swamp Annex v. White,* 561 N.Y.S.2d 609 (N.Y. App. Div. 1990).
11. *Cain v. Hyatt,* 134 F. Supp. 671, 53 EPD ¶ 40,021 (D.C. Pa. 1990); *Doe v. District of Columbia, supra,* (rejecting the "public's fear of AIDS" defense to refusal to hire an HIV-positive firefighter).
12. *Leckelt v. Bd. of Commissioners,* 909 F.2d 820 (5th Cir. 1990).
13. *Estate of Behringer v. The Medical Center at Princeton,* 56 EPD ¶ 40, 779 (N.J. Sup. Ct. 1991); *see also, Estate of Gary Urbaniak v. Frederick H. Newton,* 226 Cal. App. 3d 1128, 227 Cal. Rptr. 354 (1991) (doctor improperly disclosed patient's HIV infection).
14. *Chalk v. U.S. District Court,* 840 F.2d 201 (9th Cir. 1988).
15. *See* (ERISA) 29 U.S.C. § 1140, (ADA) 42 U.S.C. § 12101
16. *McGann v. H.H. Music Co.,* 946 F.2d 401 (5th Cir. 1991), *cert. denied sub nom. Greenberg v. H&H Music,* 121 L.Ed.2d 387 (1992). In denying benefits to AIDS victims, the employer must still observe

fiduciary duties such as notification imposed elsewhere by ERISA. *Rocker v. Pacific FM, Inc.*, 1992 U.S. Dist LEXIS 13633, 15 Empl. Ben. Cas. BNA 2353 (N.D. Cal. 1992).

17. *See* Determination of EEOC New York regional director EEOC Charge No. 160-93-0419, Jan. 8, 1993.

18. In order to amend ERISA to prevent retroactive reduction of benefits and elimination of benefits once medical treatment begins, Representative Hughes (D-N.J.) and Brehlent (R-N.Y.) introduced H.R. 6147 "Group Health Non-Discrimination Plan of 1992" to the 102d Congress.

19. *See* C. Koop, "The Surgeon General's Report on Acquired Immune Deficiency Syndrome," Centers for Disease Control 1992 Study of the "Second 100,000 Cases" of AIDS.

20. *See* 56 Fed. Reg. 64004, OSHA regulations regarding the healthcare industry; *see also* Ogletree, *et al.*, *Americans with Disabilities Act: Employee Rights and Employer Obligations* (Jan. 1993 Supp.) (citing National Commission on AIDS, Preventing HIV Transmission in Health Care Settings (1991)).

21. Ariz., Opinion of Attorney General 12/4/87; Cal. Ann. Code sec. § 199.20; Colo. Rev. Stat. § 10-3-1104.5(1-6); Haw. Rev. Stat. § 325-101(a-c); Iowa Code § 1351.1.; Ky. Rev. Stat. § 49(2)(a)(b); Me. Rev. Stat. tit. 5, § 19205-B(1); Mass. Gen. L. ch. 111, § 70F; Mo. Ann. Stat. § 191.650; Neb. Rev. Stat., § 1, 2; N.M. Stat. Ann. § 1(A)(B); N.C. Gen. Stat. § 130A-148(i), (j); R.I. Gen. Laws, § 23-6-22; Tx: Stats. § 81-101: Wash. Rev. Code § 914(1)–(4); Wisc. Stat. Ann. § 895.50.

22. *E.g.*, *Estate of Behringer*, *supra*, note 13 *Cronan v. New England Telephone*, 1 IER Cas. BNA 651 (Mass. Super. Ct. 1986).

23. *See* chapter 4.

24. *Willoughby v. Anonymous Fireman v. City of Willoughby*, 7 IER 17 (N.D.C. OH 1991).

25. *See Leckelt v. Bd. of Commissioners*, *supra* note 12.

26. Ogletree, *et al.*, *supra* at 24–25.

27. *Hummer v. Unemployment Appeals Commission*, 573 So. 2d 135 (Fla. App. 1991).

28. *Urbaniak v. Newton*, *supra* note 13.

XVI

Sexual Orientation

Until recently, the harm gay men and lesbians suffer due to discrimination went largely unnoticed. This has changed in recent years as the public has become better educated about the myriad forms of discrimination based on sexual orientation (also sometimes called sexual or affectional preference). The call to lift the ban on gays in the U.S. military has drawn intense national attention as have efforts locally to end discrimination in the workplace. This chapter is concerned with discrimination in employment based on sexual orientation.

Sexual orientation discrimination takes many forms. One is to deny gay men and lesbians jobs because of their status. The armed forces' age-old ban of gay men and lesbians has led to successful legal challenges by officers discharged because of their sexual preferences and to political efforts to repeal the policy entirely.[1] Some law enforcement agencies have used their state's sodomy statutes to effectively ban gay men and lesbians, yet these policies are eroding under challenge.[2] The forceful argument causing this rethinking is that people should be judged by their conduct in the workplace, not by their status.

Besides being denied jobs, promotions, and security, many other less blatant forms of prejudice plague gay men and lesbians. A chief "bread and butter" concern has to do with the refusal of employers to extend employee benefits to the partners of their gay and lesbian employees because such partnerships or marriages are usually not considered a legal "family" structure, as discussed below.

Generally, governmental employers may not discriminate against employees on the basis of sexual orientation. Governments are subject to constitutional requirements that they act fairly and rationally toward all citizens, including employees. In some situations, gay and lesbian employees may claim due process and equal protection under the Fifth and Fourteenth Amendments to the United States Constitution.[3] Additionally, the governors of nine states have issued executive orders prohibiting discrimination in state employment based on sexual orientation.[4] Private employers are not, however, subject to those constitutional strictures and are not covered by the current executive orders.

For a fuller discussion of the rights of gay men and lesbians in public employment and in many other areas, see *The Rights of Lesbians and Gay Men*, a book in this series. Additional information is available from the Lambda Legal Defense and Education Fund (LLDEF)[5] and the National Gay and Lesbian Task Force (NGLTF).[6]

Do federal antidiscrimination laws protect me based on my sexual orientation?

No. As discussed in preceding chapters, Title VII of the Civil Rights Act of 1964 forbids discrimination in employment on the basis of race, color, religion, national origin, and sex. It has been consistently held that Title VII's prohibition against discrimination on the basis of sex does not include sexual orientation; the ban on sex discrimination covers practices based on gender, not sexual practices and preferences.[7] Similarly, it is clear that neither Title VII nor the Americans with Disabilities Act cover discrimination against transsexuals or bisexuals[8] or against a male because he is effeminate.[9] Although numerous bills have been introduced in Congress to outlaw discrimination on the basis of sexual orientation, none has passed.[10]

Do any laws prohibit discrimination against gay men and lesbians in private employment?

Yes, and the number is growing. For a complete list contact the LLDEF or the NGLTF. Wisconsin, Massachusetts, Hawaii, New Jersey, Vermont, Connecticut, and Washington, D.C. have passed statutes banning discrimination on the basis of sexual preference in public and private employment.[11] At least eleven states prohibit discrimination based on sexual orientation in public employment only.[12] Private-sector discrimination is also prohibited in many counties and cities.[13] At least 71 cities and counties have gay anti-bias laws.[14]

Do I have any other protections as a gay or lesbian employee?

Not many. However, gay and lesbian rights activists are

working hard to change this. Some corporations have established policies against discrimination on the basis of sexual orientation in hiring and advancement. The most recent comprehensive survey, completed in the early 1980s by the then National Gay Task Force, showed that at least 150 of the *Fortune* 500 companies, including ABC, AT&T, and Chase Manhattan Bank, had announced such policies.[15] As explained in chapter 3 of this book, the value of such policies depends on the law of your state; in some states they form binding contractual obligations but in others they do not. Even if the policies are binding, however, they generally cover only hiring, firing, and promotion decisions and not other terms and conditions of employment.

The availability of employee benefits to spouses and family members in gay and lesbian families is an emerging area of litigation. With fringe benefits often accounting for up to 40% of employment compensation, health insurance, vacation plans, and other benefits are often considered essential parts of the compensation package. These benefits, when available at all, are routinely available to spouses of heterosexual employees but are rarely available to the partners of gay and lesbian employees. As a result, these employees are effectively earning less than their heterosexual married counterparts. Employers maintain that they are not obligated to recognize homosexual relationships and provide benefits to such partners where such relationships are not recognized as legal marriages and where, in some states, consensual intimate acts between two members of the same sex are still considered criminal offenses.

Recently, several cities have recognized domestic partnerships between gay and lesbian couples as legally equivalent to marriages with respect to employment benefit entitlements. Cities with ordinances that consider gay and lesbian partnerships as "families" for health benefits purposes include Berkeley, Cal.; Madison, Wis.; Santa Cruz, Cal.; Seattle, Wash.; and West Hollywood, Cal. In the following cities, sick and bereavement leave policies include gay and lesbian partnerships: Ithaca, N.Y.; Los Angeles, Cal.; Madison, Wis.; Seattle, Wash.; Tacoma Park, Md.; and New York, N.Y. (city employees only).[16]

Until such ordinances are adopted more widely, gay and lesbian employees will continue to challenge the denial of benefits on other grounds. Benefits generally are considered part of wages, and many state labor laws provide a claim for nonpayment of wages when these benefits are withheld. Additionally, arbitrary denials of benefits to the marital families of gays and lesbians may be prohibited where the benefits flow from employee welfare benefit plans that are protected under the provisions of ERISA, the Employee Retirement Income Security Act. Yet, if the plan provides benefits for "legal spouses" only, the court may deny eligibility to gay or lesbian partners. In one case, a professional lesbian couple had lived together for 12 years, raised two children and considered themselves married. The surviving partner and children who were denied about $50,000 in death benefits sued under ERISA claiming the denial was arbitrary and discriminatory, especially in light of the company's antidiscrimination policy. The judge ruled, however, that the couple was not legally married, as called for by the death benefits plan, and thus the denial was proper.[17]

In light of the foregoing, it is easy to understand why advocates for gay and lesbian rights have taken the position that, until legislation that criminalizes private consensual acts by members of the same sex has been overturned, states will be able to justify discriminatory treatment in areas such as employment. As Supreme Court Justice Harry A. Blackmun wrote in a dissent from a ruling upholding Georgia's sodomy statute: "Only the most willful blindness could obscure the fact that sexual intimacy is a sensitive, key relationship of human existence, central to family life, community welfare, and the development of human personality. . . . The fact that individuals define themselves in a significant way through their intimate sexual relationships with others suggests, in a Nation as diverse as ours that there may be many 'right' ways of conducting those relationships, and that much of the richness of a relationship will come from the freedom an individual has to *choose* the form and nature of these intensely personal bonds."[18]

NOTES

1. *E.g.*, *Meinhold v. U.S. Dept. of Defense*, 1993 U.S. Dist. LEXIS 726 (C.D. Cal. Jan. 29, 1993) (court ordered reinstatement of sailor discharged for being gay because the Navy's "justifications for its

policy banning gays and lesbians from military service are based on cultural myths and false sterotypes."); *Pruitt v. Cheney*, 963 F.2d 1160 (9th Cir. 1991) (court allowed a discharged lesbian Army reservist's equal protection claim to proceed).

2. *See* Newcombe, M., *The Military's Crumbling Gay Ban: The Year In Review*, The Lambda Update (Spring, 1992) at 20.

3. *See, e.g., Webster v. Doe*, 486 U.S. 592 (1988); *Watkins v. United States Army*, 875 F.2d 699 (9th Cir. 1989); *see Buttino v. F.B.I.*, No. C-90-1639 SBA (N.D. Cal. Feb. 21, 1992).

4. California, Exec. Order No. B-54-79; Minnesota, Exec. Order No. 86-14; New Mexico, Exec. Order No. 85-15; New York, Exec. Order No. 28; Ohio, Exec. Order No. 87-30; Pennsylvania, Exec. Order No. 1975-5; Rhode Island, Exec. Order No. 85-11; and Washington, Exec. Order No. 85-09.

5. Lambda Legal Defense and Education Fund, Inc., 666 Broadway, New York, New York, 10012, (212) 995-8585.

6. National Gay and Lesbian Task Force, 1517 U Street, N.W., Washington, D.C., 20009, (202) 332-6483.

7. *See De Santis v. Pacific Telephone and Telegraph Co.*, 608 F.2d 327 (9th Cir. 1979); *Plattner v. Cash & Thomas Contractors, Inc.*, 908 F.2d 902 (11th Cir. 1990).

8. *Ulane v. Eastern Airlines*, 742 F.2d 1081 (7th Cir. 1984), *cert. denied*, 471 U.S. 1017 (1985) (Title VII); *Holloway v. Arthur Andersen & Co.*, 566 F.2d 659 (9th Cir. 1977); 29 C.F.R. § 1630.3(d)(1) (the ADA definition of "disability" does not include transvestism, transsexualism, pedophilia, exhibitionism, voyeurism, gender identity disorders not resulting from physical impairments, or other sexual behavior disorders.) State law also has failed to provide protection for transsexuals. For instance one transexual, discharged for wearing pink pearls and using the women's restroom, failed to persuade the court that his dysphosia constituted a handicap under Washington law. *See Doe v. Boeing Co.*, 64 Wash. App. 235, 823 P.d 1159 (1992), *rev'd*, 1992 Wash. LEXIS 65 March 4, 1993.

9. *Smith v. Liberty Mutual Insurance Co.*, 395 F. Supp. 1098 (N.D. Ga. 1975), *aff'd*, 569 F.2d 325 (5th Cir. 1978).

10. *E.g.*, S. 574, introduced by Senator Cranston would amend Title VII to prohibit employment on the basis of "affectional or sexual orientation."

11. Wisc. Stat. Ann. §§ 111.31 *et seq.*; Mass. Gen. L., ch. 151B, § 4(b); D.C. Code Ann. §§ 1-2541; Haw. Rev. Stat. §§ 368.1, 378.2. Vermont's statute, Act 733 was passed in 1992. Effective Jan. 1, 1993, California's Labor Code was amended to prohibit bias in employment

on the basis of actual or perceived sexual orientation in companies with five or more employees. Cal. Lab. Code § 1102.1.

12. These states are Illinois, Louisiana, Maryland, Michigan, Minnesota, New Mexico, New York, Ohio, Pennsylvania, Rhode Island, and Washington.

13. Fla: Hillsborough; Haw.: Honolulu; Me.: Portland; Md.: Montgomery, Prince George's; Mich.: Ingham; Minn.: Hennepin; N.C.: Orange; Ohio: Cuyahoga; S.D.: Minnehaha; Wash.: Clallam, King; Wis.: Dane.

14. *E.g.*, Ariz.: Tucson; Cal.: Berkeley, Cupertino, Davis, Laguna Beach, Los Angeles, Mountain View, Oakland, Sacramento, San Francisco, San Jose, Santa Barbara, Santa Cruz, West Hollywood; Colo.: Aspen, Boulder; Conn.: Hartford; D.C.: Washington; Fla.: Tampa; Ga.: Atlanta; Haw.: Honolulu; Ill.: Champaign; Chicago, Evanston, Urbana; Iowa: Iowa City; Md.: Baltimore, Rockville; Mass.: Amherst, Boston, Cambridge, Malden; Mich.: Ann Arbor, Detroit, East Lansing, Lansing, Saginaw; Minn.: Minneapolis, Mankato, St. Paul; N.Y.: Alfred, Buffalo, Blighton, Ithaca, New York City, Rochester, Syracuse, Troy; N.C.: Carrborro, Chapel Hill, Durham, Raleigh; Ohio: Columbus, Yellow Springs; Or.: Portland; Pa.: Harrisburg, North Hampton, Philadelphia, Pittsburgh; Tex.: Austin; Wash.: Olympia, Pullman, Seattle, Tacoma; Wis.: Madison, Milwaukee.

15. The NGTF Corporate Survey (1981).

16. *Domestic Partnership: Issues and Legislation*, an LLDEF publication, 1992.

17. *Rovira v. AT&T*, 90 Civ. 5486 (S.D.N.Y. Mar. 26, 1993). This case is being handled on behalf of Ms. Rovira by LLDEF, whose address is found *supra* note 5.

18. *Bowers v. Hardwick*, 478 U.S. 186, 205 (1986).

XVII

Veterans and Reservists

Those leaving military service often encounter difficulties reentering the civilian labor market. To ease this burden, Congress has enacted laws giving veterans various employment-related rights and benefits. For a discussion of other rights, see the ACLU handbook *The Rights of Veterans* by David F. Addlestone, Susan H. Hewman, and Frederic J. Gross.

This chapter discusses the rights of those who have served on active military duty, whether as members of a regular or reserve force.

As a veteran—someone who has enlisted or was drafted into any branch of the armed forces—you are generally entitled to job counseling, training, and placement services; to reemployment by your preservice employer; and possibly to preferential treatment in getting a job. To qualify for these rights and benefits, you must be an "eligible" veteran; that is, you either (1) served on active duty in the armed forces for more than 180 days and were discharged or released with other than a dishonorable discharge, or (2) were released or discharged from active duty because of a service-connected disability.[1] Congress has also expressly extended reemployment rights to reservists, those individuals who are members of a reserve unit of the armed forces.[2]

All eligible veterans are generally entitled to the rights and benefits described above. Depending on your classification as an eligible veteran, (e.g., disabled veteran or special disabled veteran), you may also be entitled to preferential treatment. You qualify as a disabled veteran if you are entitled to receive compensation under laws administered by the Veterans' Administration or were discharged or released from active duty because of a service-connected disability.[3] If you suffered a disability rated at 30% or more, you qualify as a special disabled veteran.[4]

Which employers are covered by the federal laws concerning reemployment rights?

The federal law is all-inclusive. It covers all private employ-

ers, regardless of size. It covers any "successor in interest" of
that employer. Whether a subsequent employer is a "successor
in interest" is determined on a case-by-case basis. Additionally,
the federal law applies to the federal government, its territor-
ies, possessions, and political subdivisions, to all the states and
their political subdivisions and to the District of Columbia.[5]

**Do the federal laws concerning reemployment cover all
jobs?**
No. Under the federal law, the position you left for military
service must be "other than a temporary position."[6] Generally,
employment will be considered "other than a temporary position" if it was reasonably expected to be continuous and for an
indefinite period.[7] The mere labeling of a position as "temporary" or "probationary" is not in and of itself conclusive. For
example, one court found that a probationary employee had
not left a temporary position where he could show that it was
reasonably foreseeable that he would have received permanent
status at the completion of his probationary period and that,
in hindsight, he had in fact received permanent status.[8] You
should check with an attorney regarding the "temporary" nature of your employment.

**As a veteran, do I have a right to my old job when I am
discharged from the service?**
Yes. You must be restored to your previous position or to a
position of equal status, seniority, and pay if you are an eligible
veteran who left a permanent job to perform military service.
Additionally, once reinstated you cannot be discharged without
good cause for one year after reemployment. You are entitled
to the protections of these provisions whether you enlisted or
were drafted.[9]
To assert your statutory rights to reemployment, you need
a certificate showing satisfactory completion of military service,
and you must reapply with your preservice employer within
90 days after discharge from active training and service or from
hospitalization that continued up to one year after discharge.[10]

**As a veteran, can the length of my military service affect
my reemployment rights?**
Yes. You are not entitled to reemployment rights if (1) you

enlisted and your total service (other than in a reserve component) exceeded five years (unless involuntarily extended)[11] or
(2) you were drafted and your total active duty exceeded four
years (unless any additional period served was a result of your
inability to obtain orders relieving you from active duty).[12]

Do I have reemployment rights as a member of the reserve?
Yes. Members of a reserve unit cannot be discriminated
against because of their military obligations.[13] Your employer
may not deny you your job or any promotion on that basis.[14]

You are entitled to all reemployment rights and benefits
afforded by the statute if you are ordered to an initial period
of active duty for training of at least 12 consecutive weeks. To
assert these rights, you must apply for reemployment within
31 days after (1) your release from active duty for training after
satisfactory service, or (2) your discharge from hospitalization
incident to such active duty for training or within one year
after your scheduled release from training, whichever is earlier.
Once reemployed, you may not be discharged without cause
for up to 6 months after reinstatement, but your reemployment
rights will not entitle you to retention, preference, or displacement rights over any eligible veteran with a superior claim.[15]

At your request, you are entitled to a leave of absence if
ordered to an initial period of active duty for training or inactive
duty training of less than 12 weeks. Upon your return to work,
you are to be reinstated with the same status, pay, seniority,
and vacation rights as you would have enjoyed without such
absence. To assert these rights, upon your release or your
discharge from hospitalization incident to such training, you
must report for work at the beginning of your next regularly
scheduled work period following the last calendar day needed
to return from your place of training or hospitalization to your
place of employment (or within a reasonable time thereafter,
if delayed due to reasons beyond your control) or within one
year after your scheduled release, whichever is earlier. Failure
to report for work as stated will subject you to your employer's
disciplinary rules and regulations regarding absence from
scheduled work.[16]

If you are a reservist who voluntarily or involuntarily enters
into active duty (other than for the purpose of determining
physical fitness and other than for training) you are not entitled

to reemployment rights if your total active duty exceeded 4 years (unless any additional period served was a result of your inability to obtain orders relieving you from active duty). Your service time period is generally extended by the period of your active duty.[17] In addition to the above, reservists who voluntarily enter into active duty or whose active duty is voluntarily extended are not entitled to reemployment rights unless the additional active duty was at the request of and for the convenience of the federal government.[18] If you are a reservist who is ordered to active duty for not more than 90 days under the applicable law,[19] the service time limitation is extended by the length of your active duty.

The Supreme Court has held that the Vietnam Era Veterans' Readjustment Assistance Act of 1974 does *not* require an employer to provide preferential scheduling of work hours for an employee with military obligations if such scheduling accommodations are not made for other employees.[20] Furthermore, the Court held that the reservist was not entitled to all "incidents or advantages of employment," such as regular and overtime pay, received by other employees during the reservist's absence from work.

In addition to the federal laws that protect the reemployment rights of former reservists, many states have laws that afford additional reemployment protection and that prohibit discrimination.[21] You should check your state's law for additional rights and requirements.

As a veteran or a reservist, does my right to reemployment include retention of benefits offered by my preservice employer?

Yes. In accordance with your employer's rules and procedures which were in effect when you entered the armed forces, both veterans[22] and reservists[23] are entitled to be reemployed without loss of seniority and to participate in insurance or other benefits to the same extent as you would have enjoyed had you been employed continuously. This means that generally, benefits based on length of service (such as vacation and sick days) must be restored, and your job status (such as eligibility for promotion, job classification, or pay raises) must be calculated as if you had worked continuously and had not been ordered to active duty. Pension plan benefits and vesting rights must be administered as though you had worked continuously. If your employer provides health benefits, you may not be required to go through a waiting period (often required of new employees) before you are covered.

Do I have any reemployment rights if I was rejected for military service?

Yes. If you enlisted or were inducted into military service but were subsequently rejected (e.g., for a physical impairment), your employer must treat your time away from work as a leave of absence. You are entitled to reinstatement provided you report for work at the beginning of your next regularly scheduled work period following the last day needed to travel back from the place of preinduction or other examination to the place of your employment following your release or discharge from hospitalization incident to such rejection or examination or within one year after your scheduled release therefrom, whichever is earlier.[24]

What procedures must I follow in applying for reemployment?

You should apply to the employer or an agent of the employer who has the authority to receive applications. Your application may be written or oral; however, merely inquiring about "conditions" at your former employer's, without more, may be considered insufficient. Therefore, you are better protected if you make a written application expressly requesting reinstatement to your former position. While there is no special form for the application, you must be sure to apply within the proper time limit. These time limits are discussed elsewhere in this chapter.

If I receive an other-than-honorable discharge, am I entitled to reemployment?

Generally, not. To be entitled to reemployment and the accompanying rights you must have received a certificate evidencing your satisfactory completion of military service.[25] You may, of course, challenge and overturn an other-than-honorable discharge; in that case, you will be entitled to full reemployment rights.[26]

Do I have a right to reemployment as a conscientious objector?

Yes. You are entitled to reemployment rights and benefits if you are a conscientious objector unless you refused to perform military duty, wear the uniform, or obey lawful orders of competent military authority.[27]

Do I have reemployment rights if I am a disabled veteran?

Yes. As a former member of the armed services, national guard, or reserve, your reemployment rights are protected if you are still qualified to perform the duties of that position or are able to become requalified with reasonable efforts by the employer. If you sustain a disability that prevents you from performing your old job but are qualified to perform the duties of any other position, you must be offered employment and, upon your request, be employed in a position that is equivalent to your former position in terms of status, seniority, and pay (or the nearest approximation thereof).[28]

If I qualify for reemployment, can I still be denied my preservice job?

Yes. An employer can contest your right to reemployment if circumstances existing at the time you apply for reinstatement have "so changed as to make it impossible or unreasonable" to reemploy you.[29]

This exception has been narrowly construed by the courts. It can be applied (1) where reinstatement would require the employer to create a useless job;[30] (2) where there has been a reduction in force that reasonably would have included you;[31] or (3) where there has been a sale of the business in circumstances that constitute a real change.[32] On the other hand, an employer who has reorganized its business cannot refuse to reinstate you on the grounds that such reimbursement might result in a loss in some efficiency in its operation.[33]

Is it possible for me to waive my rights to reemployment?

Yes. You can waive your statutory reemployment rights, but only if the waiver is unequivocal and you understand what you are giving up.[34] However, you can be *assumed* to have waived your reemployment rights if, for example, you fail to apply for reinstatement within the statutory period, you refuse to accept your prior position, or you voluntarily quit a job after reinstatement. The courts have also found a valid waiver where a veteran voluntarily consented to final and binding arbitration of his reemployment rights, knowing that he could not contest the arbitrator's decision, and the arbitrator decided that he had no right to the position.[35] On the other hand, one court found no waiver where a veteran refused to accept from his former employer a temporary position that did not approximate his premilitary status.[36]

What do I do if my reemployment rights have been violated?
You should contact your local field office of the Labor Management Services Administration of the Department of Labor for information and assistance. You may also contact the national Veterans' Employment and Training Service (VETS) at

U.S. Department of Labor
Veterans' Employment and Training Service
200 Constitution Ave., N.W., Rm. S1316
Washington, D.C. 20210
(202) 523-8611

Once you make a claim, VETS and its field compliance officers will investigate the facts regarding your military and employment history and attempt to resolve the dispute between you and your preservice employer. (You may also pursue your claim through any grievance procedures contained in your employer's collective bargaining agreement, but you are not required to do so).[37] If your dispute is not resolved by VETS, VETS can refer your case to a United States attorney or comparable official in the judicial district where your preservice employer is located. If the United States attorney or other official is reasonably satisfied that you are entitled to the benefits you seek, you will be represented without costs or fees in any action instituted in federal court on your behalf.[38]

Can I be discriminated against by a prospective employer because I was given a less-than-honorable discharge?
Veterans discharged under less-than-honorable conditions frequently experience discrimination when applying for private employment. Unfortunately, there is no federal law that pro-

hibits an employer from disqualifying a job applicant because he received an unsatisfactory discharge, even if the underlying reason for the discharge does not affect the person's ability to do the job.

Under certain circumstances, however, you may be able to prevent an employer from discriminating against you because of the character of your discharge. First, if a prospective employer has contracts in excess of $10,000 with the federal government, it may only consider that portion of your discharge papers and military record that relate to the specific job requirements of the position for which you applied.[39] Second, if you are a member of a minority group, you can challenge your disqualification on the ground that it constitutes illegal employment discrimination under Title VII of the Civil Rights Act of 1964. The EEOC and at least one federal court have held that, because members of minority groups are given less-than-honorable discharges in disproportionate numbers, the use of this criteria in the selection of employees has an illegal disparate impact upon minority group members.[40] Finally, some states have regulations that forbid a preemployment inquiry into the character of a job applicant's military discharge. Generally, these regulations permit an employer to ask only about skills acquired during military service that are relevant to performance of the job. You should check your state's law in this regard.

Am I entitled to preferential treatment?

Under certain circumstances, eligible veterans are entitled to preferential treatment in job training and placement.

If you are an eligible disabled or Vietnam era veteran (or an eligible person requesting assistance, e.g., the spouse of any person who suffers from a total and permanent service-connected disability or who died of or from a service-connected disability), you can benefit from the Veterans' Benefits law, which emphasizes the goal of promptly offering you job placement, development, or employment counseling services.[41] Eligible disabled veterans, especially from the Vietnam era, can benefit from an outreach program designed to provide jobs and job training opportunities.[42] In addition, both the federal government and private employers who contract with the federal government on jobs exceeding $10,000 must take affirmative steps to hire qualified disabled, Vietnam era, and special disabled veterans.[43]

The federal government is required to have affirmative action plans in effect for the hiring, placement, and advancement of disabled veterans. As a qualified Vietnam era veteran or special disabled veteran, you may receive preference for employment as veterans' benefits counselors, claims examiners, and representatives in the outreach services programs.[44]

Private employers who contract with the federal government in excess of $10,000 are required to take affirmative steps to employ and advance in employment qualified Vietnam era and special disabled veterans. In this regard, the employer is required to (1) file a statement with the Federal Office of Contract Compliance giving the employment status of veterans under its employ; (2) consider the veteran's status a positive factor in decisions to hire, promote, or transfer the employee; and (3) list available positions with local employment service offices so that veterans may easily learn of job openings. If you believe a contractor of the United States has not complied with such affirmative requirements, you may file a complaint with the Secretary of Labor for investigation and appropriate action.[45] Eligible veterans may not enforce their rights by private action.[46]

NOTES

1. 38 U.S.C. § 4211(4).
2. 38 U.S.C. § 2021(b)(3).
3. 38 U.S.C. §§ 4211(1), 4211(3).
4. 38 U.S.C. § 4211(1).
5. 38 U.S.C. § 2021(a)(2)(A)(i).
6. 38 U.S.C. § 2021(a).
7. *Akers v. Arnett*, 597 F. Supp. 557 (S.D. Tex. 1983), *aff'd*, 748 F.2d 283 (5th Cir. 1984).
8. *Brickner v. Johnson Motors*, 425 F.2d 75 (7th Cir. 1970).
9. 38 U.S.C. § 2024.
10. 38 U.S.C. § 2021(a).
11. 38 U.S.C. § 2024(a).
12. 38 U.S.C. § 2024(c).
13. 38 U.S.C. §§ 2021(b)(3); 2024(c)–(g).

14. 38 U.S.C. § 2021(b)(3).
15. 38 U.S.C. § 2024(c).
16. 38 U.S.C. § 2024(d).
17. 38 U.S.C. § 2024(b)(2). The period of active duty may not exceed the period during which the President was authorized to order you to active duty.
18. 38 U.S.C. § 2024(b)(2).
19. 10 U.S.C. § 673b.
20. *Monroe v. Standard Oil Co.*, 613 F.2d 641 (6th Cir. 1980), *aff'd*, 452 U.S. 549 (1981).
21. States with laws protecting reservists include Alabama, Arkansas, California, Colorado, Connecticut, Indiana, Iowa, Kentucky, Louisiana, Maine, Massachusetts, Montana, Nebraska, New Jersey, New Mexico, North Dakota, Ohio, Rhode Island, South Dakota, Texas, Vermont, Washington, West Virginia. In addition, many more states have laws protecting veterans and members of the National Guard. You should be sure to check your state's law.
22. 38 U.S.C. § 2021(b)(1).
23. 38 U.S.C. § 2021(b)(3).
24. 38 U.S.C. § 2024(e).
25. 38 U.S.C. § 2021(a).
26. *Robertson v. Richmond, Frederiksburg and Potomac R.R. Co.*, 178 F. Supp. 734 (E.D. Va. 1959).
27. 38 U.S.C. § 5303(a).
28. 38 U.S.C. §§ 2021(a)(2)(B)(ii); 2024(d).
29. 38 U.S.C. § 2021(a)(2)(B)(ii).
30. *Davis v. Halifax County School System*, 508 F. Supp. 966 (E.D.N.C. 1981).
31. *Id.*
32. *Anthony v. Basic American Foods, Inc.*, 600 F. Supp. 352 (N.D. Cal. 1984); *Chaltry v. Ollie's Idea, Inc.*, 546 F. Supp. 44 (W.D. Mich. 1982).
33. *Loeb v. Kivo*, 77 F. Supp. 523 (S.D.N.Y. 1947), *aff'd*, 169 F.2d 346 (2d Cir.), *cert. denied*, 335 U.S. 891 (1948).
34. *See, e.g., U.S. ex rel. Reilly v. New England Teamsters and Trading Industry Pension Fund*, 737 F.2d 1274 (2d Cir. 1984).
35. *Wright v. Ford Motor Co.*, 196 F. Supp. 538 (E.D. Mich. 1961).
36. *Chaltry v. Ollie's Idea, Inc.*, 546 F. Supp. 44 (W.D. Mich. 1982).
37. *McKinney v. Missouri-Kansas-Texas R.R. Co.*, 357 U.S. 265 (1958).
38. 38 U.S.C. § 2022.
39. 41 C.F.R. § 60-250.5(d).
40. EEOC Dec. No. 74-25 (Sept. 10, 1973); *Dozier v. Chupka*, 395 F. Supp. 836 (S.D. Ohio 1975).

41. 38 U.S.C. §§ 3201, 4100 *et seq.*
42. 38 U.S.C. § 4104A.
43. 38 U.S.C. §§ 4212; 4214.
44. 38 U.S.C. § 4214.
45. 38 U.S.C. § 4212(b).
46. *Harris v. Adams*, 873 F.2d 929 (6th Cir. 1989).

PART 4
The Unionized Workplace

XVIII
Collective Bargaining

A little less than 20% of the American workforce is represented by unions and covered by collective bargaining agreements. The questions and answers below address how union representation and collective bargaining come about, how collective bargaining works, what can be accomplished through collective bargaining, and what are its limitations.[1]

BACKGROUND

In earlier chapters we told you about workplace benefits and safeguards that are available to all workers, whether or not they are represented by a union. These include the right to be free from discrimination on account of race, gender, age, disability, and other irrelevant factors, the right to a healthy and safe workplace, guarantees of minimum wages and payment for overtime hours, protections for pension benefits that have been established by employers, and so on. Most of these packages of protections are relatively new, the product of legislation enacted in the last three decades.

During the first part of this century our country did not set basic workplace rights through legislation, except in limited areas such as hours of work and child labor. The labor movement distrusted government involvement, and concentrated its energies on collective bargaining rather than on workplace legislation. When our legislatures did act, courts often struck down the laws on the ground they interfered with an employer's freedom to make his own contract with his employees.[2]

At the same time there was remarkable judicial hostility toward unions and collective activity. Union activity was thought to be a conspiracy in restraint of trade, interfering with the operation of the free market. Legislation designed to correct that view did not influence the courts. Union organizing was often the target of criminal action[3] or of injunctions that put an end to strikes and picketing.[4]

In the 1930s, a time of industrial unrest and depression, Congress made a fundamental choice about the direction of workplace rights. Congress was unwilling to enact legislation that would give workers additional substantive rights, a course taken in many other industrialized nations. It preferred instead to leave the terms of employment to the free market and to private parties. However, in 1935 it passed legislation that recognized and protected the right of workers to join labor unions and bargain collectively and attempted to equalize bargaining power between workers and employers. This law, the National Labor Relations Act, popularly known as the Wagner Act, set out basic procedures for establishing a collective bargaining relationship, gave workers protection against discharge for engaging in union activity, and established an administrative agency for its enforcement.

Congress twice amended the NLRA. The Taft-Hartley Amendments in 1947 placed substantial limitations on the powers of unions, especially by making it hard for them to put pressure on employers who were are not directly involved in a labor dispute (the secondary boycott). Although Taft-Hartley was condemned as an antilabor statute and was passed over the veto of President Truman, it contains some provisions that enhance collective bargaining, such as granting federal courts the authority to enforce collective bargaining agreements. In 1959 the Landrum-Griffin Amendments began to regulate the internal affairs of unions. Some of these restrictions are discussed in chapters 21 and 22. The 1959 amendments also severely limit the picketing of unorganized workplaces, requiring unions to use the procedures for obtaining recognition that are discussed later in this chapter. The entire act, consisting of the original Wagner Act and the two amendments, is sometimes referred to as the Labor Management Relations Act (LMRA) and sometimes as the National Labor Relations Act (NLRA). We will generally refer to the overall statute as the NLRA.

How is the National Labor Relations Act administered and enforced?

The National Labor Relations Act is administered by an agency, the National Labor Relations Board (NLRB). The board, which has a complex administrative structure, has its headquarters in Washington, D.C., where it makes its major policy decisions. However, the day-to-day administration of the NLRA is carried out by the various regional offices of the board, located in a number of cities in the United States. If you want to enforce your rights under the NLRA, you initiate your case by filing a charge with the regional director of the regional office that covers your workplace. You must file within 6 months of the incident you complain about. The regional director's staff will investigate your charge, and if it decides your charge has merit, it will issue a complaint and will act as your counsel. A legal claim under the NLRA is not litigated directly in court. It is first heard by an administrative law judge at a hearing. His or her decision is then reviewed by the board. The board's decision may then be appealed in the federal circuit court of appeals in the appropriate jurisdiction. The board cannot enforce its own orders but must turn to the court of appeals.

Is the NLRB required to pursue my claim?

No. The board has absolute discretion to decide whether to issue a complaint and pursue your claim. If the regional director decides that the facts don't support your claim, or that your claim doesn't involve a violation of the act, that is the end of it. You have a right to appeal the regional director's refusal to issue a complaint to the board's general counsel in Washington,[5] but these appeals are seldom successful. The courts cannot make the board proceed with your case. The board's enthusiasm for your case may depend on its political composition. The board's position on issues shifts back and forth, sometimes favoring unions and sometimes favoring management, depending on the backgrounds of its five members, who are appointed by the President with the advice and consent of Congress.

What workers are covered by the NLRA?

Not every worker is covered by the NLRA. It applies only to private employers.[6] Employees of federal, state, and local governments are covered by separate statutes that vary from jurisdiction to jurisdiction. Federal employees are covered by the federal Labor Management and Employee Relations Law, administered by the federal Labor Relations Authority.[7] Employees in the railroad and airline industries are covered by the Railway Labor Act, which was passed much earlier, in 1926.[8] Certain categories of workers, such as agricultural laborers, managerial employees, independent contractors, and supervisors, are excluded from the NLRA.[9] Many of these workers have no other statute to turn to for protection of their organizing rights. Our discussion of collective bargaining is generally confined to rights under the NLRA although we will make occasional reference to the other statutes.

The NLRA protects all covered workers from unlawful acts of the employer, such as discharging the employee for engaging in union activity, and it gives all covered workers the right to choose a union and to bargain with their employer through that designated representative. However, the benefits of collective bargaining extend only to those workers who select a union to represent them and who negotiate a collective bargaining agreement.

Does coverage under the NLRA and under collective bargaining agreements extend only to union members?

No. The protections of the NLRA extend to all covered workers, whether or not they support or join a union. And the benefits of the collective bargaining agreement extend to all workers in the covered workplace as defined in the agreement, whether or not they belong to the union. While it may be to your advantage to join a union, you do not have to do so to enjoy these protections. You have significant rights under the law to influence the governance of the union, as we will explain in more detail below in this chapter and in chapters 21 and 22, but generally you have to be a union member to exercise those rights.

What are the benefits of union representation and collective bargaining?

Union representation and collective bargaining give you many important rights. Once the workers in your workplace have selected a union to represent them through the procedures set out in the NLRA, that union has the right to negotiate with management over the terms and conditions of employment. Management is required to meet with the union and discuss the union's proposals, as long as the proposals are among the *mandatory subjects of bargaining*, a term discussed further below. However, the employer is not required to agree to any of the union's proposals.[10] The law does not prescribe the terms of the collective agreement and leaves that entirely to negotiations between the union and the company. The right to bargain gives you a voice, through your union, in determining the wages, hours, and other benefits of employment.

Collective bargaining gives you the right to bring economic pressure on your employer to agree to your proposals. The principal weapon at your disposal is the strike—the right to withhold your services if you are not satisfied with the employer's position in bargaining.[11] However, your right to strike is tempered by your employer's right to hire permanent replacements in order to operate the business. The recent Caterpillar strike demonstrates that the right to replace is a powerful antidote to the strike. Once a contract is negotiated, however, it usually provides that the employees will not strike while the contract is in effect because employee claims can be resolved through grievance arbitration, as discussed below.

Once the union and the employer reach an agreement, it becomes the primary source of your rights in the workplace and governs such things as wages, leave time, holidays, vacations, health insurance and pensions, and the right to be promoted to better jobs, usually on the basis of seniority. The agreement usually provides that the employer cannot discharge you or otherwise discipline you except for "just cause," which means that the employer must demonstrate to the satisfaction of a neutral arbitrator that the employer had good grounds for the discipline or discharge. This is usually a much stronger safeguard than the rights provided by state law, as discussed in chapter 3. The just-cause provision generally gives more comprehensive protection against unfair treatment than do the laws against discrimination discussed in part 3 of this book.

Along with the rights provided by your agreement, you have all the rights of workers who are not represented by a union, as discussed in previous chapters. When your rights under the collective bargaining agreement overlap with public rights, you may have to follow some procedures that determine which rights govern. In general, however, the employee covered by a collective bargaining agreement enjoys both public rights and those rights conferred by the agreement.

How is the collective bargaining agreement enforced?

Your rights under a collective agreement are enforced by a process known as *grievance arbitration.* This is another major benefit of union representation. If you believe that you are entitled to a benefit under the collective bargaining agreement, for example, the right to a promotion based on your seniority, you may file a grievance. This is an informal document that states your claim under the contract. Your union representative will usually take up that claim on your behalf if he believes it has merit under the agreement. There are generally several stages in the grievance process, working up to discussions with the personnel director or a vice president in charge of labor relations. You have the right to represent yourself in discussions with management at any stage of the grievance process except the final one. However, you will usually turn to your union representative, who is an expert in the administration and enforcement of the contract. Usually the grievance is resolved through these discussions, although perhaps not entirely as you had wished since sometimes claims must be compromised.

If a satisfactory solution is not reached in the grievance procedure, the union may advance your claim to binding arbitration. This decision is the union's alone. If the union decides that your claim should not be taken to arbitration, that is, if the union decides not to challenge management's position, you have only limited recourse. Unions are the experts in interpreting the agreement, and the law provides that the union has the final power to make adjustments with management over the interpretation of the agreement and in the settlement of claims. If individuals could challenge their union's decision to settle a grievance, this would disrupt the orderly process of grievance settlement. However, the union must process your grievance in good faith and without discrimination, for it owes you a duty of fair representation. If the union decides unfairly not to take your case to arbitration, you have a limited right to pursue your claim on your own in court. However, your chances of success are slim since courts seldom disagree with a union's decision. These matters involving the union's duty of fair representation are discussed in detail in chapter 20.

If the union does take your case to arbitration, it will present your claim before a neutral arbitrator. *Arbitration* is an informal proceeding somewhat like a court of law. The union presents your case, and management presents its case. You may be asked to tell your story, and your supervisor or other representatives of management will give their position. After the presentation is over, the arbitrator studies the evidence and arguments and issues a written decision, usually within a couple of months. That decision is final and binding and may be enforced in the courts. The grounds for overturning an arbitrator's decision are very limited. This means that if you win your arbitration it is unlikely that the employer can have that award reversed in court. By the same token, if you lose you will have little chance to have the award set aside, although if your claim also involves a statutory right you may be able to pursue that right separately before the appropriate agency or in state or federal court.

Arbitration is also used to enforce rights that affect the bargaining unit as a whole. For example, if the company fails to give a scheduled wage increase, the union can enforce the wage scale through arbitration.

Is arbitration the only method for enforcing my rights under a collective bargaining agreement?

No. In the normal situation your collective bargaining agreement provides that arbitration is the only way to enforce your contractual rights. Usually, the arbitration process replaces the strike as a means for enforcing worker rights. In a few contracts, however, arbitration is not provided as a means of dispute resolution, and the union is free to strike. The Supreme Court recently held that even if the collective agreement doesn't provide for arbitration, the contract may be enforced in federal court under Section 301.[12] The holding in that case turned on the fact that the union didn't exercise its right to strike and reflected the Court's understanding of a preference under our statutes for peaceful resolution of disputes over recourse to the strike weapon.

Are there any disadvantages to being represented by a union?

Yes. But we assume that most workers will conclude they are outweighed by the benefits of collective bargaining. One disadvantage is that when a union is selected to represent the workers in the unit, it alone has the power to speak for all the workers. No other union or representative may negotiate a different agreement, and the individual worker is not allowed to negotiate his own arrangement. This is known as the *doctrine of exclusivity.* It represents the dominant philosophy of collective bargaining, which the Supreme Court long ago said looks with suspicion upon individual advantages.[13] The duty of fair representation requires the union to negotiate fairly on behalf of all those in the unit, but the courts have said that the union has a wide range of choices to decide what bargain to make.[14]

Some agreements do provide that individual workers may negotiate their own terms, for example, in highly visible occupations like sports. In general, however, the bargain is made on behalf of all workers. Collective bargaining inevitably involves some trade off of individual advantage so that the group as a whole may gain. The union needs to have a broad base of support, so you can be confident that the union will look after your interests while it advances the interests of the group. In addition, you can influence the union's bargaining agenda by active participation in the union's governance. These matters are discussed in chapters 21 and 22.

Exclusivity also means that if you try to negotiate your own bargain and put pressure on the employer through picketing and similar action—taking a position different from the union's—in extreme cases you are not protected from being fired by the employer.[15]

Under the doctrine of exclusivity, the union determines whether to take your contract claims to binding arbitration, although it is required to represent you fairly in making this decision and may not act in bad faith or in an arbitrary or capricious way.[16] The duty of fair representation is discussed in detail in chapter 20. As a practical matter, if you have a strong claim under the collective bargaining agreement, the union is likely to advance it to arbitration, although the ultimate judgment call belongs to the union.

On the other hand, you are entitled to meet with your employer to attempt to enforce the terms of the collective bargaining agreement. But the union is entitled to be consulted about the terms of the agreement you reach and can oppose any adjustment that is inconsistent with the collective agreement.[17] If your employer doesn't agree with you, your only recourse is arbitration, but as indicated in the previous paragraph, only the union has the right to advance the claim in arbitration.

To illustrate, if you think you are entitled to a promotion on the basis of your skills, you may meet with management to convince them of your case. But the union is entitled to oppose your claim, for example, because it thinks the job should go to a more senior employee. If the employer gives the job to the more senior worker, it is up to the union whether to take your case to arbitration. But since, in this example, the union has already opposed your position, it is unlikely to take your case to arbitration.

Another seeming disadvantage of union representation is that it will cost you money. Unions charge periodic dues, initiation fees, and occasional assessments. Dues generally run in the neighborhood of $20 or more per month. These dues support the staff expertise the union provides to your workplace and pay the cost of arbitrations and of legal help that may be needed to enforce the contract. Dues also go to the national organization to pay for its overall activities, including its lobbying efforts for protective legislation and its attempts to organize other workers and for union conventions and other functions.

As we will explain further below and in chapter 19, you are not required to join a union even though it is required to represent you as a member of the bargaining unit. However, if you chose not to join, in most cases you must still pay the union your fair share of the union's cost of representing you. This is usually less than the full union dues. While this may seem to be a financial burden, bear in mind that the union is obliged to represent you whether or not you join the union, and the protections it negotiates benefit you even if you don't join. It is only fair that you pay for the costs of this representation.

In trying to persuade you not to select a union, your employer may tell you that a union will result in high wages and inefficient operations that will put the company out of business. Some workers may fear this and vote against the union. However, a responsible union will be aware of management's competitive limitations and will not impose terms or rules that would hurt the company's competitive position. On the other hand, this means that your union may not always be able to achieve the benefits you seek. Your employer's ability to provide desirable benefits is limited by the realities of the market in which it competes.

The employer may also tell you that having a union will result in strikes. As we will explain in a question below, the strike is an important weapon in securing contract benefits. However, it is up to the union to decide whether a strike is necessary or wise. If you join the union and participate in its governance, depending on what the union's constitution provides, you will probably have a voice in whether the union uses this weapon.

Am I required to join the union that represents me at my workplace?

No. Section 7 of the NLRA gives you the right to refrain from union activity. While another provision of Section 7, when read along with Section 8(a)(3), appears to say that you may be required to join a union,[18] the Supreme Court has held that you cannot be required to join a union as a condition of employment.[19] The most the union may require you to do is pay its costs of providing you with representation through collective bargaining. This means, according to the Court, that the requirement of membership in a union is "whittled down to its financial core."[20] The procedures for determining the amount of such payments is discussed in chapter 19.

Why should I join the union that represents me at my workplace?

The union at your workplace is required to represent and protect you. Many workers would agree that if the union is required to represent them, they ought to join and support it. As indicated in the previous question, you probably will be required to pay the union the costs of representing you, and it will not cost much more to pay the full cost of membership. A union's ability to represent you depends on having the support of the entire workforce. This is the only way it can convince management that it will take the necessary lawful steps, such as a strike, to secure its demands. Your membership in the union is an important sign of your union's economic strength. Union membership is also essential if you wish to have a voice in the union's governance. If you are not a member, you will not have a say in many of the important decisions made by the union. These rights of membership are discussed in chapters 21 and 22.

If I am hired in a workplace that already has a union, am I entitled to representation and must I join the union? Do I have any say about this?

If you are hired in a workplace that already has a union, you are immediately represented by the union. You will automatically come under the terms and conditions of the collective bargaining agreement that is in place. However, depending on the wording of the agreement, for the first couple of months of your employment you will probably be considered a probationary employee; this status is not affected by whether or not you join the union. While most of the provisions of the agreement apply to you during this probationary period, you will not be protected against discharge. The purpose of a probationary period is to allow the employer to determine whether you are likely to be a successful employee, without having its decision reviewed by an arbitrator.

The collective agreement usually provides that you must join the union within 30 days of your hire. However, as we explained above and will explore in detail in chapter 19, you cannot be required to actually join the union; the most the union may require is your payment of the equivalent of that portion of union dues that covers its expenses of representing you through collective bargaining. If and when you join the union, you are entitled to participate in its internal governance. That is discussed in chapters 21 and 22. If you don't want union representation, your only recourse is to vote against representation during those limited periods in which an employee can challenge the union's status.

How can I obtain union representation?

The following procedures apply where a union is not currently recognized as the representative of the employees at a particular workplace.

The early stages. The process usually begins when workers who are interested in union representation contact a union representative. Workers usually rely on word of mouth and the experience of friends and relatives to find a good union to represent them. Sometimes a union organizer visits the workplace and attempts to interest workers in representation. You should not try to organize until you have consulted with a union and have the union's commitment that it will advise and back you in the organizing campaign. You should get the professional assistance of the union at every stage of the organizing process, for it is a complicated procedure with high risks for the employee.

Once union involvement has been secured, the union begins to contact the workers in order to explain the benefits of unionization to them. The union normally uses a professional organizer, employed by the union and trained in the conduct of organizing campaigns. It also relies heavily on interested workers to carry its message; these workers usually set up an organizing committee. The film *Norma Rae*, although somewhat dated, gives a vivid and fairly accurate picture of both the positive and discouraging sides of how the organizing process works.[21] The union will insist on a strong showing of support by the workers before it proceeds further. It will ask workers to sign an authorization card that says the worker designates the union to represent him for collective bargaining purposes. The card may also say that the worker authorizes the union to seek an election conducted by the NLRB. Some unions will not go further until they are sure of the support of substantially more than 50% of the eligible workforce.

The petition. When the union has authorization cards signed by at least 30% of the eligible voters, it may petition the NLRB to hold a secret ballot election, where voters can vote for or against union representation. Usually the union will not take this step until it has substantially more than 50% of the workers signed up. The union often sends a letter to the employer at this point stating that a majority of the workers have selected the union to represent them and asks the employer to begin negotiations. The employer seldom agrees to recognize and deal with the union at this point, but if it does, the union is entitled to the status of certified bargaining representative. Normally, however, the employer insists that the matter be resolved by an election.

The regional office of the NLRB (or board) then examines the authorization cards, keeping the identity of the signers secret. If the union has authorization cards from 30% of the eligible work force, the board begins the election process. This consists of two stages. The first determines exactly which workers in the workplace are entitled to vote on the question of representation. This is known as determining the *appropriate bargaining unit*.[22] If the employer and union agree on the composition of the appropriate unit, this stage may take only a week or two. The election is then scheduled about three weeks after that. This means that in a situation where the unit composition is not contested, an election may be held within about five weeks of the time the petition is filed. However, considerable time may have already gone by before the union filed its petition, depending on how quickly the union is able to muster the necessary support. A campaign of a month or longer before filing the petition is not unusual. So you should be prepared for a wait of between one and two months, at the very least, from the time you initiate your interest in the union to the time the question is decided by an election.

If the employer disputes the composition of the unit, the board holds a hearing on that question. The hearing and the issuance of the board's decision can add another month or two to the process. In some cases, where a regional office's decision is appealed to the full board (the board determines whether to hear such an appeal; it is rare), the process can be delayed even further. We explain all this because the election process can be a period of great stress for the worker, and the worker should be prepared for a potentially long haul.

The appropriate bargaining unit. In determining the appropriate bargaining unit, the board looks at two sorts of issues. One is whether the worker is covered by the NLRA. Supervisors, management, and confidential employees are excluded from the NLRA and are therefore eliminated from the voting and from subsequent union representation.[23] Sometimes this is a hotly contested issue, for example, in the case of lead workers or "straw bosses." Often these are key union supporters, and the employer will claim they are supervisors and members of management who, as such, are not entitled to vote.

The other issue is concerned with the appropriate *community of interest*, which means, in very general terms, workers with roughly the same working conditions who can all be effectively represented by the same union. A common appropriate bargaining unit consists of all the production and maintenance employees at a single facility. If there are office/clerical employees in the same building, that raises a question as to whether both production and office employees may be represented in the same unit. Also the employer sometimes claims the appropriate unit must include not only the employees of the facility where the organizing drive has taken place but other facilities that may not even be in the same geographic area. If the union has not organized the workers at these other facilities and the board agrees that they are part of the appropriate unit, that usually kills the organizing drive.

Congress has provided special rules for determining appropriate units in the healthcare industry, and the board has recently promulgated regulations to govern similar situations. These regulations as well as the board's procedures for determining them, were recently upheld by the Supreme Court.[24]

The union has one strong point going for it in determining the correct unit. The board recognizes that many different sorts of units may be appropriate and does not insist that the election be held in the ideal, most appropriate unit. The only question is whether the union has picked an appropriate unit out of the many possibilities. This gives the union some flexibility in deciding the scope of the unit it wishes to organize.[25]

Unit determination questions are very complicated and cannot be adequately treated in the space given in this book. The union organizer is trained to handle these issues and will usually receive professional advice from the union's legal staff in order to get through this process successfully. The union organizer can explain the particular unit issues in your workplace to you. We have tried to simply set out the general issues and how they affect the overall election process.[26]

The election campaign. Once the election petition has been filed, and often even before that, the union and the employer each bring their message to the employees about why they think union representation is good or bad. The union is limited in its opportunity to communicate since the employer may lawfully prohibit the union organizer from entering company property. The union organizer has to stand on public property, perhaps near an entrance gate, in order to talk to workers and distribute literature. The union organizer must rely on mailed literature and on home visits and scheduled meetings in other facilities, such as union halls or churches. The employer is required to give the union a list of the names and addresses of eligible workers, so the union can make contact at homes. In a recent decision the board held that where other opportunities for communication are limited, the organizer is permitted to enter the employer's property, and therefore, it granted a union the right of access for organizing activities in a parking lot at a small strip of stores.[27] However, the Supreme Court more recently overruled the board's approach to these cases, holding that the employer's property rights outweigh the union's right of access in all but extraordinary cases, such as a remote lumber camp cut off from other access.[28] In such a case, the board may order the employer to grant the union organizers greater access if the election is rerun, but the union doesn't usually win the second time around.

Because the professional organizer's access is so limited, the union relies heavily upon its organizing committee—that is, key workers from within the plant—to carry on the organizing campaign under the direction and with the advice of the professional organizer. Some observers believe that the organizing effort works only if the union has a strong and active in-house organizing team.[29] Employees are entitled to talk to one another about unionization at any time they are not actually scheduled for work, for example, during break periods or meals, even if they are paid for that time. And they are entitled to distribute literature at any time, as long as it does not disrupt work. These restrictions are usually set forth in employer rules.[30]

The employer, meanwhile, often distributes its message through memos and letters to employees. The employer is also allowed to call meetings on company time and with pay, but it cannot require employees to attend these meetings.

The election and certification. Depending on whether the bargaining unit is contested, the election is held within several months of the time the petition is filed. If the union wins the election, it becomes the certified bargaining representative, and the employer must meet with the union in an effort to negotiate an agreement in good faith. If the union loses the election, it is not permitted to file another petition for a period of one year. However, if there was improper conduct during the election, the election may be set aside and a new one held in less than a year. In rare cases, the union can obtain bargaining rights as a remedy for employer misconduct without the need of another election. The employer, too, may have the election set aside if it can show union misconduct.

What will the arguments of the union and the employer be, and are there any limitations on what they may say?

What each side says varies widely, depending on its sophistication and resources. You can expect the union to tell you the kinds of benefits it has obtained for other unionized workers in similar plants, such as higher wages and fringe benefits. The union will stress that your contract will give you job security against unfair dismissals by providing that no employee may be discharged without just cause. The union will say that it will give you a voice in the terms of your job and will provide you with a grievance and arbitration machinery to enforce your rights. Some unions emphasize their ability to help enforce your rights to a safe and healthy workplace.

The employer will tell you that you are already enjoying a good package of benefits. It will list them in detail and say that it can only improve these benefits, as it always has, if competitive conditions permit and that the union will inhibit the company's competitiveness. It will tell you that you have always enjoyed good relations and communications with the company and that the union will only get in the way of this good relationship. It will say that unions often introduce rigid work restrictions that make the workplace noncompetitive. And it will point out that unions often call strikes and that strikes sometimes put a company out of business.

The board assumes that workers can decide what statements to believe and no longer polices the content of statements for accuracy. Its theory is that if the union or the employer makes a misstatement of fact, it is up to the other side to correct it.[31]

However, there are some limits to what each side may say, and these limits usually affect the employer's speech more than the union's. The NLRA prohibits either party from interfering by restraint or coercion with the workers' right of free choice.[32] This means that the employer may not threaten employees with loss of jobs or benefits if they select a union,[33] nor may it promise employees better conditions if they reject the union.[34] By the same token the employer cannot take benefits away or grant additional ones if they are based on the outcome

of the election.[35] These are hard concepts to apply, because
the free speech provision of the act[36] also provides that the
employer is entitled to express his views about the consequences of unionization. For example, it is hard to draw the
line between a lawful prediction that a costly union contract
will force the company out of business and an unlawful threat
that if the union comes in the employer will close the plant.
Most employers will keep their communications on the lawful
side of the line, but talk of strikes, economic security, and
competitiveness, even if lawful, may make the worker fear that
selection of the union will jeopardize his job security.

The union's communications usually do not involve restraint
or coercion. Since the union does not control the job, it cannot
use job security or job benefits as a threat or promise. However,
the union violates the NLRA if it threatens workers. In a recent
case the board held that verbal threats as well as actual physical
contact interfere with the workers' Section 7 rights.[37]

The professional organizer is trained to identify unlawful
communications and to pass them along to the legal staff for
possible use in setting aside the election. You should rely
on the organizer for guidance in this phase of the campaign.
Detailed caselaw on permissible communications during an
election goes beyond the scope of this book. However, as
illustration, we give two examples of conduct or statements
that violate the act.

Normally the grant of a raise during an election campaign
is a violation of the act, even if the employer does not say that
the raise is conditioned on defeating the union. The Supreme
Court observed that the employer is not likely to miss the
implication that there may be more of this treatment if the
worker votes against the union, calling it "the fist inside the
velvet glove."[38] On the other hand, if the employer can show
that a raise was planned for this particular time (for example,
if raises are given every six months or pegged to a rise in the
cost of living) it is not a violation to give the raise during the
organizing campaign; indeed, it would be a violation to withhold a benefit that would otherwise be given.

In a leading case,[39] the employer stressed that the petitioning
union was "strike happy" and that the company might not
survive a strike. The Court held that these statements over-
stepped the line: "Any balancing of these rights must take into

account the economic dependence of the employees on their employers" and the tendency of workers "because of that relationship, to pick up intended implications . . . that might be more readily dismissed by a more disinterested ear."[40] The Court went on to say that while an employer may make a prediction about the effect of unionism on the health of the company, "the prediction must be carefully phrased on the basis of objective fact to convey an employer's belief as to demonstrably probable consequences beyond his control or to convey a management decision already arrived at to close the plant in case of unionization."[41] The employer may not take advantage of the economic dependency of his employees to overstate the possibility of the plant closing; when in doubt, he should not overstep the line between prediction and threat.

In addition to these rules prohibiting the use of threats or coercion by either side, some more technical rules govern the conduct of the election. Once the election petition is filed, the board views the remaining time up to the election as the "critical period" in which "laboratory conditions" must be observed to insure employee free choice. Some of these rules include forbidding the employer to call a meeting within 24 hours of the election and requiring the employer to provide the union with the names and addresses of voters. The employer may also violate these election conditions by less serious acts than threats, such as polling employees about their union sentiments or spying on union meetings.

What remedies does the law provide if the employer or union violate the law during the election campaign?

The board's basic remedy for violations of the NLRA during the election campaign is to declare the election void and set the results aside. The board will set the election aside even if it is not shown that the misconduct altered enough votes to change the outcome; the board simply presumes that election misconduct affects the result. The remedial process takes several months and has been criticized as ineffective because it provides no deterrent to misconduct since if the union loses the first election it seldom wins the rerun election.

Does the board impose tougher remedies for serious election violations?

Yes. A much more meaningful remedy may be imposed if

the board concludes that the employer's violations of the act are extremely serious, for example, if it fires several key union adherents because of their union activity or threatens to close down the plant if the union wins. Those egregious violations are said to destroy the conditions for a free election. In those circumstances, the board may order the employer to bargain with the union on the basis of the authorization cards that the union obtained during the election campaign. The board reasons that in these circumstances the showing of support through the authorization cards is a better indicator of employee choice than the results of an election tainted by extreme employer misconduct. The bargaining order gives the union essentially the same legal rights as if it won the election. [42]

As a practical matter, the bargaining order may not be such an effective remedy. The employer normally appeals a bargaining order in court and is not be obliged to bargain until the appeal is resolved. It may take two years or more for the union to obtain bargaining rights this way. By this time the union's support may have eroded, particularly if there is high employee turnover. Not only that, but since a majority of the workers did not vote for the union in the first place, the union may have a very difficult time getting enough workers to support a strike if one must be called. The employer knows this and can take a tougher position in bargaining as a result.

The board has refused to implement even stronger remedies, such as imposing a contract on an employer who refuses to bargain or issuing an injunction as soon as the violation occurs ordering the employer to bargain. Many commentators have criticized the election process, although one writer suggests that unions must use more effective campaign techniques if they want to be successful in winning elections. [43] Some urge adoption of the Canadian model, which imposes a bargaining obligation as soon as the union can show majority support through authorization cards. [44]

May I be fired for supporting the union during an organizing campaign?

In theory, no. The law states clearly that the employer may not fire a worker for engaging in union activity, such as campaigning for and supporting the union during an election. But this does not guarantee that you will not be fired. The burden is on the employee to convince the board that he was fired because of his union activity and not for some other reason. Employers seldom come out and say they are firing a worker because of his union activity. Usually they will give some other reasons for his termination, such as excessive absenteeism or a poor work record. There is no guarantee that you will be able to convince the board that you were fired because of your union activity.

The risks of discharge during a union campaign are high. One commentator has estimated that one in twenty workers are fired during an organizing campaign (some of these terminations may of course be unrelated to union activity).[45] Because of this risk, it is important for the worker to keep up his productivity and attendance during an organizing campaign and not give the employer any pretext to terminate him. The worker should keep careful notes of any conversations with or unusual activities by his supervisors. At the outset of the campaign, the union may actually send management a list of employees who support the union. This is done so that if a worker is later fired for what he claims was union activity, it is impossible for the employer to say that it did not know the worker was a union supporter.

In order to prevail in a claim of unlawful discharge, you must first convince the regional office of the NLRB that there is probable cause to support your claim. You have only six months to file such a claim before the board, so it is important to act quickly. An agent in the regional office will interview you and take a statement of your claim, and will then investigate the claim by meeting with the employer. The regional office's decision whether to proceed with the claim is final; if it is dropped, there is nowhere else for you to turn. You can only get redress if you can find support under a law not tied to collective bargaining, for example, a claim of discharge in retaliation for filing a health and safety claim. It is therefore very important that you present a detailed statement and as much documentation as possible when you file your charge.

Even if you are successful in proving unlawful discharge, it may be a matter of several years before you get your job back. The board requires the employer to give the worker full backpay. Some workers fear that even if they are reinstated the employer will be out to get them. This is less of a problem if the union is successful, for the worker will then have the union to defend him under the contractual protection against dismissal that is not for just cause.

Do I have the right to engage in collective activity that is not related to a union campaign?

Yes. The act protects you against discharge for any lawful concerted activity directed at improving or protecting your workplace situation. This includes going to an agency to protest a situation at your plant or even in some cases walking off the job because of an obviously dangerous condition. These activities do not have to be tied to a union organizing campaign, and are protected even if undertaken in a workplace that is not unionized. However, an essential requirement for protection is that the activity be concerted, that is, undertaken by two or more workers. The board does not accept the idea that when you complain about a workplace condition you are in fact speaking for your fellow workers. In addition, your activity must be related to conditions in the workplace in order to be protected; for example, the act gives you no protection against discharge for taking a stand on a political issue unrelated to your work.[46]

Even if your activity is concerted and directed at a workplace problem, there are circumstances in which it is not protected under the NLRA. Illegal activity, such as trespassing, sitting in, or criminal assault, is not protected. The board also views some activity as unprotected under the vague label of "indefensible," and it is hard to give concrete advice as to what this encompasses. In general, if your activity violates established plant rules, you run the risk that it will be considered unprotected. For example, if you walk off the job in protest, the board may treat this as unprotected and grounds for discharge.[47] If you continue on the payroll and make public statements harmful to your employer, the board may consider this indefensible and unprotected as well.[48] This means that you have no protection under the NLRA if the employer fires you for this activity.

You also may find your conduct unprotected if you work in a unionized workplace and engage in conduct that is inconsistent with the position taken by your union. For example, in a leading case[49] black workers distributed handbills urging shoppers not to patronize their employer because it discriminated against minority workers. The Court held this activity unprotected because the union that represented these workers was attempting to resolve the problem through other channels.

However, if you walk off the job to protest an obviously dangerous workplace condition, you will probably be protected under the NLRA.[50] OSHA, the federal statute that deals with workplace health and safety, also protects you if you walk off your job because of legitimate health and safety concerns. Protection for drawing attention to hazardous workplace conditions and other workplace problems is discussed extensively in chapters 24 and 25. Further protections under state law are discussed in chapter 3. These activities are protected under laws apart from the NLRA even if they are done individually and not in concert with other workers.

Can I select a union to represent me if there is already a union in the plant? Can I get rid of a union that I don't want?

If there already is a union at your plant, that is, one that has been recognized or certified in accordance with the procedures we have been discussing, then it is a tricky business to bring in a new union or drop representation altogether. A collective bargaining agreement that has been negotiated by an existing union is known as a *contract bar*, and it prevents the holding of a new election for most of the term that it is in effect. A contract of up to 3 years will serve as a bar for its duration; if the contract is longer than 3 years, it will only be a bar for the first 3 years. The board will only allow an election petition during the brief period between the sixtieth and ninetieth days prior to the expiration date of the old agreement (or the same period before the end of the third year if the agreement is longer than 3 years). While this may seem like an awfully technical requirement, remember that the union already in place needs some protection so that it can effectively represent employees. If there is no challenge by 60 days before the expiration of the agreement, the incumbent union can go about its business of renegotiating its agreement without fear of challenge by a rival union looking over its shoulder. This takes away the temptation to the employer to take a hard bargaining position in the hope that the workers will get rid of the existing union.

If a petition is filed within this open period, the procedures described above for an election will be followed. The incumbent union will usually resist the claims of a rival and seek to remain the bargaining representative. In that case, the ballot will contain the names of two unions, as well as the choice of no union at all. If none of these choices receives a majority, there is a run off between the two top choices.[51]

You may also bring a proceeding to remove the incumbent union, through a decertification petition.[52] This too must be initiated within the brief period described above. The board will investigate your petition to see if it is supported by 30% of the workers in the bargaining unit.[53] The employer is not permitted to initiate or support a decertification proceeding. If that happens, the petition will be thrown out. If the petition is valid, the board will schedule a decertification election.

May the employer deal with some kind of employee group other than a union?

Only under limited circumstances. In many workplaces today there may be an informal structure for groups of employees to meet with the employer on workplace issues. This structure is usually set up by the employer and goes by a variety of names, such as worker circles, quality of worklife groups (QWL), or worker participation programs. These groups are not unions in the traditional sense understood under the act, for they cannot require the employer to deal with them, and they usually have no legal power to enforce any agreements they make with the employer. Their key role is to provide for communication between worker and management and to give the workers some additional input and say about his or her job.

The act says that it is unlawful for an employer to "dominate" or "support" a labor organization.[54] This provision was designed to deal with "company unions," unions that were set up by the employer to give the workers very weak protection, and to discourage the workers from turning to a more aggressive union. An employer who deals with such a "dominated" union violates the act, and recognition of such a union will not block a petition by a rival union for an election under the act. Nor can the dominated union stand for election.

In a long-awaited decision, *Electromation, Inc.*,[55] the board held that an employer violated Section 8(a)(2) when it set up "action committees" that were designed to discuss various workplace problems involving both economic and other issues and to make recommendations on those issues to management.

Initially, members of the management team participated on these committees, but when a union filed a demand for recognition, the employer withdrew its representatives from the committees but allowed the committees to continue to function. The union ultimately petitioned for an election, which it lost. The union challenged the election outcome on the ground that the employer had unlawfully established the action committees under Section 8(a)(2). In a carefully qualified decision, the board held that the establishment of the committee violated Section 9(a)(2).

The board's majority opinion broadly defined a "labor organization" in Section 2(5) of the act,[56] and in a three-part test held that a committee meets that test if employees participate in the organization, if it exists in part for the purpose of "dealing" with the employer, and if it deals with conditions of employment. The group need not have a formal structure, elected officers, or a constitution to meet this test of coverage. The board said, however, that an employer would not be barred from dealing with "an organization whose purpose is limited to performing essentially a managerial or adjudicative function."[57] The board also suggested that the act does not prohibit an employer from dealing with committees whose primary purpose is to achieve quality or efficiency. Finally, the opinion leaves open the question of whether a committee that doesn't purport to act on behalf of other employees in a representational capacity can be considered a labor organization under the statutory definition.

Once the committee in *Electromation* met the test of constituting a labor organization, the board easily concluded that the employer "dominated" it, in violation of the act. The key test of domination is that the "structure and function are essentially determined by management" and that the committee's continued existence "depends on the fiat of management."[58] The board made clear that the employer's motive in setting up the committee is not relevant to finding a violation of the act. On the other hand, unlawful domination would not be shown if the employees set up the committee on their own.

The other three members of the board who heard the case wrote separate opinions emphasizing the narrowness of the *Electromation* holding. These opinions stressed that programs designed to improve efficiency, solve problems, and improve communications do not violate the act.

Since *Electromation* was decided by a 4-person board, and the board's composition will change when President Clinton appoints a fifth member as well as fills any vacancies that arise during his term, the reach of the decision is somewhat unclear. Further, the decision will be reviewed by the courts, which will have to apply the leading Supreme Court decision on this point[59]—which held an employee participation program to violate the act—as well as lower court decisions that have held that dealing with an employee group that doesn't perform traditional collection bargaining functions does not violate the act.[60] At this writing, however, it is fair to say that the decision hinders employee participation programs because of the risk that they will be challenged through litigation.[61] Depending on how case law develops, worker participation programs may be seriously inhibited unless Congress clearly amends Section 8(a)(2) of the act to permit them.

What rights does the union have as the certified or recognized bargaining agent?

Once certified or recognized, the union may compel the employer to bargain with it over the terms and conditions of employment. This means that the employer must meet with the union regularly and bargain in good faith over a contract. The law does not require the employer to agree with the union's demands or to make any concessions.[62] In enacting the NLRA, Congress took the a hands-off position on what goes into the contract. All the law does is lead the parties to the bargaining table. Although the law requires the employer to bargain in good faith with the union, it is hard for the union to prove that the employer has not bargained in good faith. Furthermore, the remedies for not bargaining in good faith are almost meaningless; the employer is simply ordered to bargain in good faith. And it usually takes a couple of years to obtain such an order.

The employer must provide relevant information at the bargaining table. This includes information about the benefits it presently provides to its employees. The employer is not required to give data about its profits and losses, unless it puts its profitability into issue by claiming at the bargaining table that it is unable to afford the union's demands. Because so many companies are publicly held and their financial records a matter of public record, the union may not need to use the NLRA to obtain this information. The union is also entitled to information about health and safety, minority composition of the workforce, and to some extent data about tests that are used to determine who gets better jobs.[63] It can get some of this information through other laws, such as OSHA's right-to-know law, discussed in chapter 24. The union may also be entitled to information under the terms of the collective bargaining agreement.

The employer may not make changes in working conditions without first trying to reach agreement with the certified union. This means the employer cannot put a wage increase into effect until the union agrees. If the negotiations have truly stalled, a situation known as an *impasse*, then the employer is free to make changes.[64] But if a collective bargaining agreement is in effect, the terms of that agreement hold for its duration, and the employer is not allowed to make changes without the union's actual agreement.

Upon certification the union is in a position to make the most effective use of the economic weapons discussed below. It can use the strike or the threat of a strike in support of its bargaining demands. It can also pressure the employer through picketing, a weapon that is available to the union only in limited circumstances prior to certification.[65]

Do these bargaining rights extend to all topics my union may raise at the bargaining table?

No. The board and courts have held that the NLRA requires the employer to bargain in good faith and to provide information only on the *mandatory subjects of bargaining*. Important economic decisions that affect the direction of the employer's business are not mandatory subjects of bargaining. The employer doesn't have to respond to the union's demands on these non-mandatory subjects, and more importantly, is free to take unilateral action without violating the act. The Court says that "Congress had no expectation that the elected union representative would become an equal partner in the running of the business."[66] Accordingly, it has construed the NLRA as not requiring bargaining about "the scope and direction of the enterprise." This includes decisions about whether to go out of business or to transfer operations to another locality.

For many years the board interpreted the Court's decision as defining the scope of mandatory subjects narrowly. But in a recent decision, *Dubuque Packing*,[67] the board modified its approach and has indicated it will define the scope of the duty to bargain more broadly than it has in previous decisions. The board held in *Dubuque Packing* that a decision to relocate unit work is a mandatory subject of bargaining under the facts of that case and indicated that relocation is normally a mandatory subject.

Whether or not the Court agrees with the board's approach in *Dubuque Packing*, the Court has affirmed that the employer is required to bargain about the effects of a nonmandatory decision. This means, for example, that the employer must respond to a demand for severance pay for employees who are terminated when the employer transfers its operations.[68]

This notion that some subjects are beyond the duty to bargain has been criticized as unsupported by the statute and legislative history and as at odds with the modern reality of negotiations.[69] However, even if a subject is not mandatory, the act does not prohibit the parties from bargaining about it. This has led, for example, to employers agreeing that union officials will sit on the corporate board of directors, clearly not a mandatory subject of bargaining under existing law.

What are the economic weapons the union may use in support of its bargaining position?

The union first attempts to convince the employer to agree to its demands. It shows how its position is fair, would improve employee morale and productivity, and would not make the employer noncompetitive. The employer may not be convinced. The union must then evaluate the employer's responses, and if it is not willing to accept them it must turn to economic pressure to support its demands. A union may not actually use these weapons; sometimes the threat is enough to achieve agreement.

The strike. The primary economic weapon used by unions is the strike. This means the withholding of your labor. The employer is unable to continue production unless he finds replacements, uses his supervisory staff, or has the work performed elsewhere. The strike is expressly protected under the act, and you may not be discharged for striking.[70] However, you may be replaced by the employer in order to continue production. You may think there is no meaningful distinction between being fired or replaced, and in many cases you are right.

Your right to strike is protected only if the strike is a total stoppage of work. If you engage in an intermittent work stoppage, that is, you work for a few hours, strike, and then come back to work, the employer may be able to fire you.[71] Strikes that involve unlawful activity, such as sitting in on private property, trespassing, violence or other criminal activities, are not protected. This means you can lose your job permanently if you engage in such activity. You may even lose your protected status if your activity falls into the very nebulous category of *indefensible conduct*. For example, in one case technicians employed by a television station took out ads criticizing their employer for putting on second class television productions. Their aim apparently was to put consumer and advertiser pressure on the station. The Supreme Court upheld the station's right to fire these technicians on the ground that they had been "disloyal."[72] Your union should look carefully at these issues if you decide to call a strike. Ask the union staff person advising the union during the strike if the strike will constitute protected activity under the act. It is important to note that, depending on the governing statute, most public employees do not have the right to strike and can be subject to discharge or other penalties for striking.

There is one important procedural hurdle before you are protected as a striker under the NLRA. Your union must give proper notice to the Federal Mediation and Conciliation Service 60 days prior to the expiration of the collective bargaining agreement and may not strike until that 60-day notification period has expired. A worker who strikes before the notice period has run loses his protection under the act and may be fired.[73]

What are the employer's lawful economic responses to a strike?

The employer will attempt to operate its plant during the strike, either with supervisory and other managerial personnel or by hiring outside workers. The political and economic climate in our country is such that workers are often willing to take the place of strikers, even though in earlier times strikebreaking was looked upon as a terrible act, and the strikebreaker was called a "scab." In the widely publicized Caterpillar strike in 1992, not only was the employer able to secure strike replacements, but it persuaded a great many strikers to abandon the strike and come back to work. Many said that they had no choice, given their long years with Caterpillar and the terrible state of the economy.

The union has little recourse to prevent the hiring of replacements. It may use the persuasion of a picket line and social pressures, including choice namecalling, to discourage replacements from crossing the picket line. While once only physical intimidation of replacements was outlawed, now the pickets may not use even verbal threats.[74] Further, as discussed in chapter 19, even a member of the union who may have initially supported the strike is free to cross the picket line and go to work, for he can escape any disciplinary action by the union, including fines, by resigning from the union.[75]

The employer may also take the economic initiative by engaging in a lockout. This is usually done when the timing of the shutdown is important. For example, if the parties are at an impasse in negotiations, and the employer is afraid the union will call a strike at its busiest season, the employer may lockout the workers when the impact on its business is less harsh. There are few legal restrictions on the employer's right to lockout,[76] and current law appears to allow the employer to hire at least temporary if not permanent replacements as well.[77] However, a recent decision holds that an employer may not lockout and replace employees before it has bargained to impasse.[78]

The employer may turn to various companies that provide temporary replacement workforces. Or it may attempt to have its work done by another company, in effect subcontracting the work during the strike. The union may continue its striking and picketing. It is entitled to take its picket lines to the location of the employer doing the struck work; the theory is that such an employer is not neutral and is not entitled to the protection of the secondary boycott laws.[79]

Finally, particularly if the company is part of a large conglomerate, the company may decide to weather the storm and shut down operations during the strike so that other operations of the conglomerate will absorb economic losses. Or it may attempt to shift production to facilities overseas. The structure of the modern corporation makes it more difficult for the union to apply economic pressure.

What is the difference between being fired and being replaced as the result of a strike? Does my replacement have any rights to my job?

You cannot be fired for engaging in a lawful strike. However, the Court has held that your employer is entitled to continue to operate its business during the strike, and this means it can hire permanent replacements to do your work.[80] The employer doesn't have to show that it needed to hire permanent replacements, for example, that it was unable to hire replacements on a temporary basis. As long as the replacement is clearly hired on a permanent basis, then the job belongs to the replacement as long as he wants it. You cannot bump your replacement. This right enjoyed by the replacement even extends to workers who were initially union supporters and joined the strike but later abandoned the strike and returned to work. By "crossing over," such a worker can replace a striker who has greater seniority. Even though this device has great potential for weakening the union, the Court has upheld its use.[81]

However, if you notify your employer that you want to return to work, in effect giving up your strike, then the employer must reinstate you as soon as there is a vacancy. This is the real practical difference between being replaced and being fired. If you are replaced, there is a chance you will get your job back. If you are fired, there is little or no such chance. As a replaced striker you have some modest procedural protections. For example, the employer is required to notify you if a vacancy arises on your job or on one for which you are qualified.[82]

As a practical matter, if the strike is successful, the union will insist as part of the settlement that the permanent replacements give way to the returning strikers. This used to be a fairly routine resolution of the strike. Now, however, because of the doctrines we discussed in chapter 3, your replacement may also have legal rights in his job. The employer may not be able to comply with the union's demand to give you your job back if there is already a replacement on the job. This is a complex problem that the union and employer must resolve in their strike settlement, one that may be subject to legal challenge. The Supreme Court even went so far as to suggest in the case involving this clash of conflicting rights, that the employer tell permanent replacements before hiring them that their job is subject to the recall rights of unfair labor practice strikers or to a strike settlement with the union. [83]

If your union can establish that the strike was caused or prolonged by the employer's unfair labor practices, for example, by the employer's refusal to provide information for bargaining, then the picture changes drastically. You now become an "unfair labor practice striker" rather than an "economic striker," and you are entitled to your job back at any time, even if this means getting rid of your replacement. [84] This potential clash between the legal rights of unfair labor practice strikers under the NLRA and the legal rights of replacements under state law may make your employer think twice about using permanent replacements in a strike. As suggested in the previous paragraph, an employer may protect itself against such a dilemma by telling the replacement in advance of hiring that her job is permanent unless the strike is an unfair labor practice strike or unless the union and company reach an agreement of the sort indicated in the previous paragraph to reinstate all strikers.

Union and aligned interest groups have continued to press Congress for legislation that would limit an employer's ability to displace strikers with permanent replacements. At this writing, with the change in administrations, the prospects for passage of such legislation are much stronger than during the Reagan and Bush administrations. [85]

Am I entitled to unemployment compensation during the strike?

This depends on the law of your state. The Supreme Court has held that a state is permitted to decide whether to allow or not allow strikers to collect unemployment insurance. [86] In the leading case on this point, New York State granted strikers unemployment benefits for a limited number of weeks during the strike. Some states distinguish between the strike and the lockout, allowing unemployment benefits only in the latter situation. [87]

The picket line. Another frequently used weapon is the picket line. The purpose of the picket line is to convey to consumers, to other workers, and to suppliers that the employees of the company are on strike and seek outside support. The support the union seeks includes refusing to trade with the employer, either as a customer or supplier, and refusing to work for the employer as a striker replacement. While the picket signs appeal to outsiders to make up their own mind, the union hopes for automatic support of its picket line, especially by suppliers who are themselves union members, such as truck drivers making deliveries to the plant. Picketing does not enjoy quite the same legal protection as the strike. For example, courts may limit the number of pickets and their location and may insist that the pickets are limited to the truthful communication of information and are not coercive.

Courts may also prohibit picketing on private property. While the recent Supreme Court case that tightly limited union access to private property was decided in the context of a union organizing drive, and the court made no mention of other union activity on private property, there is every reason to expect the Court to take the same limited view of the union's right of access in cases involving union economic pressure.[88]

In addition, there is a complex set of rules that limits the lawful purposes of picketing. In particular, unions may not use picketing to apply pressure on an employer that is neutral in a labor dispute, a tactic known as a *secondary boycott*. However, union handbilling is not covered by these rules, and as a result we can expect to see a shift from picketing to handbilling.[89] This distinction is discussed further in later questions.

If I work for one company, am I legally entitled to honor a picket line set up at another company?

Yes, with qualifications. As a general rule you are protected under the act if you honor a picket line at another company. You cannot be fired. But as with the right to strike itself, the employer may insist that you do your job, and if you persist in honoring other picket lines, the employer may replace you. Further, your right to honor another's picket line may be covered by your own collective bargaining agreement, which may require you to carry out all your assignments. There is nothing unlawful about a provision in your agreement that says you may be disciplined or even fired if you fail to carry out your own job responsibilities in the course of honoring another picket line.[90]

Consumer boycotts. The union may also engage in an appeal to consumers not to purchase the products of the company with which it has a labor dispute. This is known as a *consumer boycott* and is often the most effective weapon at the union's disposal because usually the employer cannot effectively counter it. There is no limit on the union's right to use advertising or other verbal appeals to urge a consumer boycott. It may also picket stores that sell the product as long as the picket signs make clear that the union wants customers to boycott the product and not the store itself.[91] However, if the only product the store sells is the product made by the employer involved in the labor dispute, then the union will not be allowed to use pickets to urge a consumer boycott.[92] The reason for this is that the store is not really involved in the union's labor dispute with the company that makes the product, and the law does not permit unions to picket neutral stores. While the union may not be allowed to use pickets, it can get its message across through handbills.[93]

Secondary pressure. The union may attempt to put pressure on the employer with whom it has a labor dispute by making other companies stop dealing with the employer. It hopes this pressure will cause the employer to settle with the union. However, because these other employers are neutral in the dispute, the law limits the kinds of pressures the union may apply to them. These questions are governed by the law on *secondary boycotts.*[94] As a very general rule, you may set up a picket line at your own company even if its purpose and effect is to stop other, neutral companies, such as suppliers and repairmen, from dealing with your employer. However, you generally cannot take your picket line to the site of the neutral company. For example, if you are on strike against an automobile manufacturer, you cannot set up a picket line at the plant of a manufacturer of the radios that go into the car. On the other hand, it is not unlawful to set up a picket line at your automobile plant, even if that causes the radio manufacturer to stop its deliveries.

The Court has upheld these restrictions on secondary picketing because it considers them as involving something more than just free speech since picket lines are also a call to action. While picketing of a secondary employer may be prohibited, handbilling is considered a form of free speech that may not be regulated, even if it involves a neutral, secondary employer.[95]

The union is permitted to put pressure on the other employer if that employer is not truly neutral. For example, if your company "farms out" its work to another company during a strike, that other company loses its neutrality and may be picketed.[96]

Pressure against a conglomerate. The structure of the modern corporation complicates the picture considerably. These companies are often conglomerates, consisting of a number of operating subsidiaries whose operations may have nothing to do with one another. When a union has a dispute with one subsidiary, the employer may be better able to absorb a strike since it can continue to operate all its other units and generate profits for the overall corporation. Unions have attempted to combat this by putting pressure on other units of corporate conglomerates in order to win a strike at one unit. In one case, *Pet, Inc. v. NLRB.*,[97] the union was on strike at a refrigerator plant owned by Hussman, a subsidiary of the Pet Corporation. It engaged in handbilling and picketing against all Pet products. The court held that the Pet corporation was entitled to immunity from the pressures placed on the Hussman subsidiary. However, a recent Supreme Court decision indicates that the union could have accomplished its objectives by handbilling as opposed to picketing.[98] Unions have also engaged in "corporate campaigns,"[99] bringing pressure to bear upon banks that lend money to employers involved in labor disputes[100] or on companies whose directors are also on the board of the offending company. Such companies are generally considered neutral, and the union violates the secondary boycott provisions if it engages in picketing. However, it may be able to accomplish its objectives through handbilling and other forms of publicity.

Do I have the right to strike while a collective bargaining agreement is in effect?

Generally, no. Most collective bargaining agreements provide that there shall be no strikes during its term. The idea is that in their most recent negotiations the parties made the best bargain they could, and they must abide by those terms until the contract expires and a new one is negotiated. As far as interpreting the terms, the parties can use the arbitration process. Thus there is no need for a strike during the term of the contract. Even when the contract doesn't explicitly say there shall be no strikes, a court will usually imply a no-strike provision.[101]

A union that calls a strike in violation of a no-strike clause may be liable to the employer for any damages it causes. Sometimes a strike will be a spur of the moment action caused by something that upsets the workers, such as the firing of a coworker. If the union does not approve of the strike, it is considered an unauthorized or wildcat strike. In that case the union may not be liable for damages.[102] Nor will the individual worker be liable, for the no-strike promise is made by the union, and the law makes clear that individual workers cannot be held for damages for a union's breach.[103] The individual worker may be subject to discipline, including discharge, for engaging in an unauthorized work stoppage. This depends on the wording of the contract; any disciplinary action is normally subject to review by an arbitrator under the contract's just-cause provision.

In many cases the employer will be able to obtain a court injunction against a strike that violates a no-strike clause. Even though the Norris-LaGuardia Act prevents a court from issuing an injunction in a labor dispute, the Court has held that an injunction against a strike is proper if the purpose of the injunction is to force the union to use the arbitration provisions of the contract rather than strike.[104] The injunction will be upheld if the strike is over something that could be submitted to arbitration, such as a dispute over the meaning of the contract, but the injunction will not issue if the dispute is about something not covered by arbitration, for example, a sympathy strike to support another union.[105] Under this principle, an injunction against a strike has been upheld where the strike is over the company's failure to provide a safe workplace since the union could have challenged this through arbitration.[106]

If I am called in for disciplinary action, may I insist that my union representative be present?

Yes. If you are questioned by your employer about activities that you think may lead to disciplinary action, you have a right to remain silent until your union representative, such as the shop steward, can be with you. This right derives from Section 7 of the NLRA. Under the board's interpretation of that section, upheld by the courts, the worker is entitled to have her representative present "at an investigatory interview that the employee had reasonably believed might result in discipline."[107] This right is known as your *Weingarten right,* named after the case that affirmed it, and is analogous to the right to counsel in a criminal proceeding. The representative, however, may have only a limited right to speak on your behalf. The board has recently held, reversing an earlier decision, that a worker is not entitled to union representation where there is no certified or recognized union in the plant.[108] This means you can't insist on the presence of a union representative if you are disciplined during an organizing campaign.

The Weingarten right only means that you cannot be disciplined for refusing to participate in the investigation until your representative is present. You are still subject to discipline, including discharge, on the basis of any evidence that the employer obtains against you from other sources than the interview.[109] It also appears that the employer can discipline you for any information you give at the interview if you go forward without your union representative. The only thing the employer may not do is discipline you for insisting on your Weingarten rights.[110]

If I have a claim that is protected by the NLRA as well as by the collective bargaining agreement, do I have to use the grievance and arbitration process, or may I take my claim before the board?

This depends on the nature of the claim. If you have a claim under the NLRA that involves an interpretation of the contract, the board will require you to first take your case to arbitration. For example, suppose your employer subcontracted janitorial work. If you filed a charge with the board that this violated NLRA Section 8(a)(5), the board would require you first to take your claim to arbitration.[111] The theory is that your dispute involves a question of interpretation of your collective bargaining agreement, and that is most appropriately resolved through arbitration. After the arbitration is completed, you may ask the board to review that award to make sure it is consistent with the act. However, the board will take a very narrow approach to review, overturning the award only if it is "palpably wrong," that is, "not susceptible to an interpretation consistent with the Act."[112] The board, under some rather complex rules, will only defer to the arbitrator's award if the arbitrator had the opportunity to determine the issue now raised before the NLRB, but it generally finds that such an opportunity existed.[113]

Even if your claim involves an individual right under the NLRA, such as the right not to be disciplined for filing grievances, the board will probably insist that you first go to arbitration, reversing an earlier decision that cases involving individual rights should not be deferred to arbitration.[114] However, the board will not defer a claim to arbitration if your interests are in conflict with those of the union or if there is any other reason why the union will not be able to represent you adequately in arbitration.[115]

What if my claim involves a public right under some law other than the NLRA?

Where your claim involves any other public law, such as a claim under Title VII or a claim of wrongful termination under state law, the general rule is that you have the right to proceed in court without having to first challenge management's action through the grievance procedure and arbitration.[116] However, if your claim also turns on an interpretation of the collective bargaining agreement, then you must resolve the claim through arbitration. The test, according to the Supreme Court, is whether your claim is "inextricably intertwined" with the collective agreement.[117] The NLRB recently held that an employer may not insist to the point of impasse on a clause in the collective agreement that would prohibit an employee from arbitrating a grievance if the employee also pursued the same claim before a federal state agency.[118] But if you arbitrate your claim before you get to court, the court may admit the arbitration award into evidence and give it whatever weight it thinks appropriate.[119]

The Supreme Court has recently made an important exception to this rule. In a workplace with no union representation, if you knowingly agree as part of your employment relationship to submit disputes to arbitration, this may bar you from pursuing your claim in the courts. The Supreme Court reached this conclusion in a case involving a claim of age discrimination under the ADEA (discussed in chapter 13) where the employee had signed an agreement to arbitrate termination disputes as part of his employment as a stock broker.[120] While the full reach of this decision is hard to assess, the Court indicated that its reasoning does not apply if the agreement to arbitrate was made by a union as part of a collective bargaining agreement. Thus, the worker represented by a union may continue to pursue his statutory claims even if the collective bargaining agreement calls for such disputes to be resolved through arbitration.

NOTES

1. There are some excellent reference books that cover your rights under the NLRA. The most comprehensive is *The Developing Labor Law*, Patrick Hardin ed., compiled by the American Bar Association's Section on Labor and Employment Law, 3d ed. (BNA Books, 1992). A shorter reference, but with less cited authority, is Gorman, *Labor Law* (1976). We also recommend the very readable Getman and Pogrebin, *Labor Relations* (Foundation Press, 1988). For a more critical analysis of the labor movement, by a practicing attorney who has represented unions and individual union members, see Thomas Geoghegan, *Which Side Are You On?* (Farrar, Straus, & Giroux, 1991).

2. *E.g.*, *Coppage v. Kansas*, 236 U.S. 1 (1915). The vast array of such cases is collected and discussed in Forbath, *The Shaping of the American Labor Movement*, 102 Harv. L. Rev. 1109 (1989). An appendix listing the critical cases begins at page 1253 of his article.

3. The earliest use of the criminal conspiracy doctrine is the Philadelphia Cordwainers Case, *Commonwealth v. Pullis*, in 1806. The decline in the use of that weapon against unions is traced to *Commonwealth v. Hunt*, 45 Mass. 111 (1842).

4. *Vegelahn v. Guntner*, 167 Mass. 92 (1896) is an early example of the use of an injunction to put an end to picketing. Justice Holmes's dissent was the precursor of the modern view, culminating in the Norris-LaGuardia Act of 1932, which sharply limits the use of injunctions in labor cases.

5. Lawyers should be familiar with the board's rules and regulations, which govern procedures for bringing cases. NLRB Statements of Procedure, 29 C.F.R. pt. 101.

6. NLRA § 2 (2).

7. 5 U.S.C.A. 7101 *et seq.*

8. Railway Labor Act, 45 U.S.C.A. § 151 *et seq.*

9. NLRA § 2 (3). Managerial employees are excluded by a board ruling based on its interpretation of the policy of the NLRA, *NLRB v. Bell Aerospace Co.*, 416 U.S. 267 (1974).

10. NLRA § 8(a)(5).

11. NLRA § 13.

12. *Groves v. Ring Screw Works*, 111 S. Ct. 498 (1990).

13. *J.I. Case v. NLRB*, 321 U.S. 332 (1944).

14. *Ford Motor Co. v. Huffman*, 345 U.S. 330 (1953), *Litton Financial Printing Div'n v. NLRB*, 111 S. Ct. 2215 (1991).

15. *Emporium Capwell Co. v. Western Addition Community Organization*, 420 U.S. 50 (1975).

16. *Vaca v. Sipes*, 386 U.S. 171 (1967).

17. NLRA § 9(a).

18. Section 7 says you may refrain from union activity "except to the extent that such right may be affected by an agreement requiring membership in a labor organization as a condition of employment as authorized in section 8(a)(3)," and a proviso to Section 8(a)(3) says the collective agreement may lawfully require membership in the union "as a condition of employment."

19. *NLRB v. General Motors*, 373 U.S. 734 (1963).

20. *Id.* at 742.

21. There is also a vivid account of an actual organizing campaign in R. Fantasia, *Cultures of Solidarity*, 121–79 (U. Cal. Press, 1988), which covers many of the legal issues discussed here.

22. NLRA § 9(a) sets out the requirement of an appropriate bargaining unit.

23. NLRA § 2(3) excludes supervisors, and § 2(11) defines the term. Other exclusions are listed in § 2(3) as well. On the exclusion of managerial employees see *NLRB v. Bell Aerospace*, 416 U.S. 267 (1974).

24. *American Hospital Ass'n v. NLRB*, 111 S. Ct. 1539 (1991).

25. On the other hand, the board may not give controlling weight to the actual extent of the union's organizing drive, NLRA § 9 (c)(5).

26. There is a good discussion of the ins and outs of an election campaign in Getman and Pogrebin, Labor Relations (Foundation Press, 1988).

27. *Lechmere, Inc. v. NLRB*, 914 F.2d 313 (1st Cir. 1990), *reversed, Lechmere v. NLRB*, 112 S. Ct. 841 (1992).

28. *Lechmere v. NLRB*, 112 S. Ct. 841 (1992). For later cases applying *Lechmere*, see, e.g., *Sparks Nugget, Inc. v. NLRB*, 968 F.2d 991, 140 LRRM 2747 (9th Cir. 1992); *Oakwood Hospital v. NLRB*, 142 LRRM 2121 (6th Cir. 1993).

29. Getman, *Ruminations on the Organizing Process*, 53 U. Chi. L. Rev.

45 (1986); Hurd, *Bottom-Up Organizing: Here in New Haven and Boston*, 8 Labor Research Rev. 5 (1986).

30. *See St. Joseph's Hospital*, 263 NLRB 375 (1982)(employer bears the risk of ambiguity of the rule).

31. *Midland National Life Ins. Co.*, 263 NLRB 127 (1982).

32. NLRA § 8(a)(1).

33. *Sertafilm*, 267 NLRB 682 (1983), *enf'd.*, 753 F.2d 313 (3d Cir., 1985).

34. *E.g.*, *Collectramatic*, 267 NLRB 866 (1983). Compare *LRM Packaging, Inc.*, 308 NLRB No. 117, 141 LRRM 1107 (1992).

35. *Associated Milk Producers*, 255 NLRB 750 (1981).

36. NLRA § 8(c). The expressing of views is protected only if "such expression contains no threat of reprisal or force or promise of benefit."

37. *Clear Pine Mouldings, Inc.*, 268 NLRB 1044 (1984). Compare *KI (USA) Corp.*, _____ NLRB No. 169, 142 LLRM 1105 (1993), where the board held the union had not made racial remarks that might otherwise overturn the election.

38. *NLRB v. Exchange Parts*, 375 U.S. 405 (1964).

39. *NLRB v. Gissel Packing Co.*, 395 U.S. 575 (1969).

40. *Gissel Packing*, 395 U.S. at 617.

41. *Id.*

42. *Gissell Packing, supra* note 39.

43. Getman, *supra* note 29.

44. Weiler, *Promises to Keep*, 96 Harv. L. Rev. 1769 (1983).

45. *Id.* at 1781.

46. *Meyers Industries (Meyers II)*, 281 NLRB No. 118 (1986), review denied, 835 F.2d 1481 (D.C. Cir. 1987). Compare *Mike Yurosek and Son*, 306 NLRB No. 210, 140 LRRM 1001 (1992) where the board found implied concealed activity. See *Harrah's Lake Tahoe Resort Casino*, 307 NLRB No. 29, 140 LRRM 1036 (1992), holding a campaign regarding a stock option plan is not protected.

47. *Bird Engineering*, 270 NLRB No. 1415 (1984).

48. *NLRB v. IBEW (Jefferson Standard)*, 346 U.S. 464 (1953); *New River Industries v. NLRB*, 138 LRRM 2572 (4th Cir. 1991); *George A. Hormel & Co. v. NLRB*, 962 F.2d 1061, 140 LRRM 2324 (D.C. Cir. 1992).

49. *Emporium Capwell Co. v. Western Addition Community Organization*, 420 U.S. 50 (1975).

50. *NLRB v. Washington Aluminum Co.*, 370 U.S. 9 (1962). *Compare TNS, Inc.*, 309 NLRB No. 190, 142 LRRM 1046 (1993).

51. NLRA § 9(c)(5).

52. NLRA § 9(c)(1(A).

53. NLRB Statements of Procedure, § 101.18(a)(4).

54. NLRA § 8(a)(2).

55. 309 NLRB No. 163, 141 LRRM 1001 (1992).
56. Section 2(5) of the act defines a "labor organization" as "any organization of any kind, or any agency or employee representation committee or plan, in which employees participate and which exists for the purpose, in whole or in part, of dealing with employers concerning grievances, labor disputes, wages, rates of pay, hours of employment, or conditions of work."
57. Slip op. at 12.
58. Slip op. at 13.
59. *NLRB v. Cabot Carbon*, 360 U.S. 203 (1958).
60. *E.g., NLRB v. Streamway Div., Scott & Fetzer Co.*, 691 F.2d 288 (6th Cir. 1982), a decision that attempts to distinguish the Supreme Court's earlier *Cabot Carbon* decision, cited in the previous footnote.
61. *See* Piskorski, *Electromation: A Setback to Employee Participation Programs*, 9 Labor Lawyer (1993).
62. NLRA § 8(d).
63. *Detroit Edison v. NLRB*, 440 U.S. 301 (1979).
64. *NLRB v. Katz*, 369 U.S. 736 (1962).
65. NLRA § 8(b)(7)(C).
66. *First National Maintenance Corp. v. NLRB*, 452 U.S. 666 (1981).
67. *Dubuque Packing Co.*, 303 NLRB No. 66, 137 LRRM 1185 (1991).
68. *First National Maintenance, supra* note 66.
69. Atleson, *Management Prerogatives, Plant Closings, and the NLRA*, 11 N.Y.U. Rev. L. & Soc. Change 83 (1983).
70. NLRA § 13.
71. *Audubon Health Care Center*, 268 NLRB 135 (1983); *compare NLRB v. Pace Motor Lines*, 703 F.2d 28 (2d Cir. 1983), holding a one-time strike of short duration protected.
72. *NLRB v. Local 1229 (Jefferson Standard)*, 346 U.S. 464 (1953); *see* the recent decision in *New River Industries v. NLRB*, 138 LRRM 2572 (4th Cir., 1991), following the *Jefferson Standard* approach.
73. NLRA § 8(d).
74. *Clear Pine Mouldings, Inc.*, 268 NLRB 1044, *aff'd.* 765 F.2d 148 (9th Cir. 1985).
75. *Pattern Makers League v. NLRB*, 473 U.S. 95 (1985).
76. *American Shipbuilding Co. v. NLRB*, 380 U.S. 300 (1965).
77. *Harter Equipment*, 280 NLRB 597 (1986), *aff'd.* 829 F.2d 458 (3d Cir. 1987).
78. *Teamsters v. NLRB*, 136 LRRM 2329 (D.C. Cir. 1991).
79. *NLRB v. Business Machines and Office Union (Royal Typewriter)*, 228 F.2d 553 (2d Cir. 1955).
80. *NLRB v. MacKay Radio*, 304 U.S. 333 (1938).
81. *TWA v. Flight Attendants*, 109 S. Ct. 1225 (1989). *See* Westfall,

Striker Replacements and Employee Freedom of Choice, 7 Labor Lawyer 137 (1991).

82. *Laidlaw Corp. v. NLRB,* 414 F.2d 99 (7th Cir. 1969); *Waterbury Hospital v. NLRB,* 139 LRRM 2005 (2d Cir. 1991).

83. *Belknap v. Hale,* 463 U.S. at 503 (1983).

84. *Id.*

85. *See* the discussion of such proposed legislation in Westfall, *Striker Replacements and Employee Freedom of Choice,* 7 Labor Lawyer 137–39 (1991).

86. *N.Y. Telephone Co. v. N.Y.S. Dept. of Labor,* 440 U.S. 519 (1979).

87. *See Baker v. G.M.,* 478 U.S. 621 (1986).

88. *Lechmere v. NLRB,* 112 S. Ct. 841 (1992).

89. *DeBartolo Corp. v. Florida Gulf Coast Council,* 108 S. Ct. 1392 (1988).

90. *See NLRB v. Browning-Ferris,* 700 F.2d. 385 (7th Cir. 1983); *cf. Business Services v. NLRB,* 784 F.2d 442 (2d Cir. 1986).

91. *NLRB v. Warehousemen's Union (Tree Fruits),* 377 U.S. 58 (1964).

92. *NLRB v. Retail Store Employees Union (Safeco),* 444 U.S. 1011 (1980).

93. *DeBartolo Corp. v. Florida Gulf Coast Council, supra* note 89.

94. NLRA § 8(b)(4).

95. *DeBartolo v. Florida Gulf Coast Building Council, supra* note 89.

96. *NLRB v. Business Machine Union (Royal Typewriter Co.),* 228 F.2d 553 (2d Cir. 1955).

97. *Pet, Inc. v. NLRB,* 641 F.2d 545 (8th Cir. 1981).

98. *DeBartolo v. Florida Gulf Coast Building Council, supra* note 89.

99. The various techniques of the corporate campaign and employer responses are discussed in Brown and Bass, *Corporate Campaigns: Employer Responses to Labor's New Weapons,* 6 Labor Lawyer 975 (1990), and Kosanovich, *Dispute Resolution in the 1990s: The Return of Strikes and the Consideration of Other Alternatives,* 6 Labor Lawyer 991 (1990).

100. *Food and Commercial Workers Union (Hormel & Co.),* 281 NLRB No. 135 (1986).

101. *Gateway Coal Co. v. United Mine Workers,* 414 U.S. 368 (1974).

102. *Complete Auto Transit v. Reis,* 451 U.S. 401 (1981); *Carbon Fuel Co. v. Mine Workers,* 444 U.S. 212 (1979).

103. NLRA § 301(b); *Atkinson v. Sinclair Refining Co.,* 370 U.S. 238 (1962); *Complete Auto Transit v. Reis,* 451 U.S. 401 (1981).

104. *Boys Markets v. Retail Clerks Union,* 398 U.S. 235 (1970).

105. *Buffalo Forge Co. v. Steelworkers,* 428 U.S. 397 (1976).

106. *Gateway Coal, supra* note 101. Issues relating to health and safety are discussed in chapter 24.

107. *NLRB v. Weingarten*, 420 U.S. 251 (1975). See *U.S. Postal Service v. NLRB*, 969 F.2d 1064, 140 LRRM 2639 (D.C. Cir. 1992).

108. *Sears, Roebuck & Co.*, 274 NLRB 230 (1985).

109. *Taracorp Industries*, 273 NLRB 221 (1984).

110. See N. Bernstein, *Weingarten: Time for Reconsideration*, 6 Labor Lawyer 1005 (1990).

111. *Collyer Insulated Wire*, 192 NLRB 837 (1971).

112. *Olin Corp.*, 268 NLRB 573 (1984).

113. *Id.* This approach hasn't been warmly accepted by the courts. *See, e.g., Taylor v. NLRB*, 786 F.2d 1516 (11th Cir., 1986).

114. *United Technologies Corp.*, 268 NLRB 557 (1984).

115. *Hendrickson Bros.*, 272 NLRB 438 (1984). The board has been severely criticized for deferring claims that involve basic individual rights under the NLRA. *See, e.g., Taylor v. NLRB*, 786 F.2d 1516 (11th Cir. 1986), and there is a good chance this aspect of the rule will be changed.

116. *Alexander v. Gardner-Denver*, 415 U.S. 36 (1974); *Lingle v. Norge*, 108 S. Ct. 1877 (1988). *Lingle* leaves open how specific the public right must be in order to allow the individual to go to court rather than use the collective agreement.

117. *Lingle v. Norge Division*, 1486 U.S. 399, 408 (1988). *See also Schlacter-Jones v. General Telephone*, 6 IER Cas. 897 (9th Cir. 1991)(while question of employee's right to avoid mandatory drug testing raises constitutional issues, those issues can't be resolved without interpreting the collective bargaining agreement; thus the state court claim is preempted).

118. *Athey Products Corp.*, 303 NLRB No. 8, 138 LRRM 1319 (1991).

119. *Alexander v. Gardner-Denver, supra* note 109.

120. *Gilmer v. Interstate/Johnson Lane Co.*, 11 S. Ct. 1647 (1991).

XIX
Union Membership

Chapter 18 explained how the workers in an appropriate bargaining unit determine whether they wish to be represented by a union for collective bargaining. Most workplaces are not unionized since less than 15% of the workforce has chosen union representation. In this chapter we discuss your rights if you work in a company where the employees are represented by a union. The subject is whether you are required to join the union in a company that is represented by a union, to what extent you may be required to give financial support to the union, and what effect union membership or nonmembership may have on your job.

Once the workers in a bargaining unit have selected union representation, all workers in the unit are bound by that choice. That means that if you are hired in a workplace that is unionized, you are automatically represented by that union. It is required to represent you in administering the collective bargaining agreement and in negotiating new contracts. All workers in the bargaining unit are entitled to the same rights on the job and to the same representation by the union whether or not they belong to the union. No worker is required to join the union in order to get or keep her job or to enjoy the benefits of union representation.

Most workers in an organized workplace choose to become members of the union. They do so because they think it is right to support the union that represents them, because they want to present a united front to management, and in order to have a voice in the governance of the union. However, some workers may belong to the union only because of a mistaken belief that they must join in order to keep their job. In this chapter we explain that a worker is not required to join a union in order to keep his or her job.

A worker who decides not to join the union may be required to pay for the union's cost of representing him or her. Not every dollar of union dues is spent on the costs of collective bargaining. Some portion goes to representation at other units, general organizing, and lobbying and political activity. This proportion of the union's dues may not be charged to the objecting nonmember. The nonmember must pay only for the direct costs of union representation, referred to as his or her "fair share."

We do not deal in this chapter with the rights of union members within their union. Later chapters[1] discuss such internal union matters as the right to speak out in union meetings and to elect officials of the union. This chapter is concerned only with the requirements of union membership and its effect upon a person's job.

Can I be required to join a union in order to get or keep a job?

No. In 1947 Congress outlawed the closed shop. Under the closed shop, an employer and union lawfully could agree that the employer would hire only those employees who were already members of the union. Congress felt that this rule limited workers' rights of free choice, so it allowed the union and management to agree to a union shop.[2] The text of Section 8(a)(3) of the National Labor Relations Act (NLRA) says that in a union shop a person may be required to join a union within 30 days of her hire as a condition of keeping her job. However, the Supreme Court has stated explicitly that the statute does not require a person to actually join the union in order to keep her job, but merely requires her to pay the appropriate dues and initiation fees. Membership, says the Court, is thus "whittled down to its financial core."[3]

NLRA Section 8(a)(3) prohibits discrimination by an employer against an employee on the basis of that employee's membership or lack of membership in a union. However, a proviso to this section permits a union and employer to agree to a contractual provision that "require[s] as a condition of employment membership [in the union] on or after the thirtieth day following the beginning of such employment or the effective date of such agreement, whichever is the later." Most collective bargaining agreements contain such a provision, usually referred to as a *union security clause*. A typical one such as you might find in your collective bargaining agreement provides:

> It shall be a condition of employment that all employees covered by this agreement shall become and remain mem-

bers of the union in good standing on or before the thirtieth day after this contract is signed, and all new employees covered by this agreement shall become and remain members of the union in good standing on or before the thirtieth day after their first day of work.

Employees whose membership in the union is terminated by reason of the failure of the employee to tender the periodic dues and initiation fees uniformly levied against all Union members in conformity with the Constitution and By-Laws of the Union shall not be retained in the employ of the Company.[4]

The Court's conclusion that such required membership is limited to the "financial core" is derived from another portion of Section 8(a)(3), which provides that the employer may not terminate employment on grounds of nonmembership in the union if membership is denied "for reasons other than the failure of the employee to tender the periodic dues and the initiation fees uniformly required as a condition of acquiring or retaining membership." The Court concluded that since the proviso only protects the union's interest in the payment of dues and initiation fees, the employer and union may not require actual membership in the union as a condition of employment.

Isn't the text of the typical union security clause misleading, since it appears to require me to join the union as a condition of employment, while the Court has said that I needn't join?
Some have argued that such a clause is indeed misleading. It can be especially misleading if it is explained to the worker, for example, by a personnel director who informs the worker that he must join the union within 30 days of his hire. Defenders of such a clause reply that the typical union security clause does no more than repeat the language of the proviso of Section 8(a)(3), quoted above, and there can't be anything unlawful about that. There is no definitive caselaw on whether such a clause violates the act or whether it is unlawful or a violation of the union's duty of fair representation for the company or union to tell a worker that he must join the union to keep his job.[5]
Whether or not the union and the employer are required

to correctly explain the obligations under a union security clause, you now know from this discussion that you need not join the union as a condition of employment but may limit your membership to financial core support of the union. It may be in the best interests of the union to give workers an accurate explanation of their obligations, for in the long run a union's bargaining position may be stronger if its membership is comprised of workers who make a knowing and voluntary choice to join. We will discuss the advantages and disadvantages of union membership in a later question below.

What is my obligation to join a union in a "right to work" state?

In some states even the limited form of "financial core" support of the union is prohibited. These are known as *right-to-work states*.[6] In such states it is unlawful for a union and employer to make union membership a condition of employment. Since the union and employer cannot compel membership in the union at all in such states, the Supreme Court ruling that limits that membership to its financial core simply does not apply. Some right-to-work states outlaw agreements that require union membership as a condition of employment but permit the union and employer to agree to an agency fee arrangement.[7] The agency fee arrangement is quite common in the public sector in many states.[8] In an agency shop the employee is not required to join the union but is required to pay his share of the costs of representation. The amount of such payment is discussed in a question below on the nonmember's fair share obligation.

What are my obligations of membership in other sectors such as public employment or the construction or maritime industry?

Most states provide that public employers and public employee unions may agree upon an agency fee arrangement, in which the worker is required to contribute to the costs of representation but is not required to join the union. Such a result is dictated by the fact that the public employer is governed by the United States Constitution, and a requirement of membership in a union would violate the worker's right of association under the First Amendment.[9]

In the construction and maritime industries, hiring is often done through a "hiring hall." While you are not required to join a union in order to use its hiring hall, as a practical matter union membership may affect your ability to get a job in those industries.

Separate provision is made under Section 19 of the NLRA for individuals whose religious convictions prevent them from joining or supporting labor unions. Such employees may pay the equivalent of dues and initiation fees to a charitable organization.[10]

Is my decision whether or not to join a union important? What factors should I consider?

Your decision is very important. As we saw in chapter 18, when a union is selected by the majority of the workers in the bargaining unit it becomes the representative of all the workers in the unit. It speaks for all employees in the bargaining unit, whether or not they supported or joined the union. Even if you are opposed to union representation and voted against the union during the election or were hired after the election, that union now has a duty to represent you. You in turn have an obligation to pay the union your fair share of the costs of representing you. Since the union is going to be your advocate in the workplace and since you are going to pay for it, it may be to your advantage to join the union in order to have a voice in its governance. We will see in chapters 21 and 22 that union members have important rights in the governance of their union. However, those rights of participation are almost always limited to union members. Another reason for you to join the union is that the union may be able to do a more effective job of representing you if it can show the employer that it has the strong support of the bargaining unit. The most convincing measure of this may be the percentage of workers who are members of the union.

If you join the union, you must pay the full amount of valid union dues and initiation fees.[11] This is usually a larger sum than if you do not join the union but limit your obligation to payment of your fair share of representation. We will discuss this further in the next question.

If you join the union, you are also bound by the union's rules and regulations as contained in its constitution and bylaws. A common union rule that may affect your employment requires members to honor valid picket lines during a strike. Under such a rule you may be fined if you cross a valid picket line, and under typical union procedures a fine of up to the amount you earned during the strike may be imposed and collected in court. However, such a rule is not binding on nonmembers. The Court has recently held that you may resign from the union at any time in order to avoid the force of such a rule.[12]

What is the extent of my fair share obligation if I choose not to join the union?

In its recent decision in *Beck v. Communications Workers*,[13] the Court held that for workers covered by the NLRA the "financial core" obligation of membership is limited to union activities "germane to collective bargaining, contract administration, and grievance adjustment."[14] The Court held that the union could not collect dues from objecting employees for costs of organizing employees of other employers, lobbying for labor legislation, and participating in social, charitable, and political events. In the *Beck* case, about 79% of the dues normally collected could not be charged to objecting nonmembers, but this may be an atypically high percentage.[15] A later Supreme Court decision has drawn the same sorts of lines for unions in the public sector.[16]

The Court held first that the public sector union may not charge objecting dissenters for the costs of the union's lobbying and political activities. The union in the *Lehnert* case represented public school teachers. Even though the union's lobbying and political efforts were aimed at increasing public funding and support of teaching, which might ultimately benefit the dissenting teachers, the Court concluded that the First Amendment precluded the union from charging the dissenters for these activities.

As for those activities that are not political, the Court held that they could be charged to objecting members even if they are not directly related to their bargaining unit, as long as they have some indirect benefit that may inure to the bargaining unit. The Court recognized that these are difficult lines to draw. It upheld the lower court's allowance of charges for costs concerning general professional development, participation in union conventions, and even expenses in another unit in preparation for a possible strike that would have been illegal under Michigan law.

The Court has also decided the same sorts of issues for employees covered by the Railway Labor Act (RLA). While the earlier Railway Labor Act cases protected nonmembers from being charged for the costs of the union's political activities,[17] later cases focused on the propriety of charging nonmembers for union activities that did not involve political activity or lobbying. The *Ellis* case[18] prohibits unions from charging nonmembers for costs of activities that, while not political, go beyond the narrow costs of representation in the particular bargaining unit.[19]

While each of the three major Supreme Court cases deals with a different segment of the workplace (*Lehnert* with the rights of public employees under the Constitution, *Ellis* with the rights of railroad workers under the RLA, and *Beck* with the rights of most other employees under the NLRA), the principles are essentially the same, even if the statutory and Constitutional texts, and the theories, are different. Under all three tests there are close factual questions as to whether certain activities are germane to collective bargaining and therefore chargeable to employees who are not full union members or who object to charges under an agency fee system. Political activities, however, may not be charged to objectors under any of these systems.

In addition to the restrictions that derive from labor relations statutes or the Constitution, a union is prohibited under the Federal Election Campaign Act from contributing to candidates in federal elections, although it can accomplish this objective by establishing political action committees (PACs) to which members may contribute voluntarily.[20]

Are there any guidelines that help me determine what charges the union may impose on a nonmember?

Yes. The general counsel of the NLRB has issued guidelines for determining the proper scope of expenditures for unions covered by the NLRA.[21] The guidelines follow the decisions developed under the Railway Labor Act and in the public sector, both as to the scope of expenditures that may properly be charged to objecting nonmembers and as to the procedures that the union must follow in allowing nonmembers to challenge expenditures. The guidelines divide expenditures into two classifications. "Representational" expenditures may be charged to nonmembers. They include "expenses relating to collective bargaining, contract administration, and grievances. . . . National conventions, and union business meetings and social activities open to members and nonmembers are also chargeable." "Non-representational" expenditures, not chargeable to nonmembers, include "organizing expenses, and those litigation expenses that do not directly concern the bargaining unit. . . . Union publications are chargeable only to the extent they report on the union's representational activities. Expenditures for political campaigns and lobbying are not chargeable to non-members."

Unions contend that these guidelines are too restrictive since many union activities such as organizing competitors and lobbying for legislation that affects the workplace have a direct impact on the bargaining unit and ought to be chargeable to nonmembers. It remains to be seen whether unions will be able to persuade the board and the courts to enlarge the area of activities properly chargeable to a nonmember under *Beck*.[22]

A few lower court decisions since *Beck* have provided some guidance on the scope of the fair share dues of nonmembers. For example, a court held that it was permissible for the airline pilots' union to charge nonmembers with the expenditures to pay flight attendants who honored a picket line against another airline, to pay striking pilots at other airlines their lost wages, to set up a strike fund, and to support certain litigation. The court felt this was for the legitimate purpose of "creating a strong union" that could perform its duties as bargaining agent.[23]

What procedures must a union follow in determining the fair share payments of an objecting nonmember?[24]

Because it is so hard to draw lines between expenditures that are or are not germane to collective bargaining, the courts have insisted upon adequate procedures within the union for determining the proper fair share.

The leading case dealing with procedures for determining fair share payments is *Teachers Union v. Hudson*.[25] While *Hudson* involved a public sector union and was decided under the First Amendment, the procedures and principles validated by the Court will probably apply to arrangements under the

NLRA and the RLA. Indeed, the NLRB general counsel's guidelines state that the board will follow the procedures validated by the Court in *Hudson*.

In *Hudson*, the Supreme Court ruled on the use of an arrangement between the Chicago Teachers' Union and the Chicago Board of Education for determining the appropriate dues payments of objecting nonmembers. The procedure that was challenged in *Hudson* allowed the union to first determine the appropriate "proportionate share" of union dues that it could charge a nonmember; in *Hudson* the union set this figure at 95% of the normal dues. The nonmember was required first to pay the stated dues and then to object to the proportionate share by a written appeal to the union president. The objection would then be heard by the union's executive committee, with an appeal to an arbitrator selected and paid for by the union. The appeal to the Supreme Court did not call for the Court to decide whether the amount collected was proper; the Court's consideration was limited to the adequacy of the procedures agreed to by the parties.

The Court found the procedures invalid in several respects. First, because the nonmember had to pay dues before her challenge could be heard, the union might use her funds for improper purposes. Second, the procedure failed to provide the challenging employee with adequate information about the basis for the union's charges. The Court concluded that once the nonunion employee raises an objection, the burden is on the union to justify the share rather than on the individual to challenge it. Third, the arbitration procedure did not provide a "reasonably prompt decision by an impartial decisionmaker"; the Court was especially critical of the union's control over the selection of the arbitrator.

In striking down this arrangement, the Court established the groundrules for proper procedures: "[T]he constitutional requirements for the Union's collection of agency fees include an adequate explanation of the basis for the fee, a reasonably prompt opportunity to challenge the amount of the fee before an impartial decisionmaker, and an escrow for the amounts reasonably in dispute while such challenges are pending."[26]

The Court observed that "a full-dress administrative hearing, with evidentiary safeguards" was not required and that "an expeditious arbitration" might be adequate. The Court also stated that the arbitrator's decision would not "receive preclusive effect in any subsequent Sec. 1983 action,"[27] thus indicating that courts will examine arbitrators' awards in these cases more closely than they normally do; as explained in chapter 18, arbitration awards are usually immune from extensive judicial review. The case was remanded for the lower courts to pass upon the precise form of the new arrangement, and the Court did not give a definitive model of a proper mechanism for determining fair share. Therefore, other lower court decisions are useful in evaluating fair share agreements. Some recent cases applying the *Hudson* guidelines are noted in the accompanying footnote.[28]

One of the most significant requirements imposed by lower courts is that before a public sector union may impose charges on a nonmember it must provide a detailed breakdown of all union expenditures, listing those that are chargeable to nonmembers and those that are not. The breakdown must include a certification by an accountant that the amounts listed are actually expended. However, the accountant is not required to determine whether the various categories are appropriate charges. If the nonmember questions those allocations, he or she may then challenge them under the procedures outlined in *Hudson*.[29]

The guidelines for fair share procedures established by the NLRB's general counsel may be more stringent than those imposed by the Court in *Hudson*.[30] Under the NLRB guidelines, the union must notify nonmembers once a year of the percentage of union dues spent for nonrepresentational activities; those nonmembers who object need not pay for such expenditures. If a nonmember objects to this allocation, the union must follow the procedures outlined in *Hudson* and provide the objector with detailed information about the expenditures of the previous accounting year as verified by an independent accountant. In addition to the right under *Hudson* to challenge these expenditures before an independent arbitrator, the general counsel's guidelines provide that the nonmember may file his challenge with the NLRB. However, if the union has in place an arbitration system that complies with the *Hudson* standards, the board may defer considering the challenge until the arbitration is completed. As under the *Hudson* rule, the union must place the disputed amounts into an interest-bearing escrow account until the matter is resolved.

Some courts have held that the *Hudson* procedural requirements do not apply to cases that are not in the public sector. Thus, the Railway Labor Act may require procedures that are less stringent than those under *Hudson*.[31] Cases under the NLRA may also be exempt from those procedures; however, they would be governed by the more stringent guidelines of the NLRB general counsel.[32]

What can happen to me if I don't pay my periodic dues and initiation fee or fair share equivalent?

You can lose your job. Therefore, you must take very seriously your obligation to pay your dues or fair share equivalent. As indicated earlier, Section 8(a)(3) of the NLRA allows a union and company to make an agreement that conditions your employment on your membership in the union. While this obligation has been narrowed so that you may limit your membership obligation to payment of your fair share of the initiation fee and periodic dues, if you fail to make these payments on a timely basis the employer may fire you. Most collective bargaining agreements have such a provision, and most unions will insist that the employer enforce it.[33] Once you fail to make these payments on a timely basis, you cannot save your job by later paying what you owe. This rule has been followed because otherwise an employer might continually grant extensions to delinquent employees, and this might undermine the union's legitimate interest in prompt enforcement of union security arrangements.

Because of these serious consequences of not paying your dues or fair share on a timely basis, it may be to your advantage to agree to a dues deduction arrangement as discussed further below.

What defenses do I have if the union and employer attempt to discharge me under a union security clause?

You have several defenses to being discharged under a union security clause. First, the employer may discharge you only for nonpayment of the regular periodic dues and initiation fees. Failure to pay anything else is not grounds for discharge. For example, if the union fines you and you refuse to pay the fine, the employer may not discharge you. Nor may the employer fire you for not paying some other charge, such as a special assessment. Those fines and charges may be legitimate under the terms of your membership in the union, but the only way the union can enforce them is to suspend or expel you from the union or bring a court action to collect them.[34] Finally, the union and employer must follow any procedures agreed to in the collective bargaining agreement or under the union constitution before they may invoke a union security clause. These procedures may include a notice of the charges and a hearing.

While the union security clause may oblige you to pay your initiation fee as a condition of employment, NLRA Section 8(b)(5) prohibits excessive initiation fees.

You may be able to avoid the effects of a union security clause if you can show that the union and employer have enforced it inconsistently. For example, if the employer normally provides a grace period to delinquent employees and doesn't give you such leeway, the employer may not fire you. This is especially so if you can show that the employer changed the rules on you because of some reason unrelated to your failure to pay dues. And, as a leading Supreme Court case has established, if there is any doubt as to exactly what the union security clause requires, it will be interpreted in your favor. For example, if the language of the clause can be construed to allow you an extension, the court will read it that way.[35] The union's duty of fair representation may also limit its ability to invoke a union security clause to cause your discharge.[36]

Finally, the NLRA provides explicitly that the employer may not terminate an employee who is denied union membership for any other reason than nonpayment of periodic dues and initiation fees.[37] This means, for example, that an employee cannot be fired if he was expelled from the union for supporting a rival union. Section 8(a)(3) provides that the employer may not terminate the employee if the employer has "reasonable grounds for believing" that the employee was denied membership in the union for reasons other than nonpayment. The "reasonable grounds" provision is designed to protect the employer who is caught in the middle of a claim by the union that the employee did not pay his dues and a claim by the employee that there is actually some other reason why the union is insisting that he be fired, for example, because of his political activities within the union.

If you believe your termination under a union security clause was improper, you may challenge it under Section 8(a)(3) of the NLRA by filing a charge with the regional office of the NLRB. Bear in mind that you must file such a charge within 6 months of the time you learn that the employer is firing you. If the NLRB agrees with you, it may order your reinstatement to your job and require the employer or the union to pay you your lost earnings.

What is a dues authorization and how does it work?

The law permits the union and employer to agree to a "check-off" provision under the NLRA.[38] Under such an arrangement, if an employee voluntarily signs a dues authorization form, the employer will withhold from her paycheck her regular dues and pay those directly to the union. As a safeguard to the employee, such an authorization must be in writing and the employee must have the option to terminate it at least once a year. Such an arrangement is entirely voluntary. The employee may find it to her advantage to authorize withholding of dues or fair share amounts. Since she is required to pay them anyway, the authorization eliminates any danger of termination for failure to pay dues.

A recent Supreme Court case, discussed in a question below, permits a union member to resign membership at any time in order to avoid the imposition of a union fine. That case does not discuss whether the member may terminate an otherwise irrevocable checkoff authorization upon resignation from the union or may modify the authorization to cover only the payment of the nonmember's fair share rather than payment of full union dues.

The NLRB has taken the position that normally when a member resigns from his union, that terminates any dues authorization clause that he signed. This is based on the assumption that normally the employee's dues authorization was intended to be effective only for so long as he remained a member of the union. The board will hold the employee to the full year of his dues authorization when he resigns only if there is explicit language in the checkoff provision that shows that the authorization goes beyond the period of membership in the union.[39]

Does the union have the right to discipline me because of the way I perform my job?

Yes, if you are a member of the union. Under limited circumstances, the union may discipline you because of the way you perform your job. However, the union can only fine you, expel you, or take other actions against you as a member. It cannot affect your job status. The union may only discipline you if you are a member of the union, and if the offense is clearly stated in the union constitution and bylaws. The union must follow its stated procedures for imposing such discipline. There also may be some public policy limitations on the kinds of conduct for which the union may impose discipline.[40] As discussed below, you may avoid further union disciplinary action by resigning from the union.

A common example of a union restriction on the way you perform your job is a provision that a member must be loyal to the union during a strike and may not cross a lawful picket line and report to work. Many union constitutions provide that you may be fined an amount equivalent to what you earned by crossing the picket line. While such a rule might seem to discriminate against an employee for not engaging in union activity, a right protected in Section 7 and Section 8(b)(1)(A) of the NLRA, a proviso to the latter section preserves "the right of a labor organization to prescribe its own rules with respect to the acquisition or retention of membership." In a leading case, the Supreme Court has upheld the union's power to enforce through fine or expulsion a union prohibition on crossing a picket line. The Court stated:

> Integral to . . . federal labor policy has been the power in the chosen union to protect against erosion its status under that policy through reasonable discipline of members who violate rules and regulations governing membership . . . . Congress was operating within the context of the "contract theory" of the union-member relationship which widely prevailed at that time. The efficacy of a contract is precisely its legal enforceability.[41]

Under such reasoning, the courts have upheld a variety of disciplinary provisions in union constitutions. For example, the Supreme Court upheld a provision that fined a member who exceeded stated production quotas without banking his excess earnings.[42] On the other hand, some disciplinary provisions have been struck down as contrary to public policy, for example, a provision that required a member to exhaust internal union remedies before filing an unfair labor practice charge, or before initiating a decertification proceeding to remove a union as bargaining agent.[43]

In order to collect such a fine or expel the member for his offense or failure to pay the fine, the union must follow the procedures spelled out in the union constitution. In addition, the offense must be clearly stated so that the member knows what is expected of her. Finally, the union's procedures must comply with the LMRDA—for example, Section 609, which provides safeguards against improper discipline. These required procedures include adequate notice of the charges and provision of a fair hearing. Some of these points are discussed further in chapter 21.

However, the union may not enforce its disciplinary actions by causing the employer to terminate the employee. Section 8(a)(3) permits an employer to honor a union's request to terminate an employee only for the failure to pay periodic dues and assessments. The Court has held that termination from a job may not be used to enforce any other internal union obligation.[44]

The rules discussed here also apply to union discipline for matters that do not relate to the worker's job, for example, prohibitions against supporting a rival union. Such discipline must be imposed in accordance with proper procedures and may not affect the worker's job. Some of these issues are discussed in chapter 21.

May I resign from a union in order to avoid discipline?

Yes. Even if union discipline cannot affect a worker's job it can have a substantial impact on the worker. For example, if a union can impose and enforce a large fine, this may be a real deterrent to the member's conduct. A union may attempt to fine a member who crosses a picket line the full amount of his earnings during the strike. If the worker knows the union can collect that fine in court, this may convince the worker not to cross the picket line. As a result, the fine may inhibit the worker's right under Section 7 not to engage in concerted activity.

The Court has dealt with this problem by holding that the union member can avoid the imposition of a fine by resigning from the union. In a recent case involving a fine for crossing a picket line,[45] the Supreme Court held that a member may resign from the union at any time, even if the union constitution attempts to restrict the times when a member may resign. The Court said, "By allowing employees to resign from a union at any time, Section 8(a)(3) protects the employee whose views come to diverge from those of his union."[46] In the case in question, the former member resigned before he crossed the picket line. It is unclear whether the member may be fined for any violation committed before he tendered his resignation.

The board has taken the position that a union violates Section 8(b)(1)(A) of the act if it threatens a person who has resigned from the union with disciplinary action for crossing a picket line.[47]

Are there any industries in which membership in a union is required as a condition of hiring?

No, but there are industries in which membership may be a factor in your getting a job. In some industries, such as construction and maritime, where the length of employment may be short and seasonal, it may be impractical for the employer to do the hiring. In those industries, the employers and union may agree that hiring will be done, sometimes exclusively, through a hiring hall operated by the union.[48] Typically, jobs are posted as they arise, and priority goes to employees with greatest seniority in the industry or to those who have been out of work the longest. The Supreme Court has upheld the use of hiring halls in these industries, even though the very existence of the hiring hall may encourage union membership. The Court found that absent proof that the hiring hall was used to favor union members, it would not be deemed unlawful.[49]

Under the terms of Section 8(a)(3) of the act, the hiring hall arrangement may not be limited to union members, for that would violate the prohibition against discrimination in hiring based on union activity. Nonunion members must be allowed to use the hiring hall and to receive referrals on a nondiscriminatory basis, but the union may charge the nonmember a service fee for the use of the hiring hall.[50] In operating the hiring hall, the union may provide for classifications among employees, giving priority to those who have already been employed in the industry over those who have not. Such classifications have been challenged as favoring the hiring of union members since most employees who have prior experience probably have also become union members, but for the most part these classifications have been upheld.[51] Some hiring hall arrangements are specifically validated in Section 8(f) of the act.[52] A union's obligation to run its hiring hall fairly goes beyond not making referrals on the basis of union membership. The union is required to refer all workers on a fair and systematic basis and can get into trouble when it violates any of its normal rules.[53]

May the union and employer give favored treatment to union stewards?

Yes, in certain cases. Many collective bargaining agreements provide that union stewards have top seniority in their department. This benefit is designed to reward the steward for her extra efforts and as an incentive for other employees to assume this responsibility, which usually does not carry extra pay. The NLRB has approved of granting such seniority for purposes of determining layoff and recall rights but not for other purposes, such as vacation benefits and bidding on other jobs. The board reasons that since all members of the bargaining unit benefit from the steward's work, limited preferences may be given the steward even if this tends to reward employees who actively engage in union activities.[54]

NOTES

1. Internal union matters are discussed in chapters 21 and 22, below.
2. The history of the legislative shift from the closed shop to the union shop is discussed in *Communications Workers v. Beck*, 487 U.S. 735, 748–50, 108 S. Ct. 2641, 2650 (1988).

   A similar arrangement is in effect under the Railway Labor Act. Until 1951 there was no such thing as even an open shop; under that statute workers were free to join or not join unions as they saw fit. In 1951 the Railway Labor Act was amended to provide for the same sort of open shop system as under the 1947 NLRA amendments. Thus the two statutes moved to the same point but from very different directions. In the *Beck* case, the Court held that the similar language of the two statutes after the 1947 and 1951 amendments should be given the same interpretation.

3. *NLRB v. General Motors*, 373 U.S. 734, 742 (1963).

4. This clause is patterned after one in an agreement between Kinetic Dispersion Corporation and Local 55, United Auto Workers. The company is no longer in operation. The agreement may be found in the statutory supplement to Rabin, Silverstein, and Schatzki, *Labor and Employment Law* 186, 188 (West, 1988).

5. *See Pacific Bell*, 283 NLRB No. 163, 125 LRRM 1251, *enf'd without opinion*, 841 F.2d 1128 (9th Cir. 1988).

6. Section 14(b) of the NLRA allows states to prohibit collective bargaining agreements that require membership as a condition of employment. Twenty-one states have some form of a right to work provision, *See* 2 Dev. Lab. Law 1391–92 (1983), and Fifth Supplement 591 (1988).

7. The right to work measures of 13 states plainly outlaw even the payment of a fair share of the costs of representation, by prohibiting the payment of an agency fee, that is, the equivalent of union dues. Six other states have construed their statutes to prohibit such payments, 2 Dev. Lab. Law 1394 (1983). The right of a state to prohibit the agency shop was upheld in *Retail Clerks v. Schermerhorn*, 373 U.S. 746 (1963).

8. The constitutionality of agency shop arrangements in the public sector was affirmed in *Abood v. Detroit Board of Education*, 431 U.S. 209 (1977). These arrangements are discussed, and some indication given of their frequency, in Kelly, Union Security in Public Sector Contracts, in *The Evolving Process—Collective Negotiations in Public Employment* 148–65 (Labor Relations Press, 1985).

9. *Abood v. Detroit Bd. of Ed.*, *supra* note 8, at 240–41; *Lehnert v. Ferris Faculty Association*, 111 S. Ct. 1950, 1960–61 (1991).

10. We do not discuss this area further in this chapter. For an excellent overview, see Weinstock, *The Union's Duty to Represent Conscientious Objectors*, 3 Labor Lawyer 163 (1987).

11. The leading case on the obligation of nonmembers to pay their fair share of the costs of representation, *Communications Workers v. Beck*, *supra* note 2, was concerned only with the rights of employees who choose not to join the union. The rights of employees who willingly assume full membership obligations are not affected by the

decision. *Id.* at 758–60, 108 S. Ct. at 2655–56. *See also Kidwell v. TCIE*, 138 LRRM 2537 (4th Cir. 1991); *NLRB v. Associated Diamond Cabs, Inc.*, 702 F.2d 912 (11th Cir. 1983). Those workers who join the union are required to pay whatever dues, initiation fees, and assessments are required by their union in accordance with the union constitution and by-laws. However, such consenting members can only be terminated from their job for failure to pay dues and initiation fees.

It is not clear whether a worker who chooses to join the union may terminate that arrangement at any time and limit his obligations to payment of his fair share of the costs of representation. A leading case holds that a member may resign from the union at any time and terminate his obligation to abide by union rules, *Pattern Makers v. NLRB*, 473 U.S. 95 (1985). However, this case dealt with the resigning member's right to escape a union rule that prohibits him from crossing a picket line. It was concerned with the impact of union membership upon a worker's job. This issue is raised in a question below.

12. *Pattern Makers v. NLRB*, 473 U.S. 95 (1985).
13. *Beck v. Communications Workers, supra* note 2.
14. *Id.* at 745, 108 S. Ct. at 2648.
15. *Id.* at 740, 108 S. Ct. at 2645. The district court concluded that the union had failed to show by "clear and convincing" evidence that more than 21% of its funds were expended on collective bargaining matters.
16. *Lehnert v. Ferris Faculty Association*, 111 S. Ct. 1950 (1991).
17. *Machinists v. Street*, 367 U.S. 740 (1961). *Compare Railway Employees v. Hanson*, 351 U.S. 225 (1956).
18. *Ellis v. Railway Clerks*, 466 U.S. 435 (1984).
19. A similar conclusion is reached in the more recent decision of *Lehnert v. Ferris Faculty Association*, 111 S. Ct. 1950 (1991).
20. 2 U.S.C. § 441(b), formerly LMRA § 304.
21. NLRB General Counsel Memorandum (Nov. 15, 1988), 129 LRRM 399–400. This looseleaf reference is generally bound and appears in the Annual Yearbook published by BNA.
22. It is possible that unions and other interested parties will be able to refine the criteria for determining fair share obligations by further litigation before the NLRB. Although the general counsel has issued guidelines, these have not been tested by litigation before the NLRB. The *Beck* case, *supra* note 2, for example, was reviewed by the Court on the theory that the union breached its duty of fair representation in charging nonmembers for more than their fair share. Such claims are cognizable in the courts and are not confined by the doctrine of primary jurisdiction to litigation before the NLRB. While the union

in *Beck* defended its charges under the language of Section 8(a)(3) of the NLRA, the scope of that statute was considered by the Court and not by the NLRB. It may be that courts will follow guidelines that are developed by the board after litigation.

23. *Pilots Against Illegal Dues v. ALPA*, 131 LRRM 2514 (D. Colo. 1989). *See also Paid v. Air Line Pilots*, 137 LRRM 2963 (10th Cir. 1991), for an example of the deference a court may give to a union's judgment about the appropriateness of charges. *See* Rhode, *Section 8(a)(3) Limitation to the Union's Use of Dues-Equivalents: The Implications of* Communications Workers of America v. Beck, 57 Cinc. L. Rev. 1567 (1989).

24. Two excellent articles on this subject are Matsis, *Procedural Rights of Fair Share Objectors after* Hudson *and* Beck, 6 The Labor Lawyer 251 (1990), and Florey, *Fair Share Arbitration: A Case for Common Sense*, 44 Arb. J. 35 (1989).

25. 475 U.S. 292, 106 S. Ct. 666 (1986).

26. *Hudson*, 475 U.S. at 310, 106 S. Ct. at 1078.

27. *Id.* at 308, n.21, 106 S. Ct. at 1077, n.21.

28. *See Ping v. NEA*, 131 LRRM 2082 (7th Cir. 1989); *Gilpin v. AFSCME*, 131 LRRM 2636 (7th Cir. 1989); *Tierney v. Toledo*, 824 F.2d 1497 (6th Cir.1987); on remand, 131 LRRM 26684 (N.D. Ohio 1988); *Pilots v. ALPA*, 131 LRRM 2514 (D. Colo. 1989); *Paid v. Air Line Pilots*, 137 LRRM 2963 (10th Cir. 1991). On recovery of counsel fees under 42 U.S.C. § 1988, see *Dixon v. Chicago*, 138 LRRM 2925 (7th Cir. 1991). *Compare Mitchell v. Los Angeles Unified School District*, 963 F.2d 258, 140 LRRM 2121 (9th Cir. 1992) (nonunion members must give union written notice of their objection to paying for nonrepresentational activities; otherwise they must pay an agency fee equal to full union dues).

29. *Dashiell v. Montgomery County*, 925 F.2d 750, 136 LRRM 2550 (4th Cir. 1991); *Hudson v. Chicago Teachers Union*, 922 F.2d 1306, 136 LRRM 2153 (7th Cir. 1991).

30. NLRB General Counsel Memorandum 88-14 (Nov. 15, 1988). *See* the reference in note 21 *supra*.

31. *See Price v. Auto Workers*, 927 F.2d 88, 136 LRRM 2738 (2d Cir. 1991); *EEOC v. Univ. of Detroit*, 701 F. Supp. 1326 (E.D. Mich., 1988); *Hohe v. Casey*, 130 LRRM 2682 (3d Cir. 1989).

32. *Compare Price v. Auto Workers*, 927 F.2d 88, 136 LRRM 2738 (2d Cir. 1991)) *with Crawford v. ALPA*, 870 F.2d 155, 160 (4th Cir. 1989). We are indebted to W.V. Siebert and Mary S. Vick, attorneys in Denver, Colo., for the identifying some of these sources. Their research is contained in a paper on *Beck* and its progeny prepared for a meeting of the American Bar Association's Section of Labor and

Employment Law, Committee on Developments under the NLRA, March, 1990.

33. *See Amalgamated Ass'n. of Ry. Employees v. Lockridge,* 403 U.S. 274 (1971). The union and employer are probably required to treat full members and fair share payers the same when enforcing a union security clause. *See Hospital Employees,* 228 NLRB 1500 (1977), *enf'd* 567 F. 2d 831 (8th Cir. 1977).

34. A lawsuit by a union to collect a fine is subject to ordinary contract defenses under state law; for example, you may be able to establish that the basis for collecting the fine or the procedures followed are not those prescribed in the union constitution, which is the contract between you and your union. You may be able to show that the fine is unconscionable under state law. For a suggestion that your defenses may also be raised in federal court, *see Wooddell v. IBEW,* 112 S. Ct. 494 (1991). And you may have a defense that the fine is unreasonable under the NLRA. In such a case you would move to dismiss the suit for collection of the fine on grounds of federal preemption. *See NLRB v. Allis-Chalmers,* 388 U.S. 175 (1967). Of course, as we point out in a question below, you may avoid exposure to fines entirely if you resign from the union before committing the acts in question.

35. *Amalgamated Ass'n. of Ry. Employees v. Lockridge,* 403 U.S. 274 (1971).

36. *See Brand Mid-Atlantic, Inc.,* 304 NLRB No. 110, 139 LRRM 1039 (1991).

37. Section 8(a)(3) states:

> Provided further, That no employer shall justify any discrimination against an employee for nonmembership in a labor organization (A) if he has reasonable grounds for believing that such membership was not available to the employee on the same terms and conditions generally applicable to other members, or (B) if he has reasonable grounds for believing that membership was denied or terminated for reasons other than the failure of the employee to tender the periodic dues and the initiation fees uniformly required as a condition of acquiring or retaining membership.

Part (A) of this proviso has limited practical significance now that the Court has ruled that the membership obligation that may be enforced under Section 8(a)(3) is limited to "the financial core," that is, payment of periodic dues and initiation fees.

38. Such an arrangement is permitted under LMRA Section 302(c)(4), provided "that the employer has received from each employee, on whose account such deductions are made, a written assignment which

shall not be irrevocable for a period of more than one year, or beyond the termination date of the applicable collective agreement, whichever occurs sooner."

This text applies only to employees covered by the NLRA. The statutory rules governing dues authorization clauses for public sector employees are different from state to state and in the federal sector and are beyond the scope of our discussion. Postal employees are covered by a different arrangement too, discussed in note 39, *infra*. Railway employees are governed by provisions of the RLA.

39. *Woodworkers (Weyerhauser Co.)*, 304 NLRB No. 6, 139 LRRM 1033 (1991); *Affiliated Food Stores*, 303 NLRB No. 19, 138 LRRM 1035 (1991); *Electrical Workers (Lockheed Space)*, 302 NLRB No. 49, 136 LRRM 1321 (1991); *Teamsters Local (Stone Container Corp.)*, 302 NLRB No. 139, 137 LRRM 1137 (1991); *UFCW Local One*, 304 NLRB No. 49, 138 LRRM 1346 (1991). In cases involving postal workers, the board holds that in view of the language of the Postal Reorganization Act, a dues authorization is irrevocable for a period of one year even if the member resigns from the union, *U.S. Postal Service and Thomas Dalton*, 302 NLRB No. 50, 137 LRRM 1132 (1991).

Under the board's reasoning, it would appear that the nonmember who agrees to the checkoff of his fair share equivalent will probably be bound for the full term of his written authorization, up to one year, since, unlike the resignation cases, union membership is not a condition of his authorization.

40. Such limitations are suggested by the Supreme Court's decision in *Schofield v. NLRB*, 394 U.S. 423 (1969). In upholding a union fine for exceeding production quotas, the Court was very careful to find no violation of public policy in such action. Such discipline is clearly unlawful if it interferes with a worker's rights under law. For example, a union may not impose a fine on a member for attempting to file a petition with the NLRB to decertify the union, *NLRB v. Marine and Shipbuilding Workers*, 391 U.S. 418 (1968). Similarly, a fine levied pursuant to a union's constitution for suing the union without first exhausting internal procedures was struck down in *Pawlak v. Teamsters*, 628 F.2d 826 (3d Cir. 1980).

41. *NLRB v. Allis-Chalmers*, 388 U.S. 175, 181, 192 (1967).

42. *Schofield v. NLRB*, 394 U.S. 423 (1969).

43. See *American Broadcasting Companies v. Writers Guild*, 434 U.S. 995; 98 S. Ct. 627 (1978); *NLRB v. Marine and Shipbuilding Workers*, 391 U.S. 418, 88 S. Ct. 1717 (1968); *Rasmussen v. NLRB*, 131 LRRM 2557 (9th Cir. 1989); *Molders Local 125*, 178 NLRB 208, *enf'd* 442 F.2d 92 (7th Cir. 1971); *Tawas Tube Products, Inc.*, 151 NLRB 46 (1965). See also *Machinists v. Loudermilk*, 444 F.2d 719 (5th Cir.

1971) (court found fine imposed on a member for joining and becoming president of a rival union violated the members' free speech rights under the Labor Management Reporting and Disclosure Act [LMRDA]).

44. *Allis-Chalmers, supra* note 34, at 184; *Pattern Makers v. NLRB*, 473 U.S. 95, 106 (1985).

45. *Pattern Makers v. NLRB*, 473 U.S. 95 (1985).

46. *Pattern Makers v. NLRB*, 473 U.S. at 106.

47. *Chicago Truck Drivers*, 305 NLRB No. 158, 139 LRRM 1088 (1991).

48. The most recent Supreme Court decision discussing the union's right to use a hiring hall and its obligation to administer it fairly is *Breininger v. Sheet Metal Union*, 493 U.S. 67, 110 S. Ct. 424 (1989).

49. *Teamsters v. NLRB*, 365 U.S. 667, 672–73 (1961).

50. *E.g., Mountain Pacific Chapter of Assoc. of General Contractors*, 119 NLRB 883 (1970).

51. *See, e.g., Interstate Electric Co.*, 227 NLRB 1996 (1977). *But compare Teamsters Local 174*, 226 NLRB 690 (1976) (union must apply same rational standard of referral; arbitrary referrals will not do); *Iron Workers Local 433*, 228 NLRB 1231 (1977) (union owes duty of fair representation to employees in making referrals—threat to pound employee's head in the pavement interferes with his protected rights!). *See* Goldberg, *The Maritime Story* (1958). *Compare NLRB v. Electrical Workers Local 322*, No. 92 Daily Labor Report page D-1 (BNA) (10th Cir. 1979).

52. NLRA Section 8 (f)(3) allows employers and unions in the construction industry to allow unions to make job referrals. Section 8 (f)(2) also modifies the union security provision in the construction industry to require membership within 7 days of employment.

53. *Breininger v. Sheet Metal Union*, 493 U.S. 67, 110 S. Ct. 424 (1989). Unfair failures to refer workers are treated as breaches of the duty of fair representation and not as violations of the LMRDA. *See also Brand Mid-Atlantic, Inc.*, 304 NLRB No. 110, 149 LRRM 1039 (1991); *NLRB v. Barge Workers*, 600 F.2d 770, 776–77 (9th Cir. 1979); *Carpenters Local 537*, 303 NLRB No. 67, 137 LRRM 1249 (1991).

54. *See, e.g., Automobile, Aerospace and Agricultural Implement Workers v. NLRB*, 756 F.2d 482, 488 (7th Cir. 1985); *Foti Construction Co., Inc. v. Building and Construction Laborers' Union*, 742 F.2d 994, 1003 (6th Cir. 1984); *Cronin v. Oscar Mayer Corp.*, 633 F. Supp. 159 (E.D. Penn. 1986); *Dairylea Cooperative Inc.*, 219 NLRB 656 (1975).

XX

The Duty of Fair Representation

What is the duty of fair representation, and where does it come from?

When the employees in your workplace selected union representation, they made a decision that the interests of the group as a whole would sometimes take precedence over the interests of individual workers. For as we saw in chapter 18, when a union is selected to represent workers in an appropriate bargaining unit, under the doctrine of exclusivity the union alone speaks for the workers. This means no other union may represent workers in the bargaining unit, and the individual worker does not have the right to make his or her own bargain with the employer. This power of exclusivity gives the union the right to advance the interests of the group over those of the individual.

Because the union's right of exclusive representation has the potential for abuse, the courts created the *duty of fair representation,* a doctrine designed to make a union exercise its power in a fair manner. As the Supreme Court has put it, the duty of fair representation is the "bullwark" of fair treatment.[1] The Court recently characterized the duty of fair representation as "akin to the duty owed by other fiduciaries to their beneficiaries. . . . Just as these fiduciaries owe their beneficiaries a duty of care as well as a duty of loyalty, a union owes employees a duty to represent them adequately as well as honestly and in good faith."[2]

The doctrine originated in 1944 in *Steele v. Louisville Railroad,*[3] which involved blatant racial discrimination by a union. When *Steele* was decided, the various laws that now outlaw racial discrimination did not exist, so the Court had to find a way to forbid what it considered unacceptable conduct by the union. It concluded that the bargaining agent must exercise the exclusive powers given to it by statute on behalf of all employees in the bargaining unit, "without hostile discrimination, fairly, impartially and in good faith."[4] Under this standard, the negotiation of separate benefits based on race obviously could not stand.

The modern duty of fair representation was set out in a case decided 20 years after *Steele, Vaca v. Sipes.*[5] Although hundreds of fair representation cases have been decided since *Vaca*, the basic rules remain relatively unchanged.

What is the rule of fair representation under *Vaca v. Sipes?*
Vaca v. Sipes involved the familiar situation of a worker who believes his rights under the collective bargaining agreement have been violated. An employee named Owens had been out of work on disability. When Owens presented his employer with a statement from his doctor that he was fit to return to work, the employer's doctor disagreed, and the employer refused to allow Owens back. Owens filed a grievance with his union. The union processed Owens's grievance, assisted him in getting additional medical evidence to back up his position, and tried to work out a settlement with the employer. But the company still refused to put Owens back to work.

The union now had to make a critical decision on whether to bring Owens's case to arbitration and let an arbitrator decide whether the company had good grounds for refusing to reinstate him. The NLRA allows the worker to try to adjust his grievance on his own behalf with his employer but does not give him the right to take the grievance to arbitration.[6] While some collective bargaining agreements provide that the individual may bring his own case to arbitration, Owens's collective agreement, like most, gave the union the sole right to decide whether to take a case to arbitration. The union decided that Owens's grievance was weak and did not want to expend its resources on a losing case. So it refused to take Owens's grievance to arbitration.

Owens sued his union in state court for refusing to advance his grievance to arbitration. The jury agreed that Owens had a valid grievance, and the state court awarded damages to Owens's estate to compensate for Owens's wrongful loss of a job (by the time the case came to trial, Owens had died). However, the Supreme Court held that the state court applied the wrong rule. The issue, said the Court, is not whether the grievant has a meritorious grievance. For even if the grievance is a strong one, the union has no duty to advance it to arbitration. The Court held that while "a union may not arbitrarily ignore a meritorious grievance or process it in perfunctory fashion, we do not agree that the individual employee has an absolute right to have his grievance taken to arbitration."[7] The Court said a union breaches its duty of fair representation only if its conduct towards the employee is "arbitrary, discriminatory or in bad faith."[8] The Court reasoned that the grievance adjustment machinery would not function properly unless the union can make good faith decisions about the relative merits of grievances, and reach settlement with the employer without worrying about a lawsuit claiming that the grievance was valid.

If the union's decision not to advance a grievance to arbitration withstands a duty of fair representation challenge, the employee has no further claim under the collective bargaining agreement. This led Justice Black to conclude in his dissent in *Vaca* that the Court has shut the door in the face of the worker who tries to vindicate his contract rights. Of course, if the claim also involves rights completely apart from the collective bargaining agreement, for example, a statutory prohibition against wrongful dismissal, then the worker may have an independent forum for his claim even if the union doesn't take his case to arbitration. This is discussed in chapter 18.

What employees does the duty of fair representation protect, and what kinds of union decisions does it cover?

The duty of fair representation extends to employees covered by the National Labor Relations Act and the Railway Labor Act. Most other statutory labor relations systems, such as state public sector bargaining laws, have a similar duty of fair representation. Our discussion will focus primarily on the National Labor Relations Act.

A union owes a duty of fair representation to all the employees it represents within the bargaining unit. Theoretically, the bargaining unit is configured so that the union represents workers with common interests, but in reality a wide diversity of interests may appear in a single unit.[9] The union's duty extends only to worker rights that derive from the collective bargaining relationship, that is, that may be the subject of negotiations at the bargaining table or may be contained in the collective bargaining agreement. Worker rights that come from laws apart from the collective bargaining relationship do not appear to be covered by the duty of fair representation. Internal union matters present separate issues, which are addressed in

chapter 21.[10] The union owes the same duty of fair representation to a worker whether or not he is a member of the union.

The duty of fair representation extends to three basic phases
of union representation. First, it applies to the negotiation of
the collective bargaining agreement. The courts have given
unions wide leeway in determining what provisions will appear
in the collective bargaining agreement. A landmark case in
which the union negotiated a seniority preference for returning
World War II veterans over existing workers contains what is
still the controlling standard: "A major responsibility of negotiators is to weigh the relative advantages and disadvantages of
differing proposals. . . . The complete satisfaction of all who
are represented is hardly to be expected. A wide range of
reasonableness must be allowed a statutory bargaining representative . . . subject always to complete good faith and honesty
of purpose in the exercise of its discretion."[11]

This standard was reiterated in a recent Supreme Court case
in which the Court upheld the union's settlement of a strike
against Continental Airlines, holding that a union's actions in
negotiating an agreement are arbitrary only if "in light of the
factual and legal landscape at the time of the union's actions,
the union's behavior is so far outside a 'wide range of reasonableness' as to be irrational."[12]

Despite the wide discretion the union enjoys under this
standard, we will illustrate later that there is some limitation
on the union's leeway to negotiate the terms of ageement.

Second, the duty of fair representation applies to the union's
decision whether or not to take a case to arbitration, as in *Vaca
v. Sipes*. While the union has broad discretion to determine
the terms of the collective bargaining agreement, once that
agreement is reached, the individual has a strong claim to
have the agreement enforced on his behalf. The union has less
leeway to reject a meritorious claim under an existing collective
agreement than to decide not to pursue a particular demand
as part of its bargaining agenda.

A third area subject to challenge under the duty of fair
representation concerns the union's conduct in presenting a
grievance in arbitration. This topic will be discussed separately.

While the lower court cases suggest that a union may be
subject to different standards of review in the negotiation,
grievance, and arbitration stages, a recent Supreme Court deci-

sion makes clear that (at least theoretically) the standards apply in similar fashion to all phases of the union's work and that negotiation is not subject to a less stringent standard of review.[13] However, the opinion leaves open the possibility that courts may review decisions that involve the administration of the agreement, such as deciding whether to take a case to arbitration, in a more exacting way than in the negotiating phase. The Court's decision underscores that some cases are on the borderline between negotiating new terms of an agreement and applying existing ones.

What are the union's obligations in negotiating an agreement?

A union has a wide range of discretion in negotiating the terms of a collective bargaining agreement. This general rule is inevitable, for there is no realistic way for a court to review the wisdom of the various choices a union must make in negotiating a contract. Still, there are a number of cases in which the union's conduct in negotiations has been subject to close judicial scrutiny and occasionally overturned.

The cases in which the union's conduct is tested often involve corporate changes. When one company acquires or merges with another, provision must be made for the employees who find themselves in the newly merged company or who are put out of a job as a result of the merger. For example, what will be the order of seniority at the new corporation? Will each employee be credited with her full seniority as with her previous employer, and will these seniority lists be merged in strict order of seniority, a process called *dovetailing?* Or will the employees of one company be placed at the bottom of the seniority list, behind the employees of the other company, a system called *endtailing?* What package of benefits must the union negotiate for the employees who lose their jobs in the merger or acquisition? Courts are reluctant to substitute their judgment for the union's.[14] But a union may get into trouble if it fails to consider the interests of all affected employees or if it makes its decision on the basis of impermissible grounds, such as union membership or political activity within the union.

A recent airline merger case, *Bernard v. ALPA,*[15] illustrates these propositions. Alaska Airlines, whose pilots were represented by the airline pilots' union (ALPA), merged with Jet

America, whose pilots were not unionized. In mergers where both airlines are represented by ALPA, ALPA consistently followed a policy of requiring the two affected employee groups to negotiate with each other. If they could not work out an acceptable merger arrangement, the matter was referred to mediation and then binding arbitration, and ALPA would abide by the result. However, in *Bernard,* the pilots at the weaker of the two airlines, Jet America, were not represented by ALPA, even though they would be after the merger. ALPA did not follow its normal policy of allowing the two groups to negotiate with each other.

The court recited the familiar test that a union has wide latitude in negotiations and that its action will not be upset unless arbitrary, capricious, or in bad faith. However, the court concluded that the union had discriminated against the non-union pilots of Jet America in its refusal to permit any representative of Jet America to participate in ALPA's negotiations with Alaska Airlines and in the union's departure from its own merger policy for ALPA-represented groups. The court disagreed with ALPA that it had the right to choose the makeup of its team in negotiations with Alaska Airlines. It also rejected ALPA's explanation that its merger agreement had nothing to do with the nonunion status of the Jet America pilots but turned on the equitable consideration that because of Jet America's failing economic condition Jet America's pilots were entitled to less benefits than Alaska Airline's pilots.

The court directed ALPA to apply its normal merger policy to this situation and allow Jet America pilots to participate in the negotiations and to utilize the mediation and arbitration procedures. The court set aside the seniority integration agreement that ALPA had reached with Alaska Airlines.

The outcome in *Bernard* should be contrasted with another airline case, *ALPA v. O'Neil,* recently decided by the Supreme Court.[16] In a bitter dispute with the airline pilots union (ALPA), Continental Airlines declared bankruptcy in 1983 and in the process declared its collective bargaining agreement invalid. As a result of the Continental bankruptcy, Congress changed the law so that it is now more difficult for an employer to escape its collective bargaining obligations through bankruptcy. As the strike with the ALPA continued, Continental hired replacement pilots. Sensing defeat, ALPA reached a settlement with Continental that gave striking pilots the option of returning to work or accepting a severance package. Those who chose to return to work were placed below the striker replacements on the seniority list, which put them in an inferior position for bids on assignments and gave them less protection against layoff. After the settlement was reached, a group of former striking pilots brought an action against ALPA, claiming it breached its duty of fair representation by reaching a settlement that arbitrarily deprived the striking pilots of their seniority status.

ALPA resisted the lawsuit, contending that in negotiating an agreement the union must only act in good faith and treat its members equally and without discrimination. The union argued that the law doesn't require the union to provide adequate representation, and an agreement may not be challenged as arbitrary just because it is a bad settlement. The Court disagreed with the union and held that the union has a duty of adequate representation in the negotiating phase as well as in the administration and enforcement of an agreemement.

The Court assumed that the settlement was, as the striking pilots contended, worse than if the union had surrendered entirely to Continental. Still, said the Court, it has a limited role in reviewing the union's conduct: "any substantive examination of a union's performance . . . must be highly deferential, recognizing the wide latitude that negotiators need for the effective performance of their bargaining responsibilities."[17] The Court upheld the settlement as reasonable, even though in retrospect it turned out to be a bad settlement.

In another case,[18] a failing company was sold to a group of employees. Before the sale, the union agreed to modify certain contractual pension and severance benefits, within the limits permitted by ERISA.[19] This agreement adversely affected the interests of employees who were not hired by the new company, particularly with respect to the funding of the employer's obligations. The court upheld the agreement against a fair representation challenge: "It is inevitable in the give-and-take of collective bargaining that some employees will fare worse than others. But a union may compromise to achieve long-term advantages, even though individual employees may be affected differently by the resulting agreement."[20]

May a union take account of political considerations in negotiating an agreement?

No. In a controversial case, *Barton Brands,* a larger company acquired a smaller one at a time when expansion was anticipated. The employees of both companies had been represented by the same union in different bargaining units, and the union agreed initially to a dovetailing of seniority in which employees from each facility were credited with their full seniority. But when business slowed down, the employees who had formerly been employed by the larger company pursuaded the union to negotiate an endtail seniority system, which would give them a seniority advantage over the employees of the smaller company. The court held this was a breach of the duty of fair representation. "Such decisions may not be made solely for the benefit of a stronger, more politically favored group, over a minority group."[21] This approach has cast doubt on the validity of an earlier, landmark decision that upheld a seniority agreement that was based on political considerations.[22] One commentator has criticized *Barton Brands* as taking an unrealistic view of the decision-making process. "It is difficult to imagine a more or better principled basis for a democratic union than majority will."[23] Another observer agrees with the result, saying a union may not "pander" to the majority and ignore the interests of the minority.[24]

What obligation does the union have to consult its members and keep them advised of the progress of negotiations?

First, the union must follow whatever procedures are spelled out in the union constitution. If the constitution calls for regular reports to the membership or for membership ratification meetings before an agreement is finalized, then failure to comply can constitute a breach of the duty of fair representation, as well as a separate violation of the LMRDA.[25] If the constitution does not require ratification or notification, courts are generally unwilling to impose such a requirement, but may provide relief in extreme cases.[26] One commentator has suggested that participation in the ratification process is essential to union democracy.[27]

The courts generally agree that the right to participate in a ratification vote contained in the union constitution may properly be limited to union members.[28] There are suggestions in some opinions that courts may extend the right of ratification to nonunion members if their exclusion from the vote will prejudice their interests, or if such an obligation may be found in the union's constitution.[29]

Does a union have a duty to advise employees it represents of the consequences of actions those employees may take?

Generally, no, but in some cases the courts will find such an obligation. Courts are reluctant to impose on unions a duty to advise employees, particularly on matters of common knowledge, even if they involve rather technical points like the law that applies to a strike situation. For example, in *Swatts v. Steelworkers*,[30] a number of workers lost their jobs when they were replaced by workers hired during the strike.[31] The aggrieved workers claimed that during the strike the company threatened to hire replacements, but the union dismissed this as "lies" and "garbage" and urged its members to "pay no attention." The aggrieved members also complained that the union didn't warn them of the risks of a strike, particularly that the strike might cost them their jobs. The court concluded that the members' claims were isolated and exaggerated. It held that while the union may have made some misstatements, this did not violate the duty of fair representation. In a strike situation, said the court, "decisions and statements are made in haste. . . . Union leaders, in exhorting the membership, may voice opinions that later prove inaccurate, or make claims that turn out to be hyperbole. So long as such statements "are not intentionally misleading and are not of a nature to be reasonably relied upon by the membership" they are not actionable.[32] The court thought that the union did not have a duty to warn its members of the dangers of striking and that a different rule would have a chilling effect on the union's right to strike because of the fear of unjustifiable lawsuits by its members.

However, in another case[33] the court held that the duty of fair representation may be considered violated in a strike situation whenever a union misstatement, even if unintentional, "is sufficiently egregious to be considered 'arbitrary' or in 'bad faith.'"

On the other hand, mistatements of facts or failure to disclose information known only to the union are actionable. For example, where a union leader falsely stated that there was a security fund to protect workers in the event of bankruptcy or failed to tell the workers of a company plan to shut the plant if the union persisted in its demands the duty was violated.[34]

Consistent with its hands-off approach to negotiations, the court will not find fault with a union that insists on a nonmandatory subject of bargaining, as long as it drops it before impasse.[35]

What do the key terms in the *Vaca* decision—*arbitrary, discriminatory, bad faith,* and *perfunctory*—mean?

As we said earlier, there have been hundreds of fair representation cases since *Vaca*, and each one presents unique facts. The key terms in *Vaca* can only be examined meaningfully in the context of specific cases. In general, the terms *discriminatory, bad faith,* and sometimes *arbitrary* cover situations where the union intentionally disadvantages an employee. For example, if the union refuses to pursue a grievance because the employee once ran against the incumbent president of the local, this would be arbitrary, bad faith, or even discriminatory conduct. In contrast, in *Vaca* the Court concluded that there was no evidence that the union was "personally hostile" to Owens. Similarly, it might be discriminatory or arbitrary for the union to take one person's case to arbitration but not another's in exactly the same situation. Employees are seldom able to show that the union has engaged in such intentional conduct.

The terms "perfunctory" and "arbitrary" in *Vaca* include conduct that harms the individual even where the union's motives are not hostile. In its most recent fair representation case, involving the negotiating phase, the Court equated the term "arbitrary" with "inadequate" representation.[36] Most fair representation cases involve union mishandling of a grievance that is not intentional but reflects careless treatment, poor judgment, or indifferent conduct. For example, the Court in *Vaca* said the union violated its duty if it "ignored" Owens's grievance or processed it in a perfunctory manner. This means that if the union fails to consider the grievance on its merits or is extremely careless in its handling, it may violate the duty. For while the individual cannot insist that the union agree with him on the merits of the grievance, he is entitled to have the union make a careful investigation of the claim. The courts have been unwilling to stretch this concept too far. Most courts will not find a breach of the duty of fair representation just because a union has been careless or negligent. The carelessness must be unusually severe.

What are some examples of careless grievance handling that will give rise to a breach of the duty of fair representation?
In one case,[37] the contract provided for extra seniority for union stewards. The company posted a list of employees who were about to be laid off on the basis of seniority. Galindo asked the union to notify the company that he was a union steward, which would have entitled him to hold on to his job. The union forgot to tell the company, later admitting that it had "goofed." Its failure caused Galindo to be laid off. The court concluded that the union's failure to notify the company that Galindo was a steward was a breach of the duty of fair representation. The court explained that while it would not find a violation for "mere negligent conduct," some omissions by a union "may be so egregious and unfair as to be arbitrary, thus constituting a breach."[38] While acknowledging that this is a "vexing" line to draw, the court said that a failure to perform a ministerial act, which requires no exercise of judgment, will normally constitute a violation.

In another case,[39] reminiscent of *Vaca*, the grievant was injured on the job. In the face of conflicting medical evidence about the grievant's fitness to return to work, the parties agreed to submit the case to a third doctor and to be bound by his findings. That doctor examined the grievant and concluded that he had reached his maximimum level of improvement; however, the doctor did not state explicitly whether the grievant was fit to return to work. The company interpreted his diagnosis as meaning the employee was not able to return to work and discharged the grievant. The union agreed with this interpretation and did not challenge the discharge.

The court held that the union breached the duty in failing to question the third doctor as to whether his diagnosis meant the grievant could not return to work. The third doctor in fact meant that the grievant could return to work, and the company conceded that it would have reinstated the grievant had it known that. The court reiterated that while negligence alone is not grounds for recovery against the union, the union's failure need not be intentional in order to suffer liability. The court thought the union's conduct so perfunctory as to violate the duty. It said "the *Vaca* perfunctory standard permits courts to insure that unions represent individuals fairly by delineating a minimum standard of fair representation."[40]

While under the Court's language in *Vaca* an individual does not have an absolute right to arbitration, the stronger the grievant's underlying claim, the more closely the court will scrutinize the union's decision. For example, in a case involving a closing and consolidation of depots, the union initiated an arbitration seeking severance pay for all the employees who lost work because of the closings. However, on the eve of the arbitration it withdrew the claims of one group of employees because it concluded they might be treated as if on layoff status rather than out of work and therefore would not be entitled to severance pay under the contract. The union thought that advancing the claims of this group might weaken some of the other claims before the arbitrator. The court concluded that the union had no right to abandon the grievance in the face of a fairly strong contractual claim. "The more important and meritorious the grievance, the more substantial the reason must be to justify abandoning it."[41] The court felt the union's reasons for abandoning the grievance were insubstantial, for the arbitrator could sort out the grievances so that any weak ones would not hurt the meritorious ones. The court's analysis also turned on the union's hasty consideration of the claim of the disadvantaged employees.

Most circuit courts have tried to draw similar distinctions. They are unwilling to hold unions liable for mere carelessness because one cannot expect the grievance process to be error free. On the other hand, some mistakes are so extreme that the court concludes that the individual had no representation at all and imposes liability.[42] The Supreme Court has provided very little guidance on this distinction, giving conflicting directions in one case that might have addressed the issue.[43]

The seventh circuit, on the other hand, has refused to attempt these fine distinctions and will only find a breach of the duty where the union acts intentionally against the individual. For example,[44] in a case where a waiter was discharged for leaving work early and his discharge was upheld in arbitration, the waiter charged the union with extreme carelessness in the presentation of the grievance. The court concluded, however, that even gross negligence is not actionable under the duty of fair representation. It said a union is not liable for "careless or bone headed conduct," and that "any other approach would embroil courts in the merits of employment decisions."[45]

What is the union's obligation when conflicting employee interests are involved?

Many employee claims involve potential conflicts with other employees. For example, in a bidding dispute, only one employee can get the job. In the negotiating arena, we have seen that the union is given wide discretion to resolve those interests. However, in the phase of administration of the contract, the union must be more careful where conflicting interests are involved. Potential trouble areas include two employees in a fight, seniority cases where two employees vie for a job, sexual harassment cases where both the aggressor and victim are represented by the union, cases involving disabled employees who seek accommodation by being placed on a job held by a more senior employee, and plant closings in which scarce resources must be allocated.

The courts generally allow a union to choose between conflicting interests, provided it has investigated both positions carefully and has a rational basis for its choice. Where a union breaches the duty by advancing one interest over another, it is usually because it fails to consider adequately the position of the party whose cause it did not pursue. For example, in a public sector case, a school board selected a less senior teacher as a department head. The union filed a grievance and went to arbitration on behalf of a more senior teacher under a clause that awards the job to the senior employee if both candidates are equally qualified, despite the claim of the junior teacher that he was the more qualified. When the arbitrator awarded the job to the senior teacher, the junior teacher brought a fair representation lawsuit against the union for not championing his cause. The court agreed, holding that the union must investigate the competing claims before deciding which one it will back.[46]

The proposition that courts will not look at the merits of the union's choice, but will scrutinize its procedures, is illustrated by a case discussed earlier, in which a company closed three depots and reduced the number of drivers at the fourth.[47] The collective bargaining agreement provided for severance pay for employees who lost their jobs because of a closing but not for employees who were put on layoff because they lacked seniority. The union filed grievances for all employees who were affected by the closings and reductions but on the eve of the arbitration withdrew the grievances of the employees who had been assigned to the one remaining depot and then laid off, apparently concluding that they were on layoff and not entitled to severance pay. The union claimed this was a rational, tactical decision because pursuing their grievances might weaken the others. The court sustained the fair representation claim, not simply because it disagreed with the union's choice but because the union had considered and rejected the plaintiffs' position too hastily.

How does the duty of fair representation apply to cases presented in arbitration?

The union owes the same duty of fair representation to the individual in advocating his claim in arbitration as in processing the claim through the grievance procedure. However, unlike the cases where the union decides not to take the case further, when the union represents an employee in arbitration it aligns itself with the individual. The union is given a wide range of discretion in deciding how to present the case, and the courts are reluctant to second guess the advocate's tactics and judgments, particularly since many cases are presented by nonlawyers. The individual employee rarely succeeds in cases challenging the union's handling of the arbitration.[48] However, a breach has been found where the union is ignorant of the contract provisions, fails to prepare adequately or to make what the court thinks is an obvious argument, or doesn't give the grievant notice of the hearing. [49]

May the individual employee have her own attorney at the arbitration?

No. The individual grievant does not have a right to be represented by her own attorney at the arbitration. This is because the collective bargaining agreement is between the union and the company, and the union has the right to determine who will present its case and how it will be presented. As a practical matter, however, the arbitrator will probably allow the grievant to have her attorney in the hearing room, and may even allow minimal participation by the attorney. The union may decide to permit the individual to have her own attorney present the case, for this may insulate the union from further claims of unfair representation.

Does the individual have any remedy if she is unfairly represented in arbitration?

Yes. As we saw in chapter 18, an arbitration award is final and is rarely overturned by the courts. In *Hines v. Anchor Motor Freight*,[50] the Supreme Court carved out a major exception to this rule of finality where the union fails to represent the employee fairly in arbitration. The Court said that the bar of finality is removed if the union's breach of the duty of fair representation "seriously undermines the integrity of the arbitral process. . . . [I]t is quite another matter to suggest that erroneous arbitration decisions must stand even though the employee's representation by the union has been dishonest, in bad faith, or discriminatory."[51]

The Court in *Hines* was not explicit about the kind of union conduct in arbitration that would support a fair representation claim. The Court accepted the findings of the lower court that the union failed to investigate certain leads suggested by the grievants. On the other hand, there was evidence that the union was politically hostile to the grievants. The case is complicated by the fact that the decision was made by a joint union-management committee rather than a neutral arbitrator. This practice, common in the trucking industry, has been criticized as an inadequate forum.[52]

Is the fair representation doctrine wasteful, and if so, what may be done to control it?

There is an enormous volume of fair representation litigation. This presents a great drain on the resources of unions, which could be used in better ways. Since so few plaintiffs prevail in fair representation cases, one may question whether the rule is worth it. On the other hand, the very existence of the doctrine may force unions to be more careful and less arbitrary in their processing of grievances.

The amount of fair representation litigation can be controlled if unions use greater care in the processing of grievances, base their decisions on rational interpretations of the collective bargaining agreement, and avoid decisions that turn on political or other invidious considerations. Unions should train their representatives to follow careful and fair procedures. The individual employee must also realize that not every claimed contract right can be vindicated through arbitration and that a union must make hard choices in order to protect the interests of all the employees it represents.

What are the procedures for bringing a fair representation lawsuit?

A fair representation lawsuit is usually two lawsuits in one—the Supreme Court has described it as a *hybrid suit*. Where the employee complains about the union's failure to enforce through arbitration a provision of a collective bargaining agreement, his underlying dispute is really with the employer, for he claims that the employer has breached the collective bargaining agreement. His basic suit is therefore one to enforce a collective bargaining agreement under Section 301 of the NLRA. But because most collective bargaining agreements have a provision to resolve all disputes through binding arbitration, arbitration is the exclusive forum for resolving this dispute. If the case is taken to arbitration, that is usually the end of the matter, for once the parties use the contractual provisions the courts generally do not review the merits of the arbitrator's award. This limited judicial review is discussed in chapter 18 and is subject to the exception for cases in which the arbitration itself was tainted by the union's unfair representation, as discussed above.

However, when the union decides not to take the case to arbitration, that too is normally considered a resolution of the grievance under the collective bargaining agreement, for the voluntary resolution of the dispute is considered part of the grievance and arbitration process.[53] A grievance that is settled by the union and the employer is considered closed, and the employee has no further rights under the agreement. The only exception is if the individual can show that the union did not fairly represent her in the grievance process, for in such a situation the individual has not had the benefit of a fair settlement of the contract dispute. Thus, in order to be able to vindicate her claimed right under the collective agreement, the individual must first show that the union breached its duty of fair representation. She does this by suing her employer under Section 301 and her union for a breach of its duty of fair representation, and the two actions are combined. Even if the individual chooses to sue just one party, whether the union or the employer, the suit against one cannot succeed unless it is shown that the other is in breach as well.[54]

There may be cases, however, where the individual's claim is only against the union and does not also involve a claim that the collective bargaining agreement has been violated. In such a case, for example, where the individual claims that the union has run its hiring hall in an unfair manner that violates the duty of fair representation, the suit may be brought against the union alone, and not the employer.[55]

The individual may also raise her claim with the NLRB. The NLRB has taken jurisdiction over fair representation suits under Section 8(b)(1)(A) of the NLRA, concluding that a union's unfair representation restrains the individual's rights under Section 7. While the Supreme Court has never squarely upheld this construction of the NLRA, its continued acknowledgement of this procedure suggests that the Court has accepted it. The Court in *Vaca* held that the existence of a right to fair representation under the NLRA did not preempt a court action under the same theory.[56] Most fair representation suits are brought in court, presumably because of the potential for recovery against the employer under the contract.

What are the remedies if the employee wins her fair representation lawsuit?

If the court agrees with the individual that the union breached its duty in failing to take the case to arbitration, the court has two procedural choices. It can treat the arbitration phase as exhausted and decide the merits of the grievance on its own. It is suggested that if the court decides the merits of the grievance on its own, this deprives the parties of the use of arbitration, which they bargained for under the contract. Alternatively, the court can order the parties back to arbitration. In the latter situation, courts occasionally order that the individual be allowed to have his own attorney and that the union pay attorney's fees. The theory is that once the union unfairly turns down the individual's grievance, it is hardly capable of representing her fairly in arbitration.

What are the time limits for bringing a fair representation lawsuit?

Because the duty of fair representation was created by the courts, and not by statute, there is no explicit statute of limitations for bringing such claims. The Supreme Court had to borrow the most appropriate statutory limit and adopted the very tight time limit of six months for bringing a fair representation lawsuit under the NLRA.[57]

While this is an unusually short time limitation, several factors may keep the case alive. One is that the time clock starts to run when the aggrieved party knows or should have known of the breach of the duty. Where the claim is that the union failed to take a case to arbitration, such as Owens's grievance in *Vaca v. Sipes*, the time limit is usually measured from the point that the union notifies the individual that it will not take the case. In a case like *Galendo*,[58] discussed earlier, where the union failed to notify the company that Galendo was a steward, thus costing him his seniority, there were several ways to compute the six month period. It could have begun when Galendo should have realized that his name was not submitted or when he lost his position as a result of the union's omission. The court took a third approach. Because Galendo tried to get his seniority back through the arbitration process, the court held that the time clock started to run only after the arbitrator denied his grievance. Most courts hold that the clock is stopped where the individual tries to vindicate his claim through the grievance and arbitration process and only begins to run when that process terminates. If this were not so, individuals would be forced to file lawsuits before the contractual dispute resolution machinery ran its course, and this would defeat the purpose of the grievance and arbitration machinery.[59]

The clock also stops running when the individual tries to get the union to reverse its decision. There is a procedural doctrine that requires a union member to exhaust his internal union remedies—that is, to follow whatever internal union appeals machinery is available—before getting the courts involved in his dispute. Obviously, this doctrine wouldn't work unless the time clock were stopped while the internal procedures are pursued, and most courts have applied this approach and held the clock suspended during internal appeals of duty of fair representation cases. [60]

Does the individual have a duty to first exhaust his internal union procedures?

As we point out in other portions of this book, Section 101(a)(4) of the LMRDA, which protects an individual's right to sue his union, also provides that the individual may first be required to exhaust any internal appeals procedures within the union, as long as they don't exceed four months. The purpose behind this provision is to allow unions to straighten out their own matters and to keep courts from intervening unnecesarily in internal union affairs. This obligation to exhaust internal union remedies has also been applied to duty of fair representation suits but with some important qualifications.

The most significant exception is that the exhaustion requirement does not apply where the union cannot provide the relief sought by the individual. The most obvious example is where the union has refused to take the individual's case to arbitration, and, because of time limitations in the collective bargaining agreement, it is now too late to initiate arbitration. Even if the individual could convince the union that it should have taken his claim to arbitration in the first place, the union cannot provide the individual with the relief he seeks. For example, in a discharge case the union can give him damages but cannot restore him to his job. In deciding not to require exhaustion in this situation, the court said it declined "to impose a universal exhaustion requirement, lest employees with meritorious Section 301 claims be forced to exhaust themselves and their resources." [61] The court ruled that exhaustion would not be required in three situations: where the union could not provide the relief sought, where the union officials who would hear the case are hostile to the grievant, or where exhaustion would unreasonably delay relief.

In cases where the union can provide the relief sought, for example, where the time limit for initiating arbitration has not run, the individual who wishes to avoid internal union procedures may argue that the union is hostile to his interests. Since the union has already decided against the individual, she will contend that further internal appeal is futile. While the policy of the law is to allow unions to resolve their disputes internally, this may be overcome by a strong showing of antagonism, particularly if the persons who hear the internal appeal are the same persons who made the adverse decision in the first place.[62]

What happens to the time limits for filing a fair representation lawsuit while the individual attempts to exhaust his internal union procedures?

While the Supreme Court has not addressed this question, lower courts have held that if the individual chooses to go through the internal union procedures, the time limits for bringing a fair representation action are "tolled," that is, suspended while the internal union procedures take place. One court has held that the individual is entitled to attempt to exhaust his internal procedures even if they appear futile—for example, as in the previous question, where the union cannot afford the individual the complete relief he seeks. The court thought that the choice should be up to the member, for otherwise he would be in a catch-22 of either being charged with failure to exhaust internal remedies or failure to file a timely fair representation lawsuit.[63] The individual must be very careful about the application of this rule: The statute of limitations for fair representation suits is very short—six months. If the individual waits four months before initiating his internal union procedures, he only has two months left on the fair representation clock once the internal union procedures run their course. Further, if the internal procedures appear to be futile, the individual must initiate his fair representation lawsuit promptly.

Is the individual employee entitled to attorney's fees in a fair representation lawsuit?

When the individual prevails on his claim that the union should have taken his claim to arbitration or failed to represent him adequately in arbitration, there is a good chance he will recover attorney's fees. A prevailing plaintiff is not normally entitled to attorney's fees unless a statute expressly provides for this;[64] there is no such statute in the case of fair representation suits. Sometimes the employee can utilize other theories for recovery of attorney's fees, for example, when his lawsuit confers a common benefit on the union and its members or when the union's conduct is frivolous. The most promising avenue for recovering attorney's fees, however, is where an employee can show that the union unfairly refused to take his case to arbitration, or that he required separate counsel in order to vindicate his rights under the collective agreement. For example, if the court agrees that the union failed to represent the individual properly in arbitration, it may conclude that the union must pay for independent counsel as part of the individual's damages. Some courts have held that the individual is entitled to counsel fees even if he does not prevail in his underlying claim in arbitration. The Sixth Circuit disagrees, holding that the individual can recover attorney's fees only if he prevails in the arbitration. An individual should not receive attorney's fees if he would not have won the underlying grievance; this would be a breach with no injury. The contrary rule, says the court, would encourage frivolous actions.[65]

Is the plaintiff in a fair representation suit entitled to a trial by jury?

Yes, at least where the fair representation action is based on a grievance claim under the collective bargaining agreement. The right to a jury trial derives from the Seventh Amendment to the Constitution. It turns on a historical distinction between actions to enforce legal rights and actions to enforce equitable rights. A jury trial is not required if the case involves only equitable rights. The Supreme Court[66] has analogized the union's handling of a grievance to the obligations of a trustee. While this involves equitable considerations, the Court also concluded that the underlying relief involves a claim under the collective bargaining agreement, which is in the nature of a legal right. Thus, at least where the worker seeks relief that vindicates his contractual rights, he is entitled to a jury trial in a fair representation lawsuit.

NOTES

1. *Vaca v. Sipes*, 386 U.S. 171 at 182 (1967); *Hines v. Anchor Motor Freight*, 424 U.S. 554 at 564 (1976).

2. *Airline Pilots v. O'Neill*, 111 S. Ct. 1127 (1991).

3. *Steele v. Louisville Railroad*, 323 U.S. 192 (1944).

4. *Steele*, 323 U.S. at 204.

5. *Vaca v. Sipes*, 386 U.S. 171 (1967).

6. NLRA Section 9(a). The individual may make his own adjustment with his employer, but the settlement must not be inconsistent with the collective bargaining agreement. The union has the right to be present at the adjustment; as a practical matter, if the union objects to the proposed settlement, the employer is unlikely to agree.

7. *Vaca v. Sipes*, 386 U.S. at 191.

8. *Vaca v. Sipes*, 386 U.S. at 190.

9. *See Emporium Capwell Co. v. Western Addition Community Organization*, 420 U.S. 50, 64 (1975). The configuration of bargaining units is discussed in chapter 18 above.

10. *But see Wooddell v. IBEW*, 112 S. Ct. 494 (1991) for the situation in which a union member's claim against his union also involves a question of interpretation of the collective bargaining agreement and thus may be heard under Section 301 of the LMRA.

11. *Ford Motor Co. v. Huffman*, 345 U.S. 330, 338 (1953).

12. *Airline Pilots v. O'Neill*, 111 S. Ct. 1127 (1991).

13. *Airline Pilots v. O'Neill, supra* note 12.

14. *Ackley v. Teamsters*, 138 LRRM 2751 (6th Cir. 1991).

15. *Bernard v. Airline Pilots*, 873 F.2d 213 (9th Cir. 1989).

16. *Airline Pilots v. O'Neill, supra* note 12. On remand, the court of appeals upheld the earlier decision of the lower court, *O'Neill v. Airline Pilots*, 138 LRRM 2213 (5th Cir. 1991).

17. *Airline Pilots v. O'Neill, supra* note 12, at 1135.

18. *Sutton v. Weirton Steel*, 724 F.2d 406 (1983).

19. ERISA is discussed in chapter 5 above.

20. *Weirton, supra* note 18, at 412.

21. *Barton Brands Ltd. v. NLRB*, 529 F.2d 793, 798–99 (7th Cir. 1976); *see also NLRB v. General Truck Drivers*, 545 F.2d 1173, 1175 (9th Cir. 1976); *Strick Corp*, 241 NLRB 210 (1979).

22. *Humphrey v. Moore*, 375 U.S. 335 (1964); *compare Ackley v. Teamsters*, 910 F.2d 1295, 135 LRRM 2201 (6th Cir. 1990), where the court was especially protective of seniority rights and upheld a fair representation challenge that urged that the seniority rights of a small group of employees were ignored.

23. J. Getman and B. Pogrebin, *Labor Relations* 110 (Foundation Press, 1988).

24. M. Malin, *Individual Rights Within the Union* 375 (BNA Books, 1988).

25. *Smegal v. Gateway Foods*, 763 F.2d 354, 360 (8th Cir., 1985)(court

upholds the union's narrow construction of its constitutional provision requiring ratification). *See also, Alexander v. Operating Engineers,* 624 F.2d 1235 (5th Cir. 1980); *Deboles v. Trans World Airlines,* 552 F.2d 1005 (3d Cir. 1977), *cert. denied,* 434 U.S. 837 (1977). The right to participate in a ratification vote is also protected by Section 101(a) of the LMRDA, but the right depends on the language of the union's constitution.

26. *See Brown v. Electrical Workers,* 137 LRRM 2747 (6th Cir. 1991).

27. Hyde, *Democracy in Collective Bargaining,* 93 Yale L.J. 793 (1984).

28. Compare *NLRB v. Financial Institution Employees,* 475 U.S. 192, 205 (1986).

29. *Letter Carriers and Teamsters v. NLRB,* 587 F.2d 1176 (D.C. Cir. 1978); *National Letter Carriers v. NLRB,* 595 F.2d 808, 813 (D.C. Cir. 1979); *But compare Postal Workers Local 2885 v. Postal Workers,* 113 LRRM 2433 (D.C. 1982), *aff'd. mem.,* 766 F.2d 1566 (D.C. Cir. 1985), *and Maurer v. Auto Workers,* 105 LRRM 2883 (M.D. Pa., 1980), both suggesting that plaintiffs had no ratification rights. *Compare NLRB v. Financial Institution Employees,* 475 U.S. 192, 205 (1986).

30. 808 F.2d 1221 (7th Cir. 1986).

31. The company's right to replace strikers is explained in chapter 18, *supra.*

32. *Swatts v. Steelworkers,* 808 F.2d at 1225 (7th Cir. 1986).

33. *Alicia v. Suffield Poultry, Inc.,* 902 F.2d 125 (1st Cir. 1990).

34. *Anderson v. Paperworkers,* 641 F.2d 574, 578 (8th Cir. 1981); and *Warehouse Union v. NLRB,* 652 F.2d 1022, 1025 (D.C. Cir. 1981). Both cases are cited and distinguished in *Swatts, supra* note 32, at 1224. *Compare Alicia v. Suffield Poultry,* 902 F.2d 125 (1st Cir. 1990).

35. *Swatts v. Steelworkers,* 808 F.2d 1221, 1226 (7th Cir. 1986). The distinction between mandatory and permissive subjects of bargaining is discussed in chapter 18, *supra.*

36. *Airline Pilots v. O'Neill, supra* note 2.

37. *Galindo v. Stoody Co.,* 793 F.2d 1502 (9th Cir. 1986).

38. *Galindo,* 793 F.2d at 1514.

39. *Carpenter v. West Virginia Flat Glass, Inc.,* 763 F.2d 622 (4th Cir. 1985).

40. *Carpenter,* 763 F.2d at 624.

41. *Gregg v. Teamsters Local 150,* 699 F.2d 1015 (9th Cir. 1983).

42. For additional examples of cases involving careless handling of a grievance, *see Young v. Postal Service,* 907 F.2d 305 (2d Cir 1990), *Peters v. Burlington Northern R.R.,* 931 F.2d 534 (9th Cir. 1991).

43. *Hines v. Anchor Motor Freight,* 424 U.S. 554 (1976)(*Compare* "The

grievance processes cannot be expected to be error free," *with* "Congress . . . anticipated . . . that the contractual machinery would operate within some minimal levels of integrity," both at page 571. For a useful and extremely thorough review of the verbal standards applied by each circuit, see M. Malin, *Individual Rights Within the Union* 360–71 (BNA Books, 1988).

44. *Camacho v. Ritz Carlton*, 786 F.2d 242 (7th Cir. 1986).

45. *Camacho*, 786 F.2d at 244.

46. *Belanger v. Matteson*, 115 R.I. 332, 346 A.2d 124, 132 (R.I. S. Ct. 1975); *Compare Smith v. Hussman Refrigerator Co.*, 619 F.2d 1229 (8th Cir. 1980) *and Automotive Etc. Employees v. Gelco Corp.*, 758 F.2d 1272 (8th Cir. 1985).

47. *Gregg v. Teamsters*, 699 F.2d 1015 (9th Cir. 1983).

48. *Barr v. United Parcel Service*, 868 F.2d 36, 130 LRRM 2593 (2d Cir. 1989); *Lucas v. Leaseway Multi Transportation*, 738 F. Supp. 214 (E.D. Mich. 1990). *See* Rabin, *Fair Representation in Arbitration*, in McKelvey, *The Changing Law of Fair Representation* 173, 177–80 (ILR Press, 1985).

49. These propositions are illustrated respectively by *Milstead v. Teamsters*, 580 F.2d 232, 235 (6th Cir. 1978); *Holodnak v. Avco Corp.*, 514 F.2d 285, 287 (2d Cir. 1975); and *Smith v. Hussman*, 619 F.2d 1229, 1241–42 (8th Cir. 1980).

50. 424 U.S. 554 (1976).

51. *Hines v. Anchor Motor Freight*, 424 U.S. at 567, 571 (1976).

52. *See* Azoff, *Joint Committees as an Alternative Form of Arbitration under the NLRA*, 47 Tul. L. Rev. 328 (1973).

53. *Republic Steel v. Maddox*, 379 U.S. 650 (1965).

54. *Hines v. Anchor Motor Freight*, 424 U.S. at 570–71.

55. *Breininger v. Sheet Metal Union*, 493 U.S. 67 (1989). *See also Wooddell v. IBEW*, 112 S. Ct. 494 (1991).

56. *See Vaca v. Sipes*, 386 U.S. at 185–86.

57. *DelCostello v. Teamsters*, 462 U.S. 151 (1983). The other rules having to do with time limits, such as time for service of a timely complaint, are still governed by the federal rules; *see West v. Conrail*, 481 U.S. 35 (1987).

58. *See supra* note 37.

59. *See Adkins v. Electrical Workers*, 769 F.2d 330 (6th Cir. 1985).

60. *Fransden v. Railway Clerks*, 782 F 2d 674, 681–84 (7th Cir. 1986).

61. *Clayton v. Auto Workers*, 451 U.S. 679, 689 (1981).

62. *Dean v. Trans World Airlines*, 924 F.2d. 805 (9th Cir. 1990); *Lewis v. Laborers' Union*, 750 F.2d 1368 (7th Cir. 1984).

63. *Frandsen v. Railway Clerks*, 782 F.2d 674 (7th Cir. 1986).

64. Chapter 21, *supra*.

65. *Wood v. Teamsters*, 807 F.2d 493 (6th Cir. 1986). Because the union failed to represent the individuals properly, the district court ordered that they have their own attorney in the arbitration. The opinion collects the decisions of the other circuit courts on the issue of attorney's fees.
66. *Teamsters v. Terry*, 494 U.S. 558 (1990).

XXI

Rights Within the Union

Given the substantial power the union has to affect your working conditions, it is to your advantage to have a say in the way the union exercises that power. The only effective way to do that is to become a member of the union and participate in its governance. That is not the only reason, of course, for joining the union. Even if you are not interested in participating in day-to-day decision making, your membership in and support of the union increases its strength and therefore its ability to represent you properly.

This chapter discusses your rights to participate in the union's governance.[1] The questions cover your right to join the union, your right to attend and participate in meetings, your rights if you are disciplined by the union, your right to terminate your membership in the union, the imposition of a trusteeship, your rights in the union's assets, and your rights of free speech. One of the important rights of membership is the right to vote, in order to elect those officials most responsible for union governance. This right to vote is covered separately in chapter 22.

THE STRUCTURE OF UNION GOVERNANCE

How is a union normally governed, and what are my opportunities to influence its governance?

Most unions have a national or international headquarters that operates the union and charters individual local unions that may cover one or more work localities. Sometimes there may be intermediate bodies between the international union and your local. In many unions, most of the important day-to-day decisions in your workplace are made by the local union, so this is the arena in which your participation can be most critical. Your dues are usually divided between the local union and the parent or an intermediate body where one exists, although the apportionment varies substantially from union to union.

The parent union usually decides questions of general policy, such as what kinds of legislation to support, what kinds of general directions to take in negotiations, and questions of internal union governance and structure, including setting dues and allocating them between parent and local. Your opportunity to influence decisions at that level is usually limited to participating in the election of the officers of the parent organization and in the selection of delegates to conventions at which major decisions are made. You can learn about the policy questions involved at the national level by reading your union's international newspaper and by attending local union meetings, where reports are made of activities at the national level. Your rights to nominate candidates, run for office, and to vote in those elections are discussed in chapter 22.

You will probably be far more interested in the day-to-day governance of your local union, for it is at this level that the specific bargaining agenda is usually set, critical decisions are made about negotiation strategies and goals, and priorities are set and decisions made as to how the agreement shall be enforced and, more importantly, as to what grievances shall be pursued and taken to arbitration.

The governance of each local varies from union to union, and is determined in large part by the constitution of your parent union and the bylaws of your local. In most cases, the important decisions are made by local elected officials, who usually comprise some kind of executive body, consisting, for example, of the president, vice president, secretary, treasurer, and other elected members such as shop stewards and chairs of the negotiating or grievance committees.

In addition, tremendous influence may be exercised by the business agent, who is usually a paid employee of the local union or, where employed by the parent, is assigned to represent your local and often several others. The business agent may be an elected officer or an appointed official; chapter 22 on union elections discusses the circumstances in which the business agent must be elected rather than appointed to office.[2] Because of the business agent's professional training and experience, he or she usually plays an important role in affecting decisions at the local level.

Important decisions are often made on the shop floor level by union stewards, who are fellow employees elected or appointed to represent you in handling problems that arise in the workplace. Other elected or appointed officials can also play a large part in affecting your working conditions. For example, the grievance chairperson may have great discretion and influence in deciding which grievances are pursued. And the negotiating committee will play the major role in reaching an agreement through collective bargaining.

Finally, depending on your union's constitution and bylaws, provision is usually made for membership governance at periodic membership meetings. These may include meetings to decide whether to ratify or reject a collective bargaining agreement that has been reached on a tentative basis by your negotiating committee. This is one of your best opportunities to play a part in the governance of your union.

We cannot stress too strongly that your rights to participate in local governance depend in very large measure on the wording of the union constitution. The law allows unions wide leeway to structure their internal governance, and the forms of governance vary tremendously from union to union. Once the union sets up such a structure, the law requires the union to abide by it. In determining your rights to participate in local governance, the first place for you to turn is your union constitution and bylaws.

THE RIGHT TO PARTICIPATE IN UNION GOVERNANCE

What are the sources of my legal rights to participate in union governance?

The primary source of your legal rights to participate in union governance is the Landrum-Griffin Act, a 1959 enactment that regulates internal union governance. This law, which goes under the technical and cumbersome name of the Labor Management Reporting and Disclosure Act (LMRDA), is organized into six parts or titles. The most important, for purposes of this chapter, is Title I, "Bill of Rights of Members of Labor Organizations." The other major provision of the LMRDA dealing with union governance is Title IV, "Elections," which is discussed in the next chapter. Other titles of the LMRDA that also affect internal union governance are discussed at several points in this chapter.

Before Landrum-Griffin was enacted, legal regulation of unions was handled in the state courts under a variety of common law theories. For the most part, courts viewed labor organizations as voluntary associations, much like social clubs, and were reluctant to interfere with their governance. Some state law doctrine still is important in this area, and we will discuss it when relevant; a recent Supreme Court decision suggests that some rights grounded in state common law may be enforceable in federal court.[3] Landrum-Griffin explicitly provides that state law rights and remedies are not diminished by the federal law.[4]

Landrum-Griffin gives unions wide leeway to shape their internal governance through their constitutions and bylaws. For example, two of the key provisions of Title I—the right of every member to participate in governance and elections and the right of freedom of speech and assembly—are both subject to "reasonable rules and regulations" in the union's constitution and bylaws.[5] This is part of the general compromise in the LMRDA to regulate internal union affairs but still respect some degree of union autonomy. A respected authority, judge, and former professor, Harry Edwards, has observed that "Title I of the LMRDA is not a mandate for courts to impose on labor unions whatever procedures or practice they regard as 'democratic.'" Rather, courts are limited to enforcing those rights specifically enumerated in the statute.[6] In order to determine your legal rights it is therefore essential that you consult the terms of your union constitution and any applicable bylaws.

Are all unions covered by the LMRDA?

No. The LMRDA defines labor organizations in Section 402(i) and (j) to exclude unions consisting solely of employees in the public sector. Where an international union is comprised of some locals that are in the private sector and others in the public sector, LMRDA coverage of the public sector locals depends on whether the parent excercises control over the local funds or activities in question. For example, in a case where a public sector local spent funds to promote a candidate for office, the court held that while the funds came from the parent union as part of the distribution of dues collected by the parent, the local had complete autonomy in spending the money. As a result, even though the parent was covered by the LMRDA, the local's expenditures were not regulated by LMRDA Section 401(g).[7] A union not covered by the LMRDA may be subject to state regulation.

Must I belong to a union in order to participate in its governance?

Yes. The critical provisions of the LMRDA that give you the right to participate in union governance and elections apply only to members. For example, the bill of rights in Title I extends to "every member," and the voting rights in Title IV are applicable to "every member." The common law prior to Landrum-Griffin generally held that rights of governance applied only to union members. If you want to exercise the rights conferred by law to influence the governance of your union, you must join the union.

This right to participate in internal union governance, which is limited to union members, must be distinguished from the right of all workers—members or not—to the benefits of union representation. So even if you do not join the union, you are entitled to be represented by it. (See chapter 19.) But while you needn't join the union to be entitled to full representation, you must join if you wish to influence its governance.

Do I have the right to join the union that represents me?

Technically, no. But as a practical matter, it is doubtful that you will be denied admission to the union. You have no absolute legal right to join a union, even if it is authorized and required by law to represent you at the bargaining table. This is surprising since you need to belong to the union in order to effectively shape the way it represents you in setting the terms and conditions that apply in your workplace. However, because courts traditionally treated unions as voluntary associations, they were reluctant to tell unions that they must admit someone to membership.

With the enactment of Title VII and other laws prohibiting discrimination, unions can no longer deny membership on grounds of race, gender, age, disability, or other protected grounds. The LMRDA prohibits a union from expelling or disciplining a member for exercising a right protected by that statute, so a refusal to admit a worker to new membership because he exercised his previous rights of membership in a union may be outlawed.[8] While that still leaves a few areas in which a union may refuse to admit a person to union membership, the union cannot prevent that person from obtaining or keeping a job and cannot affect a term or condition of employment on account of his lack of union membership.[9]

Given the importance of union membership in enabling a worker to control the governance of a union that represents him, the current law, which allows a union to refuse to admit a worker to membership, is indefensible. As a practical matter, however, it is doubtful that in these days of declining membership many unions will take the political risk of refusing a person union membership.

Once I am admitted to membership, does the union have an unlimited right to terminate my membership?

No. While the union needn't admit you to membership, once it does admit you you are entitled to the full protections of the LMRDA and the common law. This means that you can be disciplined or expelled from the union only for reasons that are clearly spelled out in the union's constitution and bylaws and are in accordance with procedures set out in the constitution and bylaws or prescribed by law.

What rights does the LMRDA give me to participate in the governance of my union?

Title I of the LMRDA gives you two basic sets of rights to participate in your union's governance. The first is the "Equal Rights" provision.[10] It gives every member equal rights "to vote in elections or referendums of the labor organization, to attend membership meetings, and to participate in the deliberations and voting upon the business of such meetings." These rights are "subject to reasonable rules and regulations in such organization's constitution and bylaws."

It is important to understand that this provision doesn't require a union to conduct elections or referenda or to hold membership meetings, but if the union does so, then all members have equal rights of participation.

The second set of rights is entitled "freedom of speech and assembly."[11] It provides that every member "shall have the right to meet and assemble freely with other members; and to express any views, arguments, or opinions; and to express at meetings of the labor organization his views, upon candidates in an election of the labor organization or upon any business properly before the meeting."

This set of protections is also subject to a proviso, that they shall not "impair the right of a labor organization to adopt and enforce reasonable rules as to the responsibility of every member toward the organization as an institution and to his refraining from conduct that would interfere with its performance of its legal or contractual obligations."

Like the equal rights provision, the freedom of speech and assembly section of the LMRDA does not require that there be meetings and assemblies unless the union constitution and bylaws call for them. Some courts have construed the statute to require a union to hold at least some meetings.[12] If the union does hold meetings, then all members are entitled to attend and speak out and may not be disciplined for doing so.

Because of the approach of both these sections, it is important for you to consult your union's constitution and bylaws to determine when the union is required to hold meetings and referendums. When meetings and voting are required, you are entitled to the protections of Title I.

Are unions required to hold elections, referenda, and meetings?

Yes as to elections, yes as to referenda involving dues increases or other assessments, and generally no as to meetings, unless the union's constitution and bylaws call for them.

Title IV of the LMRDA regulates elections in detail. You will see that international unions are required to hold elections for officers at least every five years, intermediate bodies every four years, and locals at least every three years.[13]

Referenda, which are votes on specific issues rather than votes to elect officers, are not required to be held, unless the union constitution or bylaws require them. There is one important exception. Any increase in dues and any general or special assessment must be accomplished by majority vote in a secret ballot. Increases at the local level require direct vote by the affected members, while increases by the parent organization may be accomplished through voting by delegates.[14]

The LMRDA contains no express requirement that a local union hold meetings, and workers have not succeeded with the argument that such a requirement may be implied in the freedom of speech and assembly provision.[15] However, if a union's constitution and bylaws require that meetings be held, then members are entitled to participate fully in such meetings in accordance with Title I.

Are unions required to hold membership votes on whether to ratify a negotiated collective bargaining agreement?

Only if required by the union's constitution and bylaws. A vote on whether to accept or ratify a collective bargaining agreement negotiated by the union's bargaining team is one of the most important issues that can be submitted to the membership. However, the law on this question is no different than on any other question of whether the membership is entitled to a referendum vote. If the union's constitution and bylaws call for such a vote, then it must be held. In that case the union must provide the member with adequate information about the proposed contract.[16] Otherwise, it is entirely up to the union's negotiating team to decide whether or not to accept a contract proposal.[17] When a union does hold a ratification vote, the prevailing view is that it may exclude nonmembers from the vote.[18]

A union is not required to give access to the membership mailing list to members who oppose the union's position on ratification. While a candidate has the right to the union's membership mailing list under Section 401(c) as part of his right to a fair election under Title IV (elections are discussed in chapter 22), a similar right is not found in Title I. One court has held that such a right should not be inferred by a court as part of its notion of what is desirable union democracy.[19]

What procedures must the union follow when it seeks an increase in dues, initiation fees, and assessments?

If the increase is proposed at the local level, the union may either conduct a secret ballot on the question at a general or special meeting (as long as reasonable notice is given of the intention to vote on that question) or the union may submit the question to a membership referendum.[20]

In either case, the union must present the question fairly

and clearly, so the members can make an informed choice. For example, in a case where the vote on a dues increase was linked to a vote for a new contract, the member could not vote against the dues increase without also voting against a wage increase. The court held this deprived the member of a "meaningful vote."[21]

The requirements controlling referenda for dues increases at the parent level are more complex, and the text of the LMRDA should be consulted.[22] The law does not require that every member of the union be given an equal vote in a referendum on dues increases at the parent level. The law allows the voting to be by delegates, and the union constitution may properly provide for the weighting of delegates' votes.[23] This means, for example, that if each local is allowed one delegate, members in larger locals are underrepresented in the voting.

What safeguards must a union provide when it conducts a referendum on other subjects?

The only referenda required by law are those pertaining to increases in dues and assessments, and the LMRDA sets out the appropriate safeguards as described in the previous question. If the union constitution and bylaws call for referenda, then they must be held in accordance with the union's own rules. For example, if the constitution calls for a secret ballot vote, then a voice vote will not do.

If the union constitution requires a referendum on a particular subject, then the equal rights and freedom of speech provisions of the LMRDA will apply. In addition, LMRDA Section 501(a), which states that union officers and agents occupy a position of trust in relation to the union's members, has been construed to impose standards of fair procedure in union referenda.

Fair and open debate. Members are entitled to a "free and informed vote"[24] on referendum issues. This means they are entitled to hear the opposition point of view, which may require the union to give opposing members the right to comment, and are entitled to access to union publications[25] and perhaps to mailing lists[26] for the purpose of expressing an opposing viewpoint. Where the union asks members to vote on a complicated issue, such as a merger with another union, it must provide them with all the details; this may require sending them the text of the proposed merger agreement.[27]

A fair choice. The ballot must be framed to give the voting members a meaningful choice. It must be clear and concise and cannot involve multiple or complex issues voted on simultaneously. Although the union is not required to follow a specific ballot format, the membership must clearly be made aware of the issues and alternative views.

For example, shortly after passage of the LMRDA, the machinists union held a referendum on 47 amendments to its constitution. Although the ballots were accompanied by a circular stating that the changes were required by the LMRDA, in fact many were not. The court held that the changes required by the LMRDA should have been voted on separately from the others.[28]

In another case, in which the union constitution gave members the right to decide whether to ratify a negotiated agreement, the court held the membership is entitled to adequate information about the terms of the contract. In this case the court concluded the union must provide a full text of the proposed contract.[29]

Fair balloting and an honest count. Courts will insist that all those who are entitled by the union constitution to vote in the referendum, and no others, may cast their votes and may supervise the process to make sure this occurs.[30] Just who is entitled to vote on a particular issue is governed by the union constitution. The courts will generally uphold the constitution requirements as long as they are reasonable. Courts have upheld restrictions barring those not working in a particular trade from voting on wage scales. However, one court did not uphold a restriction denying supervisor members a vote on a death benefit fund that included them.[31] Counting of ballots improperly cast or miscounting ballots properly cast may violate express or implied provisions of the union constitution and would violate the equal rights clause of the LMRDA and the fiduciary obligation of union officials to protect members' rights to vote.[32]

May a union member insist that his local union hold a meeting?

Yes, but generally only if the union constitution requires

this. Most union constitutions provide that the local union will hold meetings at specified times. In addition, many provide that special meetings can be called by a petition of a certain number of members. These constitutional provisions are enforceable, and the courts may order officers to hold the requested meetings.[33] But if the union constitution and bylaws cannot be reasonably construed to require such meetings, the courts will generally not find an obligation to hold meetings in the text of Title I of the LMRDA.[34]

THE RIGHT TO SPEAK OUT
AND THE LIMITS OF UNION DISCIPLINE

Are members entitled to speak out at union meetings?

Yes. The equal rights provision of the LMRDA, as well as the free speech provision, give every member the right to speak out, to make motions, and to have motions voted upon at the union meeting.[35] Under the free speech guarantees of the LMRDA, the union may not silence a member because it disagrees with his point of view.[36] The presiding officer must maintain order so that members can be heard, and may not allow other members to attempt to silence the speaker through shouts or physical threats.[37] Of course the union may place some limits on debate in order to get through its agenda, under its right in the provision to LMRDA Section 101(a)(2) to apply "established and reasonable rules pertaining to the conduct of meetings."

Is there a conflict between my rights of free speech and my obligation to support my union?

In a sense, yes. The LMRDA broadly protects the rights of union members to free speech and assembly, as set out in Title I. However, the proviso to Section 101(a)(2) recognizes a union's right to make and enforce reasonable rules to maintain its institutional unity. The next set of questions and answers illustrate the tension in balancing the member's free speech rights against his obligation to support his union.

Does the union constitution define my rights of free speech?

To some extent. The union's constitution and bylaws are a primary source for determining the limits a union may place upon your free speech rights. Where a member is disciplined for activities that do not involve free speech, it is not as critical for the union to point to a provision in the constitution that enables it to impose the discipline. For the Supreme Court has held that the due process guarantees of Title I, in Section 101(a)(5), do not require that an offense be spelled out in the union constitution in order that discipline may be imposed.[38] But where a member's free speech rights are involved, Section 101(a)(2) says explicitly that free speech rights to meet, assemble, and express views may be curtailed only by the adoption of "reasonable rules as to the responsibilities of every member toward the organization." Thus, a union will probably not be able to discipline a member for exercising his free speech rights unless the constitution clearly spells out a rule that curtails those rights and only if the union can show good institutional reasons for the rule.[39] Further, the union constitution and bylaws set out the procedural requirements that a union must follow before discipline may be imposed.

Are members entitled to criticize union officers and union policies?

Yes. The free speech clause of the LMRDA is worded extremely broadly: "Every member . . . shall have the right to meet and assemble freely with other members; and to express any views arguments and opinions." The LMRDA qualifies this guarantee by declaring "that nothing herein shall be construed to impair the right of a labor organization to adopt and enforce reasonable rules as to the responsibility of every member toward the organization as an institution and to his refraining from conduct that would interfere with its performance of its legal or contractual obligations." However, the courts have not allowed this proviso to unduly limit the broad rights guaranteed by the free speech provision. The union can no more curtail the speech and assembly of it members than government can curtail the speech and assembly of its citizens.[40]

Section 609 of the LMRDA makes it unlawful for a union to "fine, suspend, expel, or otherwise discipline any of its members for exercising any right to which he is entitled" under the LMRDA. This means the member cannot be disciplined for organizing an opposition group, since that is an exercise of free assembly guaranteed by Title I. The same holds for a member who campaigns for an insurgent candidate for union office, for she is exercising rights protected by Title IV.

On the other hand, members can be disciplined for assaulting a fellow member, disorderly conduct, embezzling union funds, or engaging in a wildcat strike, since these activities do not involve rights specifically protected by the LMRDA. The LMRDA places no other limits on union discipline.

Members may criticize union officers even if their criticism can be regarded as "personally motivated vindictive statements of untruth," and members may freely advocate changes in union policies, even though this creates discontent, dissension, and turmoil in the union.[41] As for the LMRDA proviso, one court has said, "this court does not believe . . . challenge to a union official's integrity to be an act of disloyalty to the union. Just the opposite, it is the duty of the individual union member to speak out about apparent and possible improprieties."[42] One court has said that the protection of democratic processes within the union outweighs any union interest in promoting solidarity in its dealing with employers.[43] In another well-known case a member of the musicians union was expelled for urging members not to pay their union dues on the grounds their levy was unlawful. The union defended the expulsion on the grounds that urging members not to pay their dues would "undermine the very existence of the Local." The court, however, held this was protected speech. It said, "a member's responsibility to his union as an institution surely cannot include any obligation that he sit idly by while the union follows a course of conduct which he reasonably believes to be illegal."[44]

May a union member be disciplined if his criticism defames union officers or union members?

No. In this respect the LMRDA gives union members greater leeway in speaking out than the First Amendment affords a private citizen. Defamatory statements are remarks that hurt the integrity and reputation of the person who is the target of the remarks. The First Amendment allows individuals to make such statements without liability to the person harmed, as long as the statement is true. But if the statement is false, the person making it may be liable for damages. The courts, however, have refused to allow unions to punish defamatory statements, even if they are false, because union tribunals are not qualified to determine whether or not a statement is defamatory. As one court put it, unions are not "disinterested tribunals," and are "peculiarly unsuited for drawing the fine line between criticism and comment." A member who wishes to criticize his union should not be forced "to draw, at the peril of union discipline, the tenuous line between what is libelous and what is not."[45] The union may not discipline the member for a defamatory statement even if the statement was malicious and without any foundation in fact.[46]

While defamation has thus become absolutely privileged against union discipline under the LMRDA, the union may still have a claim in court for defamation under traditional common law theories.[47]

May a union member be disciplined for violating the union's collective bargaining policy?

Yes. Conduct that violates established collective bargaining policy, as opposed to speech that merely advocates such conduct, may be the subject of proper union discipline. A union member may be expelled from the union, or fined, for crossing the union's picket line and working during a strike, for exceeding production quotas established by the union, or for engaging in a wildcat strike, that is, a strike unauthorized by the union. But while the union may discipline the member for such conduct, it may not affect his rights in his job. Further, the member may be able to resign from the union in order to avoid such discipline.

But a member cannot be disciplined for protesting the union's collective bargaining policy, so long as the protest does not involve actual conduct. Even public criticism of the union's conduct of a strike is protected against union discipline. However, the NLRB recently held that a member's announcement that she would not honor a picket line was a repudiation of the union's legitimate bargaining position rather than the protected expression of a dissenting view and that she could be disciplined for these remarks.[48]

May a union member be disciplined for supporting a rival union in a representation election?

Yes, but only through expulsion, suspension, or similar discipline. The union cannot enforce a fine levied against the member for such activity. Dual unionism is traditionally recognized as grounds for expulsion from the union. Any support of a rival union has been considered a violation of the member's responsibility to the union as an institution. The union may thus rightfully protect itself from having someone loyal to a competing union within its ranks by expulsion or other discipline such as barring him from participating in union decisions.[49]

However, the union may not enforce a fine against a member for supporting a rival union. The policy under the NLRA of encouraging employee free choice in the selection of a bargaining representative requires that a union member be free to urge the replacement of an incumbent union with another union. If unions could fine members for such activity and collect such fines in court, this would discourage members from exercising their rights under the NLRA.[50]

Do members have the right to form factional groups or caucuses within the union?

Yes. Title I of the LMRDA guarantees "the right to meet and assemble freely with other members." This has been construed to protect members who form opposition groups within the union. As one court put it, "to permit a union to punish its members for meeting and discussing affairs of the union would be to deny the very purpose of the Bill of Rights."[51] The board has recently held that a union violates NLRA Section 8(b)1(A) when it threatens dissident union members.[52]

Are a union's broad or vague disciplinary provisions void because of their "chilling effect" on freedom of speech and assembly?

No. Union constitutions and bylaws frequently describe offenses in general terms such as "undermining wage standards"[53] or "conduct unbecoming a union member."[54] Such vague language may in fact discourage members from certain conduct because they cannot be sure if that conduct violates the rule. However, the courts will uphold the enforcement of the rule as long as the rule is not applied in a manner directly violating the LMRDA. Thus, the courts will enforce the rule if the conduct punished threatens union interests intended to be protected by the statute. But if the union repeatedly uses a vaguely worded rule to punish protected conduct, the court may enjoin any further enforcement of the rule.[55]

As an example of an impermissible rule, officers of the mine workers union filed a series of disciplinary charges against supporters of opposing candidates under a clause prohibiting "dishonest or questionable practices to secure the election or defeat of a candidate." The court held that this clause was so vague that a member would be in peril of violating the clause and "might well refrain from taking full advantage of his rights" under the LMRDA. The union administration had demonstrated its determination to harass and intimidate the opposition, so the court enjoined prosecutions under this provision.[56]

What forms of discipline may a union impose?

Union discipline usually takes one of three forms. The most extreme is to expel the member from the union. Expulsion means the worker is no longer entitled to participate in union governance. However, expulsion from the union cannot affect the worker's rights on her job.

Second, the member can be suspended from membership for a limited period of time. During that time he cannot participate in internal union governance, but his suspension is not allowed to affect his job status. More specifically, he cannot be fired from his job on the ground he has been suspended from the union, no matter how valid the grounds for suspension. Depending on the wording of the union constitution, the suspended member may be required to continue to pay his dues even while denied his union franchise. While we know of no case law on this point, we think that under the principles discussed in chapter 19 on the effects of union membership upon your job, the suspended member who fails to pay his union dues may be subject to termination from his job.[57] While this may seem unfair to the member, because he is being taxed by the union without the opportunity to participate in its governance, it must be remembered that the suspended member is still entitled to full union representation as a worker in the bargaining unit, and a good portion of his union dues covers that service. The discussion in chapter 19 of the obligation of a worker to pay his fair share of the costs of union representation, suggests that if the worker wants to resign from the union he can avoid the payment of full union dues; however, so long as he remains a member he must abide by the rules in the union constitution governing members who are suspended.

Third, the union may levy a fine against the member. It can enforce this fine either by expelling or suspending the member if he doesn't pay the fine or by attempting to collect the fine through a lawsuit. We will discuss the union's power to collect a fine in a later question.

All of the provisions of the LMRDA against improper discipline apply to these three forms of discipline—expulsion, suspension, and fines. However, the Supreme Court held recently that a union's abuse of the hiring hall procedure, when it refused to refer an employee for employment because he had opposed the union leadership, could not be considered disciplined under the LMRDA. But the Court held that such conduct violates the union's duty of fair representation.[58]

Do the LMRDA safeguards against improper discipline apply to union officers as well as to union members?

Generally yes if the union officers are elected. However, an appointed union officer may be subject to discipline, including removal, if he fails to carry out the policies of the administration that appointed him. An appointed officer, such as a business agent, is generally understood to serve the elected union leader who appointed him so that he can effectuate the policies that the elected official is supposed to carry out. In the leading case of *Finnegan v. Leu*,[59] the Court held that the union president could remove appointed union business agents who had campaigned for the union president's rival. The Court reasoned that the elected leadership needs freedom to choose a staff whose views are compatible with its own, thus carrying out the wishes of the membership. The Court left open whether under this rationale the union could remove officials who did not make policy or who were not confidential employees. *Finnegan* makes clear, however, that the union may not deprive the officer of his rights as a union member. For example, it cannot strip him of his membership or deny him the right to vote or the right to speak out. But it can remove him from his appointed job, and this means that he must choose between his job and his right to speak out.

Several terms later, in *Sheet Metal Workers v. Lynn*, the Court dealt with an elected business agent who spoke out against a dues increase proposed by the union trustee in a situation where the local was placed in trusteeship (trusteeships are discussed below).[60] The Court stressed the difference between elected and appointed officials, but it is not clear that the case turned on the fact that the officials in question were elected. The Court pointed out that in removing the elected officials the union deprived the members of their voting choice, which suggests that there are stronger reasons to protect the elected official than the appointed official against removal. However, the Court also emphasized that in speaking out, the business agent was exercising the rights that go with union membership and that his ouster on account of his views would chill the free speech rights of other members. While the Court in *Lynn* acknowledged that *Finnegan* also involved chilling members' speech, it concluded there is a more pressing need for a president to have a loyal appointed staff, which may outweigh the concern about chilling members' speech.

THE LIMITS ON UNION DISCIPLINE

Must a union member pursue his internal union appeals procedures before a court will hear his claim of improper discipline?

Generally yes. But where freedom of speech and assembly are at stake, courts will generally not require exhaustion of internal union remedies. Normally courts will not intervene in union discipline before the internal union appeals procedures have been exhausted. Section 101(a)(4) of the LMRDA, which protects the member's right to sue, expressly allows a union to require members to exhaust "reasonable" hearing procedures, not to exceed four months. This follows the general policy of the LMRDA that unions should be allowed to correct their own wrongdoings without judicial interference. But where the appeals procedure is futile because the appeal is to the very officers who were criticized by the member being disciplined[61] or where the discipline, if not stopped immediately, would bar the member from participating in an election or union meeting,[62] courts will not require exhaustion. Some courts hold that whenever free speech rights are involved exhaustion will not be required.[63]

Is the right of free speech protected against threats and other misconduct by union members?

Yes. Usually the union attempts to curb members' speech by disciplinary action or threats of such action. Such discipline is prohibited unless it complies with the standards discussed shortly in another question. But free speech can be chilled by other means, which are also prohibited. For example, the National Maritime Union arrested a member for criminal trespass when he distributed leaflets in the hiring hall protesting the policies of the union president. The court rejected the union's claim that it was trying to preserve order in the union hall and held that its actions violated the member's free speech rights.[64]

A member's free speech is also protected against threats of violence or other coercive action. Courts have held unions liable for violation of free speech rights when evidence suggests that an attack by other union members was at the direction of union officials or part of a prearranged plan to stifle dissent within the union.[65] The union member will not only have a claim against the union for violation of free speech rights under the LMRDA but may also claim assault and battery as well. However, even in cases where the beating was carried out by a union official, it must clearly have been for the purpose of suppressing speech in order to be actionable under the LMRDA. The courts will not impose liability on the union if the attack was the result of personal animosity.[66]

What procedures must a union follow in expelling or otherwise disciplining a member?

First, the union must follow any procedures for discipline that are spelled out in its own constitution or bylaws. This follows from the contract theory of union membership, which looks at the union constitution as part of an agreement the member makes with the union when he joins it. Union constitutions often contain detailed rules for union discipline. The union constitution may require that charges be signed by the accusing member, that a trial be held before a union tribunal constituted in a certain way, or that a transcript be made of the proceedings. Failure to follow these procedures may render the discipline invalid, although if the member goes ahead with the proceedings without protesting an improper procedure, he may be barred from later complaining about it.

Second, the union must meet the minimum standards of fairness spelled out in the LMRDA. These require that the member be "(A) served with written specific charges; (B) given a reasonable time to prepare his defense; (C) afforded a full and fair hearing."[67]

No offense except nonpayment of dues[68] may be punished until the union has followed these procedures and the member has been tried and found guilty. A member cannot be temporarily suspended pending trial even if the offense is a highly visible one such as working during a strike, where there seems to be no doubt that a violation occurred.[69]

Does the LMRDA impose upon unions minimal procedural standards for disciplining a member?

Yes. Some of the key standards are discussed here.

Notice of charges. The statute calls for the service of written, specific charges upon the member. In his legislative remarks in support of the LMRDA, Senator McClellan said the charges must be "specific enough to inform the accused member of the offense that he has allegedly committed."[70] The Supreme Court has held that the member must not be "misled or otherwise prejudiced in the presentation of his defense."[71]

The charge must do more than simply quote the constitutional provision that the member is alleged to have violated. It must state the factual circumstances and the time and place of the claimed violation.[72] For example, it was not enough to charge that a union officer "on several occasions collected dues and did not turn in the money" without specifying the time and the person from whom the money was collected.[73] The actual trial must be confined to the offenses spelled out in the charges.[74]

Time to prepare a defense. LMRDA Section 101(a)(5)(B) allows the accused member "reasonable time to prepare his defense." This of course varies with the complexity of the charges. If the member can make a reasonable showing of a need for more time, a union will seldom be upheld in rushing ahead with the trial.[75]

Right to appear and present evidence. The right to a "full and fair hearing", now protected by the LMRDA, was construed at common law to allow the accused to appear and present evidence. Thus trials in distant cities where the member and his witnesses could not appear usually invalidated the proceedings.[76] There is little case law on the more difficult questions of whether the accused member can require the union to turn over the evidence in its possession or to compel members to appear as witnesses. While the union is not required to make a transcript, a member is entitled to record the hearing at his own expense.[77] An accused member should draw upon the analogies to criminal trials in claiming rights to a "full and fair hearing" although some courts have rejected the notion that a union trial is the equivalent of a criminal proceeding.[78]

Right to know the evidence and cross-examine witnesses. An accused member is entitled to hear all the evidence against him and to confront his accusers' witnesses and cross-examine them.[79]

Right to counsel. A union member usually does not have the right to use outside counsel such as a lawyer. The LMRDA does not give the member the right to counsel, and courts have deferred to provisions in the union constitution that do not permit outside counsel. Most unions permit the member to have another member as counsel, but few allow the use of an outside representative or lawyer. This reflects a desire to keep problems within the house, as well as unions' traditional distrust of lawyers. Courts have held that the right to a full and fair hearing doesn't require legal counsel.[80] However, if the union utilizes a lawyer in its prosecution, some courts will require that the accused member be placed on an equal footing by being allowed to use his own lawyer.[81]

An unbiased tribunal. A member is entitled to a trial before an unbiased tribunal. This means one whose members have not made up their minds before hearing the case.[82] This may disqualify persons who were present at the incident under trial.[83] This is a hard concept to apply when the hearing tribunal is made up of members who are loyal to the incumbent officers, and the member on trial is opposed to the current leadership. Courts generally will not be overly strict on this point, and a hearing panel will not be disqualified unless the member can show that members of the panel were actually biased against him or were unable to give him a fair hearing, for example, because they were his political opponents in a recent election.[84] In cases of extreme divisiveness within the union, courts may invalidate a hearing held before a tribunal appointed by the leadership.[85]

GETTING RELIEF

What relief will the court give the member who has been wrongfully disciplined by the union?

The LMRDA gives the courts wide discretion to tailor the relief to fit the particular case.[86] For example, if a member has been wrongfully fined, the court will refuse to enforce the fine. If the fine has already been collected, the court will order that it be returned to the member. If the member has been wrongfully suspended or expelled, the court will order him reinstated and his record cleared.[87]

The court can also award money damages, which may include compensation for earnings lost if discipline resulted in discharge or blacklisting by employers,[88] injuries to reputation, mental suffering, humiliation, or other emotional distress.[89] Punitive damages may be awarded when the unions acts in malicious and reckless disregard of the member's rights.[90] The total damages can thus be quite substantial. For example, a member of the Painters Union was awarded $9,900 for loss of wages, $42,500 for mental suffering, and $6,000 as punitive damages.[91] The union may be required to pay for the wrongful and even malicious conduct of its officers even though it was not authorized or ratified by the union membership, although a recent Supreme Court decision suggests the union is not responsible for extreme misbehavior by an officer outside the ordinary course of his duties.[92]

Am I entitled to a jury trial on my claims against the union?

Generally, yes. The Supreme Court has recently held that a union member who sues his union for money damages under Title I of the LMRDA is entitled to a jury trial.[93] It would appear from this decision that the member's claim must include a substantial monetary component in order for him to be entitled to a jury trial. If the relief is primarily equitable, for example, if he seeks an injunction against the union, he may not be entitled to a jury trial under the principles of this decision.

May a court award attorney's fees?

Yes, in some cases. In general, courts do not award attorney's fees to the successful party unless the applicable statute expressly provides for it. Attorney's fees are provided for under the LMRDA only in certain sections not applicable here. However, you can obtain attorney's fees in special circumstances under several theories. The theory most often used is the *common benefit theory*, where the individual can show that in protecting his own rights he serves the common benefit of the union by vindicating the rights of all other members. The individual can usually prevail under this theory.[94] The member may also get attorney's fees if he can show that the union acted in bad faith, at least in the way it conducted the litigation.[95] Sometimes you can get attorney's fees if you succeed at a preliminary stage, such as an injunction, even if you don't win in the end.[96] Your attorney will tell you how these fees are calculated if he or she is successful in collecting attorney's fees from the union.[97]

How much time do I have to bring a lawsuit?

The Supreme Court recently held that the statute of limitations for relief under Title I, in Section 101(a)(2), is the applicable state statute of limitations for personal injury actions.[98] This is usually several years, much longer than the 6-month statute of limitations under the NLRA, which the courts have sometimes borrowed for other employment law litigation, for example, in fair representation suits.[99]

UNION FINES

Under what circumstances may a union impose a fine on a member?

A union may impose a fine only if the offense and the fine are spelled out in the union constitution and bylaws, if the union follows its own procedures for imposing a fine, and if the fine does not violate public policy.

While the standards for imposing a fine must be spelled out

with some clarity, they needn't have the specificity of a criminal statute. Union fines have been upheld for such behavior as dual unionism (that is, supporting a rival union), coming late to union meetings, working with a nonunion employee, and serving temporarily in a position outside the bargaining unit.[100] Courts have sustained fines for crossing a picket line and reporting to work and drawing regular pay.[101] In one case, the Supreme Court upheld a fine on a member for exceeding stated production quotas and then drawing pay, rather than banking his excess earnings as required by union rules.[102]

Certain conduct is, however, protected on public policy grounds from union discipline imposed through fines. For example, a union may not fine a member for failing to exhaust internal union remedies before filing an unfair labor practice charge.[103] Nor may the union fine a member for dual unionism, that is, supporting a rival union in a representation election or initiating a decertification petition to oust the union as the bargaining agent, though it may suspend or expel that member.[104] In these instances the member is entitled to vindicate the public rights guaranteed by the NLRA, and imposition of a fine would inhibit the member from exercising those rights. However, the union may expel the member for these offenses since expulsion does not have as chilling an impact on the exercise of public rights. On the other hand, a union may fine a member for belonging to another union where the member has not attempted to use the board's processes to have that union certified. The theory is that unless the member actually tries to have the rival union certified, no public policy is served by protecting his activities.[105]

Once again the fine is only valid if it complies with the union constitution. If the underlying union directive is itself invalid, any fine for not following the directive is invalid. Thus, if a strike is called improperly by the union, any fine for strike breaking would be unenforceable.[106]

How may a union enforce a fine imposed upon a member?

A union may enforce a fine in two ways. First, the union may suspend or expel a member for nonpayment of fines. Like any other penalty, the validity of this measure depends on whether it is spelled out in the union constitution and whether the procedures for its implementation are fair and in accordance with its constitution and bylaws. Since expulsion deprives the member of the right to participate in union governance, Section 609 of the LMRDA provides safeguards against this form of enforcement of fines.

Expulsion is not necessarily an effective way for the union to enforce a fine. An employee cannot be discharged from his job just because he was expelled from the union for not paying the fine. Thus, a member may not even care if she is expelled from the union. The Supreme Court has recognized that expulsion may be an ineffective means of fine enforcement: "Where the union is weak, and membership therefore of little value, the union faced with further depletion of its ranks may have no real choice but to accept its member's disobedience."[107]

A union may not avoid this barrier to expelling the member by insisting that the member pay his fine before he is allowed to pay his dues. The courts see this as improper coercion of the employee to pay his fine so that he won't be discharged from his employment for nonpayment of dues.[108]

An alternative method of enforcing fines is the civil lawsuit. These suits proceed on the theory that union membership is a form of contract, and the member is therefore obliged to pay any fine validly imposed under the union constitution. The individual who is fined often responds that the fine violates his Section 7 right to refrain from concerted activities. However, the Supreme Court has said that the enforcement of fines through a lawsuit does not violate the NLRA.

> Integral to . . . federal labor policy has been the power in the chosen union to protect against erosion its status under that policy through reasonable discipline of its members who violate rules and regulations governing membership . . . Congress was operating within the context of the "contract theory" of the union-member relationship which widely prevailed at that time. The efficacy of a contract is precisely its legal enforceability. A lawsuit is and has been the ordinary way by which performance of private money obligations has been compelled.[109]

What if the fine is unreasonably large or imposed through unfair procedures?

Since the union's right to fine is based on a contract between the member and her union, both the courts and the NLRB will generally not strike down a fine as interfering with Section 7 rights even if the fine appears unreasonably large or the procedures are questionable. So long as the union complies with its own standards and procedures, the board and courts will usually leave the fine alone under the NLRA.[110] Thus, a fine equaling the money a member earned while working during a strike after crossing a picket line does not violate the NLRA.[111] However, if the union seeks to collect the fine in state court, the amount of the fine and the fairness of the procedures can be legitimate defenses to collection of fines under ordinary principles of state contract law.[112]

In an action in court to collect the fine, the disciplined member may raise the same considerations discussed previously on the propriety of union discipline. These may include the degree to which the offense was spelled out in the union constitution, the adequacy of notice, and other due process concerns. If the member claims the fine to be unreasonably large, the member may argue that the union constitution did not make clear that such a large fine could be imposed, and that judicial enforcement would be unconscionable.[113]

May an employee avoid a fine by not joining a union or by resigning his membership in the union?

Since the right to fine is based on a contract between the union and its members, the employee who does not join the union is not subject to union fines or other discipline. This is one reason employees exercise their right not to join the union. NLRA Section 8(a)(3) makes clear that employees need not join the union even under a union security clause that appears to require union membership as a condition of employment. The Supreme Court has stated that the union has the right to fine a member even if he joins under the mistaken belief that a union security agreement required union membership to obtain employment.[114]

Since most employees find it advantageous to join the union despite potential discipline, the real question is whether a member may avoid a fine and its enforcement by lawsuit by resigning membership in the union. The Supreme Court has now made clear that the union member has the right to resign his union membership at any time, and by doing so may avoid any further liability for fines imposed by the union under its constitution.[115] The NLRB has taken this a step further by holding that a union member may avoid a fine by converting his status to a financial core member, rather than resigning entirely, before undertaking the activity prohibited by the union.[116] Finally, the board has held that a union member who has received strike benefits from his union during a strike cannot be forced to repay those benefits if he later resigns from the union and abandons the strike.[117] While the law is not entirely clear on this point, it appears that a member who wishes to resign his union membership to avoid a fine must do so before he engages in the prohibited conduct. If he violates the union's rule while still a member, a subsequent fine is enforceable even if the member resigns before the union holds a hearing, imposes the fine, or brings a lawsuit for its enforcement.[118] For example, if a union calls a strike, the member is subject to a fine if he crosses the picket line before he resigns his membership. The NLRB has rejected the union argument that the member must resign prior to the strike vote, as opposed to the actual strike, in order to avoid discipline for ignoring the union's decision.[119] If the member wishes to rejoin the union, the union may require that the member pay a fine imposed, even for activitities after resignation.[120]

Since resignation procedures were not considered important until the use of union fines became prevalent, many union constitutions do not provide for specific resignation procedures. But even if there is no specific time limitation on the right to resign, under current law the member is still free to resign at any time in order to avoid union discipline and fines.[121] It is less clear whether he is free to resign at any time other than those specifically provided in the union constitution in order to avoid other obligations of union membership, such as the payment of full union dues. This question was not addressed in the Supreme Court's leading case on the right to resign.

TRUSTEESHIPS

Under the union structure, the international union charters a local union, and gives it considerable autonomy and powers under the international's constitution and bylaws.

Normally, the International may not interfere with regular local activities such as election of officers, administration of funds, establishment of bargaining priorities, and administration of a collective bargaining agreement.[122] However, through the imposition of a trusteeship, the international may suspend the local's control over some of these activities.

There are valid reasons for a parent to impose a trusteeship, for example, corruption and waste of assets by the local or failure to administer properly the collective bargaining agreement. On the other hand, the parent may have improper motives, such as raiding a local treasury or getting rid of a local officer who challenges the national leadership.

Trusteeships were generally upheld at common law, as long as they were established in accordance with the union constitution and bylaws. But the McClellan committee found that the trusteeship device had been abused by a handful of unions. These abuses included an undue frequency of trusteeships of unreasonably long duration and for improper purposes. This evidence led to the enactment of Title III of the LMRDA.[123]

The Supreme Court has said that the precise scope of a trustee's powers when a trusteeship is imposed is "relatively unchartered territory."[124] However, the courts are very reluctant to allow a trustee to interfere with the basic rights of union members under Title I. The trustee clearly may not raise dues without the normal referendum procedures,[125] and it is doubtful that the trustee can suspend any of the voting rights provisions in Title IV.[126] The Supreme Court has said that a Trustee must ordinarily act consistently with the protections of Title I, but it has declined to say whether there are ever situations in which a Trustee can override Title I rights.[127]

How is a trusteeship established?

Title III of the LMRDA sets out the procedures and circumstances under which a union may impose a trusteeship upon a local.

> Trusteeships shall be established and administered by a labor organization over a subordinate body only in accordance with the constitution and bylaws of the organization which has assumed trusteeship over the subordinate body and for the purpose of correcting corruption or financial

malpractice, assuring the performance of collective bargaining agreements or other duties of a bargaining representative, restoring democratic procedures, or otherwise carrying out the legitimate objects of such labor organization.[128]

This statutory provision imposes two restrictions on the union. First, the trusteeship must be in accordance with the constitution and bylaws of the parent organization. This means that the trusteeship must comply with any procedural requirements in the constitution and bylaws, and, if the constitution and bylaws limit the purposes of a trusteeship, it can only be for those stated grounds. Second, the trusteeship can only be for the grounds listed in the provision quoted above, although the final term, "[for] otherwise carrying out the legitimate objects of such labor organization," is so broad that the union may have considerable leeway in deciding to impose a trusteeship.

There is a third requirement, imposed by another provision of Title III, which says that a trusteeship will be presumed to be valid only if it is authorized or ratified "after a fair hearing either before the executive board or before such other body as may be provided in accordance with its constitution or bylaws."[129] Some courts require a union hearing before imposing a trusteeship, except in an emergency, for example, where the local is misspending funds. Other courts hold that the prior hearing is not an automatic requirement and will uphold a trusteeship if the facts warrant it prior to a union hearing and if the trusteeship is finally approved by a vote. This line of reasoning rests on the term "ratified" in LMRDA Section 304(c).[130]

How may I challenge a trusteeship?

The LMRDA makes it fairly easy for a member to challenge a trusteeship. He may file a written complaint with the secretary of labor, who then investigates. If the secretary finds probable cause, he must bring an action in federal court. The court may grant injunctive relief, which means the trusteeship may be suspended.[131] In the alternative, the individual member may bring his own action. An employee may be able to recover attorney's fees, at the discretion of the court, if he can show that his efforts conferred a common benefit on the membership, or on other grounds normally recognized as the basis of attorney's fees.[132] The employee may be less likely to recover attorney's fees for a victory at the preliminary stages, for example, where he holds off imposition of a trusteeship until the union holds a hearing under LMRDA Section 304(c).[133]

Is a court likely to uphold a trusteeship?

The LMRDA provides that if a trusteeship is established in accordance with the union's procedures set out in its constitution and bylaws, and after a fair hearing before the parent union's executive board or other body provided in its constitution and bylaws, there is a presumption that the trusteeship is valid for a period of 18 months. It is not subject to attack during this period "except upon clear and convincing proof that the trusteeship was not established or maintained in good faith" for the purposes listed in LMRDA Section 302, quoted above. On the other hand, after 18 months the trusteeship is presumed invalid, and the burden shifts to the union to show by clear and convincing proof that the trusteeship should be continued.[134]

What are valid grounds for imposing a trusteeship?

Despite the strong presumption in favor of the trusteeship, it is hard to generalize as to what grounds will support its imposition. In one leading case,[135] the international imposed a trusteeship on a local that refused to go along with the international's directive that all locals representing Lockheed employees vote in a combined vote on a proposed contract that would cover all the facilities. In the past the locals had voted separately on the contract for their own facility. The other locals voted to reject the contract, but one local, which wished to accept, insisted on a separate vote. The court enjoined the international from imposing a trusteeship. Although the international contended that it was assuring the furtherance of the local's bargaining obligations, a purpose spelled out in the LMRDA, the court disagreed. It concluded that if the local members had to go along with the combined strike vote, its members would be placed on the horns of a dilemma of being disciplined by the union if they disobeyed the strike vote and went to work or being replaced by the employer if they honored the strike vote. The court thought the international would suffer less harm if it was not allowed to impose the trusteeship than would the local if forced to obey the strike vote. The court was swayed by the long history of separate voting by the locals.

On the other hand, an international may not impose a trusteeship solely to prevent the local from severing its connection to the international.[136] It can do so, however, if the local is diverting funds to a rival union that is engineering the disaffiliation.[137] And it may impose a trusteeship if disaffiliation will jeopardize a bargaining relationship.[138] Trusteeships have been upheld where there is evidence that the local is corrupt and squandering its assets.[139]

Courts will not usually second guess the union's judgment and will uphold the trusteeship if there is "substantial evidence" to support the union's determination and if the trusteeship is part of an honest, good faith effort to achieve legitimate goals. Thus, a court upheld a trusteeship where the international president concluded that political rivalry within the local made it impossible for the local to function.[140]

What happens when a trusteeship is imposed?

The parent union will probably take control of the local's treasury and monitor its receipts and expenditures. However, the LMRDA provides that the parent may not siphon funds out of the local and into the parent's treasury except for the normal per capita tax and assessments normally payable.[141] To achieve this monitoring the parent may impose its own set of officers on the local and manage its day-to-day affairs. It appears that a parent union has this right under Title III, even though its conduct would seem to violate the provisions of Titles I and IV dealing with conduct of meetings and election of officers.[142]

The parent union may not attempt to control the local's political influence on the parent—for example, by putting its own representative into office so that he will vote in favor of the parent's interests at a delegate convention. This was a common abuse of the trusteeship, and Congress made clear in Section 303(a)(1) that a parent union may not count the votes of any delegate of a local in trusteeship if that delegate was not chosen fairly in a secret ballot election.

During the trusteeship, the labor organization must file periodic reports with the secretary of labor. These must spell out the purposes of the trusteeship, report on the manner in which the union is carrying out its day-to-day affairs, and contain a complete financial report.[143]

FIDUCIARY DUTIES
AND OTHER SOURCES OF MEMBERS' RIGHTS

Are there any other provisions of the LMRDA that protect my rights of union membership and participation?

Yes. Title V of the LMRDA contains a strong statement of the obligation of union officers. It says "the officers, agents, shop stewards, and other representatives of a labor organization occupy positions of trust in relation to such organization and its members as a group."[144] While the remaining text of this title appears to be concerned primarily with the official or representative's obligations to handle the union's money and property, Title V has been used to impose this obligation of trust in a variety of other situations.[145]

Title V is unusual among the provisions of the LMRDA in providing for attorney's fees, although this is left to the court's discretion, and may be confined to payment out of any recovery of misspent funds.[146] Most courts have held that a union official who is sued under Title V must provide and pay for his own legal representation and that the union may not defend or pay for the official's defense.[147] A union official who handles union funds or property is required to be bonded in an amount not exceeding $500,000.[148]

In addition, the duty of fair representation may be a successful basis to challenge union misconduct not covered by the LMRDA. For example, the Supreme Court ruled that a member could use the duty of fair representation but not the provisions dealing with discipline in Title I to challenge the operations of a hiring hall.[149]

Finally, Title IV, governing union elections, provides other ways to protect a member's rights within the union. Title IV is discussed further in chapter 22.

Are there other ways the government may intervene in the governance of a union?

Yes. The government has moved increasingly to use criminal statutes to deal with extreme cases of corruption within unions.

In the most celebrated case, the government brought an action under the Racketeering Influenced and Corrupt Organizations Act (RICO) to stop members of the Provenzano crime organization from interfering with the internal affairs of a teamsters union local, to oust the currrent leadership, and to impose a trusteeship under court supervision.[150]

Does a union member have any rights regarding the assets of the union?

The question of who owns the union's assets, including its treasury, requires an examination of both the union constitution and bylaws and applicable state law. If the union constitution and bylaws are silent, the union's assets probably belong to the membership, and if the union is dissolved, each member would be entitled to a proportionate share. But in an ongoing union, the constitution and bylaws vest control of the union's assets in its officers. Further, the constitution is likely to provide that upon dissolution of a local its funds revert to the parent union.

In a broader sense, the member does have a recognized right and interest in his union's funds and in the way the union is run. Congress, in imposing certain financial disclosure requirements upon unions (contained in LMRDA Title II), observed:

> The members of a labor organization are the real owners of the money and property of such organizations and are entitled to a full accounting of all transactions involving such money and property. Because union funds belong to the members they should be expended only in furtherance of their common interest. A union treasury should not be managed as though it were the private property of the union officers, however well intentioned such officers might be, but as a fund governed by fiduciary standards.[151]

This obligation underlies Title V of the LMRDA, entitled "Fiduciary Responsibility of Officers of Labor Organizations."

THE RIGHT TO ENGAGE IN POLITICAL ACTIVITY

May I be disciplined for political speech?

No. We have already seen that the LMRDA and case law protect most aspects of a member's right to engage in political activities. A member is entitled to express his views under LMRDA Section 101(a)(2). If these views involve political issues, they cannot be grounds for union discipline; it is unlikely that a member's expression of political opinion would be subject to discipline under the proviso to that section.

The extent of this protection is illustrated by a case in which members of the union campaigned for the enactment in their state of a right-to-work law.[152] The union expelled them for violating a provision of the union constitution that condemned "conduct unbecoming a member." The court recognized a number of situations in which a member's conduct would not be protected because it jeopardized the union's existence as an institution—for example, engaging in spying on the union on behalf of an employer, dual unionism, violation of work rules, and wildcat strikes. While the campaign to enact a right-to-work law might not have been in the union's best interests as an institution, the court nevertheless held that the union could not expel the members on this basis.

> We are not called upon to decide what the result would be if a member was expelled for advocating repeal of the Wagner Act or the abolition of unions. Only the right-to-work law is here involved. The union argues that it may reasonably consider such a law seriously inimical to its interests. This is certainly not an unreasonable position, and . . . many authorities agree. But there is substantial respectable opinion to the contrary. [Professor] Cox says, "The member who acts as a strikebreaker may be guilty of treason, but one can believe in right-to-work laws and remain a good trade unionist."[153]

May my dues be used to support political activities?

As noted in chapter 19, a union may not compel a worker to pay dues that are used for political purposes such as lobbying. The worker who opposes such use of her dues may resign from the union and continue to pay dues under a fair share arrangement. The fair share payer's obligations are limited to expenditures directly related to collective bargaining.

May my union make political contributions?

No. The Federal Election Campaign Act limits the right of a labor organization to make political contributions or expendi-

tures for any election to federal office.[154] These provisions generally place unions under the same kinds of limitation as corporations with regard to political spending. The union may not
use its general funds to make contributions in connection with
a federal election or to make expenditures directed at the
general public. For example, the union may not purchase television time to conduct a get-out-the-vote campaign directed
to the public at large. On the other hand, the union may spend
money to communicate with its own members on any subject,
including electioneering on behalf of candidates for public office. It may conduct registration and get-out-the-vote drives
aimed at its members and their families. The union may also
use its funds for general educational campaigns directed at the
public—for example, a campaign urging repeal of the right-to-
work provision of the Taft-Hartley law.

State laws may also have a bearing upon union expenditures.
Thus, a state law may limit union contributions and expenditures for state and local elections in the same way that the
federal law regulates spending for federal elections. If there
is no such law, the union is free to make expenditures and
contributions for state and local candidates.

But even if the state or federal law permits the union to
make election expenditures, the individual union member still
has the right to object to the expenditure of his dues for political
purposes.

**May the union engage in political activities through volun-
tary fundraising?**

Yes. The Supreme Court has held,[155] and the Federal Election Campaign Act provides,[156] that a union may set up an
independent fund, wholly separate from the union's regular
treasury, for the purpose of supporting political candidates and
issues. However, contributions to these funds must be wholly
voluntary and cannot be a condition of employment or of union
membership. In one case, a union required employees who
joined the union to agree to a deduction of $1.00 per year for
political contributions. The member could have the contribution refunded if he filed a separate written request. Such a
reverse check-off system was held unlawful under the Federal
Election Campaign Act.[157]

While the political fund must be a fiscally separate entity, it may be administered by officials of the union, and general union funds may be used to establish and maintain the fund. Under the Federal Election Campaign Act, there are some limitations on the expenditures that may be made through these funds—for example, there is a dollar ceiling on contributions that may be made on behalf of each candidate.[158]

NOTES

1. We owe a great debt in the preparation of this chapter to Professor Clyde Summers, who was the author, along with Robert J. Rabin, of the earlier ACLU volume, *The Rights of Union Members* (Avon Books, 1979). Professor Summers was responsible for the chapters in that book on the right of union membership and the right to participate in union governance. The questions and structure of the present chapter are influenced by the earlier work. In addition, Professor Summers wrote most of the early leading articles in this field, such as Summers, *Legal Limitations on Union Discipline*, 64 Harv. L. Rev. 1049 (1951); Summers, *The Law of Union Discipline: What the Courts Do in Fact*, 70 Yale L.J. 175 (1960); Summers, *Preemption and the Labor Reform Act—Dual Rights and Remedies*, 22 Ohio St. L.J. 119 (1961).
2. There seems to be no doubt that a union may appoint officers, for the Supreme Court dealt with the express question of the union's right to remove appointed officers in *Finnegan v. Leu*, 456 U.S. 431 (1982).
3. *Wooddell v. IBEW*, 112 S. Ct. 494 (1991).
4. LMRDA § 603 (a). The full citation is 29 U.S.C. § 523(a). For purposes of this chapter, we will use the popular citation to the numbering of the LMRDA, in which Title I is Section 101, etc., Title IV is Section 401, etc., and so forth. The statutory compilation is 29 U.S.C. §§ 401–531. Some of the literature on the common law of union democracy, mostly by Professor Summers, is cited in *supra* note 1.
5. LMRDA § 101(a)(1) and (2). In contrast, Title IV, which deals with union elections, contains no analogous provision preserving the internal autonomy of unions. The Supreme Court has held that this distinction is deliberate, and in Title IV cases will not defer to union rules. *Masters, Mates and Pilots v. Brown*, 111 S. Ct. 880, 136 LRRM 2473 (1991).
6. *Carothers v. Presser*, 818 F.2d 926, 934 (D.C. Cir. 1987).

7. *Brock v. CSEA Local,* 808 F.2d 228 (2d Cir. 1987). The case involves Title IV of the LMRDA, discussed in chapter 22, but the principle applies to all aspects of LMRDA coverage.

8. LMRDA § 609. This section makes it unlawful for a union to "fine, suspend, expel, or otherwise discipline any of its members" for exercising a right protected by the LMRDA. The argument may be made that a refusal to admit a worker to membership because of his activities when he was previously a union member violates the "otherwise discipline" language of this section. There is no controlling case authority on this point.

9. NLRA § 8(a)(3).

10. LMRDA § 101(a)(1).

11. LMRDA § 101(a)(2).

12. The leading case holding that the free speech provisions of Title I do not require a union to hold membership meetings in the absence of a constitutional provision is *Yanity v. Benware,* 376 F.2d 197 (2d Cir. 1967), a case that continues to be followed and cited with approval, *e.g., Grant v. Chicago Truck Drivers,* 806 F.2d 114 (7th Cir. 1986); *Cotter v. Helmer,* 692 F. Supp. 313 (S.D.N.Y. 1988). The strongest case authority for the proposition that the failure to hold meetings deprives a member of his free speech rights is *Wade v. Teamsters,* 527 F. Supp. 1169 (E.D. Mich. 1981). *See* Klare, *The Public/Private Distinction,* 130 U. Pa. L. Rev. 1358, 1375 (1982), criticizing this decision. In consulting the cases on this point, the reader must be careful to determine to what extent the decision turns on the language of the union's constitution and bylaws. A few courts hold that even if the constitution and bylaws require meetings, failure to hold them is not a violation of the equal rights provisions of the LMRDA since all members are equally denied the opportunity for meetings. *See Rodonich v. Laborers,* 115 LRRM 2482 (S.D.N.Y. 1983), *aff'd,* 817 F.2d 967 (2d Cir. 1987); and *Linder v. Berge,* 567 F. Supp. 913 (D.R.I. 1983), *aff'd,* 739 F.2d 686 (1st Cir. 1984). *But see Moran v. Walsh,* 139 LRRM 2092 (1991) (finding the abrogation of customary meeting scheduling coupled with lack of notice deprived members of rights to attend membership meetings in violation of LMRDA § 101(a)(1)).

13. LMRDA § 401(a) and (b).

14. LMRDA § 101 (a)(3).

15. *See* note 11.

16. *O'Neill v. ALPA,* 886 F.2d 1438 (5th Cir. 1989). This case was reversed by the Supreme Court on other grounds, *ALPA v. O'Neill,* 111 S. Ct. 1127 (1991), but the point made in the text as supported by the Fifth Circuit decision appears to be accepted by the Supreme Court,

see footnote 3 of the Court's decision and accompanying text. *See also Sako v. Teamsters*, 125 LRRM 2372 (N.D. Ill. 1987).

17. *See, e.g., Walker v. Teamsters*, 714 F. Supp. 178, 131 LRRM 3185 (N.C. 1989), aff'd (as to contract interpretation discretion) and rev'd (on other grounds), 932 F.2d 376 (4th Cir. 1991) *cert. denied*, 112 S. Ct. 637; *Cumiskey v. Seafarers*, 128 LRRM 3248 (E.D. Pa. 1988); *Carothers v. McCarthy*, 705 F. Supp. 687, 130 LRRM 2751 (D.C. 1989). For a very persuasive argument that the LMRDA ought to require membership ratification of contract negotiations, but conceding that it does not, *see* Hyde, *Democracy in Collective Bargaining*, 93 Yale L.J. 793 (1984).

18. *NLRB v. Financial Institution Employees*, 475 U.S. 192, 205 (1986); *NLRB v. Eastern Connecticut Health Services*, 815 F.2d 517 (2d Cir. 1987); *Maurer v. Auto Workers*, 487 F. Supp. 731 (M.D. Pa. 1979). *See also Stolz v. Carpenters*, 655 F. Supp. 192 (D. Nev. 1987).

19. *Carothers v. Presser*, 818 F.2d 926 (D.C. Cir. 1987).

20. LMRDA § 103(a)(3)(A). *See Berger v. Iron Workers*, 843 F.2d 1395 (D.C. Cir. 1988), clarified on reh'g, 852 F.2d 619 (D.C. Cir. 1988) (holding that courts have no power to intervene in a union referendum that complies with this section), *cert. denied*, 490 U.S. 1105.

21. *Sertic v. Carpenters*, 423 F.2d 515 (6th Cir. 1970). *But see Stolz v. Carpenters*, 655 F. Supp. 192, 124 LRRM 3222 (D. Nev. 1987), which takes a much less restrictive view than *Sertic*, suggesting that as long as the union makes a reasonable effort to explain and separate out the issues, the combining of issues on a single referendum ballot is not necessarily a violation. *Stolz* contains an extensive listing and discussion of the leading cases on this subject.

22. LMRDA § 101(a)(3)(B).

23. *See Denov v. Musicians*, 703 F.2d 1034 (7th Cir. 1983).

24. *Cefalo v. Moffett*, 449 F.2d 1193, 1199 (D.C. Cir. 1971).

25. *Carothers v. McCarthy*, 705 F. Supp. 687, 130 LRRM 2751 (D.D.C. 1989); *Rural Letter Carriers, Knox County Local v. Rural Letter Carriers*, 720 F.2d 936, 114 LRRM 3300 (6th Cir. 1984).

26. *Id. See also, Brown v. Lowen*, 857 F.2d 216, 129 LRRM 2363 (4th Cir. 1988). There appears to be a split of authority on this point, as the D.C. Circuit has held there is no right to a mailing list in a referendum, *Carothers v. Presser*, 818 F.2d 926 (D.C. Cir. 1987).

27. *Blanchard v. Johnson*, 388 F. Supp. 208, 215 (N.D. Ohio 1974); *Cefalo v. Moffett*, 449 F.2d 1193, 1199 (D.C. Cir. 1971).

28. *Young v. Hayes*, 195 F. Supp. 911, 916 (D.C. 1961). *See also Schlosser v. Flight Attendants*, 121 LRRM 2358 (D. Minn. 1985), involving the wording of a referendum on whether to pay a consulting fee to establish an Employee Stock Ownership Plan (ESOP).

29. *Carothers v. McCarthy*, 705 F. Supp. 687 (D.D.C., 1989). *Compare Baker v. Newspaper Union*, 628 F.2d 156 (D.C. Cir. 1980) *Gilliam v. Independent Steelworkers*, 572 F. Supp. 168 (N.D. W. Va. 1983).

30. *Vestal v. Teamsters*, 245 F. Supp. 623 (M.D. Tenn. 1965).

31. *See generally, Rosario v. Ladies Garment Workers, Local 10*, 605 F.2d 1228, 101 LRRM 2958 (2d Cir. 1979), *cert. denied*, 446 U.S. 919, 104 LRRM 2096 (1980).

32. *Wade v. Teamsters Local 247*, 527 F. Supp. 1169 (E.D. Mich. 1981). *See also Aguirre v. Automotive Teamsters*, 633 F.2d 168 (9th Cir. 1980) (suggesting a greater standard of care where there is a "labor dispute" as opposed to the ordinary administration of union activities).

33. *Bausman v. NCR Independent Union*, 74 LRRM 2950 (Ohio Ct. App. 1970).

34. *Grant v. Chicago Truck Drivers*, 806 F.2d 114 (7th Cir. 1986); *compare Wade v. Teamsters*, 527 F. Supp. 1169 (E.D. Mich. 1981) for a distinctly minority view.

35. *Parker v. Steelworkers*, 642 F.2d 104 (5th Cir. 1981); *compare Dole v. Service Employees Union*, 950 F.2d 1456 (9th Cir. 1991), 139 LRRM 2070, involving a union challenge under the First Amendment against the secretary of labor for interfering with the internal affairs of the union.

36. *Id. Compare Petramale v. Laborers*, 736 F.2d 13 (2d Cir. 1984), *cert. denied*, 469 U.S. 1087.

37. *Parker v. Steelworkers*, 642 F.2d 104 (5th Cir. 1981).

38. *Boilermakers v. Hardeman*, 401 U.S. 233 (1971) ("Sec. 101(a)(5) was not intended to authorize courts to determine the scope of offenses for which a union may discipline its members."). *Compare Bise v. Electrical Workers*, 618 F.2d 1299 (9th Cir. 1979), *cert. denied*, 449 U.S. 904 (1980).

39. *See Bise v. Electrical Workers*, 618 F.2d 1299, 1303 (9th Cir. 1979), *cert. denied*, 449 U.S. 904 (1980) (citing *NLRB v. Shipbuilding Workers*, 391 U.S. 418, 428 (1968)). *See also Mitchell v. Machinists*, 16 Cal. Rptr. 813 (1961).

40. *Bise v. Electrical Workers*, *supra* note 38.

41. *Burns v. Painters Local 1503*, 90 LRRM 2824, 2827 (D.C. Conn. 1975).

42. *Nix v. Machinists Union*, 83 LRRM 2478, 2480 (N.D. Ga. 1972), *aff'd*, 479 F.2d 382 (5th Cir. 1973).

43. *Salzhandler v. Caputo*, 316 F.2d 445 (2d Cir. 1963), *cert. denied*, 375 U.S. 946 (1964).

44. *Farowitz v. Associated Musicians of Greater New York*, 330 F.2d 999, 1002 (2d Cir. 1964).

45. *Salzhandler v. Caputo*, 316 F.2d 445, 451 (2d Cir. 1963). The case

is still good law; *see, e.g., Petramale v. Laborers,* 736 F.2d 13 (2d Cir. 1984), *cert. denied,* 469 U.S. 1087.

46. *Cole v. Hall,* 339 F.2d 881 (2d Cir. 1965), *Salzhandler v. Caputo, supra* note 42; *Petramale v. Laborers Union,* 736 F.2d 13 (2d Cir. 1984), *cert. denied,* 469 U.S. 1087.

47. *Nix v. Machinists Union,* 83 LRRM 2478 (N.D. Ga. 1972), *aff'd* 479 F.2d 382 (5th Cir. 1973).

48. *Distillery Workers Union,* 296 NLRB No. 72, 132 LRRM 1129 (1989), discussing the leading cases on this point.

49. *Local 1199 v. Retail, Wholesale & Department Store Union,* 671 F. Supp. 279 (S.D.N.Y. 1987), *aff'd, Johnson v. Kay,* 860 F.2d 529 (2d Cir. 1988).

50. *Id.*

51. *Kuebler v. Lithographers,* 473 F.2d 359, 364 (6th Cir. 1973). *See also Shimman v. Frank,* 625 F.2d 80 (6th Cir. 1980), *reh'g denied,* 633 F.2d 468.

52. CWA Local 9431, 138 LRRM 1483 (1991).

53. *Kuebler v. Lithographers,* 473 F.2d 359, 364 (6th Cir. 1973).

54. *International Brotherhood of Boilermakers v. Hardeman,* 401 U.S. 233 (1971).

55. *Clothing Workers Rank & File Comm. v. Clothing Workers Philadelphia Joint Bd.,* 473 F.2d 1303 (3d Cir. 1973).

56. *Semancik v. Mine Workers Dist. 5,* 466 F.2d 144, 154 (3d Cir. 1972).

57. *See Ferguson v. Iron Workers,* 129 LRRM 2131, 2137 (1988) (citing 29 U.S.C. § 158(a)(3)(b)).

58. *Breininger v. Sheet Metal Workers,* 493 U.S. 67 (1989).

59. *Finnegan v. Leu,* 456 U.S. 431 (1982).

60. *Sheet Metal Workers v. Lynn,* 488 U.S. 347 (1989).

61. *Guidry v. Operating Engineers,* 882 F.2d 929 (5th Cir. 1989), *modified,* 907 F. 2d 1491, 1493 (5th Cir. 1990) (specifying that officer's actions complained of "must be 'undertaken under color of the union's right to control the member's conduct in order to protect the interests of the union or its membership,'" and "not [be] purely 'ad hoc retaliation by individual union officers.'" (citing *Breininger, supra* note 57)).

62. *See Wrightson v. General Motors,* 126 LRRM 2948 (W.D.N.Y. 1987); *But see Clift v. UAW,* 881 F.2d 408 (1989); *Leguto v. Teamsters,* 853 F.2d 1046 (2d Cir. 1988); *Truck Drivers v. Traweek,* 867 F.2d 500 (9th Cir. 1989).

63. *Kowaleviocz v. Longshoremen,* 138 LRRM 2107 (4th Cir. 1991); *Dessler v. Teamsters, Chauffeurs, Warehousemen & Helpers, Local* 251, 686 F. Supp. 977 (D.R.I. 1988).

64. *Morrisey v. National Maritime Union,* 397 F. Supp. 659 (S.D.N.Y. 1975), *aff'd in part* (upholding member's free speech claim) and *rev'd*

in part (rejecting lower court's ruling that the union could not be held liable for punitive damages under Landrum-Griffin), 544 F.2d 19 (2d Cir. 1976), 92 LRRM 3211 (1976). *Cf. Black v. Ryder/P.I.E. Nationwide*, 970 F.2d 1461, 140 LRRM 2904. (6th Cir. 1992).

65. *Shimman v. Frank*, 625 F.2d 80 (6th Cir. 1980).

66. *Maier v. Patterson*, 553 F. Supp. 150 (E.D. Pa. 1982).

67. LMRDA § 101(a)(5).

68. This is expressly excepted from LMRDA § 101(a)(5).

69. *Caravan v. Typographical Union*, 381 F. Supp. 14 (E.D. Pa. 1974). The text of LMRDA § 101(a)(5) says no member may be disciplined "unless" he has been afforded the protections of that section. The question of what actually constitutes "discipline" may be problematic for union members attempting to invoke this protection. *See MacAuley v. Boston Typographical Union*, 474 F. Supp. 344 (D. Mass. 1979); *Turner v. Boilermakers*, 528 F. Supp. 1008 (N.D. Ala. 1981).

70. Quoted in *Boilermakers Union v. Hardeman*, 401 U.S. 233, 245, n.12 (1971).

71. *Id.* at 245. For later authority, see *Frye v. Steelworkers*, 767 F.2d 1216 (7th Cir. 1985), *cert. denied*, 474 U.S. 1007. *See also Hurley v. Steamfitters*, 131 LRRM 2048 (1988); *Bollitier v. Teamsters*, 133 LRRM 2554 (1991).

72. *Lacy v. Freight Employees*, 99 LRRM 2403 (W.D. Tenn. 1978), *aff'd without op.*, 620 F.2d 303 (6th Cir. 1979). *See also Strom v. Basketball Referees*, 564 F. Supp. 250 (E.D. Pa. 1983).

73. *Gleason v. Chain Service Restaurant*, 422 F.2d 342 (2d Cir. 1970), *aff'd*, 497 F.2d 401 (1974).

74. *See, e.g., Waring v. ILA*, 653 F. Supp. 374 (S.D. Ga. 1986); *Eisman v. Clothing Workers*, 496 F.2d 1313 (4th Cir. 1974).

75. *Reilly v. Sheet Metal Union*, 488 F. Supp. 1121 (S.D.N.Y. 1980).

76. *Hart v. Carpenters*, 341 F. Supp. 1266 (E.D.N.Y. 1972), *aff'd*, 497 F.2d 401 (1974).

77. *Rosario v. Garment Workers*, 605 F.2d 1228 (2d Cir. 1979).

78. *Tincher v. Piasecki*, 520 F.2d 851, 854 (7th Cir. 1975) ("the union member need not necessarily be provided with the full panoply of procedural safeguards found in criminal proceedings"); *Gustafson v. Train Dispatchers*, 788 F.2d 1284 (7th Cir. 1986). *See also Frye, Hurley* and *Bollitier, supra* note 70.

79. *Kiepura v. Steelworkers*, 358 F. Supp. 987 (N.D. Ill. 1973).

80. *Winterberge v. Teamsters*, 558 F.2d 923 (9th Cir. 1977); *Mandoglio v. Carpenters*, 575 F. Supp. 646 (E.D.N.Y. 1983).

81. *Cornelio v. Carpenters*, 243 F. Supp. 126 (E.D. Pa. 1965), *aff'd* 358 F.2d 728 (3d Cir. 1966). But *Cornelio* seems to emphasize the idea that the union should be allowed to keep the matter "in the family,"

rather than focusing on the notion that the union should afford the member outside counsel if the union seeks outside help.

82. *Goodman v. Laborers,* 742 F.2d 780 (3d Cir. 1984).

83. *Kiepura v. Steelworkers,* 358 F. Supp. 987 (N.D. Ill. 1973).

84. *See, e.g., Myers v. Affiliated Craftsmen Union,* 667 F.2d 817 (9th Cir. 1982); *Mayle v. Laborers,* 886 F.2d 144 (6th Cir. 1988).

85. *See Cotter v. Helmer,* 132 LRRM 2351 (S.D.N.Y. 1988); *Franza v. Teamsters,* 869 F.2d 41 (2d Cir. 1989); *Johnson v. Kay,* 860 F.2d 529 (2d Cir. 1988).

86. *Hall v. Cole,* 412 U.S. 1, 83 LRRM 2177 (1973).

87. *Kuebler v. Lithographers, Local 24-P,* 473 F.2d 359, 82 LRRM 2717 (1973).

88. *Murphy v. Operating Engineers, Local 18,* 99 LRRM 2074 (N.D. Ohio 1978).

89. *Keeffe Bros. v. Teamsters, Local 592,* 562 F.2d 298, 96 LRRM 2267 (4th Cir. 1977); *Guidry v. Operating Engineers,* 882 F.2d 929 (5th Cir. 1989). *Rodonich v. Laborers,* 817 F.2d 967 (2d Cir. 1987)(recovery for emotional distress granted only if member can show physical injury as well).

90. *Boilermakers v. Braswell,* 388 F.2d 193 (5th Cir. 1968), *cert. denied,* 391 U.S. 935; *Parker v. Steelworkers, Local 1466,* 642 F.2d 104, 106 LRRM 3038 (1981); *Guidry v. Operating Engineers,* 132 LRRM 2563 (1989); *Woods v. Graphic Communications,* 136 LRRM 2660 (1991).

91. *Ryan v. Electrical Workers,* 387 F.2d 778 (7th Cir. 1967).

92. *Breininger v. Sheet Metal Workers,* 110 S. Ct. 424 (1989). The international union will be held responsible for the acts of a local, and its treasury available to pay any damages, only if it can be shown to have ratified the conduct in question, *Rodonich v. Laborers Union,* 817 F.2d 967 (2d Cir. 1987).

93. *Wooddell v. Electrical Workers,* 112 S. Ct. 494 (1991).

94. The leading case is *Hall v. Cole,* 412 U.S. 1 (1973). More current cases are collected in *Markham v. Iron Workers,* 901 F.2d 1022 (11th Cir. 1990) and in *Johnson v. Kay,* 742 F. Supp. 822, 137 LRRM 2354, 2363 (S.D.N.Y. 1990). *See Goldberg v. Hall,* 131 LRRM 2112 (S.D.N.Y. 1988) and *Guidry v. Operating Engineers,* 882 F.2d 929 (5th Cir. 1989). Attorney's fees may also be granted for litigation that is needed in order to collect attorney's fees, *Kinney v. Electrical Workers,* 137 LRRM 2866 (9th Cir. 1991).

95. *Shimman v. Frank,* 744 F.2d 1226 (6th Cir. 1984), *cert. denied* 469 U.S. 1215 (1985). *Contra Lear Siegler v. Lehman,* 842 F.2d 1102, 1117–18 (9th Cir. 1988), criticizing *Shimman* and suggesting that bad faith beyond actual conducting of litigation should subject party to liability for attorney's fees.

96. *But see Markham v. Iron Workers*, 901 F.2d 1022 (11th Cir. 1990), where the court held that a party obtaining a preliminary injunction was not a "prevailing party" entitled to attorney's fees.

97. She or he might tell you about *Delaware Valley I*, 478 U.S. 546 (1986).

98. *Reed v. U.T.U.*, 488 U.S. 319 (1989).

99. *See* Stein, *10(B) or Not 10(B): A Critical Overview of Court-Selected Limitations Periods in Labor Law*, 6 Labor Lawyer 331 (1990).

100. *Minneapolis Star and Tribune Co.*, 109 NLRB 727 (1954); *Paperworkers Local 5*, 294 NLRB No. 84, 131 LRRM 1545 (1989). *See generally*, Atleson, *Union Fines and Picket Lines: The NLRA and Union Disciplinary Power*, 17 UCLA L. Rev. 681 (1970); Gould, *Some Limitations upon Union Discipline under the NLRA*, 1970 Duke L.J. 1067.

101. *NLRB v. Allis-Chalmers Mfg.*, 388 U.S. 175 (1967). The board recently applied this doctrine to uphold a fine against a worker who announced she would not honor a picket line, despite her claim that she was exercising her right of free speech, *Distillery Workers' Union*, 296 NLRB No. 72, 132 LRRM 1129 (1989).

102. *Scofield v. NLRB*, 394 U.S. 423 (1969). *Compare Meat Cutters, Local 593*, 99 LRRM 1123 (1978).

103. *NLRB v. Industrial Union of Marine and Shipbuilding Workers*, 391 U.S. 418 (1968).

104. *American Broadcasting Companies v. Writers Guild*, 434 U.S. 995 (1978); *Ballas v. McKiernan*, 35 N.Y.2d 14, 87 LRRM 2961 (1974), *cert. denied*, 419 U.S. 1034; *Machinists v. Loudermilk*, 444 F.2d 719 (5th Cir. 1971). *Cf. Ferguson v. Iron Workers*, 854 F.2d 1169, 1173 (9th Cir. 1988), upholding fines where district court found that dual unionism was undertaken by plaintiffs to destroy union rather than reform it, and fines imposed by the union were defensive in nature.

105. *Sheet Metal Workers*, 269 NLRB No. 150, 132 LRRM 1354 (1989).

106. *Posner v. Utility Workers*, 47 Cal. App. 3d 970, 121 Cal. Rptr. 423, 90 LRRM 2515 (1975).

107. *NLRB v. Allis-Chalmers, supra* note 98.

108. *Plumbers Local 631*, 197 NLRB 267, 133 LRRM 1001 (1989). The right to have a worker terminated by his employer for nonpayment of dues is discussed in chapter 19.

109. *Id.* at 181–82.

110. *NLRB v. Boeing Co.*, 412 U.S. 67 (1973). For the suggestion that the fine may be challenged in federal court as well, see *Wooddell v. IBEW*, 112 S. Ct. 494 (1991).

111. *NLRB v. Granite State Joint Bd., Textile Workers*, 409 U.S. 213 (1972).

112. *NLRB v. Boeing Co.*, 412 U.S. 67, 76 (1973).

113. *See* the examples of lower court fine enforcement discussed by the Supreme Court in *NLRB v. Boeing Co.*, 412 U.S. at 76, n.12. *See also Electrical Workers v. Bradley*, 149 Ill. App. 3d 193, 499 N.E. 2d 577, 124 LRRM 2099 (1986).

114. *NLRB v. Allis-Chalmers, supra* note 98, at 196.

115. *Pattern Makers v. NLRB*, 473 U.S. 95 (1985).

116. *NLRB v. Hotel Employees Union*, 887 F.2d 28, 132 LRRM 2625 (3d Cir. 1989), *cert. denied*, 110 S. Ct. 1922 (1990).

117. *United Mine Workers (Canterbury Coal)*, 305 NLRB No. 56, 138 LRRM 1329 (1991).

118. This is certainly implied in the decision. *See, e.g., NLRB v. Hotel Employees Union*, 887 F.2d 28 (3d Cir. 1989), discussing the implications of *Pattern Makers* on financial core members. *See also Distillery Workers' Union*, 296 NLRB No. 72, 132 LRRM 1129 (1989)(Stephens, Chairman, concurring).

119. *NLRB v. Granite State Joint Bd., supra* note 111.

120. *Local 1327, Machinists v. NLRB*, 725 F.2d 1212 (9th Cir. 1984); *Local 1255, Machinists v. NLRB*, 456 F.2d 1214 (5th Cir. 1972).

121. *NLRB v. Granite State Joint Bd., supra* note 111.

122. *See Navarro v. Gannon*, 385 F.2d 512 (2d Cir. 1967); *Amirault v. Shaughnessy*, 749 F.2d 140 (2d Cir. 1984).

123. For a general discussion of trusteeships prior to the LMRDA, see Beaird, *Union Trusteeship Provision of the LMRDA*, 2 Ga. L. Rev. 469, 471–74 (1968). For a general discussion of the incidence and purposes of trusteeships in the early years of the LMRDA, see *Secretary of Labor, Union Trusteeships: Report to the Congress upon the Operation of Title III of the LMRDA 5–11 (1962)*, submitted to Congress pursuant to Section 305 of the LMRDA. *See also* Anderson, *Landrum-Griffin and the Trusteeship Imbroglio*, 71 Yale L.J. 1460 (1962).

124. *Sheet Metal Workers v. Lynn*, 488 U.S. 347, 358 n.9, 109 S. Ct. 639, 646 n.9 (1989).

125. *Sheet Metal Workers v. Lynn, supra* note 124.

126. Title IV is discussed separately in chapter 22.

127. *Sheet Metal Workers v. Lynn, supra* note 124.

128. LMRDA § 302.

129. LMRDA § 304(c).

130. *See* authorities collected in *Markham v. Iron Workers*, 134 LRRM 2375 (11th Cir. 1990).

131. LMRDA § 304(a).

132. *Markham v. Iron Workers*, 901 F.2d 1022 (11th Cir. 1990).

133. *Id.*

134. LMRDA § 304(c). On the question of the fair hearing required by this section see *Markham, supra* note 130.

135. *Benda v. Machinists*, 584 F.2d 308 (9th Cir. 1978), *cert. dismissed*, 441 U.S. 937 (1979). For another case involving an attempt to control the local's bargaining practices, see *Markham, supra* note 130.

136. *C.A.P.E. v. Painters Union*, 598 F. Supp. 1056 (D.C.N.J. 1984); *Boilermakers v. Local Lodge*, 694 F. Supp. 1203 (D.C. Md. 1988). But the presumption that a trusteeship is properly imposed by international must be overcome to prevail on a bad faith argument.

137. *Boilermakers v. Local Lodge*, 845 F.2d 687 (7th Cir. 1988).

138. *See Boilermakers v. Local Lodge*, 673 F. Supp. 199 (W.D. Tex. 1987).

139. *Laborers v. Nat'l Post Office Div.*, 128 LRRM 3178 (D.C. 1988).

140. *Teamsters v. Crane*, 848 F.2d 709 (6th Cir. 1988).

141. LMRDA § 303(a)(2).

142. *Blassie v. Poole*, 58 LRRM 2359 (E.D. Mo. 1964).

143. LMRDA § 301.

144. LMRDA § 501(a).

145. *E.g., Lorentangeli v. Critelli*, 692 F. Supp. 380, 387 (D.N.J. 1987) ("The fiduciary principle under [LMRDA] Section 501 extends to all of the activities of union officials. Under this interpretation, actions which violate the union's constitution are a breach of the fiduciary duty imposed by Section 501."); *Sabolsky v. Budzanoski*, 457 F.2d 1245 (3d Cir. 1972)(holding that a charge against union officers for failing to disband locals with less than ten members as required by union's constitution was a viable claim for breach of fiduciary duty imposed by Section 501). *Cf. Head v. Railway Employees*, 512 F.2d 398 (2d Cir. 1975)(restructuring of union organization to eliminate local lodges not controlled by Section 501 absent union officers' misappropriation of union funds or property).

146. LMRDA § 501(b). "The trial judge may allot a reasonable part of the recovery in any action under this subsection to pay the fees of counsel prosecuting the suit at the instance of the member of the labor organization and to compensate such member for any expenses necessarily paid or incurred by him in connection with the litigation."

147. *Wood v. Georgia*, 450 U.S. 261 (1981); *In re Gopman*, 531 F.2d 262 (5th Cir. 1976).

148. LMRDA § 502(a).

149. *Breininger v. Sheet Metal Workers*, 493 U.S. 67 (1989).

150. *U.S. v. Teamsters Local 560*, 754 F. Supp. 395, 136 LRRM 2165

(D.N.J. 1991), implementing *U.S. v. Local 560*, 780 F.2d 267 (3d Cir. 1985). *See also U.S. v. Teamsters*, 138 LRRM 2945 (2d Cir. 1990). The litigation is discussed in detail in Goldberg, *Cleaning Labor's House: Institutional Reform Litigation in the Labor Movement*, 1989 Duke L.J. 903 (1989).

151. H.R. Rep. No. 741 on H.R. 8342. 86th Cong, 1st Sess. 7–9 (1959).
152. *Mitchell v. International Ass'n of Machinists*, 16 Cal. Rptr. 813 (1961).
153. *Id.* at 819.
154. Federal Election Campaign Act Amendments of 1976, Pub. L. No. §§ 94-283, § 101, 90 Stat. 475, 486-92, 2 U.S.C.A. §§ 431 *et seq. See* Comment, *The Regulation of Union Political Activity: Majority and Minority Rights and Remedies*, 126 U. Pa. L. Rev. 386 (1977).
155. *See Pipefitters Local 562 v. United States*, 407 U.S. 385 (1972).
156. *See* Federal Election Campaign Act, 2 U.S.C.A. §§ 431–56, especially §§ 432, 433, 434.
157. *Federal Election Comm. v. National Education Ass'n*, 457 F. Supp. 1102, 99 LRRM 2263 (D.C. 1978).
158. *See Walther v. Federal Election Commission*, 82 F.R.D. 200, 101 LRRM 2360 (D.C. 1979).

XXII

The Right to Fair and Open Elections

The integrity of the electoral process is a cornerstone of union democracy.[1] Title IV of the LMRDA regulates union elections. It provides that elections shall be held at regular intervals, that members shall have the right to nominate and vote for candidates, that candidates shall have access to voting lists and reasonable use of the channels of communication within the union, and that the election itself shall be fair. Other provisions of the LMRDA, including Title I, Title V, and Section 609, insure that candidates do not suffer reprisals for challenging the incumbent leadership. In addition, the secretary of labor has promulgated rules explaining and interpreting several of the provisions of the statute, although these rules do not have the binding legal effect of the statute itself.[2] As with other areas we have discussed, the provisions of the union constitution may significantly affect voting rights.

The voting rights section of the LMRDA is unique in that the enforcement of these rights is left almost exclusively to the secretary of labor.[3] Thus, much of the law in this area is developed initially by administrative decisions—subject, of course, to review and enforcement in the courts.[4] An individual usually cannot move directly into the court to protect his right to vote but must rely upon the secretary of labor. As with other sections of the LMRDA, the complaining member must first exhaust his internal review procedure, but if an acceptable decision is not reached by the union within three months, he is free to file a complaint with the secretary of labor.[5]

The complaining member should understand that there is no assurance that the secretary of labor will find merit in his complaint. The secretary of labor's function is not only to enforce the rights of union members but to screen out those complaints which he or she deems frivolous, in order to protect unions from unnecessary litigation and judicial interference with their elections. As the Supreme Court has said, the secretary has the obligation to protect the "vital public interest in assuring free and democratic elections that transcends the narrower interest of the complaining union member."[6] The complaining member may not be satisfied with the way in which the secretary handles his complaint, for, as the Court also observed, "[e]ven if the Secretary is performing his duties, broadly conceived, as well as can be expected, the union member may have a valid complaint about the performance of 'his lawyer.'"[7]

The voting rights provisions in Title IV only apply to unions covered by the LMRDA. Unions that are comprised of employees solely in the public sector are not covered by the LMRDA but may be regulated by state law. Where a local union consists solely of public sector employees, but the parent union has private sector employees, local union elections will not be subject to the LMRDA if the local may spend its funds and conduct its elections without control by the parent.[8]

HOLDING ELECTIONS

Must a union hold elections?

Yes. The LMRDA requires that the officers of a labor organization be elected.[9] An *officer* is generally considered to be a person who exercises executive functions or who determines policy.[10] In many unions important functions are undertaken by the *business agent*, usually a person who is employed by the international union on a full-time basis to assist local unions in negotiating contracts, administering their agreements, and attending to other matters at the local level. There has been some disagreement as to whether a business agent must be treated as an officer who is required to be elected or as an employee of the union who may be appointed.[11]

In one case, a candidate for the elected position of *zoneman* complained to the secretary of labor about its election irregularities. The secretary concluded that the zoneman is not an officer under Section 402(n), which defines the term as "any person authorized to perform the functions of president, vice president, secretary, treasurer, or other executive functions . . . and any member of its executive board or similar governing body."[12] The zoneman serves as a backup to the shop chairman to funnel grievances. The zoneman does not sit on the executive committee, set policy, or undertake administrative or executive functions. A court will generally accept the secretary of labor's judgment on close factual questions of this sort.[13]

How often must elections be held?

At least once every three years in the case of officers of the local union, every four years for officers of intermediate bodies, and every five years for national or international officers.[14] Examples of an *intermediate body* include a system board or a joint board that operates on a level between the local and the national or international union.

Is secret balloting required?

A secret ballot election is required only for elections in a local labor organization.[15] Officers of the national or international union may be elected by secret ballot or, depending upon the union constitution, may be chosen at a convention by delegates who are in turn elected by a secret ballot.[16] If a labor union has an intermediate body, its officers may be elected by secret ballot election of the members or by officers who have been elected by secret ballot.[17]

RIGHTS OF CANDIDATES

What eligibility requirements may a union impose for holding office?

The union has a limited right to impose eligibility requirements for holding office. The LMRDA provides that "every member in good standing shall be eligible to be a candidate and to hold office." However, the Act qualifies this right by allowing the union to establish "reasonable qualifications uniformly imposed."[18] This is a double requirement. The qualification must be reasonable and must be applied even-handedly to all potential candidates. As you would expect, there has been much litigation on the question of what is a "reasonable" qualification for office.

In a leading case,[19] a bylaw of a local union limited eligibility for major elective offices to those union members who had previously held some lesser elective office within the union. The union argued that this requirement insured that those elected would be familiar with the workings of the local. The Court declared the rule invalid, stating that it was up to the voter and not the union to decide whether a particular candidate was qualified for office. The Court also noted that the union's rules would make some 93% of the members ineligible for office and that such a massive disqualification could hardly be considered reasonable. The Court explained:

> Congress plainly did not intend that the authorization in Sec. 401(e) of "reasonable qualifications uniformly imposed" should be given a broad reach. The contrary is implicit. . . . unduly restrictive candidacy qualifications can result in the abuses of entrenched leadership that the LMRDA was expressly enacted to curb. The check of democratic elections as a preventive measure is seriously impaired by candidacy qualifications which substantially deplete the ranks of those who might run in opposition to incumbents.[20]

In another case,[21] the union constitution limited eligibility for office to members who had attended at least one-half of the regular meetings of the local for 3 years prior to the election. In the particular local involved, only 23 of the local's approximately 660 members satisfied this requirement, and 9 of those were incumbent officers. Thus, the eligibility requirement disqualified over 96% of the union's members. The union argued that the rule served valid union purposes, was not burdensome, and had not served to entrench the existing leadership. The Court disagreed, holding that the "antidemocratic effects" of this eligibility rule outweighed any justification for it and that the disqualifications of so many members "obviously severely restricts the free choice of the membership in selecting its leaders."[22]

The courts have thrown out other eligibility requirements that unreasonably hamper the right to run for office. In one case a union restricted eligibility for high union office to those under age 65, asserting this would prevent "entrenchment in office." The court disagreed, holding there was no connection between the age requirement and fitness for office, citing regulations of the secretary that prohibit age discrimination in union elections.[23]

In another case a union rule required a candidate to transfer from a branch local to the parent local, at an additional cost of from $75 to $90, to be eligible to run for office. The court found no legitimate purpose for this requirement, which imposed an unreasonable financial burden on the right to run for office.[24]

But a union may bar a person from running for office if he belongs to a rival labor organization or holds a supervisory position on his job, since either status may be inconsistent with the union's best interests.[25] In addition, the LMRDA expressly provides that a union may deny the right to run a member who is barred from holding office on one of the grounds listed in Section 504 of the act—for example, conviction for certain crimes.[26]

What are the procedures for nominating candidates?

The LMRDA requires that "a reasonable opportunity shall be given for the nomination of candidates."[27] The actual procedures for nominating candidates may be determined by the union, as long as they do not unreasonably burden the members' right to nominate candidates and run for office. For example, a union constitution required that a candidate secure nominating petitions from five local unions and submit them by a certain date. The union barred the candidacy of a member when the secretary of one of the locals failed to send the member's petition to the parent union on time. The court held that the member could not be denied the right to run for office where the delay was the fault of a union officer and not the individual. The court went further and declared the procedure defective on its face because of the potential for abuse by local union officials in not transmitting petitions to the parent union.[28]

The union must give members reasonable and timely notice of when and where nominations must be made. It may not require potential candidates to declare their candidacy before the actual nominations are due, nor may it require candidates to pay a filing fee.[29] Similarly, the procedures for placing names in nomination must not be manipulated or designed to frustrate potential candidates. Thus, a union violated the act by locking the doors and starting a nominating meeting precisely on time when it knew that a member standing in the hall wished to nominate a candidate.[30]

What right does the LMRDA give a candidate to campaign for office?

The union is required to maintain a list of the names and

last known addresses of all persons who are members of the union in all cases in which a collective bargaining agreement requires union membership as a condition of employment. A candidate is entitled to inspect this list once within 30 days of the election.[31] However, the candidate may not copy the list, except under circumstances as discussed below. Congress was reluctant to require full copying of the list because unions expressed a fear that the lists might be used by rival employers and others to harm the union.

The candidate may require the union to distribute her campaign literature by mail or otherwise to all members in good standing, at the candidate's expense.[32] The union does not have the right to censor or reject any of this material, even if it believes it to be untrue or slanderous.[33] In a recent decision,[34] the Supreme Court held that the union may be required to distribute this material even before the nominating process is completed. In that case, involving the maritime industry, the union had a rule that a candidate could not have the literature mailed in advance of the union's nominating convention, when nominations were first made. The Court concluded that in the maritime industry, where members are widely dispersed, it is essential for the candidate to reach supporters prior to the nominating convention. The Court concluded that the judicial inquiry "should focus primarily on the reasonableness of the candidates request rather than on the reasonableness of the Union's rule."[35] The Court noted that Section 401(c) requires the union to comply "with *all* reasonable requests," and, unlike Section 401(e), which governs the right to run for office, this provision is not subject to reasonable qualifications imposed by the union. Failure to comply may warrant a rerun election.[36]

The candidate's right to inspect the membership list helps insure that the union will provide for full distribution of campaign materials. Some courts hold a candidate has this right even before the nomination process is completed, for otherwise incumbents will have an unreasonable advantage.[37]

In addition to the two specific rights of inspection and distribution just discussed, the LMRDA provides the candidate with the right of equal treatment of all candidates in using membership lists and in distributing literature.[38] This means that if one candidate, such as an incumbent officer, copies or uses the membership list to distribute his materials, the union must give all other candidates the same right to use the list.[39] More significantly, if the union permits one candidate to publish campaign materials free of charge in the union newspaper, it must provide the same right to other candidates.[40] This is a vital safeguard where the union is actively promoting the candidacy of a particular person.

Does the election process favor incumbents?

The incumbent has some inherent advantage. For example, unions usually give their leadership wide publicity in the union newspaper. In this respect the incumbent enjoys the same election advantage as an incumbent President of the United States. Yet the courts have not hesitated to find a violation where the coverage of the incumbent's activities went beyond normal newsworthy items and was really a device to promote his candidacy. This is well illustrated by the election in the Mine Workers Union between the incumbent Boyle and the challenger Yablonski. While conceding that at bottom a "judgement decision" is involved, the court stated: "A line must be drawn between the use of the Journal to report the activities of defendant Boyle as President, which is permissible, and the use of the Journal, in such a way in reporting such activities, as to promote the candidacy of said defendant."[41] The Court found excessive coverage of Boyle's activities in relation to their newsworthiness and an unexplained absence of any reference to Yablonski, who held an important position within the union.

In another case, which strangely enough involved a claim of excessive publicity for the challenger, the court held that while the LMRDA favored extensive coverage of campaign issues, many of the articles shaded too far from expressions of opinion on current issues into unwarranted personal attacks on the union president. The court held that the use of union funds for this publicity violated 401(g). So did the use of the union logo, which the court considered the equivalent of money under the statute.[42]

These decisions involve delicate judgments affecting freedom of the press, and courts are reluctant to infringe upon First Amendment rights. Thus, in the Yablonski-Boyle litigation the court very carefully avoided a remedy that would interfere with the union's freedom of the press. It merely ordered the union to provide Yablonski with an equal right to space whenever it gave coverage to Boyle as a candidate; it rejected Yablonski's requested relief that the union be compelled to print specific materials concerning his candidacy.[43]

May the union spend money to support a particular candidate?

No. The LMRDA provides that no monies received by the union in the form of dues, assessments, or similar levy may be utilized to promote the candidacy of any person. This prohibition is very broad and reaches even minimal expenditures. Thus, it bans union officers or paid union employees from campaigning for a candidate (even for themselves) during paid working time and prohibits the use of an office duplicating machine to produce campaign literature. It even outlaws the use of union stationery and typewriters. Violations of this rule may invalidate the election.[44] Candidates, whether or not they are presently union officers, may of course raise campaign funds by soliciting union members, but the contributions must be voluntary. Union officers can engage in such fundraising only on their own time. Outsiders may contribute money or effort to a candidacy, but an employer is not permitted to contribute.[45] At the other end of the spectrum, one court has held that a union may bar candidates from accepting contributions from persons who are not members of the local union, on the theory that it is reasonable for the union to try to prevent undue outside influences.[46]

A delicate line is again required between actual support of candidates and mere accommodation of their campaign needs. For example, if a union gives all candidates free space in its newspaper, this would satisfy the requirement of equal treatment of candidates but would technically violate the prohibition against the use of union monies to support candidates. Most courts have allowed unions, within reason, to give all candidates free space in union newspapers. This serves the basic purpose of Section 401(c) of the statute in providing a fair election with free and open debate that enables members to cast a knowledgeable vote.[47] However, one court has said that even if these funds are made available to all candidates, the section is still violated.[48]

THE VOTING PROCESS

May a union impose restrictions upon the right to vote?

Generally, no. The LMRDA provides that "each member in good standing shall be entitled to one vote."[49] While a union is generally not compelled to admit anyone to membership, once it admits a person it may not restrict her right to vote, except in limited circumstances. Unlike the right to run for office, the statute does not allow for "reasonable qualifications" upon the right to vote. The union is permitted under Section 101(a)(1) of the LMRDA to make "reasonable rules and regulations" concerning voting rights, but its discretion is much more limited than when it prescribes qualifications for holding office. Generally, the union may impose a brief membership requirement—usually under a year—as a condition of voting.[50] And it may require the member to have paid up his dues in order to vote.[51] Naturally, to be valid, these rules must be applied uniformly.

What rules govern the conduct of the balloting?

The LMRDA contains both general and specific provisions insuring that the election will be conducted fairly. The general requirement is that "adequate safeguards to insure a fair election shall be provided."[52] The specific protections include the following:

- Each member of the union must be mailed an election notice not less than 15 days prior to the election.[53]
- The election must provide for a secret ballot.[54]
- A candidate may have an observer at the polls and at the counting of the ballots.[55]
- Ballots and records of the election must be preserved for one year.[56]
- Votes must be cast and counted separately within each local and the results must be published separately.[57] This is designed to make it easier for a member to determine whether election misconduct may have occurred, for if there is misconduct that affects the vote, it is likely to show up in the count of the particular local ballots.

Does the member have to actually vote by secret ballot or is it enough that he is given the opportunity to vote by secret ballot?

While the LMRDA is not entirely clear on this point, the prevailing case law holds that it is not enough that a secret ballot is available to the member; rather, the union must make sure that all voters use that procedure. This is a sensible rule, for a secret ballot is defined in the act as one that insures that the voter's choice cannot be identified.[58] In one case voters were allowed to mark their ballots in the open, in the presence of other voters and observers. While provision was made for a voter to mark his ballot in private, the court concluded that a voter who wanted to do this would probably call attention to himself and indicate to others how he intended to vote.[59]

Must the union provide absentee ballots for those unable to vote in person?

The LMRDA makes no provision for absentee ballots, and the case law is unsettled on this subject. Where a substantial number of members are away from the polling place for long periods of time and where it is physically impossible for large numbers of them to vote in person, an absentee ballot will be required.[60] But where the member may vote in person without too much inconvenience or has voluntarily moved away (as in the case of retirees) an absentee ballot will not be required, particularly if the polls are kept open for several days to allow those on out-of-town assignments, such as truckdrivers, to return to vote.[61] Of course if the union constitution or bylaws require that absentee ballots be provided, this requirement must be followed.

What if the instructions on the ballot are confusing or the ballot is not marked clearly?

The courts have attempted to decide these issues on the basis of common sense and fairness, after examining the facts carefully. Confusing instructions might void the election if the court is convinced that voters were misled.[62] As for marking of ballots, in one case an impartial committee in charge of counting ballots decided to count all choices on the ballot that were clearly marked and to reject all choices not clearly marked. It decided not to reject a ballot altogether where only some of the choices were unclearly marked. The court upheld this as reasonable.[63] In another case a court set aside an election where the union mistakenly provided space for write-in candidates. The court concluded that the write-in votes were wasted since there was no real option to select a write-in candidate. The write-in option may have misled some voters, who would have otherwise voted for other candidates. The number of write-in ballots was large enough that it may have affected the election chances of other candidates.[64]

What is entailed by the right to have an observer at the polls?

The candidate is entitled to an observer of his own choosing. The union may limit observers to members of the union,[65] but it is unsettled whether other candidates may serve as observers.[66] Basically, the observer must be given the opportunity to verify that only eligible voters cast a ballot and that all ballots of eligible voters, and no other ballots, are counted. The observer is entitled to a list of eligible voters. He has a right to be present when voters receive ballots and place them in the box and must be given the opportunity to challenge those ballots that he thinks are cast by ineligible voters.[67] These challenged ballots must be kept apart from other ballots.[68] The observer has a right to oversee the sealing of the ballot box at the conclusion of voting, to observe that it is placed in custody, to be present when the ballot box is opened, and to see each ballot as it is counted. Evidence of tampering with the ballot box is grounds to invalidate the election.[69]

ENFORCING THE RIGHT TO A FAIR ELECTION

What procedures are available to enforce the right to a fair and open election?

Two procedures are available. First, in certain limited situations you may bring a suit prior to an election to correct or prevent certain existing or threatened violations. In this situation, you proceed on your own, without involving the secretary of labor. Second, you may file a complaint with the secretary of labor after an election, challenging the validity of the election. If the secretary agrees with your position, she will bring a lawsuit to set the election aside and direct a new one.

In what situations can I bring a suit prior to an election?
This procedure is limited to three types of situations.

1. Failure of the union to distribute campaign literature at the request of the candidate.
2. Refusal by the union to give a candidate access to the membership lists where there is a union-shop agreement.
3. Discrimination by the union among the candidates by giving them unequal access to mailing lists, allowing unequal distribution of campaign literature, or giving special coverage in the union newspaper to the activities of the incumbent but not a similar amount of space to the challenger.[70]

In these cases the objecting candidate may bring suit immediately in the district court. The court may not only enjoin the violation, but it may stop the election until the violation has been corrected. Whether the court will hold up the election or allow it to go forward, leaving it to the secretary of labor to later determine whether the completed election was valid, is up to the discretion of the court. Because postponing an election is disruptive and expensive, the court will not delay the election unless it is satisfied that violations of the act have occurred and that they are serious enough to affect the outcome of the election. On the other hand, postponement may be less disruptive than having a completed election challenged and subsequently rerun; therefore, if the court is convinced that violations will invalidate the election, it may halt the election.[71]

As with other provisions of the LMRDA, a candidate who succeeds in a preelection suit may be entitled to have counsel fees paid by the union, according to the discretion of the court. When these fees are awarded, it is usually on the theory that the plaintiff has conferred a "common benefit" on the union by securing a fair election, and the union should therefore pay for legal costs.[72]

Will an election be allowed to go forward even though violations have occurred that will clearly invalidate the election?
Yes. If the violations are not among those that allow a suit

to be brought prior to an election, there is no authority under the LMRDA for a court to intervene before the election. And even if the violations fall within those categories, only a candidate may challenge them in court. If the challenge does not allege violations that fall within those categories or the complaining member is not a candidate for office, the election must go forward. Examples of violations that cannot be rectified prior to the election include the failure to conduct an election by secret ballot, the failure to insure adequate safeguards at the polling place, the failure to send an election notice to a member, or the union's expenditure of money to support a candidate. After the election, the complaining member may file a complaint with the secretary of labor challenging the election on these or any other grounds covered by the LMRDA. If the candidate does not challenge the violations in advance of the election, once the election is held, the only way to challenge it is through the secretary of labor.[73]

To illustrate how narrow the preelection remedies are, in a leading case the union had a restrictive eligibility requirement for becoming a candidate. Members of the union brought suit to enjoin the union from holding the election until this requirement was eliminated. The Supreme Court held that however unfair the eligibility requirement might be, the exclusive route for challenging it is through a postelection suit by the secretary of labor. "Reliance on the discretion of the Secretary is in harmony with the general congressional policy to allow unions great latitude in resolving their own internal controversies, and, where that fails, to utilize the agencies of Government most familiar with union problems to aid in bringing about a settlement through discussion before resort to the courts."[74]

What are the procedures for challenging an election after it is held?

First, the complaining member must exhaust any election appeal procedures provided by the union constitution that are available within three months.[75] This gives the union the opportunity to first correct its mistakes. Failure to exhaust these appeals will normally bar the member from any legal relief, but if he can show that the internal appeal would have been futile—for example, because it would have to be made to the officers who won the contested election—then failure to resort to these procedures will be excused.[76]

The second step is to file a complaint with the secretary of labor, which must be done within one month from the time the union turns down the final appeal or within one month from the time the three-month exhaustion period expires, whichever comes first.[77] The secretary is required by the statute to investigate the claim within 60 days (a time limit often not met) and determine whether there is probable cause to believe that a violation occurred.[78] If the secretary does not find probable cause to proceed, a court has extremely limited grounds to overrule the secretary.[79] If she finds probable cause, she brings suit in the federal district court to set aside the election and hold a new one. The secretary presents her evidence at a trial, and the court must decide whether there has been a violation and whether a new election should be held.

Once the secretary of labor initiates her action in court, does the complaining member or any other affected person have any right to intervene in the court proceeding?

Yes. The Supreme Court has held that members affected by the election may intervene in the secretary's suit. They may want to present evidence or develop arguments that they feel the secretary will not adequately cover. But they are limited to dealing with those violations that are part of the secretary's suit and may not raise matters not covered in the secretary's complaint.[80]

Is the secretary limited in her suit to those complaints raised by the complaining union members?

Yes. The secretary can pursue only those violations that were raised by the union member in his internal appeals and in his complaint filed with the secretary or violations closely related to those in the member's complaint. Even if the secretary's investigation reveals other violations, these may not be part of the lawsuit unless the complaining member could not have known of them at the time he filed his complaint with the secretary of labor. For example, a union member filed a complaint with the secretary of labor charging that union facilities had been used to promote the candidacy of the incumbent.

The secretary investigated the complaint and added the charge that the union had imposed an unreasonable meeting attendance requirement as a condition of candidacy. The Supreme Court held that the secretary could not rely upon this additional ground in his suit, for this would defeat the purpose of the exhaustion requirement in the act by not giving the union a chance to change the attendance requirement.[81]

Will the secretary of labor move to set aside the election in all cases in which she finds a violation of the LMRDA?
No. The secretary must also find that the violations "may have affected the outcome of the election." That is, she must conclude that the election might have been won by the losing candidate if it had not been for the violations. For example, if 50 members are not sent a notice of the election, and the winner's margin of victory is only 40 votes, then the violation might have affected the outcome. But if the winner's margin is 60 votes, then the violation could not have affected the outcome, and a new election will not be sought by the secretary.[82]

If the secretary charges that a member was wrongfully disqualified from running, the election will be set aside even though realistically there was little chance that the disqualified candidate would have won had he been allowed to run. The courts will not weigh the political factors in an election in determining whether the violation may have affected the outcome.[83] Similarly, a refusal to send out mailings, misuse of the union newspaper, or other campaign violations will generally be treated as likely to have changed the outcome of the election, unless the union can show convincingly that the violations could not have made a difference.[84] Most courts conclude there is a heavy presumption that such activities as well as other violations affect the outcome of the election and impose a heavy burden on the union to produce tangible evidence that the violations didn't have this impact.[85]

Who governs the union while the election is being challenged?
While an election is being challenged, the officers who were elected in the challenged election will govern. The LMRDA

specifically provides that the challenged election shall be presumed valid until there is a final court decision invalidating the election; this decision comes only when the court certifies the results of the rerun election.[86] Because of the time spent investigating and trying to work out a settlement with the union, the secretary often does not bring suit until months or even years after the complaint is filed. The litigation, with appeals, may be very lengthy. In a number of cases the full term of office has run and another election has been held before the validity of the earlier one is finally settled. The union is permitted to hold subsequent elections in regular course, even though an earlier one has been challenged. This is permitted because the first election may be upheld, and the union's regular processes should not be disturbed.

If an election is held to violate Title IV, will this invalidate the results of a subsequent election?

Not always. LMRDA Section 402(c) says the secretary shall declare an improper election void and direct the conduct of a new one under her supervision. Even though the secretary has taken the position that she is obliged to order a new election under these circumstances, some courts have held that where the union holds a subsequent election that is fair, further remedial action is unnecessary. Thus, in one case, the secretary brought suit that eventually declared an election invalid. While the suit was pending, the union offered to allow the secretary to supervise the union's next regularly scheduled election. The secretary refused, and the union then hired an independent consultant, a respected neutral, to oversee the election. Under his supervision, the union corrected the deficiencies that had made the earlier election invalid. The court held it had the discretion to reject the secretary's demand for a rerun election under her supervision. It concluded that the union had remedied its own wrongdoing and that the LMRDA was designed to encourage unions to restore democratic procedures on their own.[87]

But even if the subsequent, regular election is entirely fair, the court may still allow the suit challenging the first election to go ahead. If the first election is declared invalid, a rerun election will be ordered even if the later election was valid.[88]

Does the LMRDA permit a union to remove an officer who is improperly elected?

It is not clear from the statutory language and reported cases whether a union may utilize its internal disciplinary procedures to remove an officer whom it thinks was improperly elected.[89] It certainly may be argued that the only remedy for unlawful campaign conduct is through a suit by the secretary of labor under Title IV. However, the secretary of labor cannot remove an officer until the results of the rerun election are certified by a court. If a union could remove an elected officer while Title IV proceedings are pending, this could jeopardize insurgent candidates who have ousted the established leadership much more than it threatens the incumbent candidate who wins an election by improper means. A recent Supreme Court decision protecting elected union officials against removal supports this conclusion.[90] On the other hand, the LMRDA seems to contemplate removal of an officer for misconduct not related to the election.[91]

Nor may a union use the trusteeship device to remove an elected officer, although under a valid trusteeship the activities of the union may be severely restricted. Trusteeships are discussed in chapter 21. On the other hand, in extreme cases of corruption, the federal government has taken over unions through criminal proceedings and has installed court appointed trustees to run the union until the problems are corrected.[92]

What is involved when the court orders a rerun election?

The court generally directs that the election be held under the supervision of the secretary of labor. The secretary will generally follow the election procedures set forth in the union's constitution and bylaws but will make any changes she thinks necessary to insure an open and fair election. The secretary's oversight may be quite detailed and intensive, depending upon the situation. As the nomination procedures and election campaign develop, the challengers and the incumbents may ask the secretary for new rules and may go to court to obtain what they believe is needed for a fair election. The court has the ultimate authority and responsibility for determining the conditions for holding the new election.[93]

OTHER AVENUES OF RELIEF

Is the present method of enforcement effective in protecting the right to fair and open elections?

Many think that the existing procedures don't discourage election violations because the limited availability of preelection intervention and the slowness of postelection remedies allow the victor to enjoy the fruits of his violations. The Yablonski-Boyle election is often cited as an example of this, for the violations began six months before the election was held, but Boyle continued as president of the Mine Workers Union for four years after the election. However, the magnitude of that litigation, which involved dozens of separate legal proceedings, was due in part to the unusual complexity of the problems involved. It was also attributable to the relative uncertainty of the law at that time; the litigation itself was responsible for the development of much of the law in this area.[94]

The temptation to violate the law is lessened, however, by the onus and expense which come with a challenged election and the uncertainty that is created until the matter is adjudicated. One reason to leave the present system of remedies alone is that more extensive use of preelection remedies could get the courts so deeply involved in complex issues that elections might be repeatedly postponed, leaving the incumbent officers in control.

Another source of the perceived inadequacy in the existing procedures is the feeling of some of those challenging union elections that the secretary of labor will not enforce the law impartially and vigorously. Perhaps this view derives from the secretary of labor's traditionally close ties with incumbent union leadership. This lack of confidence, along with the delays and burdens attached to litigation, may discourage challengers from asserting their legal rights.

Are there other ways I can challenge and remedy union practices that interfere with a fair election?

Yes. There are other ways to challenge the union's election processes that do not directly involve Title IV. For example, in the Yablonski-Boyle Mine Workers' election, Yablonski was ousted from his union office during the election campaign. He challenged this removal under Title I as a denial of his free speech rights and under Section 609, which prohibits discipline of members for exercising any right protected under the act and permits direct judicial intervention to protect such rights. Yablonski was awarded punitive damages.[95] In addition, union members brought suit against the union for restoration of funds improperly spent in support of the incumbent candidates.[96] Other lawsuits spawned by this election dealt with the improper creation of trusteeship of locals, a matter discussed in chapter 21.[97] Finally, and perhaps most significantly, Yablonski's attorneys were able to recover attorney's fees for the entire litigation.[98] However, this litigation was unusual, and the more conventional and limited remedies of Title IV will control in most cases. Where a union conducts an election that is not regulated by Title IV, for example, an election to recall an officer, the challenge to election improprieties proceeds under Title I, not Title IV.[99] Criminal law may also be useful in dealing with campaign irregularities. For example, in a recent case the government succeeded in a prosecution under the Hobbs Act against a candidate who engaged in threats and violent conduct against his opponent.[100]

NOTES

1. The literature on this subject includes Summers, *Democracy in a One-Party State: Perspectives from Landrum-Griffin*, 43 Md. L. Rev. 93 (1984).
2. These regulations are found in volume 29 of the Code of Federal Regulations, cited in these footnotes as 29 C.F.R., followed by the appropriate regulation number.
3. LRDDA § 402; compare LMRDA § 401(c).
4. LMRDA § 402(b),(c).
5. LMRDA § 401(a).
6. *Trbovich v. Mine Workers*, 404 U.S. 528, 539 (1972) (quoting *Wirtz v. Glass Bottle Blowers*, 389 U.S. 463, 475 (1968)).
7. *Id.*
8. LMRDA § 402(i) and (j). *See also Brock v. O'Connor* 808 F.2d 228 (2d Cir. 1987) (applying LMRDA § 401(g)).
9. LMRDA § 401 (a),(b).
10. LMRDA § 402(n).
11. LMRDA § 3(q); 29 C.F.R. § 452.16–21. *E.g.*, *Marshall v. Machinists*, 509 F. Supp. 90 (D.C. Md. 1981).

12. *Perreault v. Electronic Workers Union*, 823 F.2d 35, 36 (2d Cir. 1987).

13. *Perreault v. Electronic Workers Union*, 823 F.2d 35 (2d Cir. 1987). *See also* LMRDA § 3(q), 29 C.F.R. § 452. 16-25, *Marshall v. Machinists*, 509 F. Supp. 90, 95 (D. Md. 1981).

14. LMRDA § 401(a),(b),(d).

15. LMRDA § 401(b).

16. LMRDA § 401(a). *Theodus v. McLaughlin*, 852 F.2d 1380 (D.C. Cir. 1988).

17. LMRDA § 401(d).

18. LMRDA § 401(e). *See* 29 C.F.R. § 452.36(b).

19. *Wirtz v. Hotel Employees Union*, 391 U.S. 492 (1968).

20. *Id.* at 499.

21. *Steelworkers v. Usery*, 429 U.S. 305 (1977). *See also Doyle v. Brock*, 821 F.2d 778 (D.C. Cir. 1987).

22. *Steelworkers v. Usery*, 429 U.S. 305, 310 (1977).

23. *Dole v. AFSCME*, 715 F. Supp. 1119 (D.C. 1989). The regulation is 29 C.F.R. § 452.46. The opinion, by Judge Gesell, provides a good review of leading cases in eligibility requirements.

24. *Hodgson v. Operating Engineers*, 440 F.2d 485 (6th Cir. 1971).

25. 29 C.F.R. § 452.44, 47. *See Martin v. Letter Carriers Branch 419*, 965 F.2d 61 (6th Cir. 1991).

26. LMRDA §§ 401(e) and 504. In *United States v. Brown*, 381 U.S. 437 (1965), the Supreme Court declared Section 504 unconstitutional, as a bill of attainder, for imposing criminal sanctions on communist party members who hold union office. The Court held that Congress in effect made an adjudication that certain persons were incapable of holding office, and an adjudication is the function of the courts, not the legislature. *Compare Driscoll v. Operating Engineers*, 484 F.2d 682 (7th Cir. 1073) (upholding a union rule disqualifying from office a member who declined to sign an affidavit of nonaffiliation with the communist party).

27. LMRDA § 401(e).

28. *Hodgson v. Mine Workers*, 474 F.2d 940 (6th Cir. 1973).

29. 29 C.F.R. §§ 452.52, .56, .57.

30. *Garrett v. Dorosh*, 77 LRRM 2650 (E.D. Mich. 1971).

31. LMRDA § 401(c).

32. LMRDA § 401(c). 29 C.F.R. 452.67 *et seq.* For a good analysis of this section, *see Brock v. Hotel Employees*, 706 F. Supp. 175 (N.D.N.Y. 1989).

33. *Backo v. Carpenters Union*, 438 F.2d 176 (2d Cir. 1970).

34. *Masters, Mates and Pilots v. Brown*, 111 S. Ct. 880 (1991).

35. *Id.*

36. *Brown v. Lowen*, 889 F.2d 58 (4th Cir. 1989), *aff'd, Masters, Mates and Pilots v. Brown*, 111 S. Ct. 880 (1991); *Brock v. Hotel Union*, 131 LRRM 2803 (N.D.N.Y. 1989).

37. *Brown v. Lowen*, 857 F.2d 216 (4th Cir. 1988), *aff'd en banc*, 889 F.2d 58 (4th Cir. 1989). This case was affirmed by the Supreme Court on a related point in *Masters, Mates and Pilots Union v. Brown*, 111 S. Ct. 880 (1991). A contrary view is taken in *Donovan v. Carpenters Union*, 797 F.2d 140 (3d Cir. 1986).

38. LMRDA § 401(c).

39. *Shultz v. Radio Officers Union*, 344 F. Supp. 58 (S.D.N.Y. 1972). *Brock v. Plumbers Union*, 632 F. Supp. 103 (S.D. Ill. 1985).

40. *Hodgson v. Liquor Salesmen's Union*, 444 F.2d 1344 (2d Cir. 1971); *Dole v. Postal Service*, 744 F. Supp. 413 (E.D.N.Y. 1990). See also 29 C.F.R. §§ 452.75, .76; LMRDA § 481(g).

41. *Yablonski v. Mine Workers Union*, 305 F. Supp. 868, 871 (D.C. 1969).

42. *McLaughlin v. Musicians Union*, 132 LLRM 250 (S.D.N.Y. 1988). The case has extensive citations on the extent to which these types of violations may have affected the outcome of the election, thus warranting relief. See the question later in this chapter on whether the secretary of labor will move to set the election aside where she finds violations of the LMRDA.

43. *Yablonski v. Mine Workers*, 305 F. Supp. 868, 872 (D.C. 1969).

44. *Brock v. Auto Workers*, 128 LRRM 2188 (E.D. Mich. 1988); *Brock v. Engineers Union*, 790 F.2d 508 (6th Cir. 1986). *Shultz v. Steelworkers*, 426 F.2d 969 (9th Cir. 1970), aff'd, 403 U.S. 333 (1971); *Hodgson v. Liquor Salesmen's Union*, 444 F.2d 1344, 1350 (2d Cir. 1971).

45. LMRDA § 402(g).

46. *Izykowski v. IBEW*, 139 LRRM 2395 (D.D.C. 1991).

47. 29 C.F.R. §§ 452.73–.75.

48. *Shultz v. Steelworkers*, 426 F.2d 969 (9th Cir. 1970), *aff'd*, 403 U.S. 333 (1971).

49. LMRDA § 401(e).

50. *Donovan v. Sailors' Union*, 739 F.2d 1426 (9th Cir. 1984); 29 C.F.R. § 452.88.

51. 29 C.F.R. § 452.86,.88. Admission to membership is discussed in chapter 19. LMRDA § 3(o) defines a member in good standing as one who has "fulfilled the requirements for membership" and who has not voluntarily withdrawn from membership. One of the requirements of membership is normally the payment of dues and other periodic assessments.

52. LMRDA § 401(c).

53. LMRDA § 401(e).

54. LMRDA § 401(a),(b),(d).

55. LMRDA § 401(c).
56. LMRDA § 401(e).
57. *Id.*
58. LMRDA § 3(k); 29 C.F.R. § 452.97.
59. *Brennan v. Steelworkers*, 520 F.2d 516 (7th Cir. 1975). *See also Marshall v. Steelworkers*, 591 F.2d 199 (3d Cir. 1978); *Donovan v. Graphic Arts Union*, 118 LRRM 2092 (D.C. Ill. 1984).
60. *Goldberg v. Marine Cooks Union*, 204 F. Supp. 844 (N.D. Cal. 1962); *Donovan v. Teamsters*, 598 F. Supp. 710 (W.D. Mo. 1984).
61. *Hodgson v. Teamsters*, 327 F. Supp. 1284 (E.D. Tex. 1971); *Hodgson v. Plumbers*, 350 F. Supp. 16 (C.D. Cal. 1972); *Donovan v. Plumbers*, 2 LRRM 2983 (S.D. Fla. 1982). *See also* 29 C.F.R. §§ 452.94, .95.
62. *See Hodgson v. Teamsters*, 327 F. Supp. 1284 (E.D. Tex. 1971).
63. *McDonough v. Operating Engineers*, 470 F.2d 261 (3d Cir. 1972).
64. *McLaughlin v. CSEA*, 132 LRRM 2522 (N.D.N.Y. 1988).
65. 29 C.F.R. § 452.107(a).
66. *Compare Shultz v. Independent Employees Union*, 74 LRRM 2137 (W.D. Wis. 1970) and *Marshall v. Machinists*, 108 LRRM 2590 (W.D. Wash. 1981).
67. *Marshall v. Laborers*, 106 LRRM 2500 (E.D. Penn. 1980). *See also Hodgson v. Teamsters*, 336 F. Supp. 1243 (N.D. Ill. 1972).
68. 29 C.F.R. § 452.97(b).
69. *Hodgson v. Teamsters*, 327 F. Supp. 1284 (E.D. Tex. 1971); LMRDA § 402(c). *See also Beckman v. Iron Workers*, 314 F.2d 848 (7th Cir. 1963); *Marshall v. Laborers*, 106 LRRM 2500 (E.D. Penn. 1980).
70. LMRDA § 401(c). The rights listed in the seemingly endless first paragraph of this section are the only ones "enforceable at the suit of any bona fide candidate . . . in the district court of the United States." The remaining rights spelled out in Section 401(c) and in the other sections of Title IV are not directly enforceable in court by the candidate but are protected by initiating a complaint with the secretary of labor, as described in Section 402. For a discussion of the competing avenues of relief under Titles I and IV, see *Teamsters v. Crowley*, 467 U.S. 526 (1984).
71. *Compare Sheldon v. O'Callaghan*, 335 F. Supp. 325 (S.D.N.Y. 1971); *New Watch Dog Committee v. Taxi Drivers*, 438 F. Supp. 1242 (S.D.N.Y. 1977), (where the court denied preelection relief), with *Yablonski v. Mine Workers Union*, 305 F. Supp. 868 (D.D.C., 1969), (where the court granted relief, observing that the machinery for later setting aside an election is "cumbersome, doubtful and calls for delay").
72. *Bliss v. Holmes*, 130 LRRM 2919 (6th Cir. 1988); *Mims v. Teamsters Union*, 821 F.2d 1568 (11th Cir. 1987).
73. LMRDA § 403.

74. *Calhoon v. Harvey*, 379 U.S. 134, 140 (1964). *See also Laski v. Masters, Mates and Pilots Union*, 502 F. Supp. 134 (S.D.N.Y. 1980).

75. LMRDA § 402(a).

76. *Brock v. Auto Workers*, 128 LRRM 2188 (E.D. Mich. 1988). This case has extensive citations of authority on this point.

77. LMRDA § 402(a).

78. 29 C.F.R. § 452.136.

79. *Dunlop v. Bachowski*, 421 U.S. 560 (1975); *Shelley v. Brock*, 793 F.2d 1368 (D.C. Cir. 1986). For cases where a court found inadequate the secretary's reasons for not going forward, see *Doyle v. Brock*, 821 F.2d 778 (D.C. Cir. 1987); *Donovan v. Teachers Union*, 747 F.2d 711 (D.C. Cir. 1984).

80. *Dunlop v. Bachowski*, 421 U.S. 560, 568–70 (1975); *Trbovich v. Mine Workers Union*, 404 U.S. 528 (1972).

81. *Hodgson v. Steelworkers Union*, 403 U.S. 333 (1971); *Donovan v. Maintenance of Way Employees*, 737 F.2d 445 (5th Cir. 1984).

82. *Dunlop v. Bachowski*, 421 U.S. 560, 568–70 (1975); *Wirtz v. Hotel Employees Union*, 391 U.S. 492, 505–9 (1968). However, the mere statistical possibility that a different outcome might have occurred if all challenged votes were cast for one candidate will not, standing alone, suffice. *Shelley v. Brock*, 793 F.2d 1368, 1575 (D.C. 1986).

83. *Shultz v. Radio Officers Union*, 344 F. Supp. 58, 64–65 (S.D. N.Y. 1972).

84. *Shultz v. Radio Officers Union*, 344 F. Supp. 58, 69–70 (S.D.N.Y. 1972). *Compare Marshall v. Steelworkers*, 664 F.2d 144 (7th Cir. 1981).

85. *See McLaughlin v. Musicians Union*, 132 LRRM 2509, 2516–17 (S.D.N.Y. 1988) and cases cited and discussed therein.

86. LMRDA § 402(a).

87. *See McLaughlin v. Boilermakers*, 131 LRRM 2529 (8th Cir. 1989) and cases cited therein. *Compare Brock v. Hotel Union*, 131 LRRM 2801 (N.D.N.Y. 1989) (concluding that setting aside a valid election held subsequent to the election which gave rise to the secretary's complaint would unduly burden the union "while being of little value" but holding that the secretary would be allowed to supervise the next regular union election).

88. *Wirtz v. Glass Bottle Blowers Ass'n.*, 389 U.S. 463 (1968). *Compare Usery v. Masters, Mates and Pilots Union*, 538 F.2d 946 (2d Cir. 1976).

89. *See, e.g., Collins v. Pennsylvania Tel. Union*, 418 F. Supp. 50 (W.D. Penn. 1976); *Int'l Reform Committee v. Sytsma*, 802 F.2d 180 (6th Cir. 1986).

90. *Lynn v. Sheet Metal Workers*, 488 U.S. 347 (1989).

91. LMRDA § 401(h).
92. *U.S. v. Teamsters Local 560*, 754 F. Supp. 395, 136 LRRM 2165 (D. N.J. 1991), implementing *U.S. v. Local 560*, 780 F.2d 267 (3d Cir. 1985). *See also U.S. v. Teamsters*, 138 LRRM 2945 (2d Cir. 1990). The litigation is discussed in detail in Goldberg, *Cleaning Labor's House: Institutional Reform Litigation in the Labor Movement*, 1989 Duke L.J. 903 (1989).
93. LMRDA § 402(c).
94. The key cases in the Mine Workers litigation are summarized in *Yablonski v. Mine Workers Union*, 448 F.2d 1175 (D.C. Cir. 1971) and *Yablonski v. Mine Workers Union*, 466 F.2d 424 (D.C. Cir. 1972), both crucial cases in the litigation. For critical commentary on the failure of the secretary of labor to intervene in this election, see Hopson, *The 1969 UMW Election: Why No Pre-Balloting Investigation?*, 18 Vill. L. Rev. 37 (1972).
95. *Yablonski v. Mine Workers Union*, 80 LRRM 3435 (D.C. 1972).
96. *Yablonski v. Mine Workers Union*, 448 F.2d 1175 (D.C. Cir. 1971).
97. *Blankenship v. Boyle*, 329 F. Supp. 292 (D.D.C. 1971).
98. *Yablonski v. Mine Workers Union*, 466 F.2d 424 (D.C. Cir. 1972); *see also Donovan v. AFSCME*, 784 F.2d 98 (2d Cir. 1986).
99. *Int'l Reform Committee v. Sytsma*, 802 F.2d 180 (6th Cir. 1986).
100. *U.S. v. Debs*, 138 LRRM 2910 (6th Cir. 1991).

PART 5
Other Workplace Protections

PART

XXIII
Privacy and Testing

Broadly speaking, this chapter discusses your right to "be let alone" by your employer.[1] That includes your right to be free of unwarranted intrusions and your right to control the flow of information about yourself that passes through your place of work.[2]

In the past, employers invaded employees' privacy by rifling through their desks, lockers, or clothes. With current technology, however, employers are "searching" employees in far more sophisticated ways. With computer data banks, some employers track employees' past records, financial status, and medical histories. Monitoring devices provide employers with an "electronic keyhole" through which they can listen to conversations, time trips to the bathroom, and count computer keystrokes.[3] Instead of examining the employee's work product, employers are increasingly examining the employee, exploring the contents of employees' bodily fluids, measuring their retinal reflexes, identifing illicit substances in the molecules of their hair, and even probing the recesses of their minds.

Why are managers amassing so much sensitive information about employees?

Employers believe that it pays to get to know you. Managers rely heavily[4] on information as a tool to match employees to jobs and to control a host of workplace problems such as drug abuse, theft, sabotage and other forms of employee misconduct.[5] Society is discovering, however, that collecting intimate information can be a double-edged sword. At the same time that it helps managers, it unleashes a host of undesirables including stress, low productivity, low morale, job unfairness, fatigue, health problems, and an Orwellian threat to our privacy. Courts today are struggling to strike the right balance between your right to privacy and the right of employers to know more about you.

How much protection does the law provide against privacy intrusions by employers?

Unfortunately, not very much. Info-gathering technology has leaped far ahead of the law's ability to create protective barricades around our personal privacy.

The privacy rights of employees are generally weak. Privacy is not mentioned explicitly in the United States Constitution. (Moreover, in the workplace the Bill of Rights extends its implied privacy protections only to government employees.) Consequently, most employees must pick through a hodge-podge of state statutes and court decisions to find any privacy guarantees that protect them from their employers.

In addition to constitutional protections, federal employees are the beneficiaries of Congress's first privacy law. The Federal Privacy Act of 1974[6] provides federal employees with some privacy protections. For example, it requires federal agencies to (a) inform their employees of personnel records containing information about them, (b) permit those employees to examine, copy, and challenge that information, (c) maintain only accurate, relevant, and current information, and (d) limit access to that information by outsiders. About one-third of the states have similar acts pertaining to their public employees. But these statutes are of little value to the private sector employee.

As of 1993, Congress is considering an electronic monitoring bill, the Privacy for Consumers and Workers Act (S. 516, H.R. 1218), that would grant some privacy protections to all employees. It would permit electronic monitoring but limit it. Under the PCWA monitoring is confined to the employees' work; no monitoring in bathrooms or locker rooms is allowed; employers must inform employees of the kind of monitoring it uses and the scheduled times (not to exceed two hours per week) when it takes place. However, employers need not tell employees precisely when they are being monitored. Employees have the right to see the data collected about them through electronic monitoring, and disclosure of the data to others is restricted. Employees with a certain number of years of seniority could not be monitored at all. But lacking any other statutory or constitutional protection, most private sector employees can only fight intrusions based on their common law rights. Though common law protections are spotty, when these cases succeed they send a jolting message. The average jury verdicts in such common law workplace privacy cases exceed $316,000. It is clear that public sentiment is in favor of using the law to punish snooping employers, and as technology advances, so will stronger enforcement of privacy rights in the law.[7]

METHODS OF GATHERING INFORMATION

Can I be required to take a "lie detector" test to get or keep a job?

In most cases you may refuse. Federal law prohibits the use of polygraph devices, although there are several notable exceptions which we will discuss below.

Until recently, many employers used polygraph (lie detector) tests and other truth verification tests (such as a psychological stress evaluator) to screen job applicants or to examine employees periodically.

These tests work on the principle that lying causes psychological conflict, which produces stress. Polygraph tests purport to detect and record certain measurable physiological changes, such as blood pressure, rate of breathing, and electrical conductivity of skin, produced by the stress of lying. Psychological stress evaluators (PSE), sometimes called voice stress analyzers, purport to detect and record fluctuations in your voice produced by the stress. Unlike the polygraph, PSE tests do not require that you be connected to the machine and thus can be conducted without your knowledge (e.g., by hiding the machine or using it over the telephone).

Concerns about the unreliability and intrusiveness of polygraph devices finally led to the enactment of the federal Employee Polygraph Protection Act of 1988, which bans their use with the following exceptions.[8] Under the EPPA, federal and state government employers are allowed to test their applicants and employees with polygraphs, private employers are permitted to test employees whom they suspect of theft, and security and pharmaceutical companies may test more broadly. Stricter state laws may further narrow polygraph usage in your state. In general, therefore, employees not protected by EPPA must look to their states' laws[9] and, if they work for the government, to constitutional[10] protections as well if they wish to avoid such testing.

What happens if I am asked or told to submit to a truth verification test?

The answer depends on whether, in your particular circumstances, the EPPA or state law bans polygraph testing where you work. Based on the EPPA, as mentioned above, you can refuse to take a mechanical truth verification test if you work in the private sector, unless you work in the security or pharmaceutical industries or are being investigated for workplace theft. If you are covered by the EPPA and your employer wrongfully tests you with a polygraph or retaliates against you for refusing to submit to one, you may sue your employer to get your job back or for backpay if you can show that your employer used a polygraph test to screen you (a) in particular, (b) as part of a random sampling, or (c) in the course of an "investigation," but without having stated in writing its basis of "reasonably suspecting" you of theft, embezzlement, misappropriation, industrial espionage, or sabotage.[11]

If you are not protected by the EPPA, the laws of your state may "close the loopholes" in the federal law. For instance, twenty-one states have coupled their polygraph bans with fines and sometimes even imprisonment for violators. They are Alaska, California, Connecticut, Delaware, District of Columbia, Hawaii, Idaho, Iowa, Maine, Maryland, Massachusetts, Michigan, Minnesota, Montana, Nebraska, New Jersey, New York, Oregon, Rhode Island, Washington, and West Virginia.[12] Seven other states merely place licensing requirements on polygraph operators: Arizona, Arkansas, Illinois, Indiana, Louisiana, New Mexico, and Texas.[13] States with statutes that merely place restrictions on the questions that polygraphs operators may ask are Georgia, Nevada, Tennessee, Utah, Virginia, and Wisconsin.[14]

Violation of these prohibitions is typically a misdemeanor, punishable by a small fine. You may therefore report a violation to the state prosecutor, though the laws are seldom enforced. Some of the statutes specifically provide a private right of action for an aggrieved employee or job applicant, such as those of Alaska, Minnesota, and the District of Columbia.[15] Some employees who have been discharged on the basis of polygraph tests conducted in violation of state law have succeeded in asserting wrongful discharge claims based on public policy grounds.[16] Often union contracts also provide protection.

If you work for the government, the Fifth Amendment of the United States Constitution[17] and some state constitutions[18] may protect you from having to give self-incriminating answers to your employer's questions.

If truth verification tests are permitted in your state and you are fired or disciplined for refusing to take a test or for failing one, you may have trouble getting unemployment benefits, even though you are otherwise eligible; your employer may assert that your discharge was for misconduct. But some states have rejected such assertions and allowed unemployment benefits.[19] (See chapter 7 on unemployment insurance.)

Must I answer prying questions about my personal life in a job interview or on the job?

You may have to. Many employers are protecting themselves against being sued for negligent hiring by digging deep into their applicants' past to unearth misdeeds that may later resurface. Employers are therefore asking ever more probing questions in order to uncover possible violent or sexual behavior aberrations.[20]

Humiliating or not, employers generally have the right to ask these personal questions, if (a) it is not done in conjunction with a prohibited lie detector or other truth verification test, or (b) the questions are not discriminatory (as they would be if their impact were different on men and women, for instance). Private sector employees normally have little recourse unless the questions are extremely outrageous, in which case they may have a claim of intentional infliction of emotional distress under state law.[21] But if the question relates to the employer's legitimate concerns, such as your ability to do your job, the question usually will be considered permissible. There are a couple of exceptions to these general guidelines. In California, private sector workers enjoy enhanced privacy protections by virtue of that state's constitution, which may limit the employer's range of legitimate questions.[22] In Massachusetts, a state privacy statute may also protect private sector employees against invasive questioning.[23]

In the public-sector context, employees enjoy Constitutional protections, yet it is often difficult to tell when employees may successfully challenge overly intrusive questions that go "too far" and bear no relation to the employer's legitimate concerns.[24] For a private sector employee to state a claim for invasion of privacy due to prying questioning, he or she would have to show that the employer intentionally asked questions that would be highly offensive to the reasonable person in order to invade his or her privacy. Few employees can do this and prevail. For a further discussion of interview questions, see chapter 2 on the hiring process.

Must I submit to a pencil-and-paper honesty test if it is required by my employer?

Yes, except in Massachusetts, and perhaps in California. Now that polygraph use has been generally outlawed, many private sector employers are resorting to written integrity tests to determine whether their job applicants or employees are dishonest or harbor other undesirable psychological traits. A congressional study estimates that five to six thousand businesses use honesty and integrity tests to aid them in screening and selecting job applicants.[25]

These written psychological exams are sometimes called personality assessment programs, integrity tests, or honesty tests. Despite their widespread use, there is little or no conclusive evidence proving that they accurately predict dishonest behavior.[26] Unfortunately, their unreliability may cause honest employees to be falsely deemed dishonest.

Psychological tests frequently include questions that explore deeply personal matters. For instance, 2,500 job applicants recently received a $2 million total settlement from a discount department store chain that required them to answer a widely used battery of 701 questions called "Psychscreen" when they applied for the job of security guard. The questions asked included: "Do you often think about sex?," "Are you attracted to members of the same sex?," "Do you believe in the Second Coming?" The employees sued under California's unique constitution, which affords public and private sector employees privacy protection. In a landmark decision, the court held that employers must have a "compelling interest" in order to impose such tests.[27]

Nevertheless, most private sector workers have no recourse against such tests. Only Massachusetts explicitly restricts the use of preemployment written integrity tests.[28] But rampant misuse of these influential yet unreliable tests may, at some point, lead to a prohibition or restriction of their usage, like that of polygraphs, by the legislatures and courts.

Can I refuse to be tested for drugs or alcohol when I am being hired or on the job?

It depends on where you work and upon the kind of test being conducted. Until Congress enacts uniform drug testing legislation, employees will continue to face a maze of federal and state drug testing regulations. The trend, however, is to allow employers greater latitude to test for drugs, in response to growing public sentiment against drug use at work.

Employers generally test applicants and employees for drugs because they perceive that those who test positive are more likely to be fired, injured, disciplined, or absent than are those who test negative. The public, for the most part, agrees that eliminating workplace drug use can lower injuries and costs. The drug testing juggernaut has gained further momentum from the "domino effect" fueled by employers' fear that, unless they test, their organizations may become havens for drug users who cannot obtain employment with competitors who do test.

Recent studies, however, have cast doubt on earlier statistics that showed a very high correlation between drug use and workplace injuries.[29] Uncertainty also lurks within the drug tests themselves; many are said to yield inaccurate results.[30] By testing only for substances in bodily fluids, most drug tests cannot determine if the employee has been drug- or alcohol-impaired on the job. Rather, these tests reveal what the employee may have ingested on a weekend or while on a vacation or at some other undetermined point. Drug tests therefore lay bare the employee's private life without providing the employer with any performance-related information. Drug testing humiliates the employee who hands over specimens of bodily fluid or waste for inspection. Blood or saliva tests are favored for tracing alcohol, but most drug tests are performed by urinalysis, which requires the subject to collect and hand over samples of urine for analysis. Even those who generally support the aims of drug testing bridle at this affront to human dignity.[31]

Whether the drug or alcohol test actually violates the law usually depends upon a number of factors such as the employment context, the type of drug testing program, the reasons

for testing, and the manner in which the testing is administered. Drug testing programs take many forms. The least intrusive type of drug testing is *voluntary testing*, in which the
employee agrees to urinalysis. More intrusive are tests conducted without consent on urine samples routinely collected
for other medical diagnostic purposes during a routine physical
examination of the employee. Intrusive in another way are
reasonable-suspicion tests, in which the employer claims that
the employee's behavior or appearance or a report by a reliable
informant indicates that the employee might be using drugs
on the job. The employer then singles out the employee for a
spot check, based on what it contends is reasonable, individualized suspicion.

Related to such tests are *post-accident* tests conducted by
employers after serious accidents to determine whether drugs
were the cause. The suspicion usually is individualized to the
extent that only a certain group of employees involved in the
accident is tested. With certain limitations, these types of tests
have generally been held to be permissible, although many
overbroad programs have been struck down.[32]

The type of testing most often challenged successfully is
mandatory and random urinalysis, which is the most intrusive
type of testing. Because these tests are usually not triggered
by an event that indicates drug use, and are not based on
individualized suspicion, they are considered the most intrusive. Public sector workers in federal, state, or local government or any workers subject to government agency drug testing
programs have the best chance of succeeding when challenging
such random drug testing.

If I work in the public sector, must I comply with drug or alcohol tests?

It depends on the circumstances, specifically the type of
work you do and the intrusiveness of the drug testing program.
The Supreme Court has held that, under the Fourth Amendment to the Constitution, public sector employees are guaranteed the right to be free of unreasonable searches and seizures
by their employers. Since drug testing is a "search," the key
question is When do drug tests become "unreasonable"?[33] Although the Supreme Court has yet to rule on whether random
drug testing would be considered "reasonable,"[34] many lower

courts have applied the Supreme Court's balancing test to mandatory, random drug testing and have found them reasonable. The lower courts have weighed the government's purposes for drug testing against employees' expectations of privacy. Generally, courts uphold random, suspicionless drug tests where the safety and/or security stakes are high and where there is evidence of a drug problem that is causing harm in the workplace.[35] Courts have struck down drug testing, however, where drug use by employees is only speculative and poses no threat to human life.[36] Nevertheless, by stretching the "reasonableness" standard to its limit, several influential courts have approved mandatory testing for the sake of efficiency—that is, in order to protect the economic interests of the employer rather than public safety or security.[37] This disturbing trend could easily lead to universal mandatory testing since the government can claim an interest in cost-effectiveness and efficiency in every civil service job.

The more universal drug testing becomes, the more likely it is that it will achieve constitutional acceptability. The more widespread workplace testing becomes, the fewer expectations employees can have of resisting it—and using the Supreme Court's somewhat circular logic—the more reasonable the testing will become.[38] Thus, employees who feel their privacy has been taken hostage in the "war on drugs" are turning their attention to federal legislation or to their states for protection from drug testing encroachments on their right to privacy.[39]

Certainly, employees in safety-sensitive or security-sensitive positions will continue to be vulnerable to random drug testing, although several courts maintain that even police and firefighters, who work in highly regulated fields in which safety is paramount, still retain expectations of privacy that can be "unreasonably" violated by drug testing.[40] Nevertheless, the first federal law approving mandatory drug testing in the transportation industry was enacted in 1991;[41] other proposed legislation would permit mandatory drug testing in all safety-sensitive jobs while allowing reasonable-suspicion testing in all other jobs.[42]

In lieu of constitutional protection, public sector employees can turn to their states' statutes for regulations that may protect them from drug testing. The laws of at least nineteen states place restraints on public employee drug testing.[43]

If I do not work for the government, does the law protect me from drug testing?

Usually not. Private sector employees who feel their rights have been violated by a drug test must turn to their states' laws for relief, until Congress acts in this area. At least seventeen states regulate private sector drug testing, but none bans it altogether.[44] Roughly half of these states' statutes require employers to have reasonable or probable cause to believe that employees are using drugs on the job before imposing drug tests. Many of these laws also require employers to post written policies for drug testing in places where employees and applicants will see them.

At least ten states bar or place restrictions on random drug testing by employers. Those states are Connecticut, Florida, Louisiana, Maine, Minnesota, Mississippi, Montana, Nebraska, Rhode Island, and Vermont. Mississippi requires private sector employers to have reasonable suspicion before testing employees.

The laws of at least twelve states require that the employee be given a confirmatory test if the first drug test yields positive results. Those states are Connecticut, Florida, Hawaii, Maine, Maryland, Minnesota, Mississippi, Montana, Nebraska, Rhode Island, Utah, and Vermont.

If the tests are positive, the laws of nine states limit the kinds of disciplinary action the employer can take against the employee. Those states are Florida, Iowa, Louisiana, Maine, Minnesota, Montana, Nebraska, Rhode Island, and Vermont.

In addition, the test results must remain confidential under the laws of twelve states: Connecticut, Florida, Hawaii, Iowa, Louisiana, Maine, Minnesota, Mississippi, Montana, Nebraska, Utah, and Vermont.

In addition to these state laws, several states offer private sector employees some protection against random drug testing in their constitutions or in their body of wrongful discharge-based tort law.

In California, a computer operator dismissed for refusing to submit to mandatory urinalysis won her privacy-invasion suit against her employer under that state's constitution, which provides privacy protection to nonpublic employees. Louisiana's constitution offers somewhat similar protection.[45] In

Pennsylvania, West Virginia,[46] and Alaska,[47] employers who discharged employees because they refused to take drug tests have been held to violate public policy.

Union contracts often deal with drug testing. Thus if you are represented by a union, you should consult with your representative on these questions.

What if I test "positive" for drugs but the test results are false?

Employees in such situations have sued the employer or laboratory for negligent testing and/or defamation. A court in Wichita, Kansas, has held a drug-testing laboratory liable in the amount of $4.1 million for falsely deeming an employee a "user," which led to his employer firing him.[48]

If you are adversely treated due to a false positive, the Americans with Disabilities Act may protect you. It provides that those who are wrongfully regarded as drug users as a result of prior drug testing may be considered "disabled" for the purposes of the act and may not be discriminated against because of it.

Can I be required to take impairment tests on the job?

Yes. Since drug testing rarely establishes the employee's actual ability to safely perform the job, employers are increasingly turning to motor-coordination impairment tests that do measure a person's level of performance.

Compared to drug testing, motor-skills impairment tests are more accurate, inexpensive, reliable, and easy to use. Before beginning the day's work, the employee is typically seated before a video screen and asked to manipulate computer-game-like controls. The particular motor skills tested are akin to those the employee actually uses on the job. Instead of opening irrelevant and intrusive windows into your private life, the impairment test provides a useful assessment of your present ability to do the job safely.

Unlike drug or polygraph tests, motor impairment tests do not invade your body or purport to measure "honesty." As a result, employees are unlikely to be successful in bringing legal claims against job-related impairment tests that are administered fairly.

What about genetic testing?

There is presently no law prohibiting employers from (a) ascertaining an employee's genetic make-up, (b) storing such information, or even (c) basing decisions on it. If, however, the genetic information is used to detect a person's latent disease or propensity for disease then use of it might support an inference of unlawful disability discrimination. Furthermore if collecting the genetic information entails drawing blood, saliva, or urine specimens, the genetic testing might also constitute a privacy invasion.

Despite the fact that only 20 of the Fortune 500 admitted, in 1991, to genetically screening employees, it is expected that when it becomes economical, companies will expand such screening in order to determine the likelihood of applicants and employees developing chronic illnesses. A proposed federal bill, known as the Human Genome Privacy Act (H.R. 2045) would extend Privacy Act protection to genetic information. This law would give federal employees the right to determine what genetic records are collected, maintained, used, and disseminated by both government and private agencies, prohibit disclosure of such information without an individual's written consent, and establish criminal penalties for violations. Several states are currently considering bills that would extend genetic privacy rights to their citizens; they are Wisconsin, Pennsylvania, Rhode Island, and Texas.

May I be asked at a job interview whether I filed workers' compensation claims at my last job?

No. The Americans with Disabilities Act (ADA) of 1990 expressly forbids employers from inquiring into their applicant's history of filing workers' compensation claims. Should an employer do so and then treat the employee adversely, the employee may have a right of action for disability discrimination under the ADA.[49]

May an employer refuse to hire me based on my arrest or conviction record?

The law generally discourages the use of arrest records, but the use of your conviction records is more likely to be permitted. An arrest that does not result in a conviction is of questionable value because it does not establish that the applicant committed a crime. Accordingly, several states restrict an employer's acquisition and storage of information about prior arrests; they include California, Connecticut, Hawaii, Illinois, Maryland, Massachusetts, Michigan, Missouri, Minnesota, New York, Ohio, Oregon, and Virginia.[50] Some of the statutes (e.g., New York and California) prohibit an employer asking about or using any information about an arrest that did not result in a conviction. Some statutes require that you have taken action within a certain period of time to expunge the arrest record; in others, you need not take any action. Some statutes even authorize you to say that you have no arrest record in certain circumstances. Connecticut requires that any arrest record information be viewed only by the employer's personnel office. Michigan does not prohibit asking about arrests but does require that such information be kept separate from other personnel records.

A few states even restrict the use of information about convictions. In New York, for example, an employer may ask about convictions but may not penalize an exoffender solely because of a conviction unless (1) there is a direct relationship between the offense and the job sought or (2) the applicant continues to pose an "unreasonable risk" to society. In Pennsylvania, on the other hand, employers can consider both arrests and convictions that relate to job suitability.[51] A few states prohibit certain other kinds of inquiries: Maryland (psychiatric or psychological problems, unless they have direct bearing on fitness for the job); Massachusetts (treatment or institutionalization in a mental hospital); and Michigan (political associations or nonemployment activities).[52]

Employers sometimes obtain information about applicants and employees from government sources. For example, criminal justice record systems that receive federal funds through the Law Enforcement Assistance Administration are permitted to disseminate conviction records to employers, though dissemination of arrest information is supposedly restricted.[53] Many states regulate storage of and access to criminal justice records, particularly regarding investigations and arrests.

Can I be required to submit to fingerprinting, blood tests, and other similar procedures?
Usually, yes. Employers often ask job applicants and employ-

ees to submit to fingerprinting for identification or for background investigations. Unless fingerprinting results in the discriminatory exclusion from employment of a protected group,
the practice will be unobjectionable.[54]

Only two states limit the use of fingerprints. In New York,
your employer cannot require you to be fingerprinted to get or
keep a job, and California prohibits employers from requiring
fingerprints or passing them on to other employers to your
detriment.[55] Yet these states also join the majority of states in
requiring fingerprinting in certain occupations, such as teaching, crime detection, and gambling. In view of this, employers
in most jurisdictions probably will *not* violate your privacy
rights under the laws when demanding or using fingerprints
for a job-related purpose.

Can an employer do a credit check on me?

Generally, yes. As mentioned in chapter 2 on hiring, however, it has been ruled that denying you a job because of a
poor credit rating may violate antidiscrimination laws because
the number of nonwhites with poor credit ratings is disproportionately greater than the number of whites.

In any event, if an employer does gather credit information
on you, it must comply with the federal Fair Credit Reporting
Act. The Fair Credit Reporting Act (FCRA) (which is Title VI
of the Consumer Credit Protection Act of 1970), recognizes
two types of reports. The first, a *credit report*, concerns your
eligibility and standing to obtain credit based on your past
credit experience. The second kind of report is called an *investigative consumer report*, and it bears on your character, general
reputation, characteristics, and lifestyle. Agencies obtain these
investigative reports by personally interviewing your neigh-
bors, friends, and associates. If an employer seeks to obtain
either a credit or consumer report, it must certify that it is doing
so strictly for employment purposes.[56] Additionally, when your
employer requests an investigative consumer report, it must
notify you if you are seeking a job or promotion. Your employer
need not notify you when ordering a credit report or a consumer
report when you are not seeking a job.[57] Your employer must
inform you, however if he or she has used the credit report to
deny you a job or promotion.

In such cases, your employer must also provide you with

the name and address of the credit agency that compiled the report. You may then request from the agency "the nature and substance" of all information in your file and ask the agency to disclose to you the names of all the recipients of any report on you within the preceding six months.[58] Furthermore, you have the right to have disputed information in your file reinvestigated and to have your version of the facts included in subsequent reports.

Employers who willfully or negligently fail to comply with FCRA regulations (for example, obtaining credit reports for nonemployment purposes) will be liable for the employee's damages and attorney's fees.[59] However, the FCRA prohibits employees from suing employers for defamation or invasion based on the employer's misuse of credit information, unless the employer maliciously furnished others with false information.[60]

Under the civil rights laws, employers who use credit information that affects any group of protected employees may be liable for disparate impact discrimination if the credit report serves no job-related purpose.

Can an employer inquire into my medical records when I apply for a job?

Probably not. With the enactment of the Americans with Disabilities Act of 1990, employers in companies of 25 or more employees (15 or more after 1994) may not inquire into or consider medical information about you unless the employer has reason to think that you have a medical condition that interferes with your ability to perform your job or that poses a safety risk to yourself or others. Any other medical information will be considered irrelevant to your job performance under the ADA, and your employer is not permitted to collect or use it.

Medical records that are relevant to job performance concerns and are thus permitted to the employer by the ADA must be kept confidential. They must be maintained on separate forms in separate files and may be shared with supervisors and managers only for the purpose of identifying necessary restrictions on your work, or with emergency first aid personnel when you require emergency treatment. On request, government officials investigating ADA compliance may see your records. Your medical information may be used for insurance purposes but not for the purpose of limiting health insurance eligibility.[61] Your employer may submit medical information about you to your state's workers' compensation officers.[62] Should a permissible drug test reveal any drug you take for a medical condition, this information would require confidential treatment as well.

Can my employer eavesdrop on my private phone conversations?

No. Employers who use a phone extension or otherwise tap the phones in order to listen secretly to their employees' private phone calls violate federal law. The Omnibus Crime Control and Safe Streets Act of 1968 (Title III) prohibits all private individuals and organizations, including employers, from intercepting the wire or oral communications of others. An oral communication is entitled to protection if it is "uttered by a person exhibiting an expectation that such communication is not subject to interception under circumstances justifying such expectation."[63] Interception is permitted, however, when it is carried out by a person who already is a party to the communication or if one of the parties has given prior consent.[64] Accordingly, your employer could tape a direct conversation with you without your knowledge but not your conversation with someone else (unless that other person consented). Sometimes, employers monitor employees' conversations with customers or clients to evaluate performance. Since such conversations are business-related, monitoring is permitted especially if you are aware that your employer has that practice. Nevertheless, your employer should hang up the phone once it becomes clear that you are engaged in a personal conversation.[65]

Despite the threat of penalties imposed by the Omnibus Crime Control and Safe Streets Act, few employers have been charged with illegal phone monitoring. The practice, however, is said to be widespread.

If your employer intercepts, discloses, or uses any communications in violation of Title III, he or she may be liable for criminal penalties. In addition, you have a private right of action for your actual damages (at least $100 per day or $1,000, whichever is higher) and punitive damages; you are also entitled to reasonable litigation costs and attorney's fees.[66] You do not have to prove malice or bad faith to recover these awards.

Legislators, responding to employees' rights groups, have called for stricter enforcement of the antimonitoring law and have introduced bills in Congress that would strengthen privacy rights in this area.[67]

Most states also have statutes restricting wiretaps and eavesdropping. Many of these statutes provide protections and remedies comparable to Title III.[68] In Pennsylvania, moreover, private wiretapping or eavesdropping is forbidden without the consent of *both* parties.[69]

Title III does not cover photographic surveillance, such as the use of cameras to monitor your performance or honesty, though such surveillance can be quite intrusive and offensive. State laws provide no protection in this respect either, except that Connecticut prohibits employer use of sound or photographic equipment in "areas designated for health or personal comfort."[70]

Similarly, no federal or state law regulates the use of human agents, such as "spotters" posing as customers, except that both California and Nevada prohibit discharge or discipline of an employee based on a spotter's report unless the employee is afforded notice, hearing, and the right to confront the "spotter."[71]

Can my employer search me or my personal effects?

Generally, yes, unless you work for the government, in which case you may be protected by the U.S. Constitution.[72] Employers sometimes search employees or their personal effects (e.g., purses, desks, lockers) to obtain evidence of suspected theft, to prevent contraband (e.g., drugs) from getting onto company premises, and to deter theft. In the private sector there is not much you can do about such searches.

Nevertheless, you may have some protection. Your union contract might limit your employer's right to search; on-the-job searches are part of the "working conditions" that your union can seek to restrict. Further, your employer may be liable to you, for any assault or battery committed against you as well as for common law tort claims such as invasion of privacy;[73] defamation;[74] false arrest or imprisonment;[75] and intentional infliction of emotional distress.[76] For instance, bodily searches are considered highly intrusive under both constitutional and common law standards due to their personal nature. An employer carrying out a body search runs a significant risk of being penalized with tort damages for outrageous conduct unless the search is justified. Thus, a store manager was held liable for strip searching a female cashier accused by a customer of stealing.[77]

Even without a bodily search, a store manager was held liable for $100,000 in damages for searching an employee's locker for missing goods when the employee had established an expectation of privacy in the locker, which management had acknowledged.[78] As in public employment, employees' expectations of privacy are lowered in the eyes of the law by employers who announce that inspections of private areas will be made periodically, for example, where notification is made that cars will be randomly searched. Employees' expectations of privacy can also be outweighed where the employer conducts a search prompted by a strong suspicion of the employees' wrongdoing, particularly possession of drugs or stolen property.[79] But, if your employer *improperly* detains you on suspicion of theft, you may have an action for false arrest.

In addition, your state constitution or statutes may provide privacy protection against searches. Public sector employees, however, have been held to have a constitutionally protected right of privacy in their offices, desks, and file cabinets—indeed, in any place where their expectation of privacy is strong and the government's reason for conducting the search is weak.[80]

If the government employer notifies employees at the outset that their lockers or drawers may be searched at random, and the subsequent search is considered reasonable, then the search probably will not violate the employees' rights.[81] But a police officer's expectation of privacy in his locker was deemed paramount when the inspection was deemed unreasonable, even though the employer owned the lockers and retained a master key.[82] Employees' expectations of privacy will be minimal in a workplace where the employer has established a formal policy or course of conduct in which searches of personal effects and areas are routinely conducted or prior notice is given.[83]

In the private sector, employees are not protected from

searches by the Fourth Amendment to the United States Constitution, although a few state constitutions and privacy statutes have applied Fourth Amendment-like privacy protections to the private workplace.[84]

Can evidence be used to fire me if it was gathered by my employer in an unconstitutional search?

Yes. The rule that excludes evidence at criminal trials that was obtained unconstitutionally does not apply to workplace dismissals. Thus a tax auditor could be fired based on documents found in a search of his briefcase,[85] and narcotics and paraphenalia found in a corrections officer's van could be used against him at an administrative hearing[86] even if both searches were warrantless and would have violated the employees' Fourth Amendment rights in a criminal proceeding.

Are my rights being violated if my employer monitors my computer terminal activity?

No. Employers may lawfully use electronic means to monitor employees' activities at their computer terminals, even without the employee's knowledge or consent. Such monitoring may include counting the number of keystrokes the employee enters per hour or tracking other activities. Many employers have implemented monitoring in the pursuit of increased productivity. Yet surveillance of this type has been found to be stressful and demoralizing, and an electronic monitoring bill to regulate such surveillance is pending before Congress.[87] Until legislation is enacted, however, employees will only be able to convince employers to end monitoring by pointing to its hidden cost in terms of higher employee absenteeism and medical bills and lower productivity.

Can my employer intercept my electronic mail messages?

Generally, yes. While monitoring E-mail is usually legal, rules regarding privacy rights in electronic mail and other computer files are just beginning to be discussed. The opening of ordinary mail addressed to another party is a federal crime,[88] but important legal questions regarding such information in electronic form have yet to be answered. Until then, it can be reasonably anticipated that bitter controversies will emerge when electronic message users have their expectations of privacy violated by their employers.

MAINTAINING AND DISSEMINATING INFORMATION

Do I have the right to see my personnel file?

It depends on where you work. Federal employees are able to demand an inspection of their personnel files under the Privacy Act of 1974.[89] Some state and local government employees are covered by similar record disclosure provisions in states that have privacy laws. Most private sector employees do not enjoy a similar right to access their files, although at least twelve states have statutes that grant employees access to view, duplicate, and amend their employee records.[90] The federal law and most state laws granting employees access to their files contain exceptions that limit the range of disclosable records. Generally, employers are able to withhold from employees information in their files that was compiled in a criminal investigation or for law enforcement purposes. Letters of reference may also be shielded from disclosure in many jurisdictions. But these laws commonly provide the employee with the opportunity not only to view the file but to copy and correct it by inserting a protest or alternative explanation or by removing irrelevant or stale information.

A large number of employers in the private sector have established in-house rules that also permit employees access to their files.[91] Unlike most public sector statutes, however, these rules need not assure the employee the right to copy or correct his or her files. If your employer has not provided for access to your files you probably will be unable to view them.

Are there limits on disclosure of information about me to people inside my company?

Generally there are few restrictions on an employer's right to disseminate information about you *within* the company. The federal Privacy Act and similar state statutes applicable to public employees limit disclosure of personnel information to officers and employees who "need to know" the information to do their job.[92] Similarly, a few enlightened private employers have adopted privacy policies that limit disclosure to those who, in the course of business, need to know information about you.

In a few cases, the courts have limited the right of a union to obtain sensitive material from the employer about you. In *Detroit Edison Co. v. N.L.R.B.*, the union asked the employer for the scores of certain employees on psychological aptitude tests that were taken in connection with their applications for promotions. In refusing to require the employer to disclose this information, the court took official notice of the "sensitivity of any human being to disclosure of information that may be taken to bear on his or her basic competence."[93] It has been held that the federal Privacy Act's ban on the disclosure of employees' records without their consent constitutes a defense to a union's request for certain employee personnel data of a sensitive ature.[94] If your employer "publicizes" false information about you to coworkers or staff members who do not need to know such information, you may be able to state a claim for defamation as described below.[95]

Are there limits on disclosure of information about me to people outside the company?

Yes. Generally, the sources of protection against the disclosure without consent of information about you to persons outside your company are federal and state statutes and the common law of torts. The federal constitutional guarantee of a right to privacy offers little protection in this area since action by government is a prerequisite for its application

As mentioned earlier, federal and some state employees may sue for damages up to $5,000 when an official makes a knowing and willful disclosure of personnel information to outsiders, unless the disclosure falls within certain authorized categories. Private employees and other public employees have no such statutory protection.

Some states have enacted statutes that prohibit private employers from disclosing particular kinds of information. For example, in California employers may not release medical information about you without your express written approval.[96] If your employer violates this statute, you can sue for compensatory and punitive damages, plus litigation costs and attorney's fees. Some states have statutes that allow the employee to limit the information an employer may release without his or her prior authorization.[97]

The common law of torts provides limited protections against the disclosure of information. All states recognize a cause of action for defamation (i.e., libel and slander), and many states recognize causes of action for intentional or negligent infliction of emotional distress and for invasion of privacy. Thus, depending upon the common law of your state, you may have grounds under one or more tort theories to sue your employer for disclosing information about you if this disclosure has caused you to suffer some type of harm.

The tort of defamation usually comes into play in an employment setting when the employer tells an outsider (often a prospective employer or a creditor) something negative and false about the employee. Information that is untrue and lowers your reputation in the eyes of others is defamatory, but your employer may avoid liability if he or she is responding in good faith to an inquiry from someone who has a legitimate interest in the information. In such cases, employer's communication is generally covered by a "qualified privilege." To overcome this qualified privilege, you must demonstrate "malice" (that is, the employer knew of, or recklessly disregarded the falsity of, the statement or otherwise acted with wanton disregard for your rights) or you must show that the recipient of the information did not share a common interest or did not need to know the defamatory information, in which case the qualified privilege dissolves and your employer is liable.[98]

Your employer can also be held liable for defamation if you are forced to disclose derogatory statements about yourself to a third party. This occurred when an exemployee was asked by a prospective employer to state the reason why her former employer had fired her. The reason her previous employer had given was "gross insubordination." She repeated this false reason to her prospective employer who then refused to hire her, thus she essentially defamed herself. Because she was compelled to do so, however, the court held the original employer liable for defamation, even though it was the employee who "self-published" the slander.[99]

If you learn that your employer is providing inaccurate information about you to an outsider, for example to a prospective employer, you should attempt to correct the employer's information. If the employer continues to disclose the false information your claim of malice will be bolstered by this proof of your employer's willful disregard for the truth. Additionally, you should explain the facts to the prospective employer and provide him or her with favorable references from coworkers or from another employer to support your statement. Furthermore, an employer who promises you a good reference and then gives a bad one may be liable for fraud.[100]

If you learn that your employer is communicating false information about you in a credit report, you can challenge it by asking for a review under the federal Fair Credit Reporting Act (see above). If the dispute cannot be resolved, you can go to court.

The tort of invasion of privacy has been recognized in various forms in some states. The forms of this tort which are most applicable to employment are "public disclosure of private facts" and "placement of an individual in a false light before the public eye." Under the tort of public disclosure of private facts, you can sue your employer if he or she discloses to a large number of people (e.g., in a broadcast or news article) true but embarrassing private facts about you. For example, it is likely that your personnel file contains a substantial number of private facts about your health, salary, job performance, and similar matters. If an employer discloses these types of facts to an outsider, you may have a claim under this tort. You may even have a claim if the disclosure is made to numerous coworkers. For instance, one employee claimed that her employer caused her severe mental and emotional distress by letting her coworkers know that she had had a mastectomy. The court held that she stated a valid claim of public disclosure of private facts claim.[101]

There are two major problems, however, in making out a claim for public disclosure of private facts. First, your employer's conduct in disclosing the facts about you must be extreme and outrageous. In an Arizona case, the court held that while an employer's disclosure of facts about an employee's health certainly invaded the employee's right to privacy, the invasion was not sufficiently outrageous to warrant the granting of relief since the facts were disclosed to the employee's doctor.[102] Second, the private facts disclosed must be communicated to a significant number of people.[103] In one interesting case, a Michigan court held that an employer's disclosure of facts about an employee's health to his army reserve officer satisfied the "public disclosure" requirement in that this information would be spread throughout the army reserve office.[104] Generally, however, this element of the tort will be difficult to prove since employers rarely disclose this type of information to large numbers of persons.

The tort of "interference with prospective economic advantage" may be a basis for relief if a prospective employer decides not to hire you based on false statements or inappropriate facts disclosed to him by your former employer. Generally, in order to make out this cause of action you must demonstrate (1) a valid contractual relationship between you and the employer; (2) knowledge of the relationship on the part of the interferer; (3) intentional interference, inducing a breach or termination of the relationship or expectancy; and (4) resulting damage.[105]

Finally, some courts have held that an employer has a duty to keep and maintain employment records carefully and that a breach of this duty gives rise to a cause of action in negligence.[106] In one case, a plaintiff alleged that his former employer negligently maintained and disclosed to a credit company inaccurate information about the circumstances of the termination of his employment. The court held that the employer, in gratuitously supplying references, had a duty to supply accurate information.[107]

PERSONAL LIFESTYLE

Can I be fired for my off-the-job relationships?

Usually the answer is yes. In states where the employment at will rule is strong, companies can limit the range of their employees' relationships without violating the law unless the basis is discriminatory. Accordingly, employers have fired employees for consorting with coworkers, supervisors, subordinates, and competitors. Similarly, employees have been terminated for carrying on extramarital affairs, for living with others, or for procreating out of wedlock. Employers who apply such policies nondiscriminatorily (i.e., both women and men are fired for such behavior) will not run afoul of the privacy or discrimination laws.[108]

Only when the employer has previously guaranteed that such personal affairs will *not* be the basis for adverse action,[109] or when the employer is especially vindictive, will possible liability attach.[110] Thus, when a California executive was fired after his employer discovered that in his private life he was hosting homosexual group sex, which the company considered inappropriate executive behavior, the jury awarded him $5.3 million.[111]

Most states have statutes that protect the political activities of some class of employees, either public sector, private sector, or both. Only thirteen states have no such provisions.[112]

Can I be fired because of my political affiliation?

The answer is no if you work for the government. According to the Supreme Court the essence of the First Amendment's protection of free speech is the guarantee that citizens can express political ideas and vote their choice.[113] This is defeated, however, when, for instance, a politician takes office and "cleans house" by sweeping out officials or other government employees who belong to a different political faction. In such cases the court has protected the jobs of terminated employees by making the officials who discharge them personally liable for damages incurred in the violation of their First Amendment rights.[114]

If you work for a private-sector employer, however, your boss may be able to discharge you—or not hire you in the first place—based on your political activities or views.

Can I be denied work because I smoke on or off the job?

Rules restricting where you can smoke on the job are rampant, indeed, they may be required by law. Unless the rules of your workplace say otherwise, there is no legal right to smoke on the job. You can be told where to smoke on the job or not to smoke at all.

In addition to restricting smoking on the job, many employers want their employees to abstain from smoking *off* the job as well. Employers of smokers face higher medical insurance costs, higher absenteeism due to illness, and decreased life expectancies in their workforce. Hence employers have begun rejecting applicants and firing employees for smoking off the job.

Smokers' rights groups, civil liberty interests, and tobacco interests have allied to lobby state legislatures for declarations that what employees do on their own time is their own business, including smoking. A popular sentiment is growing which says that employers should not be able to tell employees what they can and cannot do on their own time. Thus, many of the same statutes that compel employers to bar or segregate smokers on the job now also forbid employers from requiring employees to abstain from smoking or using tobacco products outside of their employment.

The states that essentially force employers to recognize their employees' right to smoke in private are Indiana, Kentucky, Maine, Mississippi, New Hampshire, New Jersey, New Mexico, North Carolina, North Dakota, Oregon, Rhode Island (exempt are nonprofit antismoking organizations), South Carolina, Tennessee, and Virginia. The sudden and rapid proliferation of smoking rules, both pro and con, finds many personnel managers realizing that smoking policies are a major concern and should prompt you to check the rules where you work if you want to be sure of your rights.

Do I have the right not to breathe other's smoke on the job?

The right not to breathe the smoke of others on the job has been accorded greater legitimacy ever since the surgeon general's 1986 report, *The Health Consequences of Involuntary Smoking.* Certainly the avalanche of state and local laws and ordinances compelling employers to create nonsmoking zones seem to support the right of the employee to work in a smoke-free environment.[115] Yet around the country, the courts are divided as to whether employees can force the issue or win damages for the injuries they suffer as a result of breathing the smoke of others on the job, although at least four U.S. district courts have interpreted smoke sensitivity a disability under the Rehabilitation Act of 1973 and will continue to do so, presumably, under the Americans with Disabilities Act.[116]

Can I be fired for not complying with a dress or grooming code?

Yes, especially if your employer has a legitimate reason for imposing one, such as when a television station requires its news anchor people to wear clothes compatible with its image and the studio lighting.[117] Generally, it is legal for your employer to prescribe how you wear your hair, whether you wear a beard or moustache, and how you dress. The only grounds on which employees are likely to prevail when challenging a dress code is that the code demeans or otherwise discriminates against the protected class to which they belong. Thus, employers could not force employees to wear sexually provocative clothing such as "low-cut and slinky" cocktail dresses[118] or revealing uniforms with split sides[119] because the clothes invited sexual harassment and were not required of men.

The usual rules against disparate impact discrimination (as discussed in chapter 8) apply to dress and grooming codes. Yet at times these rules do not apply smoothly. For instance, males who wear earrings insist that they should not be fired or reprimanded since earrings are permitted to females. An Oregon man failed to convince a court of this argument, just as, for the most part, men have generally failed to overturn workplace regulations concerning the length of their air.[120] Since men can easily change their length of hair or other elements of personal appearance to conform to an employer's reasonable code, such codes, say the courts, are not barriers to employment opportunity and thus are not prohibited by the antidiscrimination laws.[121]

When a personal appearance code affirmatively requires the employee to make a significant adjustment, the reasonableness of the employer's request will be scrutinized, if not in the courts, then perhaps by the public at large. A female airline ticket agent attracted nationwide attention when she refused to wear make-up as required by the company's code. Despite the airline's legitimate purpose in maintaining its businesslike image, the fact that its rule only affected women and placed on them a potentially onerous burden (since some woman are allergic to make-up) caused the company to back down.[122] Yet a black female airline ticket agent was justifiably prohibited from wearing a braided "corn-row" hairstyle, a court held, since hairstyle is an easily changed characteristic and the employer's purpose in projecting a conservative image was bona fide.[123] "No-beard" policies have been held to disparately impact against blacks who suffer from a condition called *pseudo follicu-*

litis barbae (PFB), which makes it necessary to refrain from shaving. Similarly, the air force had to allow a Jewish chaplain to wear a beard[124] but could force him to remove his skullcap.[125] In short, where an employee can reasonably control his or her appearance to conform to a dress or grooming code, the courts are likely to find no discrimination.

In the public sector, the right to maintain one's choice of personal appearance has been recognized as a constitutionally protected liberty interest.[126] Nevertheless, a village public department could reprimand two officers for wearing earrings off-duty. The two never argued that they should be allowed to wear earrings on the job since the appearance codes of law enforcement forces have been strongly upheld. Rather, the two officers claimed that they should be permitted to wear earrings publicly when off-duty. Yet the court held that in a small village, their being seen wearing earrings off-duty would have a negative impact on police effectiveness.[127] When an employee in the public sector asserts the constitutional right of individuality or privacy to protect his or her appearance, the court will balance that interest against the competing interests asserted by the public employer.[128]

Can my employer monitor what I do off the job and fire me for it?

Employers can observe employees off the premises as long as the intrusion on the solitude or seclusion of the employee would not be considered highly offensive to the reasonable person.[129] One employer was permitted to post investigators outside an employee's house and to take movies of the employee through the window with a high powered lens when the employee had made disability claims.[130] As regards the off-premises romantic conduct of employees, employers generally are permitted to restrict relationships they consider a conflict of interest unless they do so discriminatorily or in violation of their own rules.[131]

Public sector employees who are called to task for their off-duty conduct may have a constitutional claim to invasion of privacy if government purpose for the intrusion is unreasonable or in bad faith. If the off-duty conduct in question relates to job-performance, however, the government's regulation of it may be valid. A firefighter could therefore be fired for smoking a cigarette or a policeman for any illicit sexual relations.[132] But another police officer could not be fired for cohabiting with a married woman absent a showing that the relationship affected the performance of his duties.[133]

The fact that the constitution may protect the off-duty conduct of public sector but not private sector workers underscores yet again that the right of privacy considered fundamental to the founding fathers still eludes most Americans at work, prompting the American Civil Liberties Union to assert, "The time has come to extend the Bill of Rights to the biggest remaining group of forgotten people—America's workers."[134]

NOTES

1. *Olmstead v. United States*, 227 U.S. 438, 478 (1928) (Brandeis, J. dissenting). Justice Brandeis termed the right to be let alone—"the most comprehensive of rights and the right most valued by civilized men."

2. A. Westin, *Privacy and Freedom* 32 (1967). For a fuller discussion of the right to privacy generally, *see* E. Hendricks, et al., *Your Right to Privacy*, an ACLU handbook (Southern Illinois University Press 1990).

3. According to a federal study as of 1987, about 6 million workers were under surveillance, including as many as 66% of all computer operators. *See* testimony June 11, 1991, before Subcommittee on Labor Management Relations, regarding H.R. 1218.

4. According to a 1990 survey, 47% of responding U.S. companies believed that soliciting information from job applicants, increased data retention, and effective security measures can limit the risk of employee misconduct. Two-thirds, however, reported that searches and electronic surveillance techniques to monitor employee behavior are ineffective and counterproductive. *See* Conference Board Survey on Employee Personnel Data (1990), cited in 107 *Human Resources Management* 1, CCH (Nov. 27, 1990).

5. In 1991 the Department of Justice reported that employee theft costs businesses an estimated $40 billion annually and is increasing 15% a year. Cited in 115 *CCH Personnel Practices Guide* 431–39 (1991).

6. 5 U.S.C. § 552A.

7. *See* E. Hendricks, *Your Right to Privacy*, *supra* note 2, at 98.

8. 29 U.S.C. §§ 2001 *et seq.* (1990). The law took effect Dec. 27, 1988.

9. Employees have asserted a variety of state common law claims when

challenging polygraph testing. Successful claims have aimed at employers' misuse of polygraph results or malpractice against the polygraph operator. *E.g.*, *O'Brien v. Papa Gino's of America, Inc.*, 780 F.2d 1167 (1st Cir. 1986) (employee award of $450,000 partially based on a finding that a polygraph test was offensive and an invasion of privacy); *Kairys v. Douglas Stereo*, 83 Md. App. 667, 557 A.2d 386 (Md. Ct. App. 1990) (polygraph results used to prompt a criminal investigation); *Bucko v. First Minnesota Savings Bank*, 471 N.W.2d 95 (Minn. Sup. Ct. 1991) (bank violated state polygraph statute by conducting examination of employees).

10. By and large, public-sector employees have failed to establish constitutional violations for denial of due process, based on polygraph testing. *See, e.g., Jackson v. Hudspeth Center*, 6 IER Cas. BNA 108 (Miss. Sup. Ct. 1990); *Anderson v. City of Philadelphia*, 669 F. Supp. 441 (E.D. Pa. 1987), or for violation of the Fifth Amendment's prohibition against self-incrimination, *Reynolds v. Sheet Metal Workers, Local 102*, 498 F. Supp. 952; (D.D.C. 1980), *aff'd*, 702 F.2d 221 (D.C. Cir. 1981).

11. *See* 29 U.S.C. §§ 2001, *et seq.*

12. Alaska Stat. § 23.10.37(a)(1986); Cal. Lab. Code § 432.2(a)(1971); Conn. Gen. Stat. Ann. § 31–51g(b)(1)(1987); Del. Code Ann. tit. 19, § 704(b)(1985); D.C. Code Ann. § 36-802(a)(198); Haw. Rev. Stat. § 378-26.5 (1985); Idaho Code § 44-903 (1977); Iowa Code § 730.4 (1987); Me. Rev. Stat. Ann. tit. 32, § 7151 (1986); Md. Ann Code art. 100, § 95(c) (1987); Mass. Ann. Laws ch. 149 (f) (1985); Minn. Stat. Ann. § 181.75(1)(1987); Mont. Code Ann. § 39-2-304(1) (1987); Neb. Rev. Stat. § 81-1932 (1981); N.J. Stat. Ann. § 2c: 40A-1 (1987); N.Y. Lab. Law § 735(1) (1987) (prohibits voice stress analyzers only); Or. Rev. Stat. § 659.225 (1985); R.I. Gen. Laws § 28-6.1-11 (1986); Wash. Rev. Code Ann. § 49.44.120 (1987); W. Va. Code § 21-5-56 (1985).

13. Ariz. Rev. Stat. Ann § 32-2713 (1986); Ark. Code Ann. § 71-2217 (1979); Ill. Stat. Ann. ch. 111, § 246 (1987); Ind. Code Ann. § 25-30-2-1 (1987); La. Rev. Stat. Ann. §§ 37.2831 (1987); N.M. Stat. Ann. § 61.26.9 (1983); Tex. Rev. Civ. Stat. Ann. art. 4413 (29cc) (1976).

14. Ga. Code Ann. § 43-36-1 (1987); Nev. Rev. Stat. Ann. § 648.187 (1986); Tenn. Code Ann. § 62-27-123 (1986); Utah Code Ann. § 34-37-1 (1977); Va. Code Ann. § 54-918 (1982); Wis. Stat. Ann. § 111.37(1)(a) (1987).

15. *See supra.*

16. *E.g.*, Delaware, *Heller v. Dover Warehouse Mkt., Inc.*, 515 A.2d 178 (Del. Super. Ct. 1986); Maryland, *Moniodis v. Cook*, 64 Md. App. 1, 494 A.2d 212, *cert. denied*, 304 Md. 631, 500 A.2d 649 (1985);

Pennsylvania, *Molush v. Orkin Exterminating Co.*, 547 F. Supp. 54 (E.D. Pa. 1982).

17. See the line of cases employing rules by the U.S. Supreme Court in *Garrity v. New Jersey*, 385 U.S. 493 (1967); *e.g.*, *Knebel v. Biloxi*, 453 So.2d 1037 (Miss. 1984); *Eshelman v. Blubaum*, 114 Ariz. 376, 560 P.2d 1283 (Ct. App. 1977).

18. *Texas State Employees Union v. Texas Department of Mental Health and Mental Retardation*, 746 S.W.2d 203 (Tex. Sup. Ct. 1987); *Woodland v. City of Houston*, 731 F. Supp. 1304 (S.D. Tex. 1990) (examinations of uniformed civil servants held "arbitrary" and "unreasonable").

19. *E.g.*, *Dallas v. Texas Employment Comm'n*, 626 S.W.2d 549 (Tex. Ct. App. 1981).

20. *See, e.g.*, *Smith v. Orkin Exterminating Co.*, 540 So.2d 363 (Cal. Ct. App. 1989).

21. *See, e.g.*, *Ellis v. Buckley*, 790 P.2d 875 (Colo. Ct. App. 1989), *cert. denied*, 111 S. Ct. 296 (1990).

22. Art. I § 1 of the California Constitution; *see, e.g.*, *Long Beach City Employees Association v. City of Long Beach*, 41 Cal. 3d 937, 719 P.2d 660, 227 Cal. Rptr. 90 (1986).

23. Mass. Gen. Laws. Ann. ch. 276 § 100A (1980).

24. *See, e.g.*, *Hedge v. County of Tippecanoe*, 890 F.2d 4 (7th Cir. 1989) (applicant for office job in law enforcement agency was improperly asked about her sexual affairs); *Thorne v. City of El Segundo*, 726 F.2d 459 (9th Cir. 1983), *cert. denied*, 469 U.S. 979 (1984) (female police officer's constitutional right of privacy violated by inquiries into her sexual activities).

25. The Use of Integrity Tests for Pre-employment Screening, Congress of the United States, Office of Technology Assessment (OTA) (1989).

26. *Id.*

27. *Soroka v. Dayton Hudson Corp.*, 6 IER Cas. BNA 1491 (Cal. Ct. App. 1991).

28. Mass. Ann. Laws ch. 149, 19B (1987).

29. *See* Harvard School of Public Health study of 2,537 Boston postal workers reported in 82 *American Journal of Public Health* (1992).

30. False positive results have been found when cheap drug testing units are used. Even sophisticated tests fail due to a wide range of accuracy problems including equipment sterilization, broken chains of custody, and general ineptness. *See* Larson, *Employment Screening*, (1990).

31. According to one court, "There are few activities in our society more personal or private than the passing of urine." *National Treasury Employees Union v. Von Raab*, 816 F.2d 170, 175 (5th Cir. 1987).

32. *See, e.g.*, *National Fed'n of Fed. Employees v. Cheney*, 742 F. Supp.

4 (D.D.C. 1990) (reasonable suspicion drug testing program based on the off-duty conduct of Defense Mapping Agency employees was struck down because it was unrelated to on-the-job impairment); *National Treasury Employees Union v. Sullivan*, 744 F. Supp. (D.D.C. 1990) (reasonable suspicion testing of all Health and Human Services employees held to be too broad).

33. *See Skinner v. Railway Labor Executives Ass'n*, 489 U.S. 602 (1989); *National Treasury Employees Union v. Von Raab*, 489 U.S. 656 (1989).

34. *Id.*

35. *See, e.g., Willner v. Thornburgh*, 929 F.2d 1185 (D.C. Cir. 1991); *Teamsters v. Department of Transportation*, 6 IER Cas. BNA 593 (6th Cir. 1991).

36. *See, e.g., American Federation of Government Employees v. Cavazos*, 721 F. Supp. 1361 (D.D.C. 1989) (striking down mandatory compulsory drug testing of automatic data processors).

37. *See, e.g., Willner v. Thornburgh*, 928 F.2d 1185 (D.C. 1991); *also, Dimeo v. Griffen*, 924 F.2d 664 (7th Cir. 1991).

38. Many constitutional guarantees could be gutted by the tautology, adopted by many courts in drug testing challenges, that says foreseeability of the denial of a right justifies the denial. *But see Willner v. Thornburgh*, 928 F.2d 1185 (D.C. Cir. 1991) (Henderson, J., dissenting). In 1992 the Congress began considering the Quality Assurance in the Private Sector Drug Testing Act (S. 2008, H.R. 33). *See note 42, infra.*

39. *See* Omnibus Transportation Employee Testing Act of 1991; the first law to mandate drug testing in certain federally regulated transportation industries also sets certain standards that programs must conform to. The effective date of this law was October 1992.

40. *See, e.g., Beattie v. City of St. Petersburg Beach*, 733 F. Supp. 1455 (D.C. Fla. 1990).

41. *See Omnibus Transportation Employee Testing Act of 1991, supra.*

42. In 1992 the Congress began considering the Quality Assurance in the Private Sector Drug Testing Act (S. 2008, H.R. 33). The draft of this bill sets federal standards for employer drug testing programs. Random testing could be undertaken if the test were part of a universal program in locations where drug abuse has been identified as a problem or in cases concerning "safety or security sensitive" positions. Post-accident tests, reasonable suspicion "for cause" tests, and preemployment tests would also be permitted. Testing would be performed in specified laboratories, and other procedural safeguards for accuracy would be set.

43. See note 44 for a list of states with drug testing laws. All of these apply

to public sector employees except Connecticut and Rhode Island. In addition four states have laws pertaining only to public sector employees. They are Kansas, Kan. Stat. Ann. § 75-4362(a)(f)(1990); Nevada, Nev. Rev. Stat. § 456 32-12 (1991); New Mexico, N.M. SPB R. 14 (1989); Tennessee, Tenn. Comp. R. & Reg. tit. 41, ch. 1 (1988) (applies to corrections employees only).

44. Ariz. Rev. Stat. Ann. § 15-513 A-G (1990) (applies to transportation employees only) and § 28-414.01(c) (1990) (applies to school bus drivers); Conn. Gen. Stat. Ann. § 3151t-31-51aa (1990) (applies to private sector employees only); Fla. Stat. Ch. 112.0455 (1991) and 1990 Fla. Laws Ch. 201 § 12; Iowa Code Ann. § 730.5 (1990); La. Rev. Stat. Ann. § 23-1601(10)(1991); Me. Rev. Stat. Ann. tit. 26, ch. 7 § 681 (1990); Md. Code Ann. § 17-214.1 (1990); Minn. Stat. Ann. § 181.950 (1991); Miss. Code Ann. ch. 610, §§ 1–16 (1991); Mont. Code Ann. § 39-2-304(1) (1990); Neb. Rev. Stat. §§ 48-1901-14-1910 (1990); N.H. Rev. Stat. Ann. §§ 1–5 (1990) (establishes a study committee only); N.C. Sess. Laws §§ 95-230 and 95-234 (1991); Or. Rev. Stat. § 438.435 (1)–(6) (1990); R.I. Gen. Laws § 28-6.5-1 (1990) (protects private-sector employees only); Utah Code Ann. §§ 34-38-1 through 34-38-15 (1988) (only allows private sector testing where the employer agrees to be tested as well); Vt. Stat. Ann. tit. 21, §§ 512–20 (1990).

45. *See, e.g., Luck v. Southern Pacific Transportation Company,* 267 Cal. Rptr. 618 (Cal. Ct. App. 1990) (a private employer is bound to observe the constitution's privacy provisions; *Semore v. Pool,* 217 Cal. App. 3d 1087, 266 Cal. Rptr. 280 (Cal. Ct. App. 1990) (employee terminated for refusing to take a pupillary reaction eye test for drugs states a constitutional claim); *Kelley v. Schlumberger Technology Corp.,* 849 F.2d 41 (1989) (Louisiana constitution protects private sector worker).

46. *See, e.g., Pennsylvania, Borse v. Piece Goods Shop, Inc.,* 963 F.2d 611 (3d Cir. 1992); West Virginia, *Twigg v. Hercules Corp.,* 406 F.2d 52 (W.V. Sup. Ct. 1991) (West Virginia's public policy against drug testing gives terminated employee a wrongful discharge tort claim); Alaska, *Luedtke v. Nabors Alaska Drilling, Inc.,* 768 P.2d 1123 (Alaska Sup. Ct. 1989).

47. *See Dick v. Koch Gathering Systems,* 90C1825 (Dist. Ct. Sedgwick Co. Ka 1991) Nat. Law Journal, at 1, Dec. 16, 1991. $4.1 million jury verdict to employee whose erroneous drug test results led to his discharge. *Also see Ellenwood v. Exxon Shipping Co.,* 6 IER Cas. BNA 1623 (Me. D.C. 1991) (employee discharged for alcohol-abuse stated an oral contract claim based on the employer's change in alcohol-rehabilitation policy); *Harris v. Hirsh,* 555 N.Y.S.2d 735 (Sup. Ct.

App. Div. 1990) (statement that employee was "on drugs" may be defamatory where employer uttering it knew that it was false and drug tests were negative).

48. 42 U.S.C. 12114(b)(3).

49. 29 C.F.R. 1630 (13)(a).

50. Cal. Lab. Code §§ 432.7 and 432.8; Conn. Gen. Stat. Ann. appendix pamphlet 1980; Haw. Rev. Stat. § 731-3.1; Ill. Admin. Code tit. 68 § 2-104; Md. Ann. Code art. 27, § 292; Mass. Gen. Laws Ann. ch. 1513 § 4, ¶ 9; Mich. Comp. Laws Ann. § 423.501; Minn. Stat. Ann. § 364.04; Mo. Ann. Stat. § 610.100; N.Y. Exec. Law § 296.16; Ohio Rev. Code Ann. tit. 21 § 2151.358; Or. Rev. Stat § 652-750; and Va. Code §§ 19.2-392.4(a) and (c).

51. N.Y. Exec. Law § 296.15; Pa. Ann. Stat. tit. 78, § 9122 *et seq.*

52. Md. Ann. Code art. 100, § 95A; Mass. Ann. Laws ch. 151B, § 4; Mich. Comp. Law Ann. §§ 423.501 *et seq.*

53. 42 U.S.C. § 3771; 28 C.F.R. 1.

54. *See* in this book chapter 2 on the hiring process and part 3 on discrimination.

55. N.Y. Lab. Law § 201-1 (1981), Cal. Lab. Code § 1051 (1971).

56. 15 U.S.C. § 1681(b)(3)(B).

57. 15 U.S.C. § 1681 (2)(a)(b) and § 1681(d)(a)(2).

58. 15 U.S.C. § 1681(g)(a)(1), (3).

59. 15 U.S.C. § 1681(n) and (o).

60. 15 U.S.C. § 1681(h)(e).

61. 29 C.F.R. § 1630.14(a).

62. EEOC Regulations to the Americans with Disabilities Act, 42 U.S.C. §§ 12101 *et seq.*; 29 C.F.R. pt. 1630, app., § 1630.14(b) and § 1630.14(d). If you are not covered by the Americans with Disabilities Act because your company employs less than 25 persons (or less than 15 after July 26, 1994) your state may provide you with medical privacy protection. Several states restrict an employer's use of a job applicant's medical records. With few exceptions, however, these statutes offer weaker coverage than does the ADA. Where the ADA provides employees with stronger protection than does state law, the ADA governs. California, Connecticut, and Maryland prohibit inquiries into an applicant's physical or mental condition that do not directly relate to the applicant's capacity to perform the work in question. *See, e.g.,* Md. Ann. Code art. 100, § 95A (1985).

63. 18 U.S.C. § 2510-20; *see Watkins v. L. M. Berry,* 704 F.2d 577 (11th Cir. 1983). A call may be intercepted in the ordinary course of business to determine its nature but not its content. If the call is private the employer must hang up.

64. *Briggs v. American Filter Co.,* 630 F.2d (5th Cir. 1980) (employer

who suspected an employee of revealing confidential information to a competitor was permitted to listen to the employee's call on a phone extension as this was held to be in "the ordinary course of business").

65. *Id.*, *Watkins v. L. M. Berry, supra.*

66. 18 U.S.C. § 2510-20.

67. *See* Privacy for Consumers and Workers Act S. 516, H.R. 1218. This legislation would not forbid workplace monitoring but would set guidelines for employers. For instance, employees would have to be notified immediately upon commencement of monitoring. The bill would require that all monitoring be work related and that employees have access to collected data. The bill would also limit disclosure and use of data collected by employers.

68. *See, e.g.*, Fla. Stat. Ann. § 934.01; Kan. Stat. § 22-2514; Minn. Stat. Ann. § 626A.01; Neb. Rev. Stat. § 86-701; Nev. Rev. Stat. § 200.610; N.H. Rev. Stat. Ann. § 570-A:1; N.M. Stat. Ann. § 40A-12-1, N.Y. Crim. Proc. Law § 700.05; S.D. Codified Laws Ann. § 23-13A-1; Va. Code Ann. § 19.2-61; Wis. Stat. Ann. § 968.27.

69. 18 Pa. Cons. Stat. Ann. § 5701.

70. Conn. Gen. Stat. § 31-48b(b).

71. Cal. Lab. Code § 2930; Nev. Rev. Stat. § 613.160.

72. *See O'Connor v. Ortega*, 408 U.S. 709 (1984) (discussed in note 80, *infra*).

73. *See Love v. Southern Bell Telephone and Telegraph Co.*, 263 So.2d 460 (La. Ct. App.), *cert. denied*, 262 La. 1117, 266 So.2d 429 (1972) (forced entry into trailer home of absent employee); *K-Mart Corp. Store No. 7441 v. Trotti*, 677 S.W.2d 632 (Tex. Ct. App. 1984).

74. *See Holloway v. K-Mart Corp.*, 113 Wis. 2d 143, 334 N.W.2d 570 (1983) (employee accused of stealing candy).

75. *General Motors v. Piskor*, 277 Md. 165, 352 A.2d 810 (1976) (security guards accosted employee and took him to a guardhouse for questioning).

76. *Smithson v. Nordstrom, Inc.*, 63 Or. App. 423, 64 P.2d 1119 (1982) (questioning employee for three hours and threatening criminal prosecution where evidence of wrongdoing was insufficient).

77. *Bodewig v. K-Mart, Inc.*, 54 Or. App. 480, *rev. denied*, 292 Or. 450, 644 (1982).

78. *K-Mart Corp. Store No. 7441 v. Trotti*, 677 S.W.2d 652 (Tex. Ct. App. 1984).

79. *Gretencord v. Ford Motor Co.*, 538 F. Supp. 331 (D. Kan. 1982).

80. *O'Connor v. Ortega*, 480 U.S. 709 (1989). (The Supreme Court applied the Fourth Amendment of the United States Constitution's guarantee against unreasonable search and seizures to the workplace. Hence, a hospital may have violated a psychiatrist's right of privacy

by ransacking his office based on alleged improprieties.) *Also, Scho-wengerdt v. General Dynamics Corp.*, 823 F.2d 1326 (9th Cir. 1987); *Shields v. Burge*, 874 F.2d 1201 (7th Cir. 1989)(a "fishing expedition" through a police officer's desk based on an unsubstantiated rumor that he possessed narcotics violated his constitutional rights).

81. *Postal Workers v. Postal Service*, 871 F.2d 566 (6th Cir. 1989).

82. *United States v. Speights*, 557 F.2d (3d Cir. 1977).

83. *Id.*

84. *But see* Louisiana, *Julien v. South Central Telephone Co.*, 433 So.2d 847 (La. Ct. App. 1983); California, *Rulon-Miller v. IBM*, 162 Cal. App. 3d 241, 208 Cal. Rptr. 524 (1984); Maine, *Jackson v. Liquid Carbonic Corp.*, 863 F.2d 111 (1st Cir. 1988); *see also*, Mass. Gen. Laws Ann. ch. 204.

85. *Finkelstein v. State Personnel Board*, 5 IER Cas. BNA 231 (Cal. Ct. App. 1990); *but see State v. Helfrich*, 600 P.2d 816 (1979) (Montana Supreme Court relied on Montana's constitutional privacy guarantee to exclude evidence obtained in a private search.).

86. *Sheetz v. Mayor & City Council of Baltimore*, 553 A.2d 1281 (Md. Ct. App. 1989).

87. *See* Privacy for Consumers and Workers (Electronic Monitoring) Act, S. 516, H.R. 1218.

88. 18 U.S.C. § 1702 (1982) (Violations for opening another's mail carries a penalty of up to five years in prison and a $12,000 fine.).

89. 5 U.S.C. § 552a(d), 552a(g)(i) (1982). (The federal Privacy Act of 1974, which applies to employees of the federal government, provides government agencies to maintain in their records only such information as is relevant and necessary to accomplish a recognized purpose of the agency; that act also requires such records to be accurate, relevant, timely, and complete and to be kept secure and confidential. About one-third of the states have similar laws that govern the records of public employees. These protections do not extend to private employees.)

90. *Cmp.* 5 U.S.C. § 552 a(d), 552 a(g)(i) (1982) and Cal. Lab. Code § 1198.5 (1987); Conn. Gen. Stat. Ann. § 31-1286 (1987); Me. Rev. Stat. Ann. tit. 26, § 631 (1986); Mass. Gen. Laws Ann. ch. 149 § 52c (1987); Mich. Stat. Ann. § 1762(1)–(5) (1982); N.H. Rev. Stat. Ann. § 275.56 (1986); Ohio Rev. Code Ann. § 4133.23(A) (1973); Or. Rev. Stat. § 652.750(2) (1981); Pa. Stat. Ann. tit. 43, § 1322 (1986); Vt. Stat. Ann. tit. 1 § 317(b)(7) (1985); Va. Code Ann. § 6.1-377 (1983); Wis. Stat. Ann. § 103.13(2) (1986).

91. *See* Hendricks, *Your Right to Privacy, supra* note 2.

92. *See* 5 U.S.C. § 552(a)(b)(1).

93. 440 U.S. at 318.

94. *See American Federation of Gov't Employees v. Defense General Supply Center*, 423 F. Supp. 481 (E.D. Va. 1976), *aff'd*, 573 F.2d 184 (4th Cir. 1978).

95. *Cary v. AT&T Technologies, Inc.*, No. W-027817-87 (N.J. Sup. Ct. 1991) (A supervisor incurred liability for making negative statements in a written performance appraisal that cost a worker her job.).

96. Cal. Civ. Code § 56.

97. *See, e.g.*, Conn. Gen. Stat. § 31-128(f); Mich. Comp. Laws Ann. § 423.501; Colo. Rev. Stat. § 24-50-127.

98. *See, e.g.*, *Kenny v. Gilmore*, 195 Ga. App. 407, 393 S.E.2d 472 (1990); *but see Wirig v. Kinney Shoe Corp.*, 5 IER Cas. BNA 1562 (Minn. 1990).

99. *Lewis v. Equitable Life Assurance Society*, 389 N.W.2d 876 (Minn. 1984).

100. *See, e.g.*, *Silver v. Mohasco Corp.*, 94 A.D.2d 820, 460 N.Y.S.2d 97 (1983), *aff'd*, 62 N.Y.2d 741, 476 N.Y.S.2d 822 (1984).

101. *Miller v. Motorola, Inc.*, 202 Ill. App. 2d 976, 148 560 N.E.2d 900 (1990); *see also, Cronan v. New England Tel. & Tel. Co.*, 41 FEP Cas. BNA 1273 (1986) (employer's disclosure that plaintiff had AIDS violated Massachusetts' privacy statute); *Bratt v. IBM*, 392 Mass. 508, 467 N.E.2d 126 (1984).

102. *Valencia v. Duval Corp.*, 645 P.2d 1262 (1982).

103. *See, e.g.*, *Beard v. Akzona, Inc.*, 517 F. Supp. 128 (E.D. Tenn. 1981).

104. *Beaumont v. Brown*, 401 Mich. 80, 257 N.W.2d 522 (1977).

105. *See, Collincini v. Honeywell*, 7 IER Cas. BNA 51 (Pa. Sup. Ct. 1991)(company intentionally interfered with former employee's contract by sending letters to competitor that had hired him threatening legal action if the competitor did not stop employee from soliciting company's customers which caused the competition to fire the employee); *Mason v. Funderbuck*, 446 S.W.2d 543 (1969).

106. *Bulkin v. Western Kraft East, Inc.*, 422 F. Supp. 437 (E.D. Pa. 1976); *see also, Quinones v. United States*, 492 F.2d 1269 (3d Cir. 1974).

107. *Bulkin v. Western Kraft East, Inc.*, supra; *Bratt v. IBM Corp.*, 392 Mass. 508, 467 N.E.2d 126 (1989) (psychiatrist's disclosure about plaintiff's condition to others within the company violated the Mass. privacy statute).

108. *E.g.*, *Parr v. Woodman of the World Life Ins. Co.*, 791 F.2d 888 (11th Cir. 1986); *Reiter v. Conf. Consol. School Dist.*, 618 F. Supp. 1458 (D. Colo. 1985). For a fuller discussion of antidiscrimination

laws that protect an employee's relationship with people of race, national origin, age, gender, religion, or disability, see chapters 8 through 17.

109. *Salazar v. Furs Inc.*, 629 F. Supp. 1403 (D.N.M. 1986).
110. *Saldana v. Kelsey-Hayes*, 178 Mich. App. 230, 443 N.W.2d 382 (1989); *see also Rulon-Miller International Business Machines Corp.*, 162 Cal. App. 3d 241, 208 Cal. Rptr. 524 (1989).
111. *Collins v. Shell Oil Co.*, 56 FEP Cas. BNA 440 (Cal. Sup. Ct. 1991) (The jury awarded Mr. Collins $2.5 million in lost incomes, $800,000 for noneconomic injuries, and $2 million in punitive damages.).
112. The thirteen states with no statutory protection of political activities are Alaska, Arkansas, District of Columbia, Georgia, Hawaii, Illinois, Kansas, Maine, New York, Oregon, Vermont, Virginia, and Washington.
113. *Rutan v. Republican Party of Illinois*, 111 L. Ed. 2d 828, 111 S. Ct. 13 (1990).
114. *Hafer v. Melo*, 112 S. Ct. 358, 116 L. Ed. 301(1991).
115. *See Smith v. Western Electric Co.*, 643 S.W. 2d 10 (Mo. Ct. App. 1982) applying the rule articulated in *Shimp v. New Jersey Bell Telephone*, OSHD para. 21,421 (1977).
116. *See generally* Commercial Clearing House Human Resources Reporter at para. 2415. Some states and municipalities have adopted laws and ordinances that protect the rights of those who are sensitive to smoke. *See, e.g., County of Fresno v. Fair Employment and Housing Commission of the State of California*, F012316, where the county should have moved sooner to bar smoking in a clerical unit in response to a worker's hypersensitivity to smoke.
117. *Craft v. Metromedia*, 766 F.2d 1205 (8th Cir. 1985) cert. denied, 475 U.S. 1058 (1986).
118. *Priest v. Rotary*, 634 F. Supp. 571 (N.D. Cal. 1986).
119. *EEOC v. Sage Realty Corp.*, 507 F. Supp. 599 (S.D.N.Y. 1981).
120. *Lochhart v. Louisiana*, 5 IER Cas. BNA 1464 (Or. Ct. App. 1990).
121. *See* Note, *Employer Dress & Appearances Codes and Title VII of the Civil Rights Act of 1964*, 46 S. Cal. L. Rev. 965–1002 (1983).
122. *See generally*, Larson, *Employment Discrimination*, § 40.10.
123. *Rogers v. American Airlines, Inc.*, 527 F. Supp. 229 (S.D.N.Y. 1981).
124. *Geller v. Secretary of Defense*, 423 F. Supp. 16 (D.D.C. 1976).
125. *Goldman v. Weinberger*, 475 U.S. 503 (1986).
126. *Police Officers for Equal Rights v. City of Columbus*, 644 F. Supp. 393 (S.D. 1985).
127. *Rathert v. Village of Prestone*, 903 F.2d 510 (7th Cir. 1990).
128. *Roberts v. United States Jaycees*, 468 U.S. 609 (1989).

129. *See* Prosser; § 652B-E. The Restatement (Second) of Torts (1977).
130. *See Saldana v. Kelsey-Hayes*, 178 Mich. App. 230, 443 N.W.2d 382 (1989).
131. *Bryant v. Automatic Data Processing, Inc.*, 151 Mich. App. 424, 390 N.W.2d 732 (1987) (unlawful to discriminate on the basis of race of spouse); *Rulon-Miller v. International Business Machines Corp.*, 162 Cal. App. 3d 241, 208 Cal. Rptr. 524 (1984) (firing employee for dating competitor's employee violated in-house policy assuring privacy protection); *but see Federated Rural Elec. Inc. Co. v. Kessler*, 131 Wis. 2d 189, 388 N.W.2d 553 (1986) (company may prohibit the romantic association of any employee with a married employee where the policy is applied equally to married and unmarried employees).
132. *Grusendorf v. Oklahoma City*, 816 F.2d 539 (10th Cir. 1987); *Fugate v. Phoenix Civil Service Bd.*, 791 F.2d 736 (9th Cir. 1986).
133. *Briggs v. North Muskegon Police Department*, 746 F.2d 1475 (6th Cir. 1984).
134. ACLU Public Policy Report Liberty at Work: Expanding the Rights of Employees in America, 46 (1988).

XXIV

Occupational Safety and Health

Nearly 6.8 million American workers suffered on the job accidents and illnesses in 1990.[1] In many cases these injuries and illnesses were disabling or fatal.[2] Most employers are as acutely concerned as you are about workplace health and safety and have their own health and safety programs in place. Still, the range of workplace hazards is vast, and it takes the combined efforts of the employer, workers, and government to achieve a safe and healthful workplace. In this chapter we tell you about the kinds of workplace hazards you may face, your legal rights to a safe and healthful workplace, and the steps you should take to protect your rights.

The hazards of work are not as obvious as you may think. We are familiar with the visible physical dangers of the workplace and the various safety precautions that may be taken to avoid them, such as the use of safety goggles, protective shoes, helmets, sound deadeners, emergency shutoff devices on machines, and safety standards for equipment and for ladders and walkways. But other dangers are not so apparent. Workers may be exposed to all sorts of toxic substances that are manufactured or used in the workplace, many of which are carcinogenic and life threatening. It is often difficult to know what toxic substances are present and exactly what risks they present. As you will see in questions below, there is a great deal of medical controversy over the measurable risks of exposure to such toxins as benzene and cotton dust. We have no hard answers about the dangers of sitting all day before a computer video display terminal or working in the vicinity of electromagnetic facilities. We are just beginning to understand the toll taken on the body and even on the spirit by repetitive work involving the continued, unvaried use of fingers, wrists, hands, and arms. These repetitive tasks may cause arthritis, carpal tunnel syndrome, and related disorders. Repetitive motion trauma is estimated to cause up to half the industrial illnesses in the United States. It is the subject of much publicity and of recent regulatory activity.[3]

Not until 1970 did the United States have a comprehensive

national policy assuring workers of a safe and healthy work-place. Responding to widespread evidence of workplace haz-ards, Congress enacted the Occupational Safety and Health Act (OSHAct). The OSHAct is administered by a division of the Department of Labor, under the direction of an assistant secretary of labor. In this text we refer to the department as the Occupational Safety and Health Administration (OSHA).[4] The act was designed "to assure so far as possible every working man and woman in the Nation safe and healthful working condi-tions and to preserve our human resources."[5] The testimony that led to this legislation included the estimate that 14,500 workers were killed and 2.2 million disabled each year in indus-trial accidents. As an example of an extreme abuse, the evi-dence showed that 40% of the workers who did insulation work would die of asbestosis or lung cancer.[6]

Prior to the enactment of OSHAct, workers could recover damages suffered through occupational injury primarily through worker's compensation, but the amount of damages is limited under that system. In only a few industries did law actually regulate workplace health and safety by requiring the employer to meet certain workplace standards.

Many states have their own laws regulating worker health and safety. OSHA will defer to state systems that meet essential standards.[7] There are also laws regulating specific industries, for example, the federal Mine Safety and Health Act.[8] Cities are not required by the Constitution to provide their employees with minimal levels of health and safety.[9] Our discussion will be confined to OSHAct unless otherwise indicated. The statutory references are to that act. We will also refer to a number of the extensive regulations that OSHA has promulgated, which are codified in 29 C.F.R. part 1910. You or your attorney should be sure to consult this essential resource.

At this writing, various legislative proposals for reform of OSHA are pending before Congress. The reforms include faster setting of standards, improved abatements of hazards by em-ployers, and increased worker participation, 22 OSHR 1393, 1616 (1993).

What are my rights to a safe and healthful workplace?

Your rights come under the following general categories. First, your employer is required under the *general duty clause* of the OSHAct to furnish you employment "free from recognized hazards" that are "likely to cause death or serious physical harm."[10] Second, your employer must comply with certain workplace standards that are promulgated by OSHA from time to time.[11] Both these obligations can only be enforced by OSHA, so the key to your protection is your ability to get OSHA to move on your behalf. Third, you have a right to certain information about the kinds of hazards you are exposed to in the workplace.[12] Fourth, in certain, rare occasions you are permitted to walk off the job rather than expose yourself to an imminently dangerous situation. Fifth, you may be entitled to recovery in damages if you are harmed by unsafe and unhealthy workplace conditions. Sixth, your employer may be subject to criminal liability if he maintains an unsafe workplace.

What is the employer's general duty?

The "general duty" section of the OSHAct is said to be a catchall provision to cover conditions of employment that are not the subject of specific health and safety standards.[13] The duty only applies with respect to hazards that cause "death or serious physical harm."[14] An example of a hazard that creates such a risk is illustrated by a case in which the employer stored acids and cyanides in two separate portions of a common indoor area. If the two compounds ever came together, lethal hydrogen cyanide would be formed. The court concluded that because it was recognized in the industry that this manner of storage presented a risk, it violated the general duty clause; however the court would not impose liability where the risk is not generally known in the industry.[15]

The employer's general duty applies only to "recognized hazards." This raises close questions where the risk of danger is uncertain. For example, in the case discussed in the previous paragraph, the employer argued that the potential formation of a lethal gas could not constitute a recognized hazard and that the probability of such an occurrence was too remote to fit the standard. The court was reluctant to read the term "recognized hazard" so broadly that it would reach any potential danger, no matter how remote. It decided the case instead on the basis that most other manufacturers who used the chemicals stored them in a different manner that would better prevent the formation of the lethal gas. This indicated to the court that the manner of storage used by this employer was "generally recognized" as hazardous.[16]

The cases hold that the employer does not violate the general duty clause if there is no feasible method of abating the hazard, either by physical controls or an upgrading of employee training. This qualification is not explicitly stated in the text of the OSHAct. For example, in one case[17] an employer was cited for violation of the general duty clause because it permitted an employee to ride on the running board of a moving front-end loader. The employee was killed when the loader stopped short. The court held that "Congress quite clearly did not intend the general duty clause to impose strict liability; the duty was to be an achievable one."[18] In other words, unless the hazard is preventable, the employer does not violate this aspect of the statute. This idea seems to be consistent with the statutory language that Congress intended a safe and healthful workplace "to the extent feasible," a concept discussed further in questions below. The court concluded that the employer had done all it could to prevent the accident since it had given instructions to employees not to ride on the equipment.

The general duty clause has been the source of OSHA's recent regulatory activity in attempting to reduce traumatic stress disorders caused by repetitive motions. Repetitive motion disorders are the subject of pending standards, as discussed below.

Does the general duty clause apply to conditions that are the subject of specific OSHA standards?

OSHA has established a number of detailed standards that regulate specific workplace hazards. OSHA takes the position that if a substance is governed by a specific existing standard, the employer has no additional obligations under the general duty clause. This position is cast in doubt by a recent court decision that under the general duty clause the employer is obliged to correct a condition if he knows that an existing standard is inadequate to protect his workers. This obligation does not apply if the employer does not know that the existing standard is inadequate.[19]

However, the general duty clause may require the employer to limit exposures to hazardous substances that are not covered by specific standards, even where such standards are pending.

But in a recent case on this point, the OSHA Review Commission concluded that the degree of hazard was too uncertain to justify a finding of violation of the general duty clause.[20]

What are occupational safety and health standards and how are they established?

OSHAct Section 5 (a) (2) requires your employer to comply with all occupational safety and health standards promulgated under the act. When the act was first passed, numerous health and safety standards, known as *consensus standards* had been established by private industry. The secretary of labor, who is charged with administration of OSHAct, was instructed to adopt those standards initially unless he concluded they "would not result in improved safety or health for specifically designated employees."[21] After that, the secretary was to determine whether additional or modified standards are necessary. The secretary is assisted in the technical aspects of setting standards by an expert advisory commission known as NIOSH (National Institute for Occupational Safety and Health), comprised of "representatives of management, labor, occupational safety and occupational health professions, and of the public."[22] In addition, specific advisory committees may be appointed to assist the secretary in his standard-setting function.[23] When a new or modified standard is proposed, the secretary must provide notice to the public and allow for the filing of written data or comments, as well as for a public hearing.[24] The data submitted can be voluminous and highly technical. For example, when OSHA recently reconsidered the standard for benzene, the record ran some 36,000 pages and included over 280 exhibits.[25] The act provides for judicial review of standards.[26]

OSHA has established hundreds of occupational safety and health standards. Bokat and Thompson in *Occupational Safety and Health Law* 59-107 (BNA, 1988) list and discuss some of the key safety standards, which are grouped by OSHA under such general headings as personal protective equipment, structural protection (walking and working surfaces, means of egress, powered platforms and lifts, electrical), machine protection, protection against hazardous materials such as flammable gases, and fire protection. Health standards cover ventilation, noise, radiation, and sanitation. Bokat and Thompson list 26 standards OSHA has promulgated under Section 6(b) of the OSHAct for toxic and hazardous substances.[27] All the OSHA standards may be found in 29 C.F.R. § 1910.1001 and subsequent sections, grouped by subparts, e.g., Subpart E: Means of Egress.

OSHA is in the process of putting out regulations through rulemaking that would establish guidelines for all industries for reducing ergonomic hazards.[28]

How tough do these standards have to be?

This is a tough question. Congress recognized that it was impossible to require a totally safe and healthful workplace. There are always risks and hazards that can't be avoided, and there is a great deal of medical and scientific uncertainty about the potential hazards of certain substances. But the act requires that the standards come close to assuring complete health and safety. The basic definition requires that a safety and health standard be "reasonably necessary or appropriate to provide safe or healthful employment."[29] However, the secretary of labor has a stronger mandate when he promulgates a standard dealing with toxic materials or harmful physical agents. He must set "the standard which most adequately assures, to the extent feasible, on the basis of the best available evidence, that no employee will suffer material impairment of health or functional capacity even if such employee has regular exposure to the hazard . . . for the period of his working life."[30]

The Supreme Court interpreted these provisions in the benzene case, where OSHA set a standard for benzene in light of uncertain scientific evidence.[31] OSHA proposed a drastic reduction in the allowable concentration of benzene in the workplace, from the existing standard of 10 parts of benzene per million parts of air (10ppm) to 1 part per million (1 ppm). There was ample evidence that a concentration of benzene in excess of the existing 10 ppm standard caused serious risk of cancer. In addition there was evidence from animal studies, as well as from isolated reports on workplace experiences, that exposures above 1 ppm but below 10ppm would also produce significant risks, although this could not be shown conclusively. OSHA had taken the position with respect to all carcinogens that "whenever a carcinogen is involved, OSHA will presume that no safe level of exposure exists in the absence of clear proof establishing such a level and will accordingly set the exposure limit at the lowest level feasible."[32] By "lowest level feasible" OSHA meant a standard that was technologically possible to obtain without threatening "the financial welfare of the affected firms or the general economy."[33] OSHA established that it would cost the affected industries several hundred million dollars to make the necessary changes to achieve the new level, which the Court agreed was feasible for the industry. But OSHA could not show with certainty that any measurable benefit would be gained by the more stringent standard. The Court refused to uphold the new standard. "We think it is clear that the statute was not designed to require employers to provide absolutely risk-free workplaces whenever it is technologically feasible to do so." Rather, the act only requires "the elimination, as far as feasible, of significant risks of harm."[34] The Court concluded that OSHA had failed to produce substantial evidence showing that the proposed tougher standard would "at least more likely than not" significantly improve worker health. Several years later, however, OSHA set a new standard at 1 ppm, based upon new evidence that showed risks associated with exposures below 10 ppm.[35]

In the term following the benzene decision, the Court reviewed an OSHA standard limiting the exposure to cotton dust, a substance known to cause brown lung disease. This time the secretary was able to show that the proposed tougher standard would appreciably benefit worker health. However, the employers argued that the secretary was required to weigh the costs of the new standard against the benefits it produced. The Court rejected the requirement of a cost-benefit analysis, stating that "Congress understood that the Act would create substantial costs for employers, yet intended to impose such costs when necessary to create a safe and healthful working environment."[36]

While the earlier cases usually involved employer claims that the OSHA standards were too tough, recent litigation involving OSHA standards, usually brought by unions and employees, tends to involve claims that the standards are not stringent enough. Some courts have held that OSHA is required to adopt a stringent enough standard to reduce or eliminate significant risks; that is, it *must* adopt a tougher standard if it is feasible and will produce some measurable improvement in health and safety.[37]

An employer need not comply with a standard, however, if

it can establish that it is not feasible to do so either through adopting the required engineering changes or through alternative means of protection.[38] Some standards specifically provide exemptions. A recent standard on asbestos removal exempts small scale, short duration operations from the more stringent rules, presumably on economic grounds;[39] the lead exposure standard makes an exception for one sector of the industry—nonferrous foundries—where the tighter controls for everyone else would put them out of business.[40]

What must the employer do to comply with these standards?

With respect to safety standards, compliance generally involves installing the required equipment or controls. Generally the employer must eliminate the condition that causes violation of the standard. For example, if the standard requires the installation of certain safety devices, the employer can comply only by their installation.

If the standard involves the abatement of toxic substances, the preferred OSHA strategy is to require the employer to take whatever engineering steps are necessary to eliminate the hazard, for example, by installing new ventilation systems. Sometimes, however, the employer is permitted to achieve compliance by minimizing worker exposure to the offending substance. This can be accomplished by monitoring the employee's exposure, removing employees who have been exposed too long, training employees to avoid hazards, and having employees wear protective devices, such as respirators. Often these arrangements are done on a temporary basis, until the employer can complete the engineering work necessary for permanent compliance.

For example, the final cotton dust standard relied heavily upon the use of respirators, particularly during a four year interim period necessary to install engineering controls.[41] Similarly, the original benzene standard utilized the strategy of providing medical examinations to workers exposed to levels above .5ppm and requiring engineering controls when levels reach 1 ppm.[42] The 1987 benzene standard places even greater reliance upon monitoring, medical surveillance, worker removal and personal protective equipment. If such strategies keep employee exposure below the tolerable level, the employer need not use the more extreme engineering controls.[43]

May the employer affect my working conditions in order to comply with OSHA standards?

In many cases, yes. The employer may come into compliance in certain cases by minimizing your exposure to toxic substances rather than by changing workplace equipment and methods. These actions fall into three basic categories: medical testing and monitoring, the removal or transfer of employees among jobs to avoid overexposure, and the use of protective clothing and devices.

The authority for these actions is contained in Section 6 (7) of the act, which prescribes the content of OSHA standards. It states that "where appropriate, such standard shall also prescribe suitable protective equipment . . . and shall provide for monitoring or measuring employee exposure." In addition, the standard shall "prescribe the type and frequency of medical examinations or other tests which shall be made available, by the employer at his cost, to employees exposed to such hazards."

Protective equipment, such as respirators and safety shoes, is often covered by detailed regulations.[44] Sometimes specific standards provide for safety equipment; an entire subpart of OHSA's regulations, subpart I, sets individual standards for personal protective equipment. But even if safety equipment is not required by a specific standard, it may be covered by the catchall provision in the regulation, which requires it "wherever it is necessary by reasons of hazards of processes or environment."[45] The employer normally makes the initial decision whether to require safety equipment, but may be cited for an OSHA violation for failure to do so. According to a leading authority, these requirements are construed fairly broadly.[46]

The act does not normally require the employer to pay for safety equipment. However, some OSHA standards require the employer to provide certain equipment at no cost to the employee.[47] If the employee is covered by a collective bargaining agreement, it may require the employer to pay for any safety equipment mandated by OSHA.

May my employer remove me from my job or transfer me to another job if my exposure levels are too high?

Generally, yes. Sometimes when the employer cannot reduce exposure levels to an absolutely safe minimum, the employer will monitor the exposure levels of employees assigned to the job. If those levels become too high, the employer will transfer the worker to another job. The OSHAct does not appear to prohibit such strategies, although they are not always an acceptable alternative means of compliance. Generally, OSHA insists on engineering controls as the method of compliance, with other strategies as secondary.[48] OSHA is considering generic rules for monitoring and for medical surveillance; a proposed policy in 1989 would allow the employer to use alternatives to engineering controls on a temporary basis while such controls are being installed, in emergencies, or where engineering controls yield only negligible benefits.[49]

Some standards actually encourage such worker removals, by explicitly providing for monitoring as an alternative to engineering controls.[50] This monitoring determines whether exposures have reached an unacceptable level and may trigger other compliance strategies, such as more stringent controls or protective clothing. The act also requires that the employer notify employees of the results of such monitoring.[51] In addition, the employer must make medical exams available to employees, at no cost to them, to determine the effects of exposures.[52]

At least two of the standards expressly provide that an employee may be transferred where the employee is unable to wear a respirator and as a result his exposure levels exceed the minimum.[53] In the cotton dust case, the Supreme Court refused to uphold the requirement of pay maintenance because there was no evidence to support the secretary's conclusion that preservation of wage levels was necessary.[54] However, OSHA has made findings to that effect with respect to other standards. For example, the lead standard contains a medical removal protection program (MRP), which calls for employees to be transferred to other jobs if available, or even sent home, if their exposures exceed permissible levels. The employer must protect earnings for 18 months. This requirement has been upheld by the courts.[55]

Do I have any basis outside of the OSHAct to challenge my removal from a job because of exposure to toxic substances?

Yes, in some cases. In those industries where no standard expressly governs worker monitoring and removal, nothing in

OSHA appears to prohibit the employer from removing workers with unacceptably high exposures and even terminating them. However, while there is no authority on this point, the Americans with Disabilities Act might support the argument that a worker with unacceptably high exposures is disabled and that the employer must make an accommodation to him. If you are in such a position, you should consult an attorney.[56]

Employees have challenged removal strategies where they discriminate against protected groups of workers. For example, several employers have used "fetal protection programs" to remove women of child bearing age from hazardous jobs. These strategies have been challenged as gender discrimination, based on the assertion there is no evidence that men are at less risk or that there is less risk of transmittal of toxic substances through the genes of the father than through the mother. The Supreme Court has held in a landmark decision that such a policy discriminates against women under Title VII of the Civil Rights Act and that the employer may not justify the practice under the bona fide occupational qualification (BFOQ) provision of that statute.[57] The Court even suggested that an employer who warns employees of the potential hazards of the job may not be liable to them in state court tort actions; thus the decision may avoid the quandary for the employer of being unable to remove female workers yet remaining liable to them in tort.[58]

Similar claims of discriminatory protective strategies have been raised by black workers on the basis of established evidence that because of a skin condition many more black workers than white workers are unable to wear respirators that are required on jobs.[59]

What is my role in enforcing the OSHAct?

As a worker, you have a very important role to play. The act authorizes the secretary of labor to inspect workplaces, but OSHA relies heavily on workers to be the eyes and ears for triggering many of these inspections. OSHA has a number of inspection programs, ranging from immediate investigation of imminent dangers, catastrophes, and fatal accidents to periodic inspections in high-hazard occupations, follow-ups, and reviews of employers whose records show excessive lost workdays dues to occupational accidents or illness.[60] However, the Labor Department is understaffed, and periodic inspections under these programs are inadequate.

Effective enforcement can only be achieved if you bring workplace health and safety violations to the attention of your local OSHA office. The act provides that "any employees or representative of employees who believe that a violation of a safety or health standard exists that threatens physical harm, or that an imminent danger exists, may request an inspection."[61]

If you believe that a dangerous condition exists in your workplace, you should contact your local OSHA office. There are two kinds of complaints you can file, formal or informal. The formal complaint must be in writing and signed by a current employee or by a union steward. If you contact OSHA, they will send you a form to fill out and sign, or you can simply state what you perceive as the problem in a signed letter. Be as specific and detailed as possible. You must, however, be truthful in your complaint. The OSHAct provides for a stiff fine or imprisonment for making a false statement.[62]

When OSHA receives your complaint, it will determine if "there are reasonable grounds to believe that such violation or danger exists."[63] If the OSHA office agrees with you, it will make an inspection of your workplace. If the office determines there is no reasonable ground to believe a violation exists, it will notify you in writing. You do not have a right of appeal to the courts if the OSHA office doesn't agree with you, but you can ask for an informal appeal to the regional administrator of OSHA.

As a practical matter, when OSHA receives a complaint from an employee, it usually discusses the matter informally with the employer, and this results in abatement of the violation in the majority of the cases. If this cannot be accomplished, then OSHA will move to the inspection stage. Your name will not be disclosed to your employer if you file a complaint or even ask OSHA for assistance.

The informal complaint does not have to be signed. All that OSHA will do with an informal complaint is send a letter to the employer advising it of the problem and asking the employer to correct it. OSHA does not inspect and will only follow up through random, infrequent sampling.

How does the inspection work?

If OSHA concludes from your complaint that there is reasonable likelihood of a violation, it will send an inspector to inspect the workplace. It will not give the employer any advance notice. Usually the employer agrees to allow the inspection. If the employer refuses to allow it, OSHA may not proceed until it obtains a warrant. Section 8(a)(1) and (2) of OSHAct authorize the secretary to enter workplaces and conduct inspections. However, the Supreme Court has held that because of the Fourth Amendment's prohibition against searches, these sections must be read so that they do not authorize a search without a warrant. As the Court said, "the owner of a business has not, by the necessary utilization of employees in his operation, thrown open the areas where employees alone are permitted to the warrantless scrutiny of Government agents."[64]

There is some dispute over whether an employee complaint triggers a "wall to wall" inspection of a company, or whether the inspection is limited to the terms of the employee's complaint.[65] The courts are also split as to whether OSHA also needs a warrant to obtain employer health and safety records, for example, of employee injuries. Here, OSHA argues, the employer's claim of privacy is less compelling.[66]

Am I entitled to participate in the inspection?

Yes, through an employee representative. The act provides that "a representative authorized by (the) employees shall be given an opportunity to accompany the Secretary . . . during the physical inspection of any workplace."[67] *Authorized representative* generally means your union if you work in a unionized workplace. If you are not represented by a union, the act provides that the secretary "shall consult with a reasonable number of employees concerning matters of health and safety in the workplace."[68] However, our information indicates that the investigator does not usually consult with employees in a nonunion workplace, although the OSHAct and regulations make clear that employees have the right to participate in the inspection.[69]

You are entitled under OSHA to form health and safety committees in your plant, and a representative of the committee may serve as your workplace representative in workplace inspections.[70]

The act does not require that you be paid for the time you spend on an OSHA inspection; in other words, you can be docked pay if you miss work during the inspection. An earlier regulation providing that the refusal to pay wages during the walkaround violates Section 11(c) was invalidated because OSHA had not followed the proper procedures in making the regulation.[71] Under the Mine Safety and Health Act, however, workers are entitled to their regular pay during the walk-around.[72]

What happens if the secretary determines that the employer has violated the act?

If after his investigation or inspection the secretary determines that the employer has violated the act, he will issue a citation to the employer, describing the standard, rule, or regulation that has been violated and fixing a reasonable time to eliminate the violation. If the situation involves an imminent danger, OSHA will ask the employer to abate the hazard immediately and remove endangered employees from exposure. If the employer refuses to do so, OSHA may go to court for immediate relief. You may bring a legal action to compel the secretary to go to court to seek abatement of an imminent danger.[73]

The secretary will notify the employer of any proposed penalty for the violation. The act provides for a series of penalties for violations of the act. For example, willful or repeated violations may result in civil penalties of up to $70,000.[74] A citation for a "serious violation" of a requirement, standard, rule, or order, may result in a civil penalty of up to $1,000 for each violation. Under a new enforcement strategy, where OSHA finds that an employer's violations are egregious, it will treat each infraction as a separate violation, which can drastically increase the size of the penalty. For example, OSHA used this policy in 1988 to fine Morrell and Co. $4.33 million (later reduced in a settlement) for failing to prevent cumulative trauma disorders among its meatpacking employees[75] and to fine USX $7.3 million.[76] There is some question as to whether this strategy has been put into place properly since the agency did not follow formal rule-making procedures.[77]

The employer is required to post the citation prominently although he may omit the proposed penalty. The purpose is to inform employees of the alleged hazard.

The employer has fifteen days from the receipt of the notice of the citation to contest the citation or proposed penalty. If the employer does not contest the citation or penalty, the citation becomes a final order, not subject to any further judicial review, and the employer must comply with the citation. Employees have no right to appeal OSHA's refusal to issue a citation. The only point on which employees have a legal right to intervene is the length of the abatement period that OSHA gives the employer to correct the violation.[78]

May I refuse an assignment to hazardous work?

Yes, under very limited circumstances. You have the right not to perform your assigned task if you have "a reasonable apprehension of death or serious injury coupled with a reasonable belief that no less drastic alternative is available."[79] This is a very risky course to take because if a court disagrees with the reasonableness of your judgment you will not be protected if you are fired or otherwise disciplined.

In the leading case upholding the right to refuse hazardous work, two workers were ordered to do maintenance work on a section of screen that was used to protect employees from falling objects on the assembly line. An employee had previously fallen to his death through this screen. The workers continued to bring the matter of the unsafe screen to their employer's attention. While the employer made some changes and instituted new safety procedures, the Court agreed that these workers had a genuine fear of death or bodily harm if they followed the order.

Other refusals have been upheld under this regulation, but you are urged to use the right only in extreme cases. According to the regulation, you must establish the following four elements in order to be protected in refusing an assignment: (1) a reasonable employee would conclude that there is a real danger of death or serious injury, (2) there is no reasonable alternative to refusing the assignment, (3) there is not enough time to eliminate the danger through the normal statutory procedures, and (4) the employee where possible must first ask his employer to correct the condition.[80] You don't have to be correct in your assessment of the danger; it is enough if a reasonable employee in your situation would have thought the assignment hazardous. Still, you have to convince a court that this is what a reasonable employee would do under the circumstances. You are in a much stronger position if you first report the situation to your employer and to OSHA.

You may be protected under the National Labor Relations Act if you walk off the job to protest an unsafe condition. Under this law the condition need not be life-threatening.[81] However, to gain the protection of the NLRA, you must act together with at least one other employee. If you act by yourself, you will not have the protection of the NLRA.[82] We advise workers to be cautious about relying on this law since it is seldom applied to protect employees who walk off the job.[83] There is an agreement between the NLRA and OSHA that avoids duplicative claims under both statutes.[84]

How does a collective bargaining agreement affect my right to refuse a hazardous assignment?

If you are disciplined or fired for refusing a hazardous assignment, you may challenge that discipline through the grievance and arbitration process as discipline without just cause. Surprisingly, arbitrators have not been very supportive of these refusals, insisting on strong objective evidence of the danger before they uphold the employee's right to refuse the assignment.[85] While there is no Supreme Court decision on this point, the lower courts generally hold that your statutory rights under OSHA are not affected by your collective bargaining agreement or by your use of arbitration.[86]

You cannot be fired if you and other employees walk off the job because of a hazardous condition, for Section 502 of the NLRA provides that the quitting of work "in good faith because of abnormally dangerous conditions for work" is not considered a strike. Without Section 502 your strike would be unprotected under the NLRA, for most contracts contain a no-strike clause that prohibits work stoppages, and you could be fired. However, Section 502 will protect your job action if several conditions are met. First of all, the work condition must be abnormal; if you have worked on a job that is considered inherently dangerous, you may have some trouble establishing that the danger is abnormal.[87] Also, you must have "ascertainable, objective evidence" supporting your belief that an abnormally dangerous condition exists.[88] In the leading case on this point, three mine foremen were brought up on state criminal charges for falsifying records about airflow in the mines. When the company sent two of the foremen back to the mine pending the outcome of the criminal charges, the miners refused to work. The Court held that it was not enough that the miners had an honest belief that their foremen were incompetent but that some objective evidence was required: "If the courts require no objective evidence that such conditions actually obtain, they face a wholly speculative inquiry into the motives of the workers."[89]

If you are working under a collective bargaining agreement that contains a no-strike clause, your employer will be able to enjoin any strike over health and safety conditions, unless you can establish the defense discussed above under Section 502.[90] However, as a condition of obtaining an injunction against the strike, the employer will be required to arbitrate the underlying health and safety dispute, and you may be able to achieve relief that way.[91]

May I hold my union responsible for workplace injuries?

Generally not. Employers and workers have tried to shift liability for workplace injuries to unions on the theory that the union has agreed to the safety standards that are in place or has undertaken the job of monitoring and enforcing these standards. These claims have usually not been successful, for under common law a union is not responsible for workplace health and safety unless it has specifically agreed to undertake this burden. The question of whether the union has agreed to that undertaking involves interpreting the collective bargaining agreement, which is a question of federal law that can probably only be decided by an arbitrator. The Supreme Court has held that in such a situation the state law claim is preempted.[92] The Court has also indicated that normally the union's only obligation under the collective agreement is one of fair representation but that the union might agree to assume a more encompassing negligence standard of care.[93]

Can I be disciplined for trying to correct unsafe or unhealthy conditions in my workplace?

No. Section 11(c) of the act provides that no person may be discriminated against because he has filed a complaint, instituted a proceeding under the act, testified, or "because of

the exercise . . . of any right afforded by this Act." This provision has been interpreted very broadly, to include almost any
kind of activity, including complaints to your employer.[94] This
statutory provision is also the authority for the secretary's regulation protecting the right to refuse hazardous work. Of course,
your employer may claim you were fired for another reason,
which is a problem you face with any law protecting you against
discriminatory discharge. If you attempt to exercise this statutory right, you should keep careful notes of anything that happens to you in the workplace, so you can prove discrimination
if that later becomes necessary. If you have a questionable
work record, you run the risk that the employer will use your
work record as a pretext for firing you when his real motive is
that you exercised your protected rights.

**How do I proceed if I was disciplined for exercising a pro-
tected right under OSHA?**
    You have to move fast and you have to go to the right place.
Section 11(c) of OSHA says you must file a complaint with the
secretary of labor within 30 days of any violation. If you have
been discharged or disciplined for reasons you think violate
OSHAct, contact your regional OSHA office immediately. If
you file a complaint, the secretary will investigate, and if he
thinks your rights were violated, he will bring an action on
your behalf. This will be an action in federal court, and the
relief can include backpay and restoration of your job. The
secretary must notify you within 90 days of the disposition of
your complaint.[95]
    If the secretary of labor does not agree with you, that is the
end of your rights under OSHA. The provisions for judicial
review do not include an appeal of the secretary's decision not
to proceed with a retaliation claim.[96] However, you may have
a cause of action under state law for an unlawful discharge.[97]

**Am I entitled to information about health and safety dangers
in my workplace?**
    Yes. There are several provisions that entitle you to informa-
tion and several ways to enforce your rights. First, under the
OSHAct, you are entitled to have the results of any monitoring
undertaken by your employer turned over to your physician.
This information must also be turned over to your union for

purposes of enforcement of the act. This includes records of monitoring required by the OSHAct and records voluntarily generated by the employer.[98] Your employer is obligated to report to OSHA on accidents and fatalities that occur at the jobsite.[99]

The OSHAct also contains a *hazard communication standard*, which requires the use of labels or other warnings for particular substances and requires the employer to develop a program for communicating this information.[100] OSHA requires employers who manufacture or use chemicals to determine if they are hazardous and to label each container with the identity of the chemical and give appropriate hazard warnings. In addition, manufacturers and employers who use chemicals must provide a material safety data sheet (MSDS) that lists the chemical names of the ingredients and gives information about safe use of the product. You will discover, if you ever see an MSDS, that it doesn't always provide much help for the average worker who is not trained in chemistry. In fact, OSHA is surveying representative companies to determine if workers understand the warnings on MSDSs.[101] The hazard communication standard was limited to the manufacturing sector, but in the leading case reviewing the standard, the court instructed the secretary to consider a broader application.[102]

The hazard communication standard also has a troublesome provision entitling the manufacturer or employer to withhold information that it considers a "trade secret." This refers to chemical formulas and manufacturing processes that are known only by the manufacturer and give the manufacturer a competitive edge. In the leading case reviewing the standard, the court defined trade secrets narrowly, and made it somewhat easier to obtain this information. In particular, unions are now entitled to the information; the original standard provided that only health professionals could have access to it.[103]

There are also state right-to-know laws. Some of these are preempted by the OSHA standard, in which case the federal and not the state standard controls.[104] However, there is also state right-to-know legislation that makes this information available to the general public, and this may be a good way for workers to get useful information.

Finally, if you are represented by a union, your union will be able to obtain information about health and safety as part of the employer's general duty to provide information for bargaining purposes under Section 8(a)(5) of the National Labor Relations Act (which is discussed in chapter 18).[105]

Can my employer be prosecuted criminally for unsafe working conditions?

Yes. First, the OSHAct contains its own provisions for criminal sanctions of fine and imprisonment where willful violations cause death to an employee.[106] In addition, there have been some widely publicized prosecutions at the state level of employers who have allowed unsafe workplace conditions, and employers have been convicted of manslaughter in some cases.[107] It is an open question whether the OSHAct was intended by Congress to preempt local prosecution, that is, whether an action under OSHA is the only way to stop such conditions. At this writing the courts are split on this issue, and it may have to be resolved by the Supreme Court.[108]

Can I recover damages from my employer for unsafe or unhealthy working conditions?

The OSHAct does not create new rights to recover damages from your employer. You are limited to whatever existing state tort laws permit you to recover damages for harms caused by unsafe conditions. In most states, however, you are forced to bring such claims under the workers' compensation laws, which can severely limit your damages and can cut off your rights through strict time limits. The Supreme Court has yet to determine the extent to which workers' compensation systems can close off further damage actions.[109] Judicial developments in some states have permitted workers to get around these limitations. You can avoid them altogether if you bring an action against the manufacturer of a hazardous substance rather than against your employer.[110] The Supreme Court has let stand a lower court ruling that the OSHAct does not preempt a related state tort action.[111]

NOTES

1. There are some excellent reference books on workplace health and safety. We recommend the recent publication of the ABA section on labor and employment law, Bokat and Thompson, eds., *Occupational*

Safety and Health Law (BNA Books, 1988), and the first supplement, (Collins and Gombar, eds., BNA Books, 1990). Rothstein, *Occupational Safety and Health Law*, (3d ed West, 1990), (with 1992 Pocket Part) is also a classic. B. Mintz, *OSHA, History, Law and Policy* (BNA, 1984) is another excellent reference. Some of the leading cases and a good overview of the area may be found in Finkin, Goldman, and Summers, *Legal Protection for the Individual Employee* (West, 1989). For weekly reports of developments in the area, consult the Occupational Safety and Health Reporter, a publication of the Bureau of National Affairs (BNA), also available on LEXIS. We make frequent references in these notes to this service, citing it as OSHR.

2. The Bureau of Labor Statistics reports that 6.8 million workers suffered workplace illness or injury in 1990, 21 OSHR 837 (1991). In 1991 the figure dropped to 6.3 million workers, 22 OSHR 1233 (1992). The National Safety Council estimates that 10,500 employees were killed on the job in 1990, 21 OSHR 1087 (1992). In 1991 this figure dropped below 10,000 for the first time since such records were kept, 22 OSHR 563 (1992). *See* J. Stellman and S. Daum, *Work is Dangerous to Your Health* (Vintage Books, 1973).

3. For recent cases in which OSHA or state agencies were able to bring about ergonomic changes in the way work is structured so as to avoid repetitive motions, see 20 OSHR 158, 183, 206, 277, 285, 286–87 (1990), and 21 OSHR 403 (1992) (Occupational Safety and Health Reporter, BNA, a weekly publication), respectively describing changes in use of VDTs, grocery store checkout systems at Kroger Co., laser scanners at Shoprite supermarkets, in Ford automotive plants, and in a Swift-Ehrich turkey processing plant, and in manufacturing facilities at Anchor Hocking Glass Co. and the Stanley Works, and in a Samsonite luggage manufacturing plant. A state probe of cumulative trauma disorders affecting some 20% of the workers in Perdue chicken plants was the subject of much recent publicity. See 19 OSHR 1750, 2162 (Feb. 28, 1990), (May 9, 1990). Thirty-one unions recently petitioned OSHA to promulgate an emergency temporary standard to protect workers from repetitive motion injuries, 21 OSHR 273 (1991).

4. 29 U.S.C. § 651 *et seq.* We will refer to these sections by their popular numbering; Section 651 is the equivalent of Section 1, Section 652 the equivalent of Section 2, and so on. At this writing, an OSHA Reform Bill is pending in Congress. *See* 21 OSHR 1483, 1361 (1992).

5. § 1(b).

6. Legislative History of OSHA, 92d Cong., 1st Sess. (1971) 142-44, discussed in Finkin, Goldman, and Summers, *supra* note 1, at 366.

7. § 667.

8. *Collins v. Harker Heights*, 112 S. Ct. 1061 (1992).

9. Federal Mine Safety and Health Act, 30 U.S.C. § 801 *et seq.* (1977). This is the cumulation of a series of acts that have protected mine safety going back to 1891. *See* Bokat and Thompson, chapter 26.

10. § 654 (a)(1).

11. § 654(a)(2) and § 655. These standards are constantly updated. For example, OSHA has scheduled publication of 17 final rules in 1992, 21 OSHR 1576 (1992).

12. Section 6(b)(7) of the OSHAct directs the secretary of labor to promulgate standards, including "labels or other appropriate forms of warning as are necessary to insure that employees are apprised of all hazards to which they are exposed." Pursuant to this directive, the secretary has promulgated a hazard communication standard, that appears at 29 C.F.R. § 1910.1200 *et seq.* The standard identifies certain toxic substances and requires the manufacturer or employer to adequately label them. The manufacturer or employer must also make certain information available on a material safety data sheet (MSDS). Exception are made for processes that the manufacturer deems to be trade secrets, and this has become a hotly contested issue, *e.g.*, *Steelworkers v. Auchter*, 763 F.2d 728 (3d Cir. 1985). OSHA has also promulgated a records access rule, 29 C.F.R. § 1910.20, which gives employees and their representatives access to records voluntarily created by employers with regard to employee exposure to toxic substances, and a medical access rule, 29 C.F.R. § 1913.10, which protects employee privacy in this information.

13. *Pratt & Whitney Aircraft v. Secretary of Labor*, 649 F.2d 96 (2d Cir. 1981).

14. § 5(a)(1). There is a parallel definition in § 17(k), part of the provisions for civil and criminal penalties, that a "serious violation" is one involving "a substantial probability that death or physical harm could result." This provision triggers liability for a civil penalty under § 17(b).

15. *Pratt & Whitney*, 649 F.2d at 98. *Compare R. L. Sanders Roofing Co.*, 620 F.2d 97 (5th Cir., 1980). For a very recent case finding a general duty clause violation, see *Secretary of Labor v. Tampa Shipyards, Inc.*, OSHRC No. 86-360, 21 OSHR 1394 (Mar. 10, 1992).

16. *Pratt & Whitney*, 649 F.2d at 98.

17. *National Realty v. OSHRC*, 489 F.2d 1257 (D.C. Cir. 1973).

18. *Id.* at 1265–66.

19. *UAW v. General Dynamics Land Systems Division*, 815 F.2d 1570 (D.C. Cir. 1987), *cert. denied*, 108 S. Ct. 485 (1987).

20. *Kastalon, Inc.*, 12 OSHC 1928 (Rev. Comm. 1986). This question is discussed in Collins and Gombar, eds., *First Supplement to Occupational Safety and Health Law* 17–19 (BNA 1990).

21. § 6(a).
22. § 7(a)(1).
23. § 6 (b)(1); § 7(b).
24. § 6(b)(2–4).
25. Collins and Gombar, eds., *First Supplement to Occupational Safety and Health Law* 157 (BNA, 1990). OSHA § 6(5) calls for the secretary to consider "the best available evidence," including "research, demonstrations, experiments, and such other information as may be appropriate." He shall consider "the latest available scientific data in the field."
26. § 11(a).
27. Bokat and Thompson, 98–99. The list continues to grow. For example, OSHA issued a bloodborne pathogens rule in December 1991; see 21 OSHR 892 (1991). It is considering a much more stringent standard that would lower worker exposure level to methylene chloride by 20-fold, 21 OSHR 676 (1991).
28. 20 OSHR 795 (1990). See BNA Special Report, 22 OSHR 1616 (1993).
29. § 3 (8).
30. § 6(b)(5).
31. This standard was challenged in *Industrial Union Department, AFL-CIO v. American Petroleum Institute*, 448 U.S. 607 (1980).
32. 448 U.S. at 624.
33. 448 U.S. at 637.
34. 448 U.S. at 641.
35. 52 Fed. Reg. 34460. The new standard is discussed in Collins and Gombar, *supra* note 20, at 156–61.
36. *American Textile Manufacturers Institute v. Donovan*, 452 U.S. 490, 518 (1981).
37. *Building and Construction Trades Department v. Secretary of Labor*, 838 F.2d 1258 (D.C. Cir. 1988).
38. *Dun-Par Engineered Form Co.*, 12 OSHC 1949 (Rev. Comm. 1986), *rev'd.*, 843 F.2d 1135 (8th Cir. 1988).
39. 19 OSHR 1851 (1990).
40. 19 OSHR 1451 (1990).
41. 452 U.S. at 536.
42. *Industrial Union Dept. v. American Petroleum Institute*, 448 U.S. 607, 627 (1980).
43. 52 Fed. Reg. 34,547–58. *See* Collins and Gombar, *supra* note 20, at 156–61.
44. 29 C.F.R. p. 1910. *See* especially § 1910.132.
45. § 1910.132.
46. Bokat and Thompson, *supra* note 1, at 68–69.

47. *E.g.* 29 C.F.R. § 1910.1018(h)(2)(i),(j)(1) (inorganic arsenic; 1910.1025(f)(i)(g)(1) lead).

48. 29 C.F.R. § 1990.111(h).

49. 54 Fed. Reg. 16,836 (1989), 20 OSHR 184 (1990).

50. *See* the benzene standard at 52 Fed. Reg. 34460.

51. § 8(a)(3). "The Secretary . . . shall issue regulations requiring employers to maintain accurate records of employee exposures to potentially toxic materials or harmful physical agents which are required to be monitored or measured under Section 6. . . . Such regulations shall also make appropriate provision for each employee or former employee to have access to such records as will indicate his own exposure to toxic materials or harmful physical agents. Each employer shall promptly notify any employee who has been or is being exposed to toxic materials or harmful physical agents in concentrations or at levels which exceed those prescribed by [applicable standards]."

52. Section 6(b)7 of OHSAct requires the secretary to provide in any standard "where appropriate" that the employer provide medical examinations at no cost to the employee. *See* 29 C.F.R. § 1990.152(e),(m)(1).

53. *See* the asbestos and cotton dust standards, at 29 C.F.R. §§ 1910.1001(g)(3)(iv) and 1910. 1043(f)(2)(iv), respectively.

54. *American Textile Manufacturers Institute, Inc., v. Donovan*, 452 U.S. 490 (1981).

55. 29 C.F.R. § 1910.1025(k), upheld in *Steelworkers v. Marshall*, 647 F.2d 1189, 1228–38 (D.C. Cir. 1980), *cert. denied* 453 U.S. 913 (1981). OSHA has also made such provision in its new benzene standard, 52 Fed. Reg. 34,557. *See* Mintz, *Medical Surveillance of Employees Under the Occupational Safety and Health Administration*, 28 J. Occupational Med. 913, 917–20 (1986).

56. Such an argument would rest on the definition of a "qualified individual with a disability," and of the obligation to make a "reasonable accommodation," in Americans with Disabilities Act § 101(8) and (9), and of "discrimination" in § 102.

57. *UAW v. Johnson Controls*, 111 S. Ct. 1196 (1991). A parallel challenge to such a program under the OSHAct, on the theory that a fetal program is a hazard that violates the general duty clause, was rejected in *OCAW v. American Cyanamid Co.*, 741 U.S. 444 (D.C. Cir. 1984).

58. *Johnson Controls*, 111 S. Ct. at 1208–9.

59. The disease is known as pseudofolliculitis barbae, *see EEOC v. Greyhound Lines*, 635 F.2d 188 (3d Cir. 1980).

60. *See* Bokat and Thompson, *Occupational Safety and Health Law* 197–206 (BNA, 1988).

61. § 8(f)(1).
62. § 17(g).
63. § 8 (f)(1).
64. *Marshall v. Barlow's*, 436 U.S. 307, 314–15 (1978).
65. *In re Cerro Copper Products*, 12 OSHC 1153, and *In re Kohler Co.*, No. 90-1990, 20 OSHR 279 (7th Cir. 1990).
66. *Compare Brock v. Emerson Electric Co.*, 834 F.2d 994 (11th Cir. 1987) *with McLaughlin v. A.B. Chance Co.*, 842 F.2d 724 (4th Cir. 1988).
67. OSHA § 8 (e).
68. *Id.*
69. *See* C.F.R. § 1903.8(a) and (b). Pending OSHA reform bills would provide for greater employee participation, 22 OSHR 1393,1579 (1993).
70. OSHA Bulletin 3035.
71. *Chamber of Commerce v. OSHA*, 636 F.2d 464 (D.C. Cir. 1980).
72. *Monterey Coal Co. v. Federal Mine Safety Review Comm'n.*, 743 F.2d 589 (7th Cir. 1984). *See* Bokat and Thompson, 782–84.
73. *Secretary of Labor v. Master Metals*, 20 OSHR 3 (BNA, 1990); OSHA Bulletin 2056 at 19–21 (1985).
74. The penalties are set out in § 17. OSHA has toughened its policies on repeat violations and will take into account the employer's safety record at any of its other facilities, 21 OSHR 1388 (1992).
75. Collins and Gombar, 48–50; *John Morrell & Co.*, 18 OSHR 1099–1100 (1988). The final settlement called for a $990,000 fine in exchange for Morrell's commitment to ergonomic improvements, plus payment of $260,000 to NIOSH for research, 19 OSHR 1893.
76. 19 OSHR 1936 (BNA, 1989). In addition, OSHA has proposed a $3.9 million dollar penalty against a Maine paper mill that allowed its workers to be exposed to chlorine, 21 OSHR 427 (1991). Other penalties as high as $5 million have been proposed by OSHA, 22 OSHR 1578 (1993). OSHA imposed over $100 million in fines in 1992, 22 OSHR 1434 (1993).
77. 19 OSHR 1396 (BNA, 1990).
78. OSHA Bulletin 2056, at 30 (1985).
79. *Whirlpool Corp. v. Marshall*, 445 U.S. 1 (1980), upholding the secretary of labor's authority to promulgate regulation 29 C.F.R. § 1977.12, permitting an employee to refuse a work assignment under limited conditions. The regulation was upheld as a reasonable implementation of § 11 (c) of OSHA, which prohibits discrimination against a worker for exercising any right under the act. The full text of the pertinent part of the regulation is quoted in the next footnote.
80. 29 C.F.R. § 1977.12 (1979). Here is the full text of the regulation:

"Occasions might arise when an employee is confronted with a choice between not performing assigned tasks or subjecting himself to serious injury or death arising from a hazardous condition at the workplace. If the employee, with no reasonable alternative, refuses in good faith to expose himself to the dangerous condition, he would be protected against subsequent discrimination. The condition causing the employee's apprehension of death or injury must be of such a nature that a reasonable person, under the circumstances then confronting the employee, would conclude that there is a real danger of death or serious injury and that there is insufficient time due to the urgency of the situation, to eliminate the danger through resort to regular statutory enforcement channels. In addition, in such circumstances, the employee, where possible, must also have sought from his employer, and been unable to obtain, a correction of the dangerous condition." This regulation was upheld in *Whirlpool Corp. v. Marshall*, 445 U.S. 1 (1980), which is where you will find the language quoted in the text.

81. *NLRB v. Washington Aluminum Co.*, 370 U.S. 9 (1962).

82. *Meyers Industries*, 281 NLRB No. 118 (1986), review denied, 835 F.2d 1481 (D.C. Cir. 1987); *NLRB v. City Disposal Systems Inc.*, 465 U.S. 822 (1984).

83. The danger is that walking off the job will be viewed as insubordination or may lose the protection of the NLRA if it happens repeatedly, see *Bird Engineering*, 270 NLRB No. 1415 (1984). *Compare Martin Marietta Corp.*, 293 NLRB No. 89, 131 LRRM 1715 (1989) and *Asbestos Removal, Inc.*, 293 NLRB No. 32, 131 LRRM 1304 (1989), where employee activity was protected.

84. *See* Bokat and Thompson, 672–73.

85. *See* Gross and Greenfield, *Arbitral Value Judgments in Health and Safety Disputes: Management Rights Over Workers' Rights*, 34 Buff. L. Rev. 645 (1985). This is a study of numerous arbitration awards involving this issue.

86. *E.g.*, *Marshall v. N.L. Industries*, 618 F.2d 1220 (7th Cir. 1980). We think this point is not settled. If you arbitrate your claim and lose, the arbitration award may be given some weight in the later judicial proceeding, under the Court's *Alexander v. Gardner-Denver* decision, 415 U.S. 36, n. 21 (1974). *See also* the strong language in *Gateway Coal Co. v. Mine Workers*, 414 U.S. 368 (1974), about the primacy of arbitration in resolving safety disputes, although that case was decided in the context of whether an injunction could issue against a strike over safety violations. If your union has agreed in collective bargaining that employees may not refuse work assignments, or has imposed a tougher standard as to when an employee may refuse work,

this may be upheld as waiver of the statutory right to refuse work, see *NLRB v. Magnavox Co.*, 415 U.S. 322 (1974).

87. *Anaconda Aluminum Co.*, 197 NLRB 336 (1972).
88. *Gateway Coal Co. v. Mine Workers*, 414 U.S. 368 (1974).
89. *Gateway Coal*, at 386.
90. *Gateway Coal*, at 387.
91. *Gateway Coal, supra.* Some contracts provide for expedited arbitration of certain disputes, so it is possible you can get a quick order from an arbitrator ordering that the dangerous condition be rectified immediately.
92. *Steelworkers v. Rawson*, 110 S. Ct. 1904 (1990).
93. *Steelworkers v. Rawson*, 110 S. Ct. 1904 (1990); *IBEW v. Hechler*, 107 S. Ct. 2161 (1987).
94. Bokat and Thompson, 665–66. However, there is some pressure to include specific whistleblower protection in a pending OSHAct reform bill; see 21 OSHR 1368 (1992).
95. § 11(3).
96. § 11 (a) and (b) refer to judicial review and enforcement of certain orders under previous sections of the act. § 11(c), which deals with the procedures for an employee to file a complaint with the secretary for retaliatory discharge, has no explicit provision for judicial review.
97. *See* chapter 3.
98. § 6(b)(7). The regulation, known as the records access rule, is contained at 29 C.F.R. § 1910.20 *et seq.* The employee's concern for privacy is dealt with in the medical access rule, 29 C.F.R. § 1913.10.
99. *See Hackney, Inc.*, 13 OSHC 1901 (Rev. Comm. 1988).
100. 29 C.F.R. § 1910.1200. OSHRC has recently issued rulings specifying the kind of information required under the hazard communication standard, 21 OSHR 1255 (1992).
101. 200 OSHR 211 (BNA, 1990).
102. *Steelworkers v. Auchter*, 763 F.2d 728 (3d Cir. 1985).
103. *Id.*
104. The hazard communication standard expressly provides that it preempts any state or local requirement that pertains to the subject of the standard, 29 C.F.R. § 1200(a)(2); 52 Fed. Reg. 31,860–61. However, there are still open questions as to the preemptive reach of this standard, see *N.Y. v. G.T.E. Valeron Corp.*, 19 OSHR 2088 (1990); *Pymm Thermometer*, 20 OSHR 1408 (1991).
105. *OCAW v. NLRB*, 711 F.2d 348 (D.C. Cir., 1983).
106. § 17(e). That provision does not state whether it preempts state criminal actions. Proposed amendments to the OSHAct criminal provision would broaden the standard to include willful violations that result in serious injury as well; some of these proposals would

state clearly that OSHAct preempts state criminal prosecutions. *See* 19 OSHR 1683.

107. *See Ice Film Recovery Systems*, 19 OSHR 1939, where murder and manslaughter convictions for cyanide poisoning were overturned; *Maine v. Moores Neron, Inc.*, summarized at 19 OSHR 2187; 20 OSHR 123, for an account of an 18 count federal grand jury indictment against a building contractor when a methane gas explosion killed three construction managers. Some states have separate statutes dealing with corporate criminal liability, e.g., the California Corporate Criminal Liability Act, 21 OSHR 1206 (1992), and the Maine Workplace Safety Law, 21 OSHR 789 (1991). Congressman William Ford seeks a provision in pending OSHA legislation that would allow prosecution of individual company managers and supervisors, 21 OSHR 1515 (1992); a recent federal court ruled that such persons could not be prosecuted. *U.S. v. Doig*, 950 F.2d 411 (7th Cir., 1991).

108. *See, e.g., Illinois v. Chicago Magnet Wire Corp.*, 534 N.E. 2d 962 (1989), for what appears to be the majority view that OSHA doesn't preempt state criminal actions.

109. In the *Chicago Magnet Wire* case, after the corporation was found innocent of criminal charges, it settled the civil litigation against it; 21 OSHR 1231 (1992).

110. These cases can involve massive damages. For example, 8 journalists brought a $330 million suit against Eastman Kodak claiming the use of its computer equipment results in cumulative trauma disorders, *Harrigan v. Electronic Pre-Press Systems*, discussed at 20 OSHR 7 (1990). For recent discussions of the massive asbestos litigation, see 200 OSHR 182, 209. A recent decision holds that OSHA safety standards may be used as evidence of the safety of a machine in a civil lawsuit, *Hansen v. Abrasive Engineering, Inc.*, No. Or. Ct. App., 21 OSHR 1594 (1992). However, another decision holds that portions of an OSHA investigatory report may not be introduced into evidence in a wrongful death suit against an employer, *Hines v. Brandon Steel Decks*, 886 F.2d 299 (11th Cir. 1989), *cert. den.* 112 S. Ct. 1587 (1992).

111. *Pedraza v. Shell Oil*, 942 F.2d 48 (1st Cir. 1991), *cert. denied, Shell Oil Co v. Pedraza*, 112 S. Ct. 993 (1992).

XXV

"Blowing the Whistle"

What is "whistleblowing"?

Whistleblowers bring to light evidence of wrongdoing taking place within an organization and, more often than not, get punished for it. Fired whistleblowers often claim that their discharge was wrongful because it violated public policy (see chapter 3). Wrongful discharge remedies, however, are often inadequate to protect the interests of the whistleblower. This is especially true where public policy guidelines fail to address the subject matter of the whistleblower's complaints or where the whistleblower has not been terminated. Because the law in this area is still being formulated, the fate of anyone who obeys his or her conscience instead of an employer's wishes is often hard to predict.

Consider, for instance, how blowing the whistle changed the lives of two people. John Michael Gravitt, a foreman at General Electric, announced at a plant "rap session" that his supervisors were ripping off Uncle Sam by padding employee timeslips.[1] Meanwhile, George Geary, a salesman of plastic pipe, complained that the product his company was shipping posed a health risk due to its failure to meet specifications.[2] Both Gravitt and Geary alleged company wrongdoings. As a result, both lost their jobs, but then their lives took dramatically different turns.

In Gravitt's case, the United States Government joined his suit against General Electric. Together they sued under the federal False Claims Act of 1863, a law that provides rewards to citizens who save the federal government from being cheated.[3] Under the "bounty-hunter" provision of this law, Gravitt, a $35,000-a-year foreman, stood to win an astounding $55 million dollars for his efforts once GE's penalties were added up. Salesman Geary, however, discovered that the whistleblower protection laws of his state, Pennsylvania, did little to protect him. Despite his laudable attempt to prevent inferior and possibly hazardous pipe from being sold and laid in the ground, the court held that Geary had stuck his neck out too far because quality control was not his job. The court did not award Geary any relief. Because he disobeyed his supervisor, Geary lost his job, ran up legal bills, and faced blacklisting—even though he was sure that what he had done was right.

As the cases of Gravitt and Geary make clear, whistleblowing laws around the country are inconsistent and sometimes arbitrary. While the impulse to save fellow human beings from harm and expense is a universal one, the legal safety net for whistleblowers who take the plunge is, today, ridden with holes. For that reason, whistleblowing should not be undertaken impulsively but only after a sober consideration of the consequences.

Why do employees take the risk of "blowing the whistle"?

As Mark Twain once wryly observed, when we do right, some people are pleased and the rest are astonished. To be sure, it often seems amazing that people would risk their livelihoods to satisfy their consciences. Yet, to observe or participate in wrongdoing can be one of life's most devastating experiences. One who suppresses knowledge of a wrongful deed feels like an accomplice to it. Feeling caught in such a bind can make work unbearable.

Blowing the whistle may soothe the employee's conscience, but it often leads to harsh, swift retaliation by the employer. At the very least, the employer can be expected to hurl invectives at the whistleblower, such as "snitch," "saboteur," "traitor," "malcontent," or "crackpot." Studies show that after having blown the whistle virtually all whistleblowers feel powerless, anxiety-ridden, angry, isolated, and depressed. Their careers, family life, and peace of mind often disintegrate. Only recently have courts begun to recognize that the level of mental anguish suffered by whistleblowers generally exceeds that of any other plaintiff in employment causes of action.

Are most whistleblowers protected by the law?

Usually not. In most cases, the legal protections are at best uncertain. At the outset, the employer is likely to claim that it is justified in penalizing whistleblowers. Employees, under the age-old law of masters and servants, owe their employers the duties of obedience, loyalty, and confidentiality. The law, then, would seem to require that employees refrain from whistleblowing, an act that smacks of being disloyal, disobedient, and a breach of confidentiality. Paradoxically, society urges us to enlist in its wars against crime, corruption, drugs, pollution, and other perceived evils. The law has long-championed individuals who expose hidden wrongdoing. Nevertheless, few protections exist for the employee who reveals misconduct on the job because until recently, the employers' right to fire-at-will has been preeminent.

What kinds of wrongdoing do whistleblowers report?

Wrongdoing is committed in degrees. When whistleblowers level charges of wrongdoing, the organization often seeks to blunt the allegations by minimizing the wrongfulness of the exposed conduct. The employer faults the whistleblower for exaggerating the circumstances. At times, the employer may be right. The employee who perceives misconduct may not see the whole picture.

There is no failproof way to tell whether the wrongdoing that one perceives is worth "blowing the whistle" over. Ultimately, your conscience must be your guide. Nevertheless, the law is more likely to protect the whistleblower who reveals conduct that tends to "shock the conscience" of the public.

Three such issues are defective products (ranging from "O" rings in space shuttles to the side effects of medications), improper healthcare services (such as the clandestine practice of strapping elderly patients to their beds), and gross misuse of public funds (including fraud, embezzlement, overbilling, and graft).

Less blatant forms of wrongdoing may attract media attention, but unless health, safety, and/or general welfare are at stake, the whistleblower may end up jobless and without a legally recognized claim. For example, if an oil company spills a million gallons of crude oil into a populated bay, the employee who was fired because he complained about the faulty valve that caused the spill may win his or her job back. The inevitable public outcry might even force legislators to enact new whistleblower protections that prevent further accidents in that industry. But if the same oil company "loses" a few million gallons of crude oil "on paper," in an illegal accounting maneuver, the employee fired for exposing that impropriety may find no public outcry and no law protecting him.

Similarly, the law generally fails to meet employees' expectations where codes of ethics are concerned. Many employees possess a strong set of personal ethics. Others are bound by formal professional codes, such as in medicine, accounting, or law. Most employers, however, are under no duty to play by their employees' private or professional rules. They contend that if a company had to abide by the individual codes of ethics of every employee, it would be hamstrung and could never clear a profit. Again, courts tend to bow more often to the corporate goal of smooth management than to the ethical leanings of its employees.

If I report wrongdoing, will they believe me?

At some point, whistleblowers may have to argue that misconduct has actually taken place, even against strong evidence to the contrary. Unless a "smoking gun" can be found, the whistleblower may face an uphill battle trying to prove the allegations to employers, governmental agencies, or the courts. Here the most credible whistleblower is likely to be the one who has been forced to engage in patently criminal conduct. In such cases, the whistleblower's direct knowledge and understandable motivations lend credibility to the allegations.

In most cases, however, the whistleblower only observes wrongdoing at a distance. Questions are then raised as to what actually has taken place and what has caused the whistleblower to step forth.

Indeed, the law tends to take a jaundiced view of employees who step out of the scope of their employment to gather harmful information or who set off alarms without possessing hard proof of their claims. For instance, a Pennsylvania inventory-taker claimed his company was illegally dumping toxic chemicals. After he was fired he found, to his chagrin, that his state's whistleblower protection laws did not protect him—even though his complaint affected public health and safety. The reason? Investigating pollution was not his job, counting inventory was. Had he been a safety investigator who discovered the dumping in the course of his normal duties, he might have been protected by the law. But based on the case of *Geary* mentioned above, the court held he was not protected because he was acting outside the scope of his duties.[4] That is how narrowly some whistleblower laws are interpreted.

Employers have even sued for defamation employees who "go public" with falsehoods, although these claims will generally fail where public policy favors the whistleblower.[5] As a general rule, whistleblowers must use all possible diligence in nailing down the truth of their allegations before going forward. Virtually all states with laws that protect whistleblowing, require that the employee first reasonably, and in good faith, believe that the wrongdoing exists before stepping forward with damaging allegations.

I know of a wrongdoing. To whom should I report it?

Your fate as a whistleblower may depend on how you disclose what you know. First look for an outlet within your organization. Utilize any anonymous hotline, complaint box, open door policy, ombudsman, or "bitching session" your employer offers, as long as it is bona fide. A survey of over 1,000 businesses found that more than half had a whistleblower policy.[6] Certain laws require that the whistleblower exhaust any and all internal remedies before relief in the courts can be sought.

Of course, many employers give lip service to internal dispute resolution methods but do not follow through. Unfortunately, internal complaint procedures often are simply facades or even shams in which complaints go unanswered or, worse, prompt an investigation of the complainant rather than of the complaint itself. If this is the case where you work, you may be justified in turning directly to a sympathetic ear elsewhere.

If going up the chain of command appears futile, a whistleblower will have to find the best place to lodge the complaint outside of the organization. One choice is the media. This may be the most dramatic prospect but not the most realistic. Going to the media first can ultimately be self-defeating. By seeking publicity, the whistleblower may cast doubt on the sincerity of his or her motives. Government agencies may be a better place to go first, instead. Of course, your choice of where to bring a complaint may be limited by any whistleblower laws that govern your situation. The law may direct you to a government complaint board if you work in a regulated industry or to some other intermediary. Unless you are faced with an emergency, it is prudent to consult the laws that may govern your complaint before deciding where to submit it.

What if I find out that the laws won't protect me?

To avoid retaliation, you may be left with the choice of bringing your complaint to the attention of the appropriate authorities anonymously. This may be accomplished by writing unsigned letters to people within the company or to outsiders. It can also be accomplished using silent forms of protest. For instance, a nuclear materials worker protested lax safety standards by encircling, with red tape, a heap of radioactive waste that had been improperly left on a table overnight. Despite her anonymous approach, she was discovered and terminated. The United States Supreme Court ultimately granted her the right to sue for the emotional distress caused by her discharge.[7] Her case points out the justifiable concern whistleblowers have that their identities remain undisclosed, especially where the law provides scant protection against retaliation.

Several states, as well as the federal law, have recognized the need for keeping the identity of whistleblowers confidential. The laws of California, Connecticut, Illinois, Oregon, and Tennessee require that state agencies protect the identities of whistleblowers from whom they receive reports of wrongdoing. The federal Whistleblower Protection Act, described in more detail below, also provides for confidential reporting when government workers lodge complaints within their agencies.

I've been fired for blowing the whistle. What do I do?

First realize that you are not alone. Retaliation against whistleblowers is almost a given. A recent survey found that 99 out of 100 whistleblowers suffer some form of retaliation. It can come in the form of harassment, demotion, discipline, or discharge. It may even follow the whistleblower beyond the company in the form of blacklisting.

In one sense, an employee may stand a better chance of regaining his or her position if retaliation is direct and strong, such as where there is a prompt dismissal. Subtler varieties of retaliation, such as being assigned demeaning tasks, being passed over for promotion, or being ostracized socially will all cause economic and emotional hardship but may not register as retaliation in the eyes of the law and thus may be harder to combat.

Any employee who is subjected to disciplinary action should

check to see if the company followed its own procedures in meting out the punishment. Unless your company has a genuine, fair complaint system, however, it is probably in your best interest to consult a lawyer, particularly one who is familiar with the laws mentioned in the next section. As in every case, it is best to try to remain as objective and honest as possible when telling your attorney the facts as you know them.

Do any whistleblower protection laws protect me where I work?

The whistleblower protection laws of this country have been called a "patchwork," a "crazy quilt," and a "mishmash." The reason for the chaos is that these relatively recent laws are being enacted on an industry-by-industry, state-by-state basis. Until a single, national whistleblower protection law is enacted (a remote prospect in light of the failure of a recently proposed Uniform Health and Safety Whistleblowers Protection Act to attract support), the law will remain chaotic. Today there are so few laws providing whistleblower protection that the employee must act at his or her own risk, even in those states in which the law appears to be favorable.

The best place to start is to determine whether your job is within the public or private sector. Federal, state, or local government workers are more likely find some sort of whistleblower protection covering them.

Private sector employees may also enjoy civil servant-type protection if they work in industries that are heavily regulated. The regulatory fields that currently provide some whistleblower protection for private sector employees are discussed below. If your industry is not government regulated, you may find that your state nevertheless offers you some whistleblower protection. These state laws are also discussed briefly below. If none of these options applies to you, your only source of whistleblower protection may be your state's common law which may provide a common law cause of action for wrongful discharge. These causes of action are discussed in the sections below and in chapter 3 on wrongful discharge. Keep in mind, however, that new legislation is constantly being proposed to strengthen whistleblowers' rights. In 1992, Congress began deliberating on the Occupational Safety and Health Reform Act (H.R. 3160/S. 1622) that would add new protections for workers who blow the whistle on safety violators. Check with knowledgeable authorities in your area on the latest developments in the law that may strengthen your rights in this fast-changing area.

Are there any state statutes protecting private sector employees who blow the whistle?

Few states protect whistleblowers who work in the private sector. Minnesota, Hawaii, and New Jersey, however, have enacted statutes that protects employees who speak up about a wide range of employer wrongdoing and also offer incentives for blowing the whistle.[8] Private sector employees in these states who report violations of law to their superiors or to government agencies can recover their lost wages and their costs, and stand to win other damages, including punitive damages, as well. In Connecticut, Maine, and Michigan,[9] however, private sector employees merely have the right to get back their jobs and recover their attorney's fees if indeed they have been fired in retaliation for their whistleblowing. Again, the coverage of these state laws usually extends only to whistleblowers who catch their fellow employees breaking specific statutes. States that offer similar protections but do not necessarily provide attorney's fees to complaining employees are New Hampshire, Rhode Island, and Tennessee.[10] California does not designate any form of compensation for discharged whistleblowers who uncover their employers' unlawful conduct. Rather it specifies a misdemeanor penalty for the employer.[11] Louisiana is unique in that it offers a generous award of possible treble damages plus emotional distress damages, but its statute applies only to whistleblowers who report environmental law violations.[12] Other states with whistleblower protection statutes similarly restrict the scope of their coverage to certain wrongdoings. These states include New York (the reported violation must create substantial and specific damage to the public health and safety),[13] Ohio (violations must be either criminal or likely to cause imminent risk of physical harm or a hazard to public safety),[14] and Wisconsin (applies only to violations of state labor laws).[15]

State statutes protecting public sector employees.

Since Watergate, politicians have responded with legislation to the public's outrage at governmental corruption. These laws

sometimes protect whistleblowers. The broadest of these statutes protect those who report abuses stemming from illegality,
such as fraud, mismanagement, waste, and abuse of authority.[16]

For instance, in one of the largest whistleblower verdicts
ever, a Texas architect was terminated for reporting that his
state agency was being shortchanged by contractors. He reported that one contractor failed to properly insulate a warehouse. The jury found that under Texas civil law, the state
illegally retaliated against the architect and awarded him $3
million in compensatory damages and $10 million in punitive
damages.[17]

States with less hospitable statutes may confine their legal
protection to public employees who report on a narrower range
of employer wrongdoing. If the employee is fired, the remedy
may be reinstatement at best. Or if the statutes are vague, as
some are, it may be left up to judges to determine the breadth
of the coverage and of the remedies.[18]

What federal laws protect public or private sector employees who blow the whistle?

If you work for a private company in a federally regulated
industry, such as for a defense contractor, you may find that
the regulations governing your industry include antireprisal
provisions that protect you if you blow the whistle. The list of
federal regulations that contains such provisions is continually
being expanded.[19]

Statutes protecting federal employees. The Whistleblower
Protection Act of 1989 (WPA) grants federal employees who
blow the whistle some procedural protections.[20] It charges the
Merit System Protection Board (MSPB) with the responsibility
of handling complaints of retaliation coming from whistleblowers in the federal workplace. Specifically, the MSPB's special
counsel is authorized to investigate agencies accused of retaliation against whistleblowers, to inform and protect whistleblowers while the investigation is proceeding, and to prosecute
meritorious cases.

The Whistleblower Protection Act offers few guarantees to
the employee. It specifically requires that federal employees
disclose confidential information to members of Congress only,
and accords no protection to those who disclose information

to others within their agency.[21] It leaves the ultimate fate of the employee to the hearing officers, review boards, and administrative judges who will rule based on past administrative decisions. If the employee prevails, the WPA does provide the employee with the right to attorney's fees and may allow for a preferential transfer of the whistleblower who fears more retaliation.

Common law protections. As a last resort, those who blow the whistle may find protection or relief in the common law.

For example, these claims are generally classified as wrongful discharge actions and, accordingly, are discussed further in chapter 3 of this book. Common law is court-made law that is largely based on past court precedents in the areas of contract and tort law. Some state courts are more hospitable to these types of suits than are others. These courts often protect whistleblowers under the so-called public policy exception to the employment at will doctrine. This doctrine applies where the firing of an at-will employee tends to offend or thwart a public policy. Where the employee is fired for promoting the health and safety of others, for instance, then the firing is itself unlawful. In such cases, the court may order the discharge rescinded or award compensatory and punitive damages to the employee.

Sometimes the level of wrongdoing is not considered important in determining whether a whistleblower will prevail under the public policy exception doctrine. For example, an employee of a discount store reported an apparent theft by his supervisor of an admittedly paltry sum. The court held that the employee nevertheless stated a claim for retaliatory discharge, in that public policy favors the reporting of all possible crime, regardless of the amount involved.[22]

More sensational wrongful discharge claims may involve much bigger stakes. For instance, in *Martin Marietta Corp. v. Lorenz*, the courts of Colorado heard the claim of a rocket scientist who insisted that NASA was permitting inferior quality aluminum to be used in the fabrication of a space shuttle vehicle.[23]

Most states now recognize some public policy exceptions to employment at will rule, which may protect whistleblowers. The eight jurisdictions that have declined to recognize such claims are Alabama, District of Columbia, Florida, Georgia,

Mississippi, Missouri, New York, and Ohio. Three states have not yet ruled on the issue; they are Iowa, Maine, and Utah. As of yet the courts in these states have not recognized the existence of a public policy tort in their common law. Anyone resting his or her hope for whistleblower protection in states with stronger common law are still well advised to seek a lawyer's help in determining whether such protection applies, and if so, how he or she can take advantage of its protections.[24]

NOTES

1. Wall Street Journal Feb. 23, 1989, at 1. *Note* several other whistleblowers have succeeded in pursuing "bounties" against General Electric under the False Claims Act. One whistleblower won $7.5 million and another's claim was for $17.5. *See* Wall Street Journal, July 22, 1992, at 1.
2. *Geary v. United States Steel Corp.*, 456 Pa. 171, 319 A.2d 174 (Pa. Sup. Ct. 1974).
3. 31 U.S.C. §§ 3729 *et seq.* Among its provisions, the False Claims Act, as amended in 1986, permits persons to bring civil actions against those who knowingly make or use a false record or statement to get the U.S. government to pay a false or fraudulent claim or bill. Violators can be assessed treble damages, of which a percentage goes to the whistleblower. *See* "It Can Pay to Be Whistleblower in Health Fraud," Wall Street Journal, September 2, 1993, at B1.
4. *Smith v. Calgon Carbon Corp.*, 917 F.2d 1338 (3d Cir. 1990).
5. *U.S. v. Lockheed Missiles and Space Co.*, 7 IER Cas. BNA 142 (N.D. Cal. 1991) (The employers could not bring counterclaim of defamation against whistleblowers who brought suit under the False Claims Act. The court held that permitting the employer to pursue claims of breach of loyalty would allow wrongdoers to retaliate against whistleblowers, which contravenes legislative intent.).
6. Survey conducted by HR Magazine, cited in CCH Personnel Policy/ Communications, Sept. 1991.
7. *English v. General Electric, Inc.*, 496 U.S. 72 (1990).
8. Haw. Rev. Stat. § 378-61 (1988); Minn. Stat. Ann. § 181.931 (1989); N.J. Stat. Ann. §§ 34.19-1 (1987).
9. Conn. Gen. Stat. Ann. § 631-51m (1989); Me. Rev. Stat. Ann. tit. 26, § 831 (1989); Mich. Comp. Laws. Ann. § 15-361 (1989).
10. N.H. Rev. Stat. Ann. § 275-E:1 (1988); R.I. Gen. Laws §§ 36-15-1 (1989); Tenn. Code. Ann. § 50-1-304 (1990).

11. Cal. Lab. Code § 1102.5 (1989).
12. La. Rev. Stat. Ann. § 2027 (1989).
13. N.Y. Lab. Law § 740 (1989).
14. Ohio Rev. Code Ann. § 4113.51 (1989).
15. Wis. Stat. Ann. §§ 101.01 (1990).
16. States with broader whistleblower protection coverage (that goes beyond reports of statutory violations) and that may also offer a broader spectrum of remedies: Arizona (state/local government employees reporting violations or abuse) Ariz. Rev. Stat. Ann. §§ 38–531 *et seq.* (1989); Connecticut (state/local government employees reporting violations, corruption, or abuse) Conn. Gen. Stat. Ann. § 631-51m (1989); Delaware (state employees reporting violations of laws or regulations) Del. Code Ann. tit. 29, § 5115 (1989); Hawaii (full remedies for public sector employees reporting violations of laws) Haw. Rev. Stat. §§ 378–61 (1988); Illinois (state employees who report violations) Ill. Ann. Stat. ch. 127, para. 63b119Col (1989); Indiana (state employees reporting violations of law or misuse of funds) Ind. Code Ann. § 4-15-10-4 (1989); Iowa (state employees reporting violations or abuse) Iowa Code § 379.28 *et seq.* (1989); Kansas (state employees reporting violations) Kan. Stat. Ann. § 75-2973 (1988); Louisiana (full remedies for public sector employees reporting environmental violations) La. Rev. Stat. Ann. § 2027 (1989); Maryland (state employees reporting violations or abuse) Md. Ann. Code art. 64A 12F *et seq.* (1983); Missouri (state employees who report violations or abuse) Mo. Rev. Stat. § 105.055 (1989); New Hampshire (state employees reporting any information) N.H. Rev. Stat. Ann. § 98-E: 1 (1988); New York (public sector employees reporting violations relating to public safety or health hazards) N.Y. Lab. Law § 740 (1989); Ohio (full remedies for public employees reporting violations, either criminal or hazardous to public safety (Ohio Rev. Code Ann. §§ 4413.51 *et seq.* (1989); Oklahoma (state employees reporting any information) Okla. Stat. tit. 74 §§ 841.7 *et seq.* (1989) Oregon (state/public corporation employees reporting violations or abuses) Or. Rev. Stat. § 240.316 (5)(1983); Rhode Island (state/local government employees reporting violations) R.I. Gen. Laws §§ 6-15-1 *et seq.* (1989); Texas (state employees reporting violations) Tex. Rev. Civ. Stat. Ann. art. 6252-16a (1989); Wisconsin (state employees reporting violations and abuses) Wis. Stat. Ann. §§ 230.80 *et seq.* (1988).
17. *Green v. Texas Department of Human Services*, Texas Dist. Ct. No. 480,701 (Sept. 13, 1991).
18. States specifying remedies of at least reinstatement and backpay for whistleblowers who may report on a wide range of employer illegality and wrongdoing: Alaska (covers state and local government employ-

ees) Alaska Stat. § 39.90.100 (1989); California (state government and state university employees) Cal. Gov't. Code §§ 10540 *et seq.* (1989); Colorado (state employees) Colo. Rev. Stat. §§ 24-50.5-101 *et seq.* (1989); Florida (state/local government employees) Fla. Stat. Ann. 112.3187 (1989); Kentucky (state employees) Ky. Rev. Stat. Ann. §§ 61.101 *et seq.* (1989); Maine (state/public utility employees) Me. Rev. Stat. Ann. tit. 26, §§ 831 *et seq.* (1989); Michigan (public sector employees) Mich. Comp. Laws. Ann. §§ 15.361 *et seq.* (1989); Minnesota (public sector employees) Minn. Stat. Ann. §§ 181.931 *et seq.* (1989); New Jersey (public sector employees) N.J. Stat. Ann. §§ 34:19-1 *et seq.* (1987); North Carolina (state employees) N.C. Gen. Stat. 126-84 *et seq.* (1989); Pennsylvania (state/local government employees) 43 Pa. Cons. Stat. §§ 1421 *et seq.* (1989); South Carolina (state/local government employees) S.C. Code Ann. §§ 8-24-10 *et seq.* (1988); Tennessee (state education employees only) Tenn. Code Ann. §§ 49-50-1401 *et seq.* (1989); Utah (state/local employees) Utah Code Ann. § 67-21-1 (1986); Washington (state employees) Wash. Rev. Code 42-40.010 (1989); West Virginia (state/local government employees) W. Va. §§ Code § 56C-1-1 *et seq.* (1989).

19. Age Discrimination in Employment Act. 29 U.S.C. § 621 (1988); Asbestos Hazard Emergency Response Act of 1986, 15 U.S.C. § 2641; Asbestos School Hazard Detection Act of 1980, 20 U.S.C. § 3601; Clean Air Act (CAA), 42 U.S.C. § 9601 (1988); Department of Defense Authorization Act of 1984 10 U.S.C. §§ 1587, 2409 (1988); Employee Retirement Income Security Act 29 U.S.C. § 1001 (1988); Energy Reorganization Act of 1974, 42 U.S.C. § 5801; Equal Employment Opportunity Act (Title VII), 42 U.S.C. § 2000e (1988); Fair Labor Standards Act, 29 U.S.C. § 215(a)(3)(1988); Employers' Liability Act, 45 U.S.C. § 51 (1988); Mine Safety & Health Act, 30 U.S.C. § 801 (1988); Water Pollution Control Act of 1972, 33 U.S.C. § 1251 (1988); Hazardous Substances Release Act, 42 U.S.C. § 9601 (1988); International Safe Containers Act, 46 U.S.C. § 1501 (1988); Jurors' Employment Protection Act, 28 U.S.C. § 1861 (1988); Longshoremen's & Harbor Workers' Compensation Act, 33 U.S.C. § 901 (1988); Migrant Seasonal and Agricultural Workers Protection Act, 29 U.S.C. § 1801 (1988); Occupational Safety and Health Act, 29 U.S.C. § 651 (1988); Public Health Service Act, 42 U.S.C. § 201 (1988); Railroad Safety Authorization Act of 1978, 45 U.S.C. § 421 (1988); Safe Drinking Water Act, 42 U.S.C. § 300f (1988); Solid Waste Disposal Act, 42 U.S.C. § 6901 (1988), Surface Mining Control and Reformation Act, 30 U.S.C. § 1201 (1988); Surface Transportation Assistance Act of 1978, 49 U.S.C. § 2301 (1988); Toxic Substances Control Act, 15 U.S.C. § 2601 (1988).

20. 5 U.S.C. § 2302.
21. *Haley v. Department of Treasury*, 977 F.2d 553 (Fed. Cir. 1992).
22. *Belline v. K-Mart Corp.*, 6 IER Cas. BNA 1121 (7th Cir. 1991).
23. 7 IER Cas. BNA 77 (Co. Sup. Ct. 1992).
24. For a fuller discussion of wrongful discharge, see chapter 3.

XXVI

Job Security and the Law

Our legal system does not provide you with significant economic security in your job. By economic security we mean protection against losing your job because of changing economic conditions, such as a cutting back in the workforce, a closing of your plant, or a merger with or acquisition by another company. These circumstances, which usually affect many workers, should be contrasted with terminations that affect only a single worker. In chapter 3 we saw that the law does protect individuals against termination or other discipline that is based on improper reasons. However, those protections seldom cover employment decisions that are based on economic factors.

The failure of the law to protect economic job security probably reflects a reluctance to intervene in the workings of the free market. Advocates of this position say that in the long run we are better off if through the natural effects of competition weaker employers disappear and stronger ones survive.

Despite this gloomy introduction, you will find that the law gives you some protection against termination or other dislocation caused by economic factors. The most direct regulation is under the recently enacted federal WARN statute (Worker Adjustment and Retraining Notification Act of 1989),[1] which we will discuss in some detail. You'll see that WARN affords only temporary, short-term protection. Some states have similar statutes that augment the protection of WARN. Workers represented by unions may have additional protections under their collective bargaining agreements and through limitations imposed by the National Labor Relations Act (NLRA) upon the employer's ability to make economic changes. Finally, there are other strategies that a worker can use to try to avoid economic displacement and to get his job back if terminated. They generally require the advice and assistance of a lawyer. We will touch on some of them briefly.

PROTECTION UNDER WARN

The reader or her attorney should consult the text of WARN, although the text of WARN doesn't fully answer all questions. The secretary of labor has published regulations that give interpretive guidance.[2] And the courts will further shape the meaning of the statute.

What protection does WARN provide?

For all the publicity that went along with its enactment, WARN does not prevent an employer from terminating you for economic reasons. It is primarily a notification statute that requires the employer to notify you or your union and the appropriate state and local agencies 60 days before an anticipated plant closing or a termination of a substantial number of the employees in the workplace. If the employer fails to give this notice, it is obliged to give you backpay for the period you would have been employed during the 60-day notification period had the employer not shut down, up to a maximum of 60 days, but not to exceed one-half the total number of days you've worked for your employer, and all other benefits to which you would normally be entitled, including all medical expenses that the employer would normally have paid during that period.

In addition, there is a civil penalty of not more than $500 per day of the violation. This does not help you since it goes to the state, but it may be a deterrent to the employer's closing. Finally, it may be easier for you to use a lawyer to enforce WARN since the statute provides for attorney's fees in some situations.

What employers does WARN cover?

WARN applies only to relatively large employers, that is, any business enterprise that employs 100 or more full-time employees, or a roughly equivalent number of full- and part-time employees figured out under a formula of hours of work.[3]

What situations does WARN cover?

WARN defines two basic situations in which the employer must provide notice and otherwise comply with the act. The first is a *plant closing*.[4] This is any temporary or permanent shutdown of a "single site of employment, or one or more facilities or operating units within a single site of employment" that results in an employment loss for 50 or more employees during any 30-day period.

The other situation is a *mass layoff.*[5] This is a reduction in force that is not the result of a plant closing and results in an employment loss at a single site of employment for at least 33% of the full-time employees, if that amounts to at least 50 employees. In larger plants, the provision comes into play if at least 500 full-time employees lose employment, even if this is less than 33% of the workforce.

The final qualifying definition is *employment loss,*[6] used in the previous two paragraphs. This means a termination, a layoff exceeding 6 months, or a reduction of hours of more than 50% during each month of any 6-month period.

WARN provides that where several closings or mass terminations occur within any 90-day period, they may be aggregated for purposes of determining whether the statute applies.[7] For example, if the employer terminates 20% of the workforce on March 1 and another 15% on March 15, the two figures may be combined to satisfy the 33% requirement discussed above.

Can an employer manipulate the timing of job losses and avoid coverage of WARN?

Yes, this is a possibility. As you can see, these are very complicated provisions, and application of the act can easily be avoided by minor variations in the numbers. For example, if employees are brought back from layoff at any time during the 6-month period or if the reduction of hours doesn't exceed 50% during any single month of the 6-month period, the employer is not required to comply with WARN. It remains to be seen whether an employer is allowed to deliberately manipulate hours of work in order to avoid coverage under WARN, although our reading of the statute suggests that the employer may not do this.[8]

What is an employer obligated to do under WARN?

The basic limitation is that the employer may not close its plant or implement a mass layoff until the end of the 60-day notice period. The notice must be given to each affected worker or, if there is one, to the union that represents the workers.

In addition, the employer must give notice to the appropriate state or local agency designated to help dislocated workers.[9] The idea behind the notice provision is to give workers a chance to prepare for the blow and to obtain assistance from the state or local agency in retraining and in finding new work.[10] Even though the statute says the employer may not close without giving the requisite notice, a court does not have the authority to enjoin the closing or mass layoff where the notice is not given. Instead, the statute provides for the limited remedies discussed in the question and answer following the next one. However, there is some authority that a court may issue an injunction against closing for the limited traditional purpose of protecting a potential damages award.[11]

Are there any exceptions to the application of WARN?

Yes, plenty of them. The one with the greatest potential for avoiding WARN's application allows the employer to reduce the notification period if it was actively seeking capital to allow it to avoid or postpone the shutdown, and the employer reasonably thought that giving notice under WARN would defeat its ability to obtain the capital. This exception applies only to plant closings, not to layoffs.[12] Similarly, the notice period may be reduced if the closing or layoff "is caused by business circumstances that were not reasonably foreseeable as of the time that notice would have been required."[13] These are commonly known as the "faltering company" exceptions.[14] It is not clear whether in either case the employer may reduce the notice period down to zero. Finally, the employer is excused from obligations under WARN if the loss of employment is the direct result of an act of God or other act beyond its control.[15] If the loss of employment is only an indirect result of such an act, then it may be treated under the "business circumstances" exception.[16]

The employer's obligations may be modified if the loss of employment is caused by the sale or consolidation of a business. In a sale, the new employer takes over the notice obligation as of the date of the sale.[17] If the employee loses his job because of a relocation or consolidation of the business, the employer avoids any liability if it offers the displaced worker employment at a different site within a reasonable commuting distance and with no more than a 6-month break in employment.[18] The employer may also offer a transfer to a site beyond reasonable commuting distance, and while the worker isn't obliged to accept such an offer, if he does, that eliminates any liability under WARN.[19]

What is the employer's liability under WARN and how is WARN enforced?

If WARN applies and the employer fails to give the requisite notice, it is liable for backpay for each day the worker was out of work during a period when notice should have been given, subject to a maximum of 60 days, but not more than half the days the employee has worked for the employer.[20]

The employee is also entitled to any benefits under an employee benefit plan protected under ERISA, including any medical expenses that would have been covered had the employee still been at work.[21] The same ceiling applies, but it is not clear how it applies to medical expenses. We think that it means that the employer must pay any medical expenses you incur during the 60-day period on the assumption that any medical insurance that the employer normally provides would have been in effect on the days you would have worked and would have covered you for any illness that occurred on days you did not work.[22]

In appropriate cases, a parent corporation may be liable for the failure of its subsidiary to give proper notice under WARN.[23]

There is no government agency designated to help you enforce your rights under WARN. If you think your employer has violated the act, you or your union must bring a lawsuit in federal court on your own behalf or on behalf of everyone similarly affected. If you win your lawsuit, the court may allow you to recover attorney's fees.[24]

OTHER STATUTES GOVERNING JOB TERMINATION

Do any state laws require the employer to give notice or otherwise affect the employer's decision to go out of business?

Yes. A number of states have enacted laws that require the employer to give advance notice of a termination or reduction of business, in much the same fashion as WARN, or that provide other forms of protection against plant closings.[25] Where the notice period is longer than under WARN, the employer must comply with the longer notice requirement.[26] Some state statutes place substantive restrictions on corporate acquisitions, for example by requiring the new employer to honor the provisions of any collective bargaining agreement in effect at the company that is acquired.[27] Other state statutes inhibit corporate takeovers by requiring that certain benefits be provided to affected employees, such as severance pay,[28] or by requiring the continuation of existing health insurance plans.[29] In the event of a corporate takeover, you should also seek legal counsel on whether the takeover is in compliance with applicable corporate laws. The state laws that go beyond a notice requirement are subject to challenge on the ground they are preempted by ERISA or the NLRA,[30] and it is not clear whether they will survive such challenges.

PROTECTION OF ECONOMIC SECURITY THROUGH COLLECTIVE BARGAINING

A worker who is represented by a union or who is involved in union organizational activities may have additional rights if he loses a job because of economic changes. The reader who is interested in pursuing this aspect of economic job security should consult chapter 18, which explains in detail the way collective bargaining works, and provides the necessary background for understanding the next set of questions and answers. These questions parallel some of the materials covered in chapter 18, but are collected here for the convenience of the reader.

May my union prevent a loss of work through the collective bargaining agreement?

Yes. The extent of the protection it obtains usually depends on the language it has been able to secure in the collective bargaining agreement. Many collective bargaining agreements have language that may be construed as a guarantee of job security. Thus, if you are confronted with the loss of a job, you should ask your union to enforce any such provisions through the grievance procedure and arbitration.[31] Generally, it is up to an arbitrator to determine what the contract means and whether to order the employer not to carry out the intended work changes.[32] The arbitrator's decision is not enforceable by itself, and if the employer does not abide by the award the union must seek to enforce it through a judicial order. In general, courts will enforce an arbitrator's award.

The union in some cases may be able to obtain a court order enjoining the sale or other change in the business until the union is able to bring the case before an arbitrator.[33]

Finally, even if there is no express clause in the agreement preventing the employer from making the change in question, the employer may be required as a matter of its statutory obligation under the NLRA to bargain with the union about the decision, or at least about the impact of the decision, before carrying it out.[34] The duty to bargain about the impact of the decision could include such matters as severance pay and other benefits to be paid upon termination and retraining and rehiring procedures if these are raised by the union. This obligation to bargain about the effects of the closing, or even about the decision itself, does not require the employer to agree with the union, and thus bargaining may not reverse the employer's decision. But it can have the effect of slowing down the employer's decision. Further, the employer may be concerned about a decline in productivity if it gives notice because of employees leaving work or losing motivation, and in order to make sure that productivity continues, the employer may be willing to bargain for severance benefits that are keyed to attendance and production.[35]

If I am not covered by a collective bargaining agreement, does the employer have the right under the NLRA to terminate my job for economic reasons?

Yes, if that is the true reason for the termination. However, if you can establish that the employer terminated you not for economic reasons but in order to discourage union activity at your plant, then you may have a claim under the National Labor Relations Act (NLRA) for discrimination on account of union activity.[36] But the employer has the right to shut down its entire business even for the purpose of avoiding a union.[37] If you want to challenge an employer shut down of only a part of its business, you have a tough burden of proving that this was intended to chill unionism at the employer's other facilities.[38]

If my company is taken over by another company, does that company have the obligation to bargain with my union or to honor the collective bargaining agreement that was in place at my old job?

This depends on whether the new company performs work substantially similar to the work performed by the old company and whether a majority of the new company's work force consists of employees of the old company. If both these conditions are met, there is "a substantial continuity of identity" between the old and the new company. In those circumstances, the new employer is required to bargain with the union that represented the employees at the predecessor company. However, the law does not require the parties to come to terms. Further, the new employer is not required to honor any of the contractual provisions of the old agreement, although an older case, probably no longer good law, says that it may be possible to impose the terms of the old agreement upon the new employer through arbitration.[39]

The new employer may be liable, however, for any unfair labor practices committed by the predecessor. If the remedy for those unfair labor practices includes reinstatement, a restoration of benefits, or a duty to bargain with the union, these obligations may be enforced against the successor.[40]

If my company is taken over by another company, does that company have the obligation to hire me?

Generally not. The new employer is free to hire any employees it wishes, even if it would seem to make sense to hire the employees who already work at the job. However, if the employee can show that the only reason he was not hired by the new company was that the new company was trying to avoid workers who might force union representation on the new company, then the worker may be protected under the NLRA.[41] This may entitle the worker to backpay and to reinstatement with the new employer. If enough workers are required to be hired under this approach, this may in turn require the employer to bargain with the union that represented those workers at the predecessor plant.[42]

How does WARN work if I also have rights against the employer under my collective bargaining agreement or under a state statute?

WARN expressly provides that its remedies are in addition to any remedies you have under state law or under a collective bargaining agreement.[43] This means you do not waive any rights under WARN if you also have rights through your union, nor do the remedies under WARN take away any of your rights through collective bargaining.

However, the timing of the employer's notification obligation may be affected by the existence of rights through collective bargaining. For example, your collective bargaining agreement may call for advance notification and bargaining by the employer, or such notification and opportunity to bargain may be required by the NLRA. In both situations, the employer is not free to make a decision to close until it has satisfied its bargaining obligation. This may mean the employer must complete the bargaining process before it may give the required notice under WARN. For example, if it takes two months for the employer to satisfy its obligation to bargain under the NLRA, that may be the earliest time it may give notice under WARN, in effect requiring the employer to give four months' advance notice. A similar argument may be made if the union is able to enjoin the employer from closing or moving the business until an arbitration is completed.

None of this is clear, for at this writing there is no definitive case law dealing with the interaction of the NLRA and WARN. Further, the WARN statutory language, that "the period of notification required by this Act shall run concurrently with any period of notification required by contract or by any other statute,"[44] suggests that the timing of the employer's obligation under WARN is not affected by any contractual or statutory right.

OTHER RIGHTS OUTSIDE WARN AND THE NLRA

Are there other theories I can use to prevent the employer from eliminating my job?

Yes, although success under these theories is limited. In one case employees won a claim of interference with prospective economic advantage where a company purchased the stock of their employer without observing the required reporting and waiting period under state law.[45] In another case, workers convinced a court that their employer had promised to invest in restructuring the plant and to use best efforts to keep the plant open in exchange for union concessions.[46] In another well-known case, a union was able to show that in exchange for union concessions the employer promised to remain in business if it was profitable. The court would have required the employer to stay in business under that theory, but the court disagreed with the union that the business was profitable.[47] Sometimes you may be able to delay or stop a takeover on grounds the transaction violates statutes regulating the environment or involves the improper use of federal funds.[48]

What if the closing affects older workers?

An employer may shut down one of its plants or operations in order to save costs. Or it may reduce the workforce within a single plant for economic reasons. If your employer closes down an operation which employs a large proportion of older workers, or if the reduction in force within a single plant hits older workers the hardest, the employer may be in violation of the laws prohibiting discrimination on account of age. This is a very difficult area of the law, for the employer will contend that it was only taking into account economic considerations, such as the level of salaries in a particular unit relative to that unit's productivity, or that it selected those employees who had the best cushion against layoff, for example, a pension program. The trouble with these defenses is that they generally affect older workers, for older workers tend to have the highest salaries and the most cushioning against loss of work. The courts are still sorting out the way these interests must be balanced and what kind of proof the plaintiff must present in order to win.[49] Age discrimination issues raised in plant closings are discussed in chapter 13. Such a closing might also be challenged as an attempt to deprive older workers of their pension rights in violation of ERISA.[50]

RIGHTS TO SUBSTANTIVE BENEFITS PROMISED BY YOUR EMPLOYER

In many employment settings your employer provides benefits that it or its successor must honor even if your employment is terminated. In general, these are benefits that you have already earned, much the same as wages. If you are not represented by a union, you will have to rely on plant manuals and other documents given to you by your employer that spell out such benefits as severance pay, vacations, sick leave, and health insurance. For example, in one case a group of employees was able to show that their employer had promised to continue their health and life insurance benefits after retirement. The court concluded that these employees relied upon those representations in choosing early retirement and allowed them to recover under several theories.[51] You may find that the employer has made no commitment to any such benefits and that once your employment is terminated the employer has no further obligation to provide them to you. On the other hand, as we explained at the beginning of this chapter, WARN provides that all employment benefits must continue during the statutory notification period and that the employer is liable to provide you with at least part of these benefits if it terminates you prior to the completion of the statutory notification period.

If you are represented by a union, the benefits you are entitled to are normally spelled out in a collective bargaining agreement. Ironically, the new employer is not required to honor any obligations of a collective bargaining agreement. However, some benefits provided by the agreement, such as pensions and health insurance, may be protected under the general approach of earned benefits as discussed here. With respect to benefits provided solely by the collective bargaining agreement, your best remedy is to have your union proceed against the predecessor employer, usually through arbitration.

Some of the benefits that you have already earned, such as wages and accrued vacation pay, are covered by state statutes that provide for their collection. These accrued benefits will be given priority in bankruptcy and in at least one state are enforceable against the company's officers and agents.[52] Health insurance and pension benefits are the subject of separate questions and answers below.

PROTECTION OF PENSION BENEFITS

Are my pension benefits protected if my employer goes out of business or is merged with another company?

Yes. Congress has provided comprehensive protection of

your pension benefits under the Employee Retirement Income Security Act of 1974, popularly known as ERISA.[53] Pension benefits are discussed separately in chapter 5, and that chapter should be consulted as well if you have a problem in this area. ERISA requires your employer to accumulate sufficient funds to take care of all its pension obligations. If your employer should go out of business, the assets of its pension plan must be used to satisfy all existing pension claims. If those assets are not sufficient, a federal agency known as the Pension Benefit Guaranty Corporation (PBGC) will provide the funds to pay off all the pension claims. The PBGC is funded by payments made by all employers with covered pension funds.

This protection only extends to the portion of your retirement program that is vested, which occurs after a stated minimum period of employment, usually 5 years. Further, if your employer goes out of business, this means it will make no further contributions to your pension program, and your pension benefits will be frozen at the level they were when the employer went out of business.[54]

If the employer is taken over by another company, that company is then obliged to take over the pension plan that is in effect and to provide for the funding of vested benefits. If it fails to do so, PBGC will continue to guarantee payment of the pension. However, the new employer is not required to continue the pension program, so you may find that the level of benefits does not increase.[55]

If your pension program has been established as the result of collective bargaining, the employer may not terminate it without bargaining with the union and obtaining its consent. However, PBGC may terminate such a plan "involuntarily" if it determines that the plan will be unable to meet its funding obligations. In that case, your pension will not continue to grow, but PBGC will guarantee the payment of vested benefits.[56]

If your pension program is not the result of collective bargaining, the employer is free to terminate the plan provided its assets are sufficient to pay all benefits. If the assets are not sufficient, and the employer can demonstrate financial distress, it may terminate the plan and PBGC will take over funding.

If the employer's economic situation again becomes healthy, PBGC may order the company to resume payment of pension obligations. However, PBGC cannot order the company to reinstitute the plan itself. This can actually work against you. In the leading case on this subject, LTV terminated its ongoing pension program following bankruptcy, and PBGC assumed the obligation for outstanding pension obligations. Then the union and LTV negotiated a supplemental pension program designed to restore some of the benefits that were lost when the original pension program was terminated. PBGC refused to continue to fund the old pension obligations on the ground that the "follow-on" pension program showed that the company was now able to fund its program.[57]

Can the existence of a pension plan discourage a company from going out of business or from being acquired by another company?

Yes. Since the corporation is obliged to honor all vested pension obligations under ERISA, it may find it to its advantage to continue in operation in order to keep its pension plan funded. And if a company acquires an existing corporation, it is required to assume all the vested pension obligations of the former company. This obligation may be so great that the acquiring company will not go through with the takeover.[58]

HEALTH INSURANCE BENEFITS

Are my health insurance benefits protected in the event I lose my job?

Yes, to a limited extent. If your health insurance program is part of a pension program protected by ERISA, then the funding of it is guaranteed. However since most health insurance programs cover only workers who are actively employed, ERISA will not help you to continue your health insurance coverage. It will only safeguard the funding of benefits that you were entitled to while employed. For example, if you suffered a major illness while employed, ERISA will see to it that the costs of the illness normally covered by your employer's plan will continue to be paid. Protection of health insurance benefits under ERISA is discussed in chapter 6.

Another statute, known as COBRA,[59] gives workers who are terminated the right to continue to purchase health insurance at the prevailing group rate (a rate normally much lower than for coverage purchased by an individual) for a period of three years. However, this right may be of little value to a worker who loses his job. This worker, who formerly had an income and health benefits provided by the employer, is now asked to pick up health insurance premiums on his own when he may no longer have any income. Further, the worker's right to purchase group insurance lasts only as long as the employer continues to provide group insurance. If that coverage terminates with the cessation of business, COBRA is of no help to the affected worker.[60]

May my employment benefits be terminated in bankruptcy?
Yes, but under limited circumstances. In general, unless you are protected under a collective bargaining agreement, you have no guaranteed level of salary and benefits, and your employer may cut back at any time. Benefits you have already earned, such as wages and accrued leave time, will generally be given priority in bankruptcy, that is, will be paid ahead of the bankrupt employer's other obligations.[61] Of course, if your employer has promised to keep these benefits in effect for a stated period, then you have a contractual right to their continued existence. The same holds true of any benefits the employer is required by statute to continue in effect. Some of these, such as health benefits protected under COBRA, retirement benefits under ERISA, and mandated state benefits such as the Maine law requiring severance pay, are discussed in this chapter.

May an employer avoid the obligations of a collective bargaining agreement by declaring bankruptcy?
No. The employer must satisfy a bankruptcy court that it needs relief from its collective bargaining obligations in order to survive. In contrast to nonnegotiated benefits, which usually may be cut back at any time, benefits negotiated under a collective bargaining agreement must be kept in effect during the life of the agreement. After the agreement expires, they may only be changed if the employer satisfies its obligation to bargain under the National Labor Relations Act.[62] But the employer may seek to avoid or modify its obligations under a

collective bargaining agreement by securing a discharge in bankruptcy.

Once again, the law on this subject is very difficult, and a worker in this situation should see a lawyer or make sure his union provides competent representation. A Supreme Court decision in 1984 gave bankrupt employers wide leeway to avoid the obligations of a collective bargaining agreement,[63] and it was thought that employers would jump on this device to escape their collective bargaining obligations. As a result, Congress amended the bankruptcy code to require an employer to bargain with a union before attempting to use bankruptcy to avoid a collective agreement and instructed the bankruptcy courts to give greater weight to the worker interests under a collective bargaining agreement.[64] Under the new statute the employer may get out of a collective bargaining agreement only if it can demonstrate "those necessary modifications in the employees' benefits and protection that are necessary to permit the reorganization of the debtor and assures that all creditors, the debtor and all of the affected parties are treated fairly and equally."[65]

CREATIVE CAPITALISM

May I use my pension plan or employee stock ownership plan to prevent a corporate takeover?

Yes, under limited circumstances. In cases where employees own stock in a company, especially through a stock ownership plan created to help the employer raise capital, known as an ESOP (Employee Stock Ownership Plan), the employees may be able to affect the transaction through their powers as stockholders.[66] One limitation on this device, however, is that many ESOPs do not provide shareholder voting rights for the participants.

The use of a pension fund is a little more difficult. Many pension funds own stocks in their own company, although by law that ownership is limited to 10% of the total assets of the fund. In the event of a proposed takeover, the pension fund may want to sell its shares in the corporation to the corporate raider, thus assisting the takeover. Alternatively, it may want to refuse to sell shares and even buy up outstanding shares, in order to thwart the takeover. In either case, the trustees of the fund must act consistently with their fiduciary duties under ERISA.[67] The courts have held that the primary obligation of the trustees of the pension fund is to enhance the value of the retirement benefit. This obligation may require the trustees to sell their shares to the company proposing the takeover if this will maximize the value of the stocks, even if the trustees think the workers have a greater interest in avoiding the corporate takeover.[68]

NOTES

1. Pub. L. No. 100-379, 102 Stat. 890, 29 U.S.C. 2101–9, enacted Aug. 1988 and effective Feb. 4, 1989. We will cite it by the popular section numbers, which run from §§ 1 to 11.
2. § 8. The regulations, effective May 22, 1989, are at 20 C.F.R. pt. 639.
3. § (2)(a)(1).
4. § 2 (a)(2).
5. § 2 (a)(3).
6. § 2 (6).
7. § 3 (d).
8. IERM 595:974. The position in the text is supported by *Cruz v. Robert Abbey, Inc.*, 6 IER Cas. 1225 (E.D.N.Y. 1990). *But compare OPEIU v. Sea-Land Service, Inc.*, 6 IER 1064 (S.D.N.Y. 1991), and *Oil Workers v. American Home Products*, 7 IER Cas. 673 (N.S. Ind. 1992).
9. § 3.
10. *See* regulations cited *supra* note 2.
11. § 5 (b). *IUE v. Midwest Fasteners*, 6 IER Cas. 39 (D.C.N.J., 1990).
12. § 3(b). *See, e.g., IUE v. Midwest Fasteners*, 6 IER Cas. 39 (D.C.N.J. 1990).
13. § 3 (b)(2)((A). *See, e.g., Jones v. Kayser-Roth Hosiery Inc.*, 6 IER Cas. 733 (E.D. Tenn. 1990).
14. *Carpenters v. Dillard Stores*, 6 IER Cas. 1377 (E.D. La. 1991).
15. On the question whether an order by the government to shut down an operation constitutes an exception to liability, see *Finkler v. Elsinore Shore Associates*, 7 IER Cas. 161 (D.N.J. 1992).
16. § 3(b)(2)(B).
17. § 2(b)(1); 20 C.F.R. § 639.4 (c).
18. § 2(b(2)(A).

19. § 2(b)(2)(B).

20. § 5(a)(1)(A). One court has held this means a maximum of 60 working days and not the number of working days that are normally scheduled during a 60-calendar-day period, *Carpenters v. Dillard Stores*, 6 IER Cas. 1377 (E.D. La. 1991).

21. § 5(a)(1)(B).

22. This position is supported by *Jones v. Kaiser-Roth Hosiery, Inc.*, 6 IER Cas. 733 (E.D. Tenn. 1990).

23. *IUE v. Midwest Fasteners*, 7 IER Cas. 65 (D.N.J. 1992).

24. § 5(a)(5) and (6).

25. At this writing, provisions affecting plant closings are found in Arizona, Arkansas, California, Connecticut, Delaware, Georgia, Hawaii, Indiana, Iowa, Maine, Maryland, Massachusetts, Minnesota, New Mexico, New York, Ohio, Pennsylvania, Rhode Island, South Carolina, Tennessee, Utah, Wisconsin, and Wyoming. The list is constantly changing, and the assistance of a competent attorney is urged in researching applicable provisions in your state. A good research source is the *Employment Coordinator* (Warren, Gorham, Lamont), Para. LR-35,045 and 35,046.

26. § 6.

27. *E.g.*, Cal. Lab. Code § 1127(d) (Deering); Del. Code Ann. tit. 19, § 706 (1988); Ill. Rev. Stat. ch. 48, Para. 2571-2 (1990); Mass. Ann. Laws ch. 149, § 179C; Ohio Rev. Code Ann. § 4113.30(B).

28. *E.g.*, Me. Rev. Stat. Ann. tit. 26, § 625B (1989). *See Ft. Halifax Packing Co. v. Coyne*, 482 U.S. 1 (1987).

29. *E.g.*, Conn. Gen. Stat. Ann. § 31.500 (1990)(must continue in effect for 120 days); Mass. Ann. Laws ch. 151A, § 71A-71H (establishing state health insurance benefits fund).

30. *See Ft. Halifax Packing Co. v. Coyne*, 482 U.S. 1 (1987), where a Maine statute requiring the employer to grant severance pay upon the closing of a plant was upheld against preemption challenges under both ERISA and the NLRA. However, the opinion suggests that such statutes will not always survive preemption challenges.

31. For a thorough discussion of the kinds of clauses in a collective bargaining agreement that may protect job security, see Boltuch, *Workplace Closures and Company Reorganizations*, 7 Labor Lawyer 53 (1991).

32. *See Wyatt Mfg. Co.*, 82 LA 153 (Goodman, Arbitrator, 1983), discussing prior arbitral authority.

33. For an extensive discussion of this tactic, as well as other approaches under the collective bargaining agreement, see Boltuch, *Workplace Closures and Company Reorganizations*, 7 Labor Lawyer 53 (1991).

34. The NLRA generally requires employers to bargain about "wages,

hours, and terms and conditions of employment", NLRA § 8(a)(5), 8(d). This means the employer may not make a unilateral change in conditions without first bargaining with the union. However, where the decision involves a matter at the core of entrepreneurial control, the employer is not required to bargain about the decision but is only required to bargain about its effects. *First National Maintenance Corp. v. NLRB*, 452 U.S. 666 (1981). Thus, the employer must notify the union and bargain about the effects before the decision is actually implemented, *Riedel International*, 300 NLRB No. 32, 135 LRRM 1137 (1990). An employer is generally exempt from decision bargaining about those decisions that involve a termination of work or a sale of the business but is required to bargain about the relocation of work. The distinctions are in doubt, in that the board's earlier *Otis Elevator Co., (United Technologies)*, 269 NLRB 891 (1984) has been substantially modified in *Dubuque Packing Co.*, 303 NLRB No. 66, 137 LRRM 1185 (1991). Where a collective bargaining agreement is currently in effect, however, the employer may not make unilateral changes in terms and conditions of employment, even if those terms are not contained in the agreement, but must bargain in good faith with the union until impasse is reached before making the changes; NLRA § 8(d); *Milwaukee Spring Div.*, 268 NLRB 601 (1984), *enf'd. sub nom. UAW v. NLRB*, 765 F.2d 175 (D.C. Cir. 1985).

35. *See* Boltuch, *Workplace Closures and Company Reorganizations*, 7 Labor Lawyer 53 (1991).
36. NLRA § 8(a)(3). This topic is discussed more fully in chapter 18. You will see that the employer seldom admits that it is terminating an employee for union activity and will usually give some other explanation if challenged, such as economic considerations. You will have to prove that your termination was on account of union activity and not for economic reasons to obtain relief under the NLRA.
37. *Textile Workers v. Darlington Mfg. Co.*, 380 U.S. 263 (1965).
38. *Textile Workers v. Darlington Mfg. Co.*, 380 U.S. 263 (1965).
39. *Fall River Dyeing and Finishing Co. v. NLRB*, 482 U.S. 27 (1987); *Howard Johnson Co. v. Detroit Joint Board*, 417 U.S. 249 (1974); *compare John Wiley & Sons v. Livingston*, 376 U.S. 543 (1964). Where the acquiring company simply acquires stock, and there is no change in corporate form or in operations, the new company is obliged generally to continue to honor the collective bargaining agreement in effect; *EPE, Inc. v. NLRB*, 845 F.2d 483 (4th Cir. 1988).
40. *U.S. Marine Corp. v. NLRB*, 135 LRRM 2885 (7th Cir. 1990).
41. *U.S. Marine Corp. v. NLRB*, 138 LRRM 2361 (7th Cir. 1991).
42. *Howard Johnson Co. v. Detroit Joint Board*, 417 U.S. 249 (1974); *U.S. Marine Corp. v. NLRB*, 138 LRRM 2361 (7th Cir. 1991).

43. § 6.
44. § 6.
45. *Glass and Molders v. Wickes*, 243 N.J. Super. 44, 578 A.2d 402 (N.J. Super. Ct., 1990).
46. *Local 461 v. Singer Co.*, 540 F. Supp. 442 (1982). See *Township of Ypsilanti v. General Motors Corp.* 8 IER Cas. 385 (1993).
47. *Local 1330, Steelworkers, v. U.S. Steel Corp.*, 631 F.2d 1264 (6th Cir. 1980).
48. *See* Boltuch, *Workplace Closures and Company Reorganizations*, 7 Labor Lawyer 53 (1991).
49. The subject is discussed in chapter 13. *See* Kalet, *Age Discrimination in Employment Law* 152–55 (Reduction in Force)(BNA, 2d ed. 1990); Powers, *Reductions in Force under the ADEA*, 2 Labor Lawyer 197 (1986).
50. *See* chapter 5. The Supreme Court has held that such claims are preempted by ERISA and must be brought under that statute and not under state law concerning wrongful discharge. *Ingersoll-Rand Co. v. McClendon*, 111 S. Ct. 478 (1990).
51. *Armistead v. Vernitron Corp.*, 138 LRRM 2559 (6th Cir. 1991). Plaintiffs recovered under a theory that this was a collective agreement covered by the LMRA, as well as under an ERISA theory. The opinion includes an extensive discussion of attorney fees under ERISA, although the court did not award them in this case. A leading case on this subject is *Auto Workers v. Yard-Man, Inc.*, 716 F.2d 1476 (6th Cir. 1983), which illustrates the willingness of many courts to find such commitments to retirees in representations made by the employer.
52. NYS Labor Law § 198-a provides that officers and agents of a corporation who knowingly permit the corporation to fail to pay wages commit a misdemeanor. *Compare NLRB v. O'Neill*, 140 LRRM 2557 (1992) requiring a principal shareholder to satisfy a NLRB backpay award; and *NLRB v. IMCO*, 141 LRRM 2601 (1992), imposing the same obligation on family members on a family-owned corporation.
53. 29 U.S.C. § 1301 *et seq.* For a good discussion of the operation of ERISA see *Pension Benefit Guaranty Corp. v. LTV Corp.*, 110 S. Ct. 2668 (1990). Pension plans are discussed separately in chapter 5.
54. The text of ERISA is very complicated, and we see no point in a book of this sort to cite all the sections that support the propositions in our text. The reader will find a good discussion of the statutory authority on these points in *Pension Benefit Guaranty Corp. v. LTV Corp.*, 110 S. Ct. 2668 (1990). See also *Weil v. Retirement Plan for Terson Co.*, 750 F.2d 10 (2d Cir. 1984); *Bruch v. Firestone Tire and Rubber Co.*, 828 F.2d 134 (3d Cir. 1987); *Weil v. Retirement Committee of Terson Co.*, 2d Cir., slip op. Sept. 13, 1990.

55. *See* the discussion of this topic in chapter 5.

56. *PBGC v. LTV Corp.*, 110 S. Ct. 2668, 2671–72 (1990).

57. *PBGC v. LTV Corp.*, 110 S. Ct. 2668 (1990).

58. Fruhan, *Management, Labor and the Golden Goose*, Harv. Bus. Rev. 133 (1985).

59. Consolidated Onmnibus Budget Reconciliation Act of 1985, 29 U.S.C. § 1162.

60. 29 U.S.C. § 1162(2)(B).

61. 11 U.S.C. § 507.

62. NLRA § 8(a)(5). This is discussed more fully in chapter 18.

63. *NLRB v. Bildisco & Bildisco*, 465 U.S. 513 (1984).

64. 11 U.S.C. § 1113, (1984), discussed in *Wheeling-Pittsburgh Steel Corp. v. Steelworkers*, 791 F.2d 1074 (3d Cir. 1986); *Truck Drivers v. Carey Transp. Inc.*, 816 F.2d 82 (2d Cir. 1987). *See also In re Continental Airlines Corp.*, 134 LRRM 2369 (5th Cir. 1990) for a comprehensive discussion of how this all works.

65. 11 U.S.C. § 1113(b)(1)(A).

66. *See* Kaufman, *Democratic ESOPS: Can Workers Control Their Future?*, 5 Labor Lawyer 825 (1989).

67. *See* the discussion of these obligations in chapter 5 on ERISA.

68. *Donovan v. Bierwirth*, 680 F.2d 263 (2d Cir. 1982)(Grumman Pension Fund may not refuse tender offer by LTV). *Compare Withers v. Teachers' Retirement System*, 447 F. Supp. 1248 (S.D.N.Y. 1978); *aff'd.* 595 F.2d 1210 (2d Cir. 1979)(allowing pension funds to purchase municipal bonds to stave off city's bankruptcy).

XXVII
Family and Medical Leave

When you give birth or adopt a child or when you or a member of your family is ill, you need time to be with your family without having to worry that such time will cost you your job. Until recently help for employees in this situation was provided only by state or local laws, by employer policies, or by collective bargaining agreements. On February 5, 1993, President Clinton signed into law the Family and Medical Leave Act of 1993 (FMLA).[1] These family and medical leave laws are the subject of this chapter.

How is parental and medical leave different from other kinds of leave, including maternity leave?

Parental leave grants leave to either parent to care for a newborn, newly adopted, or newly placed child. Medical leave grants the employee leave in the event of the employee's serious illness or to care for a seriously ill member of the immediate family. Parental and medical leaves usually provide job security, that is, a guarantee that the employee can return to the same or comparable job at the end of the leave without being penalized for having taken the leave. Parental and medical leaves are separate benefits from other leaves, such as time off for vacation, personal days, or sabbaticals.

The maternity leave granted by many employers is a form of disability or sick leave and is also subject to the requirements of Title VII and to state employment, disability, and insurance laws. Maternity leave is described as "leave taken by female employees to cover the period of their own actual physical inability to work as a result of pregnancy, childbirth, or related medical conditions."[2]

At a minimum, employees who seek maternity leave must be treated the same way as other employees who are similar in their ability or inability to work. If you are able and want to work, the employer must let you work. If you are unable to work, an employer who grants medical leaves for nonpregnancy-related conditions must, at a minimum, grant the same type of leave for your pregnancy-related disability.[3] This and other prohibitions on discrimination against women are discussed in greater detail in chapter 11. Maternity leave is a kind of disability leave, not a childcare leave. If your employer is covered by the FMLA and you are an eligible employee, you will also be entitled to twelve weeks leave.

In contrast, parental leave is not related to the woman's physical ability or inability to work. Rather, it is a leave granted to either parent to care for a newborn, newly adopted, or seriously ill child.

How much leave does the Family and Medical Leave Act provide?

The FMLA requires employers who employ 50 or more employees to grant up to 12 weeks of leave during any 12-month period to any eligible employee (1) following the birth or placement of an adopted or foster son or daughter; (2) to care for a seriously sick spouse, child, or parent; or (3) due to the employee's own serious health condition (an illness, injury, or impairment, or a physical or mental condition involving either inpatient care or continuing treatment by a healthcare provider).[4] *Son* or *daughter* includes a biological, adopted, or foster child, a stepchild, a legal ward or a child of a person standing *in loco parentis* who is under 18 years of age, or 18 years of age or older and incapable of selfcare because of mental or physical disability.[5] The FMLA guarantees that eligible employees who take family or medical leave will return to the same or equivalent position that they held prior to the leave.[6]

Are all employers covered by FMLA?

No. The FMLA covers employers who employ 50 or more employees for each working day during each of 20 or more calendar workweeks in the current or preceding calendar year.[7] For purposes of determining whether an employer has 50 or more employees, all full-time, part-time, temporary, and permanent employees are counted. The term *employer* covers any business entity or individual with the requisite number of employees and includes public agencies, such as state and local governments, the U.S. Postal Service, and certain other agencies of the federal government.[8] It is important to note that the calendar workweeks need not be continuous.

Does the FMLA protect all the employees of a covered employer?

No. The FMLA protects only "eligible employees" of covered employers. To be "eligible" you must have been employed by the employer for at least twelve months and performed at least 1,250 hours of service during the 12-month period prior to the requested leave.[9] This twelve-month period need not be a calendar year.

What benefits must the employer provide to the eligible employee?[10]

The employee who completes a period of leave must be returned to either the same position or a position equivalent in pay, benefits, and other terms and conditions of employment. Any employment benefits that accrued before the date the leave began cannot be lost. The employee is not entitled, however, to accrue any additional seniority or employment benefits that would have accrued during the leave period (for example, an employee who has 15 years of seniority when she leaves has 15 years of seniority when she returns, not 15 years and 3 months seniority).

There is an exception to the right to receive your job back. This exception concerns those salaried, eligible employees who are among the highest paid 10% of those employed by the employer within 75 miles of the facility of employment. An employer may deny restoration to these eligible employees if (1) the denial is necessary to prevent "substantial and grievous economic injury to the operations of the employer"; (2) the employer notifies the employee that it intends to deny restoration on that basis at the time that the employer determined that the injury would occur; and (3) where the leave has already begun, the employee elects not to return to the employment after receiving the notice that the job would not be restored. The regulations to be promulgated under this law should clarify the obvious complexities of this exemption.

In addition, an employer is required to continue health benefits throughout the employee's leave. The employer who pays the health benefits must continue paying for them. Where the employee contributes all or part of the health insurance premium money, the employee must continue those contributions. If the employee fails to return from leave, the employer may require reimbursement from the employee for the health coverage premiums that the employer paid unless the employee's failure to return from a leave is because of the continuation, recurrence, or onset of a serious health condition, or because of something beyond the employee's control. An illustration is helpful here. Suppose an employee leaves for an operation. During the operation other complications develop. The employee is out of work for 6 months instead of the anticipated 12 weeks. Even though the employee fails to return to work at the end of 12 weeks, the employer may not recover payments made for the employee's health insurance during the initial 12 weeks of leave.

It is important to note that the FMLA neither requires nor prohibits the family or medical leave from being paid leave. Rather, the matter is largely left to the employer to determine. An employer may require that the employee use up any such accrued paid leave. If the employer does not make the employee use the accrued paid leave, the employee may substitute accrued paid leave for any part of the 12-week leave period. Once any paid leave has been used, the remainder of the 12 weeks of leave may be unpaid.

Are both parents entitled to leave under the FMLA?

Yes. The law is gender neutral. Each eligible employee is entitled to 12 weeks unpaid leave for appropriate reasons. There is one exception to this.[11] Eligible employees who are employed by the same employer are limited to an aggregate 12 workweeks of leave during any 12-month period if the leave is taken (1) to care for a newborn or newly adopted or placed son or daughter or (2) to care for a parent of the employee who has a serious health condition.[12] No such limitation exists when the leave is taken because of the serious health condition of the employee.[13]

May I take my leave intermittently or by working a reduced work schedule?

It depends on the reason for the leave. Intermittent or reduced leave schedule is not available for leave taken following the birth of a newborn or the placement of a child for adoption or foster care, unless the employer and employee agree to such leave.[14] When the leave is taken because of the serious health condition of a spouse, child, parent, or for the employee's own serious health condition, such leave may be taken intermittently or on a reduced schedule, if medically necessary, without the employer's approval. If this last kind of leave schedule is foreseeable based on planned medical treatment, the employer may require the employee to transfer temporarily to an available alternative position that has equivalent pay and benefits and better accommodates recurring periods of leave. Employees are required to make reasonable efforts to schedule treatment so as not to unduly disrupt the operations of the employer and to provide 30 days' notice or such notice as is practicable.

Where both spouses are employed by the same employer, and leave is requested for the illness of a child or the other spouse, each spouse is entitled to 12 weeks leave. If leave is required to take care of the serous health condition of a parent, however, the spouses' aggregate leave is limited to 12 weeks.

The law does not say what happens to an employee who fails to provide the proper notice.

May my employer require certification of my need for leave?

Yes.[15] An employer may require an employee to provide certification of the employee's serious health condition or for the serious health condition of a family member. The certification must be provided in a timely manner and must include (1) the date on which the serious health condition began, (2) its probable duration, (3) appropriate medical facts regarding the condition, and (4) a statement that the employee is unable to perform his or her functions. In the case of intermittent leave, the certification must include the dates and durations of treatments to be given. The employer may require a second opinion but must obtain that opinion at its own expense. The second opinion may not be provided by a healthcare provider employed by the employer. If the first and second opinions conflict, a third healthcare provider must be designated or approved jointly by the employer and the employee. The employer pays the cost of the third opinion and the third opinion is binding.

The law also allows the employer to require an eligible employee to obtain subsequent recertification on a reasonable basis. The law does not define what is meant by a reasonable basis, and the regulations are expected to elaborate on this issue.

May an employer discriminate against me for my actions in connection with the FMLA?

No.[16] An employer may not interfere with or restrain your right to exercise the provisions of the FMLA. An employer may not terminate you or otherwise discriminate against you if you (1) oppose a practice made unlawful by the FMLA, (2) file charges or institute any proceeding under the FMLA, (3) give information in any proceeding, or (4) testify in a proceeding relating to any rights provided under the FMLA.

Who has the authority to enforce the FMLA?

The United States Department of Labor has the authority to investigate claims under the FMLA and to require employers to maintain compliance records.[17]

What do I do if I believe my rights have been violated?

You may bring an action in federal or state court, or an action may be brought on your behalf by the secretary of the Department of Labor. Generally, an action must be brought within two years of the last event constituting the alleged violation. If the violation is willful, you have three years in which to bring your action. Employers who violate the law are liable to any eligible employee for monetary relief including liquidated damages as well as for appropriate equitable relief such as employment, reinstatement, or promotion. Attorney's fees are also provided to successful employees. The act is modeled on the enforcement procedures under the Fair Labor Standards Act which is discussed in chapter 23.[18]

What is the relationship between the FMLA and other state and federal laws?

Nothing in the FMLA is intended to affect federal or state laws that prohibit discrimination or state laws that provide greater leave rights.[19] Moreover, nothing in the FMLA diminishes an employer's obligation under a collective bargaining agreement benefit plan or employer policy from providing greater rights than are provided by the FMLA. For example, states that have leave laws that apply to employers with fewer than 50 employees are still in effect and are not superseded by the FMLA.

Are teachers treated differently under the FMLA?

Yes.[20] The FMLA contains special provisions covering employees of public or private elementary or secondary schools.[21] For example, if a teacher wishes to take intermittent leave that would cause the teacher to be absent from the classroom for more than 20% of the time, the teacher may be required to take continuous leave or to be placed in an equivalent position that would not disrupt the classroom. In addition, the teacher may be required to extend leave through the end of the semester if the teacher would have returned within the last two or three weeks of the end of that semester.[22]

Is there anything else I need to know about the FMLA?

Yes. As this book goes to press, the regulations have not yet been adopted. Therefore, you should check with a lawyer knowledgeable in this area of law if you have questions concerning your right to leave.

Are there any state laws that protect my job in these circumstances?

Yes. By 1993, many states had enacted legislation granting public and private employees some form of parental or medical leave as defined earlier in this chapter. These laws vary from state to state in many ways, including the circumstances in which they are available, the length of the leave, and which employers are covered. In addition, because of the rapid developments in this area you should be sure to check the state and local law as well as the federal law.

As of May 1993, most states and the District of Columbia provide some form of parental and/or medical leave with job security to employees.[23] The details vary from state to state. Some provide both medical and parental leave to either parent,[24] while others provide leave to the mother only. The duration of the leave and its nature (i.e., parental or medical leave) may vary.[25] Some guarantee reinstatement to the same position, while others only guarantee return to an equivalent position, and only if it is still available.[26]

Some states[27] limit family leave to physical disability, that is, they guarantee reinstatement to the same or comparable position to women who take a leave of absence because of a physical disability related to pregnancy and childbirth. This is not a leave to take care of the newborn although it coincidentally provides some time off following the birth of the child with job security. Generally, these pregnancy disability leaves are unpaid. Finally, a small number of states (California, Hawaii, New Jersey, New York, and Rhode Island)[28] have Temporary Disability Insurance laws that pay salary replacement benefits when employees are unable to work, including disability arising from pregnancy, childbirth, and related medical conditions. These disability insurance laws should not be confused with other leave laws. They are only salary replacement laws and do not guarantee job security.

What other legal protections give me the right to family leave?

Increasingly, corporations are establishing policies for parental and medical leave. Depending on the state, these employer policies may create enforceable contractual obligations. The specifics of the policies vary greatly. For example, the Time Inc. Magazine Company offers eligible employees unpaid parental leave of up to 12 months following the birth or adoption of a child.[29] The 12-month period includes the period of paid disability leave for female employees. Employees are guaranteed their former job or a comparable position within their division. If no appropriate job is available at the end of the leave period, however, the employee is terminated and is given the applicable notice and severance pay. At the company's discretion, employees may be permitted to return to work at first on a part-time basis. Bank Street College of Education offers eligible employees up to 3 months of paid leave. Employees may request additional unpaid leave of up to 6 months with extensions for up to one year. Employees may expect to return to their former salaries and positions. Even if their position has been eliminated, they may expect to return to a position of comparable responsibility and salary.[30]

Workers represented by unions may find that they have job-protected leave. Their collective bargaining agreements may contain provisions guaranteeing reinstatement for employees caring for a newborn or adopted child or seriously ill dependents. For example, a recent contract between certain divisions of the American Telephone and Telegraph Company and the Communications Workers of America Union provides for up to one year of unpaid leave to care for a newborn or adopted child and an unpaid leave for up to 12 months within a 2-year period to care for a seriously ill family member.[31]

Even if there is no official company policy or an enforceable manual or collective bargaining agreement, you may still have some protection in the form of an individual contract or even an informal agreement with your employer. For example, unless the leave arises as an emergency, you may have had one or more discussions with your employer concerning a leave of absence for an anticipated birth or adoption of a child. Depending on the circumstances, these discussions may rise to the level of an enforceable contract.

If there is no written policy, it may be helpful if you clarify the issue of job security prior to the leave. Before any discussions with your employer, you should try to find out the employer's past practices concerning disability and medical leaves, leaves of absence for childcare, and leaves of absence for other personal reasons. This may give you some sense of what you can expect. Following any discussions, you should try to get a letter from your employer confirming the terms of your leave and your return. If you cannot get a letter, immediately following your discussions you should make notes of any conversations concerning the leave and job security. It may be advisable to send a memorandum concerning the substance of your discussion to your employer or simply to place a memorandum in your file. All of this may strengthen your position in the event you take a leave and suddenly find yourself unemployed or underemployed upon your return to work.

Finally, even if you have no contract claim, you may have a sex discrimination claim. If men who are given leaves are routinely allowed to return to their jobs but women are not, this may violate laws prohibiting discrimination based upon gender. You should check with an attorney to see whether you have a sex discrimination claim. For more information on sex discrimination claims in general see chapter 11.

NOTES

1. Pub. L. No. 103-3 (FMLA §§ 101 *et seq.*).
2. EEOC Compliance Manual § 626.5.
3. Pregnancy Discrimination Act, 42 U.S.C. § 2000e-(k).
4. FMLA §§ 101–2.
5. *Id.* at § 101.
6. *Id.* at § 104.
7. *Id.*
8. *Id.* at § 101.
9. *Id.*
10. *Id.*
11. *Id.* at § 104.
12. *Id.* at § 102.
13. *Id.*
14. *Id.*
15. *Id.*
16. *Id.*
17. *Id.* at § 103.
18. *Id.* at § 105.
19. *Id.* at § 107.
20. *Id.*
21. *Id.* at § 108.
22. *Id.*
23. These include: Alaska, California, Colorado, Connecticut, Delaware, District of Columbia, Georgia, Hawaii, Iowa, Maine, Massachusetts, Minnesota, Missouri, Montana, New Hampshire, New Jersey, New York, North Dakota, Oregon, Rhode Island, Tennessee, Vermont, Washington, West Virginia, and Wisconsin.
24. *E.g.*, Connecticut, Conn. Gen. Stat. § 5-248A (1989); Maine, 26 Me. Rev. Stat. Ann. § 849 (1989); Wisconsin, Wis. Stat. Ann. § 103.10 (1989).
25. *E.g.*, Wisconsin, Wisc. Stat. § 103.10 (1987–88); Maine, 26 Me. Rev. Stat. Ann. § 849 (1989).
26. *Compare* New Jersey, N.J. Stat. Ann. 34:11B-3 *with* Connecticut, Conn. Gen. Stat. § 46a-60(a)(7)(D).
27. Connecticut, Conn. Gen. Stat. §§ 46a-60(a)(7)(B)–(D) and 46a-82-96 (1986); California, Cal. Gov't Code §§ 12945(1)–(2) and 12960–75 (West 1980 and Supp. 1988); Hawaii, Hawaii Dept. of Industrial and Labor Relations, Sex and Marital Status Discrimination Regulations, §§ 12-23-1 to 12-23-22; 12-23-58 (FEP Manual (BNA) 453:2301–28

(1983); Kansas, Kansas Commission on Civil Rights, Guidelines on Discrimination Because of Sex §§ 21-32-6(D); 21-41-1 to 21-45-25 FEP Manual (BNA) 453:3311; 453:3318–37 (1977); Montana, Mont. Code Ann. §§ 49-2-310–40-2-311; 49-2-501–9 (1989); Montana Human Rights Commission, Maternity Leave Rules §§ 24.9.202–4; 24.9.1201–7 (1988); New Hampshire, N.H. Rev. Stat. Ann. §§ 354-A:9-10 (Supp. 1987); N.H. Code Admin. R. Hum. §§ 402.01; 201.01–212.06 (1988); Oregon, Or. Rev. Stat. § 659.340 (1989); Tennessee, Tenn. Code Ann. § 4-21-408; Vermont, 21 V.S.A. §§ 472; Washington, R.C.W. Wash. Rev. Code §§ 49-78-030 and 49.10.050 (1990).

28. California, Cal. Ed. Code § 44965 (1990); Hawaii, Haw. Rev. Stat. § 383-1 (1989); New York, N.Y. CLS Soc. Serv. Law § 132; Rhode Island, R.I. Gen. Laws § 28-39-2 (1990).

29. Time Inc. Magazines, Managers Handbook at 4-14 to 4-15.

30. *Pregnancy and Employment: The Complete Handbook on Discrimination, Maternity Leave, and Health and Safety* (BNA 1987) at 207–8.

31. Agreement between American Telephone and Telegraph Company on Behalf of Certain Business Units and Divisions and the Communications Workers of America (Effective May 28, 1989).

XXVIII
The Legal System

For many persons, law appears to be magic—an obscure domain that can be fathomed only by the professionals initiated into its mysteries. People who might be able to use the law to their advantage sometimes avoid the effort out of awe for its intricacies. But the main lines of the legal system, and of the law in a particular area, can be explained in terms clear to the layperson.

What does a lawyer mean by saying that a person has a legal right?

Having a right means that society has given a person permission—through the legal system—to secure some action or to act in some way that she or he desires. For example, a woman might have a right to an abortion, a job applicant the right to employment free from discrimination, or a person accused of a crime the right to an attorney.

How does one enforce a legal right?

The concept of enforcing a right gives meaning to the concept of the right itself. While the abstract right may be significant because it carries some connotation of morality and justice, enforcing the right yields something concrete—the abortion, the job, the attorney.

A person enforces a right by going to some appropriate authority—often, a judge—who has the power to take certain action. The judge can order the people who are refusing to grant the right to start doing so, on pain of a fine or jail if they disobey.

The problem with the enforcement process is that it will often be lengthy, time-consuming, expensive, frustrating, and may arouse hostility in others—in short, it may not be worth the effort. On the other hand, in some cases it is not necessary to go to an enforcement authority in order to implement a right. The officials may not realize that a right exists and may voluntarily change their actions once the situation is explained to them. Further, the officials may not want to go through the legal process either—it may be expensive and frustrating for them also.

Where are legal rights defined?

There are several sources. The prime sources are the constitutions of the federal and state governments. Rights are further defined in the statutes or laws passed by the United States Congress and by state and city legislatures. They are also set forth in the written decisions of federal and state judges. Congress and state and local legislatures have also created institutions called administrative agencies to enforce certain laws, and these agencies interpret the laws in decisions and rules that further define people's rights.

Are rights always clearly defined and evenly applied to all people?

Not at all. Because so many different sources define people's rights and because persons of diverse backgrounds and beliefs implement and enforce the law, there is virtually no way to enforce uniformity. Nor do statutes that set forth rights always do so with clarity or specificity. It remains for courts or administrative agencies to interpret and to flesh out the details. In the process of doing so, many of the interpreters differ. Sometimes, two courts will give different answers to the same question. Whether or not a person has a particular right may depend on which state or city he or she lives in.

The more times a particular issue is decided, the more guidance there is in predicting what other judges or administrative personnel will decide. Similarly, the importance of the court or agency that decides a case and the persuasiveness of its reasoning will help determine the impact of the decision. A judge who states thoughtful reasons will have more influence than one who offers poor reasons.

In sum, law is not a preordained set of doctrines, applied rigidly and unswervingly in every situation. Rather, law is molded from the arguments and decisions of thousands of persons. It is very much a human process, of trying to convince others—a judge, a jury, an administrator, the lawyer for the other side—that one view of what the law requires is correct.

What is a case or decision?

Lawyers often use these words interchangeably, although technically they do not mean the same thing. A *case* means the lawsuit started by one person against another, and it can refer to that lawsuit at any time from the moment it is begun until the final result. A *decision* means the written opinion in which the judge declares who wins the lawsuit and why.

What is meant by precedent?

Precedent means past decisions. Lawyers use precedent to influence new decisions. If the facts involved in a prior decision are close to the facts in a new case, a judge will be strongly tempted to follow the former decision. She is not, however, bound to do so and, if persuasive reasons are presented to show that the prior decision was wrong or ill-suited to changed conditions in society, the judge may not follow precedent.

What is the relationship between decisions and statutes?

In our legal system, most legal concepts originally were defined in the decisions of judges. In deciding what legal doctrine to apply to a case, each judge kept building on what other judges had done. The body of legal doctrines created in this way is called the *common law*.

The common law still applies in many situations, but increasingly state legislatures and the Congress pass laws "statutes" to define the legal concepts that judges or agencies should use in deciding cases. The written decisions of individual judges are still important even where there is a statute because statutes are generally not specific enough to cover every set of facts. Judges have to interpret their meaning, apply them to the facts at hand, and write a decision; that decision will then be considered by other judges when they deal with these statutes in other cases. Thus it is generally not enough to know what a relevant statute defines as illegal; you also have to know how judges have interpreted the statute in specific situations.

What different kinds of courts are there?

The United States is unique for its variety of courts. Broadly speaking, there are two distinct court systems: federal and state. Both are located throughout the country; each is limited to certain kinds of cases, with substantial areas of overlap. Most crimes are prosecuted in state courts, for instance, although a number of federal crimes are prosecuted in federal courts. People generally use state courts to get a divorce, but they must sue in federal court to establish rights under certain federal laws.

In both federal and state court systems one starts at the trial or "lower" court level, where the facts are "tried." This means that a judge or jury listens and watches as the lawyers present evidence of the facts that each side seeks to prove. Evidence can take many forms: written documents, the testimony of a witness on the stand, photographs, charts. Once a judge or jury has listened to or observed all the evidence presented by each side, it will choose the version of the facts it believes, apply the applicable legal doctrine to these facts, and decide which side has won. If either side is unhappy with the result, it may be able to take the case to the next, higher-level court and argue that the judge or the jury applied the wrong legal concept to the facts or that no reasonable jury or judge could have found the facts as they were found in the trial court and that the result was therefore wrong.

What are plaintiffs and defendants?

The *plaintiff* is the person who sues—that is, who complains that someone has wronged him or her and asks the court to remedy this situation. The *defendant* is the person sued—the one who defends against the charges of the plaintiff. The legal writing in which the plaintiff articulates her or his basic grievance is the *complaint,* and a lawsuit is generally commenced by filing this document with a clerk at a courthouse. The defendant then responds to these charges in a document appropriately named an *answer.*

One refers to a particular lawsuit by giving the names of the plaintiff and defendant. If Mary Jones sues Smith Corporation for refusing to hire her because she is a woman, her case will be called *Jones v. Smith Corporation* (*v.* stands for versus, or against).

What is an administrative agency?

Agencies are institutions established by either state or federal legislatures to administer or enforce a particular law or series of laws and are distinct from both courts and legislature. They often regulate a particular industry. For example, the Federal Communications Commission regulates the broadcasting industry (radio and television stations and networks) and the telephone and telegraph industry, in accordance with the legal standards set forth in the Federal Communications Act.

Agencies establish legal principles, embodied in rules, regulations, or guidelines. *Rules* are interpretations of a statute and are designed to function in the same way as a statute—to define people's rights and obligations in a general way but in a more detailed fashion than the statute itself. Agencies also issue specific decisions in cases, like a judge, that apply a broad law or rule to a factual dispute between particular parties.

How does one find court decisions, statutes, and agency rules and decisions?

All these materials are published and can be found in law libraries. In order to find a desired item, one should understand the system lawyers use for referring to, or citing, these materials. For example, a case might be cited as *Watson v. Limbach Company*, 333 F. Supp. 754 (S.D. Ohio 1971); a statute, as 42 U.S.C. § 1983; a regulation, as 29 C.F.R. § 1604.10(b). The unifying factor in all three citations is that the first number denotes the particular volume in a series of books with the same title; the words or the letters that follow represent the name of the book; and the second number represents either the page or the section in the identified volume. In the examples above, the *Watson* case is found in the 333d volume of the series of books called *Federal Supplement* at page 754; the statute is found in volume 42 of the series called the *United States Code* at section 1983; the regulation is in volume 29 of the *Code of Federal Regulations* at section 1604.10(b).

There are similar systems for state court decision. Once the system is understood, a librarian can point out where a particular series of books is kept so that the proper volume and page or section can be looked up. It is also important to check the same page or section in material sometimes inserted at the back of a book, since many legal materials are periodically updated with "pocket parts." A librarian will explain what any abbreviations stand for that are unclear.

Given this basic information, anyone can locate and read important cases, statutes, and regulations. Throughout this book, such materials have been cited when deemed important. Although lawyers often use technical language, the references cited usually can be comprehended without serious difficulty, and reading the original legal materials gives people self-confidence and a deeper understanding of their rights.

What is the role of the lawyer in the legal system?

A lawyer understands the intricacies and technicalities of the legal system and can maneuver within it. Thus lawyers know where to find out about the leading legal doctrines in a given area and often how to predict the outcome of a case based on a knowledge of those doctrines. A lawyer can advise a client what to do: forget about the case, take it to an administrative agency, sue in court, make a will, and so on. A lawyer also helps take the legal actions that the client wants.

How are legal costs determined and how do they affect people's rights?

The cost of using the legal system is predominantly the cost of paying the lawyer for his or her time. Since the cost has become prohibitive even for middle-class individuals, many people are not able to assert their rights, even though they might ultimately win if they had the money to pay a lawyer for doing the job.

Is legal action the only way to win one's legal rights?

By no means. Negotiation, education, consciousness raising, publicity, demonstrations, organization, and lobbying are all ways to achieve rights, often more effectively than through the standard but costly and time-consuming resort to the courts. In all these areas, it helps to have secure knowledge of the legal underpinnings of your rights. One has a great deal more authority if one is protesting illegal action. The refrain "That's illegal" may move some people in and of itself; or it may convince those with whom you are dealing that you are serious enough to do something about the situation—by starting a lawsuit, for instance.

Appendix A
Federal Antireprisal Statutes

The following statutes contain provisions prohibiting reprisals against employees reporting violations of or asserting rights under those statutes:

- Age Discrimination in Employment Act of 1967, 29 U.S.C. § 623
- Americans with Disabilities Act, 42 U.S.C. § 12203
- Asbestos School Hazard Detection & Control Act, 20 U.S.C. § 3608
- Civil Rights Act of 1964, Title VII, 42 U.S.C. § 2000e-3
- Civil Rights of Institutionalized Persons Act, 42 U.S.C. § 1997(d)
- Civil Service Reform Act of 1978, 5 U.S.C. §§ 2301, 2302, 7102, 7116
- Clean Air Act Amendments of 1977, 42 U.S.C. §§ 7401, 7622
- Comprehensive Environmental Response, Comp. & Liability Act of 1980, 42 U.S.C. § 9610
- Conspiracy to Obstruct Justice Act, 15 U.S.C. § 1985(2)
- Consumer Credit Protection Act of 1968, 15 U.S.C. § 1674
- Employee Polygraph Protection Act, 29 U.S.C. § 2002
- Employee Retirement Income Security Act of 1974, 29 U.S.C. §§ 1140, 1141
- Energy Reorganization Act Amendment of 1978, 42 U.S.C. § 5851
- Fair Labor Standards Act, 29 U.S.C. § 215
- Federal Mine Safety and Health Act Amendment of 1977, 30 U.S.C. §§ 815, 820(b)
- Federal Railroad Safety Act Amendment, 45 U.S.C. § 441
- Federal Water Pollution Control Act of 1972, 33 U.S.C. § 1367
- International Safe Container Act of 1977, 46 U.S.C. § 1506

- Jury Duty Act, 28 U.S.C. § 1875
- Longshoremen's and Harbor Workers' Compensation Act of 1972, 33 U.S.C. § 948(a)
- Migrant and Seasonal Agricultural Worker Protection Act of 1983, 29 U.S.C. § 1855
- National Labor Relations Act, 29 U.S.C. § 158
- Occupational Safety and Health Act of 1970, 29 U.S.C. § 660
- Railroad Employers Act of 1908, 45 U.S.C. § 60
- Safe Drinking Water Act of 1974, 42 U.S.C. § 300j-9
- Solid Waste Disposal Act of 1976, 42 U.S.C. § 6972
- Surface Mining Control & Reclamation Act of 1977, 30 U.S.C. § 1201, 1293
- Toxic Substances Control Act of 1976, 15 U.S.C. § 2622

Appendix B
Legal Resources for Victims of Employment Discrimination

LAWYERS IN PRIVATE PRACTICE

Equal employment law is very technical and changes frequently. It is therefore important that you find an attorney who is experienced in this area. Most EEOC offices have lists of private attorneys who work in the civil rights field. Also, civil liberties and civil rights organizations in your area may be able to refer you to an experienced private attorney. There is one national organization of attorneys who represent employees that can refer you to a specialist in your area.

National Employment Lawyers Association
535 Pacific Avenue
San Francisco, CA 94133
(415) 397-6335

NELA has a directory of over 1,100 employment law attorneys, including brief descriptions of their practices. For more information, send a self-addressed, stamped envelope.

LEGAL SERVICES ORGANIZATIONS

If you are poor or unemployed you may be eligible for free legal assistance from a local legal services organization supported by federal and local funding. These organizations, usually referred to as Legal Aid Societies or Legal Services Organizations, employ lawyers who provide legal assistance to poor people in all areas of law, including discrimination law. These oganizations exist in nearly every city and county in the country.

To find your nearest legal services organization you should look through the phone book or call a local government official for advice. If you have difficulty finding the appropriate local organizations, there are several national organizations you might want to contact.

National Legal Aid and Defender Association
1625 K Street, N.W., 8th Floor
Washington, D.C. 20006
(202) 452-0620

These legal service lawyers or their organizations are members of the NLADA. The NLADA may be able to refer you to the appropriate legal services office in your area.

Legal Services Corporation
750 1st Street, N.E.
Washington, D.C. 20002
(202) 336-8800

The Legal Services Corporation is an independent agency that provides federal funding to most legal services organizations. It should be able to refer you to an appropriate legal services office in your area.

NATIONAL CIVIL LIBERTIES AND CIVIL RIGHTS ORGANIZATIONS

Several national civil liberties and civil rights organizations have state and local offices (usually called chapters or affiliates) throughout the United States. Generally, the national offices will not be able to assist you directly, but will refer you to one of their local offices, which may assist you.

The local offices of the following major organizations are listed in your telephone directory. If you cannot find them, you should write to the national offices for referrals.

American Civil Liberties Union
132 West 43d Street
New York, New York 10036
(212) 944-9800

The ACLU specializes in free-speech law but is also involved in discrimination law. There are state affiliates and local chapters of the ACLU in nearly every state.

Asian-American Legal Defense and Education Fund
99 Hudson Street, 12th Floor
New York, New York 10013
(212) 966-5932

AALDEF offers legal services and attorney referrals for Asians and Asian-Americans.

Mexican-American Legal Defense and Education Fund
182 2d Street, 2d Floor
San Francisco, CA 94105
(415) 543-5598

MALDEF specializes in discrimination law and represents almost exclusively Mexican-Americans. Its offices are located primarily in the Midwest, the Southwest, and the West.

National Association for the Advancement of Colored People
4805 Mount Hope Drive
Baltimore, MD 21215-3297
(414) 358-8900

The NAACP, the oldest and largest of the civil rights organizations, specializes in racial discrimination law on behalf of African Americans. It has state and local chapters throughout the United States.

National Urban League
500 East 62nd Street
New York, New York 10021
(212) 310-9000

Like the NAACP, the National Urban League specializes in racial discrimination on behalf of African Americans, and has offices throughout the United States.

National Veterans Legal Services Project
2001 S Street, NW
Suite 610
Washington, D.C. 20009
(202) 265-8305

Puerto Rican Legal Defense and Education Fund
99 Hudson Street

New York, New York 10013
(212) 219-3360

The PRLDF specializes in discrimination law and particularly in bilingual education law. It maintains several offices, primarily in the Northeast.

REGIONAL, LOCAL, AND SPECIALIZED CIVIL LIBERTIES AND CIVIL RIGHTS ORGANIZATIONS

There is a large number of regional, local, and specialized civil liberties and civil rights organizations across the United States. Many of them are very small and operate primarily or solely through volunteer help. Others employ staff attorneys.

ACLU Southern Regional Office
44 Forsythe Street
Suite 202
Atlanta, GA 30303
(404) 523-2721

The ACLU Southern Regional Office specialized in voter discrimination law and jury discrimination in the South.

Center for Constitutional Rights
666 Broadway
New York, New York 10012
(212) 614-6464

The Center for Constitutional Rights focuses on many constitutional issues, including discrimination issues.

Center for Law and Social Policy
1751 N St., NW
Washington, D.C. 20036
(202) 328-5140

The Center for Law and Social Policy is involved in civil liberties, civil rights issues, and occupational health and safety issues.

Lawyers Committee for Civil Rights Under Law
1400 I Street, NW
Suite 400

Washington, D.C. 20005
(202) 371-1212

The Lawyers Committee concentrates on all aspects of racial discrimination law, primarily on behalf of African Americans. It maintains a number of regional and local offices, and often uses the volunteer services of lawyers in private law firms.

NAACP Legal Defense Fund
99 Hudson Street
Suite 1600
New York, New York 10013
(212) 219-1900

The Legal Defense Fund, an organization entirely separate from the NAACP (except for the shared name), has the largest national legal staff of any civil rights organization. It concentrates on all aspects of racial discrimination law and represents African Americans almost exclusively. Although the Legal Defense Fund has no local offices, it maintains a close relationship with hundreds of lawyers, many of whom are African American, and most of whom are in small private law firms located primarily in the South that specialize in civil rights law.

National Conference of Black Lawyers
126 West 119th Street
New York, New York 10026
(212) 864-4000

NCBL, an organization of African American lawyers, focuses on all aspects of discrimination law through its national network of African American lawyers.

National Lawyers Guild
55 Avenue of the Americas
New York, New York 10013
(212) 966-5000

The Guild, a membership organization of civil rights lawyers, focuses upon unpopular legal causes, including the rights of minorities. It maintains offices in most major cities.

Native American Rights Fund
1506 Broadway
Boulder, CO 80302

(303) 447-8760

The Native American Rights Fund specializes in Native American issues and represents indigent Native Americans exclusively. It has several offices in the West and in the Southwest.

Southern Poverty Law Center
400 Washington Avenue
Montgomery, AL 36104
(205) 264-0286

The Southern Poverty Law Center specializes in the legal problems of the poor and primarily represents poor African Americans. It focuses its efforts throughout the South.

The following organizations provide assistance in the area of sexual harassment.

9to5, National Association of Working Women
614 Superior Avenue, NW
Cleveland, OH 44113
(210) 566-9308 (General Information)
(800) 522-0925 (Hotline)

9to5 is a national nonprofit organization for office workers, affiliated with Serivce Employees International Union, with local chapters across the country.

NOW Legal Defense and Education Fund
99 Hudson Street, 12th Floor
New York, New York 10013
(212) 925-6635

Legal referrals are available through the mail.

U.S. Department of Labor
Women's Bureau
200 Constitution Avenue, NW
Room S 3311
Washington, D.C. 20210

The department provides a list of resources, including organizations, training materials, court cases, and articles.

Women's Legal Defense Fund
1875 Connecticut Avenue, NW

Suite 710
Washington, D.C. 20009
(202) 986-2600

WLDF provides assistance in the area of sex discrimination and sexual harassment.

American Federation of State, County, and Municipal Employees (AFSCME)
1625 L Street, NW
Washington, D.C. 20036
(202) 429-5090

AFSCME provides information about what public sector unions do to help women workers.

DISPUTE RESOLUTION

Several organizations can provide you with information on how to empower yourself by pursuing your legal rights without bringing a lawsuit.

American Arbitration Association
140 West 51st Street
New York, New York 10020
(212) 484-4000

The AAA is a national nonprofit organization offering mediation and arbitration services through local offices nationwide. It also can provide a wealth of education publications and services specifically relating to employee rights and alternative dispute resolution.

UNION MEMBERS RIGHTS ORGANIZATIONS

Several organizations specialize in helping union members involved in internal union discrimination disputes by providing information and/or referrals.

Association for Union Democracy
500 State Street

Brooklyn, NY 11217
(718) 855-6650

AUD provides attorney referrals, legal advice, and the assistance of union members.

Public Citizen Litigation Group
2000 P Street, N.W.
Suite 700
Washington, D.C. 20036
(202) 785-3704

Public Citizen litigates on behalf of organizations and individuals on a variety of significant test issues.